THE ROUTLEDGE HANDBOOK OF INTERNATIONAL RESILIENCE

Resilience is increasingly discussed as a key concept across many fields of international policy-making from sustainable development and climate change, insecurity, conflict and terrorism, to urban and rural planning, international aid provision and the prevention of and responses to natural and man-made disasters. Edited by leading academic authorities from a number of disciplines, this is the first Handbook to deal with resilience as a new conceptual approach to understanding and addressing a range of interdependent global challenges.

The Handbook is divided into ten sections:

- Introduction: contested paradigms of resilience;
- the challenges of resilience;
- governing uncertainty;
- resilience and neoliberalism;
- environmental concerns and climate change adaptation;
- urban planning;
- disaster risk reduction and response;
- international security and insecurity;
- the policy and practices of international development;
- Conclusion: international resilience and the uncertain future.

Highlighting how resilience-thinking is increasingly transforming international policy-making and government and institutional practices, this Handbook will be an indispensable source of information for students, academics and the wider public interested in resilience, international relations and international security.

David Chandler is Professor of International Relations, Department of Politics and International Relations, University of Westminster, UK, and Editor of the journal *Resilience: International Policies, Practices and Discourses*.

Jon Coaffee is Professor in Urban Geography, the Department of Politics and International Studies, University of Warwick, UK. At Warwick, Jon has established the Resilient Cities Laboratory, and directs the Warwick Institute for the Science of Cities.

THE ROUTLEDGE HANDBOOK OF INTERNATIONAL RESILIENCE

Edited by David Chandler and Jon Coaffee

LONDON AND NEW YORK

First published 2017
by Routledge
2 Park Square, Milton Park, Abingdon, Oxon OX14 4RN

and by Routledge
711 Third Avenue, New York, NY 10017

Routledge is an imprint of the Taylor & Francis Group, an informa business

British Library Cataloguing in Publication Data
A catalogue record for this book is available from the British Library

Library of Congress Cataloging in Publication Data
A catalog record for this book has been requested

ISBN: 978-1-138-78432-1 (hbk)
ISBN: 978-1-315-76500-6 (ebk)

Typeset in Bembo
by Sunrise Setting Ltd., Brixham, UK

CONTENTS

Contents

FIGURES

TABLES

CONTRIBUTORS

Claudia Aradau is Reader in International Politics in the Department of War Studies, King's College London, UK. Her research has developed a critical political analysis of security practices. She is the author of *Rethinking Trafficking in Women: Politics out of security* (Palgrave Macmillan, 2008) and co-author, with Rens van Munster, of *Politics of Catastrophe: Genealogies of the unknown* (Routledge, 2011). She has recently co-edited *Critical Security Methods: New frameworks for analysis* (Routledge, 2014, with Jef Huysmans, Andrew Neal and Nadine Voelkner) and a special issue of Security Dialogue on 'Questioning Security Devices: Performativity, Resistance, Politics' (2015, with Anthony Amicelle and Julien Jeandesboz). Her current work pursues a critical exploration of security and non-knowledge, with a particular focus on anticipation, devices and (big) data.

Charis Boke is a Ph.D. candidate in Anthropology at Cornell University. Her current research is focused on the intersections of climate change, race and class politics in the United States, rooted in participant-observation research conducted with community organizers and herbalists in New England. Her dissertation considers how members of these communities are integrating understandings of healing individual bodies, addressing political inequalities and healing plane-tary ecologies. Boke's scholarly commitments in anthropology are deeply entwined with her work as a social justice activist. This research has been supported by a partnership between the Atkinson Center for a Sustainable Future and Oxfam America (the Rural Resilience Research Fellows program). Additional support was provided by Cornell University's Institute for Social Sciences Land Theme Project, by the Society for the Humanities at Cornell and by the American Studies Program at Cornell.

Sophie Bond is a Senior Lecturer in the Department of Geography/Te Iho Whenua at the University of Otago. She is passionate about teaching and the possibilities of encouraging students to think critically about place, environment, nature, inequalities and justice in ways that may facilitate empowering hopeful alternative futures. Her research spans geographies of contestation and activism, environmental democracy, post politics and spaces of dissent in the current con-juncture and the implications of working in neoliberalised universities. She primarily adopts poststructural feminist approaches in her research, and seeks to engender a decolonized praxis and a feminist ethic of care in both her teaching and research.

Lee Bosher is a Senior Lecturer in Disaster Risk Reduction in the Water, Engineering and Development Centre (WEDC) at Loughborough University, UK. He has a background in disaster risk management and his research and teaching includes disaster risk reduction and the multi-disciplinary integration of proactive hazard mitigation strategies into the decision-making processes of key stakeholders, involved with the planning, design, construction and operation of the built environment. Lee is coordinator of the International Council for Building's Working Commission W120 on 'Disasters and the Built Environment'; he is a Fellow of the Royal Geographical Society and he has been involved in research projects that investigated how urban resilience can be increased in the UK, Haiti, India, Nigeria and across parts of Europe. Lee's books include *Hazards and the Built Environment* (Routledge, 2008) and the forthcoming *Disaster Risk Reduction for the Built Environment: An introduction* (Wiley 2017).

Philippe Bourbeau is Lecturer in the Department of Politics and International Studies at the University of Cambridge, UK. He holds a Ph.D. in political science from the University of British Columbia, Canada. He has expertise in the field of international relations, security studies, resilience and comparative immigration policies. Bourbeau is the editor of *Security: Dialogue across disciplines* (Cambridge University Press, 2015) and the author of *The Securitization of Migration: A study of movement and order* (Routledge, 2011). His articles have been published in *International Studies Review*, *Journal of Ethnic and Migration Studies*, *Millennium: Journal of International Studies*, *Critical Studies on Security*, *Resilience: International Policies, Practices and Discourses*, *Critique internationale* and *Revue européenne des migrations internationales*.

David Chandler is Professor of International Relations, Department of Politics and International Relations, University of Westminster and editor of the journal *Resilience: International Policies, Practices and Discourses*. His most recent books are (co-authored with Julian Reid) *The Neoliberal Subject: Resilience, adaptation and vulnerability* (Rowman & Littlefield, 2016) and *Resilience: The governance of complexity* (Routledge, 2014).

Ksenia Chmutina is a Lecturer in Sustainable and Resilient Urbanism in the School of Civil and Building Engineering, Loughborough University. Her main research interest is in synergies of resilience and sustainability in the built environment, including holistic approaches to enhancing resilience to natural and human-induced threats, and a better understanding of the systemic implications of sustainability and resilience under the pressures of urbanization and climate change. She has extensive experience of working on RCUK and EU-funded projects that focused on resilience and sustainability of urban spaces in Europe, China and the Caribbean.

Jonathan Clarke is a Post-doctoral Research Fellow in the Resilient Cities Laboratory in the Department of Politics and International Studies (PAIS) at the University of Warwick. His work considers the roles of design, planning and governance in identifying and responding to future urban challenges. His research explores the role that urban design and governance might make to enhanced city resilience, based upon on an inductive approach of learning from practice. In addition to his academic work, Jonathan is an experienced urban designer, planner and chartered landscape architect, specializing in regeneration, master-planning, environmental impact assessment and public realm design. He is a professional practice examiner for the Landscape Institute and an external tutor at the University of Sheffield's Department of Landscape.

Jon Coaffee is Professor in Urban Geography based in the School of Politics and International Studies at the University of Warwick, UK. At Warwick, Jon has established the Resilient Cities Laboratory, and directs the Warwick Institute for the Science of Cities. His research focuses upon the interplay of physical and socio-political aspects of urban resilience. Most notably he published *Terrorism Risk and the City* (Routledge, 2003), *The Everyday Resilience of the City* (Palgrave Macmillan, 2008), *Terrorism Risk and the Global City: Towards Urban Resilience* (Routledge, 2009), *Sustaining and Securing the Olympic City* (Ashgate, 2011) and *Urban Resilience: Planning for Risk, Crisis and Uncertainty* (Palgrave Macmillan, 2016). His work has been supported by a significant number of EU and UK Research Council grants. Jon is also an Exchange Professor at New York University's Center for Urban Science and Progress (CUSP).

Angela Connelly is a researcher at the School of Environment, Education and Development at The University of Manchester, where she completed her Ph.D. in 2011. Her recent research considers adaptation to extreme weather events and to the future implications of climate change, particularly through the prism of new technologies and techniques that may help cities adapt to climate change.

Raven Cretney is a Ph.D. candidate at the Centre for Urban Research, RMIT University, Melbourne, Australia. Her research approaches the social and cultural aspects of current local and global issues, particularly surrounding crisis and disaster. She has written on emerging radical articulations of resilience and is working on further projects addressing the capacity for grassroots responses to environmental and social issues. Her current research investigates the role of community-led recovery initiatives in shaping perceptions of democracy and participation in post-earthquake Christchurch in Aotearoa/New Zealand.

Simin Davoudi is Professor of Environmental Policy and Planning at the School of Architecture, Planning and Landscape, Newcastle University, and Associate Director of the university's Institute for Sustainability. She is past President of the Association of the European Schools of Planning (AESOP), Fellow of the Academy of Social Sciences and the Royal Society of Arts and has led the UK Office of the Deputy Prime Minister's Planning Research Network. Her research on urban planning, environmental governance, climate change and resilience is published widely. Recent books include: *Justice and Fairness in the City* (Policy Press, 2016), *Town and Country Planning in the UK* (Routledge, 2015), *Reconsidering Localism* (Routledge, 2015), *Climate Change and Sustainability Cities* (Routledge, 2014), *Conceptions of Space and Place in Strategic Spatial Planning* (Routledge, 2009) and *Planning for Climate Change* (Earthscan, 2009).

Cecile de Milliano currently works at the emergency operations unit of the regional office of the International Federation of the Red Cross (IFRC) in Kenya. The unit has a focus on responding to emergencies in countries in Eastern Africa and the Indian Ocean Islands. In the past ten years, Cecile has worked and performed research in numerous countries in Africa, Asia and Latin America. She specializes in the fields of resilience, humanitarian action and age- and gender-sensitive programming and is affiliated to Globalisation Studies Groningen, University of Groningen (the Netherlands).

Brad Evans is a Reader in Political Violence at the University of Bristol. He is currently leading a series of articles and dialogues dedicated to the problem of violence for the opinions section of *The New York Times (The Stone)*. He also edits the *Histories of Violence Section* of Los Angeles Review of Books. Brad's latest books include *Disposable Futures: The Seduction of Violence in the Age* *of the Spectacle* (with Henry Giroux, City Lights: 2015), *Resilient Life: The Art of Living Dangerously* (with Julian Reid, Polity Press, 2014), *Liberal Terror* (Polity Press, 2013) and *Deleuze & Fascism* (with Julian Reid, Routledge, 2013). He is currently working on a number of book projects, including *Ecce Humanitas: Beholding the Pain of Humanity* (Columbia University Press, forthcoming 2018), *Histories of Violence: Post-War Critical Thought* (with Terrell Carver, Zed Books, forthcoming 2016) and *Portraits of Violence: Ten Thinkers on Violence – A Visual Exploration* (with Sean Michael Wilson, New Internationalist, forthcoming 2016).

Ding Fei is a Ph.D. candidate in the Department of Geography, Environment and Society at the University of Minnesota – Twin Cities. She is interested in understanding how global and national development paradigms influence local livelihood opportunities in developing countries. Her dissertation research investigates 'China–Africa cooperation', with a particular focus on company work regimes and labour agencies in different sectors of Chinese investment in Ethiopia.

Pete Fussey is a Professor of Sociology at the University of Essex specializing in a number of areas including surveillance and society, terrorism and counter-terrorism, critical studies of resilience, major-event security, organized crime and urban sociology. He has published extensively in these areas, was recently elected a director of the *Surveillance Studies Network*. He has also recently concluded working on two large-scale funded research projects analysing counter-terrorism in the UK's crowded spaces and, separately, future urbanism and resilience towards 2050. Recent books include *Securing and Sustaining the Olympic City* (Ashgate, 2011) and *Terrorism and the Olympics* (Routledge, 2011).

Kevin Grove is an Assistant Professor of Human Geography in the Department of Global & Sociocultural Studies at Florida International University. His work draws on political geography, security studies and political ecology to explore the biopolitics of disaster resilience. Kevin has conducted fieldwork in Jamaica on disaster management and development programming and is currently researching post-Sandy urban resilience in the greater New York City region. His work has appeared in a number of peer-reviewed journals in geography and related fields, including the *Annals of the Association and American Geographers, Security Dialogue, Environment and Planning D: Society and Space, Antipode, Geoforum* and *Geopolitics*.

Søren Vester Haldrup is an international development professional. He has previously worked for the UNDP in Tanzania and the Danish Institute for International Studies, where he has published on capacity development, South–South cooperation and public–private partnerships and resilience. Søren is currently working as a consultant at Oxford Policy Management.

Charlotte Heath-Kelly is Assistant Professor of Politics and International Studies at the University of Warwick, UK. Her research into the reconstruction of bombsites is funded by the Economic and Social Research Council. She has published two monographs: *Death and Security: Memory and mortality at the bombsite* (Manchester University Press, 2016) and *Politics of Violence: Militancy, international politics, killing in the name* (Routledge, 2013). Her work has also appeared in the journals *Security Dialogue, The British Journal of Politics and International Relations, Politics, Critical Studies on Terrorism* and *Studies in Conflict and Terrorism*. Furthermore, she co-edited two books with Lee Jarvis and Chris Baker-Beall during their mutual convenership of the BISA Critical Terrorism Studies Working Group: *Neoliberalism and Terror: Critical engagements* (Routledge, 2015) and *Counter-Radicalisation: Critical perspectives* (Routledge, 2014).

Alf Hornborg has been Professor of Human Ecology at Lund University since 1993. He has conducted fieldwork among the Mi'kmaq of Nova Scotia, Canada, and additional field research in Peru, Brazil and Tonga. His main research interest since the early 1990s has been the cultural construction of economy and technology in the dominant modern worldview. Using insights from economic anthropology, economic and environmental history and ecological economics, he has shown how the mainstream categories of economics are the products of geographically and historically situated perspectives established in nineteenth-century Europe, which systematically ignore the fundamental role of asymmetric global resource flows and environmental load displacement in processes of economic growth and technological progress. His central contribution is the identification of a hegemonic technological fetishism obscuring the appropriation of human time and natural space on which modern society has been founded since the Industrial Revolution. His books include *The Power of the Machine* (AltaMira Press, 2001), *Global Ecology and Unequal Exchange* (Routledge, 2011) and *Global Magic* (Palgrave Macmillan, 2016).

Anne Jerneck is Professor of Sustainability Science at LUCSUS. Her research concerns processes of social, structural and institutional change in relation to poverty, gender inequality, climate change and the politics of sustainability. Her methodological contribution to sustainability science relates to knowledge structuring, interdisciplinarity and transdisciplinarity.

Jonathan Joseph is Professor of International Relations at the University of Sheffield. His current research looks at the role of the EU in promoting resilience across different policy areas such as development, humanitarian intervention, infrastructure protection, counter-terrorism, and security policy. These are compared with resilience policies in the UK, US, France and Germany and considered through the conceptual lens of governmentality. He is currently working on a book, *Varieties of Resilience*, to be published by Cambridge University Press next year. His previous monograph was *The Social in the Global: Social theory, governmentality and global politics* (Cambridge University Press, 2012). Other recent work looks at European integration as a hegemonic project (with Simon Bulmer, *European Journal of International Relations*) and *Scientific Realism and International Relations* (with Colin Wight, Palgrave 2010). He is currently an editor of *Review of International Studies*.

Jeroen Jurriens is a Disaster Manager at the Inter-Church Organisation for Development Cooperation (ICCO Cooperation) in the Netherlands, member of ACT Alliance (Action by Churches Together Alliance). He specializes in the fields of resilience, Disaster Risk Reduction and humanitarian action. He is chair of the ACT Alliance Community of Practice on Disaster Risk Reduction/Climate Change Adaptation and he is a member of the Working Group on Disaster Risk Reduction within the Voluntary Organisations in Cooperation in Emergencies (VOICE). His experience in working on humanitarian and Disaster Risk Reduction projects covers a diversity of countries in Central & Eastern Africa and South-East Asia, amongst them Indonesia, Philippines, East-Timor, Ethiopia, Uganda, Kenya, South-Sudan and Democratic Republic of Congo.

Mareile Kaufmann is a Senior Researcher at the Peace Research Institute Oslo and a member of the Nordic Centre of Excellence for Security Technologies and Societal Values. She holds a Ph.D. in Criminology from Hamburg University. Neighbouring disciplines such as critical security studies and cultural sciences equally shape her research agenda, which focuses on the meeting point between societal security and security technologies. While resilience, crisis management and different understandings of deviance are her key themes of interest, analytical concepts such as the digital, bodies, affect and regulation often serve as the entry point to explore contemporary security practices. Mareile has published on resilience theory, the use of social media during crises, drones, Internet security and humanitarian technology. She has gained project management experience and insights into applied security research in a broad range of European Commission and Research Council-funded projects.

Chuan Liao is a Post-doctoral Research Fellow in the School of Natural Resources and Environment at the University of Michigan – Ann Arbor. His research interest is situated at the intersection between people, the environment and community development. He conducts empirical research with pastoral communities in the East African savanna in Borana, Ethiopia and the Central Asian steppe in Xinjiang, China. He has published papers in development and change, risk analysis and applied geography. His current research focuses on large-scale land transactions and their socioeconomic and ecological impacts.

Sara Nelson is a doctoral candidate in the Department of Geography, Environment and Society at the University of Minnesota – Twin Cities. Her research engages the fields of political and economic geography, science studies and political theory to explore the political economy of conservation and environmental management. Her dissertation, 'The Nature of Value: A genealogy of neoliberal environmentalism', examines the political history of environmental valuation as a formative problem in the history of neoliberal capitalism. Her work is published in the journals *Antipode*, *Resilience: International Policies, Practices, and Discourses* and *Progress in Human Geography*; online at *Antipode* and *Jacobin*; and is forthcoming in the journal *Capitalism Nature Socialism*.

David O'Byrne is a Ph.D. candidate in Sustainability Science at the Interdisciplinary Research School for the Integration of Social and Natural Dimensions of Sustainability, coordinated by LUCSUS.

Paul O'Hare is a Senior Lecturer in Geography and Development at Manchester Metropolitan University. His research focuses upon urban resilience, the use of technologies for risk management and public and civil society engagement in governance. His recent work has examined the social, economic and cultural dimensions of using adaptive technologies for risk management, and the role of individuals and communities in countering urban vulnerability. His previous research has been funded by the European Union, RCUK, the ESRC and government agencies. This work has often had intense practical relevance, for instance through working with consultancies, businesses and communities to develop practice-orientated outputs such as guidance documents, decision-support frameworks and advisory notes.

Lennart Olsson is Professor and the founding Director of LUCSUS (Lund University Centre for Sustainability Studies). His research fields include human-nature interactions in the context of land degradation, climate change and food security/sovereignty. His current research focuses on the politics of climate change in the context of poverty, food insecurity and ill-health in sub-Saharan Africa and beyond.

Johannes Persson is Professor of Theoretical Philosophy at Lund University. His research fields include philosophy of science, philosophy of risk and human decision-making. His current research focuses on the integration of evidence and knowledge from different sources, such as science and personal experience.

Samuel Randalls is a Lecturer in Geography at University College London. His research explores the relationship between weather, climate and society. This incorporates both historical and contemporary settings, with a particular interest in the business management of weather risk and the politics of climate change. This research has led to papers on Victorian weather insurance, a history of climate change economics, the paradoxes of current climate politics/policy and twenty-first century weather futures markets (the subject of his Ph.D. from the University of Birmingham). He has co-edited a reader in *Future Climate Change* (Routledge, 2011) as well as special issues of the journals *Environment and Planning: A*, *Geoforum*, and *Social Studies of Science*. He is currently co-editing a new *Handbook of Political Economy of Science* (Routledge).

Julian Reid is a political theorist, philosopher, and Professor of International Relations at the University of Lapland, and is renowned for his advance of the theory of biopolitics, contributions to cultural theory, postcolonial and post-structural thought, critique of liberalism and seminal deconstruction of resilience. He has occupied the Chair in International Relations at the University of Lapland since 2010. In 2012 Reid established the very first Master's programme in Global Biopolitics in the world, at Lapland. He was Visiting Professor at the University of Bristol between 2013 and 2014. He is co-editor of the journal *Resilience: Policies, Practices and Discourses*. He is a member of the RELATE centre of excellence, based at the University of Oulu, and a member of the Advisory Board to the Histories of Violence project. His work has been funded by the Economic and Social Research Council (ESRC), the Finnish Academy and the European Union (EU). He is currently leading a research project, *Indigeneity in Waiting*, funded by the Kone Foundation. His latest book, *The Neoliberal Subject*, was published by Polity in 2016.

Peter Rogers has been researching resilience in many forms for the last decade. As a researcher, consultant and activist around resilience his work on resilient governance and urban resilience, in particular, advocates for a deeper grounded review of the interplay through, across and within complex systems when governing uncertainty. He is also a founding member of the Global Resilience Collaborative and is currently based at Macquarie University, Sydney.

Frederik Rosén is a Senior Researcher at the Danish Institute for International Studies. He has published widely on international security and facilitates policy development in the UN and NATO on resilience-related thematic areas. He is the author of the book *Collateral Damage: A Candid History of a Peculiar form of Death* (Hurst, 2016), which is an enquiry into the conceptual bedrock of our ideas of governance and authority.

Delf Rothe is Post-doctoral Fellow at the Institute for Peace Research and Security Policy, Hamburg, Germany. He received his Ph.D. in political science from the University of Hamburg in 2014 and in his post-doctoral project he is studying the influence of ecological concepts like sustainability and resilience in development and security policy. Delf has published on securitization theory, risk-management, global climate governance and discourse theory in journals such as *Security Dialogue*, *International Relations* and *Journal of International Relations and Development*. His book on the securitization of climate change was published by Routledge in 2015. He is co-editor of two volumes on *Interpretive Approaches to Global Climate Governance* (Routledge, 2013) and *Euro-Mediterranean Relations after the Arab Spring* (Ashgate, 2013).

Jessica Schmidt received her Ph.D. in International Relations from the University of Westminster, London, UK, and was a Post-doctoral Fellow at the Centre for Global Cooperation Research, Duisburg, Germany. She has published articles in various journals such as *European Journal for International Relations*, *Cambridge Review of International Affairs* and *International Relations*. Her book *Rethinking Democracy Promotion in International Relations* (2016) has recently been published by Routledge. Her research focuses on the interplay between epistemology and governance. She now conducts her research outside of academia and is currently training to become a forestry worker.

Stephanie Simon is a geographer and research associate in the University of Amsterdam's Department of Politics. Her research critically interrogates everyday practices and spaces of security and the ways in which the politics of pre-emption and resilience are negotiated in urban and transnational contexts. Current projects are focused on the sensibilities of landscape and urban design as spatial mediators of environmental risk and resilience. Her work has been published in *Antipode, Theory, Culture & Society, Social and Cultural Geography, Security Dialogue* and *Space and Polity*.

Brian Thiede is Assistant Professor of Rural Sociology in the Department of Agricultural Economics, Sociology, and Education at The Pennsylvania State University. His research uses both quantitative and qualitative methods to investigate questions about the social impacts of environmental change and development.

Henrik Thorén is a Postdoctoral Fellow in Philosophy of Science and based at LUCSUS. His research deals with concepts such as interdisciplinarity, knowledge integration and scientific pluralism, in the context of sustainability science.

Jessica West is a Ph.D. candidate in Global Governance and International Security Studies at the Balsillie School of International Affairs, Wilfrid Laurier University. Her research is focused on the emergence and evolution of resilience-based policies for national security in the United Kingdom, United States and Canada. She also does research on governance, security, and technology at Project Ploughshares where her work includes managing an international research project on space security. Jessica received her Master's of Arts at the Norman Paterson School of International Affairs, Carleton University.

Iain White is Professor of Environmental Planning at the University of Waikato in New Zealand. His research focuses upon the interface of the natural and built environments and he has written widely in this field. He has also recently published *Environmental Planning in Context* (Palgrave, 2015) and is the author of *Water and the City: Risk, Resilience and Planning for a Sustainable Future* (Routledge, 2010). His work has been supported by a significant number of research grants and he has been awarded a number of multi-million dollar projects as either Principle Investigator or Co-Investigator. He has been an invited Keynote Speaker in a number of countries, including the UK, Ireland, Taiwan, the Netherlands and New Zealand.

Chris Zebrowski is a Lecturer in Politics and International Relations at Loughborough University, UK. His research has investigated the emergence of resilience discourses and their implications for the rationalities and practices of liberal emergency governance. He is an assistant editor of *Resilience: International Policies, Practices and Discourses* and author of *The Value of Resilience: Securing Life in the Twenty-First Century* (Routledge, 2016).

PART I

Introduction

1

INTRODUCTION

Contested paradigms of international resilience

David Chandler and Jon Coaffee

Introduction

Resilience has risen rapidly over the last decade or more to become one of the key terms in international policy and academic discussions. Whatever the subject matter of concern – whether it comes to questions of conflict management, the response to economic crisis, the mitigation of climate change, the challenges of urban poverty or disaster risk management – questions of resilience will be at the forefront. Leading international institutions, such as the United Nations, the European Union, the World Bank, the International Monetary Fund, government agencies and departments, international non-governmental organisations and community groups are all promoting the importance of resilience, formulating various conceptions of what it might be and how to achieve it and developing indicators to measure it. However, with the rapid rise of resilience has come uncertainty as to how it should be built and how different practices and approaches should come together to operationalise it (Hussain, 2013).

Advocates and critics disagree over many aspects of resilience: whether it is a new approach, capable of redirecting international policy discussions or just meaningless jargon; whether it is decentralising and redistributive of agency or maintains current structures of power; whether it opens up possibilities for radical critique and transformation or merely reproduces neoliberal understandings of self-responsibility; whether it is about maintaining stability and the status quo or encouraging risk-taking and change; whether the system- and process-based conceptualisations of ecology are suitable analogies for social and political life; whether measurements and metrics can or even should be developed to enable comparisons across time and space, or whether resilience is contextually and relationally specific; and so on.

As the reader will notice from a glance at the contents pages of this edited collection, international resilience is a multi-faceted concept and a set of multiple and evolving practices. This collection focuses on international discourses of resilience and enables the reader to engage with a range of conceptual positions from a number of disciplinary approaches. Some chapters are more conceptual, some are more empirical and case study based. We hope that there will be more than enough to feed the interests and needs of both practitioners and academics, whether they are experts in the field or approaching this issue for the first time. This brief introduction serves to contextualise the discussion of resilience in the international academic and policy developments of the last decade or so, and to contextualise the Handbook itself.

Paradigms of resilience

The world before resilience was one with a greater confidence in the capacity of states and governments to secure and control events. In this confident world, it appeared that knowledge and understanding could grow and that problems could be learned from in a universalist way: that lessons could be generalised and applied elsewhere. We suggest that the world of resilience is one with less confidence in the power of securing agency and the capacity of knowledge and generalisation. It is a world that seems less certain and more complex or contingent (Chandler, 2014). A world where clarity is less possible and separations between threats and objects to be secured, between inside and outside, human and nature, problems and solutions, past and future, seem less stable than before. Resilience is often defined in relation to this new awareness of insecurity or contingency: as a capacity to prepare for, to respond to, or to bounce back from problems or perturbations and disturbances, which cannot necessarily be predicted or foreseen in advance.

For the advocates of resilience, this new approach or new set of sensitivities enables a more open and fluid approach to the world, one which attempts to rethink or to move away from traditional approaches to problems. The characteristics of a more open approach often include a more iterative or process-based approach to problems, working with difficulties, being sensitive to feedback and not assuming that there is an immediate or fail-safe cure or solution. The reason for resilience approaches often involving less hubris and more caution is a greater awareness of unintended consequences or side-effects when acting in the world; for these reasons, resilience is seen as a more experimental and more context-dependent approach, less prone to making generalisations about what works and what does not. Advocates also flag up the shift in focus, with less of a binary 'friend/enemy' understanding and more of a focus on inter-relationships and mutual feedback. Problems are not always seen as something external to us, but often as symptoms or expressions of our own lack of understanding or failure to be alert to changes and shifts in our own environment.

While the general framework of resilience approaches seems to fairly coherently presage a number of shifts in awareness and policy-making in the international arena, this does not mean that resilience approaches are not necessarily problematic: in their starting assumptions; in their application; or in their attempted goals. Many of the chapters that follow seek to engage critically with certain aspects of resilience approaches and draw out the limitations, confusions, exclusions, misappropriations and power inequalities which can be involved in resilience discourses and practices. The purpose of the Handbook is to present a wide variety of engagements with the resilience problematic, to extend thinking in this field, and to develop discussion and analysis. We have no intention of closing down or limiting this developing field by assuming that discussion and debate are over; in fact, we realise that it is precisely because resilience is understood in diverse ways that the academic and policy field is so contested.

However, we think that, by way of introduction, it may be useful to draw attention to how the rise of resilience relates to contemporary political and philosophical discussions, which have problematised modernist binaries of nature/culture, subject/object or mind/matter. By this we mean that the idea of progress (in the abstract, but also in relation to specific questions of security, the environment, development or urban planning) is no longer one where the external world is seen to be uniform, linear or law-bound and unchanging: merely waiting for human knowledge to develop adequately to solve problems. Progress today is not so much about storing up, extracting and universalising knowledge but rather about being more relationally aware of our own systems of organisation – politically, culturally, socially and economically – and about the interactive effects of these forms of organisation with the external, changing environment and international context. In this sense, resilience approaches seem to be much more about relations and contexts than about fixed essences and linear causal chains. Resilience approaches are often about how to engage in processes of interaction in more aware and reflective ways.

This enables us to articulate at least three broad and inter-related framings of resilience, ranging from more conservative approaches, which seek to maintain the status quo to more radical approaches, which see the world as a much more interactive flux.

First, the approach, which may be best known: that of maintaining the status quo or 'bouncing back'. This could be seen as a *homeostatic* approach, one that seeks to regulate a return to the pre-existing equilibrium. This is a resilience approach that seeks to organise internally to enable a smooth and efficient return to functioning after a disaster or setback. Within this broad framing, some 'bounce back' approaches might focus upon internal properties of the community or society – levels of social or communal capital; levels of redundancy, slack or spare capacity; perhaps also on questions of variety and diversity, avoiding over-reliance on particular resources, sources of supply or centres of coordination. The focus on internal properties and capacities is also sometimes connected to 'engineering' or 'psychological' vocabularies of resilience as a set of internal properties. This approach sometimes makes a distinction between the society or community – on the inside, to be made resilient – and the threat or problem – on the outside, as something to be resilient against. Here, the threat of terrorism may serve as a good example. Terrorism is often conceived as an external threat, one that is difficult to prevent and therefore necessitates ways of bouncing back to normal functioning should major infrastructural facilities be damaged or massive outrages take place.

The 'homeostatic' approach is concerned with bouncing back after an event, but nevertheless encourages changes in the present. These changes are geared less towards preventing risks, threats or problems from taking place (pre-resilience views of security) and more often towards recognising problems and addressing or responding to them and recovering with the minimum of disruption. So rather than working on the external world in a direct way, resilience tends to work indirectly, often starting with the process of working on the self. This is an important shift away from traditional or modernist approaches to problem solving. The ways in which this work on the self is understood are relationally orientated; not to achieve linear goals in themselves, but to be able to respond to external disturbance, much as a thermostat works on the basis of feedback and response to changes in the external environment (think about how our bodies regulate heat by perspiring on a hot day or shivering on a cold day). Approaches within this framework often involve the development and use of real time responsiveness, sometimes with the application of new technologies – referred to as Big Data, digital sensing, machine-learning and the Internet of Things – seeking to adapt to the emergence of conflict, infectious diseases, climate change or other problems or threats.

If the homeostatic approach is the first generation of resilience thinking, and still perhaps the dominant approach in many areas, then perhaps the second generation of resilience could be seen as an *autopoietic* approach. In this approach, bouncing back is not the aim but rather growth and development, through an increased awareness of interconnections and processes. Societies or communities are understood as being able to grow and develop through the shift towards resilience approaches, independently of whether there is a disaster, crisis or unexpected development. Resilience thereby becomes independent, standing on its own as a way of thinking about problems; creating a shift towards organising and governing on the basis of resilience per se. Here, the process of being or becoming 'self-regulating' is seen as key. Resilience is no longer about returning to the equilibrium or maintaining the status quo, but is seen to be a process of ongoing self-transformation that can be likened to 'bouncing forward'.

Resilience as transformation, or as autopoietic self-growth, presupposes a very different relationship between the self (or the society or community) and the outside world. The autopoietic approach to resilience follows the earlier homeostatic approach of not working directly on an external world but focusing on internal forms of organisation in relation to the external world. In this case, however, rather than aiming for the maintenance of stasis, the aspiration is to generate new and innovative ways of thinking and organising. Judith Rodin, for example, sees this as the 'Resilience Dividend' (2015). Thinking in resilience ways thus enables communities and societies to 'bounce back better', in terms of learning more about themselves and building new forms of interconnection and self-awareness. External or outside stimuli or disruptions are therefore vital to enable this process of self-reassessment (see also, Taleb, 2012). Even if there is no disastrous event, these sensitivities to changes and reflective approaches can be applied to improve and rethink everyday processes and exchanges, discovering new possibilities in the present.

This approach of resilience as self-transformation is taken further in Kathleen Tierney's influential book *The Social Roots of Risk* (2014), which argues that resilience approaches bring together the natural and social sciences, enabling forms of recursive governance, i.e. forms of governance based on the awareness of problems and threats that emerge out of interactions between the social order and the external environment. This approach moves well beyond pre-resilience perspectives of prevention, and the 'bouncing back' framing, as it enables a fundamental critique of modernist forms of knowing and governing that fail to take into account the unintended consequences of narrow 'problem-solving' approaches. Classic examples would be the construction of flood barriers or levees, tending to make water systems more volatile and undermining natural protections, or the case of antibiotics, held to facilitate more virulent and resistant strains of viruses. Thus governance is seen as a recursive process of governing the consequences of previous attempts to solve problems, being wary of the possibility that this stores up further problems for the future and attempting to break out of this loop through new, more imaginative, approaches. In these framings, problems are no longer considered as entirely external threats but also as products of social processes, with resilience practices and policies as, similarly, a matter not merely of technical but also of social and political adaptive change (see Pelling, 2011).

A third range of resilience approaches could be seen as quite different from the first two approaches, which are still very subject-orientated – thinking linearly about preparing for the future or learning from the past, where the subject or community seeks to either maintain the status quo or to develop autopoietically. The third generation of resilience approaches has less emphasis on temporality and direction and is often more concerned with rethinking contextual possibilities in the present. This framing is more focused on developing resilience at the level of micro-politics or life-politics, using more reflexive and self-aware approaches to repurpose or to re-envision ways of engaging communities. This approach to resilience is highlighted in the idea of public service 'jams' or civic hackathons, where Smart City Labs, the UN Development Programme or other donors invite ideas and proposals to deconstruct problems and try out prototype solutions with volunteer hackers, technologists and designers immersing themselves in the problem. These *ad hoc* forums are lauded as mechanisms for reaching out to citizens to develop new ideas, exposing governing authorities and international institutions to new tools and skill sets, and for re-envisioning problems – seeing issues in a different light. Hacking is an iterative, gradual approach to policy interventions, where each hack uses and reveals new inter-relationships creating new possibilities for thinking and acting. Here, resilience is an ongoing transformative process of building engaged communities through experimentation and grasping momentary and fluid connections and interrelations in a highly context-dependent way. International policy interventions on this basis thus neither seek to exercise hegemonic control and direction, nor do they seek to ignore and disengage from the problems. Instead, the problems themselves are reinterpreted as enabling and creating opportunities.

Resilience can thus be seen in a number of ways, which can easily overlap, or be seen as contradictory, depending upon our angle or level of analysis. Thus, we would argue, that rather than focusing on fixed definitions of resilience it is perhaps more useful to see resilience as forming the basis of – or cohering – a range of policy discussions in a number of fields that seek to rethink traditional policy approaches. For us, resilience begins with the assumption that problems cannot be prevented, ring-fenced, solved or cured in traditional ways (often described as reductionist or linear). Thus, resilience operates to frame discussions of a quite fundamental nature, of how we might rethink forms of social, political and economic organisation. These ways of reflecting upon social and organisational changes then range in focus, from preparatory policy-making to bounce back, to more radical calls for changes in structures and habits and forms of understanding, to calls for high-tech forms of awareness, real-time responsiveness or temporary hacking, all them involving fundamental questions of policy development, community engagement, feedback effects and interactive relationships.

The Handbook

This Handbook contains 30 chapters. For ease of reference, they are divided into eight sections, with three to five chapters in each: an introduction to the challenges of resilience thinking; a section on resilience thinking's relationship with uncertainty and contingency; a number of chapters on resilience and neoliberalism; how resilience relates to environmental concerns and climate change adaptation; to urban planning; to disaster risk reduction and response; to issues of international security and insecurity; and to the policy and practices of international development.

The first section of chapters concerns the challenges of resilience thinking. These chapters serve to introduce the conception of resilience from a variety of different angles. Peter Rogers engages with the etymology and genealogy of the concept of resilience and looks at the complex agential interplay shaping and contesting its meaning. Philippe Bourbeau analyses a range of approaches to resilience within the social sciences and areas for its potential development. Samuel Randalls and Stephanie Simon further stretch the challenge of resilience thinking, seeking to analyse how multiple approaches and understandings hang together as a generality and need to be forced on to the plane of specifics. Lennart Olsson, Anne Jerneck, Henrik Thorén, Johannes Persson and David O'Byrne consider the implications of resilience thinking travelling from the natural to the social sciences, arguing that we should be wary of the potential depoliticising consequences of this move. Chris Zebrowski investigates the development of resilience understandings, not as the development of science and understanding but through seeing resilience as the development of a set of knowledge practices constituting the subject of its governance.

The book continues with sections on resilience as an approach to uncertainty and with resilience in relation to the knowledge scepticism of neoliberalism. There are four chapters addressing uncertainty. Claudia Aradau analyses resilience in the context of negotiating a world understood as a series of surprise events, suggesting that there has been a shift away from the promise of security. Charis Boke's chapter is a study of how the Transition Town movement attempts to deal with the insecurity of climate change and peak oil through the use of conceptual, material and affective resources to build a bridge to the future from a romanticised past. Mareile Kaufmann analyses the application of high-tech approaches to emergency response in the digitisation of resilience, noting how this enhances existing trends towards the focus on the crowd as the source of resilience and to the pattern as the epistemological authority for resilience programming. Jessica Schmidt's chapter is essentially concerned with the temporality of resilience, suggesting that life is understood as emergent through interaction; thus, in this framing, resilience is not an attempt to tame contingency but rather to thrive with it.

The relationship between resilience and neoliberal forms of knowing and governing has been a central concern for critical theorists and three chapters provide different analyses. David Chandler analyses how resilience thinking moves beyond what are normally seen as neoliberal constructions of difference and complexity, focusing on more open-ended forms of adaptation rather than neo-institutionalist path-dependencies and problematic rationalities. Alf Hornborg's chapter argues that the system-theoretic approach of resilience enables forms of self-organisation and autonomy that can provide an alternative to a global neoliberal hegemony, while Jonathan Joseph, applying a Foucauldian framework of responsibilisation, suggests that there is a close connection between the rise of resilience and the dominance of neoliberal approaches, although operating at different levels in different international contexts.

The following two sections concern the environment and urban planning. Delf Rothe analyses resilience in relation to climate change and security, focusing on UK policy framings; arguing that resilience weaves together diverse practices and different logics of governing and should not be narrowly seen as a single discourse. Sara Nelson explores social-ecological systems approaches to resilience to climate change, arguing that the forms of power exercised under the rubric of adaptation can be resisted and subverted through drawing on the radical, ecological counter-revolutionary underpinnings of these discourses. Chuan Liao and Ding Fei question dominant assumptions about resilience in the face of climate change; from a comparative study of pastoralists they suggest that international policies of diversification can further undermine traditional practices rather than help secure them.

Urban planning is fast becoming a major thematic for international resilience policies and practices in relation to climate change, infrastructure vulnerability, poverty and welfare provision (Coaffee and Lee, 2016). In this section, Jonathan Clarke provides an overview of the development of resilience thinking within urban planning, giving emphasis to the shift from 'maladaptation' – problem-solving which gives rise to problematic side-effects – to more iterative, reflexive, holistic and open-ended approaches, which see resilience as a longer-term process of adaptation. Simin Davoudi's chapter focuses on resilience and territorial cohesion through concepts of planning and spatial justice, suggesting that both concerns have come together under neoliberal agendas which stress the autonomous potential for development rather than putting resources into areas of highest need. Paul O'Hare, Iain White and Angela Connelly close this section with an analysis of the paradox of the growth of the insurance sector as an integral part of resilience policy approaches and risk transfer, which mitigates against adaptation and maintains the status quo of neoliberal responsibilisation and is therefore a major barrier to resilience as transformative change.

The following three sections deal with disaster response, security and insecurity and resilience frameworks of international development. Opening the disaster response section, Cecile de Milliano and Jeroen Jurriens reflect on the problems faced by humanitarian non-governmental organisations on the ground, expected to follow resilience agendas often without adequate experience or support. Ksenia Chmutina and Lee Bosher analyse the use of resilience in UK Disaster Risk Management policies. Their focus is upon the 'all hazards' approach and the tensions between policy and practice, particularly the ways in which holistic visions are vitiated by prioritising top-down visions over local autonomy and response over prevention. Closing this section, Raven Cretney and Sophie Bond study the potential role of grassroots autonomous activism, with a case study from Canterbury, New Zealand, of the response to the earthquakes of 2010/2011, which radically reshaped discourses of resilience and transformation.

Jon Coaffee and Pete Fussey open the section on resilience and security, suggesting that the twinning of resilience and security in counter-terrorism policies has created a number of spatial and scalar tensions, especially when communities are seen as both a security threat and a securing resource. Charlotte Heath-Kelly's chapter examines resilience as a chimera of security, focusing on the anticipation of disaster or recovery from it but effacing the horror of the disaster event itself, as illustrated in the 'make-overs' of disaster sites. Jessica West provides an analysis of UK policy practices to build community resilience in the service of counter-terrorism, suggesting that the logics of civic resilience are to build the capacities of the state rather than to empower communities. Brad Evans and Julian Reid draw out the logic of resilience as a critique of traditional security discourses, arguing that resilience requires the acceptance of the permanent condition of vulnerability and the continual exposure to danger, thus life is reduced to a permanent process of adaptation.

The final section has three chapters concerning the application of resilience approaches to international development. Brian Thiede considers the potential clashes at spatial and temporal scales of international policy intervention to enable poverty reduction in rural Ethiopia, where international and local understandings of resilience can differ and where short-term subsistence approaches can undermine long-established community coping mechanisms. Søren Vester Haldrup and Frederik Rosén provide an analysis of how resilience approaches of process facilitation and empowerment have arisen at the same time as there has been a retreat from grand planning and a lowering of international aspirations, questioning the idea that resilience is a transformative discourse. Kevin Grove draws on post-colonial approaches and assemblage theory to draw out the 'hidden transcripts' of resilience in Jamaican disaster management, through which alternative forms of community development can emerge. The conclusion by the editors draws out the key themes of the edited collection and suggests directions for future research.

References

Chandler, D. (2014) *Resilience: The Governance of Complexity*. London: Routledge.

Coaffee, J. and Lee, P. (2016) *Urban Resilience: Planning for Risk, Crisis and Uncertainty*. Basingstoke: Palgrave.

Hussain, M. (2013) Resilience: meaningless jargon or development solution? *The Guardian*, 5 March. Available at: www.theguardian.com/global-development-professionals-network/2013/mar/05/resilience-development-buzzwords (accessed 14 July 2016).

Pelling, M. (2011) *Adaptation to Climate Change: From Resilience to Transformation*. Abingdon: Routledge.

Rodin, J. (2015) *The Resilience Dividend: Managing Disruption, Avoiding Disaster, and Growing Stronger in an Unpredictable World*. London: Profile Books.

Taleb, N. (2012) *Antifragile: Things that Gain from Disorder*. London: Penguin.

Tierney, K. (2014) *The Social Roots of Risk: Producing Disasters, Promoting Resilience*. Stanford, CA: Stanford University Press.

PART II

Challenges

2

THE ETYMOLOGY AND GENEALOGY OF A CONTESTED CONCEPT

Peter Rogers

Introduction

Resilience is everywhere; it is the idea and the encounter. It is the root and the branch. It is a travelling concept, a conceptual 'rhizome' that has risen to prominence in debates about how we seek to understand, manage and solve the wicked riddle of uncertain times. It is assembled for different purposes, by diverse actors and, as such, is used in many ways. It may be unstable as it emerges, reconfiguring and reconfigured by the particular materialities and enunciations through which it is imagined, defined and enacted.[1] In this chapter the goal is twofold. First, the origins of resilience have been widely discussed but rarely discussed well, or with sufficient attention to detail. That is both bad and easy to fix. This chapter lays groundwork for understanding resilience. It will cut across the imagined, defined and enacted in order to give the reader a better grasp of what resilience can be and what it should, perhaps, not be. The second goal is to trace from the furore of speculation a network of assemblages that show how resilience has operated as a generator of metaphor, each encounter offering up semantically related fields of understanding used by different audiences for particular ends. Resilience is complex, it is rhizomatic in that each re-emergence offers a variation; it is therefore polysemic in nature embedding diverse, and sometimes contradictory, logics into the practices it informs – each emergent understanding being thus embedded in the goals of those who encounter it. This chapter provides the greater depth, currently lacking, in how we understand the foundations of resilience thinking as a 'mode of governance' implemented by real people in real time. It shows how the generative metaphor shapes the logic of resilience that can then be implemented by particular coalitions of actors. It shows how the way in which resilience has been operationalised informs the mechanisms by which it can be implemented, and thus provides a deeper analysis of the necessarily polysemic logics embedded in the emergent politics of resilience, in its circadean rhythms, in its institutionalisation via affective relationships as the 'rules of the game' owned, supported, or subverted by numerous coalitions – some of common purpose, others of contested purpose. This lays foundations for a theory of resilience as a complex interplay acted out in our everyday lives.

The relationship of resilience to multiple fields of enquiry must be clarified to avoid further misreading of resilience. It should not be treated as 'all things to all people' or an 'umbrella' term, universalising in nature. This chapter offers a theoretically informed etymology that leads to an empirically grounded genealogy of resilience; whilst this effort can trace the trajectory of change thus far it cannot exhaustively define resilience, as that operation is in and of itself a self-defeating endeavour. Those seeking to create a self-aggrandising grand narrative on this fashionable concept are on a fool's errand and only fall prey to the dangers they critique; too much of such critical appraisal implicitly reifies the logic of neoliberalism. Yes, there is danger that the positive potential may be confined and absorbed into the established orders of capital, however that moment has not yet come. If resilience represents anything, it represents the possibility of change. This will become clearer as you read through the other chapters in this book; as some critique in order to tear down resilience in fear of what it is and may become, others support a proactive approach that expands on the greater potential of resilience to foster a deeper socialisation countering the totalising exigencies of the neoliberalising global order.[2]

To frame this battle for the soul of resilience one must frame its meaning in language, in research and show how contested meanings coalesce around particular coalitions whose mechanisms, strategies and tactics for implementing resilience shape our current and future understanding of its potential, real or imagined. By taking this approach a more forensic, fine-grain reading highlights two dominant narratives, aligned with two potential trajectories of broader social change. The broader threshold of change within which basin of attraction we finally reside will shape the institutionalised logic of resilience. We must not in our rush to critique ignore the fuller trajectory of resilience, or the nuances of this complex concept cannot be fully mobilised. The questions thus asked are where the idea has come from, how it has been (and is being) used, and why it is important.

What does it mean: etymology and polysemy

The growth of interest in resilience has proliferated definitions, each seeking to identify the grand theory of their particular field. The term has roots in the post-classical Latin *resilientia* – as 'a fact of avoiding' as early as 1540, but also an 'action of rebounding' from the classical Latin root. The Latin *resilio* (see Klien *et al.*, 2003) and the suspiciously French sounding *resiliere* (see for example Paton and Johnston, 2006) are also frequently cited. In modern English, the literal definition is 'The action or an act of rebounding or springing back; rebound, recoil' used by Francis Bacon: 'whether there be any such resilience in echoes', emphasising the percussive or rather *repercussive* bouncing of sound (Bacon, 1659, p. 330). More well known is a sense of *elasticity*, the power to resume one's original shape or position after compression or bending – not suggesting *mutability*, rather *resistance*. Born of mathematics and mechanical engineering, this was often used in reference to the amount of energy per unit of volume absorbable by a material when subjected to strain, but also the value of strain at the elastic limit of the material. Thomas Young suggested that 'the resilience of a beam may be considered as proportional to the height from which a given body must fall to break it' (1807, p. 50). Thomas Tredgold (1818; 1824) extended this definition, suggesting the 'modulus of resilience' as 'the number which represents the power of a material to resist an impulsive force' (1824, p. 82).

These are common language definitions, literal in nature. There are also more obscure, figurative roots; these are useful for flagging the variety of interpretations, thus flagging the lexical ambiguity required to establish polysemy. *Resilement* is the 'action of going back upon one's word', an obscure and rare usage traceable to Thomas Blount's (1656) mid-seventeenth century *Glossographia*. This text identified the literal meanings, but also defined resilience as 'a going from ones word'; a moral revolt or recoil with negative emotional overtones. This is an explicit sense of the negative, in terms of repugnance and antagonism verifiable in Thomas Mozley's *Reminiscences:Chiefly of Oriel College*: 'It was possibly a mutual resilience between him [*sc.* Hartley Coleridge] and people of more orderly ways that prevented him from standing at Oriel till some years after' (1882, p. 85).

A caveat is exposed in the sense of resilience as *exposure to a negative*, and as a *characteristic of persons* or, at the very least, of negative interactions between them. John F. Smith and William Howitt's (1864) *Cassell's Illustrated History of England* offer the opposite, suggesting a positive sense of resilience: 'In their struggles with the ponderous power of England [the Scotch] discovered an invincible vigour, not only of resistance, but of resilience' (1864, I. lx. 333/2). This final figurative root lays groundwork for resilience as a quality of 'speedy or easy recovery from, or resistance to the effects of a misfortune, shock or illness' and 'of being robust and adaptable under duress' in the common tongue. Etymologically the linguistic analysis establishes a contestation for dominance between the inanimate and the human. A more linear sense of resistance and 'bounce back' in materials is reconfigured to emerge as a positive elasticity of spirit in human actors resulting from exposure to negative events. One can find elements of these roots in all the subsequent reappearances of resilience across disciplines in contemporary debates.

From etymology to genealogy

Linguistics help identify the root meanings of resilience, and establish broad semantic fields from which polysemy emerges. Which of these meanings are activated when this concept is operationalised and implemented will be different depending on the context within which it is mobilised. To establish this lexical ambiguity within a logic of governance, one must bridge theory, research and practice. One must also be aware of the particular historical contexts through which the diverse re-assemblages permeate in equally diverse intellectual, ethical and political domains.

The uses of engineering resilience are drawn into a linear logic denoting resilience as a property of materials (e.g. a steel or wooden beam used in building ships or in a spiral spring). The 'constancy' of this material is understood as energy, i.e. the total quantity of work (or energy) that can be stored in materials (Thompson, 2011 [1877]). Thus our understanding of the measurement that takes place is of stability, an equilibrium of obdurate qualities inherent in the fabric itself. This was carried forward into the modern era in engineering, but was reapplied by Holling (1973), whose influential work framed engineering resilience explicitly as 'the time required for an ecosystem to return to an equilibrium or steady-state following a perturbation'. Holling used 'engineering resilience', applied not to materials but to ecosystems; the return-time to the steady-state becomes *systemic recovery* rather than *material efficiency*. This divides resilience between 'engineering' forms of 'recovery' and 'efficiency' from 'ecological' resilience as 'the capacity of a system to *absorb* disturbance and *reorganize* while undergoing change so as to still retain essentially the same function, structure, identity, and feedbacks' (Walker *et al.*, 2004, p. 6. emphasis added). In understanding the 'characteristics' of the steady-state, the material properties of a system overlap with the 'capacity' of that system to maintain its stability or equilibrium. *Stress* shifts to *shock* caused by external origin of a 'perturbation' to the natural balance within an ecosystem, resilience becomes a more complex, dynamic process.

Holling is the point of departure for many scholars, but Nicholas Garmezy (1971, 1973) was a contemporary with a different approach from within psychology, exploring how children were able to develop normal functions when raised in high-risk environments. In this approach, we refer 'to the process of [and] capacity for … outcomes of positive adaptation' (Masten *et al.*, 1990, p. 426) emerging from exposure to risk or adversity. Resilience is inferred from two fundamental judgements about an individual's life experience: (1) that a person is now or is currently 'doing okay', and (2) that there either is currently or has been in the past a significant risk or adversity to overcome in their life experience (Masten and Coatsworth, 1995). A resilient person, or subject, exhibits the 'characteristics' of resilience through 'a resilient pattern' over time when under stress within 'living systems' (Masten and Obradovic, 2008). This anthropogenic understanding designates the process as individual 'development' towards a positive outcome.

The polysemic overlap of these approaches informs a multi-disciplinary reworking of the original ecological concept through social, psychological, and biological sciences re-emerging in social ecology (Gunderson and Holling, 2002). This influential approach emphasises greater interplay between human agents and ecosystems, harnessing interactions as relational *and* procedural. Focus shifts to the 'adaptive capacity' of human *and* environmental systems, in either cooperation or contestation. These complex systems interplay in a constantly changing form of meta-stable equilibrium. The characteristics of equilibrium are defined within safe thresholds, i.e. when does recovery become impossible? (*latitude*), the *resilience* of the system to change, the *precariousness* of its current state and the cross-scale interactions – framed not as a hierarchy but as a *panarchy*.

Where we run into problems for translating these research paradigms into practice is when we acknowledge that characteristics may not lend themselves to easy quantification or measurement. They can be analysed best through the dynamics of systemic complementarities and potential fractures. Thus researchers seek to find if learning from exposure 'transforms' the system, how such adaptation occurs and at what threshold. Whether the system is better able to remain in equilibrium as a result of change prioritises learning from exposure to enhance systemic 'stability'. The analysis thus critically unpacks how disturbances lead to creative reorganisation in complex social *and* ecological systems, but there is a conceptual muddying of the resilience meaning between the animate human actor, inanimate material, non-human ecological components and processes of systemic interplay.

Somewhat separate from the research-led approaches discussed above has been an understanding of resilience emerging in what Comfort, Boin and Demchak (2010) call the *organisational* and *management* sciences. Arguably the most influential figure here is Aaron Wildavsky (1984, 1988), who suggests that 'resilience is the capacity to cope with unanticipated dangers after they have become manifest, [it is] learning to bounce-back' (1988: p.77). We see the reappearance of a linear engineering application within the organisational domain. Here the regime of anticipatory protocols and strategies for generating 'risk calculus' prediction models thus seeks to manage uncertainty in organisations. Built into this approach is a linear view of institutionalised organisational 'coping capacity' on a highly technocratic model. The rational adoption of *risk reduction* strategies emphasises issues like asset protection and overcoming vulnerability for increasing an organisation's competitive marketplace advantage. A good example of this is the work of Yossi Sheffi (2005) on 'the resilient enterprise', which emphasises the anticipation and assessment of vulnerability for building in *flexibility* to organisational structures and business strategy. Elements of this approach are strongly echoed in attempts to govern uncertainty through disaster resilience, explored below.

Some of the above meanings overlap, whilst being generated along distinct trajectories by unrelated, partially related or closely connected fields of enquiry. The rise of resilience in governance has, however, coincided with a greater global focus on the impact of crisis, disaster and security – discussed in several ways in the other chapters of this section. Through these discourses we begin to delve deeper into the historical and political context of operationalised and implementable resilience, as well as the challenges of measurement, which are increasingly a key aspect of how the term is being used in practice. In what remains of this chapter, I move from a theoretical appraisal of genealogy in research to the applied sense of genealogy in the mechanisms, strategies and tactics of governing emergencies. Through linking resilience to policy and practice, we begin to see how this is being enacted, how this usage shapes what it is becoming and what may yet be.

Linking theory, research and practice

There are a number of influential conceptual frameworks in disaster policy and practice. Walker and Cooper (2010) note the American experience under the Clinton administration, highlighting the primacy of Critical Infrastructure Protection (CIP). They also highlight the relationship between a Hayekian logic of complex systems – as mathematically realisable predictabilities of creative-destruction – and the Cold War logic of first-order cybernetics. Both conceptual frameworks are arguably given ideological fuel in governance by the prevalence of rational choice theories of human decision-making underpinning the resultant governance policy. Walker and Cooper go on to suggest that a second-order cybernetics or 'second order functionalism' may be emerging that has inculcated the resilience logic into the global capitalist logic of financial risk regulation. In this logic the 'securitization of the bio-sphere' (Chichilnisky and Heal, 2000) in the 'financialisation' of nature (Sullivan, 2012) co-opts the *all hazards* logic of resilient disaster management to embed positive *economic* growth as a positive adaptation from exposure to disorderly crises or disaster events. A counter-weight to this analysis can be offered through the UK experience, showing that the re-emergence of resilience in disaster policy did not ignore the divide between security threats and ecological or technological disasters, but, rather, was driven by comprehensive capability development across all hazards (Coaffee *et al.*, 2009; Rogers, 2012). A more important separation overlooked by this America-centric reading is that of organisational and community forms of resilience, which may more effectively reflect the neoliberalisation of resilience (Rogers, 2015). A deeper look at the development of resilience in practice through the UK experience shows the genealogy of practice to be much clearer, but one must go back to the emergence of the emergency management trade and work up to the emergence of resilience in this context to draw out the nuances of this process more clearly.

The primary responsibility for civil defence in the UK was military until after World War I. The first statutory responsibilities given to civil government agencies were embedded in the Air Raid Precautions Act of 1937, updated by the Civil Defence Act of 1948, which in turn gave only a broad obligation for planning to continue essential services during a time of war. This followed the prevailing logic emerging from the pressures of World War II, which required stringent limits on military spending. The resultant policy shift moved responsibility away from a militarised defence model to the Civil Defence Corps and an Auxiliary Fire Service – civilian and volunteer-based agencies. Higher standards of training and professionalisation saw, on the one hand, the logic move from the prevention of nuclear attack to the mitigation of recovery and support for the survivors. With the change in government came a change in policy. The then Labour government reduced spending on militarised defence further and upgraded investment and planning for domestic services in casualty prevention, sheltering and dispersal. Further economic pressure saw both organisations shifted to a 'care and maintenance' basis, before officially closing in 1968, with retention of the Warning and Monitoring Organisation (tracking fallout from nuclear events). Despite the 1971 Home Defence Review strongly suggesting that militarised defences should not be completely abandoned, the incumbent Conservative government were far more concerned with internal security threats from the Irish Republican Army (IRA), internal industrial relations and the domestic disasters arising from public order incidents, industrial accidents and transport related-events.[3] However this was more often than not driven by the perceived need to respond to specific events at the local level (Alexander, 2002, p. 209–210).

The nuclear threat was not gone, far from it. As the posturing of East–West remained a key feature of the international relations of the day – from the 1979 Iranian revolution – the 1980 election of Ronald Reagan and the invasion of Afghanistan by the Soviets all put pressure on 'defence'. Despite such pressures, a more passive approach was maintained, signposting the shift

17

from a Cold War 'civil defence' footing to peacetime 'civil protection'. The public were educated through 'protect and survive' propaganda during the 1970s, but the primary drivers of policy in the 1980s were internal threats, aligned with economic and industrial pressures of critical infrastructure privatisation by the Thatcher government.[4] Responsibility for the management of disasters moved from the military to the emergency services (divided by police, fire and ambulance as 'blue light agencies') and, due to funding restrictions and reluctance to expand civil government roles, was relegated to a back-office function of local authorities (Rockett, 1994).

Despite flaws in the lack of a comprehensive or unified response across diverse local contexts, the system was seen as largely 'fit-for-purpose'. In the UK, a review was being undertaken as early as 1990, but little was expected and there were no significant outcomes from the work. Between 2000 and 2005, this was shown to be mistaken through a string of cross-regional and international emergency crises, which stimulated a new interest through a comprehensive 'capabilities review' of those agencies tasked with responding to disaster events. As a result of this review, civil *defence* and civil *protection* were conceptually conflated into a sense of civil *contingencies* for which we needed to be prepared. The organisational capabilities for dealing with disaster were rigorously reviewed and improved to enhance the social or 'civilisational' capacity to learn from the mistakes that had been made in mitigating the fuel protests (e.g. blockades of oil refineries, go-slow convoys on motorways), the outbreak of foot and mouth disease (e.g. controlling access to affected areas and disposal of carcasses) and a number of serious flooding incidents (e.g. inadequate infrastructural defences and poor public awareness of flood plains). Furthermore, the speed of this review and the seriousness of central government attention harnessed this stimulus from the broader range of anthropogenic *risks* (man-made ecological or industrial dangers as well as those arising from social disorder) and natural ecological *hazards* (fire, flood, tsunami, volcano, earthquake) alongside the emerging *threat* of terrorism raised by the attacks on the USA in September 2001. The term 'resilience' remerged within the civil contingencies review, and the eventual Civil Contingencies Act 2004, as an umbrella within which all of the required changes to emergency management could be implemented. The policy metaphor of being more resilient was also presented politically as a means of empowering local responders, whilst also providing opportunities to attempt restructuring, imposing economies of scale on a number of key agencies – with varying degrees of success (Rogers, 2011). As investment in regional and national coordination of best practice increased, the capability to prepare for, mitigate and respond to dangerous events of a larger scale has also increased, though this is not always sustained beyond the review and implementation of change – as seen in the UK abolition of regional government offices where resilience teams were housed in the first decade of the twenty-first century. Resilience during this period was repackaged again, becoming a way to bring together multi-agency collaborations that could *mitigate the impact* of disastrous events, addressing the need to maintain *robust functions* in critical infrastructure, social order and everyday life and to shorten the *duration of perturbation* to a minimum as a kind of 'bounce-back ability', with both a sharing of responsibility for preparedness between citizen and state and an implied, but often not well documented, shared learning from the vulnerabilities identified during a crisis, often referred to as 'bouncing-forwards' (Siambabala *et al.*, 2011).

At this point the polysemic overlap and lexical ambiguities of resilience began to undermine the strength of the emergent metaphor. Disaster sciences and socio-ecological research were clearly reconnecting with the neoliberalising governance of security and disaster through integrated emergency management (IEM), a condition that enhanced the critique of neoliberalisation through resilience. This is quite true where resilience has been operationalised from the 'top-down' through hierarchical and paramilitary organisational structures it encourages passing responsibility to citizens and the creation of resilient subjects.[5] This aligns particularly well with the logic of neoliberal governance. On the other hand, where resilience has been implemented as participatory or collaborative practice through flattened, horizontal networks it offers opportunities for counter-neoliberalisation through the empowerment of citizens within their locale. The emergent metaphor was, for a time, used as a catch-all phrase for the coordination and implementation of the Civil Contingencies Act 2004 (Coaffee *et al.*, 2009), blurring bounce-back ability with a sense of learning from exposure and, where possible, pre-emptive actions enabled by rigorous risk assessment and the creation of risk registers used to prioritise action across locales and regions for Category 1 responders (civil government and 'blue light' agencies) and Category 2 responders (utilities operators, NGOs and a range of other partners in private sector, health or environmental services).[6] As such, different organisations saw resilience building in subtly different ways, leading to different types of policy experiments and funded projects, with different measurements, outcomes and outputs. This in turn has encouraged commentators to call for more developed research on the standards underpinning this emerging policy metaphor (Perry and Lindell, 2003; Alexander, 2005; McConnell, 2003), as well as widespread cynicism of the terms as an emergent form of neoliberalism (Joseph, 2013; Tierny, 2015).

In practice, the step change in modelling of these approaches has followed a roughly similar trajectory in most Western nations but has been institutionalised in different models of practice through diverse political and organisational contexts in each nation-state. Examples of these might include comprehensive crisis management, disaster risk reduction, integrated emergency management and civil contingencies, though resilience is often a common feature of the policy vernacular. Often first to be actioned as a discrete area of policy and practice enhancement, or process improvement, is *risk*, informing the drive towards comprehensive identification and assessment strategies, aligned with the *typology* and *taxonomy* of specific disaster agents (e.g. fire, flood, pandemic) and a scale of potential impact (e.g. local, regional, national). Such strategies allow for a better understanding amongst policy-makers and front-line practitioners of what vulnerabilities are most severe, what needs to be done to 'fill the gaps' in preparedness and who has the capability to deliver on particular aspects of service in a complex multi-agency organisational system as well as across the public and private aspects of critical infrastructure (transport, utilities etc.). As time has gone by, resilience has increasingly spread into other spheres of influence. Discussion of resilience in relation to global policy platforms, such as the sustainable development goals, Habitat III and the New Urban Agenda are only going to increase; however, which form of resilience will emerge from the complex overlap of contested polysemic meanings remains uncertain.

Emerging challenges

The change discussed above documents the broad trajectory of an ongoing transformation, which makes the understanding of resilience a challenge. It is a moving target. It means different things to different people depending on the context within which it is encountered. The etymology offered above traces the underpinning meaning of resilience through language to a rough genealogical appraisal of research; this offers a theoretically informed understanding of the term itself, but not much insight into how it has been used. To address this gap a genealogy of civil defence, from civil protection to civil contingencies applied the emergent polysemic overlap of the concept to resilient ways of thinking, doing and acting out, by showing how different stakeholders have approached the strategic coordination of best practice, in emergency management in particular. Significant improvements in the coordination of risk management sit at the forefront of change. The prevalence of risk management and business continuity as features of everyday organisations are exemplified in the statutory adoption of ISO31000 standards for risk management in all agencies that have a stake in critical infrastructure, from telephone and post to utilities and food supply chains, and further in the development of TC223 standards for 'societal security' now emerging to benchmark emergency management and business continuity practices (Rogers, 2013). The awareness of flexible capabilities that can be mobilised across scales (national, regional, local) have also been rolled out in tandem with the comprehensive mapping and categorisation of dangers, the prioritisation of key vulnerabilities thus identified and the comprehensive planning, testing and exercising of emergency procedures and protocols in table-top scenarios and field exercises. Such change is thus not revolution, but refinement of existing expertise and broadening of the emergency planning agenda into everyday aspects of governance, as well as those centrally tied to what we might previously have thought of as a potential disaster. By building multi-organisational capacity one can increase the resilience to particular dangers in a targeted manner, thus improving societal security as a whole. The categorisation of anthropogenic risks (both human and technological), ecological hazards and security threats creates an 'all hazards' approach to danger as a complex system with resilience to that danger as a pervasive and persuasive justification for change, though much of that change has unseen ramifications at this point.

The optimistic view of change is one that sees the empowerment of local agencies through consultation and the creation of typologies that increase ownership of danger across scales. This draws most heavily on the socio-ecological and psychological framings of resilience, but is increasingly ambiguous in terms of the strategies, tactics and mechanisms by which it is implemented in different contexts or particular policy experiments.[7] A range of tools are being brought forward that try to identify, assess and characterise risk to better understand the potential impact of an event, both the immediate sharp shock (such as flood, fire, bomb) as well as longer-term dangers (from climate change, to sustainable development to ideologies of terrorism).[8] Much of this work emphasises the identification of vulnerabilities in systems, structures, policies and practices and using this knowledge to prioritise work-streams that will allow for mitigation of the risk before the event happens through flexible and adaptive ways of working. This represents a conceptual shift in thinking about disaster from the previous defence and protection model that increases the importance of *pre-emptive* measures above and beyond the need for robust response and recovery mechanisms. It also integrates recovery and the need to identify and learn from the fragility of failures exposed during a crisis event. A stage of review and quality management of the improvement process has begun to feature more heavily in the re-assessment of risk after the fact, creating effectively a continuous loop of information for analysis, but not always embedding the lessons learned in the governance logic itself. Importantly, none of these areas of work are isolated; they cross over and inform each other across all agencies and all hazards, creating a far more comprehensive and integrated system of emergency management within a framework of organisational resilience. As Gordon (2009) has stated:

> These tools can be helpful in deepening understanding of scenarios that have unfolded. The tools can be helpful in spurring imagination concerning possible scenarios that could unfold. The tools can aid those in positions of responsibility act in ways that are far more proactive and realistic than in the past, particularly as regards catastrophic and other unprecedented events.

A more cynical view of change might see a darker side to resilience. It is possible for the broadening of the emergency planning agenda to have a knock-on effect on the relationship between the citizen and the state. Multi-agency stakeholder networks may dramatically improve the quality and flow of communication between the civil and private sectors, as well as the inter-operability and resilience of best practice; however the general public are often relegated to a largely passive role. As the passive recipients of warning and informing information, the public are not directly consulted or engaged; rather, governance fulfils its obligation to protect by providing generic information on dangers. Increasingly, the shift towards community resilience of this model seeks to engage insurance companies and critical infrastructure providers on the behalf of citizens without incorporating the citizens themselves into the process. Hard to reach members of the community, such as the young, the old and the disabled, are present in planning but absent from consultation, and competing discourses of community to some extent undermine the utility of the concept in policy circles.

Where this has been incorporated into policy, *community* resilience tends towards the enforcement of individual responsibility that follows from a minimal warning and informing of risk. This reality contrasts sharply with the implication of a policy rhetoric that suggests rather than delivers a meaningful engagement with the existing capacity of individuals in a given locale. Though increasing, this is beginning to change as the metaphor of resilience is bedded down and becomes more nuanced. Other concerns of governmentality frame the engagement with community as an attempt to manipulate agency by designing out the options for certain forms of conduct, whether through Crime Prevention Through Environmental Design approaches or increased visible and invisible forms of architectural security – enforcing certain types of actions and uses of the urban environment. The context of the encounter and the underlying assumptions drawn from polysemic overlap and lexical ambiguity are difficult to resolve. Thus what resilience, who benefits from change, what kind of change and how this informs the nature of intervention, empowerment, coordination and so on affect the variation of resilience being mobilised in each case.

Conclusions

This chapter sets up the etymological meaning of resilience as a generative metaphor that fed twentieth-century research paradigms. This is then applied to policy so that the polysemy of meaning can be drawn through disaster governance; this genealogical method draws metaphor into the practical institutionalisation of resilience in policy through the changing organisational frameworks used to implement it in practice, using the UK as a prime exemplar. It is important to note that disaster resilience in particular is not a product of the Cold War, nor of the ways in which security and emergency have been rethought since the high-profile disasters occurring in the first few years of the twenty-first century; it has a longer genealogical ancestry in the seventeenth and eighteenth century before its emergence in twentieth-century research and policy. Each of these incarnations offers particular overlapping polysemic re-assemblages, evoking elements of rebound, elasticity, resistance, adaptation or the transformative potential of resilience to differing degrees.

There is no one emergent metaphor of resilience, rather many encounters with particular configurations or assemblages. These appear in the 'politics of catastrophe' (Aradau and Munster, 2011), in the 'everyday life of resilience' (Coaffee *et al.*, 2009) and in the bio-politics of critical infrastructure and security (Lundborg and Vaughan-Williams, 2011) – also elsewhere – but as we see more fields begin to adopt a resilience metaphor more variations will continue to emerge, reconstituting the trajectory of meaning in new ways. Whilst this chapter has not interrogated these trends exhaustively, it is hoped that by linking general language meanings to the applied research and resultant policy interventions one can show the complexity and reflexivity required when encountering resilience. The etymological and genealogical framing of the concept does not universalise the term; rather, by embracing the roots of the metaphor as repercussive and elastic one highlights the linearity of engineering logics in contrast to the dynamics of more social science-oriented and socio-ecological approaches. The particular characteristics of each assemblage create an 'interplay', through which meanings are mobilised by particular coalitions of actors within a specific frame of reference. This complexity allows resilience to be deployed in different ways to achieve different goals – an institution of modernity with multiple interpretations – so the 'rules of the game' are in flux. These treatments vary by degree rather than by type, and embracing the full adaptive and transformative potential of the concept requires a fine-grain contextualisation of the terms' use *in situ* through the diverse policy experiments where resilience has been made manifest. Broad-brush, uncritical and schematic applications of a universal resilience metaphor actually limit our ability to understand the complex interplay of ideas at work, whereas an understanding that embraces the polysemic overlap and permeable re-assemblage of resilience in a contextually embedded way enhances the conceptual utility of resilience in the future. It is important to note that categorisation is a means not an end; characteristics are more useful than categories. Complexity becomes a prerequisite of any attempt to map patterns of resilience, which are often limited themselves by the context within which they are deployed. Perhaps the biggest challenge for those seeking to use the resilience concept is to avoid becoming trapped in the effort to establish one particular dominant meaning, and allowing the flexibility of polysemy to continue creating opportunities for thinking, doing, and acting differently as we stumble on through an age of uncertainty.

Notes

1 Here I am invoking the idea of assemblage as explored by Deleuze and Guattari, (1987).
2 Here I refer to the process of neoliberalisation and its alternatives discussed in depth by Brenner *et al.* (2010).
3 1985 – Fire at Bradford FC Football Stadium (50 fatalities, 300 injuries), Fire on Aircraft at Manchester Airport (54 fatalities); 1987 – Fire at Kings Cross underground station (31 fatalities), Severe Storms (21 fatalities), Ferry *Herald of Free Enterprise* capsizes (193 dead); 1988 – *Piper Alpha* oil rig explosion (167 fatalities), Clapham rail crash (32 fatalities, 120 injuries), airplane terrorist attack and Lockerbie plane crash (259 fatalities on plane, 11 fatalities on the ground); 1989 – Kegworth plane crash (47 fatalities, 79 injuries), Hillsborough football stadium riot (95 fatalities, approx. 700+ injuries).
4 See for example the Control of Industrial Major Accidents Hazards Regulations 1982, 1983 Civil Defence Regulations, and the Civil Protection in Peacetime Bill 1986.
5 See for example Reid (2012).
6 The import of the rise to prominence of metaphorical 'resilience' is particularly important to emergency management (henceforth EM) (O'Brien and Reid, 2005) and raises issues in thinking on civil contingencies (McConnell and Drennan, 2006; Boin and McConnell, 2007).
7 Examples of case studies and other research projects which address this can be found elsewhere in this volume.
8 For an interesting take on the politics of climate change and resilience see Knight-Lenihan (2015).

Bibliography

Alexander, D. (2002) From civil defence to civil protection – and back again. *Disaster Prevention and Management*, 11 (3), 209–213.

Alexander, D. (2005) Towards the development of a standard in emergency planning. *Disaster Prevention and Management*, 14 (2), 158–175.

Aradau, C. and van Munster, R. (2011) *Politics of Catastrophe: Genealogies of the Unknown*. London: Routledge.

Aradau, C., Lobo-Guerrero, L. and van Munster, R. (2006) Security, technologies of risk, and the political: guest editors' introduction. *Security Dialogue*, 39 (2–3), 147–154.

Attorney Generals Department (2010) *Critical Infrastructure Resilience Strategy*. Canberra: Attorney Generals Department.

Attorney Generals Department (2011) *National Disaster Resilience Strategy*. Canberra: Attorney Generals Department.

Bacon, F. (1659) *Sylva Sylvarum, or, A Natural History in Ten Centuries*. London: William Lee.

Beck, U. (1999) *World Risk Society*. London: Polity Press.

Blount, T. (1656) *Glossographia, or, A Dictionary Interpreting all Such Hard Words of Whatsoever Language Now Used in our Refined English tongue* (published 1661).

Boin, A. and McConnell, A. (2007) Preparing for critical infrastructure breakdowns: the limits of crisis management and the need for resilience. *Journal of Contingencies and Crisis Management*, 15 (1), 50–59.

Bonanno, G. A. (2005) Resilience in the face of potential trauma. *Current Directions in Psychological Science*, 14 (3), 135–138.

Brenner, N., Peck, J. and Theodore, N. (2010) After neoliberalization? *Globalizations*, 7 (3), 327–345.

Cabinet Office (2010) Community resilience. Available at: www.cabinetoffice.gov.uk/ (accessed on 23 September 2011).

Cash, D. W. and Moser, S. C. (2000) Linking global and local scales: designing dynamic assessment and management processes. *Global Environmental Change*, 10, 109–120.

Chichilnisky, G. and Heal, G. (2000) Securitizing the biosphere. In Chichilnisky, G. and Heal, G. (eds) *Environmental Markets, Equity and Efficiency*. New York: Columbia University Press, pp. 169–179.

Coaffee, J., Murakami-Wood, D. F. J. and Rogers, P. (2009) *The Everyday Resilience of the City: How Cities Respond to Terrorism and Disaster*. London: Palgrave Macmillan.

Comfort, L. K., Sungu, Y., Johnson, D. and Dunn, M. (2001) Complex systems in crisis: anticipation and resilience in dynamic environments. *Journal of Contingencies and Crisis Management*, 9 (3), 144–158.

Comfort, L. K., Boin, A. and Demchak, C. C. (2010) *Designing Resilience: Preparing for Extreme Events*. Pittsburgh: University of Pittsburgh Press.

Comfort, L. K., Oh, N., Ertan, G. and Schneider, S. (2010) Designing adaptive systems for disaster mitigation and response: the role of structure. In Comfort, L. K., Boin, A. and Demchak, C. C. *Designing Resilience: Preparing for Extreme Events*. Pittsburgh: University of Pittsburgh Press, pp. 33–62.

Council of Australian Governments (2009) *National Disaster Resilience Statement*. Canberra: COAG.

Cronstedt, M. (2002) Prevention, preparedness, response and recovery: an outdated concept? *Australian Journal of Emergency Management*, 17 (2), 10–13.

Deleuze, G. and Guattari, F. (1987) *A Thousand Plateaus: Capitalism and Schizophrenia*, Minnesota: Minnesota University Press.

Emergency Management Australia (2011) *Natural Disaster Relief and Recovery Arrangements: Determination 2011 (Version 1)*, Canberra: Department of the Attorney General.

Garmezy, N. (1971) Vulnerability research and the issue of primary prevention. *American Journal of Orthopsychiatry*, 41 (1), 101–116.

Garmezy, N. (1973) Competence and adaptation in adult schizophrenic patients and children at risk. In Dean, S. R. (ed.), *Schizophrenia: The First Ten Dean Award Lectures*. New York: MSS Information Corp., pp. 163–204.

Gordon, P. (2009) Some conceptual tools for understanding and addressing catastrophic challenges as well as other lesser emergencies. Available at: http://users.rcn.com/pgordon/homeland/conceptual09.htm (accessed on 15 January 2011).

Graham, S. (2010) *Cities Under Siege: The New Military Urbanism*. London: Verso.

Gunderson, L. H. (2000) Resilience in theory and practice. *Annual Review of Ecology and Systematics*, 31, 425–439.

Gunderson, L. H. and Holling, C. S. (eds) (2002) *Panarchy*. Washington: Island Press.

Holling, C. S. (1973) Resilience and stability of ecological systems' *Annual Review of Ecology and Systematics*, 4, 1–23.

Huggins, L. J. (2007) *Comprehensive Disaster Management and Development: The Role of Geoinformatics and Geo-collaboration in Linking Mitigation and Disaster Recovery in the Eastern Caribbean*. ProQuest. University of Pittsburgh, USA.

International Standards Organisation (2011) Available at: www.iso.org/ (accessed on 21 May 2011).

International Standards Organizations (2009) *ISO 31000: 2009 – Risk Management – Principles and Guidelines*. ISO: Geneva.

Joseph, J. (2013) Resilience as embedded neoliberalism: a governmentality approach. *Resilience*, 1.1 (2013), 38–52.

Klien, R. J. T., Nicholls, R. J. and Thomalla, F. (2003) Resilience to natural hazards: how useful is this concept? *Global Environmental Change: PART B: Environmental Hazards*, 5 (1–2), 35–45.

Knight-Lenihan, S. (2015) Benefit cost analysis, resilience and climate change. *Climate Policy*, 1–15.

Lundborg, T. and Vaughan-Williams, N. (2011) 'Resilience, critical infrastructure, and molecular security: the excess of 'life' in biopolitics. *International Political Sociology*, 50, 367–383.

McConnell, A. (2003) Overview: crisis management, influences, responses and evaluation. *Parliamentary Affairs*, 56, 393–409.

McConnell, A. and Drennan, L. (2006) Mission impossible? Planning and preparing for crisis. *Journal of Contingencies and Crisis Management*, 14 (2), 59–70.

Masten, A. S., Best, K. M., and Garmezy, N. (1990) Resilience and development: contributions from the study of children who overcome adversity. *Development and Psychopathology*, 2 (4), 425–444.

Masten, A. S. and Coatsworth, J. D. (1995) Competence, resilience, and psychopathology. In Cicchetti, D. and Cohen, D. J. (eds) *Developmental Psychopathology, Vol. 2: Risk, Disorder, and Adaptation, Wiley Series on Personality Processes*. Oxford: John Wiley & Sons, pp. 715–752.

Masten, A. S. and Obradovic, J. (2008) Disaster preparation and recovery: lessons from research on resilience in human development. *Ecology and Society*, 13 (1), 9. Available at: www.ecologyandsociety.org/vol13/iss1/art9/ (accessed on 13 July 2011).

Mozley, T. (1882) *Reminiscences: Chiefly of Oriel College and the Oxford Movement*, London: Longmans Green.

O'Brien, G. and Reid, P. (2005) The future of UK emergency management: new wine, old skin? *Disaster Prevention and Management*, 14 (3), 353–361.

O'Malley, P. (2000). Uncertain subjects: risks, liberalism and contract. *Economy & Society*, 29 (4), 460–484.

O'Malley, P. (2010) Resilient subjects: uncertainty, welfare and liberalism. *Economy & Society*, 29 (4), 488–509.

Paton, D. and Johnston, D. (eds) (2006) *Disaster Resilience: An Integrated Approach*, Springfield: Charles C. Thomas.

Perry, R. W. and Lindell, M. K. (2003) Preparedness for emergency response: guidelines for the emergency planning process. *Disasters*, 27 (4), 336–350.

Reid, J. (2012) The neoliberal subject: resilience and the art of living dangerously. *Revista Pléyade*, 10, 143–165.

Rockett, J. P. (1994) A constructive critique of United Kingdom emergency planning. *Disaster Prevention and Management*, 3 (1), 47–60.

Rogers, P. (2011) Resilience and civil contingencies: tensions in northeast and northwest UK (2000–2008). *Journal of Policing, Intelligence and Counter Terrorism*, 6 (2), 91–107.

Rogers, P. (2012) *Resilience & the City: Change, (Dis)order and Disaster*. London: Ashgate Publishing Ltd.

Rogers, P. (2013) The rigidity trap in global resilience: neoliberalisation through principles, standards, and benchmarks. *Globalizations*, 10 (3), 383–395.

Rogers, P. (2015) Researching resilience: Aan agenda for change. *Resilience: International Journal of Policy and Practice*, 3 (1), 55–71.

Rudd, K. (2008) *The First National Security Statement to the Parliament: Address by the Prime Minister of Australia The Hon. Kevin Rudd MP*, 4 December 2008. Available at: https://pmtranscripts.dpmc.gov.au/release/transcript-16289 (accessed on 14 July 2016).

Schrader-Frechette, K. S. and McCoy, E. D. (1993) *Method in Ecology*. London: Cambridge University Press.

Sheffi, Y. (2005) *The Resilient Enterprise: Overcoming Vulnerability for Competitive Advantage*. New Cambridge: MIT Press.

Siambabala, B. M., O'Brien, G., O'Keefe, P. and Rose, J. (2011) Disaster resilience: a bounce back or bounce forward ability? *Local Environment*, 16 (5), 417–424.

Smith, J. F. and Howitt, W. (1864) *John Cassell's Illustrated History of England: The Text, to the Reign of Edward I*. London: Cassell, Petter & Galpin.

Smith, R. (2008) Summary and conclusions: report of the review of Homeland and Border Security. Available at: http://parlinfo.aph.gov.au/parlInfo/search/display/display.w3p;query=Id%3A%22library%2Flcatalog%2F00160884%22 (accessed on 14 July 2016).

Sullivan, S. (2012) Banking nature? The spectacular financialisation of environmental conservation. *Antipode*, 45 (1), 198–217.

Thompson, J. (2011) [1887] *Collected Papers in Physics and Engineering*. London: Nabu Press.

Tierney, K. (2015) Resilience and the neoliberal project discourses, critiques, practices—and Katrina. *American Behavioral Scientist*, 1327–1342.

Tredgold, T. (1818) On the transverse strength and resilience of timber. *Philosophical Magazine Series*, 51 (239) xxxvii.

Tredgold, T. (1824) *Practical Essay on the Strength of Cast Iron and Other Metals*. London: J. Weale.

Young, T. (1807) *A Course of Lectures on the Natural Philosophy and the Mechanical Arts*. London: Taylor and Walton.

Walker, B., Holling, C. S., Carpenter, S. R. and Kinzig, A. (2004) Resilience, adaptability and transformability in social–ecological systems. *Ecology and Society*, 9 (2), 5. Available at: www.ecologyandsociety.org/vol9/iss2/art5 (accessed on 14 July 2016).

Walker, J. and Cooper, M. (2010) Genealogies of resilience: from systems ecology to the political economy of crisis adaptation. *Security Dialogue*, 42 (2), 143–160.

Wildavsky, A. (1984) *Trial without error: anticipation versus resilience as strategies for risk reduction*. Centre for independent Studies, Occasional papers: no. 13.

Wildavsky, A. (1988) *Searching for Safety (Studies in Social Philosophy & Policy)*. New York: Transaction Publishers.

Zebrowski, C. (2009) Governing the network society: a biopolitical critique of resilience. *Political Perspectives*, 3 (1), 1–38. Available at: www.politicalperspectives.org.uk/wp-content/uploads/2010/08/Vol3-1-2009-4.pdf (accessed on 20 September 2011).

3

RESILIENCE, SECURITY AND WORLD POLITICS

Philippe Bourbeau

Introduction

In recent years, a great deal has been written in the scholarly literature about the role of resilience in our social world. This scholarship has sparked vivid theoretical debates in psychology, criminology, social work and political geography about the nature of resilience and how scholars should go about studying it. Resilience is increasingly making its entries into international studies literature, shaped by these discussions. Several factors have contributed to the specificity of these debates in the international field: the infancy of the resilience research programme; the mistaken belief that some international studies scholars have 'invented' a new concept; the relative scarcity of empirical research applied specifically to the international sphere; and the perennial question of what resilience is actually about. This chapter provides a brief introduction to how the concept of resilience has been defined and deployed within social sciences, suggests a particular definition of resilience and outlines a terrain of debate and research agendas.

The first section of this chapter provides a brief introduction to how the concept of resilience has been defined and deployed within social sciences. While recognizing the importance of these contributions, I argue that they all share elements that are problematic in a study about the relationship between resilience and world politics: they fail to take into account the negative aspect of resilience and the multi-scalar dimension of resilience. In the second section, I seek to bolster research on resilience by suggesting a particular definition. In the third section, I outline a terrain of debate between resilience and current international issues including the question of change and continuity, interdisciplinary dialogue, critical junctures and the notion of progress.

Resilience in social sciences

Resilience is a concept that cuts across several disciplines. Psychology, ecology, criminology, engineering sciences, human resources studies, nursing, organizational studies, computer science, and social work have all either tackled, debunked, measured, employed, studied, tested, hypothesized or criticized resilience (Luthans 2002; Ollier-Malaterre 2010; Anaut 2005; Bruneau *et al.* 2003).

Psychologists, criminologists and social workers have been studying and theorizing resilience for a longer time than international relations scholars (Garmezy 1974; Rutter 1987). One of the main elements in this scholarship is the notion of 'bouncing back'. After all, the English word 'resilience' originated in the sixteenth and seventeenth centuries, deriving from the verb *resile*, which in turn was drawn from the Latin verb *resilire*, meaning to 'jump back, recoil'. Thus, the ability to recover from or adjust easily to misfortune, adversity, unease, conflict, failure, and/or change is central (Seery *et al.* 2010). A large strand of this scholarship aimed at uncovering the internal and external resilient qualities that help people to bounce back and to adapt positively in the face of profound adversity – that is, adaptation that is substantially better than would have been expected given the circumstances (Hauser 1999; Donnon and Hammond 2007; Bonanno 2004). A special issue of the *American Psychologist* seeking to identify and describe resilient qualities (such as happiness, optimism, wisdom, creativity, etc.) illustrates this line of research nicely (Seligman and Csikszentmihalyi 2000).

Wanting to move away from a conception of resilience as a set of dispositional qualities or protective mechanisms of the individual, several criminologists and social workers have proposed instead to 'de-individualize' resilience and to see it as a process (Rumgay 2004; Gilgun 2005; Seccombe 2002; Norris *et al.* 2008). As such, the definition of resilience was slightly modified to 'a dynamic process encompassing positive adaptation within the context of significant adversity' (Luthar *et al.* 2000: 543, see also Masten and Powell 2003). Resilience is therefore seen not as a set of predetermined qualities that an individual possesses (or not), but as a temporally and con- textually informed process (Ronel and Elisha 2011; Ungar 2004, 2011; Schoon 2006).

The fields of political geography and environmental studies have also been dynamic in studying resilience, albeit from a different angle. A large strand of literature employs resilience to analyse how co-evolving societies and natural/ecological systems can cope with, and develop from, disturbances. Stemming from the ecological sciences, this scholarship seeks to address persistence and change in ecosystems (Carpenter *et al.* 2001; Holling 1996; Gunderson 2000), socio-ecological systems (Berkes *et al.* 2003, Walker *et al.* 2006), and in terms of the impacts of natural hazards (Zhou *et al.* 2010; Cutter 2008; Klein *et al.* 2003; Renaud *et al.* 2010). Environmental change and particularly changes of environmental regime have been under- standably a central focus of attention (Young 2010; Duit *et al.* 2010).

This literature has provided several perspectives on resilience and, in spite of the fact that there appears to be no consensus on how resilience should be theorized, three main currents have emerged: engineering resilience, ecological resilience, and socio-ecological resilience. Engineering resilience is associated with the concept of equilibrium and is about studying the conditions specifying how far a system can be displaced from a fixed point of equilibrium and still return to that equilibrium once the disturbance has passed. Ecological resilience some- what moves away from the idea of equilibrium and is defined as the capacity of a system to experience disturbance and still maintain its ongoing functions and controls. In the words of one of the most important advocates, ecological resilience determines the persistence of relationships within a system and is a measure of the ability of these systems to absorb changes and still persist (Holling 1973). Unsatisfied with these perspectives, scholars have come up with 'social- ecological resilience' to emphasize that the delineation between social and ecological systems is, in fact, artificial and arbitrary. These scholars have transformed research on resilience by arguing that the focus of resilience is not only on being robust to disturbance but also on the opportunities that emerge, in terms of self-reorganization, recombination, and the emergence of new trajec- tories (Walker and Meyers 2004; Folke 2006; Berkes and Folke 1998).

These definitions share two elements that are problematic for the transference of resilience thinking to the study of world politics. First, they start with the premise that the disturbance (or the shock) is inherently negative and that resilience is about positive adjustment. There is indeed a large acceptance in this literature that resilience is good and thus must be promoted. This might simply be a disciplinary bias, as resilience is often employed to describe the capacity to react to sexual abuse, terrorist attacks or disturbances of global ecological systems. Being resilient in the face of such trauma is unequivocally a positive adaptation. Notwithstanding, resilience defined as positive adaptation eschews that resilience has a dark side, especially in societal terms. Resilience is not always a desirable feature of social, political or economic life. Being resilient might, in fact, mean being an obstacle to positive change in some cases. I am not arguing that one should find a way to interpret terrorist attacks in large cities as positive policy. However, I do argue that there might be good reasons for wanting to transform a social structure, a given situation, a regime, a norm, an economic system of exploitation, etc. and that being resilient to these changes could be considered as negative. Displaying an a priori normative bias seems rather limiting here, as adjustment may be both positive and negative. Approaches to resilience should be able to theorize situations in which endogenous or exogenous shocks could be seen as positive and in which a resilient strategy could be understood as negative.

The second element that these models have in common is their tendency to understand resilience in a binary way. Resilience is usually seen as an all-or-nothing concept: either there is resilience or there is not. One direct consequence of this is that the notion of a scalar under-standing of resilience is either under-theorized or entirely lacking in some cases. Just as there is a scale of securitization (Bourbeau 2011), there is a scale of resilience. Another consequence of treating resilience in a binary way is that it eschews the question of types of resilience. This is problematic because it creates a disconnection – in theoretical and empirical terms – between the complexity of contemporary world politics and the analytical framework proposed to make sense of the different patterns of response that world politics brings.

Definition and typology

With the limits of these definitions in mind, I suggest an alternative conceptualization of resilience as the process of patterned adjustments adopted by a society or an individual in the face of endogenous or exogenous shocks (Bourbeau 2013b, 2015).

This position has multiple advantages. First, it obviously moves away from a conception of social equilibrium; it rids resilience of the assumption of a return to equilibrium. Indeed, the underlying model of change in engineering resilience (and resilience as positive adaptation) is of a system in equilibrium disturbed by exogenous forces. In contrast, the approach adopted here underscores that the sources of change may be endogenous or exogenous and that the outcome of change is not necessarily a return to a previous equilibrium. Instead of returning to some prior equilibrium, societies often make adjustments that are best understood as moves to maintain their compatibility with the social construction of their particular collective identity and changing circumstances. Resilience is thereby grasped as an inherently dynamic and complex process.

Second, while resilience involves disturbances and adaptation, this position permits an understanding of disturbances and adjustments as differing from context to context, from culture to culture, and from individual to individual. Resilience can refer to how well a society is nav-igating through some past adversity such as 9/11 (retrospective), how successfully a society is navigating through some current adversity (concurrent), or the likelihood that a society will successfully navigate through disturbance in the future (prospective). In addition it should be noted that a society may be able to respond with resilience to a particular type of adversity (terrorist attacks) but not to another (rise in urban criminality), or at one time in its history (during the Cold War) but not in another (in a post-Cold War era).

A third, and crucial, advantage of this position is that it accepts that disturbances or shocks are interpretative moments. Disturbances do not objectively exist out there waiting to exercise influence. Endogenous or exogenous shocks rarely speak for themselves in the social world.

Agents have to interpret shock as being a security threat or a disturbance for that shock to become a security threat. The meaning of an event as a disturbance is often a social construction involving multiple directionality and constant interactions between agential powers and the social structure. Contrary to Leach *et al.* (2010), who argue that scholars focusing on resilience have so far failed to recognize that how resilience is evaluated depends on context and perspective, I argue that if resilience is about anything, it is about context and perspective. For some scholars, this is what makes resilience a useless approach. Fully accepting the importance of contextuality does in fact render difficult – if not impossible – the development of a comprehensive theory of resilience, applicable across cases and time. Yet, for those inclined to fully accept the complexity of the social world and the inherent limits that this complexity imposes on our knowledge, this is what makes resilience an especially stimulating approach. A context-informed resilience stimulates a richer dialogue between ideas and evidence.

Inspired by Stephen Dovers and John Handmer's typology (1992), I further propose to identify three types of resilience. Indeed, I distinguish between resilience as Maintenance, resilience as Marginality, and resilience as Renewal – in short the 'MMR' typology.

The first type – resilience as Maintenance – is characterized by adaptation in which resources and energy will be expended in maintaining the status quo. The importance and saliency (and 'threat-ness') of the problem will often be exaggerated in order to better justify the necessity to implement measures to uphold the status quo against changes provoked by the events. Re-affirmation of the value, benefit and importance of the status quo will be made on several occasions. A society relying strongly on this type of resilience will deal with endogenous and exogenous shocks with rigidity and will underscore the potentially negative transformative consequences brought about by these events. Disturbances or shocks are not by definition problematic or negative; they will be socially constructed as being threatening and dangerous by dominant discourses. Although the possibility that a disconnection between security discourses and security practices exists, resilience as maintenance will often see an alignment of discourse and practices. Rhetorical and discursive powers will be deployed to portray the event as a significant threat and security practices will also be either implemented or strengthened as a response.

The second type – resilience as Marginality – is characterized by responses that bring changes at the margins but that do not challenge the basis of a policy (or a society). Resilience as marginality implies responding within the boundaries of the current policy, norm and/or social structure. The nature and importance of the 'problem' will often be presented as being less salient than with the first type of resilience, but an effort to acknowledge the issue and to recognize that marginal adjustment is needed will be made. There is a danger that the minor changes implemented may delay the major changes that some may argue are required. There is also the possibility that the marginal adjustments made at one point in time (and thought of as being marginal at that time) become extremely important and influential at another point in time (and thus are not seen as marginal anymore). This type of resilience will often see a disconnection between security discourses and security practices. In some cases, discursive powers will be almost absent and marginal changes in security practices will take place. In other cases, security practices will mostly remain the same but a shift in discourse and how the event is discursively represented will constitute the source of marginal, yet important adjustments. As such, studies emphasizing the role of security practices might reveal different patterns of responses than a focus on speech and discourses – and vice versa.

The third type – resilience as Renewal – is characterized by responses that transform basic policy assumptions and, thus, potentially remodel social structures. Resilience as renewal implies introducing novel vectors of response that will (in an implicit or explicit way) fundamentally change existing policies and set new directions for governance in this field. Redefinitions, however, do not take place in a vacuum but draw on past experiences, collective memory and social history, as well as the windows of opportunity upon which agential powers decide to act (or not) (Bourbeau 2011; 2014a). As with resilience as maintenance, the importance of the disturbance (or the shock) may often be exaggerated, but unlike the objectives of the first type of resilience, which seek to maintain the status quo, the goal here is to present the option of renewal as inescapable. The disturbance has such profound ramifications that substantial reorganization of the policy is strongly desired. Redefinition often involves important shifts in interpretation and meaning, in agents' power relations, as well as in institutional and organizational configurations. The particular social mechanisms by which redefinition and renewal are carried through are multiple and could include analytic deliberation, nesting strategies, institutional variety, etc. (Dietz *et al.* 2003). This is not to argue that everything would be created anew after a disturbance, as if events and agency were unfolding in a social vacuum. Yet, resilience as renewal means that disturbances would play a triggering role in a sustained and systematic effort to change profoundly a given policy or how a society understands and interprets a particular set of issues.

These types are not mutually exclusive and they can be found in the same society diachronically and synchronically. Furthermore, a society can adopt one type of resilience in one domain and another type of resilience in another domain. By definition, resilience as maintenance is no more normatively negative or positive than resilience as renewal; as such, there is no normative continuum that starts with maintenance and ends with renewal.

The added value of resilience

Elsewhere, I have argued that the premises of resilience are threefold: (1) that resilience has a dark and a bright side, (2) that knowledge about resilience is contingent, and (3) that resilience is a socio-historically informed, dynamic and varied process (Bourbeau, 2015). Understanding resilience as a process of patterned adjustments adopted by a society, a group, or an individual in the face of endogenous or exogenous shocks and postulating the three premises aforementioned offer many kinds of added value and shed a new light on contemporary international politics. In what follows, I take a few steps in suggesting ways of broadening and deepening research agendas around issues of change and continuity in international studies, interdisciplinary dialogue, critical junctures and progress.

Issues of change and continuity in international studies

A focus on resilience can enlighten us about vectors of change and continuity in world politics, particularly as a complement to the recent focus on 'practices' in International Relations (IR) and on the new institutionalism in political science (Pouliot 2008; Hopf 2010, 2013; Neumann 2002; Adler and Pouliot 2011a; Mahoney and Thelen 2010b; Thelen 2003; Pierson and Skocpol 2002; Hall and Taylor 1996). While there is a large consensus, among 'practices' scholars and others, about the usefulness of a practices approach to explain continuity in world politics, important disagreements exist about the effectiveness of this approach in tackling the notion of change. For some, a practices approach is particularly well placed to tackle the issue of change, since 'change, not stability, is the ordinary condition of social life. . . . Stability, in other words, is an illusion created by the recursive nature of practice' (Adler and Pouliot 2011b, p. 18). For others, a practices approach makes a strong case for the enduring characteristics of the social world, but a considerably weaker case for the prevalence of change and critical junctures (Hopf 2010). Friendly critics further contend that the analysis of practices, as it is currently organized and applied, not only falls short of offering satisfying ways of theorizing change in international politics but also – and perhaps more importantly – 'generates an exaggerated sense of stability and can obscure both the social processes that generate change and the inherent instability of practices themselves' (Duvall and Chowdhury 2011, p. 337). Notwithstanding these 'in-house' disagreements, the fact remains that a practices approach has so far offered few guiding principles to distinguish practices relating to change from those related to continuity, or to make sense of key moments of change in world politics, where actors step out of boundaries and transcend the field of action in which they are normally engaged.

This is where an emphasis on resilience is particularly useful. Resilience offers anchoring devices through which practices inducing change can be discerned and distinguished from practices inducing continuity. In fact, research on resilience has already started to make inroads into these questions. Jon Coaffee and David Murakami Wood (2006) have shown that a focus on resilience allows for a revised understanding of changes in the regulation of urban order. Resilience offers one way of reconstituting change over time, space and place in order to better understand the social and practices patterns that (re)constitute everyday life and bring 'security home'. In the field of international intervention, David Chandler has recently argued that it is because the discursive power of human security stems from its articulation with the resilience paradigm, (which stresses in this field of research a programme of empowerment and capacity-building) that we are better able to grasp the recent change in dominant security discourses and practices, i.e. away from the liberal internationalist framework and towards a growing emphasis on preventive intervention (Chandler 2012, 2015).

A focus on resilience can also nicely complement a practice perspective in attempting to explain continuity in world politics. For instance, I have shown that the resilient pattern of adjustment chosen by dominant narratives in France to the so-called worldwide refugee crisis of the early 1990s led to both the diversion of detention centres from their original purposes and the re-employment of the security practice of detaining migrants in order to fight the perceived existential threat of international migration (Bourbeau 2013b; 2014b). Resilient strategies and security practices were thus employed to fight the security threat that international migration represented to France's collective identity, and were used to uphold the status quo against changes provoked by international migration. Seen in this light, detention centres for migrants are part of the state's security practice and resilience strategy, and have undergone an evolving relationship with the social forces currently at play in France.

A focus on resilience can also be very useful in explaining the endurance of institutions and regimes. It can show that, on some occasions, what seems to be an idiosyncratic institutional reproduction is, in fact, a culturally embedded pattern of adjustment to endogenous or exogenous shocks. While rationalist explanations for continuity mainly emphasize the maximization of benefit and the obtained Pareto-optimal equilibrium, a focus on resilience as a tool of explanation provides an informative alternative approach. A resilience-based analysis taps into sociological institutionalist explanations, focusing on the institutional practices, cultural frameworks and 'social resources' available to individuals and/or societies at a given point in time (Hall 2010). Jane Jenson and Ron Levi (2013) demonstrate that the international human rights regime and the social rights regime were able to endure in the face of massive pressure from neoliberalism mainly because advocates of these regimes exploited neoliberalism's ideas for their own purposes. Jenson and Levi argue that one vector explaining the continuity of these two regimes is the fact that actors within these regimes adjusted 'their practices and discourse to the changing political context in contingent fashion' (Jenson and Levi 2013, p. 71). Some variation occurred across both regimes, although adjustments in the human rights regime were less significant than in the social rights regime. Nevertheless, both these regimes maintained essential elements while actively building new approaches to social resilience along dimensions that mapped onto the prevailing political and cultural narratives of the neoliberal era.

Interdisciplinary dialogue

Resilience is an interdisciplinary bridge builder. Research into the interconnections between International Relations and other disciplines such as psychology, political geography, criminology, and urban studies should be further encouraged, both in theoretical and empirical terms. An excellent example here is Peter A. Hall and Michèle Lamont's edited volume *Social Resilience in the Neoliberal Era* (2013), which brings together an epidemiologist, political scientists, sociologists, public health specialists and psychologists. A quick look at the editorial board of the new journal, *Resilience: International Policies, Practices and Discourses*, which includes IR scholars, economists, sociologists, political geographers and urban scholars, is also indicative of the interdisciplinary nature of resilience.

The relationship between resilience and the political psychology 'turn' in IR is obvious. A number of scholars have recently emphasized the role of psychology in world politics (Mercer 2013; Rathbun 2011; Hymans 2006; Ned Lebow 2008; Fattah and Fierke 2009; McDermott *et al.* 2011; Krebs and Rapport 2012). A focus on resilience contributes to this growing area of research in several ways. A first option is to treat resilience as a psychological quality of an individual or a society. As discussed above, much of the early application of resilience in contemporary world politics followed this line of thought. Another option – the one preferred here – is to highlight the psychological underpinnings of political acts and decisions while underscoring the social, historical and psychological embeddedness of individuals and society. Notably, resilience speaks to the strand of foreign policy literature that focuses on cognition and prospect theory, by further explaining the social mechanisms by which individuals and societies seek to maintain the consistency of their 'belief systems' against novel and sometimes discrepant information as well as their tendency to organize issues around a reference point and consider options from that vantage (Levy 1997; McDermott 2004; Mercer 2005; Hudson 2005; Mintz 2004). In this way, a focus on resilience not only enhances our understanding of our multifaceted and emotionally driven social world, but also provides further ammunition to those seeking to underscore the limits of the rational choice model in the field of decision policy making.

The field of international political geography, and particularly the literature on environmental resources and climate change, is also a logical place to develop our interdisciplinary understanding of resilience. In these circles, discussions have mainly focused on the robustness of the resilience paradigm in the so-called social-ecological systems theory (Folke 2006; Berkes *et al.* 2003). Some have sought to connect this theory with the literature on IR regimes. Oran Young (2010), for example, argues that the social-ecological systems theory yields important insights that advance our understanding of state changes in environmental and resource regimes, in terms of incremental changes that actually reinforce status-quo resilient mechanisms of these regimes as well as in terms of non-linear and abrupt changes. However, critical voices have gained considerable traction of late. Mark Pelling and David Manuel-Navarrete seek to uncover the potential bias in the theory of status-quo preservation; together, they move the literature several steps forward by analysing the transformation that induces resilience and by including a wider understanding of social and political life (Pelling and Manuel-Navarrete 2011; Pelling 2010). Nevertheless, to date, the literature on social-ecological systems has remained relatively untouched by current theorization of resilience in IR. Undoubtedly, further investigating the interconnections and applications of these standpoints on resilience will significantly enhance our understanding of the sources and implications of resilience.

Critical junctures

Most studies of resilience start with the identification of what is sometimes called a 'critical juncture'. Commonly defined as 'choice points that put countries (or other units) onto paths of development that track certain outcomes – as opposed to others – and that cannot be easily broken or reversed' (Mahoney 2001, p. 7), critical junctures are slowly making their way from comparative politics (Collier and Collier 1991; Capoccia and Keleman 2007; Katznelson 2003; Mahoney and Thelen 2010a) to IR scholarship (Fioretos 2011; Bourbeau 2011, 2013a). Recent scholarship has pushed the theorization of critical junctures a few steps further. For instance, Hillel Soifer (2012) proposes to distinguish between two types of causal conditions at work during a critical juncture: permissive conditions, which refer to the easing of the constraints of structure to make change possible, and productive conditions, which, in the presence of a permissive condition, produce the outcome and ensure its reproduction. If Soifer (2012, p. 1582) is right that (1) 'the absence of the permissive condition is itself sufficient to determine the absence of change', and (2) 'even when the permissive condition is present, the absence of the productive condition is also sufficient to determine the absence of change', resilience studies will have to spell out in a more detailed and theorized fashion the conditions enabling and constraining resilience strategies. Further developing the theorization of resilience in connection with Soifer's arguments should be seen as a stimulating challenge, and advocates of a resilience approach should squarely engage with it.

Another fruitful way to strengthen the critical juncture component of resilience research would be to juxtapose it with the postcolonial perspective, and in particular with this perspective's focus on 'encounter'. In her study of norm-compliance in International Relations, Zarakol (2011) interprets the encounter between the 'East' and the 'West' as a constitutive moment that shaped power relations in a decisive and enduring way. The focus on encounter is crucial, explains Zarakol, following Goffman (1963), because it creates and establishes a stigma that individuals and groups have to cope with. Comparatively analysing how Turkey, Japan and Russia dealt with the trauma of loss of empire, she points out that dominant narratives in these countries saw their relationship with the 'West' sometimes as a weakness that needed to be overcome and sometimes as a blessing that needed to be exploited. The encounter is here understood as the key moment creating a condition that, in turn, leads to a process of formation of collective identity that is rather difficult to transform or reverse. The field of resilience studies has thus a unique opportunity to strengthen one of its components by bolstering and facilitating a dialogue with a diverse array of scholarly approaches, including comparative politics and the postcolonial perspective.

Progress

The focus on resilience speaks to the idea of progress. Some scholars who borrow from the psychological definition of resilience as 'positive adaptation' tend to argue, directly or indirectly, that resilience is a successful and progressive strategy. In his account of how two French labour organizations adjusted to the neoliberalization of the labour regime, Ancelovici (2013) argues that two pathways were available to these organizations: a successful one leading to resilience, and a less-successful one leading to stagnation. Along the same lines, one of the forms of resilience that Bouchard (2013, p. 267) identifies in his analysis of Québec society's response to neoliberalism is 'progressive resilience', by which he means that the society managed to 'reinvent [it]self through major innovations and progressive changes' – in other words, the psychologists' axiom of 'doing better than expected'. Other scholars have presented a radically sceptical view of the progressive nature of resilience (Evans and Reid 2013; Joseph 2013), while I have proposed a middle-ground position, arguing that resilience possesses both a dark and a bright side (Bourbeau 2013b). In the end, this is exactly the sort of friendly disagreement that will enliven further research on resilience.

Conclusion

This chapter has sought to deepen our understanding of the various meanings and practices that can be attached to resilience in different socio-cultural contexts. In doing so, I have (1) briefly traced the evolution of the definition of resilience; (2) put forward an alternative definition; and (3) outlined a terrain of debate.

Leaving aside both the exhilaration and the lambasting that has arisen concerning resilience, the fact remains that the emergence of resilience in the field of world politics constitutes an invitation for scholars to critically examine our social world. Resilience holds a great deal of potential for renewing and broadening the global governance research agenda. Moving beyond an understanding of resilience as a set of qualities that an individual possesses or as a process of positive adaptation in the face of threats, the threefold type of resilience presented here helps in analysing the constant and complex interplay between persistence and change, reproduction and transformation. It also provides one among several arenas for generating integrative and inter-disciplinary collaboration on issues of critical junctures, progress and interdisciplinary dialogue in the study of world politics.

Acknowledgements

I wish to thank David Chandler and Jon Coaffee for the invitation to participate in this Handbook. Some of the material presented has been revised and updated from Bourbeau, P. (2013) 'Resiliencism: premises and promises in securitization research'. *Resilience*, 1(1), 3–17. DOI: 10.1080/21693293.2013.765738.

References

Adler, E. and Pouliot, V. (eds) (2011a) *International Practices*. Cambridge: Cambridge University Press.
Adler, E. and Pouliot, V. (2011b) International practices. *International Theory*, 3(1), 1–36.
Anaut, M. (2005) Le concept de résilience et ses applications cliniques. *Recherche en soins infirmiers*, 82, 4–10.
Ancelovici, M. (2013) The origins and dynamics of organizational resilience. A comparative study of two French labor organizations. In P. A. Hall and M. Lamont, *Social Resilience in the Neoliberal Era*. Cambridge: Cambridge University Press, pp. 346–375.
Berkes, F., Colding, J. and Folke, C. (eds) (2003) *Navigating Social-ecological Systems: Building Resilience for Complexity and Change*. Cambridge: Cambridge University Press.
Berkes, F. and Folke, C. (eds) (1998) *Linking Social and Ecological Systems: Management and Practices and Social Mechanisms*. Cambridge: Cambridge University Press.
Bonanno, G. A. (2004) Loss, trauma, and human resilience. Have we underestimated the human capacity to thrive after extremely aversive events? *American Psychologist*, 59(1), 20–28.
Bouchard, G. (2013) Neoliberalism in Québec. The response of a small nation under pressure. In P. A. Hall and M. Lamont, *Social Resilience in the Neoliberal Era*. Cambridge: Cambridge University Press, pp. 267–292.
Bourbeau, P. (2011) *The Securitization of Migration. A Study of Movement and Order*. London: Routledge.
Bourbeau, P. (2013a) Politisation et sécuritisation des migrations internationales: Une relation à définir. *Critique internationale*, 61(4), 125–146.
Bourbeau, P. (2013b) Resiliencism: premises and promises in securitization research. *Resilience: International Policies, Practices and Discourses*, 1(1), 3–17.

Bourbeau, P. (2014a) Moving forward together: logics of the securitization process. *Millennium: Journal of International Studies*, 43(1), 187–206.

Bourbeau, P. (2014b) Resiliencism and security studies: initiating a dialogue. In T. Balzacq, *Contesting Security: Strategies and Logics*. London, Routledge, pp. 173–188.

Bourbeau, P. (2015) Resilience and international politics: premises, debates and agenda. *International Studies Review*, 17(3), 374–395.

Bruneau, M., Chang, S., Eguchi, R., Lee, G., O'Rourke, T., Reinhorn, A., Shinozuka, M., Tierney, K., Wallace, W. and von Winterfeldt, D. (2003) A framework to quantitatively assess and enhance the seismic resilience of communities. *Earthquake Spectra*, 19(4), 733–752.

Capoccia, G. and Keleman, D. (2007) The study of critical junctures: theory, narrative and counterfactuals in historical institutionalism. *World Politics*, 59(3), 341–369.

Carpenter, S. R., Walker, B., Anderies, J. and Abel, N. (2001) From metaphor to measurement: resilience of what to what? *Ecosystems*, 4, 765–781.

Chandler, D. (2012) Resilience and human security: the post-interventionist paradigm. *Security Dialogue*, 43(3), 213–229.

Chandler, D. (2015) Resilience and the 'everyday': beyond the paradox of 'liberal peace'. *Review of International Studies*, 41(1), 27–48.

Coaffee, J. and Murakami Wood, D. (2006) Security is coming home: rethinking scale and constructing resilience in the global urban response to terrorist risk. *International Relations*, 20(4), 503–517.

Collier, R. B. and Collier, D. (1991) *Shaping the Political Arena: Critical Junctures, the Labor Movement, and Regime Dynamics in Latin America*. Princeton: Princeton University Press.

Cutter, S. L. (2008) A place-based model for understanding community resilience to natural disasters. *Global Environmental Change*, 18, 598–606.

Dietz, T., Ostrom, E. and Stern, P. C. (2003) The struggle to govern the commons. *Science*, 302(5652), 1907–1912.

Donnon, T. and Hammond, W. (2007) Understanding the relationships between resiliency and bullying in adolescence. *Child and Adolescent Psychiatric Clinics of North America*, 16, 449–472.

Dovers, S. R. and Handmer, J. W. (1992) Uncertainty, sustainability and change. *Global Environmental Change*, 2(4), 262–276.

Duit, A., Galaza, V., Eckerberga, K. and Ebbesson, J. (2010) Governance, complexity, and resilience. *Global Environmental Change*, 20, 363–368.

Duvall, R. D. and Chowdhury, A. (2011) Practices of theory. In E. Adler and V. Pouliot, *International Practices*. Cambridge: Cambridge University Press, pp. 335–354.

Evans, B. and Reid, J. (2013) Dangerously exposed: the life and death of the resilient subject. *Resilience: International Policies, Practices and Discourses*, 1(2), 1–16.

Fattah, K. and Fierke, K. (2009) A clash of emotions: the politics of humiliation and political violence in the Middle East. *European Journal of International Relations*, 15(1), 67–93.

Fioretos, O. (2011) Historical institutionalism in international relations. *International Organization*, 65(2), 367–399.

Folke, C. (2006) Resilience: the emergence of a perspective for social-ecological systems analyses. *Global Environmental Change*, 16, 253–267.

Garmezy, N. (1974) The study of competence in children at risk for severe psychopathology. In E. J. Anthony and C. Koupernik, *The Child in his Family: Children at Psychiatric Risk: III*. New York: Wiley.

Gilgun, J. F. (2005) Evidence-based practice, descriptive research and the resilience-schema-gender-brain functioning assessment. *British Journal of Social Work*, 35(6), 843–862.

Goffman, E. (1963) *Stigma: Notes on the Management of Spoiled Identity*. New York: Simon & Schuster.

Gunderson, L. H. (2000) Ecological Resilience – in theory and application. *Annual Review of Ecology and Systematics*, 31, 425–439.

Hall, P. A. (2010) Historical institutionalism in rationalist and sociological perspective. In J. Mahoney and K. Thelen (eds), *Explaining Institutional Change. Ambiguity, Agency and Power*. Cambridge, Cambridge University Press, pp. 204–224.

Hall, P. A. and Lamont, M. (2013) *Social Resilience in the Neoliberal Era*. Cambridge: Cambridge University Press.

Hall, P. A. and Taylor, R. (1996) Political science and the three 'new institutionalisms'. *Political Studies*, 44(5), 936–957.

Hauser, S. (1999) Understanding resilient outcomes: adolescent lives across time and generations. *Journal of Research on Adolescence*, 9(1), 1–24.

Holling, C. S. (1973) Resilience and stability of ecological systems. *Annual Review of Ecology and Systematics*, 4, 1–23.

Holling, C. S. (1996) Engineering resilience versus ecological resilience. In P. Schulze (ed), *Engineering within Ecological Constraints*. Washington, DC: National Academy Press, pp. 31–44.

Hopf, T. (2010) The logic of habit in international relations. *European Journal of International Relations*, 16(4), 539–561.

Hopf, T. (2013) Common-sense constructivism and hegemony in world politics. *International Organization*, 67(2), 317–354.

Hudson, V. M. (2005) Foreign policy analysis: actor-specific theory and the ground of international relations. *Foreign Policy Analysis*, 1(1), 1–30.

Hymans, J. E. (2006) *The Psychology of Nuclear Proliferation: Identity, Emotions, and Foreign Policy*. Cambridge: Cambridge University Press.

Jenson, J. and Levi, R. (2013) Narratives and regimes of social and human rights: the Jackpines of the neoliberal era. In P. A. Hall and M. Lamont, *Social Resilience in the Neoliberal Era*. Cambridge: Cambridge University Press.

Joseph, J. (2013) Resilience as embedded neoliberalism: a governmentality approach. *Resilience: International Policies, Practices and Discourses*, 1(1), 38–52.

Katznelson, I. (2003) Periodization and preferences. In J. Mahoney and D. Rueschemeyer (eds), *Comparative Historical Analysis in the Social Sciences*. Cambridge: Cambridge University Press pp. 270–303.

Klein, R., Nicholls, R. J. and Thomalla, F. (2003) Resilience to natural hazards: how useful is this concept? *Environmental Hazards*, 5, 35–45.

Krebs, R. R. and Rapport, A. (2012) International relations and the psychology of time horizons. *International Studies Quarterly*, 56(3), 530–543.

Leach, M., Scoones, I. and Stirling, A. (2010) Governing epidemics in an age of complexity: narratives, politics and pathways to sustainability. *Global Environmental Change*, 20, 369–377.

Levy, J. S. (1997) Prospect theory, rational choice, and international relations. *International Studies Quarterly*, 41(1), 87–112.

Luthans, F. (2002) The need for and meaning of positive organizational behavior. *Journal of Organizational Behavior*, 23(6), 695–706.

Luthar, S. S., Cicchetti, D. and Becker, B. (2000) The Construct of Resilience: A critical evaluation and guidelines for future work. *Child Development*, 71(3), 573–562.

McDermott, R. (2004) Prospect theory in political science: gains and losses from the first decade. *Political Psychology*, 25(2), 289–312.

McDermott, R., Wernimont, N. and Koopman, C. (2011) Applying psychology to international studies: challenges and opportunities in examining traumatic stress. *International Studies Perspectives*, 12(2), 119–135.

Mahoney, J. (2001) *The Legacies of Liberalism: Path Dependence and Political Regimes in Central America*. Baltimore: Johns Hopkins University Press.

Mahoney, J. and Thelen, K. (eds) (2010a) *Explaining Institutional Change: Ambiguity, Agency, and Power*. Cambridge: Cambridge University Press.

Mahoney, J. and Thelen, K. (2010b) A theory of gradual institutional change. In J. Mahoney and K. Thelen (eds), *Explaining Institutional Change: Ambiguity, Agency, and Power*. Cambridge: Cambridge University Press.

Masten, A. S. and Powell, J. L. (2003) A resilience framework for research, policy and practice. In S. S. Luthar (ed), *Resilience and Vulnerability: Adaptation in the Context of Childhood Adversities*. Cambridge: Cambridge University Press, pp. 1–27.

Mercer, J. (2005) Prospect theory and political science. *Annual Review of Political Science*, 8(1), 1–21.

Mercer, J. (2013) Emotion and strategy in the Korean War. *International Organization*, 67(2), 221–252.

Mintz, A. (2004) How do leaders make decisions? A poliheuristic perspective. *Journal of Conflict Resolution*, 48(1), 3–13.

Ned Lebow, R. (2008) *A Cultural Theory of International Relations*. Cambridge: Cambridge University Press.

Neumann, I. B. (2002) Returning practices to the linguistic turn: the case of diplomacy. *Millennium: Journal of International Studies*, 31(3), 627–651.

Norris, F. H., Stevens, S. P., Pfefferbaum, B., Wyche, K. F. and Pfefferbaum, R. L. (2008) Community resilience as a metaphor, theory, set of capacities, and strategy for disaster readiness. *American Journal of Community Psychology*, 41, 127–150.

Ollier-Malaterre, A. (2010) Contributions of work-life and resilience initiatives to the individual/organization relationship. *Human Relations*, 63(1), 41–62.

Pelling, M. (2010) *Adaptation to Climate Change: From Resilience to Transformation*. London: Routledge.

Pelling, M. and Manuel-Navarrete, D. (2011) From resilience to transformation: the adaptive cycle in two Mexican urban centers. *Ecology and Society*, 16(2), 11.

Pierson, P. and Skocpol, T. (2002) Historical institutionalism in contemporary political science. In I. Katznelson and H. V. Miller (eds), *Political Science: The State of the Discipline*. New York: Norton.

Pouliot, V. (2008) The logic of practicality: a theory of practice of security communities. *International Organization*, 62(2), 257–288.

Rathbun, B. C. (2011) Before hegemony: generalized trust and the creation and design of international security organizations. *International Organization*, 65(2), 243–273.

Renaud, F. G., Birkman, J., Damm, M. and Gallopin, G. C. (2010) Understanding multiple thresholds of coupled social-ecological systems exposed to natural hazards as external shocks. *Natural Hazards*, 55(3), 749–763.

Ronel, N. and Elisha, E. (2011) A different perspective: introducing positive criminology. *International Journal of Offender Therapy and Comparative Criminology*, 55(2), 305–325.

Rumgay, J. (2004) Scripts for safer survival: pathways out of female crime. *Howard Journal*, 43, 405–419.

Rutter, M. (1987) Psychosocial resilience and protective mechanisms. *American Journal of Orthopsychiatry*, 57, 316–331.

Schoon, I. (2006) *Risk and Resilience: Adaptations in Changing Times*. Cambridge: Cambridge University Press.

Seccombe, K. (2002) 'Beating the odds' versus 'changing the odds': poverty, resilience, and family policy. *Journal of Marriage and Family*, 64(2), 384–394.

Seery, M. D., Holman, A. E. and Silver, R. C. (2010) Whatever does not kill us: cumulative lifetime adversity, vulnerability, and resilience. *Journal of Personality and Social Psychology*, 99(6), 1025–1041.

Seligman, M. and Csikszentmihalyi, M. (2000) Positive psychology: an introduction. *American Psychologist*, 55(1), 5–14.

Soifer, H. D. (2012) The causal logic of critical junctures. *Comparative Political Studies*, 45(12), 1572–1597.

Thelen, K. A. (2003) How institutions evolve. In J. Mahoney and D. Rueschemeyer (eds), *Comparative Historical Analysis in Social Science*. Cambridge: Cambridge University Press.

Ungar, M. (2004) A constructionist discourse on resilience. *Youth & Society*, 35(3), 341–365.

Ungar, M. (2011) The social ecology of resilience: addressing contextual and cultural ambiguity of a nascent construct. *American Journal of Orthopsychiatry*, 81(1), 1–17.

Walker, B. H. and Meyers, J. A. (2004) Thresholds in ecological and socio-ecological systems: a developing database. *Ecology and Society*, 9(2), 3.

Walker, B. H., Anderies, J. M., Kinzig, A. P. and Ryan, P. (2006) Exploring resilience in social-ecological systems through comparative studies and theory development: introduction to the special issue. *Ecology and Society*, 11(1), 12.

Young, O. R. (2010) Institutional dynamics: resilience, vulnerability and adaptation in environmental and resource regimes. *Global Environmental Change*, 20, 378–385.

Zarakol, A. (2011) *After Defeat: How the East Learned to Live with the West*. Cambridge: Cambridge University Press.

Zhou, H., Wang, J., Wan, J. and Jia, H. (2010) Resilience to natural hazards: a geographic perspective. *Natural Hazards*, 53(1), 21–41.

4

MAKING RESILIENCE STRANGE

Ontological politics in a 'time of crisis'

Samuel Randalls and Stephanie Simon

Introduction: resilience in a time of crisis

Our analysis is concerned with the multiplicity of resilience. We trace the concept across ecology and security, through to surgery, management and psychology. In doing so we argue that resilience can only be interrogated politically at its moments of articulation where the ontological politics, norms, values and changes in practices envisaged are named and, often, obscured. Rather than either take resilience to be a determinedly new shift in policy-making or simply an empty signifier, our analysis focuses on the different ways resilience arguments are made to enable, justify and legitimate changes in behaviours and practices that often invoke competing and contradictory visions of the good life to be lived and the bad life or death to be avoided. Armed with an array of diverse examples, the chapter makes resilience 'strange' in a Foucauldian sense and interrogates the ontological politics of resiliences, exposing common points of tension that highlight embedded political commitments.

The proliferation of resilience-speak is closely tied to the idea that we now live in a 'time of crisis'. Crisis is interpreted broadly across many domains in which the resilience ideal appears – in ecology it could refer to disturbances in a social-ecological system producing a systemic 'flip' in which a new field of attractors is established; in psychology it could refer to a traumatic experience that an individual cannot efficiently absorb, but rather pushes them into new, possibly destructive behavioural paths. Across its multiple manifestations, resilience has come to stand for the ability to absorb, withstand, persist and maybe even thrive and reorganise in the face of the shocks and disturbances of always uncertain becoming, that is now even 'more so'. It is difficult to find writings on resilience that do not in some way reference contemporary ecological, financial, political or security crises or the contingencies and anxieties of 'uncertain times'. Resilience is offered as *the solution* to incredibly challenging societal problems. Wendy Larner (2011) has critically explored the 'time of crisis' narrative in relation to qualitative changes under neoliberalism and urges that even as we must be critical of totalising neoliberal and crisis narratives that claim uniqueness and novelty, we must attend to the ways in which contemporary crisis narratives are rearranging political forms and relations, or assemblages: 'the widespread identification of crisis . . . means that existing governmental and political forms are losing their coherence and effectiveness and that new forms of understanding and acting are being invented' (2011, p. 329; see also Neocleous, 2012; Swyngedouw, 2010). In this sense, resilience-as-solution narratives work to organise, align and shape relations.

Resilience interventions also re-make connections to the future, yet retreat into the future too. Failure is remedied by greater resilience next time. This pursuit rearranges things in the present in the name of inevitable crises of the future. There is the gleaming promise of what the American Psychological Association (2008) calls the 'road to resilience' that suggests 'it' could be arrived at in the future, even while denying the possibility of completely 'having' or 'reaching' it. But can resilience be such a singular project, particularly if the road is not to a destination but to an ever-expanding horizon? What does this pursuit actually look like as it is deployed in diverse regimes, practices or assemblages? What 'new forms of acting and understanding' emerge in the name of resilience? And do these multiple enactments cohere as 'a road to resilience' ('a resilience project') or alternatively travel towards different, sometimes contradictory, and sometimes unsettling destinations?

Rather than reining in the concept of resilience and granting it a clear causal path of emergence, our analysis is inspired by the explosion of 'resilience' deployments. We are concerned with the multiplicity of resilience (as Anderson, 2015). There are multiple resilience conceptualisations and proliferating resilience assemblages. Within security, for example, there is no one security resilience: there are assemblages of resilience aimed at 'radicalising' youth; cyber systems; critical infrastructure, and so on. These have different geographies and temporalities; they have diverse effects and have different kinds of political implications. While some forms of resilience thinking mesh together, others conflict, meaning that the oft taken-for-granted *good* of resilience (everything that doesn't lead to death) is invoked in everything from psychology to counter-terrorism but recrafted in different ways.

Thus we wish to problematise and politicise resilience in ways that resonate across its multiple articulations and commitments. Resiliences 'that go by a single name' (Mol, 2002, p. 84) can be many different things, imagine many different futures, and inspire different interventions and, yet, are all drawn under the same banner. We thus argue that resilience is multiple. It is not a pre-given object but a generality with ontological flexibility, and we wish to grasp 'the coexistence of multiple entities that go by the same name' (Mol, 2002, p. 151). We seek to de-universalise notions of resilience, in order to expose it as a post-political term of art that has to be taken to task at its points of articulation. We maintain that the way in which resilience can be politicised is by forcing the question of its particulars at its points of articulation.

Conceptualising resilience multiple

Our rendering of 'resilience multiple' draws inspiration from Annemarie Mol's 'body multiple' (2002). In her ethnography of the disease atherosclerosis in a Dutch hospital, Mol details how the disease is enacted multiply in human and more-than-human ways, such as laboratory tests, clinical examinations, in genes, symptom reports, the embodied experience of patients and so on. Yet, multiple does not mean plural. As Mol writes, the body multiple is 'more than one, but not fragmented into being many' (2002, p. viii). The disease still 'hangs together' and is rendered actionable through 'forms of coordination' (2002, p. 55). Similarly, even as we argue that resilience is multiple, the 'assumption of singularity', how it hangs together amongst its many articulations, is important for how it does work, for its 'world-making effects' (Blaser, 2014, p. 54). Translating Mol's analysis of the enactment of a disease in one site to our analysis of a concept so widely wielded and dispersed, we might ask: what is the assumption of singularity in uses of resilience, how does it 'hang together' and what does this enact? We argue that resiliences hang together precisely through the generalisability and flexibility of 'resilience', which names a positive future, or desirable conditions of possibility, but does not necessarily have to actively name, promise or craft that positive future, as we elaborate below. As a 'bridging concept'

(Coaffee, 2006), resilience is offered as an organising principle and a solution that can bene-ficially connect whatever needs to be bridged across space and time. Its fundamental ambiguity stems from the fact that resilience is ultimately agnostic as to *what* it joins up, *where* it might span, *who* makes it so, *how* it might get there and *why* this is good. Through resilience generality, 'fragments of a large number of possible orders glitter separately' (Foucault, 2002, p. xix), are made potential, precisely *through* one and the same word.

Articulations of resiliences should not be seen as divorced from 'real' resilience to be found out there, say as an ecosystemic or psychological trait. Rather, these articulations make resilience what it is; they enact and grant capacities in different ways. Thus our purpose is to interrogate the ontological politics of resiliences. Ontological politics 'has to do with the way in which problems are framed, bodies are shaped, and lives are pushed and pulled into one shape or another' (Mol, 2002, p. viii). It has to do with the 'conditions of possibility', or the 'positivity', which give things their form and 'mode of being' (Foucault, 2002, p. 378). Put differently, John Law calls ontological politics: 'a politics about what there is in the world . . . what there might be in the world. An interference for the kinds of things that might exist in the world. Between the singular and the plural' (2002, p. 198). We engage with this question of interference between the singular generality of resilience and it's multiple, jostling articulations, which invoke quite different crisis politics and relations to the present and future, even as they are drawn under the same banner.

For example, consider two divergent understandings of resilience with regard to poverty. Writing about poverty amongst families, Karen Seccombe (2002) argues for understanding resilience in social and structural terms, whereby resilience to poverty should be facilitated through wealth redistribution and strong social welfare policies rather than through the study of individuals who are perceived as resilient in the face of poverty. In sharp contrast, the World Bank roots resilience to poverty in 'the rural poor', who bear the burden of developing resilience through enterprising activity (World Resources Report 2008). Or consider the divergent implications of resilience in ecological thought. While resilience has been deployed in social-ecological systems literatures as a critique of destructive resource management (Zimmerer, 2000), Phelan *et al.* (2013) argue that 'perverse resilience' can occur, for example, where a high carbon economy becomes locked in and generates its own forms of resilience that prevent more environmentally progressive policy outcomes. While there are differences in terms of the influence and reach of these different understandings, they illustrate the divergent political visions that resiliences enact.

In sketching out the ontological politics of resiliences in this 'time of crisis', we find inspiration in understandings of contemporary post-politics, which refers to a political condition defined by a lack of antagonism and, in its place, decision-making by consensus and technocratic management, and the assumed inevitability of existing capitalist relations. Post-politics takes the form of minor tweaks here and there from experts aimed at the administration of narrowly defined social matters, thus diminishing the demands, 'moments of openness', reversal, and fundamental antagonisms of the properly *political* (Žižek, 1999; 2001). Our purpose is not to simply name resilience post-political; rather we wish to draw out the productive elements these discussions provide for thinking through what resilience might or might not enact, particularly with regard to its generality and flexibility as a taken-for-granted good that does not have to name names or make promises.

In particular, we find two important lines of enquiry in Erik Swyngedouw's (2010) under-standing of post-politics. First, in reference to the 'apocalypse forever' of climate change post-politics, Swyngedouw finds a purely negative relation to the future:

> In contrast to other signifiers that signal a positively embodied content with respect to the future (like socialism, communism, liberalism), an ecologically and climatologically

different future world is only captured in its negativity; a pure negativity without promises of redemption, without a positive injunction that 'transcends'/sublimates negativity and without proper subject.

(2010, p. 224)

Resilience could be seen, in contrast, as a positive placeholder in relation to the future. We are not arguing that resilience is positive or that 'it' produces the secure relation it arouses, but that, politically, it resides in the empty space of this purely negative relation to the future that Swyngedouw describes. This is the irrefutability of resilience: who could argue against the desirability of 'being resilient'? It suggests a positive relation with the future with positive affects but it makes no demands or promises. Without the demand, 'nothing really has to change' (ibid., p. 223). This is the power of agnostic, general resilience – that it simultaneously names the 'cure' and names nothing substantial at all. Further, and in line with neoliberal resilience critiques discussed below, when it makes an appeal to the future that is rooted in the present, to minor tweaks and the 'administration of social matters' (Žižek, 1999, p. 199), its 'conditions of possibility' are located in maintaining the present condition, not in fundamentally changing existing frameworks. Thus, our concern for the 'singular' of resilience is that it arouses positive visions of the future and yet it makes no demands.

We would caution, however, against ending the story here: that 'resilience' (singular) simply reproduces the status quo or ultimately does nothing at all. 'Resilience' is multiply enacted – through widely different means and towards dramatically different ends – and this is the focus of our interrogation of ontological politics and interferences. This task is important because there is a tendency to reify resilience as, in particular, a neoliberal object, born out of and perpetuating neoliberal logics, conditions and relations (Walker and Cooper, 2011; Evans and Reid, 2014; Joseph, 2013). For example, Walker and Cooper (2011) trace resilience through the work of ecologist C. S. Holling and the uptake of complexity thinking in ecosystem science and place it in relation to contemporaneous Hayekian neoliberals' attention to irruptive and nonlinear dynamics of capital. Resilience is cast as a neoliberal term of art that buttresses a disavowal of any promise of societal security, devolution of responsibility to the individual, an ideal of self-organisation without intervention, normalisation of crisis and financialisation of moments of crisis as sites of capital accumulation. As Mackinnon and Derickson (2012: p. 254) put it: 'resilient spaces are precisely what capitalism needs—spaces that are periodically reinvented to meet the changing demands of capital accumulation in an increasingly globalised economy'. There is thus 'an intuitive ideological fit' between neoliberal philosophies and resilience logics (Walker and Cooper 2011, p. 144). This line of thought resonates with the post-politics of resilience in general, outlined above.

We do not disagree with this analysis, but we think it can give resilience a coherence that obscures the 'oscillation between singularity and multiplicity' (Law, 2002, p. 199) that is crucial for making resilience appear as an object (i.e. solution, natural trait, etc.). So our aim is not to refute these readings of neoliberal resilience, nor is it to rescue or recraft resilience for progressive ends. Rather, our aim in looking at resilience through its multiple and divergent articulations is to understand the difference that resiliences make in particular instances. The key moments lie in recognising the conditions of possibility that resilience articulations open up or foreclose; in interrogating its ontological politics at its points of articulation. We aim to show how and where resilience deployments name names – can be *made* to name names – by focusing on what we see as two key moments of tension and interference inherent in any appeal to resilience: its sitings or locations and the interventions that are meant to foster or create resilience. The following section draws out these two key tensions using examples from a variety of domains.

The ontological politics of resilience multiple: sitings and interventions

Sitings

Resilience has been described as a capability, quality, outcome, tool, ideological instrument, process, posture, and inherent property. In this section we argue that what 'resilience' *is*, is fundamentally tied to *where* it is said to be or come from, and, further, that these spatial ontologies of resilience are inherently linked to the conditions of political possibility of resiliences. As Mol emphasises, the 'question about *where* the options are is so relevant to ontological politics' (1999, p. 80).

In the case of resilience multiple, the issue of spatial ontologies is particularly important because articulations seem to suggest that what makes resilience, what it actually is, can be fashioned from almost any invocation of that which has survived or that is functioning or alive. This generality and its vague positive injunction, require denaturalisation. Consider, for example, Brian Walker's (2009) definition of resilience, where he discusses the ways in which trauma surgery is designed to move people from an indeterminate state of shock back towards life rather than death. He draws a dualistic life–death graphic on a whiteboard that represents how surgeons attempt to steer the body towards the life-pole, away from the waiting death-pole, by intervening with medical instruments, induced comas and so forth. The body's resilience is equated with survival and is proven through this trial. A failure to be resilient directly leads to death in this case.

A similar equation is found in the common tactic of using past traumas survived or the non-occurrence of crisis as 'evidence' of resilience. Psychiatrists Southwick and Charney (2012) study former prisoners of war and other individuals who survived trauma – individuals who were 'bent but not broken' – in order to make claims about the traits held by these purportedly biologically, psychologically, and socially resilient individuals – and how others might foster these same traits. In cybersecurity, that the Internet 'has not yet failed' is used as evidence of its resilience (ENISA, 2011). Past traumas survived or never realised are retrospectively or prospectively labelled as evidence of resilience. The non-resilient, the non-surviving, become the other through which resilience emerges – even those that live in arguably 'less resilient' ways are often granted the trait of resilience by surviving. If 'resilience' can be equated with anything that is functioning, then it is emptied of meaningful content. This is an important part of how its generality, its vague positive injunction, becomes productive, eliding over quite different commitments. Being attendant to the ways in which resilience is located or slides between locations, bares certain assumptions, options and possibilities of resiliences.

This question of spatial ontologies and their political effects is helpfully elaborated by considering Aranda *et al.*'s (2012) distinction between three common ontological orientations of resilience: found, made and unfinished. '*Resilience found*' locates resilience in inherent capacities of individuals or systems. In these articulations, the de facto good of resilience can be 'discovered,' as it is located a priori in the resilient subject. The most extreme examples of this locate resilience biologically or inherently, such as the growth of genetic resilience in disease treatment experimentation that suggests an inbuilt resilient trait. 'Found' framings are also evident in less overt articulations, such as encouraging indigenous groups to seek psychological connections, which 'allow communities to access the resilience of their ancestors' (Landau, 2007, p. 355). 'Found' resilience frameworks can work to reward those who 'possess' it, while also requiring strategies to cope with those less well endowed.

'*Resilience made*' is about practices rather than inherent properties; here, resilience is not discovered but nurtured (Aranda, *et al.* 2012). In 'made' framings, things and people can be made resilient through an engagement of environmental factors and hearts and minds. Consider, for example, the wealth of self-help websites geared toward fostering psychological resilience. 'MeQuilibrium' (n.d.) offers a self-help system to create internal fortitude to deal with life's little problems. 'The Climate Psychology Alliance' (n.d.) offers therapy for those struggling to become resilient to the mental anguish of a changing climate. 'Made' is also evident in the proliferating efforts to teach or train for resilience, particularly in security domains. For example, the FBI offers resilience lessons in the bureau's curriculum to teach and discipline the resilient subject through 'a training of the mind' (Larned, 2012). 'Made' suggests an active process of crafting and working toward resilience in relation to environmental factors, events, or stressors and variably assigns responsibility for obtaining it.

Aranda *et al.* (2012) argue that there is a third, more analytical resilience siting in play: '*resilience unfinished*'. This is a post-structural resilient subject, ambiguous, reflexive, and with an embodied and affective biography. The resilient subject is produced through a set of practices and behaviours, and is always already unfinished such that subjects embody, learn, instill, and generate resilience, however defined. We could think about, for example, how resilience discourses produce 'neurotic citizens' (Isin, 2004) or encourage us to focus on 'poor choice making' (Chandler, 2013); if becoming resilient is the imperative of our 'time of crisis', how can one know if one is resilient enough? Most importantly, this frame draws out the interminable horizon, the never-ending project of pursuing something called resilience.

Across domains, however, there is no *one* ontological siting. Rather, it can be variably named as found, made and unfinished. Consider for example, one of the author's test results for the 14-Item Resilience Scale™ test, which is actually used in academic psychology research. With a score of 68 out of a possible 98, part of the author's online test report stated, 'Your resilience level is on the low end but this doesn't mean you have zero resilience. Everyone is resilient to some degree.' The scale seems to be of several minds about the siting of resilience. It asks for gender, age and general health, which, along with the admission that 'everyone' is at least somewhat resilient, would seem to suggest 'found'. But it is centred on self-reported assessments of personality traits and how one might handle situations that could arise: asking how determined you are, if you believe in yourself and to what degree you 'usually manage one way or another'. This, coupled with the wealth of psychology research developing country-specific and culturally-specific versions of the test, seem to suggest 'made'. The entire enterprise, through which some psychologists identify incredibly broad self-reported traits as evidence of something called 'resilience', which is both possessed and cultivated through practice and mindfulness, demonstrates the 'unfinished' nature of it all.

A key moment in discerning the particular antagonisms and claims of resilience is to locate where it is said to reside and how it got there. For example, is it suggested that *humans* are resilient or that *some* humans are resilient (e.g. along geographic (Americans) or circumstantial ('the poor') lines). How did they come to be that way, were they born with it or did they learn to be resilient through trials, learning, necessity, or. . .? The answers to these kinds of questions offer moments of specificity for nailing down the ontological politics, demands and promises of resiliences. Who or what is asked to become resilient, who is deemed to 'be resilient', how did they obtain this, can others get it, who claims to 'give' it or teach it, and so on?

For instance, take the example of psychologist Michael Ungar's 'social ecology' approach to resilience (2011) in the case of childcare:

> One can hypothesize that if we grew the environment—for example, by providing well-subsidized quality public day care for all children under the age of 5—we could create the optimal conditions for more resilient children. . . . The day care, if culturally relevant, *potentiates* the development of resilience. Whether an individual child benefits

specifically is not the core issue; rather, the fact that the day care is there, and the possibilities for change it provides for working and socially isolated parents, creates a social ecology where more positive development can be expected.

(2011, p. 2)

Here, resilience does not reside, found or made, in day care spaces or in individual parents and children. Resilience is potentially enabled through socio-spatial relationality; it is a desired possibility that could only emerge from the production of spaces of positive development. It names the positive value: communal responsibility for and expectation of societal security and care. Further, it names how this positive value could be enabled: well-subsidised public day care. This example is somewhat rare in resilience parlance because it very openly bares its ontological locations and their political responsibilities and desired future. These elements are what must be uncovered by resilience critiques and openly articulated by those wishing to mobilise resilience politically.

Interventions

Cutting across resiliences from another angle, baring the different ways resilience might be created or fostered through interventions reveals multiple interferences and divergent political imaginations. This is again an issue of denaturalising resiliences, which is particularly important given the enduring impact of resilience conceptions drawn from ecologists such as C. S. Holling (1973), who argued that management plans focused on rigid *control* made ecosystems less resilient. Instead, he advocated adaptive management approaches that are flexible to changing circumstances and immanent properties of ecosystems, and that effectively learn by doing. If resilience is predominantly defined as an inherent property and immanent relation of self-organising systems, then how do actors, perhaps outside of these systems, intervene within them? In this section, we argue that this issue of intervention is another axis along which the politics of resiliences are revealed at points of articulation.

While systems, individuals and phenomena are said to be most resilient when left to their own devices, this has not meant that things are always or even usually left to develop without guiding interventions. For example, climate change policy still fixates on the two degrees temperature target; for all the calls to experimentation, much of conservation ecology is still determinedly preservationist in approach (Cabin, 2007); and for all the talk of cyber resilience and the desirability of letting it alone, the explosive growth of the cybersecurity industry obsessively pursues ways to rein in and guide emergent cyber relations.

Rather than the hands-off benevolence that self-organisation might suggest, we find active projects of crafting and directing relations, which is to say nothing of the just-as-political decision *not* to intervene. Resilience is rarely invoked without recommendations for how to build resilience. As the Department of Homeland Security puzzlingly reports, 'Resilient self-healing systems require a complete overhaul' (2004, p. 14). Perhaps Brian Walker sums up this tension best when he states: 'The essence of resilience . . . is to understand feedbacks *that keep it self-organizing in the way we want it to be*' (2009, emphasis added). This fundamental tension begs the questions, Who defines how 'we want it to be'? How are the 'self' and the 'inherent' actively crafted? This moment of tension is one of the key openings for interrogating the ontological politics of resiliences by revealing the political weight of what is often cast as the natural unfolding of inherent, self-organising relations.

In ecological literatures, one of the prime ways of pursuing a positive proliferation of resilience is through experimentation and the retreat from certainty when acting to conserve or restore ecosystems. For example, Gross (2010) argues that ecological restoration must embrace the unexpected; surprises are likely when reintroducing species or recovering contaminated or industrial sites. Perhaps the most complete statement of experimentation in ecology is provided by Cabin (2007), who proposes that one could allocate land plots to groups with different ecological ideas and simply see what happens. Those that function successfully will eventually be chosen as the model for recolonising the remainder of the area. This is a radical re-distribution and democratisation of expertise, in which the ultimate epistemological failure to know in advance what might work transforms experimentation into the only strategy to ensure resilient solutions. The emphasis is on positive transformations to engineer new futures rather than return to vulnerable pasts (Young, 2010; see also Nelson, 2014). But each resilience intervention contains (whether discussed transparently or not) a view of the positive, the goals sought, the ideal world to be enacted. Nonequilibrium ecology can be politically progressive or conservative (Zimmerer, 2000); experimentation can be resisted, transformed and can fail (Castan Broto and Bulkeley, 2013). Interventions in resilience multiple need to be interrogated for their specific effects in particular articulations and experiments.

If ecological resilience interventions are turning to experimentation, one rough equivalent in security is creating redundancy, or the possibility for multiple pathways of recovery to emerge during events. Here, the ideal for resilience interventions is that they might foster an 'in-built adaptability to the fluid nature of the new security threats' (Coaffee, 2006). For example, infrastructure security agendas in the US, the UK and the EU explicitly wish for self-healing systems and security that is emergent, inherent and 'designed in'. The security sector borrows quite liberally from ecological and biological concepts to argue for letting systems find their own pathways. For example, one US report states that:

> To achieve the strategic goal of self-healing, self-sustaining CI [critical infrastructure] networks, automated responses to electromagnetic disturbance, laser, and particle beam weapons will need to suppress, divert, redirect, re-profile and otherwise 'morph' the attacked system into a form that can survive the event.
>
> *(Department of Homeland Security, 2004, p. 34)*

The report longingly references traits such as 'graceful stealth' (ibid., p. 19) and outlines goals like new manufacturing processes and materials science 'that may be patterned after biological processes' (ibid., p. 14). It details the desirable traits of nanotechnology innovations that mimic the outer protection of shellfish, soil as a model of self-healing, and the productive possibilities of processes like DNA and RNA replication.

While these natural imaginaries of resilience are quite explicit, interventions to craft 'it' are often fuzzy and indistinct. Security interventions are commonly described with words such as sensing, smart, embedded, autonomous, autonomic, intuitive and inherent. Here, intervention is written out, as security seems to merely tap into 'natural' or 'found' qualities. This is not the case, however, as interventions are vital – 'suppressing, diverting, redirecting, morphing' – that comes to define 'inherent' properties. For example, the Department of Homeland Security's 'Resilient Electric Grid' initiative is testing superconductor cables that might replace existing copper wire infrastructures. The hope is that the cables would allow substations to automatically distribute excess capacity during emergencies, thus avoiding surges and major power failures. In this case, development of this inbuilt flexibility is a project that emboldens spending on private-sector research and development. The Resilient Electric Grid is partnered with the private company Consolidated Edison, but one programme manager states: 'There are a lot of components to this system so there are a lot of places for others to get in' (Michael, 2012). These places 'to get in' on the resilience security project expose the active interventions and shaping of 'self-organising' and 'self-healing' systems. One task for resilience analytics is to expose the ways in which appeals to the 'natural' can obscure political choices.

Resilience interventions have to articulate when something is 'resilient enough', which also bares assumptions about exposure, agency and responsibility for risk-taking. Consider Brian Walker's elaboration on the essence of ecological resilience with the example of exposing children to dirt and dust in their environments in order to increase their resilience to disturbances from the environment: 'The way you maintain the resilience of a system is by allowing it to probe its boundaries . . . [by] disturbing and probing the boundaries of resilience' (Walker, 2009). Active intervention is to test the boundaries. In parts of psychology, similarly, resilience is a capacity that emerges precisely as one is exposed to adversity. For example, Garmezy *et al.* (1984) posit a 'challenge model' of children's stress resistance, wherein exposure to 'stress is treated as a potential enhancer of competence' as long as it is not excessive. An American Psychological Association report on resilience and African American adolescents emphasises that young people can be considered 'at promise' as opposed to 'at risk'. In this framing, certain factors 'traditionally considered risk factors—can be reconceptualized as adaptive or protective processes' (2008, p. 3). Here, persistent risk exposures or vulnerabilities are recast as potentially positive moments for enhancing adaptability. Some trials of resilience, however, take on a rather different social and political character. Phelan *et al.* (2013) posit that 'perverse resilience' occurs where a fossil fuel economy becomes internally resilient, despite seeming to fall out-of-line with ecological health. A system that is too resilient to change for the 'better good' can have collateral damage and be destructive for some interests or living things. Interventions to prop up capitalism, in this example, can sediment internal contradictions and endemic perversity, as much as encouraging 'naturally' positive traits to flourish.

There are common frictions or interferences across the interventions of resiliences appearing in social-environmental systems, security, business and psychology interventions. There is a tension between advocating for self-determination and ownership, while simultaneously dictating the terms (or interventions) of the 'enterprise' of self-determination from without. There is also a common tension related to risk exposure and how this is intervened upon (or not). We draw on such diverse deployments precisely to illustrate the varying political 'projects' underlying specific articulations and interventions of resiliences. Rather than giving agency to 'resilience', or having faith in it, or allowing it to maintain coherence as an apparent object, we argue that analyses must explicitly trace the practices that are being re-made through these interventions in specific contexts of articulation. Calls for resilience can therefore take rather different ontological politics in terms of the interventions aimed at achieving '*it*', as they implicitly or explicitly articulate a desirable future world and responsibility (or not) for this in the present.

Conclusion

If we now live in a 'time of crisis', then fundamental questions emerge: Where does crisis originate? Who and what bear the burden of crises of oppression, insecurity, ill health, inequality, debt, and environmental degradation? What are the desired futures and how will these be enacted? Is this about accepting vulnerability, expecting security from governance mechanisms, accepting survival without political promise or qualification, to live a vulnerable life with positive projects? Do we 'learn how to die'? (Evans and Reid, 2014). What does the appeal to 'resilience' do in this context and how can we interrogate its inherent generality?

In this chapter, we have argued that resilience is multiple. Like crisis, resilience becomes an organising concept, but it does so within a variety of different ontological assumptions, which have varying geographical, temporal and political implications. Our aim is not to offer a 'right' model of resilience against other deployments. Rather we have attempted to make the concept of resilience strange in a Foucauldian sense. It is our contention that, to paraphrase Mol's discussion of atherosclerosis, the singularity of objects requires work, it is an 'accomplishment'. Competing ontological objects that are kept apart, spatially dispersed (in distinct hospital wings or across academic disciplines) belie the frictions between them: 'As long as incompatible [resiliences] do not meet, they are in no position to confront each other' (2002, p. 119). We find that there are a multiplicity of spatial ontologies and interventions amongst resiliences – and they (do not) resolve the ontological challenge of assessing and defining the resilient from the non-resilient (human, non-humans, planet, Internet, ecosystem) in different ways with different political visions.

The generality of resilience can be made to do any number of things. The politics of resiliences only appear when it is made explicit what and where 'resilience' is, where it could or should be, and how it might get there in any given context, as above: the daycare for broad communal support rather than an individual child's traits or redistribution of wealth versus individual poverty resilience. We think Walker and Cooper (2011) are right to emphasise the degree to which resilience has been and can be deployed toward profoundly conservative and systemically self-referential ends. This is one ontological siting, where resilience is supposedly found in the survival of the unavoidable and never-ending turbulence of speculative capitalism. There are, however, many other ontological locations of resilience. While we can identify that resilience is emerging as one of the organising concepts in a contemporary zeitgeist of uncertainty, critical approaches have to grapple with the geographical, political, and temporal ambiguities of the concept. We say this not necessarily to resuscitate or rescue resilience, but to offer a framework for assessing the implications of this concept so widely wielded to arrange present relations in the name of such widely divergent visions of the future. Critical assessments of resilience can cut across the generality, ambiguity and evasiveness of resilience by nailing it down, forcing the question of specifics – which we maintain is perhaps the only universal moment for politicising the concept.

References

American Psychological Association (2008) *Resilience in African American Children and Adolescents: A Vision for Optimal Development*. Available at: www.apa.org/pi/families/resources/resiliencerpt.pdf (accessed July 2016).

Anderson, B. (2015) What kind of thing is resilience? *Politics*, 35(1), 60–66.

Aranda, K., Zeeman, L., Scholes, J. and Arantxa, S.-M.M. (2012) The resilient subject: exploring subjectivity, identity and the body in narratives of resilience. *Health*, 16(5), 548–563.

Blaser, M. (2014) Ontology and indigeneity: on the political ontology of heterogeneous assemblages. *Cultural Geographies*, 21(1), 49–58.

Cabin, R.J. (2007) Science-driven restoration: a square grid on a round Earth? *Restoration Ecology*, 15(1), 1–7.

Castan Broto, V. and Bulkeley, H. (2013) Urban governance and climate change experiments. In Mieg, H. and Topfer, K. (eds) *Institutional and Social Innovation for Sustainable Urban Development*. London: Routledge, pp. 72–87.

Chandler, D. (2013) Resilience and the autotelic subject: toward a critique of the societalization of security. *International Political Sociology*, 7, 210–226.

Coaffee, J. (2006) From counterterrorism to resilience. *The European Legacy*, 11(4), 389–403.

Department of Homeland Security (2004) *The National Plan for Research and Development In Support of Critical Infrastructure Protection*. Washington, DC. Available at: www.dhs.gov/xlibrary/assets/ST_2004_NCIP_RD_PlanFINALApr05.pdf (accessed June 2014).

ENISA (European Network and Information Security Agency) (2011) *Inter-X: Resilience and the Internet Interconnection Ecosystem. Summary Report*. Available at: www.enisa.europa.eu (accessed July 2016).

Evans, B. and Reid, J. (2014) *Resilient Life: The Art of Living Dangerously*. Cambridge: Polity Press.

Foucault, M. (2002) *The Order of Things*. London: Routledge.

Garmezy, N., Masten, A.S. and Tellegen, A. (1984) The study of stress and competence in children: a building block for developmental psychopathology. *Child Development*, 55(1), 97–111.

Gross, M. (2010) *Ignorance and Surprise: Science, Society and Ecological Surprise*. Cambridge, MA: MIT Press.

Holling, C.S. (1973) Resilience and the stability of ecological systems. *Annual Review of Ecology and Systematics*, 4, 1–23.

Isin, Engin (2004) The neurotic citizen. *Citizenship Studies*, 8(3), 217–235.

Joseph, J. (2013) Resilience as embedded neoliberalism: a governmentality approach. *Resilience: International Policies, Practices and Discourses*, 1(1), 38–52.

Landau, J. (2007) Enhancing resilience: families and communities as agents for change. *Family Process*, 46(3), 351–365.

Larned, J.G. (2012) Becoming more resilient. *FBI Law Enforcement Bulletin* October. Available at: www.fbi. gov/stats-services/publications/law-enforcement-bulletin/october-2012/becoming-more-resilient (accessed October 2014).

Larner, W. (2011) C-change? Geographies of crisis. *Dialogues in Human Geography*, 1(3), 319–335.

Law, J. (2002) *Aircraft Stories: Decentering the Object in Technoscience*. Durham, NC: Duke University Press.

MacKinnon, D. and Derickson, K.D. (2012) From resilience to resourcefulness: a critique of resilience policy and activism. *Progress in Human Geography*, 37(2), 253–270.

MeQuilibrium (n.d.) www.mequilibrium.com/ (accessed July 2016).

Michael, T. (2012) Protecting the electric grid. *Innovation*, 10(5). Available at: www.innovation-america. org/protecting-electric-grid (accessed October 2014).

Mol, A. (1999) Ontological politics: a word and some questions. *Sociological Review*, 47: 74–89.

Mol, A. (2002) *The Body Multiple: Ontology in Medical Practice*. Durham, NC: Duke University Press.

Nelson, S.H. (2014) Resilience and the neoliberal counter-revolution: from ecologies of control to production of the common. *Resilience: International Policies, Practices and Discourses*, 2(1), 1–17.

Neocleous, M. (2012) 'Don't be scared, be prepared': trauma-anxiety-resilience. *Alternatives: Global, Local, Political*, 37(3), 188–198.

Phelan, L., Henderson-Sellars, A. and Taplin, R. (2013) The political economy of addressing the climate crisis in the Earth system: undermining perverse resilience. *New Political Economy*, 18(2), 198–226.

Seccombe, K. (2002) 'Beating the odds' versus 'changing the odds': poverty, resilience, and family policy. *Journal of Marriage and Family*, 64(2), 384–394.

Southwick, Steven M. and Charney, Dennis S. (2012) *Resilience: The Science of Mastering Life's Greatest Challenges*. New York: Cambridge University Press.

Swyngedouw, E. (2010) Apocalypse forever? *Theory, Culture & Society*, 27(2–3), 213–232.

The Climate Psychology Alliance (n.d.) www.climatepsychologyalliance.org/ (accessed July 2016).

Ungar, M. (2011) The social ecology of resilience: addressing contextual and cultural ambiguity of a nascent construct. *American Journal of Orthopsychiatry*, 81(1), 1–17.

Walker, B. (2009) What is resilience in people and ecosystems? Stockholm Resilience Centre Whiteboard Series. Video seminar available at: www.youtube.com/watch?v=tXLMeL5nVQk (accessed October 2014).

Walker, J. and Cooper, M. (2011) Genealogies of resilience: from systems ecology to the political economy of crisis adaptation. *Security Dialogue*, 42(2), 143–160.

World Resources Report (2008) *The Roots of Resilience: Growing the Wealth of the Poor*. Available at: http:// pdf.wri.org/world_resources_2008_roots_of_resilience.pdf (accessed October 2014).

Young, O. (2010) *Institutional Dynamics: Emergent Patterns in International Environmental Governance*. Cambridge, MA: MIT Press.

Zimmerer, K. (2000) The reworking of conservation geographies: nonequilibrium landscapes and nature-society hybrids. *Annals of the Association of American Geographers*, 90(2), 356–369.

Žižek, S. (1999) *The Ticklish Subject: The Absent Centre of Political Ontology*. London: Verso.

Žižek, S. (2001) Psychoanalysis and the post-political: an interview with Slavoj Zizek. *New Literary History*, 32(1), 1–21.

5

A SOCIAL SCIENCE PERSPECTIVE ON RESILIENCE

Lennart Olsson, Anne Jerneck, Henrik Thorén,
Johannes Persson and David O'Byrne

Introduction

Resilience is often promoted as a unifying theory to integrate social and natural dimensions of sustainability. But it is a troubled attempt of scientific unification from which social scientists may feel detached. To explain this, we first construct a typology of the many varied definitions of resilience. Second, we analyse core concepts and principles in resilience theory – system ontology, system boundary, equilibria and thresholds, feedback mechanisms, self-organisation, function – causing incommensurability between the social and natural sciences. Third, we propose that the unification ambition in resilience theory leads to scientific imperialism and undesirable political implications. In contrast, and to avoid this, interdisciplinary research for sustainability would be better served by methodological pluralism drawing also on core social scientific theories and concepts.

A typology

We acknowledge the long history of the concept of resilience with its many articulations, iterations and positive attributes. However, it is an elusive concept in need of structuring. It is clear that resilience thinking describes important attributes of ecosystems, of materials and of human beings, i.e. the ability to cope with and recover after disturbance, shocks and stress. But with popularity comes the risk of blurring and diluting the meaning (Brand and Jax, 2007). From a scientific point of view, one might think that scientists rooted in resilience research would try to safeguard the concept from inconsistency and ambiguity because conceptual accuracy and precision are of fundamental importance and are often considered a prerequisite in science (Bacon [1620], 2000).

A major point of the discussion in resilience circles is whether resilience is a normative concept or not, i.e. is resilience 'good' or 'bad', or neither? The policy use of resilience is almost exclusively normative (UNDP, 2014) and proponents of resilience theory have recently acknowledged that 'we agree that the resilience literature often treats resilience as something good' (Olsson *et al.*, 2014). But the tendency to see resilience and all that it entails as desirable is an important reason, we argue, why social science focusing on social change over stability has difficulties in accepting the resilience concept, let alone resilience theory. Given the controversy around the normativity of resilience, the notions of 'good' and 'bad' resilience need to be studied more (Béné *et al.*, 2012).

Table 5.1 Typology of resilience definitions in ecology and social-ecological systems thinking

Attributes / Meanings	Descriptive – Neutral (N)	Prescriptive – Good (G)
Bounce back	BB-N (Holling, 1973) Resilience and stability of ecological systems	BB-G (Perrings, 1998) Introduction: Resilience and Sustainble Development
Bounce back and transform	BB-T-N (Walker et al., 2006) A handful of heuristics and some propositions for understanding resilience in social-ecological systems	BB-T-G (Folke et al., 2010) Resilience thinking: integrating resilience, adaptability and transformability

Here we suggest a typology comprising two conceptual meanings, two attributes and four main types of definitions frequently used in the scientific literature (Table 5.1). The first conceptual meaning refers to the ability of a system to cope with stress and 'bounce back' (BB); the second refers to the ability of the system to 'bounce back' and 'transform' (BB–T). The first attribute is descriptive, implying that resilience is 'neutral' (N), i.e. neither inherently good nor bad; this is contrasted by a prescriptive attribute implying that resilience is desirable and 'good' (G). Each of the four distinct types is exemplified by one representative article.

Incommensurability

Resilience aspires to be an integrated framework to be used across the boundaries of the natural and social sciences (Perrings, 1998). But this causes tension in relation to core social science concepts such as agency, conflict, knowledge and power. Social scientists have therefore argued that the application of resilience to social systems requires more 'solid theoretical grounding' (Davidson, 2010) and sensitivity to theoretical development in contemporary social science. In the following five subsections we identify core concepts and principles in resilience theory that create theoretical tensions and methodological barriers between the natural and social sciences and thus stand in the way of a constructive dialogue on knowledge integration between disciplines. To evaluate the ontological compatibility of resilience theory with social science, we examine the concepts and principles deployed in resilience research in terms of their assumptions about society and the standing of these assumptions in social science. At the end of this section, we synthesise our findings.

First: system ontology

In ecology the concept of resilience is associated with a system ontology and ecosystems as the target domain. While some ecologists study ecosystems for the interactions between predators and their prey, others see ecosystems as flows of energy. Neither of these 'constructed systems' is intended as a complete account of ecosystems. In the literature on coupled social-ecological systems (SESs), the system under study commonly has a prominent ecosystem component, such as a coral reef (Adger et al., 2005), fisheries (Peterson, 2000), forests (Gardner et al., 2009), grasslands (Walker et al., 2004) or wetlands (Olsson et al., 2004). The notion of system is indispensable to resilience and having decided on the phenomenon to be explained, the system boundaries need to be defined. Beyond that, resilience is sometimes used to describe and analyse social entities such as institutions, organisations, cities or states (Scheffer, 2009). To take it even further, ecologists sometimes claim that 'ecological and social domains of social-ecological systems can be addressed in a common conceptual, theoretical, and modelling framework' (Walker *et al.*, 2006). Even if the system ontology is essential in resilience thinking, there are surprisingly few studies addressing resilience at the system level. In a recent quantitative meta-analysis of 197 published articles on resilience, Downes et al., (2013) found an overwhelming focus on the species or community level in ecological studies and on the individual level in social science studies.

In the social sciences, system ontology is not new or unknown. Researchers studying social phenomena based on social theory are reluctant to use systems as an ontological description of society but may use 'system' analytically to study a specific aspect of society, polity or the economy such as the energy system, the party system or the tax system. To be noted here, some early social system theories emanated from physics and biology. In 1935, in his book *The Mind and Society*, the renowned economist Vilfredo Pareto formulated one of the first social system theories in the form of 'General Sociology'. Here he claimed that: 'My wish is to construct a system of sociology on the model of celestial mechanics, physics [and] chemistry'(Pareto, 1935). In sociology, Talcott Parsons, as yet another proponent of system theory, was inspired by Pareto and the emerging system science in biology (Parsons, 1970). Intentionally or unintentionally, the current discourse on SESs borrows many of its ideas about society from this early view of social systems inspired by the natural sciences, which is now highly controversial in contemporary social sciences (Baecker, 2001).

The most prominent modern system theory in the social sciences, especially in sociology, is without doubt Niklas Luhmann's general system theory rooted in functionalism (Luhmann, 1982). But Luhmann's notion of system is very different from that of Parsons and also quite different from the meaning of system in resilience theory. According to Luhmann, a social system consists of nothing but communication; neither material conditions nor human beings are part of it (Blühdorn, 2000). Luhmann's systems are characterised by autopoiesis, meaning that the system creates its own basic elements that make up the system. For example, the economic system, as we know it, is based on money, and money is created by the economic system. Without an economic system that defines the value of money, it would simply be pieces of paper and without money there would be no economic system. This is very different from how we understand ecosystems.

Another characteristic of an autopoietic system is that its boundaries are determined by the system itself. In the economic system, anything that is scarce and in demand has a price and is internal to the system, while goods and services that are either ubiquitous or not in demand have no price and are external to the system. Hence, an autopoietic system has no direct links to its environment; it is closed. But under pressure from its environment the system may change by shrinking or extending its boundaries. In Luhmann's system theory, the environment (ecosystems, for example) can never become part of society and society can never become part of the environment – the notion of social-ecological systems is therefore incompatible with Luhmann's systems theory (Luhmann, 1997).

Although Luhmann's attempt to reconceptualise modern society is 'attractive, comprehensive and theoretically consistent' it is, for several reasons, highly controversial in social theory and critics have pointed out that not all systems are as (functionally) autonomous or closed as Luhmann described them (Blühdorn, 2000). As a whole, the critique points at the problem of using functional systems thinking to describe and explain relations between entities and systems (Ritzer 2011, pp. 348–349). This takes us to the next point: the problem of defining system boundaries.

Before that, we should briefly mention World System Theory (WST) as yet another well-known system theory in the social sciences, with the sociologist Immanuel Wallerstein as its most prominent theorist. It developed in the 1970s out of Marxist thought and builds on dependency theory, emerging in the late 1960s as a critique of functionalist modernisation theory in development (Wallerstein, 1974). WST is an important source of inspiration to many environmental social scientists (Roberts and Grimes, 2002) – and development thinkers alike – but it is hardly compatible with resilience theory. From our discussion below, on the similarity between resilience theory's assumptions about society and those of functionalism, it should be clear why WST and resilience seem incompatible, especially since WST is fundamentally informed by a radical rather than a conservative political agenda (Wallerstein, 2011).

Second: system boundary

The ability to define boundaries is an important prerequisite in 'system ontology', but at times this can be a challenge. Owing to its layered atmosphere, not even planet Earth is an example of a system with perfectly clear boundaries. In some cases it is easier to define the system because it may have clear boundaries, or the research focus may allow boundaries to be clearly stipulated. In psychology, the system ontology is well established and the most fundamental systems under study are (fairly) well defined such as the individual, the family, the local community, the school, and so forth. In many instances it is more difficult to settle the boundaries – both in the natural and the social sciences. A forest, for instance, may have no boundaries that can be unambiguously determined. It may be more or less well connected with other forests, lakes, and rivers in such a way that any suggested boundary will be arbitrary or artificial. At first blush, a lake ecosystem is clearly separate from the surrounding terrestrial environment. But some plants along the shoreline may be either partially submerged or rooted in the surrounding land; amphibians move between the shoreline and the water; surrounding trees drop leaves into the water, etc. (Smith *et al.*, 2006, chapter 6). To take a further, but different, example of the delineation problem, cognitive processes draw on the external world to such an extent that an individual's skin can obviously not be taken to approximate the boundaries of an individual's cognitive system (Haugeland, 2000). The delineation of a system is not just a matter of social or spatial location, and depending on the choice of theory boundaries will vary. Hence, we must rely on other properties and recognise how scales and social relations are interconnected with actors, institutions and structures beyond the 'system'.

Generally, we seem to understand a system as an entity of a given phenomenon that we want to describe, explain or interact with – and this has consequences for how we understand the system. Herbert Simon (1969) argued that the strength of connections between variables can be used to decompose systems into distinct subsystems. Moreover, it is often claimed that a system is a set of elements standing in reciprocal interrelation (Bertalanffy, 1968). But even such systems depend to some extent on pragmatic considerations (Wimsatt, 1976). As an illustration, Collier and Cumming (2011) claim that: 'The difficulty of defining an ecosystem is complicated by the fact that any description of an ecosystem is from the perspective of an observer.' This resonates with the social science perspective, arguing that boundaries, like theories, are constructed by someone for some purpose (Smith and Stirling, 2010). In case study design, researchers set boundaries based on research questions, propositions generated from theory, meta-theoretical assumptions, etc.

As regards boundaries, there is no sharp line of demarcation in reality to explain perceived differences between natural or social systems. Neither in nature nor in society are boundaries fixed unless we first decide on the phenomenon to be described or explained. Pragmatic considerations imply some degree of idealisation – in both social and natural contexts. There is thus a certain degree of reflexivity among researchers who recognise that system boundaries are constructed, and that sometimes, for various reasons, resilience is contested.

In theory and practice, systems and systems boundaries are essential components of resilience, while there are many obstacles to systems thinking inherent in contemporary social science. In particular, system boundaries depend on the assumption that there is a given set of entities and that these are universally recognised across disciplines. But in the natural sciences a given set of entities is more accepted than in the social sciences. It is tempting to downplay the conceptual requirements of systems in order to make resilience applicable to social phenomena, but that would be a clear example of blurring the concept of resilience, which should be avoided because it would result in a less scientific concept.

While the systems concept is almost universally employed in the natural sciences, institutions are axiomatic, though interpreted variously, to social science and core to understanding social continuity and change (Mahoney and Rueschemeyer, 2003; Mahoney and Thelen, 2010). The use of an institutional lens on the integration of social and natural dimensions could become a methodological linchpin to connect the social and the natural sciences for the sake of sustainability. This would require not only the use of rational choice institutionalism, as represented by Ostrom (1998) and often associated with SESs (Ostrom, 2009), but also the involvement of historical, sociological and discursive institutionalism, which stress material as well as ideational aspects (Schmidt, 2008) of society and nature and their dynamics. Different institutional theories would treat the idea of system and system boundaries differently.

Third: equilibria, thresholds, and feedback mechanisms

The idea of multiple equilibria and thresholds is central to resilience theory, as seen in this quotation: 'Social-ecological systems exhibit thresholds that, when exceeded, result in changed system feedbacks that lead to changes in function and structure'(Walker *et al.*, 2006). This dynamics is often visualised by a ball on an undulating surface with multiple concave shapes. If pushed too hard, or if the walls are lowered, the ball may move into another concave shape, illustrating that the system has exceeded some critical threshold(s) and shifted into a new equilibrium. Examples could be a lake shifting from a vegetation-dominated clear state into a turbid plankton-dominated state (Scheffer, 2009). The interesting question is whether the lake has shifted into a new system, thus a system transformation, or whether the system is basically the same but with an altered function. Using this as an analogy to social systems is problematic because here we take transformation to mean a process in which society changes not only in function but more profoundly in terms of structures, institutions or social relations: 'after a transition, the society, or a subsystem, operates according to new assumptions and rules, thus indicating a range of new practices and not just an altered function' (Jerneck and Olsson, 2008, p. 176).

The analogy of the ball and the undulating surface is problematic in relation to social phenomena because of competing explanations and paradigms in the social sciences. In ecological resilience, the undulating surface reflects the current scientific understanding, while in the social sciences there may be no consensus on the 'shape' of that 'surface'.

Feed-back is another central component of the 'system ontology' that is problematic in the study of society and social relations. In cybernetics there are two types of feed-back mechanisms: negative feed-back that stabilises the system (homeostasis) and positive feed-back that causes exponential change. Applied to social phenomena, this notion of negative and positive feed-back is overly simple. Social entities interact back and forth in norm-based processes of continuously interpreted (and re-interpreted) communication and interaction that may or may not affect behaviour – thus indicating less predictability and greater complexity than simple positive or negative feed-back (Bennett, 1975; Davidson, 2010). The structural complexity of ecological and social systems can partly be conceived of in similar terms, but the feedback processes associated with each are incomparable, since feed-back mechanisms in social systems are primarily determined by agency, or structured agency, rather than by structural forces (Davidson, 2010). This is especially so since norms influencing agency are dynamic constructs subject to continuous change rather than to static structures (Schmidt, 2008).

Fourth: self-organisation

The principle of self-organisation is a further cornerstone of the resilience discourse (Folke *et al.*, 2005). In ecology, self-organising systems are common and perceived as unproblematic because there is often an overarching driver, the attractor, providing the logic of self-organisation. To exemplify this, all leaves in a deciduous boreal forest orientate themselves towards the sun in order to optimise the amount of sunlight that they can capture, thus maximising the uptake of solar energy, which is an attractor of that system.

As regards society, the most obvious example of self-organisation would be the 'invisible hand', which was first described by Adam Smith, in 1776, stating that capitalist markets would self-regulate if left on their own (Mazzucato, 2013). According to Smith, the natural propensity of humans to 'truck, barter and exchange' leads to a situation where every man is a merchant and 'the society itself grows to be what is properly a commercial society' (Smith [1776] 2010). Even if Smith did not use the term self-organisation, what he depicts is almost a perfect illustration of such a system. The outcome (= the market) is the result of a decentralised and non-intentional process where the role of government is to guarantee freedom, property rights and security in a process that should work even if participants are unaware and have no knowledge of it (Ullmann-Margalit, 1978).

Much later, in an argument in favour of market forces and against radical (state-oriented) reformists, the economist Friedrich Hayek (1988) developed the idea of self-organisation even further. However, such views of society are contested by scholars outside the neo-classical paradigm. When Polanyi speaks of the emergence of a self-regulating market, he stresses that it relies on strong state interventions, primarily the commodification of land, labour and money (Polanyi, 1957). He also argues that Smith's claim of man's natural propensity to 'truck, barter and exchange' is a myth created during industrialisation. What appears to be self-regulating by some is thus considered the result of political forces and institutional change by others. As a further illustration, social science offers a vast literature on power as a fundamental and omnipresent force shaping and reshaping interactions, relations and social (not self-) organisation, implying various degrees and types of continuity or change (Avelino and Rotmans, 2009). The literature on agency, conflict, institutionalism, structuralism and other middle-range theories is also rich, varied and frequently used.

In fact, self-organisation is aligned with rational choice theory, as seen in the works of Elinor Ostrom (Ostrom, 1998; 2009; Ostrom *et al.*, 1999), who was a strong supporter of and contributor to resilience thinking. But rational choice is often criticised for leaning heavily on the two principles of methodological individualism – of seeing macro patterns as resulting from the aggregation of individual choices and of seeing economic change as determined by factor costs (land, labour, capital).

Resilience theory is rooted in complexity theory, wherein self-organisation is seen as the overriding organising principle (Barabási and Albert, 1999; Folke *et al.*, 2005). A conspicuous example is given by Walker *et al.* (2004), claiming that:

> a characteristic feature of complex adaptive systems is self-organisation without intent . . . and although the dynamics of SESs are dominated by individual human actors who do exhibit intent, the system as a whole does not (as in the case of a market).

Proponents of complexity theory argue that complex systems (e.g. business systems and social networks) can be understood by emergence – in terms of new configurations resulting from self-organisation (Fuchs, 2003), while others say that emergence refers to new patterns and properties resulting from iterative human interaction (McGregor, 2014). Importantly, when self-organisation is used in the social sciences it is mainly understood as a reaction to power asymmetries and structural inequality such as in the formation of social movements (Collinge 1999; Hughes 2009; Shakespeare 1993).

Fifth: the notion of function and functionalism

The understanding of function is a major source of divergence between the natural sciences and contemporary social sciences, but this was not always the case. In ecological sciences function is a central theme, often defined as the ecological mechanisms that maintain the structure and services produced by ecosystems, such as primary production, decomposition and trophic (food chain) interactions (Barnes and Spurr, 1998). The early functionalists in the social sciences, such as the sociologist Durkheim and the anthropologist Radcliffe-Brown, argued that the concept of function, when applied to society, can be seen as an analogy between social life and organic life (Radcliffe-Brown, 1935). A meaning similar to that used by the early functionalists is found in resilience theory assuming that ecosystems have four main functions (exploitation, conservation, release, reorganisation), which, according to certain dynamics, are responsible for the succession and transformation of ecosystems from one state to another (Gunderson and Holling, 2002, p. 34).

In the seminal book *Panarchy* (Gunderson and Holling, 2002, p. 107), the definition of a social system is taken from *The Social System* by Talcott Parsons (1951), a structural functionalist in sociology who argued that his principles could be applied to many systems, not just social systems. Interestingly, resilience thinking resembles Parsons' general theory wherein intra- and inter-systemic relations are defined by cohesion, consensus and order (Ritzer 2011). In particular, there are obvious similarities between the SESs discourse and Parsons' AGIL scheme describing four core functions – or functional imperatives – that serve to maintain stability and secure survival of the social system (Ritzer, 2011, pp. 241–242):

- A: adaptation – a system must adapt to the physical and social environment as well as adapt the environment to its needs;
- G: goal attainment – a system must define and achieve its primary goals;
- I: integration – a system must coordinate and regulate interrelationships of its components and strive towards a cohesive whole;
- L: latency – a system must furnish, maintain and renew itself and its individuals to perform their roles according to social and cultural expectations.

As a further description and explanation of the AGIL model, modern societies have acted on all four components according to Parsons: for adaptation, societies developed industries and markets as well as science and technology; for goal attainment, societies developed political institutions; for integration, societies developed civil society and religion; and for latency, societies developed families and schools. Parson was later criticised for overemphasising consensus, conformity, stability and reification, and to address this critique, neo-functionalists incorporated more agency, dynamics and conflict into this thinking (Geels, 2011).

A recent quotation from Landscape Ecology may serve as an example of the resemblance between resilience theory and Parsons's functionalism:

> The crux of the problem of fostering sustainable, resilient landscapes is thus the problem of designing or developing appropriate institutions that will act flexibly, proactively, and at appropriate scales to strengthen feedbacks that modify and moderate demand for ecosystem services and incorporate the trade-offs between human wellbeing, profit, and the exploitation of ecosystems.
>
> *(Cumming et al., 2013, p. 1143)*

However, the crux of the matter is not only to create functional institutions but also, as known from institutional theory, that inefficient or ineffective norms, rules and values often persist because institutions are 'sticky' and not easily replaced nor designed, developed or changed (North, 1990). There are further concerns with functional definitions of institutions. First, the emphasis on the functionality of institutions implies a conservative approach to social change (Cote and Nightingale, 2012, p. 480). Second, the existence of malfunctioning institutions is difficult to explain if their role is to perform the very function that defines them (Davidson, 2010). Third, the equilibrium tendencies in structural functionalism may not be helpful in a social science analysis (Alexander, 2013, p. 2712).

As a reaction to the incapacity of functionalism, such as the inability to explain rapid social change, various conflict theories rooted in the ideas of Karl Marx, Max Weber and George Simmel emerged in the 1960s and asked other questions about society (Jones *et al.*, 2011). According to conflict theory, institutions are shaped by existing conflicts, power (im)balances and social stratifications in society, which in itself is seen as highly dynamic rather than static as in functionalism (Dahrendorf, 1959). Based on a wealth of empirical data, the further development of sociological conflict theories has since then emphasised the importance of the detailed study of processes in society, thus moving away from the production of grand theory and what was perceived as ideologically based conflict theory (Collins, 1990). Similarly, the influence of functionalism waned substantially from the 1960s (Jones *et al.*, 2011) and some even declared it to be 'dead as a dodo' (Barnes, 1995, p. 37). Notably, and as a peculiarity, functionalism builds on a non-dynamic consensus perspective of society which echoes the state of a steady equilibrium that resilience theory reacted against and rejected in its own analysis of ecosystems (Hatt, 2013).

The most fundamental obstacle here, we argue, is the difference in how resilience theory and the social sciences understand society – in terms of social systems, social relations and social change. In essence, resilience theory is implicitly based on an understanding of society that resembles consensus theories in sociology, according to which shared norms and values are the foundation of a stable harmonious society, in which social change is slow and orderly – and where, in analogue, resilience thus becomes the equivalent of stability and harmony or the good norm. However, while previously seen as dominant in sociological theory – though strongly contested, for example, by the critical theory of the Frankfurt School – consensus theories have declined dramatically since the 1960s (Ritzer, 2011), giving more space to conflict theory and issues of diversity, inequality and power. Conflict theories emphasise conflicting interests between groups in society, meaning that social order is maintained by (material or discursive) manipulation and control by dominant and powerful groups, and that transformational change can develop from the tensions between these groups and the redistribution of power. In functional approaches, the conservatism is clear: change is understood as coming about due to continuous progressive processes such as the division of labour or differentiation, conflict arises in reaction to these and a stable society must contain the unrest. It is important though that a deeper understanding of conflict is taken into consideration in any serious attempt to bridge the social with the natural sciences, be it via resilience theory and thinking – or via other less unifying and thus more methodologically and theoretically pluralist approaches.

Whereas most disciplines seek to avoid teleological explanations, biology, and evolutionary biology in particular, is rife with functional claims (Sober, 1994). The striking similarities between resilience theory and rightly abandoned theories of functionalism (and structural functionalism) in the social sciences, as also noted by others (Alexander, 2013; Cote and Nightingale, 2012), is one reason why the resilience discourse does not fit the social sciences. Resilience theory rests on functionalism as a theoretically superseded understanding of society and, furthermore, owing to its emphasis on self-organisation, it appears to be aligned with the contemporary neo-liberal economics paradigm (Walker and Cooper, 2011; Gowdy, 1997). This entails a proliferation of market-based instruments for ecosystem management (Norgaard, 2010) as epitomised by The Economics of Ecosystems and Biodiversity initiative (TEEB), aiming to 'help decision-makers recognise, demonstrate and capture the values of ecosystem services and biodiversity' (Kumar, 2010; see also Brown, 2014).

Synthesis

Our analysis of the incommensurability results in three main synthesised reasons for why resilience is not attractive to nor easily integrated with social science thinking: (1) the ontological presupposition to see reality as a system with equilibria, feed-backs, and thresholds; (2) the principle of self-organisation overshadowing agency, conflict and power; and (3) the notion of function as foundational to resilience theory while having lost its centrality in the social sciences.

Scientific imperialism

To understand the conditions for how to build integrated knowledge across disciplinary domains, such as the natural and social sciences, we identify two distinct types of scientific knowledge integration: pluralism and unification. According to scientific pluralism, the ultimate goal of scientific inquiry is not (necessarily) to establish a single theory (Kellert *et al.*, 2006). Scientific pluralism appears when several disciplines contribute particular theories, methods and/or questions to solve a problem. Pluralism is useful in situations where no unified theories are available to explain a phenomenon, or where the phenomenon can only be explained by multiple theories (Dupré, 1991; Mitchell, 2009).

In contrast, unification can easily slip into not so useful scientific imperialism, which is usually thought of as an illicit infringement, such as when one discipline attempts to explain phenomena or solve problems in a domain belonging to or associated with another discipline (Dupré, 1994, 2001; Mäki, 2013). Serious cases of scientific imperialism are reductive in the sense that they tend to, or aim to, exclude alternative (even compatible) explanations and solutions (Clarke and Walsh, 2009; Midgley, 1984; Thorén, 2015) resulting in a situation where inferior explanations or problem solutions outcompete superior ones (Thorén, 2015). All kinds of unification are not necessarily imperialist (in this negative sense), but there is always reason to worry about imperialism in situations where a single theory is claimed to account for major or persistent social problems such as poverty, or for complex phenomena such as climate change impacts and responses in society.

The claims made in resilience theory (to close the gap to the social sciences) can be classified as an attempt of unification via disciplinary imperialism. It is partly this ambition in combination with the incommensurability that has given rise to the problems that constitute our central argument. Many of these difficulties arise from the inappropriate extension of concepts from the natural sciences to society. These concepts entail similar assumptions to both functionalism and neoclassical economics, which have been found to be highly problematic by social science, as seen already from the 1950s when development economics (and other development theories) emerged in reaction to neoclassical economics. Given the dominance of economics, and particularly neoclassical theory, in the social sciences, it is also likely that associated concepts appear as given for ecologists unfamiliar with the diversity within social science. In contrast to unification, we advocate pluralism. Rather than seeing resilience as a grand or unifying theory, it should be seen (and used) as a middle-range theory compatible with some but not with all ontologies (Geels, 2010).

In essence, we argue that there are two main barriers for resilience thinking to bridge the natural and social sciences, as it aspires to do. First, the aspiration of a unifying theory is contested because the idea of the unity of science has long been controversial – especially after the postmodern turn, which advocated diversity and criticised grand theory for suppressing alternative views and voices originating in less influential parts of society. Second, the combination of unificationist ambitions and issues of incommensurability is particularly problematic. Incommensurability of the ontological type we have focused on here effectively blocks unification. This is best represented by how resilience thinking recreates functionalism, which is now rightly outdated in contemporary social sciences (Ritzer 2011).

Politics of resilience

As resilience travels from being a descriptive – and initially a rather precise – concept in ecology to become a normative notion in society (and policy), it becomes increasingly vague and woolly, while the descriptive origin somehow gets lost (Brand and Jax, 2007). Owing to its malleability in science, combined with its popularity among powerful private or public actors, there is a risk of (un)intentional scientific justification of particular policies, projects and practices. Further, in the attempt 'to make resilience a full-scale paradigm or even a science', its explanatory power gets 'pushed to represent more than it can deliver' (Alexander, 2013). This creates a tendency in resilience theory to depoliticise social change (Reid, 2013) as in a recent article where poverty is seen as a stochastic dynamic process (Barrett and Constas, 2014) rather than the outcome of political and structural processes. In the context of poverty, it is clear that resilience has serious limitations: there is no automatic connection between resilience building and poverty reduction; efforts to reduce poverty cannot simply be replaced by building resilience, and, emphasis on system level resilience may work against the interest of people who are poor (Béné et al., 2012).

Discussion and conclusions

Despite its compelling attractiveness in terms of its original coherence, simplicity and apparent completeness, there are problems in using resilience as a universal concept. Admittedly, it has analytical potential, especially in the serious effort to promote integrated approaches across scales, sectors and spaces (Béné et al., 2012), but not everyone finds it helpful that resilience thinking seeks to combine adaptation (dynamic) with resistance (static) in one framing concept (Alexander, 2013). Whereas resilience theory aims to prevent transitions or, rather, hinder the collapse of a productive system, social theory commonly used in sustainability studies – from transition theory to political ecology – aims to locate and analyse multi-level or multi-scalar resistance against change while seeking to stimulate social transformation (Geels, 2010). This incommensurability is problematic for at least two reasons. First, sustainability research needs to consider both continuity and change while also distinguishing between them (Geels, 2011). Second, transformation for the sake of persistence of the system – rather than transformation for profound change – appears counterintuitive to social science thinking. Whereas studies building on rational choice, as often found in the literature on SESs, have difficulties in identifying and explaining change, studies drawing on, for instance, transition theory and discursive institutional theory seek specifically to identify initial change by studying agency, or the thinking and speaking that precedes agency (Schmidt, 2008). Agency, in turn, can be interpreted differently depending on the analytical perspective, be it cultural, discursive, power based or rational choice (Geels 2010).

Our analysis has illustrated the problems of using resilience as a universal and unifying concept, and it has explained why social scientists lack research-strategic incentives to fully engage with resilience theory and thinking. Below, we contribute three conclusions to the resilience debate and a final cautionary remark:

- Definitions of resilience vary from concise to comprehensive, from coherent to internally contradictory, from precise to vague, and from descriptive to normative to predictive – but can be categorised into a typology of four distinct types (see Table 5.1).
- The incommensurability between the natural and social sciences operates in two ways: core concepts in resilience theory do not fit into the social sciences, and core concepts and theories in the social sciences – such as agency, conflict, knowledge, power – are ignored by resilience theory.
- Given the lack of attention to agency, conflict, knowledge and power, and its insensitivity to theoretical development in contemporary social science, resilience is becoming a powerful depoliticising or naturalising scientific concept and metaphor when used by political regimes.

The unifying ambition in resilience theory and thinking *to go beyond* natural science is counterproductive to successful interdisciplinary and integrated research. Far reaching unification as an approach to integrated research can easily result in scientific imperialism –which is arguably how resilience theory has been perceived from the perspective of the social sciences. Approaches based on pluralism are therefore a more fruitful way forward.

Acknowledgements

This is an abridged and revised version of: Olsson, L., Jerneck, A., Thorén, H., Persson, J., and O'Byrne, D. (2015). 'Why resilience is unappealing to social science: Theoretical and empirical investigations of the scientific use of resilience.' *Science Advances*, 1(4), e1400217.

References

Adger, W. N., Hughes, T. P., Folke, C., Carpenter, S. R. and Rockström, J. (2005) Social-ecological resilience to coastal disasters. *Science*, 309, 1036–1039.
Alexander, D. (2013) Resilience and disaster risk reduction: an etymological journey. *Natural Hazards and Earth System Science*, 13, 2707–2716.
Avelino, F. and Rotmans, J. (2009) Power in transition. An interdisciplinary framework to study power in relation to structural change. *European Journal of Social Theory*, 12, 543–569.
Bacon, F. [1620] (2000) *Francis Bacon: The New Organon*. Cambridge: Cambridge University Press.
Baecker, D. (2001) Why Systems? *Theory, Culture & Society*, 18, 59–74.

Barabási, A.-L. and Albert, R. (1999) Emergence of scaling in random networks. *Science*, 286, 509–512.

Barnes, B. (1995) *The Elements of Social Theory*. London: University College London Press.

Barnes, B. V. and Spurr, S. H. (1998) *Forest Ecology*. New York: Wiley.

Barrett, C. B. and Constas, M. A. (2014) Toward a theory of resilience for international development applications. *PNAS*, 111, 14625–14630.

Béné, C., Wood, R. G., Newsham, A. and Davies, M. (2012) Resilience: new utopia or new tyranny? Reflection about the potentials and limits of the concept of resilience in relation to vulnerability reduction programmes. *IDS Working Papers*, 2012, 1–61.

Bennett, J. W. (1975) Ecosystem analogies in cultural ecology. *Population, Ecology and Social Evolution.* Polgar, S., ed, 273–303. The Hague and Paris: Mouton Publishers.

Bertalanffy, L. V. (1968) *General System Theory: Foundations, Development, Applications*. New York: Braziller.

Blühdorn, I. (2000) An offer one might prefer to refuse: the systems theoretical legacy of Niklas Luhmann. *European Journal of Social Theory*, 3, 339–354.

Brand, F. S. and Jax, K. (2007) Focusing the meaning (s) of resilience: resilience as a descriptive concept and a boundary object. *Ecology and Society*, 12, 23.

Brown, K. (2014) Global environmental change I: a social turn for resilience? *Progress in Human Geography*, 38, 107–117.

Clarke, S. and Walsh, A. (2009) Scientific imperialism and the proper relations between the sciences. *International Studies in the Philosophy of Science*, 23, 195–207.

Collier, J. and Cumming, G. (2011) A dynamical approach to ecosystem identity. *Philosophy of Ecology*, 11, 201–218.

Collinge, C. (1999) Self-organisation of society by scale: a spatial reworking of regulation theory. *Environment and Planning D*, 17, 557–574.

Collins, R. (1990) Conflict theory and the advance of macro-historical sociology. *Frontiers of Social Theory: The New Syntheses*, 68–87.

Cote, M. and Nightingale, A. J. (2012) Resilience thinking meets social theory: situating social change in socio-ecological systems (SES) research. *Progress in Human Geography*, 36, 475–489.

Cumming, G. S., Olsson, P., Chapin III, F. and Holling, C. (2013) Resilience, experimentation, and scale mismatches in social-ecological landscapes. *Landscape Ecology*, 28, 1139–1150.

Dahrendorf, R. (1959) *Class and Class Conflict in Industrial Society*. Stanford, CA: Stanford University Press.

Davidson, D. J. (2010) The applicability of the concept of resilience to social systems: some sources of optimism and nagging doubts. *Society and Natural Resources*, 23, 1135–1149.

Downes, B. J., Miller, F., Barnett, J., Glaister, A. and Ellemor, H. (2013) How do we know about resilience? An analysis of empirical research on resilience, and implications for interdisciplinary praxis. *Environmental Research Letters*, 8, 014041.

Dupré, J. (1991) Reflections on biology and culture. In Sheehan, J. J. and Sosna, M. (eds), *Boundaries of Humanity: Humans, Animals, Machines*. Berkeley, CA: University of California Press.

Dupré, J. (1994) Against scientific imperialism. PSA: Proceedings of the Biennial Meeting of the Philosophy of Science Association. JSTOR, 374–381.

Dupré, J. (2001) *Human Nature and the Limits of Science*. Oxford: Oxford University Press.

Folke, C., Hahn, T., Olsson, P. and Norberg, J. (2005) Adaptive governance of social-ecological systems. *Annual Review of Environment and Resources*, 30, 441–473.

Folke, C., Carpenter, S. R., Walker, B., Scheffer, M., Chapin, T. and Rockström, J. (2010) Resilience thinking: integrating resilience, adaptability and transformability. *Ecology and Society*, 15, 20.

Fuchs, C. (2003) Some implications of Pierre Bourdieu's works for a theory of social selforganization. *European Journal of Social Theory*, 6, 387–408.

Gardner, T. A., Barlow, J., Chazdon, R., Ewers, R. M., Harvey, C. A., Peres, C. A. and Sodhi, N. S. (2009) Prospects for tropical forest biodiversity in a human-modified world. *Ecology Letters*, 12, 561–582.

Geels, F. W. (2010) Ontologies, socio-technical transitions (to sustainability), and the multi-level perspective. *Research Policy*, 39, 495–510.

Geels, F. W. (2011) The multi-level perspective on sustainability transitions: responses to seven criticisms. *Environmental Innovation and Societal Transitions*, 1, 24–40.

Gowdy, J. (1997) Introduction: biology and economics. *Structural Change and Economic Dynamics*, 8, 377–383.

Gunderson, L. H. and Holling, C. S. (2002) *Panarchy: Understanding Transformations in Human and Natural Systems*. Washington, DC: Island Press.

Hatt, K. (2013) Social attractors: a proposal to enhance 'resilience thinking' about the social. *Society and Natural Resources*, 26, 30–43.

Haugeland, J. (2000) *Having Thought: Essays in the Metaphysics of Mind*. Cambridge, MA: Harvard University Press.

Hayek, F. A. (1988) *The Fatal Conceit: The Errors of Socialism*. Chicago, IL: University of Chicago Press.

Holling, C. S. (1973) Resilience and stability of ecological systems. *Annual Review of Ecology and Systematics*, 4, 1–24.

Hughes, B. (2009) Disability activisms: social model stalwarts and biological citizens. *Disability and Society*, 24, 677–688.

Jerneck, A. and Olsson, L. (2008) Adaptation and the poor – development, resilience, transition. *Climate Policy*, 8, 170–182.

Jones, P., Bradbury, L. and Leboutillier, S. (2011) *Introducing Social Theory*. Cambridge: Polity Press.

Kellert, S. H., Longino, H. E. and Waters, C. K. (2006) Scientific pluralism, introduction. *Minnesota Studies in the Philosophy of Science*, xix.

Kumar, P. (2010) *The Economics of Ecosystems and Biodiversity: Ecological and Economic Foundations*. London and Washington, DC: UNEP and Earthscan.

Luhmann, N. (1982) The world society as a social system. *International Journal of General Systems*, 8(3), 131–138.

Luhmann, N. (1997) Globalization or world society: how to conceive of modern society? *International Review of Sociology*, 7, 67–79.

McGregor, S. L. (2014) Transdisciplinarity and conceptual change. *World Futures*, 70, 200–232.

Mahoney, J. and Rueschemeyer, D. (2003) *Comparative Historical Analysis in the Social Sciences*. Cambridge: Cambridge University Press.

Mahoney, J. and Thelen, K. (2010) *Explaining Institutional Change: Ambiguity, Agency, and Power*. New York: Cambridge University Press.

Mazzucato, M. (2013) *The Entrepreneurial State: Debunking Public vs. Private Sector Myths*. London: Anthem Press.

Midgley, M. (1984) Reductivism, fatalism and sociobiology. *Journal of Applied Philosophy*, 1, 107–114.

Mitchell, S. D. (2009) *Unsimple Truths: Science, Complexity, and Policy*. Chicago, IL: University of Chicago Press.

Mäki, U. (2013) Scientific imperialism: difficulties in definition, identification, and assessment. *International Studies in the Philosophy of Science*, 27, 325–339.

Norgaard, R. B. (2010) Ecosystem services: from eye-opening metaphor to complexity blinder. *Ecological Economics*, 69, 1219–1227.

North, D. C. (1990) *Institutions, Institutional Change and Economic Performance*. Cambridge: Cambridge University Press.

Olsson, P., Folke, C. and Hahn, T. (2004) Social-ecological transformation for ecosystem management: the development of adaptive co-management of a wetland landscape in southern Sweden. *Ecology and Society*, 9, 2.

Olsson, P., Galaz, V. and Boonstra, W. J. (2014) Sustainability transformations: a resilience perspective. *Ecology and Society*, 19, 1.

Ostrom, E. (1998) A behavioral approach to the rational choice theory of collective action: presidential address, American Political Science Association, 1997. *American Political Science Review*, 92, 1–22.

Ostrom, E. (2009) A general framework for analyzing sustainability of social-ecological systems. *Science*, 325, 419–422.

Ostrom, E., Burger, J., Field, C. B., Norgaard, R. B. and Policansky, D. (1999) Revisiting the commons: local lessons, global challenges. *Science*, 284, 278–282.

Pareto, V. (1935) *The Mind and Society*. New York: Harcourt, Brace and Co.

Parsons, T. (1951) *The Social System*. London: Routledge.

Parsons, T. (1970) On building social system theory: a personal history. *Daedalus*, 99, 826–881.

Perrings, C. (1998) Introduction: resilience and sustainable development. *Environment and Development Economics*, 3, 221–222.

Peterson, G. (2000) Political ecology and ecological resilience: an integration of human and ecological dynamics. *Ecological Economics*, 35, 323–336.

Polanyi, K. (1957) *The Great Transformation: The Political and Economic Origin of Our Time*. Boston MA: Beacon.

Radcliffe-Brown, A. R. (1935) On the concept of function in social science. *American Anthropologist*, 37, 394–402.

Reid, J. (2013) Interrogating the neoliberal biopolitics of the sustainable development-resilience nexus. *International Political Sociology*, 7, 353–367.

Ritzer, G. (2011) *Sociological Theory*. New York: McGraw-Hill.

Roberts, J. T. and Grimes, P. E. (2002) World-system theory and the environment: toward a new synthesis. In Dunlap, R. E., Buttel, F. H., Dickens, P. and Gijswijt, A. (eds), *Sociological Theory and the Environment: Classical Foundations, Contemporary Insights*, 167–196. Lanham, MD: Rowman and Littlefield Publishers.

Scheffer, M. (2009) *Critical Transitions in Nature and Society*. Princeton, NJ: Princeton University Press.

Schmidt, V. A. (2008) Discursive institutionalism: The explanatory power of ideas and discourse. *Annual Review of Political Science*, 11, 303–326.

Shakespeare, T. (1993) Disabled people's self-organisation: a new social movement? *Disability, Handicap and Society*, 8, 249–264.

Simon, H. A. (1969) *The Sciences of the Artificial*. Cambridge, MA: MIT Press.

Smith, A. [1776] (2010) *The Wealth of Nations. The Economics Classic*. Chichester: Capstone Publishing Ltd.

Smith, A. and Stirling, A. (2010) The politics of social-ecological resilience and sustainable socio-technical transitions. *Ecology and Society*, 15, 13.

Smith, R. L., Smith, T. M., Hickman, G. C. and Hickman, S. M. (2006) *Elements of Ecology*. San Fransisco, CA: Benjamin Cummings.

Sober, E. (1994) *Conceptual Issues in Evolutionary Biology*. Cambridge, MA: MIT Press.

Thorén, H. (2015) *The Hammer and the Nail*. PhD, Lund University, Department of Philosophy.

Ullmann-Margalit, E. (1978) Invisible hand explanations. *Synthese*, 39, 263–291.

UNDP (2014) Human development report 2014: sustaining human progress: reducing vulnerabilities and building resilience. *Human Development Reports*. New York: United Nations Development Program.

Walker, B., Holling, C., Carpenter, S. and Kinzig, A. (2004) Resilience, adaptability and transformability in social–ecological systems. *Ecology and Society*, 9, 5.

Walker, B. H., Gunderson, L. H., Kinzig, A. P., Folke, C., Carpenter, S. and Schultz, L. (2006) A handful of heuristics and some propositions for understanding resilience in social-ecological systems. *Ecology and Society*, 11, 13.

Walker, J. and Cooper, M. (2011) Genealogies of resilience. From systems ecology to the political economy of crisis adaptation. *Security Dialogue*, 42, 143–160.

Wallerstein, I. (1974) *The Modern World-System, 3 Vols (1974–89)*. New York: Academic Press.

Wallerstein, I. (2011) *The Modern World-System IV: Centrist Liberalism Triumphant, 1789–1914*. Berkely, CA: University of California Press.

Wimsatt, W. C. (1976) Reductive explanation: a functional account. In Cohen, R. S., Hooker, C. A., Michalos, A. C. and Van Evra, J. (eds), *Proceedings of the 1974 Biennial Meeting Philosophy of Science Association*. Boston, MA: D. Reidel Publishing Company.

6

THE NATURE OF RESILIENCE

Chris Zebrowski

Introduction

Panic has long figured as a principle consideration guiding strategies of emergency governance. Its spectacular fall from a core operational assumption organizing emergency response well into the final days of the Cold War to its current status within academic literatures as 'myth' (Clarke, 2002; Cocking *et al.*, 2009; Johnson, 1985; Keating, 1982; Sheppard *et al.*, 2006; Tierney, 2003; Wessely, 2005) must therefore be regarded as a pivotal event in the history of emergency governance.

In stark contrast to the competitive, self-interested behaviour assumed to accompany emergencies, disaster researchers have documented the widespread cooperation (even altruism), which often manifests during disasters. Social norms, far from breaking down, not only continued to govern behaviour (Cocking *et al.*, 2009; Sime, 1983; Drury *et al.*, 2009) but proved remarkably resilient with incidences of violence and crime often subsiding significantly (Auf der Heide, 2004; Tierney, 2003). To the extent that 'irrational behaviour', or panic, was witnessed, experts argued that these were in fact rational decisions based on imperfect knowledge within a rapidly unfolding event, which only appeared to onlookers as irrational (Tierney, 2003). Panic, we are now told, is nothing more than a fallacious, culturally ingrained belief, perpetuated through its ubiquitous appearance in media portrayals of emergencies, but having no basis in reality (Clarke, 2002; Tierney, 2003). Disaster researchers have also noted the implications of this research on the organization, direction, and conduct of emergency response (Dynes and Drabek, 1994; Manyena, 2006). Government, within an unfolding emergency, should not look to direct, but to supplement and encourage the natural tendencies of those in emergency events to help themselves. Instead of withholding information, for fear of inciting panic, populations in emergencies should be provided with all the information they require to self-organize an evacuation or response (Proulx and Sime, 1991). People are to be encouraged, not directed; managed, not controlled.

The acknowledgement that panic is a 'myth' has lent support to the profound reorganization of UK emergency governance at the turn of the century. Departing radically from the disciplinary logic which guided British Civil Defence over the course of the Cold War, the resilience strategies of UK Civil Contingencies are instead oriented towards facilitating and optimizing the natural, self-organizational capacities, or 'resilience', of populations-in-emergency (Zebrowski, 2009; Kaufmann, 2013). The advent of resilience strategies within UK Civil Contingencies has thus been explained as the result of an improved conceptualization of the referents of security.

But disaster research also serves to legitimize resilience strategies by premising the introduction of these policies on an empirically validated re-evaluation of collective human behaviour within emergency events. Indeed, resilience strategies are routinely celebrated as demonstrative of the growing humanism of emergency governance. Within these narratives, resilience enjoins the positivism of social science with the emancipatory project of liberalism: knowledge of the nature of 'the social' permits less governance, less control and more 'freedom'.

This chapter seeks to advance an alternative to this positivist explanation: that the appearance of 'resilient populations' is an effect, rather the cause, of a broader restructuring of rationalities and practices comprising liberal governance. Such an explanation challenges the idea that resilience represents an objective 'discovery' of (social) science. Instead, resilient populations are taken to be a *particular* enframing of life forged and sustained through the repeated exercise of practices governance. Such an approach entails placing a priority on the constitutive effect of practices in shaping our understanding of the world around us. Moreover, it draws attention to the ontopolitical status of resilient populations as a referent of governance. To say that resilience is the correlate of neoliberalism does not mean that resilient populations are an illusion or a 'false' conception. On the contrary, such a claim invites critical inquiry into the processes through which resilient populations were rendered 'true', panic was deemed 'false', and the implications of this shift for the ways in which governmental power is exercised during emergencies.

This chapter aims to identify the conditions under which resilient populations could emerge as a referent of emergency governance. It does so by investigating transformations in the order of power/knowledge underpinning liberal governance. Our analysis begins by recognizing the importance that the 'natural' status of the market played in the historical genesis of liberalism as an art of governance. As disciplines with an authority on the composition of 'the natural', the historical co-evolution of Economics and Ecology is quickly traced with the aim of rendering explicit their common archaeological structure. Emphasis is placed on the function of equilibrium-based models (which persisted from classical studies of balance to the cybernetically inflected discourses dominant in the period following the Second World War) in providing nature with a *telos* and liberal governance with an objective. C. S. Holling's resilience theory is next examined as a radical departure from classical equilibrium-based models towards an atelic figure of nature composed of multiple, emergent equilibria. The simultaneous rearticulation of Ecology and Economics within the framework of the complexity sciences is taken as a profound shift in the order of 'the natural', enabling the development of novel forms of government. Turning to Hayek's appropriation of the complexity discourses in his later career, this study looks to identify the historical singularity of 'environmental' techniques of exercising power. Taken together, this novel account of nature, coupled with environmental techniques of government, is understood to forge a new regime of knowledge/power. The final section of this chapter accounts for the appearance of resilient populations as a function of the emergence of this regime.

The nature of nature

Before the term *oecology* was coined by German Darwinist Ernst Haeckel in 1866, references to the study of 'nature's economy' abounded. The phrase derived from Linnaeus' 1749 *The Oeconomy of Nature: A Study of the Divine Order Visible within Nature's Design* (see Worster, 1994, pp. 34–8). In the late eighteenth century the term *oeconomy* still carried a connotation with household management – the original sense of the term from which it derives the prefix *oikos*, Greek for home or habitation. Thus, the title of Linnaeus' highly influential 1749 *The Oeconomy of Nature* referred to the transcendent Creator's orderly design of nature rather than an allusion to 'political economy' in the contemporary sense. Early studies of nature's economy marvelled at the balance and harmony achieved by this divine design, which paired ends with means down to infinitely small detail (Worster, 1994). Yet, while God's infinite attention to detail was a source of marvel, it provided a problem for translating nature into a model for human governance. While man could aspire to this level of management, it was only God, with his infinite wisdom, who could achieve such perfection in design.

Ecology,[1] which emerged as a field of study at the threshold of the late eighteenth and early nineteenth centuries, was to purge the idea of a transcendent ordering of nature by a divine Creator and replace it with a model of immanent self-ordering through competition. As is well known, Darwin credited Thomas Malthus for insights leading him to the theory of natural selection, which echoed economic notions of the invisible hand as a mechanism responsible for the immanent self-ordering of the market. However, the success of classical economic liberalism was similarly based on its success in articulating market mechanisms as 'natural'. In his lecture series *The Birth of Biopolitics* Foucault discusses how from the middle of the eighteenth century the market transitions from a site of jurisdiction against fraud – a significant risk between the sixteenth and seventeenth centuries – to a site of veridiction: 'a site and a mechanism for the formation of truth' (Foucault 2008, p. 30). Integral to this shift, Foucault argues, was the 'discovery' of the market's ability, when left to its own devices, to generate a 'natural price': one which accurately represents the relation between costs of production and demand. The 'natural' status of the market was used to argue for the displacement of government intervention from ensuring justice within the market to limiting interference (and especially political interference) with these 'natural' mechanisms.

While references to ordered harmony faded as both fields became similarly conceptualized as sites of competition for scarce resources, the emphasis on balance would be preserved and given 'scientific' rigour within studies of market equilibrium. In his 1874 *Elements of a Pure Economics*, Léon Walras provided the foundations for general equilibrium theory by outlining the basic equations for a general equilibrium model and advanced a proof for the existence of a solution (Walras 2003, p. 169). Moreover, Walras sought to specify how this solution would be arrived at through the 'natural' adjustment mechanisms that exist within a competitive market. Competitive markets arrived at equilibrium prices – those which perfectly coordinate aggregate demand with supply so as to clear the market – through a process of *tâtonnement* ('groping towards') (Walras 2003, p. 170). If prices were set under equilibrium levels, so as to render supply insufficient for demand, then prices would slowly climb as markets 'groped towards' equilibrium level, and vice versa. Through a process of 'sequential' *tâtonnement*, markets would clear, one at a time, until prices converged at a general equilibrium. Likewise, destabilization of prices following an economic shock would be expected to adjust through *tâtonnement* back to equilibrium over time.

The natural tendency towards equilibrium was echoed at this time within ecological treatments of succession. By the turn of the twentieth century, ecology had become a prominent field, in large part due to its perceived insight into the integration of political and economic units, which were used to inform strategies of social, and especially colonial, administration (Anker, 2001). It is not unsurprising, then, that a primary area of study was ecological succession: the colonization of plant and animal communities within a given region over time. Succession was premised on the widespread assumption of progressive development of a biotic community, consisting of both animal and vegetal species. Of particular influence to the field were Fredric Clements' theories of succession – widely suspected of having been derived from his reading of sociologist (and social Darwinist) Herbert Spencer (Worster, 1994; Anker, 2001; Kwa, 2002). Biotic communities were thought to progress from a relatively homogeneous and undifferentiated community (in human terms: a hunter-gatherer society) to more heterogeneous 'complex' communities in which functions were harmonized into a functioning whole (modern European societies) – which for Clements, as for Spencer, functioned as a 'super-organism'. Increased harmonization of the whole would absolve the need for further adaptation, thus halting evolution at what Clements would term a climax community. A climax community refers to the ecological composition of this biotic (or human) community within the final stage in its development. The type of vegetation composing the climax stage – be it a forest, desert, marsh, grassland, or otherwise – was said to be predefined by regional climatic variables such as temperature, rainfall, and wind. While external shocks to an ecological community could disrupt this progression, nature would always rebound to continue its march through intermediary stages, known as *seres*, towards its climatically defined climax.

In 1935, Arthur Tansley outlined an inventory of systems based on the value of 'stability' (Tansley, 1935). Stability was measured by the ability of a system to maintain its composure over time. The 'ecosystem', a term appearing for the first time in this paper in distinction to the 'biotic communities' and 'complex organisms' found in the holistic theories of Clements and Smuts, was a relatively unstable system given the range of factors both internal and external which could disrupt equilibrium. Yet the natural return of the system to equilibrium was assumed almost without question. 'The universal tendency to the evolution of dynamic equilibria has long been recognized', and thus was provided no further explanation within the paper (Tansley, 1935). Kwa has suggested that this self-evidence may be related to the widespread reference in explanations of life processes at the turn of the century to Le Chatelier's late nineteenth-century experiments, which demonstrated that endogenous shocks to a chemical equilibrium would be responded to by other factors so as to restore equilibrium (Kwa, 2002, p. 33).

The scientification of ecology at this time was mirrored within the fields of economics. From the 1930s, Walrasian microeconomics would become more rigorously mathematicized as part of an overall trend in economics (Mirowski, 2002, p. 7; Weintraub, 2002). In the process, core concepts such as equilibrium, stability, and the process of *tâtonnement* would be fundamentally reinterpreted (Weintraub 2002, p. 125). *Tâtonnement* would be rearticulated during this time to make it amenable to the ascendant neoclassical synthesis of Walrasian (microeconomic) theory and Keynesian (macroeconomic) theory, which effectively displaced a number of rival theories including Institutionalist, Marxist, and Austrian perspectives during this period (Hands 2009). Walrasian sequential *tâtonnement* would be replaced within the literature by Samuelson's version of *tâtonnement*, which foregrounded speed of adjustment and more adequately accommodated Keynesian concerns regarding the 'stickiness' of some markets in adjusting to equilibrium including, especially, labour markets. Keynesian demand-management could thus be justified in assisting processes of *tâtonnement* to restore equilibrium in a more efficient and timely manner.

The common archaeological structure of the fields of ecology and economics from the time of their co-constitution was premised on a 'natural' *telos* towards a unique equilibrium following a systemic perturbation. The stability of systems to withstand shock – to move only incrementally away from equilibrium and return to it quickly thereafter – was recognized as a value with which to assess these systems and inform programmes of governance. The diagram of governance operating in relation to this ontologization of nature would operate a security logic of protection designed to protect systems from shocks in the first place and speed their return to equilibrium following a perturbation. This is what Holling would call 'engineering resilience' (Holling, 1996), the security programme advocated by systems ecologists concerned with speedily restoring a presumed 'natural' equilibrium. It was in opposition to this logic of security that Holling would advance the notion of 'ecological resilience': a programme of governance which not only reinterpreted the *telos* of security, but offered a radical re-ontologization of nature rooted within the discourses of the complexity sciences.

Transforming nature

In the 1950s, Clements' theory of a climax community would be refigured, but essentially preserved, as functional homeostasis when ecology was translated into the discourse of cybernetics. The ecosystem, understood as a cybernetic system, responded to destabilizing exogenous shocks through feedback mechanisms, which would return the system to a pre-defined equilibrium state. Written in response to these models, C. S. Hollings' highly influential 'Resilience and Stability of Ecological Systems' would challenge the notion that nature was itself organized around a unique 'natural' equilibrium and, with it, challenge the long-established belief in nature's *telos* (Holling, 1973). In doing so, Holling would draw on developments in third-wave cybernetics associated with chaos, complexity, and self-organizing autopoietic systems in order to advance a security programme for ecosystemic sustainability, which he would term 'resilience.'

Specifically, Holling took issue with the cybernetically grounded 'systems ecology' of brothers Eugene and Howard (Tom) Odum. Inspired by the writings of Alfred Lotka on the energetics of evolution, the brothers' work used systems analysis to study the function of energy flows within a system (Odum, 1953; Patten and Odum, 1981; Odum, 1983). In the process, Tansley's notion of ecosystem would be reconceptualized as a cybernetic system progressively developing towards a climax-state of 'functional homeostasis'. In *The Strategy of Ecosystem Development*, the idea of functional homeostasis is presented as both nature's *telos* and a security project:

> In a word, the 'strategy' of succession as a short-term process is basically the same as the 'strategy' of long-term evolutionary development of the biosphere—namely, increased control of, or homeostasis with, the physical environment in the sense of achieving maximum protection from its perturbations.
>
> *(Odum, 1969, p. 262)*

Achieving 'maximum protection', it is noted, may however conflict with man's emphasis on 'maximum production' – an idea that is given further development by Eugene's brother Howard in *Environment, Power and Society* (Odum, 1971). Here, H. T. Odum reflected on the implications of industrial-led growth for the sustainability of Western ecosystems, arguing that the depletion of fossil-based resources would demand a fundamental restructuring of economies along sustainable lines. Achieving such a programme would require a massive effort in the control engineering of economies, with an eye to the natural limits of ecosystems (Cooper and Walker, 2011, p. 6).

Holling's work would challenge the command and control approaches to ecosystem management advocated by systems ecologists, in favour of what he would term a resilience approach. The earliest mention of the concept appeared within 'Resilience and Stability of Ecological Systems' (Holling, 1973). The paper immediately takes aim at quantitative approaches to ecosystem management, stating that the application of systems analysis to the study of ecosystems places an excessive emphasis on equilibrium, which 'may simply reflect an analytic approach developed in one area because it was useful and then transferred to another where it may not be' (Holling, 1973, p. 1). Instead, questions of sustainability require a shift in 'emphasis from the equilibrium states to the conditions for persistence' (Holling, 1973, p. 2).

Over the course of the article, Holling progressively outlines a new ontology of ecosystems rooted in the discourse of complex adaptive systems. Critically, Holling dismisses the idea that ecosystems organize around a single equilibrium point to which a system will automatically return following systemic shock. Rather, the particular attractor around which a system is organized represents only one of a multitude of possible states, which emerge and disappear over time. A system will continue to organize around a particular attractor, given the presence of feedback mechanisms related to levels of biodiversity. The range in which a system can operate whilst organizing around the same attractor is referred to as a stability domain. Stability domains themselves evolve over time, expanding or contracting based on the size and number of the feedback loops operating around an attractor. The gradual weakening of the feedback loops operating around an attractor, for example through the loss of biodiversity within an ecosystem, can make a system more fragile and susceptible to shocks that will transfer it out of its current stability domain, towards an attractor organized around different processes. Depending on the nature of the feedback cycles within a regime, a transition may either be gradual or sudden – which accounts for the non-linear phase shifts of a system over time.

Holling was eager to emphasize the implications of this new ontology of nature for ecosystem management. He criticized efforts to protect vulnerable populations through system stabilizing approaches focused on maintaining the system in an equilibrium state. Programmes based on maintaining an optimal level of a population, such as those of Maximum Sustained Yield or protectionist policies designed to eliminate competitors and predators, have had, in some documented cases, the unintended consequences of reducing the overall resilience of a system: 'a measure of the persistence of systems and of their ability to absorb change and disturbance and still maintain the same relationships between populations or state variables' (Holling, 1973, p. 14). Eroding the resilience of a system would leave it more susceptible to even minor external perturbations – random events such as climactic change, fire, or pollution – which could flip the system into another stability domain and potentially increase the risk of wholesale species extinction (Holling, 1973, p. 9). According to Holling, for ecosystem management 'the important point is not so much how stable they are within the domain, but how likely it is for the system to move from one domain into another and so persist in a changed configuration' (Holling, 1973, p. 10). Going further, Holling suggested that in many cases what appears to be an instability within a system, such as widely fluctuating population levels of a particular species, can in fact *contribute* to systemic resilience (Holling, 1973, pp. 16–17). Again, an overemphasis on stability within equilibrium-centred approaches should in fact be reconsidered and replaced by an approach which aimed to increase the resilience of a system through a study of the dynamics underlying its domain of attraction. In his concluding paragraph, Holling characterized a resilience approach in terms of epistemological modesty, an acknowledgment of the limits of human understanding.

A management approach based on resilience would emphasize the need to keep options open, the need to view events in a regional rather than a local context, and the need to emphasize heterogeneity. Flowing from this would be not the presumption of sufficient knowledge, but the recognition of our ignorance; not the assumption that future events are expected, but that they will be unexpected. The resilience framework can accommodate this shift in perspective, for it does not require a precise capacity to predict the future, but only a qualitative capacity to devise systems that can absorb and accommodate future events in whatever unexpected form they may take (Holling, 1973, p. 21).

Over the course of his career, Holling would develop and elaborate an approach to managing ecosystems composed of multiple, emergent equilibria. Departing from equilibrium-focused techniques focused on systemic stability, a resilience approach, as outlined by Holling, would focus on optimizing the conditions for persistence of a species or ecosystem. Enhancing a system's resilience could be achieved in two ways (Holling 1973). First, one could attempt to move the system further away from a critical threshold that would send it towards an alternate attractor. However, positioning a system away from an attractor could come at the cost of systemic efficiency. Alternatively, resilience could be enhanced by expanding the stability domain around an attractor. As Gunderson and Holling have noted, this second solution – which seeks to engender resilience into a system – not only increases the capacity of a system to withstand the impact of potentially destabilizing shocks, but also permits the system to quickly and efficiently reorganize, so as to capitalize on emerging opportunities (Holling *et al.*, 2002, p. 76).

Security, within a resilience framework, was no longer a conservative enterprise. It was an opportunity to evolve. Governance, rather than maintaining systems around 'natural' equilibrium points through normative/disciplinary techniques, would be reoriented towards enhancing the conditions of a systems capacity for adaptive emergence. To appreciate the significance of this new programme for liberal governance, we should now turn to examine associated developments that were occurring simultaneously in the field of Political Economy.

The nature of neoliberalism

A year after Holling's groundbreaking paper, Friedrich von Hayek was awarded the 1974 Nobel Prize in economics. In his acceptance speech, subsequently published under the title 'The Pretense of Knowledge' (Hayek, 1989), Hayek railed against the hubris of Keynesian 'scientistism' in the context of the ongoing international stagflation crisis. Echoing Holling, Hayek charged economists with committing the 'scientist error' of naively appropriating the mathematically rigorous models of the physical sciences without sufficient regard to the differences between fields. The market, Hayek maintained, citing prominent cyberneticist Warren Weaver to lend credibility to his assertion, displayed an 'essential complexity' that precluded mathematical modelling. Despite his earlier criticism of 'slavish imitation of the method and language of science' (Hayek, 1952, p. 15) by economists, Hayek would increasingly draw upon the discourses of complexity to articulate his understanding of the market and promote a form of neoliberal economic governance sensitive to the powerful self-organizing capacities of the market (Cooper and Walker, 2011; Mirowski, 1997, 2007). Consistent with classical liberalism, Hayek interpreted the 'natural' status of the market to confer limits on the degree to which government could regulate and control its processes. Where Hayek's project increasingly diverged from classical articulations of liberalism over the course of his career was on the nature of the 'natural' itself.

Hayek singled out in his Nobel Prize speech the Club of Rome's report on *The Limits to Growth* (Meadows *et al.*, 1972) as demonstrative of the status afforded to dubious science which transgressed the limits of what it could rightfully determine (Hayek 1989, p. 6). The report had received significant attention in light of its provocative thesis that the sustainability of exponential economic growth was untenable, with the limits to this trajectory likely to be reached within the century. The MIT research group behind the report applied systems analysis to computer models to extrapolate the interaction between population growth, industrialization, pollution, food production, and resource depletion over time. Altering these variables across a range of possible future scenarios, the MIT team concluded that the rate of depletion of the finite resources upon which industrial economies were based raised significant concerns about the limits to economic growth. Echoing the prescription of Howard Odum, the report suggested that 'it is possible to alter these growth trends and to establish a condition of ecological and economic stability that is sustainable far into the future' (Meadows *et al.* 1972, p. 24) if economic growth was engineered along sustainable lines within a steady-state economy that respected ecological and biotic equilibria.

For Hayek, in such a complex field as the market, that which is important for study is rarely quantifiable. Yet, the scientific status afforded *prima facie* to quantitative studies had encouraged analysis of those factors that *can* be measured, regardless of their overall importance to the dynamics of the market. Even the positive correlation between aggregate demand and total employment may only be approximate, Hayek suggested. However, insofar as it is the only cause for which we have quantitative data, it has been taken as a scientific truth despite the fact that it may only be a partial explanation of more complex processes. What may, in fact, contribute more substantially to unemployment – namely, discrepancies between the distribution of demand for goods and services and the allocation of labour and other resources mandated for production – cannot be demonstrated in relation to quantitative evidence and, as a result, has been ignored by policy-makers.

Just as policies of Maximum Sustainable Yield (MSY) had eroded the resilience of complex ecosystems over time, Hayek purported that Keynesian demand-management approaches have had a debilitating effect on the ability of the underlying economic system to adjust to misallocations in labour and capital – the real cause of high unemployment, according to Hayek. By pumping money into sectors of the economy that only yield temporary demand, policies of Keynesian demand-management only delay necessary structural adjustment and breed dependency on a continual flow of state-finance – both of which only serve to increase inflation. What was required was, instead, a qualitative approach focused on optimizing the conditions for self-organization, adaptability, and growth. Hayek would characterize this approach as environmental:

> if man is to do more harm than good in his efforts to improve social order, he will have to learn that in this and in other fields where essential complexity of an organized kind prevails, he cannot acquire full knowledge which would make mastery of the events possible. He will therefore have to use what knowledge he can achieve, not to shape the results as the craftsman shapes his handiwork, but rather to cultivate growth by providing the appropriate environment, in the manner in which the gardener does this for his plants.
>
> *(Hayek 1989, p. 7)*

Environmental governance would invoke the nature of the market, in classical liberal fashion, to discourage interventionist state policies that might interfere with inherent processes of self-organization. However, in conceptualizing the market in terms of an open, complex adaptive system (see Mirowski, 2002), Hayek would draw upon a fundamentally different understanding of nature than that which had been classically conceived in both the fields of Political Economy and Ecology. For Hayek, the complexity of the market required a displacement of government efforts from intervening upon the processes of the economy itself to optimizing the conditions for self-organization and adaptive evolution. As an open, complex system the economy evolved most effectively in far from equilibrium conditions and productively when liberated from the stagnating control of the interventionist state. As open systems, local economies, rather than being shielded from the wider economic environment through state finance, would need to be opened to it, in order to allow processes of adaptation and co-evolution to operate. Scholarship, in turn, would need to be conducted with requisite epistemological modesty, identifying the qualitative conditions in which the self-organization of the market is optimized.

In *The Birth of Biopolitics*, Foucault would recognize the singularity of the 'environmental technology' operationalized within a neoliberal governmentality (Foucault, 2008, p. 259). These techniques, he would stress, were not the equilibrium-based mechanisms of disciplinary society based on a 'standardizing, identificatory, hierarchical individualization' (Foucault, 2008, p. 261). Rather, this is the:

> image, idea, or theme-program of a society in which there is an optimization of systems of difference, in which the field is left open to fluctuating processes, in which minority

individuals and practices are tolerated, in which action is brought to bear on the rules of the game rather than on the players, and finally in which there is an environmental type of intervention instead of the internal subjugation of individuals.

(Foucault, 2008, pp. 259–60)

The advent of environmental technologies coincided with the 'massive withdrawal [of] the normative-disciplinary system' (Foucault 2008, p.260). This is not a programme of standardization utilizing disciplinary technologies to structure the mentality of individuals in accordance with an ideal normality. Nor is it a programme of biopolitical regulation operating on the 'generality' of aleatory events which, though unpredictable in their individual occurrence, display a constancy at the mass-level of the population in relation to which regulatory mechanisms could be introduced "to establish an equilibrium, maintain an average, establish a homeostasis, and compensate for variations within this general population and its aleatory field" (Foucault, 2003, p. 246). The idea of fixed norms and 'natural' equilibria, at the level of the individual and the population, are dispensed with entirely for an 'environmentalism open to unknowns and transversal phenomena' (Foucault, 2008, p. 261). Foucault's lecture notes conclude with a provocative question: 'But does this mean that we are dealing with natural subjects? [*end of manuscript*]' (Foucault, 2008, 261).

If environmental technologies operated in relation to a 'natural' subject, this was not to suggest either that they proceeded from a more objective rendering of the political subject or that they are involved with emancipating the subject from processes of political subjectification. Rather, it was because human populations were now understood within the same 'natural' figure of the environment – characterized by non-linear emergent self-organization. This reconceptualization would have implications for liberal governance. Ensuring that the subject is capable of co-evolution with their environment cannot be achieved by structuring the mentality of the subject. Rather, governance would be directed towards acting on the subject's environment: understood as an incentive structure and thus a condition of possibility for emergent norms and behaviours. Security could thus no longer attempt to protect the subject from threat if this meant closing them off from their milieu. Instead, security would have to proceed by exposing the subject more fully to their environment so as to optimize its governmental effects in encouraging innovation and, crucially, adaptation.

The birth of resilient populations

We have now established how the discursive framework advanced within the complexity sciences, coupled with the environmental techniques of governance associated with neoliberalism, comprised a novel apparatus of power/knowledge. We may now account for the appearance of resilient populations as an effect of these transformations. Following Foucault, it is imperative to recognize how an order of power/knowledge 'marks out in reality that which does not exist and legitimately submits it to the division between true and false' (Foucault 2008, p. 19). Priority is placed on the constitutive effect of practices in determining the objects of social science. Resilient populations, as such, must be regarded as a *particular* enframing of life, which arose as the correlate to neoliberal governance. As an object constituted through the exercise of specific practices of governance, resilient populations cannot be said to properly 'exist' ontologically. Nor can they be discovered. They must instead be understood as the product of more obscure *ontopolitical* processes. This requires a shift in perspective – one that denies the existence of a fundamental logic underlying the 'being' of resilient populations, and instead attunes itself to the politics constitutive of resilient populations as a referent of governance. Resilient populations are simply the correlate of practices of governance; an interpretation of social behaviour determined by, and supportive of, neoliberalism.

These thoroughly *political* processes of objectification are what this chapter has sought to begin fleshing out. Given the immensity of the task, it would be impossible to exhaustively account for these processes here. Instead, this final section will investigate critical changes to the definition of panic, which facilitated the appearance of resilient populations.

From the 1950s, substantial American military funding was being provided to researchers at The University of Chicago, the University of Maryland, and the University of Oklahoma to investigate population behaviour in civilian emergencies.[2] The military was interested in extrapolating the conclusions of these studies to understand how civilians react to crisis both to inform the design of domestic social controls and direct offensive strategies (Quarantelli, 1987, 1990, 2004). The empirical research collected corroborated the evidence of earlier studies, including those of Mintz and Strauss, which had argued that the behaviour of populations in an emergency was better characterized as rational action, rather than irrational hysteria, based on an individual's perception of their situation (see Mintz, 1951; Strauss, 1953). This proposition was assisted by E. L. Quarantelli's popular redefinition of panic as 'actual (or attempted) physical flight' (Quarantelli, 1957, p. 188) which, though more empirically verifiable, was quite obviously a radical departure from an understanding of panic in terms of irrational social hysteria. Panic, Quarantelli concluded, is 'a relatively uncommon phenomenon', which is 'over-exaggerated' in disaster literature (Quarantelli, 1954, p. 275). To the extent that it does manifest,

> panic flight does not involve irrational thought if by that is meant anything in the way of faulty deductions from certain premises. From the position of an outside observer this may appear to be the case but, from a participant's viewpoint, given his limited perspective of only certain portions of the total situation, no such interpretation or irrationality can be made. For the fleeing of person, his action appears to him quite appropriate to the situation as he perceives it at that time.
>
> *(Quarantelli, 1954, p. 272)*

Significantly, Quarantelli warns that '[o]ne of the most important contributory conditions [to the onset of panic] is the existence of a social or group predefinition of a crisis as one that is likely to eventuate in panic flight' (Quarantelli, 1954, p. 275).

While reminiscent of earlier studies which had investigated panic as a contagion, (Orr, 2006; Pelling, 2001; Forth, 2001) Quarantelli's conception of panic displayed an important qualification. Panic's transmission mechanism would no longer be perceived in energetic terms as a contagious affect that, by exciting the body, served to undermine rationality, and by extension sociality, but in terms of an adaptive, rational response to information within a situation of perceived entrapment. This shift in the understanding of panic aligned with a broader trend in sociological research of the late 1950s in which notions of 'suggestibility' and 'contagion' were displaced by an emphasis on emergent norms and adaptive tendencies as explanations of collective behaviour (Orr, 2006, pp. 128–34). This shift was indicative of the creeping influence of cybernetics and information theory within American sociology, which would come to understand the maintenance of a stable social order as a function of information exchange.

Jackie Orr identified that by the 1970s, sociological studies of panic appeared far less frequently and were being displaced by mounting psychological research on 'panic disorder': a condition characterized by recurrent panic attacks (a sudden, uncontrollable onset of intense fear often accompanied by hyperventilation, perspiration, nausea, dizziness, and heart palpitations) triggered by no observable cause (Orr, 2006, pp. 172–75). Assisted by Quarantelli's rigorous, but ultimately far narrower, definition of panic in terms of flight, the very idea of panic was itself being transformed alongside the general trend towards cybernetic thinking taking place within American sociology. No longer understood in terms of irrational hysteria, panic was now taken to be an adaptive response exhibited by a minority of individuals within a position of perceived entrapment. Combating this behaviour required opening communication channels and assisting participants by providing them with information upon which to base their decisions.

Despite the mounting literature of disaster research, it was only at the turn of the twenty-first century that disaster research would affect a significant reorganization of emergency planning and response in Britain. True, the end of the Cold War provided an opportunity, giving impetus to a radical rethink of UK Civil Contingencies in light of the widespread acknowledgement that Civil Defence was poorly suited to the 'complex emergencies' and 'new security challenges' of the twenty-first century (Smith, 2003, p. 414). But, this reorganization of UK Civil Contingencies also indicates an important event that is much more difficult to pinpoint – the passing of panic below a particular threshold of truth and the validation of 'resilient populations' as a referent object of emergency governance. What we can, however, begin to identify are the conditions within which such determinations could not be recognized as valid.

Conclusion

The resilience of populations in emergencies is often portrayed as the discovery of a natural phenomenon by disaster researchers. This chapter offers an alternative explanation, with the aim of upsetting the predominance of this narrative. Resilient populations, I suggest, are not a socio-historical constant whose essence can be objectively determined and communicated by science. The appearance of resilient populations is the result of ontopolitical processes, rather than an objectively ontological discovery.

This chapter has sought to locate the conditions under which resilient populations could emerge as a conceptual object and referent of governance. It locates these conditions within transformations occurring in the order of power/knowledge supporting liberal governance. Specifically, this chapter demonstrated how the coupling of a novel account of nature produced by the complexity turn within the disciplines of Ecology and Economics with 'environmental' techniques of government constituted a novel apparatus of power/knowledge that underpins contemporary neoliberalism. Priority was placed on the constitutive effects of practices in rendering 'resilient populations' as an empirical object of social science, and referent object of governance is an effect of neoliberal governance. As such, the conditions under which resilient populations could appear as a conceptual object were located not in the advance of (social) science, but in the ascendance of neoliberalism as a regime of governance.

Given the important role which panic played in enabling the disciplinary and biopolitical techniques of emergency governance historically, its current problematization within resilience discourses must be regarded as a pivotal event in the history of emergency governance. But, of course, the exhaustiveness of this event should also not be overstated. Panic has proved to be a remarkably persistent idea. Indeed, the widespread assumption of panic within popular imaginaries of disaster has been identified as a recurrent obstacle to the spread of resilience strategies. Initiatives to enhance 'community resilience' have thus been accompanied by educational campaigns designed to raise public awareness of the fallacy of panic and promote good practice with regard to the governance of resilient populations (Challenger et al., 2009). In spite of these efforts, the assumption of panic remains widespread with references to panic continuing to be found even within UK emergency planning guidance (Drury et al., 2013). The persistence of panic should, I believe, alert us, firstly to the fact that resilience discourses, while ubiquitous, are far from hegemonic. Panic is not simply a relic of the past, but something which continues to be manifest to the extent that disciplinary and biopolitical forms of government persist within the social field. The colonization of this space itself represents a condition of possibility for the continued evolution and spread of resilience discourses.

Notes

1 In 1893 it was decided by the International Botanical Congress to change the name of the field to our modern spelling, 'ecology' (Worster, 1994).
2 Detailed histories of this field of research are now provided by a number of sources (see Dynes and Drabek, 1994; Quarantelli 1987, 1990, 1994, 2004).

References

Anker, P. (2001) *Imperial Ecology: Environmental Order in the British Empire, 1895–1945.* Cambridge: Harvard University Press.

Auf der Heide, E. (2004) Common Misconceptions about Disasters: Panic, the 'disaster syndrome' and Looting. In M. O'Leary (ed.), *The First 72 Hours: A Community Approach to Disaster Preparedness.* Lincoln: iUniverse Publishing, pp. 340–80.

Challenger, R., Clegg, C. W., and Robinson, M. A. (2009) *Understanding Crowd Behaviours.* London: Cabinet Office. Available at: www.gov.uk/government/publications/understanding-crowd-behaviours-documents (accessed 15 July 2016).

Clarke, L. (2002) Panic: Myth or Reality? *Contexts,* 1(3), 21–6.

Cocking, C., Drury, J., and Reicher, S. (2009) The Psychology of Crowd Behaviour in Emergency Evacuations: Results from Two Interview Studies and Implications for the Fire and Rescue Services. *The Irish Journal of Psychology,* 30(1–2), 59–73.

Cooper, M. and Walker, J. (2011) Genealogies of Resilience: From Systems Ecology to the Political Economy of Crisis Adaptation. *Security Dialogue,* 14(2), 143–60.

Drury, J., Cocking, C., and Reicher, S. (2009) Everyone for Themselves? A Comparative Study of Crowd Solidarity among Emergency Survivors. *British Journal of Social Psychology,* 48, 487–506.

Drury, J., Novelli, D., and Stott, C. (2013) Representing Crowd Behaviour in Emergency Planning Guidance: 'Mass Panic' or Collective Resilience? *Resilience: International Policies, Practices and Discourses,* 1(1), 37–41.

Dynes, R. and Drabek, T. (1994) The Structure of Disaster Research: Its Policy and Disciplinary Implications. *International Journal of Mass Emergencies and Disasters,* 12(1), 5–23.

Forth, C. E. (2001) Moral Contagion and the Will: The Crisis of masculinity in fin-de-siècle France. In A. Bashford and C. Hooker (eds), *Contagion: Historical and Cultural Studies.* London: Routledge.

Foucault, M. (2003) *Society Must Be Defended: Lectures at the Collège de France, 1975–76.* London: Penguin.

Foucault, M. (2008) *The Birth of Biopolitics: Lectures at the Collège de France, 1978–1979.* Basingstoke: Palgrave Macmillan.

Hands, D. W. (2009) The Rise and Fall of Walrasian General Equilibrium Theory: The Keynes Effect. *The First International Symposium on the History of Economic Thought 'The Integration of Micro and Macroeconomics from a Historical Perspective'.*

Hayek, F. A. (1952) *The Counter-Revolution of Science: Studies on the Abuse of Reason,* Glencoe, IL: The Free Press.

Hayek, F. A. (1989) The Pretense of Knowledge. *The American Economic Review,* 79(6), 3–7.

Holling, C. S. (1996) Engineering Resilience versus Ecological Resilience. In P. Schulze (ed.), *Engineering within Ecological Constraints.* Washington, DC: National Academy Press, pp. 31–44.

Holling, C. S. (1973) Resilience and Stability of Ecological Systems. *Annual Review of Ecology and Systematics,* 4, 1–23.

Holling, C. S., Gunderson, L. H., and Peterson, G. D. (2002) Sustainability and Panarchies. In C. S. Holling and L. H. Gunderson (eds), *Panarchy: Understanding Transformations in Human and Natural Systems.* Washington, DC: Island Press, pp. 63–102.

Johnson, N. (1985) Panic and the Breakdown of Social Order: Popular Myth, Social Theory and Empirical Evidence. *Sociological Focus,* 20(3), 171–83.

Kaufmann, M. (2013) Emergent Self-organisation in Emergencies: Resilience Rationales in Interconnected Societies. *Resilience: International Policies, Practices and Discourses*, 1(1), 37–41.

Keating, J. P. (1982) The Myth of Panic. *Fire Journal*, 76(3), 57–61.

Kwa, C. (2002) Romantic and Baroque Conceptions of Complex Wholes in the Sciences. In *Complexities: Social Studies of Knowledge Practices*. Durham and London: Duke University Press, pp. 23–52.

Manyena, S. B. (2006) The Concept of Resilience Revisited. *Disasters*, 30(4), 433–50.

Meadows, D. H., Meadows, D. L., Randers, J., and Behrens, W. W. (1972) *The Limits to Growth: A Report for the Club or Rome's Project on the Predicament of Mankind*. London: Pan Books.

Mintz, A. (1951) Non-Adaptive Group Behavior. *Journal of Abnormal and Social Psychology*, 46(2), 1950–9.

Mirowski, P. (1997) Machine Dreams: Economic Agents as Cyborgs. In J. B. Davis (ed.), *New Economics and its History*. Durham, NC and London: Duke University Press.

Mirowski, P. (2002) *Machine Dreams: Economics Becomes a Cyborg Science*. Cambridge: Cambridge University Press.

Mirowski, P. (2007) Naturalizing the Market on the Road to Revisionism: Bruce Caldwell's Hayek's Challenge and the Challenge of Hayek Interpretation. *Journal of Institutional Economics*, 3(3), 351–72.

Odum, E. (1953) *Fundamentals of Ecology*. Philadelphia, PA: W. B. Saunders.

Odum, E. (1969) The Strategy of Ecoystem Development. *Science*, 164(3877), 262–70.

Odum, H. (1971) *Environment, Power and Society*. New York and Sydney: Wiley Interscience.

Odum, H. (1983) *Systems Ecology*. New York: John Wiley.

Orr, J. (2006) *Panic Diaries: A Genealogy of Panic Disorder*. Durham, NC: Duke University Press.

Patten, B. C. and Odum, E. (1981) The Cybernetic Nature of Ecosystems. *American Naturalist*, 118, 886–95.

Pelling, M. (2001) The Meaning of Contagion: Reproduction, Medicine and Metaphor. In A. Bashford and C. Hooker (eds), *Contagion: Historical and Cultural Studies*. London: Routledge.

Proulx, G. and Sime, J. D. (1991) To Prevent 'Panic' in an underground Emergency: Why Not Tell People the Truth? In G. Cox and B. Langford (eds), *Fire Safety Science – Proceedings of the Third International Symposium*. London: Elsevier Applied Science, pp. 843–52.

Quarantelli, E. L. (1954) The Nature and Conditions of Panic. *American Journal of Sociology*, 60(3), 267–75.

Quarantelli, E. L. (1957) The Behavior of Panic Participants. *Sociology and Social Research*, 41(3), 187–94.

Quarantelli, E. L. (1987) Disaster Studies: An Analysis of the Social Historical Factors Affecting the Development of Research in the Area. *International Journal of Mass Emergencies and Disasters*, 5(3), 285–310.

Quarantelli, E. L. (1990) Thirty Years of Catastrophe Research. In P. Lagadec (ed.), *States of Emergency: Technological Failures and Social Destabilization*. London: Butterworth-Heinemann, pp. 101–19.

Quarantelli, E. L. (1994) Disaster Studies: The Consequences of the Historical Use of a Sociological Approach in the Development of Research. *International Journal of Mass Emergencies and Disasters*, 12(1), 25–49.

Quarantelli, E. L. (2004) The Origins and Impact of Disaster Research. In M. O'Leary (ed.), *The First 72 Hours*. Lincoln, NE: iUniverse Inc., pp. 318–36.

Sheppard, B., Rubin, G. J., Wardman, J. K., and Wessely, S. (2006) Terrorism and Dispelling the Myth of a Panic Prone Public. *Journal of Public Health Policy*, 27(3), 219–45; discussion at 246–9.

Sime, J. D. (1983) Affiliative Behaviour During Escape to Building Exits. *Journal of Environmental Psychology*, 3(2), 21–41.

Smith, J. (2003) Civil Contingencies Planning in Government. *Parliamentary Affairs*, 56, 410–22.

Strauss, A. (1953) Concepts, Communication, and Groups. In M. Sherif and M. O. Wilson (eds), *Group Relations at the Crossroads*. New York: Harper.

Tansley, A. G. (1935) The Use and the Abuse of Vegetational Concepts and Terms. *Ecology*, 16(3), 284–307.

Tierney, K. (2003) Disaster Beliefs and Institutional Interests: Recycling Disaster Myths in the Aftermath of 9–11. In L. Clarke (ed.), *Terrorism and Disaster: New Threats, New Ideas*. Oxford: Elsevier, pp. 33–52.

Walras, L. (2003) *Elements of Pure Economics: Or the Theory of Social Wealth*, London and New York: Routledge.

Weintraub, E. R. (2002) *How Economics Became a Mathematical Science*. Durham, NC and London: Duke University Press.

Wessely, S. (2005) Don't Panic! Short and Long Term Psychological Reactions to the New Terrorism: The Role of Information and the Authorities. *Journal of Mental Health*, 14(1), 1–6.

Worster, D. (1994). *Nature's Economy: A History of Ecological Ideas*, 2nd ed. Cambridge: Cambridge University Press.

Zebrowski, C. (2009) Governing the Network Society: A Biopolitical Critique of Resilience. *Political Perspectives*, 3(1), 1–38.

PART III

Uncertainty

7

THE PROMISE OF SECURITY

Resilience, surprise and epistemic politics

Claudia Aradau

Over the past decade in particular, resilience has become a quasi-universal answer to problems of governance, from climate change to children's education, from indigenous history to disaster response, and from development to terrorism. The proliferation of resilience is so extensive that a critic has talked about the 'gospel of resilience' (Nadasdy, 2007). Given its rapid circulation and uptake across many fields of governance, resilience has attracted intense analytical attention and extensive criticisms. From the criticism of extending resilience to socio-ecological systems (Berkes *et al.*, 2003; Holling, 1973; Levin *et al.*, 2001) to that of the absence of interest in power relations and social transformation (Pelling, 2010) or inattention to inequalities, structures and conditions of possibility of transformation (Hornborg, 2009), resilience has been critically dissected across many scholarly fields and disciplines. In International Relations and security studies, the criticism of the 'fit' between resilience and neoliberalism has been particularly prominent.

The novelty, proliferation and appeal of resilience for a whole array of social practices have often been folded back upon the continuity of liberal or neoliberal practices of governance. The political subject fostered as resilient is neoliberal and self-reliant, supportive of the status quo rather than insurgent or rebellious, agential but within the coordinates of the system (Chandler, 2012; O'Malley, 2010). In these approaches, the logic of resilience is symptomatic of an intensified neoliberal logic. For Walker and Cooper, resilience evinces an 'intuitive ideological fit with a neoliberal philosophy of complex adaptive systems' (Walker and Cooper, 2011; see also Joseph, 2013). For Evans and Reid, the boundaries of resilience expand through an ontological move: the underlying ontology of resilience, therefore, is actually vulnerability (Evans and Reid, 2013). Pat O'Malley concurs on the liberal genealogy of resilience, which he sees as a particular assemblage of 'liberalism, militarism and medicine' (O'Malley, 2010, p. 4). Resilience is therefore another instantiation of the neoliberal logic of security, with its attendant constitution of vulnerability and abjection.

Why resilience today? This chapter aims to offer a different answer to this deceptively simple question. While it is undeniable that resilience is often deployed within or resonates with neoliberal frameworks, these analyses tell us little about the difference that today makes. 'What difference does today introduce with respect to yesterday?', asked Michel Foucault (1984). Taking Foucault's question seriously, this chapter inquires into the increasing appeal and rapid circulation of resilience across so many social and political domains. Questioning the novelty of resilience is suspended when a continuous history of resilience is rendered as an expression of neoliberal practices (Walker and Cooper, 2011) or through an ontology of liberal subjectivity as 'fundamentally vulnerable' (Evans and Reid, 2013). Neoliberalism as an overarching logic does not fully capture the reformulation of UK emergency planning into UK resilience, the reframing of counter-terrorism or the supplementation of disaster reduction with disaster resilience in UN reports or the UK's humanitarian policy.

Several authors, however, have addressed the novelty of resilience by unpacking the logic of security and tracing a move from protection to prevention or from vulnerability to agency (Chandler, 2012; Duffield, 2012). Yet, this move embraces novelty at the expense of longer histories of prevention – through risk profiling, assessment and management – and agency – through fostering neoliberal, entrepreneurial subjects. This chapter argues that a more nuanced position is needed to attend to the difference that resilience makes today, while exploring historical continuities.

To this purpose, the chapter starts by unpacking the problematisation to which resilience offers a solution. The particular problematisation of future events as surprises that resilience aims to tackle shows the transformation of regimes of knowledge. Long-standing challenges for security governance, surprises are reconfigured through the knowledge of complex systems. In a second stage, I expose the political transformations that the epistemic regime of surprising events entails through a reading of the UK Department for International Development's (DFID) reformulation of humanitarian policy, which is centred on resilience. The problematisation of humanitarian policy in the face of continuously surprising events reveals a political transformation that resilience makes possible – the suspension of the promise of security. The final section then unpacks the promise of security across epistemic regimes in order to reveal the political implications of this suspension. Although the language of the promise of security is pervasive in International Relations (IR), the concept of the promise and promissory politics have remained unexplored. The promise allows us to understand the effects of the transformation that takes place: from the promise of security to the non-promise of resilience.

Resilience and changing epistemic regimes

The literature on resilience has recognised that resilience enacts a shift from problems to responses. Some commentators have noted that 'resilience thinking plays an important heuristic role in shifting the focus away from the quantitative availability of resources, and towards the scope of available response options' (Cote and Nightingale, 2012, p. 478). For instance, Cote and Nightingale argue, the problem of the 'earth's carrying capacity', which led to particular solutions of 'limits to growth', is replaced by a wider array of variable solutions, under the heading of resilience (Cote and Nightingale, 2012). The emergence of resilience as a solution and the analysis of the contours of that solution are entwined with the articulation of a particular problem. However, the formulation – and formation – of the problem to be tackled has been less discussed. In focusing on the kinds of responses that resilience entails, what it means and what kind of 'fit' with neoliberal governance it effects, less attention has been paid to the articulation of the problem that resilience purports to solve.

Rather than starting from the numerous and endlessly varied meanings of resilience, I propose to revisit the problematisation that leads to the invocation of resilience. Problematisation entails turning 'the given into a question' and 'exploring the conditions under which possible answers can be given' (Foucault, 2000, p. 118). In much of the resilience literature, it is assumed that resilience is a response to shocks, disasters, risks, threats and other disturbances. Understanding how particular things become a problem allows us to understand how particular solutions are presented as necessary and how they become truthful.

Resilience offers a solution to a particular problematisation of future events. To understand the shift that is taking place, I draw on the distinction between three epistemic regimes: ignorance/ secrecy; risk/uncertainty; surprise/novelty.[1] These three epistemic regimes are underpinned by different assumptions about what can be known, how knowledge can be acquired and how contingency can be 'tamed'.

Ignorance and secrecy entail an assumption that the unknown can be reduced and rendered tangible by making transparent, surveying and discovering secrets. It is an epistemology of depth and surface, where ignorance is simply a failure that can be remedied through better access to what is held secret, hidden or underground. Although ignorance has often been considered synonymous to non-knowledge or the unknown, its analysis in relation to knowledge that is obscured, silenced or deflected indicates a particular epistemic regime in which the relation between knowledge and non-knowledge is that of surface and depth.[2] In this epistemic regime, contingency is tamed by accessing secrets; making transparent and reducing non-knowledge.

Risk and uncertainty work within a different epistemic regime. Rather than surface and depth, knowledge depends upon the existence of parallel words. There is no deeper knowledge to be accessed. Knowledge is only produced by creating a parallel world that 'models', 'simulates' and mimics the 'real' world through statistical and computing techniques. Risk does not solve the problems of non-knowledge by probing deeper or bringing to the surface. The dynamic of risk is that between individual and mass. Risk can tell us nothing about a particular event, but only about a class of events for which frequencies can be calculated. As Mary Ann Doane (2007, p. 24) has noted, 'Statistics is an epistemological framework that works by acknowledging the intractability of the contingent, the unknowability of the individual; knowledge is displaced to the level of the mass.' Events are made governable not as singular occurrences, but as patterns that can be deciphered in populations across time with the use of statistics. Risk management creates a different reality that can be ordered; it is the reality of multiples and averages. Uncertainty is tamed through the move from the individual to the multiple and from uncertainty to risk.

Unlike the regimes of ignorance/secrecy and risk/uncertainty, surprise and novelty indicate an epistemic regime in which events are always emergent and potential.[3] As complexity theorists argue, surprise is inevitable and novelty always already in the making (McDaniel Jr *et al.*, 2003). In this epistemic regime, there is one 'flat' world where surprise is always a potentiality – the unknown is always already part of the world, but it cannot be made visible either through accessing a deeper secret or through modelling uncertainty through risk management techniques. Preparedness and resilience are the answers to the surprising event and its emergent novelty. Although surprise can function within other epistemic regimes, it takes on different meanings and functions.

The changes to the historical uses of surprise are indicative of these epistemic changes. The problematisation of surprise itself is not new, but has a longer history that includes surprise attacks in strategic thought, psychological and emotional surprise, and, more recently, climate change surprise. For instance, Handel noted in the 1980s that '[s]urprise diplomacy can be used to transcend old policies through two interrelated elements, namely, secrecy and shock' (1980, p. 61). Even as the language of surprise is used, surprise implies an epistemic regime of surface and depth, where knowledge can be accessible and brought to the surface. Similarly, surprises continue to exist in the regime of risk/uncertainty. Every individual event would contain an element of surprise. However, it is not the individual event but the frequencies and the general distribution of risk that count. In current deployments of surprise, surprise is ontologised – a given characteristic of our world: 'it is part of the natural order of things' (McDaniel and Driebe 2005, p. 7).

Surprise becomes an ontological characteristic of all complex adaptive systems rather than a lack of knowledge that can be addressed. It is its unexpected and always emergent quality that becomes the main concern for security and governance. At the same time, surprise is dehistoricised and divorced from an analysis of historical conditions and constraints. If surprises always happen and novelty is emergent, historical conditions lose their importance.

In policy discourses, the events that confront us globally today take this unpredictable, unpreventable and surprising character. Take, for instance, the UK 2009 *National Security Strategy*, which formulated resilience as an innovative response to new problems confronting contemporary societies:

> The increasingly networked, interdependent and complex nature of modern society, and the critical systems which underpin daily life will, over the coming years, increase both the UK's vulnerability and the potential impact of civil emergencies. . . . Dealing with *these widespread, complex and unpredictable events* will require greater societal resilience than we have today.
>
> *(UK Government, 2009; emphasis mine)*

For the UK government, it is not simply that we are faced with more unpredictable or uncertain events, but the complexity and interdependency of societies makes these events unknowable and unmanageable. The problematisation that calls for resilience is that of 'un-ness': unexpected, unknowable, unpredictable, unmanageable events.[4]

The role of unpredictable events has been noted in the literature on resilience. However, the epistemic difference that surprising events introduce is effaced when events are subsumed under danger, shock, emergency or disaster. C. S. Holling initially formulated the problem of events in ecological systems as 'surprises' (Holling, 1994). His theory of resilience has also been called a 'theory of surprise' (Adger, 2000), drawing attention to the importance of the problem that resilience answers. Surprises are unexpected events that appear to be unknowable, unpredictable and unmanageable. In complexity theory, surprise is 'inevitable because it is part of the natural order of things and cannot be avoided, eliminated, or controlled' (McDaniel Jr *et al.*, 2003, p. 1). Neither dangers nor emergencies have the same resonance. Holling had also noted that 'there is an inherent unknowability, as well as unpredictability, concerning evolving managed ecosystems and the societies with which they are linked' (Holling, 1996). Surprise, as inherent to our social and ecological systems, entails a different modality of governance that is attuned to the unexpected and unknowable, rather than purporting to prevent, anticipate or protect against the unexpected and the uncertain.

When the resilience literature in International Relations refers to surprises and shocks, it is without exploring the epistemic implications of this terminology.[5] Yet, surprise restructures the epistemic quality of the continuum of events that resilience responds to. Resilience captures responses to a whole array of changes that 'can be driven by shocks – sudden changes – or through long-term erosions (or increases) in capacity, effectiveness or legitimacy' (OECD, 2008). It is, however, not the duration of stresses that becomes important in this epistemic regime. Rather, it is the moment of surprise that counts, when stresses cascade and give rise to unexpected and potentially surprising events. The remit of events that require resilience extends to encompass slow erosions and everyday disruptions, by modifying their epistemic quality through the lens of surprise. Even when the long-term quality of stresses is recognised, ultimately stresses and shocks require resilience when they take the form of adverse events: 'People and systems are vulnerable when they are susceptible to, or unable to cope with, the adverse events' (Department for International Development (DFID), 2012b). Similarly, the UK Cabinet Office promotes resilience as a response to highly capacious 'disruptive challenges', particularly in the context of organisations and business continuity management (UK Cabinet Office, 2010). Disruption is an event whose occurrence is unexpected, but whose effects can be potentially absorbed.

Future surprising events – shocks, disasters, adversities, stresses, conflicts or disturbances – are seen as largely interchangeable in both policy and academic discourses. At the same time, they all share epistemic assumptions of 'surprise'. For instance, even as several authors have noted the pitfalls of 'ecological surprise' and 'climate surprise' for responding to climate change (Streets and Glantz, 2000; Kates and Clark, 1996), they have paid less attention to the epistemological assumptions of surprise. When surprise becomes the dominant understanding of future events, these are processed on the modality of unexpected and unknowable occurrences emerging, in a sense, out of nowhere. This has implications for how discourses of governance have been transformed. The next section draws attention to humanitarian governance, as formulated by DFID in the UK, in order to show how an epistemic regime of surprise shapes resilience responses.

Surprises of development: from dignity to resilience

In 2011, the DFID published a report on the UK's humanitarian policy, entitled *Saving Lives, Preventing Suffering and Building Resilience*. The report has resilience at its centre as the building stone of humanitarian action, as 'the impact of disasters can be significantly mitigated by building the resilience of nations and people, and addressing the root causes of vulnerability' (Department for International Development (DFID), 2011, p. 5). At first sight, resilience appears to supplement the promise of disaster risk reduction by incorporating community practices, based on the understanding that families and communities are the first ones to react in a disaster. The 2011 report places resilience in a shift from reactive to proactive humanitarian action, which in itself is not new. Early warning, anticipation, risk management have long informed humanitarian policy. Resilience appears to supplement and strengthen a framework of risk management for disaster prevention. However, it is instructive to compare the specification of resilience in this report with another DFID report, published in 2006, which also mentions resilience but does so more marginally. The difference in the title is also telling –*Saving Lives, Relieving Suffering, Protecting Dignity* (Department for International Development (DFID), 2006, p. 10). 'Relieving suffering' has been replaced by 'preventing suffering' and 'protecting dignity' by 'building resilience'. A turn from the present to future-oriented action is also evident in the title change.

In 2011, DFID clarified that building disaster resilience implies either to 'maintain or transform living standards in the face of shocks and stresses – such as earthquakes, drought, or violent conflict' (Department for International Development (DFID), 2011). The problem that resilience tackles is that of surprising events.[6] Underpinned by an epistemic regime of surprise, conditions of the possibility of shocks and stresses remain unquestioned. The epistemic regime of surprise assumes that knowledge is limited and the condition of future events is that of unpredictability, novelty and unknowability. Earthquakes, drought and violent conflict are all problematised as surprise events. They are reconfigured through another epistemic regime, which departs from either ignorance or risk.

Although the DFID recognises that poor countries and poor people are most affected by disasters, the problematisation of events means that improving living standards is left out in favour of downscaling (read euphemistically as 'transformation') or 'maintaining' existing living standards. Most strikingly, the language of poverty and poverty reduction is absent from the 2011 report. Ironically, poverty appears only on the report's back cover to capture the DFID motto: 'leading the UK Government's fight against world poverty' Department for International

Development (DFID), 2011, p. 10). The report itself talks about 'the poor' and the 'poorest' rather than poverty. Equated with the poor, poverty becomes a given that resilience strategies need to accommodate.

In 2006, the report saw a clear link between poverty reduction and reducing the impact of disasters. Disaster risk reduction measures were therefore expected to:

> include national systems of social security to improve the wellbeing of the most vulnerable, and to provide a safety net in times of crisis. Where governments are not willing to back a pro-poor agenda, other options for delivering social welfare and basic services will be explored.
>
> *(Department for International Development (DFID), 2006, p. 10)*

An epistemic framework of risk and uncertainty underpinned these measures, which saw the possibility of 'taming' uncertainty through risk spreading. Spreading risk through insurance practices was a mode of reducing poverty and vulnerability to disasters. Moreover, humanitarian emergencies were seen as the effects of failures in policy. Thus, political measures focused on long-term investment were needed to tackle vulnerability and poverty. Five years later, resilience responses entail a change in how poverty, development and security more broadly are envisaged:

> Humanitarian assistance should be delivered in a way that does not undermine existing coping mechanisms and helps a community build its own resilience for the future. National governments in at-risk countries can ensure that disaster risk management policies and strategies are linked to community-level action.
>
> *(Department for International Development (DFID), 2011, p. 10)*

This formulation does not specify what the mechanisms are or how the knowledge of disasters is formulated, acquired and distributed. Responses mobilise existing capacities and assume that disasters are a 'fact' in certain parts of the world. In its operational plan for 2012–2015, one of the DFID's aims is to 'Help the poorest build resilience against economic shocks such as high food prices through the provision of expert technical advice to support the scaling up of effective programmes to protect the most vulnerable using innovative technologies' (Department for International Development (DFID), 2012a, p. 3). Long-term investment has also disappeared from the more recent strategy. It also remains unclear what the technical advice or the innovative technologies to be deployed are. Moreover, economic crisis, natural disasters, and conflict are all imagined as surprise events. The rendition of economic crisis as 'shocks' does not question the conditions of possibility for the crisis or the policies that might have led to crisis.

There is an important difference in how the problem of disasters and humanitarian crises is formulated in 2006 and 2011. In 2006, disasters were seen as the effects of 'failures of development and politics' (Department for International Development (DFID), 2006, p. 7). The language of failure is that of knowledge that can locate problems and pitfalls. In 2006, the DFID translates failure into an epistemic regime of risk, where the solution is ultimately the spreading of risk. In 2011, the language of shock is that of inherent surprise, of the turn to the future and irreducible limits of knowledge. Unexpected 'shocks and stresses' call for resilience, while disasters are now seen to impede development. In this reversal of the disaster-development linkage, the failures of development need no longer be questioned.

Building resilience assumes that the unknown cannot be diminished, as with epistemologies of ignorance. It also cannot be displaced, as with risk management, even as prevention remains a desirable goal for DFID policies. These implications of the problematisation of surprise as the paradigmatic future event become explicit in the renunciation of security. Resilience answers the implicit realisation that security is not possible in complex world eliciting surprises, while its promise remains desirable for individuals and communities. This is spelled out in a series of recommendations to DFID:

> The key to security is resilience, for ecosystems, people and economies. . . . We may not be able to protect people from stresses, shocks and catastrophic events, but we can help them withstand disasters, recover and adapt.
>
> *(Toulmin, 2009, p. 1)*

Security, as governments, experts and academics keep repeating, is not what it used to be. The promise of security that underpins the liberal state is subtly rephrased – 'we may not be able to protect people'. The provision of humanitarian aid, for instance, does not just create dependency, but it also has unintended effects. According to a report for DFID on the economics of disaster resilience, emergency aid has been 'either too late or inappropriate, and . . . has further undermined sustainable development in these areas' (Cabot Venton *et al.*, 2012, p. 16).

Ultimately, it seems that what changes from 2006 to 2011 is the very promise of development and poverty reduction through mechanisms of risk spreading and protection of dignity. Surprises undo protective and preventive mechanisms. Mark Duffield, for instance, has argued that '[e]arlier modernist forms of protection have been replaced by postmodernist calls for resilience and the acceptance of risk as an opportunity for enterprise and reinvention' (Duffield, 2012, p. 475). Evans and Reid formulate the move in starker terms, as they emphasise that 'the liberal discourse of resilience functions to convince peoples and individuals that the dream of lasting security is impossible' (Evans and Reid, 2014, p. 68). While these authors are right to note the difference between resilience and earlier discourses of protection, the shift from protection to resilience does not account for the historical reconfiguration of security through prevention, pre-emption or preparedness, to name just a few. Moreover, assuming a move from 'lasting security' to the lack of security does not fully consider the illusion of 'lasting security'. After all, prevention did not cherish the dream of 'lasting security' either. As critical scholars have long pointed out, security discourses and practices reproduce insecurity, both in designating others as dangerous and in fostering anxiety and unease among populations to be made secure (e.g. Huysmans, 2006; Bigo and Tsoukala, 2006; Aradau, 2008; Peoples and Vaughan-Williams, 2011). Instead of positing a binary of security/resilience or protection/resilience, the next section shows how the political implications of resilience can be grasped through an engagement with the promise of security and promissory politics.

Resilience and promissory politics

The promise of security is often referred to in the IR literature on security and more broadly (Young, 2003; Stern, 2006). Yet the analytical focus has been on security rather than the promise itself. David Campbell (1992, p. 50) notes, for instance, that '[t]he state grounds its legitimacy by offering the promise of security to its citizens'. The promise is also the paradigmatic speech act in securitisation theory, but is quickly glossed over through integration in a continuum of baptism, marriage, betting and so on (Buzan *et al.*, 1998). I propose to analyse the *promise* of security as a critical vantage point from which to understand the political effects of resilience discourses.

The promising speech act presupposes a regime of knowledge based on the reduction of ignorance and dispelling of secrecy. Promises are felicitous if no secret plans to the contrary nullify them, if they are well intended and their consequences are carried out (Austin, 1975 [1962]). At the same time, promises presuppose a degree of control over the future, through the diminution of ignorance and the role of knowledge. To promise means to create continuity from the present to the future. Understood through the vantage point of the promise, security is primarily an epistemic endeavour, which tames contingency through the production of certainty about the future. This move drastically limits or even suspends the openness of the future and effectively closes off political possibilities. Yet, embracing untamed contingency can have deleterious political effects, as Hannah Arendt has aptly noted:

> Without being bound to the fulfilment of promises we would never be able to keep our identities; we would be condemned to wander helplessly and without direction in the darkness of each man's lonely heart, caught in its contradictions and equivocalities.
> *(Arendt, 1958, p. 237)*

Arendt's analysis of the promise is particularly useful for my purposes, as she connects promises and epistemic politics. If politics for Arendt is about common action that creates a new beginning, the fragility and unpredictability of action needs to be tamed through promises. As she puts it,

> binding oneself through promises, serves to set out in the ocean of uncertainty, which the future is by definition, islands of security, without which not even continuity, let alone durability of any kind, would be possible in the relationships between men [*sic*].
> *(Arendt, 1958, p. 237)*

Arendt's engagement with uncertainty and unpredictability has received little attention in the literature on International Relations, which has often invoked the distinction between the social and the political in Arendt's work (Owens, 2012). If security is simply a method of social governance, then it is also depoliticising, destroying the political with its 'power of potentiality by closing down futurity' (Diprose, 2008, p. 636). Yet, Arendt's conceptualisation of the promise as a way of taming the unpredictability of politics and addressing its fragility can help challenge this binary. The promise holds a paradoxical role, as it attempts to navigate the tensions between the unpredictability and surprising character of the future and need for some certainty. This paradoxical role of the promise can appear as a retreat from the contingency of the future and of politics, and Bonnie Honig cautions that the promise would 'belie the moment of contingency that . . . characterises the moment of politics' (1991, p. 104).

The paradox of the promise can be read differently and more productively, as a way of rethinking contingency/the limits of knowledge and politics. For Arendt, the promise enacts a limit to contingency and unpredictability, as promises are a necessary political supplement to the unpredictability of action. 'Taming' contingency does not necessarily imply recourse either to the production of certainty or to the calculability of risk. Arendt's conceptualisation of the promise eludes the dream of knowledge and of the reduction of ignorance. The promise of enlightened knowledge, which is the promise of the security speech act, is effectively the voice of authority and certainty. A world that is completely certain, foreseeable and predictable, is a world devoid of politics. Resisting always-emergent surprises cannot simply mean a reversal to a world of knowledge, control and predictability.

Arendt's cautionary note about the extension of promises draws attention to the fact that it is the negotiation of the boundary between uncertainty and certainty, predictability and unpredictability, that defines the possibilities of political action:

> The moment promises lose their character as isolated islands of certainty in an ocean of uncertainty, that is, when this faculty is misused to cover the whole ground of the future

and to map out a path secured in all directions, they lose their binding power and the whole enterprise becomes self-defeating.

(Arendt 1958, p. 244)

At the same time, Arendt also cautions against simply embracing contingency, as Nietzsche's critique of promises would seem to suggest. Arendt acknowledges the importance of Nietzsche's analysis of the inextricable link between control and the promise-making individual. Nietzsche sees the capacity of making promises to rely on 'the more immediate task of first making man to a certain degree necessary, uniform, a peer amongst peers, orderly and consequently predictable' (Nietzsche, 2007, p. 77). Promises require the production of predictable subjects and the promising individual needs to be first ordered according to a logic of predictability.

Yet, Arendt does not fully accept Nietzsche's critique of promises. Unlike Nietzsche, Arendt reclaims promises away from the association with individualism, sovereignty and violence that Nietzsche offers. Security promises do not just pawn us to sovereign authority. Arendt replaces individualistic promises with the collective and mutual promises, which neither forsake contingency nor embrace predictability. As Vanessa Lemm (2006, p. 163) notes in her comparison of Arendt and Nietzsche:

> On Arendt's assumption that freedom arises from the power of the 'We' rather than from the will power of the isolated individual, the figure of the sovereign individual in Nietzsche becomes the paradigmatic example of a genuine lack of freedom resultant from a devaluation of the political.[7]

Promises arising from collective action tame the contingency of the future and foster political action in the present. Thus, Arendt radically departs from the promise implied in security speech acts. Promises 'depend on plurality, on the presence and acting of others, for . . . no one can be bound by a promise made only to himself' (Arendt, 1958, p. 237). Promises can extend the power of collective action into the future by enacting some form of knowledge and stability to counter the effects of unpredictability. Unlike security speech acts, promises do not rely on epistemologies of certainty and do not embrace emergent uncertainty.

The collective dimension of promises also avoids the pitfalls of taming contingency through risk. As the first section has shown, the epistemic regime of risk/uncertainty displaces contingency from the individual to the mass by depriving collectivities of political agency. Statistical populations emerge through statistical calculation and lack the power of collective action. Yet, if statistical calculability translates the past into future 'destiny', Arendt aims to undo the strictures of the past. Alongside promises, forgiveness palliates the other predicament of action: that of irreversibility (Arendt, 1958, pp. 236–42). If unpredictability is a consequence of political action in concert and human freedom, then it can also be 'tamed' through collective action. When unpredictability is ontologised as always emerging surprise, the historical capacity of human beings to hold actions to account and act upon the future is radically diminished. At the same time, when contingency is tamed through anticipation and certainty, the past forecloses the capacity for novel political action in the future. Knowledge becomes expertise and political subjects are reconfigured as either risky or vulnerable populations. Arendt draws attention to the 'infinite improbability' that characterises human action as well as to the history of promises that tame the 'chaotic uncertainty of the future' (Arendt, 1958, p. 300). These elements disappear from the problematisation of resilience when contingency and surprise are inserted in the fabric of the social as always already there, independent of historical political events.

Through the ontologisation of surprise as always already emergent, resilience forecloses the politics of the promise, with its pitfalls, adjustments and potentials. Promises cannot but remain paradoxical, as they straddle the boundary between unpredictability and predictability, certainty and uncertainty, probability and improbability, possibility and impossibility. Promises unsettle the epistemic regimes of ignorance/secrecy, risk/uncertainty or surprise/novelty. Through promises, contingency is simultaneously tamed and embraced through the power of collective action that transforms the future. Isn't the resilience of communities an Arendtian promise for the future? The resilience of communities confronted with surprising events forsakes the unexpectedness of political action for the anticipation of resilient behaviour. Even when read through community rather than individual action, resilience ultimately enacts a displacement of contingency and unexpectedness as characteristics of political action upon contingency as a 'given' of the world. Moreover, resilient behaviour is imagined in relation to pre-given groups rather then opening up to the emergence of new collective subjects. Promises, however, can reignite the paradox of anticipation and surprise, uncertainty and certainty as political and not just epistemic questions.

Conclusion

Just like neoliberalism, resilience seems to be everywhere today. Although many of the elements of resilience appear to resonate with neoliberal principles, I have argued that the appeal of resilience today can be understood by exploring the epistemic regime underpinning resilience. Formulated as a response to the problem of surprising events, resilience draws attention to the transformation of epistemic regimes of ignorance/secrecy and risk/uncertainty. If ignorance presupposed an episteme of depth in which secrecy could be made visible, risk an epistemic regime of parallel worlds where uncertainty could be 'tamed', surprise functions in a complex, interconnected world where the novel and the unexpected are always emergent. The reference to surprise makes possible the constitution of a continuum of events, from minor adversities to shocks, and from stresses to traumatic events to capture a whole array of what the UK Cabinet Office refers to as 'disruptive challenges'. Reconfigured through an epistemic regime of surprise and novelty, all these events make possible the deployment of resilience across multiple domains of governance.

When epistemic assumptions of emergent surprise underpin calls for resilience to reformulate DFID's humanitarian policies in the UK, for example, these can be aligned with the retrenchment of the promise of security. Even as security remains desirable, the problematisation of surprising events renders its promise impossible, to be replaced by resilience. Resilience does not promise anything inasmuch as it does not purport to 'tame' contingency, but only to live through the surprising and the unexpected. It also does not aim to constitute the conditions of collective political action, but reverts back upon forms of individual or pre-given group action. I have argued that Arendt's analysis of the promise offers a vantage point from which both the promise of security and the non-promise of resilience close off political action. The promise of security stultifies the future through anticipation and expert knowledge, and disavows the limits of knowledge. Resilience withdraws from the promise, as it disavows the transformative capacity of collective political action and remains hostage to the limits of knowledge.

Acknowledgements

This chapter is a slightly revised and updated version of Aradau, C. (2014). The promise of security: resilience, surprise and epistemic politics. *Resilience* vol. 2 (2), 73–87, Abingdon: Taylor & Francis. DOI: 10.1080/21693293.2014.914765.

Notes

1 This distinction was developed in Aradau and van Munster (2011).
2 Linsey McGoey has recently argued for attention to ignorance and particularly strategic ignorance. She aptly draws attention to ignorance within a broader analysis of 'the constant policing of boundaries between the known and the unknown' (McGoey, 2012, p.13).
3 The ecological literature often tends to collapse surprise, ignorance and uncertainty (see, e.g. Faber *et al.*, 1992).
4 While discussions of resilience have focused on the assumptions of complexity, connectivity and emergence, less attention has been paid to how events are known and governed (Kaufmann, 2013).
5 Walker and Cooper do not use the term 'surprise' in their analysis of resilience. References to surprises are by and large absent from the International Relations literature on resilience (Walker and Cooper 2011).
6 There is a second problem that the DFID's endorsement of resilience responds to: that of austerity. However, it is beyond the scope of this article to analyse the role of austerity, as it focuses on the epistemic politics of resilience.
7 I disagree, however, with her assessment that the promise 'reverses the flow of time' and removes the uncertain future in favour of a 'secured past' (p. 163). Arendt' s reinterpretation of past political events would be indicative of an openness of the past rather than the possibility of securing it.

References

Adger, N.W. (2000) Social and ecological resilience: are they related? *Progress in Human Geography*, vol. 24 (3), 347–64.

Aradau, C. (2008) *Rethinking Trafficking in Women. Politics out of Security*. Basingstoke: Palgrave Macmillan.

Aradau, C. (2014) The promise of security: resilience, surprise and epistemic politics. *Resilience* vol. 2 (2), 73–87.

Aradau, C. and van Munster, R. (2011) *Politics of Catastrophe: Genealogies of the Unknown*. Abingdon: Routledge.

Arendt, H. (1958) *The Human Condition*. Chicago, IL: University of Chicago Press.

Austin, J.L. (1975 [1962]) *How To Do Things with Words*. 2nd edition. Oxford: Oxford University Press.

Berkes, F., Colding, J. and Folke, C. (2003) *Navigating Social-ecological Systems: Building Resilience for Complexity and Change*. Cambridge: Cambridge University Press.

Bigo, D. and Tsoukala, A. (2006) *Illiberal Practices of Liberal Regimes: The (In)security Games*. Paris: L'Harmattan.

Buzan, B., Waever, O. and de Wilde, J. (1998) *Security: A New Framework for Analysis*. Boulder, CO: Lynne Rienner.

Campbell, D. (1992) *Writing Security: United States Foreign Policy and the Politics of Identity*. Manchester: Manchester University Press.

Chandler, D. (2012) Resilience and human security: the post-interventionist paradigm. *Security Dialogue* vol. 43 (3), 213–29.

Cote, M. and Nightingale, A.J. (2012) Resilience thinking meets social theory: situating social change in socio-ecological systems (SES) research. *Progress in Human Geography*, vol. 36 (4), 475–89.

Department for International Development (DFID) (2006) *Saving Lives, Relieving Suffering, Protecting Dignity: DFID's Humanitarian Policy*. DIFD 2006 [cited 15 November 2012]. Available from: http://webarchive.nationalarchives.gov.uk/+/http://www.dfid.gov.uk/Documents/publications/humanitarian-policy.pdf.

Department for International Development (DFID) (2011) *Saving Lives, Preventing Suffering and Building Resilience: The UK Government's Humanitarian Policy*. DFID 2011 [cited 15 November 2012]. Available from: www.gov.uk/government/uploads/system/uploads/attachment_data/file/67468/The_20UK_20Government_s_20Humanitarian_20Policy_20-_20September_202011_20-_20Final.pdf.

Department for International Development (DFID) (2012a) *Operational Plan 2011–2015. DFID – Growth and Resilience Department (GRD)*. DFID 2012a [cited 25 May 2013]. Available from: www.gov.uk/government/uploads/system/uploads/attachment_data/file/67421/gth-res-dept-2011.pdf.

Department for International Development (DFID) (2012b) *Promoting Innovation and Evidence-based Approaches to Building Resilience and Responding to Humanitarian Crises. A DFID Strategy Paper*. DFID 2012b [cited 10 March 2014]. Available from: www.gov.uk/government/news/dfid-research-promoting-innovation-and-evidence-based-approaches-to-humanitarian-crises.

Diprose, R. (2008) Arendt and Nietzsche on responsibility and futurity. *Philosophy & Social Criticism*, vol. 34 (6), 617–42.

Doane, M.A. (2007) Imaging contingency: an interview with Mary Ann Doane. *Parallax*, vol. 13 (4), 16–25.

Duffield, M. (2012) Challenging environments: danger, resilience and the aid industry. *Security Dialogue*, vol. 43 (5), 475–92.

Evans, B. and Reid, J. (2013) Dangerously exposed: the life and death of the resilient subject. *Resilience*, vol. 1 (2), 1–16.

Evans, B. and Reid, J. (2014) *Resilient Life: The Art of Living Dangerously*. Cambridge: Polity.

Faber, M., Manstetten, R. and Proops, J.L. (1992) Humankind and the environment: an anatomy of surprise and ignorance. *Environmental Values*, vol. 1 (3), 217–41.

Foucault, M. (1984) What is Enlightenment? In *The Foucault Reader*, edited by Paul Rabinow, pp. 32–50. New York: Pantheon Books.

Foucault, M. (2000) Polemics, Politics, and Problematizations. In *Essential Works of Foucault 1954–1984*, edited by Paul Rabinow, pp. 111–19. London: Penguin Books.

Handel, M.I. (1980) Surprise and change in international politics. *International Security*, vol. 4 (4), 57–85.

Holling, C.S. (1973) Resilience and stability of ecological systems. *Annual Review of Ecology and Systematics*, vol. 4 (1), 1–23.

Holling, C.S. (1994) Simplifying the complex: the paradigms of ecological function and structure. *Futures*, vol. 26 (6), 598–609.

Holling, C.S. (1996) Surprise for science, resilience for ecosystems, and incentives for people. *Ecological Applications*, vol. 6 (3), 733–35.

Honig, B. (1991) Declarations of independence. Arendt and Derrida on the problem of founding a republic. *Americal Political Science Review*, vol. 85 (1), 97–113.

Hornborg, A. (2009) Zero-sum world. *International Journal of Comparative Sociology*, vol. 50 (3–4), 237–62.

Huysmans, J. (2006) *The Politics of Insecurity: Fear, Migration and Asylum in the EU*. London: Routledge.

Joseph, J. (2013) Resilience as embedded neoliberalism: a governmentality approach. *Resilience*, vol. 1 (1), 38–52.

Kates, R.W. and Clark, W.C. (1996). Environmental surprise: expecting the unexpected? *Environment: Science and Policy for Sustainable Development*, vol. 38 (2), 6–34.

Kaufmann, M. (2013) Emergent self-organisation in emergencies: resilience rationales in interconnected societies. *Resilience*, vol. 1(1), 53–68.

Lemm, V. (2006) Memory and promise in Arendt and Nietzsche. *Revista de Ciencia Política*, vol. 26 (2), 161–73.

Levin, S.A., Barrett, S., Aniyar, S., Baumol, W., Bliss, C., Bolin, B., Das Gupta, P., Ehrlich, P., Folke, C., Gren, I.M., Holling, C.S., Jansson, A., Jansson, B.O., Maler, K.G., Martin, D., Perrings, C. and Sheshinski, E. (2001) Resilience in natural and socioeconomic systems. *Environment and Development Economics*, vol. 3 (02), 221–62.

McDaniel Jr, R., Jordan, M.E. and Fleeman, B.F. (2003) Surprise, surprise, surprise! A complexity science view of the unexpected. *Health Care Management Review*, vol. 28 (3), 266–78.

McDaniel, R.R. and Driebe, D.J. (2005) Uncertainty and Surprise: An Introduction. In *Uncertainty and Surprise in Complex Systems: Questions on Working With the Unexpected*, edited by Reuben R. McDaniel Jr and Dean J. Driebe, pp. 3–12. Berlin: Springer.

McGoey, L. (2012) Strategic unknowns: towards a sociology of ignorance. *Economy and Society*, vol. 41 (1), 1–16.

Nadasdy, P. (2007) Adaptive Co-management and the Gospel of Resilience. In *Adaptive Co-management: Collaboration, Learning, and Multi-level Governance*, edited by D.R. Armitage, pp. 208–27. Vancouver, BC: University of British Columbia Press.

Nietzsche, F. (2007) *On the Genealogy of Morality and Other Writings*. Cambridge: Cambridge University Press.

O'Malley, P. (2010) Resilient subjects: uncertainty, warfare and liberalism. *Economy and Society*, vol. 39 (4), 488–509.

OECD (2008) *Concepts and Dilemmas of State-Building in Fragile Situations. From fragility to resilience*. [accessed 24 July 2016]. Available from: www.oecd.org/development/governance-peace/conflictandfragility/docs/41100930.pdf.

Owens, P. (2012) Human security and the rise of the social. *Review of International Studies* vol. 38 (3), 547–67.

Pelling, M. (2010) *Adaptation to Climate Change: From Resilience to Transformation*. Abingdon: Routledge.

Peoples, C. and Vaughan-Williams, N. (2011) *Critical Security Studies: An Introduction*. London: Routledge.

Stern, M. (2006) 'We' the subject: the power and failure of (in)security. *Security Dialogue*, vol. 37 (2), 187–205.

Streets, D.G. and Glantz, M.H. (2000) Exploring the concept of climate surprise. *Global Environmental Change*, vol. 10 (2), 97–107.

Toulmin, C. (2009) *Building Resilience for an Interdependent World: Why the environment matters and what DFID should do about it*. London: IIED.

UK Cabinet Office (2010) *Strategic Framework and Policy Statement on Improving the Resilience of Critical Infrastructure to Disruption from Natural Hazards*. London: Cabinet Office.

UK Government (2009) *National Security Strategy. Security in an Interdependent World* 2009 [cited 20 June 2011]. Available from: http://webarchive.nationalarchives.gov.uk/+/http://www.cabinetoffice.gov.uk/reports/national_security.aspx.

Venton, C.C., Fitzgibbon, C., Shitarek, T., Coulter, L. and Dooley, O. (2012) *The Economics of Early Response and Disaster Resilience: Lessons from Kenya and Ethiopia* 2012 [cited 4 December 2013]. Available from: www.gov.uk/government/uploads/system/uploads/attachment_data/file/67330/Econ-Ear-Rec-Res-Full-Report_20.pdf.

Walker, J. and Cooper, M. (2011) Genealogies of resilience from systems ecology to the political economy of crisis adaptation. *Security Dialogue*, vol. 42 (2), 143–60.

Young, I.M. (2003) The logic of masculinist protection: reflections on the current security state. *Signs*, vol. 29 (1), 1–25.

8

AN ETHIC OF CARE FOR RESILIENCE

Addressing resilience's problem of the present in the 'Transition Towns' model

Charis Boke

Introduction

This study examines the organizing model 'Transition Towns' and its broader social movement, one that is explicitly oriented toward building resilience. Grounded in two years of ethnographic fieldwork among Vermont and New England community organizers, this chapter sets the concept of resilience in a particular historical and social context. I demonstrate how 'resilience building' as *practice* in the contemporary United States is made complex by the contextual particularities of 'resilience' as *concept*.

I outline the ways that resilience as it is practiced in Transition Towns involve pulling objects from the idealized past forward through time to help with the social and political work of preparing for uncertain futures. I argue that resilience as a concept predisposes an explicit orientation towards the future – one which curtails organizers' ability to 'build resilience' while simultaneously working on existing socioeconomic challenges in the present moment. Here, resilience-building objects serve two purposes: one of these purposes is as a temporal suture, knitting idealized pasts with imagined futures, the purpose which has been privileged in Transition initiatives. The other purpose is the demonstrated capacity of objects to serve in processes of social mobilization, wherein resilience is both a practice of intimate human relationships and a practice of material risk-preparation.

I suggest that overlooking the particular histories of the object assemblages used to 'build resilience' serves to erase the histories of people for whom (for instance) hand-scything was slave labour in the otherwise 'ideal pastoral'. Thus, 'resilience building' becomes a set of practices in which only certain, privileged groups are able to take part. I seek neither to undermine the potential utility of models like Transition Towns for creating the conditions for good lives, nor to suggest that resilience itself is a conceptual lost cause. Rather, by addressing the histories and materialities of resilience as a *concept*, I suggest, throughout, that integrating an 'ethic of care' (Smith, 2005) into the way resilience is *practiced* may ensure that our focus on future resilience does not preclude work to ameliorate current social justice issues.

I examine first the broad histories of the concept's use, and its specific mobilization in Transition Towns organizing. Next, I articulate the ways in which resilience as a concept is limited to a particular kind of future-orientation. I turn also to the everyday emergence of resilience's practiced qualities as (1) rooted in particular kinds of object assemblages and (2) relational. This in turn allows me to articulate some challenges to communities using the term 'resilience' as a grounding logic for their work.

Resilience contextualized

An ecosystemic understanding of successful resilience might look to the 'dynamic equilibrium' approach to define the state of resilience (see e.g. Norbert Weiner's 1948 work on cybernetics and subsequent applications in the systems-theories of ecological anthropologists such as Roy Rappaport, 1968). For a psychological take on resilience, one might look for individuals' affective cues for resilience – the ability to express emotion but not be overwhelmed by it, for instance. And in the context of governance-based resilience, some signs of success in resilience building might be that the population has been given the information about the tools it needs, and has been asked to practice *feeling* the right way about a disaster, enough so that the state apparatus can be assured that there will not be a public panic in addition to a 'natural disaster', economic calamity or physical attack (Davis, 2007; Dewey, 1927; Orr, 2004).

'Resilience,' then, and by extension 'resilience building', in this historical moment, has become something of a 'total social fact' (Mauss, 2002 [1954], p. 76). Resilience as a concept links fields of economics, politics, sociality and relationality – it links the human with the nonhuman – it links ideal pasts and imagined futures. As what David Chandler calls an 'open ontology', resilience is a concept that proliferates in the scope of its possibilities and demands (Chandler, 2014, p. 50). This entanglement means that it is never entirely clear what the end-goal of resilience *is*, least of all in that most complex of domains, everyday life. It is this domain to which, as an anthropologist, I devote the most sustained attention, offering ethnographically informed data on the mobilizations of resilience in Vermont's Transition Fervill.

The notion of resilience as used by Transition Towns practitioners, particularly in the United States, as a method for organizing the future, grows directly out of affective and material links to particular social and historical contexts. For this consideration, the central such context in the United States is the national security state's efforts to articulate and prepare for future threats, crafting a relationship to the public founded on the productive logics of fear.[1]

'Transition Towns' is a community organizing model developed in Totnes, England, with the guidance of Dr Rob Hopkins' *The Transition Handbook* (2008). The model was made public in 2005, and published in the USA in 2008. Subsequent texts (Hopkins, 2008, 2011; Chamberlin, 2009) and online resource-sharing tools broadened the spread of the model in the global north, predominantly through existing ecologically concerned, politically liberal communities. The goal of Transition Towns is to 'help local communities develop resilience in the face of the triple crisis', which involves 'the growing costs of climate change, the end of the oil age, plus ongoing economic contraction'.[2] Thus, Transitioners are community organizers and activists who are aware of the intersecting challenges posed by economic instability, global climate change and habitat destruction, and a foreseeable decline in readily available energy sources. 'Transition' denotes a transition from the old normal, or the status quo, to one of many potential futures, as yet undefined. For Transitioners, this means the end of the status quo of the last several hundred years in the United States, where carbon and its products have been king and leaders have been predominantly wealthy whites. Transitioners try to weave the social fabric of a shift from this quotidian experience to whatever it is that comes next, envisioning a thriving world after this shift, enabled by its future-building work.

Transitioners worldwide strive to organize social relations under a new iteration of the old adage, 'think globally, act locally'. The model asks participants to consider what resources their local community will need for the 'triple crisis', whether that crisis manifests as a lack of fuel to run the trucks to deliver groceries or otherwise. After considering challenges, Transition Towns encourage people to consider what resources already exist in their community, guiding them through ways to network people with resources they (will) need to withstand the shocks anticipated by different facets of the triple crisis. And because the model was developed in the global north, many possible concerns articulated are rooted in a privileged, global-north perspective on risks and how to create 'good lives'.

As of November 2014, the Transition Network website registered 477 'official' initiatives in 43 countries. The majority of these are clustered in Europe, the United States and Australia, with a scattered few in South America, Asia and South Africa (see Figure 8.1). An 'official' initiative starts with a core group of five to ten people, who – using Transition's methods, frameworks, and practices as laid out in the Handbook – begin to determine how to build resilience within their community in the face of peak oil, climate change and economic instability. Transition United States was formed as a national hub for coordinating the groups scattered across the nation towards that larger goal.[3] Transition US is a 501(c)3 nonprofit as of 2009, and while some local and regional Transition groups are seeking individual official nonprofit and tax exempt status, many are not.

The regional network within which I conducted fieldwork was instantiated in 2011, and the Transition group I worked with in Fervill, Vermont, has been an official Transition initiative since 2010.[4] At the national level, as well as at local levels, 'building resilience' is understood as work that is done primarily through workshops, education, conversation and collaborative projects that imagine new ways of living. All of these involve particular materials and particular visions for what constituted the 'good' practices of the past, and how those materials and visions can be drawn forward to create a 'good', or resilient, future. I suggest that materials and practices rendered desirable for resilience building often serve to focus organizers' gazes on the future rather than on the present moment, and that this detracts from their ability to address contemporary social justice concerns.

Resilience and anticipation

Visions of economic collapse, environmental catastrophe, 'peak oil',[5] and social unrest, following the disappearance of all systems as we have come to know them, haunt the future for people involved in this model. Transition Towns' resilience-building practices shape sensibilities, enabling imaginary projections of future threats which, in turn, create the material possibilities and desires of what Joseph Masco, in reference to the post-Cold War security state, calls 'anticipatory pre-emption' (2014, p. 41) for a future of proliferating crises.

Resilience as practiced in the Transition Towns model is a future-oriented conceptual framework that is grounded in such anticipatory pre-emption. Thus, it has a low capacity for dealing with the social justice problems of the present. Following the insights of historical anthropologists (e.g. Masco, 2014; Sturken, 2007), of scholars thinking through ecosystemic relationships (Chandler, 2014; Meadows *et al.*, 1992; Meadows, 2008; Nadasdy, 2007), and of feminist geography (e.g. Gibson-Graham, 2006; Lawson, 2010; Smith, 2005), I suggest that resilience's histories curtail its usefulness as a stand-alone concept for organizing change. Indeed, resilience thinking can actively stand in the way of doing the work organizers themselves want to do – work for a 'more beautiful, more just, more sustainable world' in the present (Eisenstein, 2013).

Addressing the object assemblages of resilience building, I build on anthropological imperatives to consider nonhumans as powerful actors in human social relations (see e.g. Cruikshank, 2005; Helmreich, 2009; Kohn, 2013; Latour, 2005). The historical, social and temporal relations implied by scythes, potatoes and hand-knitted hats – as well as the practices into which they

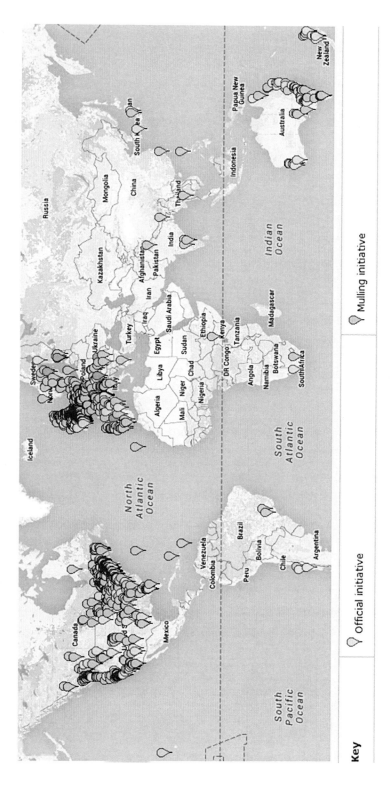

Key

♀ official initiative   ♀ Mulling initiative

Figure 8.1 The Transition Network's Google map plugin shows Transition's 'Official' initiatives and 'mullers' by pinpointing locations on a map of the world. The vast majority are clustered in the global north

Source: Google: https://transitionnetwork.org/initiatives/map (accessed 25 July 2016).

become incorporated – come into play here. How do these object assemblages reflect or call upon an imagined resilience of the past (e.g. narratives of hardy and thrifty New England small farmers)? What happens when resilience as a concept serves to suture such idealized pasts into multiple possible futures? If resilience building is to have a meaningful impact for all – which most scholars agree is a necessary goal in the face of actual climate crisis and the potential of actual economic collapse – the particular material entanglements of the concept must be taken into consideration.

In effect, the culturally prevalent notion of a New England ideal-pastoral helps frame the ways in which organizers craft 'resilience-building' practices to anticipate and pre-empt crises – unknown, proliferating potential crises. Such crises emerged most pointedly as a tool for organizing public affect in the post-Cold War United States.[6] Masco's suggestion obtains here: that the contemporary counter-terror state, as an outgrowth of the Cold War nuclear security apparatus, '[allocates] conceptual, material, and affective resources to ward off imagined but potentially catastrophic terroristic futures, [while it] also creates the conditions for those catastrophic futures to emerge' (2014, p. 13).

In other words, as we see in some Transition Towns practice, an imagined ever-pending crisis provides a continual reason for demanding hyper-vigilance and fear. It also provides an excuse for pre-emptive action – action taken in anticipation of that-which-has-not-yet-occurred, but could. In this context, these pre-emptive actions involve 'reskilling': learning how to use certain objects and practices in anticipation of a post-oil, post-crisis future. Thus, the material practices of Transition Towns' resilience-building efforts broadly participate in nuclear security history and re-enact it as part of a preparatory practice for the 'triple crisis'.

By explicitly weaving affective responses to proliferating crisis into the work it does with objects for survival and thriving, Transition Towns as a model serves to loosen the concept of resilience from its previous home as a tool of state apparatus, of ecological management, or of individual psychology. Considering the bare materials of life – food, shelter, medicine, transportation, energy – Transition's model reformulates resilience as an inchoate set of requirements for survival in a risky future. And, in fact, as an unattainable set of requirements: the ever-pending crisis produces for my interlocutors a sense that the work is never done, and therefore survival is never assured.

Resilience in this context, then, has a mandate that includes, simply put, *everything imaginable*. Every object, every practice, every human and every system is possibly at risk of collapsing – including the very state apparatus out of which the notion of resilience emerged. This typifies:

> a 'culture' of resilience that turns crisis response into a strategy of permanent, open ended responsibleness, integrating emergency preparedness into the infrastructures of everyday life and the psychology of citizens . . . [issuing] a call to permanent adaptability in and through crisis. What is resilience, after all, if not the acceptance of disequilibrium itself as a principle of organization?
>
> *(Walker and Cooper, 2011)*

By first positioning the past – 'skills and objects our grandparents had', as Transitioners often say – as the resilient ideal, Transition then creates the conditions for 'accepting disequilibrium' as an organizing principle for social relations. Hand scythes, root cellars and plant medicine as objects become an integral part of a 'strategy of permanent adaptability', which grounds anticipatory affects such as fear, hope and grief. Focused on preparing for the permanent crisis, resilience builders encounter a problem in dealing with the present moment. In fact, the mandate of resilience building in Transition Towns' work looks to a longer future, what Stewart Brand might call the 'long now' (Brand, 1999) – not to a present in which problems already proliferate and crave attention. Planning for the one-hundred-year, post-petroleum timescale that the Transition model's 'Energy Descent Action Plans' (EDAPs), for instance, call for, is not something that civil society members – among whom most Transitioners number – often find themselves doing. The timescales of resilience building are not quite geological;[7] nonetheless, they are often intended to stretch beyond the limits of one human lifetime.

It is unsurprising that it presents a challenge, for Transitioners and for others using the concept of resilience, to shuttle back and forth between a hundred-year timescale and the already existing challenges of the present moment. To be effective in its own terms, resilience-building community organizing with a long time-horizon in mind must also take into account a wide array of complex existing sociopolitical realities: for instance, the continued appropriation of land and resources from Native, First Nation and other indigenous communities (see e.g. O'Brien 2010; Wolford 2010); or the reality of communities of colour living in spaces made environmentally marginal by the byproducts of corporate industry throughout the continent (see e.g. Murphy, 2006; Kuletz, 1998). Without such an accounting, the project of resilience will go no further than benefitting those who already have the time, energy and money to acquire the skills, objects and processes which indicate a resilient life(style).

Resilience as object assemblage

Collapses and crises, and how to be materially and psychologically ready for them, are subjects constantly on the minds of Transitioners. 'Where will the food come from for me, my family, and my community once the food trucks stop running?', ask my interlocutors in a community meeting. In another conversation after a regional meeting on resilience building, an older interlocutor was vehement that the town needed to have solar panels 'isolated from the electrical grid' as a community benefit in the event of an electrical grid collapse. Such a collapse could occur, she suggested, by natural disaster as much as by the possibility of social unrest 'when everyone from New York comes up here for food'. This is one among many narratives that help to generate particular orientations towards the object assemblages – in these cases, food, petroleum products, trucks, solar panels, electrical infrastructure – in Transitioners' resilience-building work. These kinds of objects serve two purposes – as temporal sutures linking imagined pasts and anticipated futures, and as tools for the mobilization of relationships.

In this section, I address these object assemblages in their capacity, for Transitioners, as temporal sutures. What follows is a partial list of materials which Transitioners use to 'build' their own, and their community's, resilience.

- root cellars – for storing vegetables, grains and canned foods for survival when the food trucks stop running;
- medicinal plants;
- 'Energy Descent Action Plans' (EDAP) – these emerge from discussions about community-wide weaning from toxic and limited fossil fuels;
- scythe – for cutting hay and grain without using fossil fuels;
- hand-knitted hats and knitting – for making clothing once industrial manufactured clothing has fallen by the wayside;
- farm-field gleaned produce – for eating or donating to the local food bank;
- local currency – for use now, and after the 'econopocalypse,' as one person put it, in ways that circumvent national finance.

It is in these materials and others used to demarcate an imagined state of 'resilience' that I locate resilience's problem with the present. This problem emerges in these objects first because many objects identified with resilience building are rooted in a particular notion of an idealized pastoral history. Many of these object assemblages are woven into a narrative of an early United States or a nineteenth-century Europe (see e.g. Marx, 1964; Sachs, 2006, 2013; Schama, 1996). Consider the hand scythe, or the small-scale root cellar for food storage. This ideological mobilization of these objects out of such pasts enables a tendency to refer to idealized (pre-mass petroleum industry) pasts in order to attempt to create the conditions for (post-oil) futures that are insulated from the unexpected food shortages.

Other objects listed are creations of the contemporary resilience-building movement and are based partially on practices developed in other settings – like the Energy Descent Action Plan, rooted in centralized emergency management practices, and the connections between Transition's work to build local resilience and that of the United States' FEMA (Federal Emergency Management Agency) in outreach to small fire departments as emplaced emergency managers.

People take such objects up in practice in such a way that they suture pasts and resilient futures through the present. This suturing is most visible as Transitioners repeatedly cite such things as desirable elements for an ideal future – elements that emerge from past subsistence modes of life, or from present governance-based emergency management. These desires strengthen the link between pastoral histories, political structures of anticipation and imagined futures in which human communities can thrive. The material implements, which the idealized hardscrabble, subsistence farmer in New England made use of, must come back into play, for survival in a different kind of imagined hardscrabble, post-oil future. A root cellar, for example, speaks to a kind of individualistic, idealized New England thrift – one which prizes self-sufficiency and has done so for hundreds of years. Though Transitioners may not, themselves, put purchase on the kinds of isolation that were often experienced by many members of rural farming families (especially women, children and indentured labourers), the sorts of affective resonance that root cellars enable still give them a power to help shape how ideal futures may emerge.

In both sets of objects – the ideal pastoral and the contemporary preparatory – we can see a desire to allay any uncertainty or insecurity in the future. To return to Masco's analysis, he suggests that 'American national security culture' is 'enabled by the politics of shock'. This politics is a cycle of 'shock-terror-normality', which makes possible:

> the promise of a world without events—that is, a perfectly secure every day unbroken by surprise, and with the inevitable failure of that project, the continual drive to expand the security project in the name of producing a world without shock.
> *(Masco, 2014, p. 41)*

For Transitioners engaged with the material objects listed above, in attempts to be adequately enough prepared for an un-anticipatable future, it is exactly this impossible-to-achieve 'world without shock' that they attempt to build with object practices like root cellars and EDAPs.

Thus far, objects have figured as a temporal suture of pasts and futures. However, they also may serve as a tool for mobilizing relationships grounded in an ethics of care, and capable of also addressing the needs of the present. *Community* root cellars, in fact, are another iteration of this assemblage that Transitioners have articulated as desirable, perhaps as an antidote to the isolating affect of the traditional root cellar – and perhaps a well-placed example of how resilience can be at once caring and relational, as well as addressed to a future without grocery stores. An ethic of care, if used to ground resilience-building practices, can create the conditions for the necessary dimensions of humanity, intimacy, attention and relationship needed to cultivate justice for the present and the future. Not just community root cellars for a post-oil future, but a closer attention to access to food for racially and economically marginalized communities in the present moment, can be encompassed by resilience grounded in an ethics of care. This tendency is already present in the relational work of Transition's resilience, and we can learn from it to highlight an ethics of care in other domains of resilience work.

Resilience as relationship

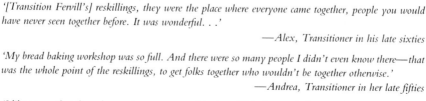

'[Transition Fervill's] reskillings, they were the place where everyone came together, people you would have never seen together before. It was wonderful. . .'

—Alex, Transitioner in his late sixties

'My bread baking workshop was so full. And there were so many people I didn't even know there—that was the whole point of the reskillings, to get folks together who wouldn't be together otherwise.'

—Andrea, Transitioner in her late fifties

'I like to say that the only way to save communities is to fall in love with them, and that's what I want to do. . .'

—Sam, Transitioner in his early sixties

The quotes offered above outline some ways that Transitioners talk about identifying a *feeling* or a *sense* of building resilience, one which is intimately connected with *relationship*: coming together with different people, 'falling in love' with communities. Resilience as a concept was often an implied, rather than explicit, part of Transition work through reskillings, free schools, community and the work of Transition Towns in this area. Gathering people together to learn a skill is a key part of the Transition model for resilience building. Gaining skills that are central to survival in a future world where all current systems have collapsed – for so the story of the future is told by Transitioners – is part of the intent. Skill-sharing also connects community members over a shared physical practice. These skills often involve particular materials, objects that become emblematic of 'resilience' writ large in this landscape – hand scythes, medicinal plants, local currency, all of which are spoken of as key to thriving in a post-oil, post-current-economic system future. Certain practices and activities done together are easy to draw under the umbrella of resilience-building work – others are not.

Alex, the Transitioner quoted above, suggested to me that: 'resilience is community, and relationship. That's what it is, at its core, relationship'. This sentiment is borne out in practice, as Transitioners gather to watch films (usually about peak oil, global climate change, economic issues or health issues) at the local public library and stay for cookies and discussion afterwards. They gather, also, to work in the local community garden that the organization helped create; between 2011 and 2013, they gathered several times every week for 'reskilling' workshops and discussions; for film screenings; for community garden workshops and more. Sam wanted to love the community deeply, to treasure relationships as the core of resilience. Andrea and Alex felt a certain effervescence at the workshops, where people 'who wouldn't otherwise get together' had a chance to connect with one another.

It is these kinds of interactions which constitute 'resilience building' for this community. In fact, the mission statement of Transition Fervill places community connections and resilience together at the heart of its work:

> [We engage] the creativity, expertise and skill-sets of our friends and neighbors in the design of a sustainable, resilient, socially just and mutually supportive community.

> We collaborate to embrace the extraordinary challenge and opportunity of climate change, peak oil and economic instability. Together we reinvent, rethink, rebuild and celebrate our community and the world around us.[8]

In this mission statement it is easy to decipher the parallel goals of 'sustainability, resilience, social justice and mutually supportive community'. As with much human experience, though, the ideals outlined here manifest in different ways in everyday life. Transition Fervill's emphasis on 'our friends and neighbors' and connecting community members, translates from the mission statement to the daily work they did on the ground. What does not translate so readily is the close correspondence between 'resilience' and 'social justice' articulated in the mission statement. Nor is it precisely clear what resilience might look like if it were achieved – instead, the open question remains for Fervill and other Transition initiatives as to what a 'reinvented, rethought, rebuilt' world looks like.

When I asked Jonathan, another local Transitioner in his sixties for his thoughts on resilience, he responded:

> all this preparation and resilience-building is good, but honestly, we're screwed—it won't do any good. And I guess I keep holding gatherings and doing this work because I'd rather go down in the company of friends, holding hands, than alone.

While building resilience – through gathering and working together in community – is still a desirable practice for Jonathan, 'resilience' as a state is a goal that will never be reached. For him, resilience, as an identifiable state, is still deeply bound up with the objects and skills with which it is associated: scythes, cellars and herbs as antidotes, or at least preparatory measures, for an unsurvivable future.

Though resilience, for Jonathan, might emerge as a set of visible social and physical processes, which people do together in relationship, there are particular objects and practices which frame the *kind of relationship* that can be called resilience building. The relationality that those objects enable is central to his notion of what shapes appropriate preparation for a risky future. In this context, community building activities, like volunteering at the Food Shelf or hosting a dance, are important, but not *directly and explicitly* about resilience. Though resilience is defined by Transitioners as necessarily relational, not all relationality counts as resilience for them. One must have the proper materials, and the proper anticipatory understanding of future crisis, to which to collectively orient.

Thus, the tension between resilience as a practice of caring relationship, of connection, and resilience as a set of materially-rooted knowledges that will ensure future survival, governs the back-and-forth work of resilience building in Transition initiatives. In practice, care and the relevance of relationship manifest intensely – and they do so via bread-baking, scything fields, connecting during workshops about using rifles, and the materials positioned as necessary for surviving the unknowable future threats of climate, economy and energy.

Some of the objects in question emerge as desirable for resilience building from narratives of a pre-industrial past of subsistence labour and low-carbon emissions. When current understandings of the progress of climate change and economic instability are projected onto the wide screen of the imagined future, this pre-industrial past allows for the possibility of eating, sleeping and being together safely. That projection carries the histories of resilience's objects with it, acknowledged or not. The assumption is that the conditions of the past – for example, reproductive manual labour and low carbon emissions – will be in place.

The social relationality that these objects enable is shaped by their cross-temporal presence as object assemblages. As objects, they are also spaces of action which carry with them understood cultural histories linking them to some kind of imagined successful past. These links serve as a kind of material suture, pulling imagined pasts into imagined futures.

How does one care? Resilience and difference beyond the scale of a human lifetime

A future threatened by lack of food because 'the trucks stop running' is a vision of a particular problem raised by a collapsing, crisis-ridden future, one often reiterated by Transitioners. Another canonical story engendering desires for anticipatory pre-emption draws a picture of a future where urban food shortages in nearby cities leads to an influx of internal 'climate migrants' from Connecticut or New York City (both connected to Vermont by shared watersheds, the Connecticut River and the Hudson River respectively).

In the midst of accumulating facts – data from scientific publications as much as popular press on environmentalist or economic websites – Transitioners also act. These actions are often understood as both for the present moment and also pre-emptive, and are underpinned by a larger conception of what *kind* of future crisis they might assist with. They build community gardens, bike-share programmes or volunteer at the Food Shelf. Still, there is a lacuna for Transitioners' resilience where the present meets the future. What is missing is the explicit connection between the resilience-building question: 'What kinds of food sources will we have when the trucks stop running?' and the present-moment social justice question: 'What do people need right now?'

Efforts like the Gleaning Program and the Vermont Food Bank's location in Fervill are referenced frequently by Transitioners as places where people work across class difference in ways that are 'related to Transition work, but are not *exactly* building resilience'.[9] However, such activities sometimes are articulated as part of organizing a workable local and regional set of systems for post-oil food and transport, or a local system of exchange – both of which are articulated explicitly as future-oriented projects under the umbrella of resilience building. Such attempts to reformulate existing social relations create the conditions of possibility for care in the present moment, in the context of resilience.

One counter to my argument that 'resilience' overlooks the crises of the moment, in fact, is that creating different socialities and politics *now* in preparation for the collapses of the future can offer relief for currently existing challenges. Actions taken in the context of the world-that-is, which are meant to foreshadow the social and political mores of the world-which-will-come, can be called 'prefigurative politics' (Juris and Khasnabish, 2013). To the extent that Transition's resilience building is engaged in working towards this reformulation – of relations of exchange, of community formation, of food distribution – it can be understood to be already engaging in a kind of prefigurative politics, merging an ethic of care with ideals of resilience. It is on the matter of reconstructing social relations, among them relations across class difference, race difference, citizenship difference and more, that resilience building needs recuperation.

There is a tension that arises in Transition Towns work that is rooted in the dual nature of how 'building resilience' is practiced. As we have seen, care manifests deeply in Transitioners' work, in how people speak about building *relationship* and *community* as key to building *resilience*. There is something at once caring and also utilitarian about such resilience-based relationship building, rooted in reskilling workshops, mobilized by certain object assemblages. By taking up care and utility together, Transitioners grapple with how to prioritize the work of building resilience across the demands of different kinds of risk and need.

Observing this tension in everyday practice, feminist geography and medical anthropology's 'ethic of care' offers a productive way of re-crafting our understanding of human relations, as much as a re-thinking of the relations themselves. Susan Smith suggests: 'this is an ethic that is already rooted in the fact that everyday life is full of ideas and practices which lean towards what is good, fair and care-full' (Smith 2005, p. 208). How, then, do we prepare for future threats with an eye, and a hand, on caring practices of the present moment?[10]

Redistributive practices like gleaning are an important element – especially when coupled with considerations of the underlying social, political and economic reasons for food insecurity, and work that aims to address those issues at both a grassroots and a policy level. Creating local currencies, again as a redistributive practice (and as a failsafe against the potential losses of 'big banking') can be very productive, but must be done in such a way as to take into consideration the broad realities of a community with vastly differing levels of economic stability. What establishments will accept the currency? Based on where it is accepted, who will be able to participate in that currency as part of their regular financial practice? Creating root cellars and growing more of a community's food are key material practices: communities and scholars need to ask themselves, though, who has the time to take part in such activities, and whether there are additional forms of caring resilience that might need to be developed before, or alongside, that garden patch or hand-scythed field.

J. K. Gibson-Graham offers a nuanced take on the relationality of currency in a capitalist context, suggesting that particular 'noncapitalist' practices of exchange need not be seen as 'outside' the monolith of capitalism but perhaps also as equally powerful, pervasive, compelling and world-making (2006). Their framing offers the opportunity to see the non-dominant practices of building relationships across class and race differences, and supporting work for small-scale economic justice in particular places like Fervill as world-making, and as necessarily bound up with resilience as a practice accessible *for all*.

In effect, an ethics of care reframes the kinds of relationships that economic processes of capitalism and ideologies of individualism have obscured. By weaving an ethics of care into the kinds of work that resilience's object assemblages can do – by attending to the social and political histories of those assemblages rather than taking them as neutral – such assemblages can serve as tools to mobilize a reframing of social relations that enables attention to current social justice needs.

Conclusion

I have described resilience-building objects in terms of sutures that knit idealized pastoral history into anticipatory, collapse-oriented practices. By unifying the pasts of these objects into a single story of simple times, unalienated manual labour, and low carbon emissions, and projecting them into a future in crisis, resilience as a concept offers no staunching of the current wounds of poverty and systemic injustice – foreclosing who may participate in 'resilience building' under these terms. I have presented ethnographic evidence and corresponding analysis that demonstrates the dual nature of 'building resilience' in Transition communities, looking both to relationship and to object assemblage as key for future preparation. This dual nature, with attention to the ways that objects carry their histories with them, highlights the 'problem with the present' that the resilience concept carries with it. By analysing the objects and social practices central to building resilience in the Transition Towns model, I unfolded a critique of the temporality of the concept of resilience itself. If we are, as scholars, intent in part on producing work that supports practices for the good in the world, we must engage in recuperative work on resilience, wresting it away from the perpetually anticipatory, anti-shock infrastructure provided by wartime logics of fear and preparation.

Resilience, after this chapter, might be best framed not merely as a checklist of necessary objects and skills, but rather as a set of relations, grounded in an ethics of care, among individuals and groups and their objects and skills. In Fervill's Transition Town, each of these characters – humans, objects, skills, administrative bodies – plays a role in producing the kind of suturing of idealized pasts to the imagined futures. In practice, it is next to impossible to formulate new, robust ways of relating across difference via a future-oriented manifestation of 'resilience' alone. Stirring an element of care for the present moment and existing human needs into resilience work is especially salient for those working in the global north. Though many communities like the ones I describe here are not (yet) fully impacted by climate change, they cannot do their work well without understanding that *right now* there are needs not being met. Right now, in a moment of relative abundance for the global north, people go hungry or are imprisoned as a result of systemic inequalities and racisms. One need not look to our 50- or 100-year climate threshold models (see e.g. the Intergovernmental Panel on Climate Change's 2012 report) of CO_2 emissions to find food deserts and suffering. In order to do work that has a meaningful impact, we must develop an ethic of care for building resilience that encompasses the timeframes of the present and the future at once.

An ethics of care tuned towards the exchanges, or interactions with objects of resilience building, would offer a stronger reformulation of what it means to be in a relationship for the future. Resilience as a framework is frequently mobilized to do this kind of work, and just as frequently fails – due, I have argued, to the facile adoption of the future-orientation of the concept. Weaving in an ethics of care may enable more room for cross-difference relationships to build and grow *today*. In the face of catastrophic climate change, global sea rise, economic instability, the shift of governance structures and the end of the era of abundance for the privileged few, it is attending to the material realities of such relationships that will make it possible to address the needs of the future.

Acknowledgements

This research was supported by Cornell University's Atkinson Center for a Sustainable Future and Oxfam through the Rural Resilience Research Fellowship, and the Department of Anthropology at Cornell University. I am grateful to those who helped develop these ideas; Marygold Walsh-Dilley, Sara Keene, Eleanor Andrews, Beth Reddy, Ashley Smith, Anaar Desai-Stephens and Hayden Kantor in particular deserve many thanks.

Notes

1 Other factors at play include the 'back-to-the-land' movement of the 1960–1970s and Vermont and New York's nineteenth-century utopian and millenarian communities.

2 Transition United States hub webpage. Accessed Feb 10, 2016. www.transitionus.org/blog/what-your-group-can-do.

3 Here is the Transition United States hub's take on resilience:

> #5: Build Resilience. This stresses the fundamental importance of building resilience i.e. the capacity of our businesses, communities and settlements to withstand shock. Transition initiatives commit to building resilience across a wide range of areas (food, economics, energy, etc) and also on a range of scales (from the local to the national) as seems appropriate – and to setting them within an overall context of the need to do everything we can to ensure environmental resilience.

4 Transition Fervill's town and participant names are pseudonyms, and direct references are obscured.

5 Peak oil is a term organizers use to refer to a decline in readily available petroleum supplies.

6 It also draws on the 'Victory Gardens' of World-War-II England. The labour of subsistence – growing and preserving food, sustaining communal connections – becomes bound up with war as a 'mode of life' (Povinelli, 2006, p. 109).

7 Unlike the 'deep time horizons', of scientists designing storage for spent nuclear fuel (Ialenti, 2014), or the Svalbard Seed Vault's holding space for 'the world's biodiversity' (Fowler, 2008).

8 Accessed online November 2015. Citation redacted for confidentiality purposes.
9 Gleaners volunteer to collect leftover produce from farm fields, bringing it to local Food Shelves and restaurants.
10 On an ethics of care in everyday practice, see e.g. Feldman and Ticktin, 2010; Held, 2006, 2014; Lawson, 2009; Garcia, 2010.

References

Brand, S. (1999) *'The Clock of the Long Now' Time and Responsibility: The Ideas Behind the World's Slowest Computer*. New York: Basic Books.
Chamberlin, S. (2009) *The Transition Timeline for a Local Resilient Future*. White River Junction, VT: Chelsea Green Publishers.
Chandler, D. (2014) Beyond neoliberalism: resilience, the new art of governing complexity. *Resilience: International Policies, Practices and Discourses*, Vol. 2: 1, 47–63.
Cruikshank, J. (2005) *Do Glaciers Listen? Local Knowledge, Colonial Encounters and Social Imagination*. Vancouver: UBC Press.
Davis, T. (2007) *Stages of Emergency: Cold War Nuclear Civil Defense*. Durham, NC: Duke University Press.
Dewey, J. (1927) *The Public and Its Problems*. Athens: OH: Ohio University Press.
Eisenstein, C. (2013) *The More Beautiful World Our Hearts Know is Possible*. Berkeley, CA: North Atlantic Books.
Feldman, I. and M. Ticktin (2010) *In the Name of Humanity: The Government of Threat and Care*. Durham, NC: Duke University Press.
Fowler, C. (2008) The Svalbard seed vault and crop security. *BioScience*, Vol. 58: 3.
Garcia, A. (2010) *The Pastoral Clinic: Addiction and Dispossession Along the Rio Grande*. Berkeley, CA: University of California Press.
Gibson-Graham, J. K. (2006) *The End of Capitalism (As We Knew It): A Feminist Critique of Political Economy*. Minneapolis, MN: University of Minnesota Press.
Held, V. (2006) *The Ethics of Care: Personal, Political, and Global*. Oxford: Oxford University Press.
Held, V. (2014) The ethics of care as normative guidance: comment on Gilligan. *Journal of Social Philosophy*, Vol. 45: 1, 107–115.
Helmreich, S. (2009) *Alien Ocean: Anthropological Voyages in Microbial Seas*. Berkeley, CA: University of California Press.
Hopkins, R. (2008) *The Transition Handbook: From Oil Dependency to Local Resilience*. White River Junction, VT: Chelsea Green Publishing.
Hopkins, R. (2011) *The Transition Companion: Making Your Community More Resilient in Uncertain Times*. White River Junction, VT: Chelsea Green Publishing.
Ialenti, V. (2014) Adjudicating deep time: revisiting The United States' high-level nuclear waste repository project at Yucca Mountain. *Science and Technology Studies*, Vol. 27: 2.
IPCC (2012) *Managing the Risks of Extreme Events and Disasters to Advance Climate Change Adaptation*. A Special Report of Working Groups I and II of the Intergovernmental Panel on Climate Change (Field, C. B., V. Barros, T. F. Stocker, D. Qin, D. J. Dokken, K. L. Ebi, M. D. Mastrandrea, K. J. Mach, G.-K. Plattner, S. K. Allen, M. Tignor, and P. M. Midgley (eds)). Cambridge and New York: Cambridge University Press, Cambridge.
Juris, J. and A. Khasnabish (2013) *Insurgent Encounters: Transnational, Activism, Ethnography, and the Political*. Durham, NC: Duke University Press.
Kohn, E. (2013) *How Forests Think: Towards an Anthropology Beyond the Human*. Berkeley, CA: University of California Press.
Kuletz, V. L. (1998) *The Tainted Desert: Environmental and Social Ruin in the American West*. New York: Routledge.
Latour, B. (2005) *Reassembling the Social: An Introduction to Actor–network Theory*. Oxford and New York: Oxford University Press.
Lawson, V. (2009) Instead of radical geography, how about caring geography? *Antipode*, Vol. 41: 1, 210–213.
Lawson, V. (2010) Dumping grounds and unseen grounds: placing race, ethnicity and poverty in the American Northwest. *Annals of the Association of American Geographers*, Vol. 100: 3.
Marx, L. (1964) *The Machine in the Garden: Technology and the Pastoral Ideal in America*. New York: Oxford University Press.

Masco, J. (2014) *The Theater of Operations: National Security Affect from the Cold War to the War on Terror.* Durham, NC: Duke University Press.

Mauss, M. (2002) *The Gift: The Form and Reason for Exchange in Archaic Societies.* London: Routledge.

Meadows, D. (2008) *Thinking in Systems – A Primer.* London: Earthscan Publishing.

Meadows, D. L., D. H. Meadows and J. Randers. (1992). *Beyond the Limits: Confronting Global Collapse, Envisioning a Sustainable Future.* White River Junction, VT: Chelsea Green Publishing.

Murphy, M. (2006) *Sick Building Syndrome and the Problem of Uncertainty: Environmental Politics, Technoscience, and Women Workers.* Durham, NC: Duke University Press.

Nadasdy, P. (2007) Adaptive Co-Management and the Gospel of Resilience. In D. Armitage, F. Berkes and N. Doubleday (eds) *Adaptive Co-Management: Collaboration, Learning, and Multilevel Governance.* Vancouver: University of British Columbia Press, pp. 208–227.

O'Brien, J. (2010) *Firsting and Lasting: Writing Indians out of Existence in New England.* Minneapolis, MN: University of Minnesota Press.

Orr, J. (2004) The Militarization of Inner Space. *Critical Sociology*, Vol. 30: 2, 451–481.

Povinelli, E. A. (2006) *The Empire of Love: Toward a Theory of Intimacy, Genealogy, and Carnality.* Durham, NC: Duke University Press Books.

Rappaport, R. (1968) *Pigs for the Ancestors: Ritual in the Ecology of a New Guinea People.* New Haven, CT: Yale University Press.

Sachs, A. (2006) *The Humboldt Current: Nineteenth-Century Exploration and the Roots of American Environmentalism.* New York: Viking Press.

Sachs, A. (2013) *Arcadian America: The Death and Life of an Environmental Tradition.* New Haven, CT: Yale University Press.

Schama, S. (1996) *Landscape and Memory.* New York: Vintage Books.

Smith, S. J. (2005) States, markets and an ethic of care. *Political Geography*, Vol. 24: 1–20.

Sturken, M. (2007) *Tourists of History: Memory, Kitsch, and Consumerism From Oklahoma City to Ground Zero.* Durham, NC: Duke University Press.

Walker, J. and M. Cooper (2011) Genealogies of resilience: from systems ecology to the political economy of crisis adaptation. *Security Dialogue*, Vol. 42: 143.

Weiner, N. (1948) *Cybernetics: or Control and Communication in the Animal and the Machine.* Cambridge, MA: MIT Press.

Wolford, W. (2010) *This Land is Ours Now: Social Mobilization and the Meanings of Land in Brazil.* Durham, NC: Duke University Press.

9

THE DIGITIZATION OF RESILIENCE

Mareile Kaufmann

Introduction

The integration of portable and wearable technologies into our everyday lives has made computing so ubiquitous that it has begun to transform emergency communication and resilience management. Already during the 2010 Haiti earthquake, large amounts of digital data were circulated via social media, a process that was later termed "knowledge sharing" (Yates and Paquette, 2011, p. 7). This information was harvested and translated into "knowledge applications" (ibid., p. 10), such as the identification of urgent cases, the coordination of resource distribution or fundraising for disaster relief (see Gao *et al.*, 2011). Since the upsurge of smart phones in the early 2010s, apps and every-ware,[1] but also social media and digital mapping tools have been identified as a "tremendous opportunity" (Crowe, 2011, p. 418) for emergency response and resilience planning. European Commission investments in the "next generation emergency services" (European Commission, 2014) endorse this trend. In light of increased digitization, this chapter asks: What are the specific properties of digital information and how do they influence resilience governance?

This chapter argues that the rapid exchangeability of digital information not only inspires new emergency communication practices for affected populations and managers. The traceability, storability and computability of digital information also allows for new resilience analytics, the identification of correlations and patterns based on big data, which affects resilience epistemologies and the contents of resilience as such. After outlining the properties of digital information and the activities they afford (Gibson, 1986), the chapter investigates how the increased production and circulation of digital information influences resilience practices and epistemologies. Based on a review of academic literature, policy papers and online emergency management tools, it identifies and discusses three aspects of resilience management that are influenced by the rise of the digital: first, practices of mapping, visualizing, and assessing the emergent situation; second, approaches to manage and change trajectories of the emergent situation, and third, post-emergency activities such as analyzing response, learning, and designing future resilience. Finally, the chapter presents overarching conclusions about the digitization of resilience, pointing to the way in which the digital fosters the focus on the crowd as the main performer of resilience activities, and the pattern as the novel epistemological rationale for "resilience programming" (Grove, 2014).

Properties and affordances of digital information

Digital information has become a key asset for emergency management and resilience practice. It is the digital format of information, which makes a difference in the way that resilience is being thought about and enacted. Both communication and analytical practices have experienced remarkable transformations with the rise of the digital. In order to trace these influences on resilience programming, it is essential to understand first what the properties of digital information are and how they render specific activities possible. Gibson argues that it is the composition of an object, a landscape or a substance that constitutes what kind of action it permits and enables (Gibson, 1986). His argument goes back to Gestalt psychology and the term "Aufforderungscharakter" (Lewin, 1969), meaning that something literally invites for a specific usage; it has "affordances" (Gibson, 1986). The way in which an object is constituted thus makes a difference in action. Affordances do not necessarily turn an object into a political subject, but it is also not just a neutral object, since it can "authorize, allow, afford, encourage, permit, suggest, influence, block, render possible, forbid, and so on" (Latour, 2005, p. 72). Its oriented form of existence—or, to put it in Galloway's words, the fact that bodies must not only always speak, but "must always speak *as*" (Galloway, 2012, p. 137)—facilitates some activities over others. Following this, it is the interrelation between the affordances of an artifact and actors that utilize and harness these affordances, which results in the mutual construction of intentional action.

Understanding digital information thus not as an abstracted, ephemeral and disembodied "pure information object" (Paul, 2009, p. 19), but as in possession of properties that enable or constrain it as an artifact (see Blanchette, 2011, pp. 1045–46; see Leonardi, 2010) with specific affordances prompts an investigation of what these properties are and what actions they permit. Only in describing them, is it possible to point to the influence digital information has on the production of resilience knowledge and practice.

Hardware has a fundamental influence in constituting digital information. The way in which information is manipulated, stored, and exchanged not only mediates material properties of digital data (Blanchette, 2011), but also establishes information as electronic. Information is codified in discrete digits, which are transformed into electronic impulses that can travel through the network. The properties of electronic data are further determined by computing language, which organizes the dual registers through which digital code operates. Digital bits are thus shaped through various languages with their own grammar and linguistic varieties that constitute the way in which digital data travel (Blanchette, 2011). As a result, digital information, whether visual, audio, or metadata, entails specific affordances: it cannot only be transmitted and circulated, but this exchange of information can happen simultaneously and over long distances at a considerable speed. As basic as these affordances may seem, they are currently important influence factors in emergency communication and resilience programming, where timely information (Meier, 2013) and data from areas with low accessibility are key assets.

Blanchette furthermore points to the fact that file formats (JPEG, TIF, etc.) constrain the mutability of bits (Blanchette, 2011), which not only defines the material property of digital information, but also makes it storable. In addition to this, metadata, such as geospatial information or IP addresses, make it possible to assign geographic locations to contents of digital information. This makes digital information traceable and searchable. These affordances influence the way in which digital information can be used for analysis. Geospatial mapping of information, for example, is increasingly used in emergency management and resilience programming for situational analysis (Committee on Planning for Catastrophe, 2007). Due to their numeric and material properties, digital data can furthermore be copied and reproduced, counted and computed. The existence of digital information in distributed networks, their simultaneous and rapid exchangeability, their storability, traceability, and computability emphasize the various options for gathering and re-assembling digital information in different contexts, online and offline.

It is through these specific affordances that analytical practices of association and correlation emerge: digital information affords analysis through forms and patterns. Amoore (2013) argues that the relevant information for political practices doesn't sit in the data nodes as such, but in the way they are being associated with each other. One example of such a form is the algorithm. The form of the algorithmic is malleable and emergent as long as the points are held together. Algorithmic form is thus characterized by mobile lines and loose associations, allowing for the disaggregation of data and for limitless amounts of re-combinations to make visible whatever resilience management practices seek to target (see ibid.). As a result, the detection of phenomena "takes place within form itself, in the links and patterns that materialize and take shape" (ibid., p. 133).

Thus, besides novel forms of communication, digital information affords big data analysis and associative practices opportunities of "connecting the dots" in order to create actionable information. Digital information enables automated analytics about complex environments through complex processes that are, due to the mere size of available information, beyond individual comprehension. The ability of the digital to install new forms of sense-making about complexity by unearthing indiscernible and emerging patterns (Andrejevic and Gates, 2014) has been identified as a big promise, especially in contexts that are characterized by indiscernible and emergent dynamics, such as disasters and crises (see Stauffacher *et al.*, 2012; Meier, 2013; Ikanow. com: "Crisis Management"). Big data analytics are thus presented as a solution for risk and resilience management, whether this concerns situational analysis, the identification of self-organizing patterns in communities, or lessons learned activities.

This promise, however, has not only encountered diverse ethical concerns regarding privacy and data protection (Crawford *et al.*, 2013). It has been criticized as a method that is only available to those with processing power: as a combination of "size, storage, medium, and analytic capability" (Andrejevic and Gates, 2014, p. 186) big data is not merely a new scale of analytics, but the analytics and its system must be reinvented, including the social and material transformations needed to conduct big data analyses (ibid.). Another key challenge that such analytics face is that big data is systematically opaque and non-transparent (ibid.), which adds speculative elements to analysis and challenges objectivity. Datasets do not just exist, ready for objective measure (Amoore, 2013) – they have to be generated: "Data creators have to collect data and organize it, or create it from scratch" (Manovich, 2002a, p. 224). This is already an act of creativity that influences the results that big data can generate. Boyd and Crawford argue similarly that digital datasets, before being analyzed, need to be "imagined": decisions have to be taken about which variables to count and which ones to ignore. The process of imagining datasets according to one's own norms and values, as well as data errors and other limitations, challenges the objectivity of the calculated result (Boyd and Crawford, 2012).

Challenges to objectivity do not only occur in the production of digital datasets, but also while reading and interpreting them. In the context of the mining of legal texts, Hildebrandt points to the difficulty of digital hermeneutics and semiotics vis-à-vis their analogue counterparts. She asks whether new and different forms of reading are needed to analyze and interpret digital data (Hildebrandt, 2012). The digital presupposes a semiotics that does not necessarily equate a sign with a letter or other literal metaphors, but it may include symbolisms, metaphors, and analogies that can be an instance of form in the mathematical or aesthetic sense. In order to ensure a meaningful reading of data, this semiotics has to be identified and implemented before reading and interpretation take place (ibid). This fundamentally influences the production of knowledge. The digital changes the way in which we engage with information altogether—it foregrounds epistemologies of the countable. Digital data can only reason numerically. Here, Boyd and Crawford emphasize the general, but important, point that numbers don't necessarily speak for themselves (Boyd and Crawford, 2012). Knowledge created through numeric models simply lacks the insights of other approaches to find out why and how people do, write and make things. This problem is not solved by augmenting the amount of digital data because it lies within the numeric nature of data itself. "Bigger data is not always better data" (Boyd and Crawford 2012, p. 6) precisely because it removes context and depends on specific tools to harvest and interpret data.

Most importantly, however, the analysis of forms and patterns draws the focus away from underlying explanations of phenomena to correlations and effects. Andrejevic and Gates (2014) criticize that big data analytics does not have sorting power, but the algorithms that search digital information simply function. What matters in the knowledge created by big data is thus the correlation, not the content itself. Unearthing new correlations can be done, for example, by mapping behavioral patterns about resilience to geographic contents, which provides conclusions about how to target specific groups. Repurposing existent digital information and continuing to unearth emergent patterns is the main goal of big data, which leads Andrejevic and Gates to conclude that "the function *is* the creep" (2014, p. 189). The purpose of big data analysis is then neither to produce an accurate or complete view of the world nor to explain phenomena, but "it's about intervening in that world based on patterns" (ibid., p. 190). It is about intervening effectively, which is, ultimately, also the purpose of resilience management.

Understanding the digital through its properties and affordances of rapid circulatability, traceability, storability, and computability does not lead to a critique of the digital altogether, neither does it encourage the adoption of the attitude that the digital is a "technology" that merely needs better design to avoid causing unintended side effects. Rather, it takes digital data out of the realm of inconspicuousness within our everyday practices (Manovich, 2002b), where it is concealed from critical study. It makes it possible to study how digital data changes resilience epistemologies and practices. Digital information on emergencies has already become interesting to private and public actors, because it seems to answer the urge to access and share actionable information during emergencies. It enables crowdsourcing, associative knowledge production, and bears the potential for rapid intervention. As such, digital modes of communication and analytics enable new resilience practices. However, they don't necessarily seek to reflect what resilience may be, but they are performative: they make, transform, and reconfigure it (on the basis of Derosières, 2014).

The digitization of resilience

Managing and dealing with emergencies is of course never exclusively digital. However, as the usage of digital technology increases, the role that digital information plays for resilience management grows, too (see IFRC, 2013). Key sources of digital information during emergencies are social media and apps. While data on platforms such as Twitter, Instagram, and Tumblr is publicly accessible, data on platforms with restricted access can in many cases be collected as well, since terms and conditions create loopholes for governments to access data, especially if related to security situations (see Rushe, 2013). Digital information refers to content data, but also audio and visual data, like photos and satellite imagery, and metadata, for example geolocations, IP addresses, or web traffic. This increased circulation of digital information, so the chapter argues, transforms resilience programming. In particular, it affects the exchange of information, fostering new communication practices to enhance resilience, as well as the collection and analysis of information, generating new kinds of knowledge about resilience as a basis for intervention.

While the scholarly discourse predominantly points to the benefits of digital information for resilience practice (Meier, 2011, 2013; Yates and Paquette, 2011; Keim and Noji, 2011; Stauffacher *et al.*, 2012), critical scholarship questions whether a state of exception (Schmitt, 1921; Agamben, 2005) legally and morally justifies the collection of potentially personal data (Buchanan and Ess, 2008; Boyd and Crawford, 2012; Crawford *et al.*, 2013). Especially big data analytics, even if conducted for benevolent purposes, raises a range of concerns. It brings about issues of ownership and protection of personal data, questions of accountabilities for conclusions drawn from collective data, the potential for rising technology dependency and the creation of new vulnerabilities in terms of hackable, but sensitive information. It is furthermore unclear as to who profits from this move towards the digital and whether the digitization of resilience inspires a privatization and commercialization of resilience management in the form of different web-based services. Vis-à-vis these concerns, Crawford *et al.* (2013) point to the need for good governance principles in data-driven projects, the informed use of technology for data collection, as well as the importance of local data and sociocultural contexts in interpreting data. These critical questions and guidelines, however, largely refer to the way in which digital practices are being executed. Implicitly and explicitly they substantiate the argument that technology development and analytical practice simply needs to get better at addressing these issues. As such, this discourse does not reflect upon the way in which the specific affordances of digital information influence resilience programming altogether, creating new practices, forms of knowledge and under-standings of resilience itself. The chapter describes and discusses these transformations in relation to three broad developments.

Mapping, visualizing and assessing the emergent situation

Due to its distributed character and rapid exchangeability, digital information about emergencies can be gathered from and sent to isolated locations within affected areas. Accordingly, resilience strategies have identified citizens as "active collection nodes" for relevant information (ikanow. com: "Social Media"). Such strategies utilize the familiarity of users with social media and the low degrees of separation between each user (Meier, 2011) to "push" information to the public in emergency situations or to "pull" information from bystanders. This allows resilience managers on the one hand to provide guidance or raise awareness by communicating through these networks. Here, smart-phone apps are currently being discussed as specified services through which guidance can be received (Meier, 2013). Social media can, on the other hand, be used for providing and collecting information, for example, about damages and losses. In accessing this information, resilience managers can visualize emergency impacts, as well as resilience and response mechanisms (Meier, 2013). Since all this information travels in the form of electronic pulses, this gathering process can be conducted at a considerable speed. The circulation of digital information is considered to be "real time" (Emergency Journalism, 2012), which means that it is possible to receive new information without perceivable delay. In programming, a real-time system is one that "controls an environment by receiving data, processing them, and returning the results sufficiently quickly to affect the environment at that time" (Martin, 1965, p.4). The real-time monitoring of emergencies has created considerable optimism about the acceleration of emergency response (Puhorit *et al.*, 2014), to the extent that real-time computing systems are already understood to be "mission critical" (Crowe, 2011) to collect information and create new forms of situational analysis and overview. Summarized under the term "neogeography" (Turner, 2006), initiatives such as the "International Network of Crisis Mappers," "Open Street Maps," and "Random Hacks of Kindness" leverage mobile platforms, geospatial technologies, and visual analytics to map emergent challenges and resilience initiatives in order to accelerate response.

Some of these services, such as the "Internet-Response-League," tackle the large amount of circulated information by embedding visual Twitter and Instagram data into online games, where players get game-rewards in return for the analysis of the material.

As these first response activities show, the digital affords new practices of creating knowledge about the emergent situation and resilience mechanisms. It enables, for example, new communication modes, which promote an increased focus on the citizen. Through crowd-tasking the public becomes part of the response network. Crowdsourcing, the act of soliciting information about emergencies from large groups of people rather than traditional emergency responders, also speaks to the idea of self-organization, which is a key characteristic of resilience. Through new communication modes, individuals are thought to become less dependent on the government, since they "turn to their virtual communities for information and assistance" (FEMA, 2011, p. 4). Public knowledge is not only produced by pulling information from social networks that users have already circulated, but also by creating incentives to mobilize help, for example by distributing rewards for sharing helpful information (*The Economist*, 2012). Initiatives such as "idisaster" and "MicroMappers" actively encourage the public to volunteer. MicroMappers' approach of "micro-tasking" very much reflects the idea of resilient self-organization as it asks people to "spend a little bit of time performing a small task. Anyone can become a MicroMapper – there are no special skills or exceptional time commitments required" (Gilbert-Knight, 2013). Communicating and mapping information inspires new forms of "watching" emergencies, but also processes of "watching out" for each other, for example by exchanging crucial information with affected parties (see Kaufmann, 2015). With the rise of digital information, knowledge about emergencies is neither exclusively produced, nor solely accessed by traditional emergency management authorities. By giving rise to the crowd as a new epistemic community, the digital is thus inductive of a shift in the status of expertise. It creates the expert status of the affected citizen, who shares information, and that of the analyst and engineer, who seeks to make this knowledge work in the emergency management system.

The latter is an instance of the second development that the digital affords, namely new forms of information analysis. Even though information created by the affected citizen is based on "convenience sampling" (Meier 2011, p. 6) and may not be statistically representative, it is used for collective and associative forms of knowledge production. The computability of digital information allows for the association and correlation of information. Patterns (Andrejevic and Gates, 2014) arise as the main mode of creating knowledge about emergencies, which gives rise to new practices of viewing emergencies. Patterns visualize any correlation of interest to resilience managers; they are key to the creation of dynamic maps and visual reports about behaviour (FEMA, 2011), hubs of action, processes over time, movements of people and goods, access to safe and dangerous areas, as well as to forecast hazards arising from the evolving situation. Through such techniques of association, the digital contributes to a new form of situational overview and expands the options for people to inform themselves about unfolding emergencies.

Knowledge and visibility created through digital modes of communication and analytical practice are, however, not only created but also restrained by their digital properties. Digital information is always selective, and at times even deceptive. The circulation of misleading or wrongful information (trolling) is a prominent challenge for big data analysis during emergencies, since time to thoroughly analyze the veracity and validity of the data is scarce. As a result, digital knowledge is ontologically tied to specific approaches to truth. Building on the insight that "false rumors tend to be questioned much more than confirmed truths" (Mendoza *et al.*, 2010, p. 8) and that wrong messages "are often corrected by other users" (Merchant *et al.*, 2011, p. 2), veracity seems to arise from a large number of people validating reports (Gao *et al.*, 2011). This means that truth can be established by consensus. The "actively listening community" (Emergency Journalism, 2012) is not only another instance of self-organized verification, as comprehended in the idea of resilience, but it is also an approach to truth that is based on clusters and mass: finding a "statistical consensus between the crowd's contributions" (ibid.) can be exercised via credibility scores. Indicators representing veracity of information have been identified and collected in tools such as the "Seriously Rapid Source Review," which specifies where the submitting user is located, whether the user was an eyewitness and what the top five entities of the user's tweet history are (Meier, 2012b). As such, the tool leaves the question of veracity to the judgment of the crowd. A similar form of judgment, so it is suggested, could be done by volunteer task forces, who establish the veracity and credibility of contents by checking inconsistencies in the user's tweeting habits, by reviewing the tweeter's followers and by triangulating the user's identity via mainstream media (Meier, 2011, p. 15). As promising as such approaches to veracity are, they are not only time-consuming, but they instantiate new forms of digital surveillance by which the traceability of a social media user inspires a particular form of establishing truth based on mass, consensus, or statistical likelihood. The truthfulness of digital information is thus scalable; it can vary from completely true to completely false. If truthfulness is established via likelihood metrics (Merchant *et al.*, 2011; Meier, 2012a), it becomes subject to probability, which injects the emergent presence with a sense of speculation. Information, however, cannot only be true or false, but most digital information is selective in the first place. The uneven distribution of digital technologies (Graham, 2011), gendered and culturally diverse usage, as well as the specifics of defining and "imagining" the information relevant to the analysis (Boyd and Crawford, 2012) produces structural invisibilities within the creation of overviews. Information that is not digitized, not sent in a specific format, or not covered by the algorithmic program, will not be mapped and is thus rendered invisible, which is particularly harmful in the emergency management and resilience context.

Managing and changing trajectories of the emergent situation

What follows from the visualization of the emergency is the possibility to respond to and intervene in the emergent situation (Crowe, 2011; FEMA, 2011). Information about hubs of action, casualties, or dangerous zones can be translated into concrete advice to control the emergency's trajectory, instigate disaster response, and save lives (see Stauffacher *et al.*, 2012; Gao *et al.*, 2011; Merchant *et al.*, 2011; Yates and Paquette, 2011; Keim and Noji, 2011). Collected information can assist in making informed decisions and reduce impacts by giving practical advice, such as pointing to road access and locations of emergency infrastructures (Lindsay, 2011). "Google Crisis Response," for example, offers alert functions and person finders to locate lost individuals based on shared data. Social computing, artificial intelligence, machine learning, and big data analysis are furthermore deployed to identify needs, allocate resources, and match both with each other to install resilience (Meier, 2013). While such services presuppose the population's technical ability and expertise to access such information, once guaranteed, it also enables them to act upon this information. Offering a digital space for mutual assistance and neighborly help, Meier argues, furthermore aids the building of common norms and trust for faster recovery: "this bonding is not limited to offline dynamics but occurs also within and across online social networks" (ibid). "Peer-to-peer feedback loops" (ibid.) not only enable resilience management, adaptation and self-organization, but they also provide data for risk analysis and techniques of anticipation which can be used to predict evolving risks and instigate anticipatory action in order to steer the course of the emergency towards normality.

This course of action describes the very idea of resilience: self-organized emergency response. Not only is the information about the emergency provided by the affected subject, but the committed subject can now also further organize itself. This self-organization not only includes practical aspects, but also the emotional facets of resilience, thus: "social media, specifically their core strengths of timely information exchange and promotion of connectedness, were able to act as sources of psychological first aid in the early stages of disaster and assist in supporting aspects of community resilience" (Taylor *et al.*, 2012).

Since the digital emphasizes the role and status of the self-organized individual in new ways, traditional emergency services are now in need of reinventing their strategies and identifying which digital services they can offer for emergency response. While big data analysis may provide new avenues for resilience management, the digital also increases the gap between the emergency setting and the emergency managers who analyze the given data. Not only may analyzers lack the experience of the context in which emergency data is produced (Boyd and Crawford, 2012), but if digital communication replaces physical presence and face-to-face communication, the relationship between managers and the affected population is increasingly mediated. This lack of direct contact may not only influence the experience of emergency for the affected population, but it can influence the relationship of professional responders towards emergencies. Screens become the interface through which resilience managers operate and their engagement is likely to become subject to gamification, the game-like experience of emergencies, which through application design triggers natural desires for mastery, competition, and achievement (for example, see the Internet Response League). In the context of drone usage, it has furthermore been discussed whether this mediated experience entails an emotional removal of the pilots from the reality of the situation (Sandvik, 2013). The digital may not only mediate the emotional relationship of the responder to the emergency situation, it also increases the physical distance between emergency populations and authorities that analyze the emergency situation from the "control room" (Duffield, 2011). As a result, the digital not only "broadens" the space for emergency intervention and brings responders "closer" to the emergency in some situations, but it also redefines physical proximity. It affords mediated closeness and physical remoteness at the same time. As such, it enhances the idea of remote management, the exercise of coordination and control during emergencies from a distance (Collinson *et al.*, 2013). Creating resilience would then be recast as a form of facilitating self-organization from a bunker (Duffield, 2011), where analysts may veer away from the physical situation.

Analyzing response, learning and designing future resilience

Since "tweets and photographs linked to timelines and interactive maps can tell a cohesive story about a recovering community's capabilities und vulnerabilities" (Merchant *et al.*, 2011, p. 2), digital information also provides insights that affect future resilience practices and policies. The storability of digital information cannot only be used to manage knowledge and organize acute emergency relief, but this information can also be analyzed to measure general vulnerabilities (Birkmann, 2006) and unearth resilience patterns in the aftermath of an emergency as a form of lessons learned. Merchant *et al.*, for example, suggest that "now is the time to begin deploying these technologies while developing meaningful metrics of their effectiveness and of the accuracy and usefulness of the information they provide" (2011, p. 2). This entails that social media cannot only be systematized as a communication tool for future preparedness, but that existing information can be used to identify and analyze recovery stories. Digital information then installs resilience in the sense of enhancing a system's "capacity to learn from past incidences"

(Holling, 1973). Through the traceability of digital information, indicators for resilient behavior can unearth resilience patterns within big datasets:

> it can also help when you want to go back and look at what happened during an emergency to see how an organization responded to data as it became available, or simply to look at how information flowed to try to optimize it for the next disaster.
>
> *(ikanow.com: Crisis management)*

Shared data furthermore provide options to identify "socio-economic, ethnic, cultural, religious, partisan, political, tribal and other patterns that help early warning, mitigation, response and recovery" (Stauffacher *et al.*, 2012, p. 5).

Tendencies to utilize digital information for future resilience practices were, for example, suggested in the report following the July 22 attacks in Norway, which recommended that information circulated via social media about efforts to contact potential victims and the experience of support should be used for situational analysis and information gathering about emergencies in the future (NOU, 2012, pp. 454–55). This information about emergencies is, however, not restricted to online sources. Many tabletop emergency exercises produce offline digital data, which also allow for the assessment of resilience patterns (BBK 2011). In sum, the traceability and storability of digital information affords the assessment of resilience practices and the creation of resilience indicators. It enables the analysis of relations between localities, events, and people and the way in which they utilize available information and communication services. By assessing behavioral patterns in past emergencies, new modes of resilience for future emergencies are being devised, which again foster expectations of self-organization towards affected populations and responders: "With an additional click, perhaps off-duty nurses or para-medics who check in at a venue could also broadcast their professional background and willingness to help in the event of a nearby emergency." (Merchant *et al.*, 2011, p. 1).

The various affordances of digital information thus transform resilience programming. Information produced during past emergencies can be reconstructed, analyzed, and translated into new forms of resilience procedures and curricula, which strategically calibrate relations within communities to enable politically desired forms of adaptation (Grove, 2014). Resilience patterns based on association, correlation, averages, and mass behavior arise as one form of reasoning and truth about dealing with emergencies, which informs resilience policies and practices of self-care. As a result, the digitization of resilience contributes to the creation of a specific resilient subject: the digital combines the discretely countable with the accountable. While resilience promotes a subject that is accountable or held responsible for its own wellbeing, the analysis of resilience patterns within digital information tie this status to the logic of calcu-lation, measurability, and mass. Resilience is then not only about individual response—personal and highly context driven—but about dividuated, pattern-based response (Deleuze, 1992) as digital information provides the associative and calculative set-up for reasoning about the resilient subjects' behavior.

Conclusions: resilience, the digital and the growing focus on the crowd

Resilient behavior has become digitally mediated and will be even more so in the future (Fine, 2013). Digital information technologies stimulate new forms of communication and self-organization during emergencies, at the same time as they enable the centralized collection and analysis of data for novel forms of pattern analysis, overview and resilience planning. This promise of the digital, however, requires a careful investigation vis-à-vis the resilience concepts, practices, and knowledge regimes it inspires. Such investigations need to focus on the way in which production, analysis, and exchange of digital information are enabled, but also restrained by a multitude of influence factors, which have been discussed above. More importantly, however, the digitization of resilience implicates two overarching developments that determine the very contents of resilience and resilience programming. The digital fosters the trend towards the crowd as the main performer of resilience activities, a characteristic already inherent in resilience thinking, and it gives rise to the pattern as the epistemological authority for resilience programming.

As a result of the increased circulation of digital information during emergencies, big data analysis has become an important aspect of resilience management. In the context of big data analytics the value of information is created by mass. And to that effect, the crowd has become the main producer of valuable information and the main target of the information market, as every sharing user contributes to the value of information. This trend concurs with an increasing focus on the inclusion of the crowd into resilience activities, whereby emergency management and security is progressively instantiated by the affected population (Joseph, 2013; Kaufmann, 2013). The digital is thus another entryway for the crowd to become an active participant of resilience management. Whether intended or not, both trends reinforce each other, to the extent that digital technologies have already become key tools for crowd-oriented resilience activities. While some digital initiatives for emergency and resilience management grow organically out of the crowd (Kaufmann, 2015), crowdsourcing and crowd-tasking are increasingly intentionally deployed by authorities to involve the citizen in resilience management. Such practices redefine the relationship between authorities and the affected population, not only in terms of the crowd's role within resilience management and the information value it creates, but digital practices furthermore mediate the relationship between resilience managers and the affected. They install remote- and self-management based on methodologies that only those with processing power have access to (Andrejevic and Gates, 2014).

A second element, which influences the relationship between resilience managers and the affected population, is that the resilient population's moves are inherently traceable. Their behavior has—within the given limits—become assessable. Unearthing patterns has become a key activity of digital resilience management, which influences the contents and practices of resilience itself. Resilience programs that suggest how affected populations should organize themselves are increasingly based on the logic of mass and association. The identification of correlations and patterns based on crowd-sourced information, however, not only neglects individual ways of coping, but also foster the already present dynamic of resilience to move away from explanatory models for the treatment of uncertainty and emergency causes towards effective intervention. Patterns and correlations, which emerge from big data analysis, serve as a basis of intervention (Andrejevic and Gates, 2014)—and effective intervention is what resilience governance seeks to install. If both resilience patterns and effectiveness indicators are derived from the same dataset, however, their significance is not only redundant, but is also restrained by the circumstances under which this dataset has been produced.

Vis-à-vis the digitization of resilience, political planners need to take into consideration that digital practices change the perception of emergencies and mediate the relationship between the affected and resilience managers. Future resilience programming needs to reflect on the key features of this shift—particularly the increased focus on the performing, information-sharing crowd, on the value of information created and the emergence of the pattern as epistemological authority, on the tendency to move from causal explanations towards intervention—and the ways in which it influences the contents of resilience management.

Note

1 "Every-ware" describes software that allows for computing in any location, on any device, in any format.

References

Agamben, G. (2005) *State of Exception.* Chicago, IL: University of Chicago Press.

Amoore, L. (2013) *The Politics of Possibility. Risk and Security Beyond Probability.* Durham, NC and London: Duke University Press.

Andrejevic, M. and Gates, K. (2014) Big Data Surveillance: Introduction. *Surveillance and Society,* 12(2), 185–96.

BBK (2011) *Leitfaden für Strategische Krisenmanagement-Übungen.* Bonn: Bevölkerungsschutz.

Birkmann, J. (2006) *Measuring Vulnerability to Natural Hazards: Toward Disaster Resilient Societies.* Tokyo: United Nations University Press.

Blanchette, J. F. (2011) A Material History of Bits. *Journal of the American Society for Information Science and Technology,* 62(6), 1042–57.

Boyd, D. and Crawford, K. (2012) Critical Questions for Big Data. Provocations for a cultural, technological, and scholarly phenomenon. *Information, Communication and Society,* 15(5), 662–79.

Buchanan, E. and Ess, C. (2008) Internet Research Ethics: The Field and Its Critical Issues. In Himma, E. and Tavani, H. (eds.) *The Handbook of Information and Computer Ethics.* Sussex: Wiley.

Collinson, S., Duffield, M., Berger, C., Felix da Costa, D., and Sandstrum, K. (2013) *Paradoxes of Presence. Risk Management and Aid Culture in Challenging Environments.* London: Humanitarian Policy Group.

Committee on Planning for Catastrophe (National Research Council) (2007) *Successful Response Starts with a Map: Improving Geospatial Support for Disaster Management.* Washington, DC: The National Academies Press.

Crawford, K., Faleiros, G., Luers, A., Meier, P., Perlich, C., and Thorp, J. (2013) Big Data, Communities and Ethical Resilience: A Framework for Action. White Paper for PopTech and RockefellerFoundation. Available at: www.rockefellerfoundation.org/report/big-data-communities-and-ethical-resilience-a-framework-for-action/ (accessed 18 July 2016).

Crowe, A. (2011) The Social Media Manifesto: A Comprehensive Review of the Impact of Social Media on Emergency Management. *Journal of Business Continuity and Emergency Planning,* 5(1), 409–20.

Deleuze, G. (1992) Postscript on the Societies of Control. *October,* 59, 3–7.

Derosières, A. (2014) *Prouver et Gouverner. Une Analyse Politique des Statistiques Publiques.* Paris: La Découverte.

Duffield, M. (2011) Environmental Terror: Uncertainty, Resilience and the Bunker. School of Sociology, Politics and International Studies. University of Bristol. Working Paper No. 06–11. Available at: www. bristol.ac.uk/spais/research/workingpapers/wpspaisfiles/duffield-0611.pdf (accessed 18 July 2016).

Emergency Journalism (2012) Wildfires: Digital Age Tools for the Reporter. Available at: http://emergencyjournalism.net/wildfires-digital-age-tools-for-the-reporter/ (accessed July 29, 2014).

European Commission (2014) Disaster Resilience: Safeguarding and Securing Society, Including Adapting to Climate Change. Topic: Communication Technologies and interoperability Topic 2: Next Generation Emergency Services. DRS-19–2014. Available at: https://ec.europa.eu/research/participants/data/ref/h2020/wp/2014_2015/main/h2020-wp1415-security_en.pdf (accessed 18 July 2016).

FEMA (2011) Universal Access to and Use of Information. Strategic Foresight Initiative. Available at: www.fema.gov/pdf/about/programs/oppa/universal_access_paper_051011.pdf (accessed 18 July 2016).

Fine, M. (2013) How Social Media is Changing Disaster Response. *Scientific American.* Available at: www. scientificamerican.com/article/how-social-media-is-changing-disaster-response/ (accessed 18 July 2016).

Galloway, A. R. (2012) *The Interface Effect.* Cambridge, MA: Polity Press.

Gao, H., Barbier, G., and Goolsby, R. (2011) Harnessing the Crowdsourcing Power of Social Media for Disaster Relief. *Cyber-Physical-Social Systems,* 26,10–14.

Gibson, J. (1986) *The Ecological Approach to Visual Perception.* New York: Taylor and Francis.

Gilbert-Knight, A. (2013) Social Media, Crisis Mapping and the New Frontier in Disaster Response. *The Guardian.* Available at: www.theguardian.com/global-development-professionals-network/2013/oct/08/social-media-microtasking-disaster-response (accessed 18 July 2016).

Graham, M. (2011) Time Machines and Virtual Portals: The Spatialities of the Digital Divide. *Progress in Development Studies,* 11(3), 211–27.

Grove, K. (2014) Agency, Affect, and the Immunological Politics of Disaster Resilience. *Environment and Planning D*, 32, 240–56.

Hildebrandt, M. (2012) The Meaning and the Mining of Legal Texts. In Berry, D. (ed.), *Understanding Digitial Humanities*. Basingstoke: Palgrave Macmillan.

Holling, C. S. (1973) Resilience and Stability of Ecological Systems. *Annual Review of Ecology and Systematics*, 4, 1–23.

IFRC (International Federation of Red Cross and Red Crescent Societies) (2013) World Disasters Report. Focus on Technology and the Future of Humanitarian Action. Available at: http://worlddisastersreport. org/en/ (accessed 18 July 2016).

Joseph, J. (2013) Resilience as Embedded in Neoliberalism: A Governmentality Approach. *Resilience*, 1(1), 38–52.

Kaufmann, M. (2013) Emergent Self-organisation in Emergencies: Resilience Rationales in Interconnected Societies. *Resilience: International Policies, Practices and Discourses*, 1(1), 53–68.

Kaufmann, M. (2015) Resilience 2.0: Social Media Use and (Self-)care during the 2011 Norway Attacks. *Media, Culture and Society*, 37(7), 972–87.

Keim, M. E. and Noji, E. (2011) Emergent Use of Social Media: A New Age of Opportunity for Disaster Resilience. *American Journal of Disaster Medicine*, 6(1), 47–54.

Latour, B. (2005) *Reassembling the Social. An introduction to Actor-Network-Theory*. New York: Oxford University Press.

Leonardi, P. (2010) Digital materiality? How Artifacts without Matter, Matter. *First Monday*, 15(6–7).

Lewin, K. (1969) *Grundzüge der topologischen Psychologie*. Posthume deutsche Ausgabe, hrsg. von R. Falk & F. Winnefeld. Bern: Huber.

Lindsay, B. R. (2011) *Social Media and Disasters: Current Uses, Future Options, and Policy Considerations*. CRS Report for Congress. R 41987.

Manovich, L. (2002a) *The Language of New Media*. Cambridge, MA: The MIT Press.

Manovich, L. (2002b) Data Visualisation as New Abstraction and Anti-Sublime. Available at: www. zannahbot.com/data_art/DataVisAsNewAbstraction.pdf (accessed May 29, 2014).

Martin, J. (1965) *Programming Real-time Computer Systems*. Englewood Cliffs, NJ: Prentice-Hall Inc.

Meier, P. (2011) Verifying Crowdsourced Social Media Reports for Live Crisis Mapping: An Introduction to Information Forensics. Available at: http://irevolution.files.wordpress.com/2011/11/meier-verifying-crowdsourced-data-case-studies.pdf (accessed 18 July 2016).

Meier, P. (2012a) Truthiness and Probability: Moving Beyond the True or False Dichotomy when Verifying Social Media. Available at: http://irevolution.net/2012/03/10/truthiness-as-probability/ (accessed 18 July 2016).

Meier, P. (2012b) Rapidly Verifying the Credibility of Information Sources on Twitter. Available at: http://irevolution.net/2012/11/20/verifying-source-credibility/ (accessed 18 July 2016).

Meier, P. (2013) Disaster Resilience 2.0. Available at: http://irevolution.net/2013/01/11/disaster-resilience-2-0/ (accessed 18 July 2016).

Mendoza, M., Poblete, B., and Castillo, C. (2010) Twitter Under Crisis: Can We Trust What We RT? 1–9. Available at: http://snap.stanford.edu/soma2010/papers/soma2010_11.pdf (accessed 18 July 2016).

Merchant, R. M., Elmer, S., and Lurie, N. (2011) Integrating Social Media into Emergency-preparedness Efforts. *The New England Journal of Medicine*, 365, 289–91.

NOU (Norges offentlige utredniner) (2012) Rapport fra 22. Juli-kommisjonen. 2012: 14. Departementes servicesenter Informasjonsforvaltning, Oslo 2012.

Paul, G. (2009) *Foundations of Digital Evidence*. Washington, DC: American Bar Association.

Rushe, D. (2013) Facebook Reveals Governments Asked for Data on 38,000 Users in 2013. *The Guardian*. Available at: www.theguardian.com/technology/2013/aug/27/facebook-government-user-requests (accessed 18 July 2016).

Sandvik, K. B. (2013) Drone Pilots, Humanitarians and the Videogame Analogy: Unpacking the Conversation, *UAV – bare ny teknologi eller en ny strategisk virkelighet? Luftkrigskolens skriftserie* volume 29, 29. Trondheim: Luftkrigsskolen.

Schmitt, C. (1921) *Die Diktatur*. Leipzig and München: Duncker & Humblot.

Stauffacher, D., Hattotuwa, S., and Weekes, B. (2012) *The Potential and Challenges of Open Data for Crisis Information Management and Aid Efficiency: A Preliminary Assessment*. ICT4Peace foundation, March 2012.

Taylor, M., Wells, G., Howell, G., and Raphael, B. (2012) The Role of Social Media as Psychological First Aid as a Support to Community Resilience Building. *Australian Journal of Emergency Management*, 27(1), 20–6.

The Economist (2012) Six Degrees of Mobilization. September 1, 2012. Available at: www.economist.com/node/21560977 (accessed 18 July 2016).

Turner, A.J. (2006) *Introduction to Neogeography*. Sebastopol, CA: O'Reilly Media.

Yates, D. and Paquette, S. (2011) Emergency Knowledge Management and Social Media Technologies: A Case Study of the 2010 Haitian Earthquake. *International Journal of Information Management*, 31(1), 6–13.

Websites

http://internet-response-league.com/ (accessed 18 July 2016).

www.ikanow.com/crisis-management/ (accessed 28 January 2014).

www.ikanow.com/five-tools-your-disaster-recovery-software-needs-to-have-when-using-social-media/ (accessed 28 January 2014).

10

RESILIENCE AND THE INVERSION OF POSSIBILITY AND REALITY

Jessica Schmidt

The truth is that we change without ceasing, and that the state itself is nothing but change. This amounts to saying that there is no essential difference between passing from one state to another and persisting in the same state.

(Henri Bergson, 1944; OECD 2013)

Introduction

It is by now widely acknowledged that resilience, the capacity of absorbing or adapting to change and disturbances, has forcefully arisen to provide the semantics of a 'pervasive idiom of global governance' (Walker and Cooper 2011, p. 144). Since resilience has established itself as a field of research for the social sciences in general but also for international relations (IR) in particular, the respective literature has taken an interesting trajectory. Initially, resilience seemed to pose few questions. Critical scholars, often concerned with the transfigurations of security, agreed upon its neoliberal nature. From this perspective, resilience seemed neither particularly new nor particularly surprising. The interpellations of resilient subjects and societies 'debased' the political subject which no longer could claim any right to security by way of naturalizing uncertainty and risk (Reid 2012). Resilience undermined the liberal artifice and reduced individuals to neoliberal, responsibilized subjects by leaving them exposed to their bare existence (Lentzos and Rose 2009; Joseph 2013; Evans and Reid 2013; Welsh 2014). It was even argued that resilience was a veiled form of Social Darwinism (Walker and Cooper 2011). The rise of resilience hence did not seem to require more differentiated reflections into whether we were observing something that we did not know (Neocleous 2013; see Chandler 2013). The answers were obvious and the issue seemed settled before the questions even arose.

While familiar features and neoliberal traits in resilience discourses can of course not be denied, increasingly skepticism has been voiced as to whether these findings really engaged the world of resilience on its own terms (Schmidt 2014). Lately, therefore, a second generation of scholars concerned with resilience has been emerging. What their contributions speak of is the discovery that digging into resilience uncovers more questions to be explored than answers provided. In effect, most recent studies, implicitly or explicitly, acknowledge an ongoing revolution (turn-around) in thought, agency, and governance that is unfolding in discourses and practices of resilience. In this context, it is argued that, for instance, the appearance of 'resilient populations' is not the grounds for changes in security governance but rather the 'effect of a broader restructuring of rationalities and practices comprising liberal governance' (Zebrowski 2013, p. 161). From this perspective, the biopolitical project of resilience was enabled by far-reaching transformations in the understanding of nature. Nature in resilience terms is no longer understood as a system in a single, optimal equilibrium but rather an inherently dynamic system with nested multiple equilibria (Zebrowski 2013).

While these approaches stay within the paradigm of liberalism when investigating and evaluating resilience discourses, another line of interrogating resilience has been extrapolated through discourses of hope (Wrangel 2014) and promise (Aradau 2014). What is interesting about these is that they challenge the treatment of resilience in terms of a dystopic discourse and instead investigate and evaluate the possibilities resilience is able to afford. That is, they are interested in what becomes epistemologically and politically possible through resilience thinking. Wrangel's argument, for instance, revolves around the observation that 'bare life', a central concept in Agamben's critique of liberalism, no longer constitutes the exclusion that enables liberal, qualified life. Instead, as the reference point of governance, hope is transferred to bare life, formerly known to 'afford no hope' (Agamben, cited in Wrangel 2014, p. 186). It is argued that bare life as the new embodiment of hope, where there was none before, becomes possible through eclipsing the present by way of constantly referring life to the future and its indeterminacy. This finding introduces an intriguing temporal element into the analysis of resilience governance: resilience governance thus inculcates 'a futural life, a present life that continuously experiences the future as promise' (Wrangel 2014, p. 193). As a result, an actually catastrophic state of being (bare life) and the hope induced by the indeterminacy of the future paradoxically collapse into each other.

A similar observation motivates Aradau's recent contribution in which she looks at the elements of surprise and novelty in resilience discourses and contrasts these with the notion of promise as a way of taming future's contingency and indeterminacy. Her finding, however, differs from the idea of a continuous promise of the future that sustains bare life as hope. Instead she argues that there is no promise possible in resilience thinking. If promise is a way of taming contingency and appropriating the future then resilience, with its emphasis on embracing a world full of surprises and novelty, ontologically eclipses the possibility of promise.

To these contributions the chapter develops in a tangential manner. That is, it does not disagree with Wrangel's and Aradau's findings but merely seeks to add something to our understanding of resilience. It concurs with Aradau's finding that resilience thinking discards the other-directed promise of a *particular* future as a way of taming contingency. Likewise, it takes into consideration Wrangel's argument that resilience is driven by an ingrained futural connotation that functions as a general substitute for the particularity of the promise (a particularity that links a graspable present to a graspable future). Yet, it seems to me that resilience thinking cannot adequately be captured and critiqued by using binary concepts, such as promise/contingency or bare life/qualified life. This inadequacy consists in always being able to also argue the opposite when critically engaging with resilience, as demonstrated in the above debate on promise, where resilience is both the absolute promise in terms of futural life or none at all or on the question of its neoliberal character, where resilience both affirms responsibilized and individualized subjects while at the same time embedding them in ever more networks that affect them.

In this chapter, therefore, I would like to suggest that resilience thinking – and consequently governance – does something more radical than to constantly inculcate future life at the expense of the present. Instead, resilience is based on the continuous creation of new realities in a temporally holistic but spatially partial sense. That is to say, it might be small, not global, realities that change at a given moment but the change is radical in the sense that it no longer links to past and future.

Any change, moreover, while it might be partial, takes place in what is understood to be an interconnected world, so that it will produce equally radical changes elsewhere. In incubating the interplay between surprise, which figures as a form of discontinuous continuity in resilience discourses, and the processes of adaptation, which are unknowable but expectable, the idea of resilience effectively describes the continuous coming-into-being of novel worlds. Such new worlds holistically become their own past possibility and indicate newly reconfigured indeterminacies in the moment of their realization.

This constant change of ontologies comes at the expense of the future rather than referring to the future. The future, in resilience thinking, is only the non-linear shift between worlds. It is a void, while nevertheless part of a holistic process of change, transformation, and adaption. Crucial here is that resilience discourses not only work with novelty and disturbances but also with the idea of a connected, networked world. As resilience is fundamentally de-centred and the instantiation of novel worlds never spatially total but never spatially separate any such reality is rendered unstable. World-creation is thus sustained as a continuous, dynamic and self-causing process. The paradigm of resilience, therefore, has no place for the promise, rather than rendering the promise impossible, nor does it simply refer to the future because there is no conventional contingency of an indeterminate future that is connected to the present. It makes little sense to reason with such notions as promise and future, which are based on some idea of the singularity, linearity and permanence of reality. Resilience, it seems, breaks with this linear course of time.

In order to demonstrate where this perspective on resilience originates, I will first draw on some of the insights in ecology and highlight some of the connections to complexity thinking in the natural sciences. In the second section, I will point to some relevant aspects in the work of vitalist philosopher Henri Bergson. It is in particular his thoughts on the inversion of reality and possibility that are of interest for an understanding of resilience as a constant process of world-creation without future. In the third section, some of the consequences for human being and action will be insinuated by drawing on the work of Hannah Arendt on the interplay between natality and orientation.

Ecology and physics: resilience as process and rupture

Ecology: transformative-adaptive processes as the essence of existence

When it initially appeared, the notion of resilience gained purchase as an area of research foremost in ecology (Holling 1973), alongside with psychology (Garmezy 1973, cited in Garcia-Dia *et al.* 2013). A central enabling condition for perceiving and thinking about such a phenomenon as resilience – the capacity to cope and adapt to changes and unforeseen events – is a systemic perspective and within this systemic perspective a primacy of relations. That is, in order to think resilience it is necessary to understand reality in terms of (interconnected) systems in which relations rather than entities matter. The idea of resilient systems, moreover, hinges upon the discovery of multiple equilibria. Whereas, before, systems had been understood to contain one optimal equilibrium, now they were understood to be able to exist in various different equilibria.

A relational systemic perspective is thus categorically different from an individualistic one. Whereas the latter conceives of entities, the former conceives of interactions. In stressing interactions, simply putting individual entities in relation to each other can never lead to the same insights as looking at the world in terms of flexible systems that can materialize in various – and ever changing – states. That is, resilience, as a phenomenon, emerges only from a global perspective at which a sufficient level of complexity allows for interactions to unfold. Resilience would be undetectable from a reductive view in which some elements and factors are hierarchically singled out, made to interact under sterile conditions and looked at individually (Gunderson and Allen 2010; Allen and Holling 2010). It is conditioned by a framing that allows for the analytical experience of multiple interactions between parts of a system as well as between multiple systems and their parts (system and environment), while the parts never take primacy over their essential imbrication in relations. As an adaptive capacity, being resilient essentially means to be in an irreducible, non-static and, in a sense, also non-defining relation to (other) environmental factors.

With this primacy of systemic interactions we see something of a mission creep in resilience as a field of research: wherever its boundaries are initially set for analytically detecting resilience, resilience thinking continuously demands of these boundaries to be taken down as untenable arbitrations. The fundamental paradox that sits at the basis of resilience systems is that, in fact, such systems with their primacy of relations and interactions neither have an outside nor a centre. It is therefore difficult, if not impossible, to speak of systems in the plural for which they would have to be bounded and definable. Rather, while resilience as a phenomenon might be accorded to whatever one looks at and wherever one finds oneself at a given moment, as a concept it almost necessarily must go global.

This mission creep is very noticeable in the understanding of resilience in ecological research. In the beginning, resilience referred to a system's 'ability to absorb change and disturbances and still maintain the same relationships' (Holling 1973, p. 14). This initial understanding is still characterized by compartmentalized thinking in which systems were considered in terms of entities and parts, fixed boundaries and identities. Systems, such as nature or society with its individuals, existed a priori and independently from the change or disturbance. Changes were carried to such systems externally and absorption or adaptation did not impact upon the identity of the system. Such compartmentalized thinking, however, was untenable from the start as it contradicted the idea of multiple equilibria and hence soon began to pose problems. If multiple equilibria are the norm, the forces and linkages inducing new equilibria gain priority over fixed identities and interdependence becomes pervasive. Modifications in the understanding of resilience therefore became necessary because initial definitions start to be considered reductive and unrealistic. From within ecology it was criticized that a reductive focus on ecological systems captured 'only part of reality' and therefore did not put adequate emphasis on those interlinked forces and effects. Rather than being considered an analytical requirement, it was now 'irrational to continue to separate the ecological and social and try to explain them independently, even for analytical purposes' (Folke *et al.* 2010, p. [2]).[1]

Once it became impossible to artificially delimit systems from a resilient perspective, the definition of resilience and its core element, that of adaptation, experienced a crucial revision. No longer singling out individual systems and thus including a human dimension, adaptability no longer meant the passive absorption of shocks. As a capacity, it was extended to include an active element of experiencing and learning. Adaptation as the capacity of socio-ecological systems therefore meant to 'learn, combine, experience and knowledge, adjust the responses to external drivers and internal processes' (Folke *et al.* 2010, p. [2]). With this active element accorded to adaptation, adaption has come to refer to a quality that was in fact excluded from Holling's initial definition: adaptation became transformability. Transformability describes the capacity of self-difference, to become something or someone different and to enter into a new state of being, initiated through changes and disturbances. It is this idea of adaptation as transformability that introduces novelty. Whereas before, resilience meant the maintenance of identity in the face of external disturbances, it now referred to the idea of identity transformation. What is more, it is considered unpredictable; what this adaptive transformation will look like cannot be pre-determined due to the complexity of factors. Radical novelty therefore means that the outcome cannot be statistically derived from existing conditions. While adaptive transformation is thus incalculable, it is – or it will have been – possible.

This mission creep of resilience in a system with no outside or centre and the expansion of its meaning, first to include an active component in the meaning of adaption and then to equate adaption with transformation, has had a major impact on the understanding of life (as well as matter). While, initially, bounded systems were imaginable as undisturbed, the focus on inter-actions and the resulting dynamism of open-boundary systems rendered such thinking unviable. With the continuous deferral of systemic boundaries to also include social (and other) systems and the general idea to look at all beings and phenomena in terms of interactive systems, such undisturbed existence can no longer be conceived. Entities, beings and systems do not enter into relationships but are already essentially imbricated in them so that change is inherently produced. Change *is* the rationale of the resilient system.

This has a crucial consequence for the quality of resilience in relation to existence. Leading resilience scholar Carl Folke and colleagues declare that resilience 'may at first glance seem counterintuitive as it embraces change as a requisite to persist' (Folke *et al.* 2010, p. [1]). The reason why it seems counterintuitive to associate change with existence is precisely that existence had previously been associated with (a priori) being. This understanding still underpins Holling's initial definition of resilience as a quality that systems and entities did or did not have (and it was better if they were resilient). Embracing change as a requisite to persist describes a radically different understanding of existence and resilience. No longer is it a quality that was good to have, but it is the essence of existence as such. Being resilient – being in a constant process of adaptive becoming – becomes a vital necessity, the promise of persistence and the manifestation of existence as such.

Physics: uncertainty and non-linearity as the new laws of nature

Whereas contingency and novelty (and hence uncertainty) were known to biology, and in extension to ecology, since Darwin's theory of evolution, physics – the knowledge of matter – remained a hard science for longer. While biology, as well as ecology, 'has come to seem a science of the accidental', physics, 'cold in its calculus, implied a deep order, an inevitability' (Kauffman 1995, p. 7). This ontological inevitability, however, is being revoked in the physics of non-equilibrium processes (Prigogine 1997).

In non-equilibrium physics and complexity science, a decisive shift has taken place: epis-temological complexity, in which uncertainty was a computational problem, has turned into ontological complexity, in which uncertainty has become, so to speak, a new law of nature. Classical science was based upon the reversibility of all physical processes. Reversibility meant that science was determined by laws: physical laws of classical science equalled certainty, necessity and predictability. In classical science, however, there always existed the dilemma between the 'intelligibility of nature' and the 'assumption of human freedom [and] creativity' (Prigogine 1997, p. 17) that had been displaced rather than solved through the epistemological separation of science and philosophy (Arendt 1998). To maintain the lawfulness of nature and the freedom of the human, a natural sphere of necessity had to be separated and an artificial realm of human freedom superimposed (Dewey 1929) which consolidated the idea of an 'anthropic exception' (Connolly 2011, p. 21; Harman 2009).

Catalytic for the emergence of non-equilibrium physics was the physics of population and dissipative structures, which was enabled by advances made on the molecular level (Prigogine 1997, p. 35). At the molecular level, dynamic systems far from equilibrium were discovered. On the level of complex microstructures, instability carries information that cannot be found at the level of individual particles independent from initial conditions (Prigogine 1997, p. 38). This information cannot be reduced to or derived from the sum of individual trajectories. And crucially, what this discovery introduces to physics, which thus far was comprised of laws, linearity and reversibility, is the event (Prigogine 1997, p. 5).

The phenomenon of the event poses intricate problems in Western philosophy as well as epistemology, precisely because it suspends the passage of time, interferes with the linearity of being or becoming and challenges causation. Events are unique phenomena; they are an interruption into normalcy and the expected course of things; they are not willed or intended (they can only be managed, as in 'event management') because events can never be the product of individual or even collective agency. Unexpected and unforeseeable as they are, events bring something new and irreversible to the world. In this sense, events are extra-ordinary as well as untimely (Davidson 2001, pp. 163–80). Events thus are non-being and non-time (Badiou 2005). They constitute a jump or void in the passage of time and the continuity of being. As such, they exceed our representative capacities.

The discovery of ontological uncertainty in non-equilibrium physics tells us that events are real rather than just computational problems. In this sense, there will be jumps that can neither be reversed nor indicate a future trajectory (because there will be events). Ontological uncertainty means that there are voids that will suspend the continuity of being and the course of time. And these moments will have been transformative. That is, there will be moments in which an ontological shift, characterized by novelty and non-representability, realizes itself. As Prigogine concludes, we now 'begin to perceive the origin and variety in nature we observe around us. Matter acquires new properties when far from equilibrium in that fluctuations and instabilities are now the norm. Matter becomes more "active"' (Prigogine 1997, p. 65).

In other words, ecology provided the process-character of change, whereas physics provided the element of void. In ecology, there is nothing external but also nothing central to transformative change and in physics change is the radical break. Resilience thinking encompasses both aspects of continuous change, that of process and that of rupture, and combines it into a whole that breaks with conventional understandings of time and existence.

Bergson: inversion of reality and possibility

Resilience as instantiations of worlds

The precondition for life and for matter to manifest itself is the event and its provocation into a changed state of being. The event, however, is not external to this, since resilience knows no outside. Instead, the disruptive event is already essential to the dynamic of resilience. Resilience – the condition of sustained existence – could not be without radical disturbance; it has become internal to the whole of life and matter. In this, resilience thinking captures both the novelty event as well as the adaptive-transformational process. Here, it is Bergson's concept of duration that is helpful because it opens up a perspective on resilience not limited to a temporal dimension (constant deferral into the future) but rather as ontic (constant instantiations of worlds).

Duration, for Bergson, is indeed a form of time but one that is holistic. He explains this with reference to the movement of a hand from A to B. This movement appears in terms of two orders. Usually such a moment is scientifically described in terms of (an infinite number of) positions at certain moments and the line is treated as their compilation. The movement itself, however, is never captured by this approach. '[B]oth mechanism and finalism would leave on one side the movement, which is reality itself.' In this sense of being reality itself 'the movement is *more* than the positions and more than their order' because the compilation of an infinite number of dots never touches upon the reality of the movement. At the same time,

> the movement is *less* than the series of positions and their connecting order, for to arrange points in a certain order, it is necessary first to conceive the order and then to realize it with points, there must be the world of assemblage and there must be intelligence.
>
> *(Bergson 2002a, p. 198)*

The movement of the arm is less than its dissection because in itself it does not form part of the conception of order, meaning or anticipation; it simply makes itself real in the moment of its execution. There can be no position of externality, that is, no description of the whole of the movement, only its enactment. Reality is therefore simultaneously more and less than any representation of it. The movement is more than infinite dots put next to each other because it is real: it is a total, singular whole without parts. This is what Bergson calls duration. The movement is less for the same reason: the dots need to be added to it since, in reality, they do not exist as part of the movement. Only the raw movement without conception and meaning makes itself real.

The fact that partitioning of the whole and the whole never meet has major consequences for understanding cause and effect and, by the same token, for possibility and reality. Further, following Bergson's reasoning, neither the entirety of positions can effect the movement nor can the movement effect the entirety of positions. 'In reality, the cause . . . cannot produce its effects except in one piece, and completely finished' (Bergson 2002a, p. 201). Resilient being – that is, adaptive transformation as sign and requisite for sustained, relational existence – is a form of indivisible duration that is simultaneously more and less than its description. Transformation will always have occurred but it will never last. Paradoxically, resilient being, as the essence of persistence, only is once and as long as it is activated but it can only be activated in the moment of the event. Resilience is radically performative. And similarly to Bergson's vitalist thinking, the movement of adaptive-transformation and change cannot be the linear effect of individual causes; it only comes into momentary being 'in one piece, and completely finished' while the process itself has no end.

Forcing linearity from cause to effect is certainly not a new problem, but Bergson argues it is one of the 'bad' philosophical problems because it should never have arisen. That it has is due to the 'idea that the possible is less than the real, and that, for this reason, the possibility of things precedes their existence' (Bergson 2002b, p. 228). Against this causal succession from possibility to existence, which renders reality but the realization of a programme, Bergson stresses that it is the real as an indivisible whole that 'makes itself possible, and the possible which becomes real' (Bergson 2002b, p. 232). By instantiating itself as reality, possibility works through a temporal loop. Possibility is that which will have been possible in the event in which it becomes a reality. As Bergson explains:

> As reality is created as something unforeseeable and new, its image is reflected behind it into the indefinite past; thus it finds it has from all time been possible, but it is this precise moment that it begins to have been always possible and that is why I said that its possibility, which does not precede its reality, will have preceded it once the reality has appeared.
>
> *(Bergson 2002b, p. 229)*

The encompassing inversion of reality and possibility[2] therefore makes the past. It is not the case that the presence works backwards but that the past is always merely a contingent causal arrangement of order that only comes into being, and thereby becomes possible, in this particular way through the present moment.[3] In this sense, the present is an event. It works like the turning of a kaleidoscope in which indeterminacy moves into place thereby forming the particular order with this particular causal path (from past into presence) that has been made possible in the very moment that it turned. Only in this moment it also has become a possibility.

In other words, modern trajectories of time, causation and becoming, which are held to be misguided, are being replaced by the constant instantiation of novel worlds. Reality is made up of events to which all that exists adapts and transforms in the moment of its realization. It is for this reason, it seems, that policy guidelines on resilience see the major problem as 'silo' thinking and programming (OECD 2013, p. I; World Bank 2013, p. x). As for instance an OECD report (2013, p. i) emphasizes:

> The risk landscape that people, institutions and infrastructure have to face is complex, and thus working in risk silos no longer makes sense. Separating the risks that people face in their daily lives into neat boxes is a bit like stuffing jellyfish into pigeonholes – it just can't be done neatly, and doesn't make sense. The risks people face are complex and interlinked. . . . Working to narrow institutional mandates no longer makes sense. . . . [A] layer of society cannot be 'selectively' resilient.

Yet, these realities are never stable. In a resilience paradigm, the parts of the kaleidoscope are not self-standing entities but relations far from equilibrium that continuously affect and destabilize each other. Novelty provokes novelty. There is no linear causal link between them, however, as each becomes a possibility and, as such, a moment in which indeterminacy is ordered in that particular fashion that excludes all other possibilities in the moment of its instantiation; this immediately opens the door for further realizations of new worlds. Event and transformative adaptation are part of a simultaneous, holistic but always unstable process. What this inversion of reality and possibility also means is that thinking in terms of ontological shifts excludes a conception of the future that is in any way linked to the presence. This link will only realize itself in the moment of novelty and then, but only then, it 'will have been'. Being thus becomes the process of performative self-differentiation, and, as such, resilient.

Arendt: natality without orientation

In this third, and last, section I would like to speculate on some possible consequences of ontological change for human existence in the world. The question, in other words, is: what are the conditions for human being in a resilience world if it is made up not of (linear) time but of (wholesale) ontological change? It seems to me that one of the core features to be affected is the role of experience. The reason for this constituting a key point is that experience previously was central for establishing permanence and calculability as well as dependent upon some form of permanence and calculability. As such, it held the promise of purposeful human action.

To ponder upon this point, I will draw on Hannah Arendt's thoughts on the role of experience for human existence. Arendt, of course, was a decidedly humanist thinker, thus the difference between an anthropocentric ontology in which the main divide is that between man and her environment composed of entities and a complex ontology (or ontology of events) in which this divide is replaced by de-centric relationality should become clear.

One of Arendt's central concepts, upon which her idea of purposeful human action in the world, that is, the idea of deliberately changing the conditions we live in hinges, is the linkage between natality and permanence. While the former rests upon newness and spontaneity, the latter grants meaning, expectation and orientation. Importantly, making experiences provides the link between newness and orientation.

Natality, for Arendt (1998, p. 247), describes the miracle of birth and constitutes the 'onto-logical root' for (political) action. Natality is a bifurcated concept. On the one hand, it fruitfully plays with the anthropological or sociological fact that humans never just encounter the world as the unattached, exceptional outsider but rather are always already embedded within it. On the other hand, being brought into a certain environment, according to Arendt, also brings with it the possibility of newness and enables spontaneity. Natality thus describes the possibility of new beginnings within conditions that precede or go beyond us. If everything was and went exactly the way we expect things to be and go, any expectation would become intuitive and habitual to the point of no longer being able to be the subject of experience. In other words, newness or unexpectedness are necessary conditions for becoming aware (Peirce 1998, pp. 194–5). Awareness, in turn, is the precondition for action that seeks to induce purposeful change.

Central to the idea of natality as the condition for inducing purposeful change is strangeness. As Arendt says, we come into a world as strangers (Arendt 1998, p. 9). Being a stranger, however, bears within it a crucial ambivalence. While it is the stranger who, in being thrown into unknown and unexpected conditions, becomes aware and is thus the catalyst for new beginnings, strangers or newcomers also are dependent on others who introduce them and who bear respective responsibility (Arendt 2006, pp. 170–93). There is, in other words, a mutual dependency between the native's need for new perspectives, in order to achieve the capacity and the freedom to change things, and the stranger's need for orientation.

What this means is that in order for natality to be the force of purposeful change, the second element of a level of predictability is necessary. Being able to estimate what we can expect is based on meaningful experiences we make in the course of our lives and in concerted actions with others. Although Arendt does not literally mention expectation, we can infer as much from her elaborations on the promise. Not wishing to advocate any form of determinism, Arendt grants, as would complexity thinkers, that the world we inhabit is complex and the outcome of our actions not foreseeable. If radical unpredictability was indeed the condition of human being, our existence would be nothing more than participation in meaningless accidents. As she puts it poetically:

> Without being talked about by men and without housing them, the world would not be a human artifice but a heap of unrelated things to which each isolated individual was at liberty to add one more object; without the human artifice to house them, human affairs would be as floating, as futile and vain, as the wanderings of nomad tribes.
>
> *(Arendt 1998, p. 204)*

Hence, in difference to complexity thinking with its emphasis on relationality – to alleviate this condition of unpredictability under which our existence would be nothing more than accidental and ultimately inconsequential floating – Arendt introduces the idea of promise. The idea of promise directly links up with experience, expectation and will, as well as with orientation and permanence. The utterance of a promise is only meaningful if what is promised generally lies within the realm of possibility (if I promise someone that tomorrow I will become a flying unicorn this promise is obviously in vain). A promise generates expectations for both the one to whom something is promised as well as for the one who promises. What lies within the realm, feasibly, of what I can meaningfully promise rests upon experience both with regard to myself as well as others and the world. Mutual or shared expectations, in turn, provide for permanence and reliability – and the more permanence there is, the better the chances of making meaningful promises.

Yet, since there is no absolute reliability and neither is the future foreseeable, the promise also hinges upon the will to make things happen (or prevent things from happening). It is this wilful alleviation from accidental existence that enables orientation to the world. But, to re-emphasize, the promise only makes sense under conditions in which experiences can be made that are drawn and collected from the past and guide further actions. Experiences must hold beyond the moment in order to allow for the promise to have significance.

Obviously, Arendt's project is indeed one of deliberately singling out humans as exceptional. Exploring this exceptionality is what drives her thinking and work. In this endeavour, she was explicit about the exceptional human capacity to relate things in the world. In this capacity to relate things she found what makes humans humans (rather than animals) and argued this power was the condition for giving meaning in an otherwise accidental world (Arendt 1998, p. 9). By way of relating things, humans were capable of introducing islands of stability and permanence.

The permanence of ontological change in a resilience world is based on exactly the opposite. Complexity, with its ontology of events, hinges upon the idea that things relate among themselves, even come into being only through such interrelation (Harman 2009). The resulting complexity of a world in constant flux challenges, if not deprives, humans of any superior role. Like any being they become resilient being: essentially imbricated with others while adapting to, and transforming through, change under conditions of uncertainty.

If we take Arendt's points on the interplay between natality and permanence, what resilient being then becomes is the eternal stranger. Again, there are indicators in international policy-making on resilience that seem to accept and incorporate this permanent condition of estrangement from both oneself as well as the world one is imbricated in. It is very noticeable that policy reports by international organizations seeking to promote resilience in development contexts are first and foremost concerned with the donors themselves. Instead of wishing to change recipient societies, suggestions for resilience programming almost exclusively refer to the self-transformation of donor organizations themselves (see, for instance, World Bank 2013, p. ix; OECD 2013, p. ii). What is more, the condition of being an eternal stranger in unknown, unpredictable worlds can even be said to be a policy goal to be promoted. At first sight, it seems peculiar that programming guidelines should focus on 'measuring resilience' and consequently develop unrealistically long lists of indicators (a good example is the 2013 OECD report on *Risk and Resilience*). However, looked at from a slightly different angle, advising to simply measure everything and pay attention to every detail will necessarily lead to confusion and disorientation. At the same time, change, surprise and novelty will be guaranteed if only enough things will be allowed to relate and interact and hence the permanent process of estrangement and self-differentiation is set in motion.

Resilient being is in an exceptional position with regard to novelty and spontaneity. It is a constant newcomer to ever-changing worlds. While natality is thus accentuated, the second element of permanence and orientation is eclipsed. What this means is that meaningful experiences cannot be made. If what one has experienced before no longer has validity for the current world, nothing really guides actions and decisions. What resilient being, forever estranged, is therefore left with is mere perception. All newness and unexpectedness vanishes into mere accidents. Arendt (1998, p. 204) seemed to have foreseen this imbalance and its consequences:

> The melancholy wisdom of *Ecclesiastes*—'Vanity of vanities; all is vanity. . . . There is no new thing under the sun . . . there is no remembrance of former things; neither shall there be any remembrance of things that are to come with those that shall come after'—does not necessarily arise from specifically religious experience; but it is certainly unavoidable wherever and whenever trust in the world as a place fit for human

appearance, for action and speech, is gone. Without action to bring into the play of the world the new beginning of which each man is capable by virtue of being born, 'there is no new thing under the sun'; without speech to materialize and memorialize, however tentatively, the 'new things' that appear and shine forth, 'there is no remembrance'; without the enduring permanence of a human artifact, there cannot 'be any remembrance of things that are to come with those that shall come after'.

Conclusion

This chapter did not intend to develop an entirely new perspective on resilience but rather tried to complicate existing accounts. In particular, it sought to further contribute to findings that emphasized the elimination of promise in resilience thinking and the transvaluation of bare life through resilience's futural orientation.

By looking at the trajectory of the understanding of resilience as well as the rise of complexity thinking, the chapter showed how adaptive transformation and learning turned into the essence and expression of life as such. This development within the notion of resilience was accompanied by a turn towards complexity in the natural sciences. Complexity thinking focuses on radical unpredictability and irreversibility and thus speaks of an ontology of events.

In referring to some of the work by vitalist philosopher Henri Bergson, the chapter argued that such an ontology of events replaced the linearity of time and cause. In a linear understanding of time and cause, time spans from past to future and the future is essentially a causal-temporal projection of its past. Instead, an ontology of events – in which it is not humans that relate things but everything that relates to all others in unpredictable ways – brings forth wholesale ontological changes. New realities come into being by becoming their own possibility in the moment of their realization, and these new realities are complete with their own temporal dimensions that are not causally connected to what was before or comes after.

In the last section, the chapter drew on Hannah Arendt's notion of natality in order to evaluate some of the consequences of ontological change for human being. Natality refers to the phenomenon of birth and, for Arendt, means the possibility of new beginnings in the otherwise circular processes of life. The section, however, highlighted that it was not the concept of natality alone that Arendt accorded with the possibility of purposeful human action, but rather its combination and dependence on the permanence of the world. Without such permanence, meaningful experiences cannot be made and resilient being becomes the eternal stranger as novelty eclipses permanence.

To the argument that it was liberalism's bare life that became resilience's highest good, through its constant deferral into the future, the chapter therefore offered an alternative reading through focusing on ontological change. The point here is that ontological change or an ontology of events does not work along a linear passing of time. While the chapter agrees with the argument that the promise is being eclipsed in resilience thinking, it argued that this problem is part of a wider, more comprehensive, development. It pointed out that the promise must, together with experience, be seen through the mutual dependence between novelty and permanence. Perhaps this is also why the rise of resilience evades easy critique. Novelty, spontaneity and adaptation per se are not necessarily problematic and they have been thought of as essentially human qualities. But when seen through the essential interplay between newness and reliability, the 'promise' of resilience might look slightly more troubling.

Of course people do not necessarily live according to the imperatives of ontological change. I would be surprised if people had resigned from making experiences and drawing conclusions for their further actions, opinions and self-conduct. In this sense, resilience as a form of governance currently perhaps constitutes more of an ideology than an analysis of really existing conditions. But this does not mean that we are not being encouraged through policies to live without the permanence-creating experiences as eternal strangers at the peripheries of our own worlds.

Notes

1 My page count.
2 I use the term 'encompassing' here because in the inversion of reality and possibility it is possibility that encompasses both. As Bergson (2002b: 230) states, 'the possible implies the corresponding reality with . . . something added, since the possible is the combined effect of reality once it has appeared and of a condition which throws it back in time'.
3 What Bergson is saying is that if someone rings the doorbell, his choice was not between ringing or not ringing (which it would be according to the idea that reality is but the realization of prior possibilities) but that infinite indistinctive potentialities (e.g. weather, the existence of a doorbell, the custom of ringing doorbells, all occurrences that led that person to be in front of that particular door, etc.) realized themselves in the moment of ringing that particular doorbell. In the moment the ringing occurred, they moved into place so that all of this became causally linked. If the doorbell had not been rung, a whole different variety of those indistinctive potentialities would have moved into a different order, forming a different past so that ringing or not ringing are fundamentally not connected.

References

Allen, C. R. and Holling, C. S. (2010) Commentary on part one articles. In Gunderson, L. H., Allen, C. R. and Holling, C. R. (eds) *Foundations of Ecological Resilience*. Washington, DC: Island Press, pp. 3–18.
Aradau, C. (2014) The promise of security: resilience, surprise and epistemic politics, *Resilience: International Policies, Practices and Discourses*, 2: 73–87.
Arendt, H. (1998) *The Human Condition*. Chicago: University of Chicago Press.
Arendt, H. (2006) *Between Past and Future: Eight Exercises in Political Thought*. New York: Penguin Books.
Badiou, A. (2005) *Being and Event*. London: Continuum.
Bergson, H. (1944) The endurance of life. In Pearson, K. A. and Mullarky, J. (eds). *Henri Bergson: Key Writings*. London: Continuum, pp. 171–86.
Bergson, H. (2002a) Life as creative change. In Pearson, K. A. and Mullarky, J. (eds), *Henri Bergson: Key Writings*. London: Continuum, pp. 191–203.
Bergson, H. (2002b) The possible and the real. In Pearson, K. A. and Mullarky, J. (eds), *Henri Bergson: Key Writings*. London: Continuum, pp. 223–32.
Chandler, D. (2013) Pre-emptive strike: a response to 'Resisting resilience'. *Radical Philosophy*, 179, 58–9.
Connolly, W. (2011) *A World of Becoming*. Durham, NC: Duke University Press.
Davidson, D. (2001) *Essays on Actions and Events*. Oxford: Oxford University Press.
Dewey, J. (1929) *The Quest for Certainty: A Study of the Relation between Knowledge and Certainty*. New York: Minton, Balch & Co.
Evans, B. and Reid, J. (2013) Dangerously exposed: the life and death of the resilient subject. *Resilience: International Policies, Practices and Discourses*, 1, 83–98.
Folke, C., Carpenter, S. R., Walker, B., Scheffer, M., Chapin, T. and Rockström, J. (2010) Resilience thinking: integrating resilience, adaptability and transformability. *Ecology & Society*, 15, 20.
Garcia-Dia, M. J., DiNapoli, J. M., Garcia-Ona, L., Jakubowski, R. and O'Flaherty, D. (2013) Concept analysis: resilience. *Archives of Psychiatric Nursing*, 27, 264–70.
Gunderson, L. H. and Allen, C. R. (2010) Why resilience? Why now? In Gunderson, L. H., Allen, C. R. and Holling, C. S. (eds), *Foundations of Ecological Resilience*. Washington, DC: Island Press, xiii–xv.
Harman, G. (2009) *Towards Speculative Realism: Essays and Lectures*. Winchester: Zero Books.
Holling, C. S. (1973) Resilience and stability of ecological systems. *Annual Review of Ecology and Systematics*, 4, 1–23.
Joseph, J. (2013) Resilience as embedded neoliberalism: a governmentality approach. *Resilience: International Policies, Practices and Discourses*, 1, 38–52.
Kauffman, S. (1995) *At Home in the Universe: The Search for the Laws of Self-Organization and Complexity*. Oxford: Oxford University Press.

Lentzos, F. and Rose, N. (2009) Governing insecurity: contingency planning, protection, resilience. *Economy and Society*, 38, 230–54.

Neocleous, M. (2013) Resisting resilience. *Radical Philosophy*, 178, 2–7.

OECD (2013) Risk and resilience: from good idea to good practice. Available at: www.oecd-ilibrary.org/development/risk-and-resilience_5k3ttg4cxcbp-en (accessed 26 July 2016).

Peirce, C. S. (1998) The seven systems of metaphysics. In The Peirce Project *The Essential Peirce: Selected Philosophical Writings*, Vol. 2. Bloomington: Indiana University Press, pp. 178–95.

Prigogine, I. (1997) *The End of Certainty: Time, Chaos and the New Laws of Nature*. New York: Free Press.

Reid, J. (2012) The neoliberal subject: resilience and the art of living dangerously. *CAIP Revista Pléyade*, 10, 143–65.

Schmidt, J. (2014) Intuitively neoliberal? Towards a critical understanding of resilience governance. *European Journal of International Relations*, 21, 402–26.

Walker, J. and Cooper, M. (2011) Genealogies of resilience: from systems ecology to the political economy of crisis adaptation. *Security Dialogue*, 42, 143–60.

Welsh, M. (2014) Resilience and responsibility: governing uncertainty in a complex world. *The Geographical Journal*, 180, 15–26.

World Bank (2013) Building resilience: integrating climate and disaster risk into development. Available at: www.worldbank.org/content/dam/Worldbank/document/SDN/Full_Report_Building_Resilience_Integrating_Climate_Disaster_Risk_Development.pdf (accessed 26 July 2016).

Wrangel, C. (2014) Hope in a time of catastrophe? Resilience and the future in bare life. *Resilience: International Policies, Practices and Discourses*, 2, 183–94.

Zebrowski, C. (2013) The nature of resilience. *Resilience: International Policies, Practices and Discourses*, 1, 159–73.

PART IV

Neoliberalism

11

RESILIENCE, COMPLEXITY AND NEOLIBERALISM

David Chandler

Introduction

Resilience, as a framework informing governance, relies on an ontology of emergent complexity. This chapter analyses how complexity operates not only as a critique of liberal modes of 'top-down' governing but also to inform and instantiate resilience as a postmodern form of governance. In so doing, resilience approaches develop upon and transform neoliberal conceptions of complex life as a limit to liberal governance and directly critique the policy-frameworks of 'actually existing neoliberalism', which seeks to govern complexity 'from below'. Whereas actually existing neoliberalism focuses governmental regimes on the 'knowledge gaps' seen as the preconditions for successful policy-outcomes, resilience asserts a flatter ontology of interactive emergence, where the knowledge that needs to be acquired can only be gained through self-reflexive approaches. This distinction will be illustrated by drawing upon recent UK government policy documents relating to the National Adaptation Programme to make the UK resilient to climate change.

As Brian Walker and David Salt argue in the preface to their influential book *Resilience Thinking*: 'We live in a complex world. Anyone with a stake in managing some aspect of that world will benefit from a richer understanding of resilience and its implications' (2006, p. xiv). In this starting assumption they reflect the growing awareness that there is an intimate connection between living in a world of complexity and the perceived relevance of resilience-thinking for informing how we might govern in this world. To analyse the demand for resilience-thinking as a potential answer or solution, it is therefore vital to grasp what is already implied in the question of the ontology of the world, or life itself, as 'complex'.

This chapter seeks thereby to analyse the assumption that emergent complexity – or life as the object of governance conceived as complex – necessarily calls forth a new 'resilience' agenda of governance. It seeks to unpack the nature of that 'life', which is seen to evade liberal forms of representation and of government and to dictate new forms of governing. The following sections clarify the ontology of emergent complex life emphasising that, while it is understood in precisely the relational terminology immune to liberal reductionist and linear understandings, complex life is also understood to demand governance through other – non-linear and non-reductionist – approaches. Complex emergent life is governable but on a very different basis to liberal and neoliberal 'life'.

The awareness of complex life, its limits and possibilities, has been driven through rethinking governance in terms of the perceived crisis of 'actually existing neoliberalism' (see Brenner and Theodore, 2002). These approaches challenged liberal modernist 'top-down' understandings of government and sought to govern from the 'bottom-up'. These neoliberal policy practices evolved into highly regulatory and interventionist regimes, seemingly at odds with neoliberalism 'in theory'. Resilience-thinking, it will be argued, is a radical critique of the knowledge claims of actually existing neoliberalism, suggesting that the hierarchical causal structure and assumptions of socially determined interactive outcomes still clings too much to a liberal modernist ontology.

The emergence of complexity

Life began to be conceived as complex, both in the natural and social sciences, in the 1920s – after the shock to liberal modernist confidence in progress caused by the carnage of the First World War (1914–1918) and the fears unleashed by the Bolshevik Revolution of 1917. Complexity theorists often locate this shift less in cultural and political sensitivities than in scientific discoveries such as Werner Heisenberg's discovery of the 'uncertainty principle' in quantum mechanics in 1927 – where at the quantum level of tiny particles it was impossible to measure both mass and momentum simultaneously, making access to full information impossible and thereby undermining the predictive promise of science (Mitchell, 2009; Prigogine and Stengers, 1984). Since the 1920s, classical mechanical understandings have increasingly given way to emphasis on the growth of 'uncertainty': the theorisation of the limits to understanding processes of interaction in order to predict outcomes.

Prior to the recent influence of complexity-thinking on the social sciences, the extension of the logic of Heisenberg's 'uncertainty principle' – chaos theory – was the most widely-cited scientific theory of the limits of knowledge. In 1987, James Gleick's *Chaos: Making a New Science*, became a bestseller, introducing the general principles of chaos theory as well as its history to the broader public (Gleick, 1998). Essentially, the fact that it was impossible to accurately measure, at the same time, the position, mass and momentum of particles was, over the long term, held to lead to unpredictable variations in outcomes. Chaos theory thus emphasised the importance of sensitivity to initial conditions, which meant that tiny, unobservable, differences could – over repeated iterations – have major effects in the long term. Simple or closed systems of complexity theory shared this ontology but were distinct in that in the latter order rather than entropy emerged from a dissipative system over many reiterations of simple processes of interconnection (as noted by Norman Farmer and J. Doyne Packard, complexity theory for this reason is the 'related opposite' of chaos theory; see Resnick, 1999, p. 14).

Both worked on the epistemological level, emphasising the impossibility of knowing interactive processes of multiple determinations, which undermined universal linear assumptions. Thus, simple complexity within a closed system can be understood to produce order through structural functionalist autopoeisis; analogous to first generation systems theory, for example, in the work of Niklas Luhmann (1995), the work on non-ergodic systems of new economic institutionalist Douglass North (1999) or the assemblage theory of Manuel DeLanda (2006). Linear or reductionist approaches, therefore, were rejected on the basis that they failed to grasp that which was crucial to understanding the chain of causation: interaction (Cilliers, 1998, pp. viii–ix). Nevertheless, the apparent randomness – caused by tiny variations in initial conditions – could still be understood as driven by an underlying mechanical conception of a law-bound world.

Whereas chaos theory and deterministic understandings of complexity pose an epistemological critique of the ability to grasp the world on the basis of law-bound determinism, emergent or general complexity approaches promise a radically different ontology of objective unknow-ability beyond merely epistemic limits. Systems of general or emergent complexity are not observable from the outside as a deterministic or autopoietic closed system is. The interaction between emergent complex life and governing intervention is held to be open and therefore full of immanent possibilities. In a closed system of complexity, the outcome of external policy intervention would be determined by the inner interactions of that system or assemblage and thereby have non-linear outcomes (unknowable in advance, but potentially knowable). In an open system of complex interaction, governance cannot 'intervene' from the outside but is already embedded within the problematic and therefore works in a constant process of self-reflexivity rather than assuming an external subject position or instrumental means–ends causality (see Byrne and Callaghan, 2014, pp. 86–106). The implications of this shift were already recognised and highlighted by Jean-François Lyotard in the late 1970s.

In Lyotard's understanding, for complicated deterministic or closed systems of interaction it is de facto impossible to have a complete definition of the initial state of a system (or all the independent variables) because of the resources this would take up. It would be analogous to an emperor wishing to have a perfectly accurate map of the empire, making the entire country devote its energy to cartography and therefore leading it to economic ruin because there are no resources for anything else (1984, p. 55). However:

> this limitation only calls into question the practicability of exact knowledge and the power that would result from it. They remain possible in theory. Classical determinism continues to work within the framework of the unreachable – but conceivable – limit of the total knowledge of a system. . . . Quantum theory and microphysics require a far more radical revision of the idea of a continuous and predictable path. The quest for precision is not limited by its cost, but by the very nature of matter.
>
> *(Lyotard, 1984, p. 56)*

It is important to emphasise the distinction between the deterministic ontology of non-linear outcomes in simple complexity and the understanding of emergent causality of general com-plexity theory. Calculation or control and direction become impossible in general complexity theory but the unknowable is not a result of hidden determinism (as in simple complexity), nor can it be the result of blind chance or luck. Lyotard insightfully flagged up how an emergent complexity approach transformed the ontology of knowledge and unknowability and its implications for modernist subject/object distinctions. In a liberal episteme there is the necessary assumption of hidden determination – as Einstein argued, it was impossible that 'God plays with dice' – problems of knowledge are epistemological, merely a matter of knowing more, in order to reveal the causal interconnections. In general complexity theory – where statistical regularities (orders) occur without 'the supreme Determinant' – nature or life reveals itself as an emergent power, neither determined nor merely arbitrary:

> If God played bridge, then the level of 'primary chance' encountered by science could no longer be imputed to the indifference of the die toward which face is up, but would have to be attributed to cunning – in other words, to a choice, itself left up to chance, between a number of possible, pure strategies.
>
> *(Lyotard, 1984, p. 57)*

The problematic of a complex emergent order is not that of knowing more, 'filling in the gaps' of knowledge, but an ontological problem, i.e. the problem exists at the level of what is to be known (it is not linear and law-bound) rather than at the level of how we might know the underlying reality.

In this way, three epistemes of knowledge and unknowability emerge in terms of governmental reasoning, which can be heuristically drawn out in the idiom famously used by Donald Rumsfeld, when serving as US Secretary of Defense in 2002:

> there are known knowns; there are things we know that we know. There are known unknowns; that is to say, there are things that we now know we don't know. But there are also unknown unknowns – there are things we do not know we don't know.
>
> *(USDoD, 2002)*

The first, modernist or liberal, episteme understands the 'known knowns' as central to governmental reason, based on linear and universal assumptions of the progressive accumulation of knowledge of laws and regularities of human affairs. The second, neoliberal, episteme regards these 'known knowns' to be less important, resulting in merely artificial and potentially counterproductive assumptions that ignore the interactive complexity of life. Where policy-outcomes depend more on the inner deterministic causal relations of the object being governed, these knowledge gaps are revealed and necessitate a greater sociological or anthropological awareness of social interaction to enable more effective policy interventions. These crucial knowledge gaps are therefore the 'known unknowns', the hidden, underlying, processes of determination, which we know we do not fully know. For resilience approaches, working on the basis of emergent causality or general complexity there is no deterministic understandings of 'known unknowns', operating underneath or at a deeper level of causation. In the more open interactive ontology of resilience it is the 'unknown unknowns' that increasingly have the central role in emergent causation, meaning that contingent outcomes only reveal concrete causality after the event and are impossible to know beforehand.

Thus, three regimes of governance emerge, each premised upon a different means of operationalising 'life' as a technology of governance. Complexity theory itself provides a conceptual field in which non-linear causality (the breakdown of modernist linear cause-and-effect assumptions) can be understood to operate at either an epistemological or at a deeper ontological level. At the most simple level, the object of governance can be understood as shaped through determinate but complex causality, often articulated in terms of cultural evolution, endogenous processes of inter-subjective understanding or socio-economic path-dependencies – which then pose a problem for governing policy intervention into these processes. In this deterministic understanding of complexity, there is still a division between the subject (the governing actor) and the object (now understood as complex). There is still a liberal subject external to the problematic – much like a scientist observing complexity in eco-systems or a liberal observer considering how to intervene in a complex social order.

In a more extended understanding of complexity, this divide between subject and object is elided through understanding that the governing/knowing subject is not external to the problematic but always and already 'entangled' or embedded in this relationship. With the crisis of modernist framings, emergent or general complexity thus appears to be the leading contender as an alternative ontological vision of the world – of how life can be alternatively conceived as the object of governance. In this sense, general complexity approaches could be seen as reinforcing the new materialist 'ontological turn' in the social sciences (for example, Connolly, 2013; Coole and Frost, 2010; Bennett, 2010), which highlights how a complex ontology constitutes radical possibilities foreclosed by liberal forms of governance.

Complexity-thinking in the social sciences could thus be understood as being on a continuum between a problematic of complexity for policy intervention with instrumental governance goals and complexity understandings that would dispute the possibility of such a subject/object separation. The two ends of this continuum will be heuristically framed in terms of the governing rationalities of actually existing neoliberalism (as a set of regulatory policy practices where the object of intervention is constructed in terms of complexity) and resilience-thinking (where governance is no longer a matter of intervening in an external problematic but of self-reflexive understandings of entanglement).

The market as the *deus ex machina*?

Resilience-thinking is thereby not novel in pitting complex life against the artifice of human social construction. As Michel Foucault states, all liberal forms of governing require the articulation of internal limits to rule as part of the process of reflective self-knowledge of what it means to govern – the construction of life as (un)governable in different ways is inseparable therefore from a study of what it means to govern in a liberal way (2008, pp. 10–22). What is distinct about resilience is that complex life is no longer seen as merely constituting the limit to the world of governmental reason, but instantiates the 'unknown unknowns' as the basis of governmental reason itself. This only became possible through a number of transformations and inversions in liberal reasoning, particularly in relation to the key sphere through which limits were internalised or brought into governmental reason: that of political economy, held to produce its own parallel mechanisms of 'truth' as a limit to those generated by liberal governmental reason (Foucault, 2008, p. 35).

Thereby resilience-thinking, which posits an ontology of general or emergent complexity, can be seen as a distinctive third governmental episteme and contrasted with liberal and neoliberal ways of conceiving life as complex. This way of grasping complex life as an object of governance and integrating complexity into governmental reasoning depended upon neoliberalism as a prior way of bringing complexity into governmental reasoning, rather than upon excluding complexity and assuming universal rational and linear modes of reasoning. It is thereby only on the basis of understanding neoliberalism as a mode of governing that the distinctive mode of governing through resilience approaches to complexity can be fully drawn out.

Empirically, the rise of complexity theorising in the social sciences, especially in political economy, can be seen as an ideological response to the extensions of state intervention from the 'top-down' in order to deal with the economic and social crisis of the inter-war period, the New Deal in the US, Keynesianism in the UK and, of course, the totalising Stalinist and Nazi regimes that came to power in Russia and Germany. In this sense, what is at stake in modern neoliberalism, according to Foucault, is not a revival of pro-market sympathies or the economic need to 'free the economy', but rather a political mistrust of the extension of a certain form of governing intervention seen as producing a crisis for liberal forms of rule (2008, pp. 68–70; 116–118; 130–134). Neoliberalism as a response, cohered theoretically in the post-war period, suggested that top-down interference could only lead to the erosion of liberal freedoms and that active governance interventions necessarily had to work on the basis of 'bottom-up' understandings that worked on the pre-conditions necessary for effective market and democratic systems. States needed to actively govern 'for' the market, not 'against' or 'over' market outcomes, facilitating and enabling outcomes from below rather than directing and controlling from above.

Neoliberal thought therefore argued that the knowledge necessary for policy interventions in complex life was not of the type acquired under the modernist social sciences, with their assumptions of universal regularities of cause-and-effect. Essentially, rather than separating the realms of governmental reason (governing over rational and autonomous subjects of rights and interests) and an external realm of self-ordering complex life (the social and economic sphere, subject to laissez-faire non-intervention), neoliberalism brings complexity into governmental reason itself (the centrality of the 'known unknowns'). For Friedrich von Hayek, often considered the archetypal neoliberal theorist, despite the technical gains of science and technology, Newtonian, or any other 'natural laws' were merely social constructions (1952). For Hayek, knowledge of reality was not that of scientific and technological laws but other forms of adaptive knowledge learnt by imitation and cultural transmission:

> Rules for his [man's, the individual's] conduct which made him adapt what he did to his environment were certainly more important to him than 'knowledge' about how other things behaved. In other words: man has certainly more often learnt to do the right thing without comprehending why it was the right thing, and he still is often served better by custom than understanding.
>
> *(Hayek, 1978a, p. 8)*

For Hayek – as for Walter Lippmann, John Dewey and today's philosophical pragmatists, new materialists, non-representational theorists, actor-network theorists and post-humanists – there was no relationship between technical and scientific progress and liberal modernist assumptions of governmental reason, which assumed that technical and scientific knowledge provided government with a greater ability to control or direct policy outcomes (see Hayek, 1960, p. 22). While Cartesian or Newtonian constructivism might work for the development of abstract technical and scientific 'laws' with some (although limited) application in the natural sciences, the human world was not amenable to understanding through such conceptual fabrications and crude tools of reasoning (Hayek, 1978b). In the face of 'real' complex life, modernist frameworks thus vastly overrated the power of human reasoning. Hayek therefore argued that complex life could not be understood and assimilated into liberal ways of 'knowing' – that the imagined world of the 'known knowns' was much less significant than policy-makers believed:

> Today it is almost heresy to suggest that scientific knowledge is not the sum of all knowledge. But a little reflection will show that there is beyond question a body of very important but unorganised knowledge which cannot possibly be called scientific in the sense of knowledge of general rules: the knowledge of particular circumstances of time and place. It is in this respect that practically every individual has some advantage over all others in that he possesses unique information of which beneficial use might be made, but of which use can be made only if the decisions depending on it are left to him or are made with his active cooperation.
>
> *(Hayek, 1945, pp. 521–522)*

For Hayek and classical neoliberal thought, while governments were denied access to knowledge of complex reality (the 'known unknowns'), the market was able to indirectly make accessible the complex interactions of socio-economic life. The market (as the 'truth' of complex interactive and epistemologically inaccessible life) was idealised as the intermediary, connecting local and specific knowledges, through prices as indicators. Prices here played a fundamental role of revealing or giving access to the plural reality of complex life and also acting as a guide to future behaviour – how one should adapt to and learn through this reality. Here, complex reality was revealed through embedded relationality – not through abstraction and the artifice of social construction – in fact, it was revealed so clearly that no theory or self-reflexivity was required to learn the 'truths' revealed by the price mechanism.

The lessons that complex life revealed, once these were understood in neoliberal frameworks, were that governmental reason should not seek to plan or direct the external world and instead should focus on more effective forms of evolutionary adaptation through properly reading market signals. For Hayek, 'the unavoidable imperfection of man's knowledge and the consequent need for a process by which knowledge is constantly communicated and acquired' depended upon the outcome of market interconnections which demonstrated 'how a solution is produced by interactions of people each of whom possesses only partial knowledge' (1945, p. 530). No new knowledge was required other than what already existed, but the market did all the work of organising this knowledge. Hayek drew upon Alfred North Whitehead (whose work is receiving much wider recognition today), citing his view that:

> It is a profoundly erroneous truism, repeated by all copy-books and by eminent people when they are making speeches, that we should cultivate the habit of thinking what we are doing. The precise opposite is the case. Civilization advances by extending the number of important operations which we can perform without thinking about them.
>
> *(1945, p. 528)*

The problem for Hayek was an epistemological one of human reason itself. The market here worked as the *deus ex machina*, resolving the problems of the limits of governmental and individual reasoning and providing indirect access to the reality of complex life, without the need for conscious reflection. Neoliberalism as a critical theoretical approach could articulate how complex life posed a limit to policy intervention but not how to go beyond these limits, in cases where policy intervention was deemed necessary. Neoliberal approaches were only confronted with the need to rethink how policy interventions might be necessary after the collapse of the Left/Right framework of politics, and the post-war consensus that supported this, in the 1980s and 1990s. It is in this period that 'actually existing' neoliberalism developed as a set of understandings of how complexity might be governed.

Perhaps the clearest expression of the problem of adapting neoliberal understandings to policy intervention is that articulated by Nobel Prize-winning economist and neoliberal World Bank policy advisor Douglass North. North acutely posed the dilemma: 'Hayek was certainly correct that our knowledge is always fragmentary at best. . . . But Hayek failed to understand that we have no choice but to undertake social engineering' (North, 2005, p. 162). Neoliberal thought found 'social engineering' deeply problematic as the policy interventions of governmental power necessarily appeared to imply the need for knowledge of how social processes operated and the development of instrumental means–ends understandings in support of promised policy outcomes. This challenge of governing necessitated a revision of classical neoliberalism because policy activism was necessary despite the limited knowability of social interactions and the constitution of institutional forms.

For Hayek, it was not possible to rationally reflect on the evolution of cultural understandings and the 'organic' institutions, which reflected these. However, for 'actually existing' neoliberal policy-approaches, access to knowledge of the 'known unknowns' became vital. As North stated, this transformation necessarily operated at the level of how neoliberal thought understood 'consciousness' and 'human intentionality' (2005, p. 162). From the position of governing, it seemed necessary that knowledge could be gained in order to intervene instrumentally in the sphere of complex social interaction. These cultural and ideational preconditions, shaping 'consciousness', became the realm of 'bottom-up' policy intervention once 'top-down', linear approaches were seen to be ineffective:

> Understanding the cultural heritage of a society is a necessary condition for making 'doable' change. We must have not only a clear understanding of the belief structure underlying the existing institutions but also margins at which the belief system may be amenable to changes that will make possible the implementation of more productive institutions.
>
> *(North, 2005, pp. 163–164)*

The market was no longer seen as integrating complexity, but merely as an outcome of further 'known unknowns': the complex social processes of interaction which themselves needed to be grasped though interventionist techniques. This active and interventionist framing of neoliberalism has been analysed well by Foucauldian governmentality theorists, and others, who have insightfully described these forms of regulatory and technical intervention, extending the role of the state in areas of socio-cultural life held to be the preconditions shaping the environmental and ideational context for social and economic decision-making (see, for example, Collier, 2005; Castree, 2007; Dean, 2010; Barry *et al.*, 1996).

Resilience and the critique of neoliberalism

Neoliberal approaches thus underwent a transformation from the conceptual approaches to complexity, constituted as an unknowable epistemological limit to governmental reason, to 'actually existing' neoliberal approaches, which sought to govern through the instrumental use of social engineering with regulatory market techniques. The key point is that in the transition from marginal critics from the sidelines in the 1950s and 1960s to governing authority in the late 1980s, neoliberal frameworks brought into sharp focus the problematic of complex life and its governance. For Hayek, this was never a problem, as complex life was constituted as a hidden process and as a boundary limit to governmental knowledge. For neoliberalism as a governing rationality the contradictions gradually became clearer as policy-makers claimed to be able to intervene in the sphere of the 'known unknowns' on the basis of 'correcting' processes of social interaction, understood as systemic path-dependencies or endogenous social, cultural and ideational constructions.

Thus while Hayek was clearly working at the level of the epistemological limits to classical liberal modernist assumptions of the 'known knowns', exemplified in the inter-war linear assumptions informing policy-interventionism, he was never forced to confront the problem of neoliberalism as a form of governance on the basis of the problematic of the 'known unknowns'. A radical and sceptical critique of liberal assumptions of knowledge was thus transformed into a search for ever-more knowledge: a constant process of filling the 'knowledge gaps' required to intervene in social processes of interaction understood as requiring ever-more social depth to work on the preconditions for the smooth and effective workings of economic and political institutions. The limitations of neoliberal frameworks, which have sought to govern ever more from the 'bottom-up', through bringing state and market rationalities together to facilitate regulatory governing agendas, is at the heart of the rise of resilience-thinking. Resilience-thinking is thereby a radically distinctive approach to governing complexity (bringing complexity into governmental reason), through reposing complexity as an ontological rather than an epistemological problem.

The increasing centrality of emergent complexity to thinking about governance beyond 'actually existing' neoliberal approaches can be illustrated by examples taken from recent developments in British government policy-making practice and policy-thinking. One example, the UK government's July 2013 document, *The National Adaptation Programme: Making the Country Resilient to a Changing Climate* (DEFRA, 2013a), usefully highlights the shift from seeking to acquire a greater knowledge of hierarchical and deterministic processes of social interaction, based on the episteme of 'bottom-up' governing techniques, to emphasising the centrality of the 'unknown unknowns', which require much more self-reflexive forms of governance.

From 1994 to 2011 the UK government operated a national programme for sustainable development, which was then replaced by the National Adaptation Programme. The final report from the Sustainable Development Commission makes sobering reading, as attempts to cohere government around the balances of sustainability and progress became increasingly seen to be problematic for their reductive understandings and the assumption that government policy-intervention was the answer. As Andrew Lee, the Chief Executive Officer of the Commission, stated in his Introduction: 'Increasingly, we face new types of problems – "wicked issues" – which will require new types of response – flexible, adaptive, using systems thinking, seeing the whole picture not just a part of it. One of the watchwords will be creating "resilience".' (Lee, 2011, p. 5)

In terms of the typology heuristically laid out in this chapter, the UK government sustainable development programme could be understood as a classic example of neoliberal governance through simple complexity analysis with the assumption that governance stood outside complexity, able to manage and direct levers of state and market direction to facilitate and enable sustainable outcomes. This approach was subsequently rejected for its reductionist, cause-and-effect understandings and reworked through an increasing attention to general complexity and resilience.

The National Adaptation Programme (NAP) involves a lot of government intervention and coordination at both national and local levels, even extending new powers to the Secretary of State to direct certain organisations, such as those with responsibilities for critical national infrastructure, to prepare reports on the steps they are taking and will take to deal with the risks from a changing climate: the so-called Adaptation Reporting Power (ARP) (DEFRA 2013a, p. 9; DEFRA 2013b). The point is not that resilience-thinking is against government intervention, but rather how policy-intervention is perceived to operate – on the basis of the natural or existing capacities available through removing institutional blockages understood as the unintended outcomes of markets and state policy-making.

The analytic annex accompanying the NAP programme report expands on the barriers to natural adaptation and 'identifies market failures, behavioural constraints, policy failures and governance failures as the most important' (DEFRA, 2013c, p. 6). Market failures are understood to be inevitable and to stem from the limits to adequate information under conditions of complexity and emergent causality, including failures to act on such information, in the belief that others will, and the exclusion of vital public goods (especially those connected with the environment) from market considerations. Even more interesting is the understanding of policy failure:

> Policy failures occur when the framework of regulation and policy incentives creates barriers to effective adaptation. This can happen in the presence of competing policy objectives. Similar to the concept of market failure, which as discussed above is a situation that prevents an efficient market solution, this concept must not be interpreted as a failure of policy, but as a systemic characteristic which prevents an efficient policy solution.
>
> *(DEFRA, 2013c, p. 7)*

Resilience-thinking tells us that policy failure is, in fact, 'not a failure of policy' but a learning opportunity with regard to the systemic process of unintended consequences and side effects in a complex world, where failure enables policy-makers to learn from the revelation of these concrete and emergent interconnections. Thus policy failure is construed as distinct from governance failure, which is the failure to reflexively learn from complex life the need to overcome reductionist understandings. Governance failure is the failure of reflexive adaptation, defined as: 'when institutional decision-making processes create barriers to effective learning' (DEFRA, 2013c, p. 7). The barriers to governing complexity are thus given full consideration, in terms of the dangers of unintentional outcomes and side effects.

Given the barriers to both policy-based and market-based decision-making, under conditions of complexity and uncertainty, the National Adaptation Programme is based upon the assumption that policy-making necessarily becomes an ongoing process of relational understanding, binding the policy-makers with the problem which they seek to govern, rather than one of discrete decisions which are then implemented: 'Uncertainty does not mean that action should be delayed. It means that decision-making should be an iterative process and incorporate regular reassessment to consider the latest available information' (DEFRA, 2013c, p. 2). In effect, the decision-making process does not take place before policy is implemented, as in the liberal and neoliberal epistemes, but rather as a continual process of self-reflection upon already existing policy entanglements.

As UK government policy-making becomes increasingly attuned to the mechanisms of governance informed by resilience-thinking – those of understanding policy-failure as part of the policy-process and the need for a constantly iterative policy-process of feedback and data gathering – the gap between government and the governed is seen to be constantly narrowing, as the unknowability of complex life itself comes to constitute the rationality of its governance. Governance is therefore no longer seen to be based upon 'supply-side' or goal-based instrumental policy-making but rather on the understanding of the processes and capacities that already exist and how these can be integrated into policy understandings. In this way, resilience-thinking should not be understood narrowly, as merely building the capacities of individuals and societies (and thereby little different to neoliberal approaches to the preconditions necessary for sustainable and effective institutions) but, more broadly, as a rationality of governing which removes the modernist understanding of government as instrumentally acting in a world potentially amenable to cause-and-effect understandings of policy-making (see also DfID, 2013, p. 8).

Conclusion

The area where resilience-thinking has gone furthest is in the rejection of modernist or liberal approaches to governance, based upon linear or deterministic knowledge assumptions of causality. For liberal universalist approaches, policy-making is constructed in 'top-down' ways, determined by the 'known knowns' of established knowledge and generalisable assumptions of cause-and-effect. For neoliberal approaches, operating on the basis of simple or deterministic complexity ontologies, the problematic of governance always lies at the level of the 'known unknowns' – knowledge gaps that require deeper or more sociological understandings of determinate relational causality – the path dependencies and cultural or inter-subjective transmissions of values and understanding.

For resilience approaches of general or emergent complexity in open systems (where there is no separation of governance from the object of governance) the key aspects of concern are the 'unknown unknowns', which are only revealed post-hoc, through the appearance of the problem. Governance thereby works 'backwards' – from the problem – not forwards to achieve some collective policy-goal. The key attributes which need to be developed in order to govern on the basis of unknowability are those of self-reflexivity and responsivity, necessary for governance in a society which is changing fast and where neither the market nor the state seem capable of directing or addressing the changes required.

Resilience can therefore be understood as an adaptation of a postmodern ontology to the problematic of governing per se, rather than merely to an understanding of its limits. More specifically, resilience-thinking demarcates itself from actually existing neoliberalism as the governing rationality of the 1980s to the 2010s, which attempted to use states and markets to govern complexity in instrumental ways from the 'bottom-up', intervening further in the sphere of social interaction. Neoliberalism as a governmentality sought to govern complexity through instrumentally intervening in interactive social processes to adjust or transform them from the position of the knowing liberal subject, able to balance the levers of the market and the state in order to direct and set goals. In rejecting simple complexity understandings that maintained the subject–object divide between governance and the object to be governed, and the deterministic understandings of causality concomitant with this ontology, resilience-thinking increasingly asserts that governance is only possible in non-instrumental ways, in ways which do not assume an external subject position and therefore reject the hubristic assumptions involved in using market and state levers to work on social processes to attain policy-goals.

Resilience-thinking therefore brings governance as a set of policy-understandings of intervention into neoliberal constructions of limits. Neoliberalism, as a body of theory, which in an age of liberal state interventionism articulated the need to respect complex life as the limit to governance, seems therefore to be undergoing a transformation, via reflections upon the problems of actually existing neoliberalism; rearticulating complex life as the positive promise of transformative possibilities. It is particularly important to note that it is only 'actually existing' neoliberal rationalities, which aim to direct market and state levers instrumentally, that are discursively framed to be the problem for resilience-thinking, not the neoliberal assumptions of complex life per se. Resilience-thinking thereby intensifies neoliberal understandings of complexity and suggests that neoliberalism – as a set of policy practices – still bears the traits of liberal 'hubris' in its contradictory or paradoxical assertions that complex life can be simplified and potentially known by governing power. Neoliberalism as a governing rationality of the last three decades is therefore criticised on the basis of its 'humanist legacies' and its inability to rethink governance on the basis of unknowability. Where neoliberalism failed to properly work through the consequences of postmodernity for governance, resilience-thinking claims to have the solution to the apparent conundrum of governing without assumptions of Cartesian certainty or Newtonian necessity.

References

Barry, A., Osborne, T. and Rose, N. (eds) (1996) *Foucault and Political Reason: Liberalism, Neoliberalism and Rationalities of Government*. Chicago: University of Chicago Press.

Bennett, J. (2010) *Vibrant Matter: A Political Ecology of Things*. London: Duke University Press.

Brenner, N. and Theodore, N. (2002) Cities and the Geographies of 'Actually Existing Liberalism'. *Antipode*, 34, no. 3, 349–379.

Byrne, D. and Callaghan, G. (2014) *Complexity Theory and the Social Sciences: The State of the Art*. Abingdon: Routledge.

Castree, N. (2007) Neoliberal Environments: A Framework for Analysis. *Manchester Papers in Political Economy*, working paper no. 04/07, 10 December.

Cilliers, P. (1998) *Complexity and Postmodernism: Understanding Complex Systems*. Abingdon: Routledge.

Collier, S. (2005) The Spatial Forms and Social Norms of 'Actually Existing Neoliberalism': Toward a Substantive Analytics. *International Affairs Working Paper* 04, June.

Connolly, W. (2013) *The Fragility of Things: Self-Organizing Processes, Neoliberal Fantasies, and Democratic Activism*. London: Duke University Press.

Coole, D. and Frost, S. (eds) (2010) *New Materialisms: Ontology, Agency and Politics*. London: Duke University Press.

Dean, M. (2010) *Governmentality: Power and Rule in Modern Society*. London: Sage.

DEFRA (2013a) Department for Environment, Food and Rural Affairs, *The National Adaptation Programme: Making the Country Resilient to a Changing Climate*. London: HM Government/DEFRA.

DEFRA (2013b) *Strategy for Exercising the Adaptation Reporting Power and List of Priority Reporting Authorities*. London: HM Government/DEFRA.

DEFRA (2013c) *The National Adaptation Programme Report Analytical Annex: Economics of the National Adaptation Programme*. London: HM Government/DEFRA.

DeLanda, M. (2006) *A New Philosophy of Society: Assemblage Theory and Social Complexity*. London: Continuum.

DfID (2013) UK Department for International Development, *Operational Plan 2011–2015 DFID Growth and Resilience Department*. London: DfID.

Foucault, M. (2008) *The Birth of Biopolitics: Lectures at the Collège de France 1978–1979*. Basingstoke: Palgrave.

Gleick, J. (1998) *Chaos: Making a New Science*. London: Vintage.

Hayek, F. (1945) The Use of Knowledge in Society. *American Economic Review*, 35, no. 4, 519–530.

Hayek, F. (1952) *The Sensory Order: An Enquiry into the Foundations of Theoretical Psychology*. Chicago: University of Chicago Press.

Hayek, F. (1960) *The Constitution of Liberty*. London: Routledge.

Hayek, F. (1978a) *The Three Sources of Values*. London: London School of Economics and Political Science.

Hayek, F. (1978b) Lecture on a Master Mind: Dr. Bernard Mandeville. In Hayek, *New Studies in Philosophy, Politics, Economics and the History of Ideas*. London: Routledge and Kegan Paul, pp. 125–141.

Lee, A. (2011) CEO's Foreword. In Sustainable Development Commission, *Governing for the Future – The Opportunities for Mainstreaming Sustainable Development*. London: Sustainable Development Commission.

Luhmann, N. (1995) *Social Systems*. California: Stanford University Press.

Lyotard, J. (1984) *The Postmodern Condition: A Report on Knowledge*. Manchester: Manchester University Press.

Mitchell, M. (2009) *Complexity: A Guided Tour*. Oxford: Oxford University Press.

North, D. (1999) Dealing With A Non-Ergodic World: Institutional Economics, Property Rights, and the Global Environment. *Duke Environmental Law & Policy Forum*, 10, no. 1, 1–12.

North, D. (2005) *Understanding the Process of Economic Change*. Princeton: Princeton University Press.

Prigogine, I. and Stengers, I. (1984) *Order Out of Chaos: Man's New Dialogue with Nature*. New York: Bantam.

Resnick, M. (1999) *Turtles, Termites, and Traffic Jams: Explorations in Massively Parallel Microworlds*. Cambridge, MA: MIT Press.

USDoD (2002) United States Department of Defense, news briefing, 12 February. Available at: www.nato.int/docu/speech/2002/s020606g.htm.

Walker, B. and Salt, D. (2006) *Resilience Thinking: Sustaining Ecosystems and People in a Changing World*. Washington, DC: Island Press.

12

RESILIENCE, POWER AND MONEY

Limitations and prospects of systems ecology in envisaging a sustainable world economy

Alf Hornborg

Introduction

It can be argued that discourses on the sustainability of human–environmental relations that ignore their political dimension are not only incomplete, but in themselves—as ideologies—manifestations of power. In this chapter, I begin by arguing that the currently burgeoning discussions on "social-ecological resilience" (Berkes and Folke 1998; Levin *et al.* 1998; Peterson 2000; Gunderson and Holling 2002; Berkes *et al.* 2003; Folke 2006) tend to mask the power relations, contradictions of interest, and inequalities that to a large extent determine how humans utilize the surface of the Earth. On the other hand, I hope to demonstrate the underexplored potential of resilience theory to radically confront such power structures by identifying some of the basic assumptions of economics as the very source of vulnerability, mismanagement, and crises. The most basic assumption of economics is arguably its faith in general-purpose money and global markets as signaling-systems that promote the most efficient allocation of resources. Contrary to this assumption, I shall argue that the logic of general-purpose money in several respects promotes *in*efficiency, if other parameters such as energy are taken into account. Of more immediate relevance in this context, however, is the inclination of general-purpose money and global markets to reduce local socio-ecological resilience. This conclusion can be derived from the systems-theoretical tenets of resilience theory itself. These tenets can be used to argue for special-purpose currencies and local markets that complement the global economy, rather than an undifferentiated globalization of resource flows. The ultimate implications of resilience theory, in other words, are vastly more radical and subversive than its current proponents imagine.

The ideological disarmament of disaster

The emergence of resilience discourse in recent years has been critically discussed from several angles, tracing its intellectual ancestry in systems ecology, its ideological affinities with neoliberal economics, and its incapacity to account for actual patterns of land use in various parts of the world (Hanley 1998; Lélé 1998; Nadasdy 2007; Brand and Jax 2007; Gotts 2007; Hornborg 2009; Kirchhoff *et al.* 2010; Walker and Cooper 2011; Park 2011; Reid 2012; Sheridan 2012;

Widgren 2012). It has also been scrutinized micro-sociologically as a social movement explicitly determined to avoid criticism (Parker and Hackett 2012), which raises questions about its solidity as a scientific endeavor.

I have previously argued that the use of the concept of resilience in public and academic discourse on human–environmental relations reflects an ideological assimilation of environmental concerns by an establishment keen to avoid alarmist messages challenging business as usual (Hornborg 2009). Although represented as a synthesis of perspectives from both the natural and the social sciences, resilience discourse generally appears to be ignorant of most of the tenets of modern social science, except for occasional contributions from economists eager to develop new mathematical models for natural resource management. Leading advocates of the resilience of traditional resource management, for instance, reveal a very superficial grasp of anthropology (Berkes and Folke 1998; Berkes 1999; Berkes *et al.* 2003). Their proposal that the modern concept of social-ecological systems has affinities with traditional eco-cosmologies is highly misleading, as is obvious from the fact that the latter tend to extend the social domain into the natural, rather than vice versa (Descola 1994). Passing references to what Lévi-Strauss (1966) has called "savage thought" (Berkes and Folke 1998, pp. 12–13) similarly miss the point of his analyses entirely. Even more problematic than its distortions of anthropology, however, is what Lélé identifies as its pervasive inattention to "major asymmetries in the interests and powers of the different actors." (1998, p. 253) The "panarchical perspective," writes Gotts, "has had little to say about social elites and the often violent and oppressive ways in which they maintain themselves" (2007, p. 6). This conspicuously ideological dimension of resilience discourse prompted Nadasdy to conclude that it "has the implicit goal of maintaining the social-ecological relations of capitalist resource extraction and agro-industry" (2007, pp. 217–18).

The key metaphor of the resilience movement is the model of the "adaptive cycle," applied decades ago by the ecologist Crawford Holling to forest ecosystems in eastern Canada. The famous horizontal figure eight recurs in countless publications on resilience theory, including the cover of the canonical 2002 volume *Panarchy* (Gunderson and Holling 2002), and seems to be the principal common denominator of resilience research. As such, its many uses deserve special scrutiny. Social scientists are commonly disturbed by claims that the model of the adaptive cycle is applied not only to ecosystems or social-ecological systems but even to social systems as such. Resilience theorists have thus proposed analogies, for instance, between old-growth forests and large corporations, and between forest fires and financial panics (Peterson 2000). Apparently, the "growth" phase of the adaptive cycle is as applicable to forest biomass as to the logging industry, or to fish stocks as to fisheries (ibid.). This obviously represents a logical contradiction when applied to social-ecological systems where the growth of societal capital is inversely related to the growth of natural capital, e.g. where the growth of the logging industry is associated with the depletion of forest biomass, or the growth of fishing fleets with the depletion of fish stocks. This contradiction can be resolved only by concluding that the social and ecological components of such systems follow separate and antagonistic cycles, where the growth phase of economic capital coincides with the release phase of natural capital. But if social and ecological systems follow distinct and contradictory cycles, it no longer seems meaningful to conceive of them as components of a single system tracing a common "adaptive cycle."

It has been observed that the concept of resilience can be more or less precisely defined in engineering and ecology, but can serve only as a vague and contested metaphor in the social and behavioral sciences (Brand and Jax 2007; Park 2011; even its use in ecology has been contested, as reflecting a particular cultural construction of ecosystems, see Kirchhoff *et al.* 2010), where it will inevitably raise normative questions about the relative desirability of different states and conditions. In order to discuss the resilience of a particular "social-ecological system," it would be necessary to define its geographical boundaries, its exchanges with the world outside those boundaries, its physical constitution (population, resources, metabolism, etc.), its social and cultural organization, the relevant physical and social parameters and their acceptable ranges of variability, the vulnerability of these parameters to disturbance, and so on. In spite of the voluminous rhetoric on the resilience of social-ecological systems, I am not aware of any case study in which all these aspects have been competently addressed. In fact, I doubt that it is at all feasible to do so.

An example of the kind of quandaries that theorists of societal resilience will run into is the problem of how to define its opposite, i.e. societal collapse. Anthropologists and archaeologists have defined this concept as a sudden loss of political or economic integration and complexity, resulting in a fragmentation into less inclusive and more autonomous social units (Tainter 1988; Yoffee and Cowgill 1988). World history can be viewed as sequences of such collapses, followed by periods of greater local autonomy and then renewed integration, but is it correct and meaningful to approach world history as an "adaptive cycle"? What does it mean to say that civilizations are "complex adaptive systems"? Can social systems "learn"?[1] At which level of social inclusiveness are the resilience theorists concerned with resilience? Was the collapse of the Roman Empire a failure of resilience, or was the survival of (some) post-imperial communities an index of adaptive success? Is the contemporary world market a similar social project destined for collapse, or is the preoccupation of neoliberal economists with resilience an indication of their commitment to preserving it? If the collapses of past civilizations are to be approached in terms of social-ecological cycles, we again need to ask why the growth of societal capital (cities, temples, roads, etc.) tends to be inversely related to the growth of natural capital (forests, topsoil, biodiversity, etc.), illustrating that social and ecological systems follow separate and contradictory cycles?

A further dilemma for systems ecologists addressing social systems is how to handle the concept of "identity" (see Brand and Jax 2007). The identity of an ecological system is a matter of objective properties remaining within a certain range, whereas social or cultural identity refers to the subjective experience of groups of people. Thus, for instance, archaeologists have seriously questioned if there really was a Maya collapse in the tenth century, as there is still a large population of people who speak a Maya language and identify with Maya culture (McAnany and Yoffee 2010). Although my response to these archaeologists would be that it is essential to distinguish between an objective historical loss of socio-political complexity and the persistence of a sense of ethno-linguistic identity, the ecologists' explicit suggestion to focus on identity raises the question of how the concept is to be used in trans-disciplinary approaches to social-ecological systems.

The theorizing on social-ecological systems by systems ecologists shows remarkably little respect for social science research, and it is difficult to imagine examples of inverse colonization of natural by social science, as if, for instance, political scientists should begin conceptualizing ecosystems in terms of power structures. The ecologists' theory of society tends to strike social scientists as highly naïve and generally at odds with elementary social theory established decades ago. It appears to conceive of disasters such as societal collapse, epidemics, starvation, and war as "adaptive" phases of more or less "natural" cycles. Most remarkable is its neglect of decades of voluminous discourse on political ecology (Blaikie and Brookfield 1987; Peet and Watts 1996; Bryant and Bailey 1997; Keil *et al.* 1998; Paulson and Gezon 2005; Biersack and Greenberg 2006; Peet *et al.* 2011). Several authors have also explicitly contrasted the approaches of resilience theory and political ecology, arguing that the latter is better equipped to account for actual patterns of land use and resource management (Sheridan 2012; Widgren 2012).

The currently expanding dominance of resilience theory within the field of sustainability research can thus not be accounted for in terms of analytical progress, but appears to reflect its capacity to ideologically defuse the challenges posed by political ecology and other conflict-conscious approaches to human–environmental relations. In the remainder of this chapter, I would like to discuss how power might be addressed within the framework of resilience theory, so as to exploit the potential of Holling's systems ecology as a *subversive* analytical framework. I offer these suggestions in response to recurrent assertions by proponents of resilience theory that they are indeed very concerned with issues of power, but have simply not yet turned their attention to them.

Towards an understanding of power in social-ecological systems

Let us begin by agreeing with resilience theorists that social and ecological systems are geared to each other, or "coupled" (Berkes and Folke 1998; Gunderson and Holling 2002; Berkes *et al.* 2003). With this established, we must conclude that a theoretical framework capable of accounting for the dynamics of such coupled systems will have to accommodate essential elements of both social and natural science. On the one hand, an indispensable element of modern social theory is the pivotal role of *culture*, understood as socially negotiated systems of meanings. Cultural systems of meanings can also be referred to as symbolic systems, or even *semiotic* systems (Sebeok 1994). Without reckoning with the specific cultural ways in which the world is perceived by the particular category of humans under consideration, there can be no social theory. A central aspect of culture, of course, is language. The way in which humans collectively classify phenomena in society and nature influences their behavior in fundamental ways. On the other hand, an account that accommodates the objective realities investigated by natural sciences must also be capable of reckoning with material factors such as flows of energy and materials. In other words, a theory of socio-ecological systems must be able to deal with both cultural and material phenomena, i.e. with flows of signs as well as flows of matter and energy.[2] If the inattention to power is indeed a glaring lacuna in theories of socio-ecological resilience, we must encourage resilience theorists to seriously engage the topic.

Power is a hybrid phenomenon involving both cultural and material phenomena. A general definition of power could be built on the observation that it universally implies unequal access to material resources of some kind, including energy. But in order to be complete, such a general definition would also have to account for how such inequalities of access are socially maintained.[3] A reasonable proposition is that the most pervasive, yet least salient, way in which social inequalities are maintained is through cultural mystification, i.e. by rendering them either invisible or self-evident and "natural." This is simultaneously a quite concise way of defining "ideology." Of course there are other means of reproducing inequalities as well, notably coercion, but I would propose that they are generally secondary to the power of ideology. The subtle power of culture or ideology tends to be encoded in our basic and seemingly self-evident categories of thought, i.e. our language.

Two examples will suffice to illustrate this point. The first is derived from the Inca Empire of early sixteenth-century Peru, where the Inca emperor persuaded his millions of subjects to invest their labor in agriculture, public architecture, warfare, and manufacturing by claiming to be the son of *Inti*, the Sun God. He and his relatives were able to claim a significant proportion of harvests and other produce by representing the unequal exchange of labor and resources as a reciprocal exchange between the emperor and his subjects. The material flows of resources hinged on the semiotic flows of words through which the former were conceived and organized, e.g. *mita* (the labor tax) and *ayni* (the ritual events in which peasants worked the emperor's land in exchange for *chicha*, i.e. maize beer). Needless to say, the volumes of maize that had been brewed into the *chicha* served at the *ayni* represented only a tiny fraction of the maize that was harvested. The power of the Inca emperor, in other words, consisted not only of flows of matter and energy converging on his many warehouses, but also on the cultural concepts (such as *mita* and *ayni*) through which the metabolism of the empire was reproduced.

The second example is much closer to home and will thus be more difficult to assimilate, but the basic argument is the same. For more than two centuries now, Europeans and their overseas dependents have learned to find it quite natural to sell their labor time and natural resources on the market for money. They have contributed to European factories and industrial machinery, built cities, fought wars, and produced commodities. The urban-industrial infrastructures that illuminate Europe on satellite images of night-time lights indicate vast investments of labor time, energy, and materials. Once again, we can observe that these asymmetric flows of matter and energy would not have occurred without the semiotic flows of words by which they were orchestrated, e.g. concepts such as *wage* and *market price*.[4]

A conclusion we can draw from these two examples is that cultural systems of meanings, encoded in language, are essential components of any social arrangements for the distribution of material resources. Inequalities in social power tend to boil down to inequalities of access to such resources, including armies with which to assert them, all legitimized by hegemonic discourses, whether concerned with the divine ancestry of the Inca emperor or with the invisible hand of the market. The phenomenon of social power includes not only unequal access to resources, but also unequal influence over the construction of mainstream discourse. To understand "social-ecological systems," it is absolutely necessary to address the political dimensions of such cultural discourses. In the modern world, this means addressing the political dimensions of mainstream economics.

The revolutionary implications of (p)anarchy

Let us now turn to a central observation in Holling's framework for understanding the operation and viability of living systems: the ideal congruity of temporal and spatial scales (Gunderson and Holling 2002). It appears that resilience in natural systems is importantly geared to the tendency toward a general correspondence between level of integration and longevity, so that, for instance, a forest is more permanent than a tree, a tree more permanent than a leaf, and so on. This nested hierarchical character of living systems safeguards the more inclusive systems from being jeopardized by the failures of subsystems, and in some contexts *vice versa*. The relative autonomy of subsystems vis-à-vis lower or higher levels can thus be regarded as a key principle for resilience and sustainability. Societies need to be able to survive the demise of individual organisms, and organisms need to be able to survive the failures of individual cells, but individual trees inversely need to be able to survive forest fires, and local communities need to survive the collapse of empires or global markets. Such cybernetic insights long ago prompted the anthropologist Roy Rappaport to define "maladaptation" in terms of communicative failures such as "over-segregation," "hyper-coherence," and "usurpation" (1979, pp. 145–72). The general understanding of socio-ecological crises as crises of communication can be traced to Rappaport's mentor Gregory Bateson (1972), who was very much involved in developing the field of cybernetics, or systems theory. If stripped of some of the metaphysical confidence in diffusely organized "wholes," which suggests significant affinities between systems ecology and neoliberal economics (Walker and Cooper 2011), the approach is of undeniable relevance for the continuing deliberations on sustainability.

It is remarkable that resilience theory has not proceeded from such central insights of systems ecology to critically scrutinize the operation of communicative mechanisms in the modern world, the most fundamental and pervasive of all of which is *money* (Weatherford 1997). It would be completely in line with Holling's emphasis on the principle of congruity of temporal and spatial scales to observe that what economic anthropologists refer to as *general-purpose money* systematically defies that principle, by making all kinds of values commensurable, regardless of which level of scale they pertain to. Goods and services pertaining to the reproduction of individual human organisms (such as food and beverages), for instance, are considered interchangeable on the world market with goods and services pertaining to the reproduction of entire ecosystems, or even the biosphere (such as technologies for deforesting Amazonia). Due to the logic of general-purpose money, people thus routinely "trade rainforests for Coca-Cola," as I have elsewhere phrased such deplorable but culturally "natural" practices.

In resilience discourse, the neglect of the destructive implications of general-purpose money is closely related to the neglect of those of global systems of exchange. In the world-view of leading resilience theorists, "social systems can be as small as a family or as large as a nation" (Gunderson and Holling 2002). Presumably, the nation represents the most inclusive social system conceivable for these theorists. Gotts' observation that "world-systems analysis could strengthen work within the resilience conceptual framework" (2007, p. 7) is thus clearly an understatement. General-purpose money has historically extended the reach of long-distance trade and is the cornerstone of today's increasingly globalized markets. Although celebrated in neoliberal ideology, economic globalization undeniably increases the dependency and vulnerability of local communities. "In recent centuries," writes Gotts, "largely European-derived changes in transport, communication, and military technologies have drastically reduced the autonomy of regional-scale systems" (ibid.). Yet, although the globalization of the market has thus increased vulnerability and reduced resilience, neoliberal advocates of this very globalization now present themselves as champions of resilience (Walker and Cooper 2011; Reid 2012).

Why is it that resilience theorists have not yet zoomed in on *money* as a culturally specific way of communication, which is quite obviously a central factor in generating unsustainable practices and increasing socio-ecological vulnerability? Would such an observation be too politically controversial, or are they simply too embedded in the cultural assumption that general-purpose money is an unquestionable feature of social life? Considering what is at stake, e.g. one billion people on the verge of starvation on a planet facing climate change and socio-ecological collapse, it is difficult to see how *any* idea could be dismissed as politically too controversial. But my main point here is that Holling's understanding of hierarchies of spatio-temporal scales in living systems, in fact, provides excellent analytical tools for identifying modern money—through its capacity to confuse scales—as a source of environmental degradation. Although the tendency of money to promote the interchangeability of values at very different spatial and temporal scales very obviously dissolves socio-ecological resilience, resilience theorists continue to approach capital as if it was as natural as biomass, and markets as if they were a kind of ecosystem.

Even if the most well-meaning advocates of sustainability are thus unable to discern the cultural peculiarities which appear to propel global society toward disaster, this is not because there are no alternatives. It is, in fact, quite conceivable to organize an economy with separate and incommensurable currencies for different kinds of values. Not only are there plenty of ethnographic examples of such "multi-centric economies" documented by economic anthropologists such as Paul Bohannan (1955), but recent financial breakdowns in countries such as Argentina and Greece have invariably prompted initiatives in the same direction (North 2007). The creation of local currencies for community cooperation and survival is a recurrent theme in the turbulent history of international finance, and is a central component in the Transition Towns movement. The myriad ephemeral experiments with so-called LETS (Local Exchange Trading Systems) illustrate the attractiveness of the idea of local currencies, but in order for this idea to generate a decisive and general break with the destructive logic of modern money, it needs to be grounded in more profound analysis and to be backed by national authorities.[5] It is not entirely impossible that the current financial turmoil in Europe and North America might provide opportunities for serious discussions about how spheres of economic commensurability could be redefined in the interests of financial, social, and ecological security.

Redefining commensurability: a strategy for socio-ecological resilience

A common denominator of the various experiments with LETS is the ambition to create an alternative, informal economy alongside the formal economy based on state-issued currencies. The main point has generally been to increase local interaction, local economic diversity, and local control over resources. Crucially, however, the alternative local currency in these experiments does not distinguish between local and non-local products, i.e. values representing different scales of socio-ecological inclusiveness. In accordance with the analysis above, this ought to be the central function of a currency system that would enhance local resilience. In order to achieve the desired effects, the new local currency would need (1) to offer consumers a superior alternative to purchasing commodities with regular money, and (2) to specify the range of (local) goods and services that it can be exchanged for. In other words, a political decision to implement such an alternative economic system would need to include a strategy (1) for persuading consumers to actually use the local currency, rather than regular money, and (2) for ensuring that its use actually promotes consumption of local goods and services. How might this be achieved?

A first consideration would be if any nation state in its right mind would really want to encourage the growth of an untaxed, informal economy in local communities. This would no doubt be unfeasible in the present political climate, but it is not inconceivable that, a few decades from now, financial or ecological crises might induce currently affluent nations to seriously consider such options. The potential benefits of localizing economies are not restricted to bio-physical consequences such as reducing transports, energy use, carbon dioxide emissions, and waste, or enhancing biodiversity through more complex patterns of land use, but would include reducing federal expenses, e.g. for transport infrastructure, environmental protection, health services, and social security; i.e. precisely the kinds of public expenditures that are already proving a heavy burden for many welfare states. Over the long term, such localization would reduce marginalization and vulnerability to various kinds of crises, enhancing cooperation, diversity, and general resilience at the local level. This is not to advocate a sudden abandonment of highly specialized, vulnerable, or disaster-prone communities, denying them the supra-local relief that they have grown used to, but to encourage a long-term increase in local self-sufficiency, autonomy, and social-ecological calibration. Carefully implemented and monitored by the federal authorities, the reform would proceed at a pace that would not risk jeopardizing human or ecosystem health.

If these benefits were acknowledged, and the authorities persuaded that such a bi-centric economy would indeed relax the pressure on fiscal resources, they might find that the most efficient way of reorganizing the economy in this direction would be print and each month distribute a certain sum of the new, special-purpose currency to all households in proportion to their size.[6] Assuming that households will wish to economize with their various resources, we can expect them to employ the new currency in purchasing local produce such as food, firewood, and building materials, and local services such as childcare, carpentry, and repairs, because in doing so they would be saving much of their regular income for non-local expenditures such as information technology and pharmaceutical products. Over the long term, of course, this shift would significantly reduce the demand for long-distance imports of commodities that can be locally produced, which is very much in line with resilience, sustainability, and any non-monetary measure of efficiency. The list of potential advantages of such a shift can be made very long, particularly if we include not only ecological and financial, but also social and existential benefits

(Hornborg 2011, pp. 157–60). As the new currency would be distributed to households without any required reciprocation, it could be regarded as a kind of citizen's allowance that guarantees a minimum level of subsistence even where no formal employment is available, or even desired.

The aim of such an intentional re-localization of social metabolism (flows of matter and energy) would be to generate a multitude of spatially restricted but overlapping spheres of exchange, in which the average transport distances of goods and services are significantly reduced. The idea would not be to create separate local currencies for separate, bounded communities, but to allow the rationality of the (single) new currency to work out its own spatial-metabolic logic in terms of overlapping geographical fields of distribution. The assumption is that it would generate incentives to both consume and provide goods and services with as short transport distances as possible. Instead of visualizing communities as bounded cells, we might anticipate their metabolic flows more as intersecting local networks. If transport distance could once again be expected to increase a commodity's price, as in the pre-railway world of von Thünen ([1826] 1966), local-ization and diversification of production would be encouraged through market competition. It would not make economic sense, for instance, to use the formal currency to purchase remotely derived ("global") inputs, such as diesel, to produce goods or services for local markets, where the potential gain is in local currency only. Until such price competition itself suffices to promote the local economy, the determination of which goods and services qualify as "local" could con-ceivably be organized in different ways, but it might initially involve some kind of certification system specifying, for instance, a maximum number of transport kilometers for different products sold at a given market, or a range of neighboring municipalities from which they may derive.

Rethinking progress, globalization, and development

The localizing consequences of dividing the market into two separate spheres of exchange will be recognized as in some respects running counter to developments that we, for centuries, have learned to celebrate as progress and modernization. In these respects, the suggested reform would appear to be a step backward, but this is an illusion, building on our cultural definition of progress. A *material* localization of the economy would not contradict a continued *communicative* globali-zation. The modern intensification of energy use, long-distance transports, and mechanization represents the historical experience of a privileged segment of global society over the past two centuries of fossil-fueled capitalism. From a global perspective, human progress should be defined not in terms of capital accumulation but of enhanced conditions for harmony, sustainability, health, communication, and security. In short: resilience. But rather than inspire resistance against the neoliberal world order against which it was launched, the concept of resilience has been incorporated as a central component of the neoliberal model itself (Walker and Cooper 2011; Reid 2012). The radical implications of Holling's recipe for resilience, which should provoke a serious confrontation with some foundational assumptions of contemporary economic science, have yet to be explored by his followers.

A very important foundational assumption, not only of economics, but of modern thought in general, is that technological capacity should be viewed primarily as a progression in time, rather than something that is (unequally) distributed in social space (Hornborg 2001; 2011). The uncritical subscription to this assumption is reflected in the way technology is discussed by resilience theorists, namely as a means of extending "the ambit for human choices from local to regional to planetary scale" (Gunderson and Holling 2002, p. 101), rather than as a means for *some* humans to extend their ambit at the *expense* of others (see further, Bauman 1998, 2011). Access to modern technology is tantamount to relative purchasing power, and the rationality of any technological system is inextricably geared to relative prices of labor and resources on the world market. Thus our cultural faith in money and the market are as essential to the material accumulation of technology as was the cultural faith in the Sun God to the material accumulation of terraces in the Inca Empire. Modern technologies cannot be made universally accessible to all humans, but represent social strategies for redistributing time and space in global society. In a long-term, inter-generational perspective, moreover, the contemporary extension—by means of fossil-fuel technologies—of the ambit of affluent humans occurs at the expense of future generations whose ambits are curtailed by exhausted oil reserves and climate change. The extent to which the accumulation of modern technological infrastructures is contingent on structures of market exchange would become very apparent if the reform sketched above were to be implemented. If the demand for long-distance imports were to subside, there would simply be no incentive to maintain massive infrastructures for transporting foodstuffs across the globe.

A predictable objection to the vision of a bi-centric economy would be that the proposal is in line with the neoliberal strategy to urge states to relinquish their responsibilities for the well-being of their citizens. I sympathize with the critiques voiced by Duffield (2008) and Reid, (2012), who argue that mainstream policies advocating community-based self-reliance may simply have the purpose of shifting "the burden of security from states to people," (Reid 2012, p. 67) and I fully share the underlying conviction that it should be the responsibility of democratically elected authorities to safeguard as far as possible the health and security of the people under their jurisdiction, which certainly means intervening in the polarizing logic of the capitalist market. Nevertheless, the problems of sustainability and security currently facing humanity require analyses and policies that transcend the conventional confrontation between right-wing advocates of the market and left-wing advocates of state intervention.

Unfortunately, the left-wing vision of a world of universally affluent, technologically advanced and egalitarian nations is no longer credible. The Scandinavian countries of the 1960s, which for many served as a model for development, now represent a privileged corner of the world, blessed by the success of their export industries on the very capitalist world market that they pretended to transcend. The levels of consumption—not least of fossil fuels—enjoyed by average Scandinavians are physically impossible to universalize among seven billion humans (Wackernagel and Rees 1996), nor are they defensible from the perspectives of global sustainability and climate change. Ambitious federal welfare programs are feasible only as long as domestic export industries do not relocate to countries with lower salaries and lower taxes, or as long as welfare and consumption can be financed through credit. The recent financial crises in the United States and Europe indicate that the capacity of developed nations to maintain a high and preferably rising standard of living for a majority of their population is seriously constrained not only by the logic of the capitalist world economy, but ultimately also by the finiteness of the biosphere of which it is a part. This is not to deny that a minority of speculators has profited enormously from these crises, but the problems of unrealistic standards of consumption and of increasing fiscal deficits are not solved simply by redistributing such profits for collective use.

It is no doubt true that concerns over resilience and sustainability have been co-opted by the very neoliberal model which prompted them to emerge in the first place (Reid 2012, p. 74), but to dismiss ecological and/or financial concerns as neoliberal mystifications is to deny real structural problems that adhere not simply to capitalism (Foster and Magdoff 2008; Harvey 2010), but to the cultural phenomenon of (general-purpose) money itself. To believe that some version of socialism would enable seven billion humans to adopt the technological comforts and levels of consumption currently enjoyed by average Americans or Scandinavians is almost as naïve as imagining that, in the distant future, "humanity will plausibly expand outward in our solar system and even further into the galaxy" (Schwartzman 2008, p. 53). Thinking realistically about the prospects for a sustainable and more egalitarian world society means navigating between the Scylla of ruthless neoliberalism and the Charybdis of high-tech utopias of solidarity. Both programmes presuppose that the money will be there to distribute, and that the critical issue is how to distribute it. Neither program seriously considers the possibility that faltering core areas of the world-system such as the United States and Europe will be unable to maintain their positions as regions of privileged purchasing power and undiminished mass consumption. In not having grasped the conditions for their own feasibility, both these political visions would in due time lead to socio-ecological disasters and unprecedented human suffering. It is against this background that I have offered the vision of a bi-centric economy.

Conclusions

In this admittedly wide-ranging discussion of the shortcomings and prospects of resilience theory, I began by recommending its proponents to engage more respectfully with social science, particularly its understandings of culture and power. They were also advised to establish a critical distance to the metaphysical assumptions of "complex adaptive systems theory," particularly when applied to social systems. Furthermore, if resilience theorists are as sincerely concerned about sustainability as I believe they generally are, they have every reason to critically scrutinize the operation of general-purpose money, the global market, and neoliberal ideology. Upon doing so, I am convinced that they would find the idea of a bi-centric economy, as sketched above, entirely consistent with the fundamental insights of resilience theory.

To conclude with one more glimpse from the ancient Andes, I would like to reflect on the historical fate of the local village communities (*ayllu*) that in the early sixteenth century were the building blocks of the Inca Empire. Although the emperor and his court were obviously adept at extracting surplus from these communities, they must have been granted a significant measure of autonomy, or many of them would not have survived the traumatic collapse of the empire, followed by centuries of colonialism and impoverishment. Many rural, Quechua-speaking communities in Peru still today practice sustainable subsistence agriculture on terraces constructed several centuries before the rise of the Inca Empire.[7] The local, socio-ecological building blocks of pre-colonial Andean civilizations were apparently sufficiently autonomous to recover from the recurrent shocks of supra-system breakdown. It is very doubtful if modern communities in Europe or North America are similarly resistant to wider systemic crises. Specialization and dependency increases vulnerability, which is tantamount to reducing resilience. It would be most useful if the resilience theorists, following the implications of Holling's observations, focused their attention on how the very foundations of current economic policies need to be radically reconsidered.

Notes

1 Most social scientists would reject the notion that social transformations can be understood as learning processes, and it is reassuring to find a forest ecologist similarly wondering "how does an ecosystem 'learn' and 'adapt'?" (Park 2011, p. 339).
2 This binary opposition approximates the conventional Cartesian dualism of Society (or Culture) versus Nature, understood as the *analytical* distinction between communicative/semiotic and material aspects. I am well aware that the two poles are ubiquitously intertwined in the real world of bodies, landscapes, and technologies, but this does not mean that the analytical distinction between features of socio-cultural versus natural (physical) *derivation* should be dissolved.
3 I realize, of course, that there have been many attempts to define "power," and that this is not the only one possible.

4 To the extent that this argument is successful in revealing the significance of our everyday vocabularies, the comparison with the Inca Empire is probably essential. This anthropological method has been referred to as "defamiliarization by cross-cultural juxtaposition" (see Marcus and Fischer 1986).

5 Rather than review the extensive literature on alternative currencies, selectively endorsing and rejecting various ideas, I have chosen to outline some fundamental requirements of a bi-centric economy that could be expected to be both sustainable and attractive. Previous deliberations relevant to the topic of alternative currencies include Schumacher 1974; Kennedy 1989; Dobson 1993; Douthwaite 1999; Hart 2000; North 2007; 2010; Nelson and Timmerman 2011.

6 A simpler way of handling the practicalities of distributing this currency might be to issue it electronically, along with plastic cards.

7 It is perhaps fitting that indigenous Quechua women are portrayed on the cover of Berkes and Folke's classical volume *Linking Social and Ecological Systems* (1998).

References

Bateson, G. (1972) *Steps to an Ecology of Mind*. Frogmore: Paladin.

Bauman, Z. (1998) *Globalization: The Human Consequences*. Cambridge: Polity.

Bauman, Z. (2011) *Collateral Damage: Social Inequalities in a Global Age*. Cambridge: Polity.

Berkes, F. (1999) *Sacred Ecology: Traditional Ecological Knowledge and Resource Management*. Philadelphia: Taylor and Francis.

Berkes, F. and Folke, C. (eds.) (1998) *Linking Social and Ecological Systems: Management Practices and Social Mechanisms for Building Resilience*. Cambridge: Cambridge University Press.

Berkes, F., Colding, J., and Folke, C. (eds.) (2003) *Navigating Social-Ecological Systems: Building Resilience for Complexity and Change*. Cambridge: Cambridge University Press.

Biersack, A. and Greenberg, J. B. (eds.) (2006) *Reimagining Political Ecology*. Durham: Duke University Press.

Blaikie, P. and Brookfield, H. (1987) *Land Degradation and Society*. London: Methuen.

Bohannan, P. (1955) Some Principles of Exchange and Investment among the Tiv. *American Anthropologist*, 57: 60–70.

Brand, F. S. and Jax, K. (2007) Focusing the Meaning(s) of Resilience: Resilience as a Descriptive Concept and a Boundary Object. *Ecology and Society*, 121, 23.

Bryant, R. L. and Bailey, S. (1997) *Third World Political Ecology*. London: Routledge.

Descola, P. (1994) *In the Society of Nature: A Native Ecology in Amazonia*. Cambridge: Cambridge University Press.

Dobson, R. V. G. (1993) *Bringing the Economy Home from the Market*. Montreal: Black Rose Books.

Douthwaite, R. (1999) *The Ecology of Money*. Totnes: Green Books.

Duffield, M. (2008) *Development, Security and Unending War: Governing the World of Peoples*. Cambridge: Polity.

Folke, C. (2006) Resilience: The Emergence of a Perspective for Social-Ecological Systems Analyses. *Global Environmental Change*, 16, 253–67.

Foster, J. B. and Magdoff, F. (2008) *The Great Financial Crisis: Causes and Consequences*. New York: Monthly Review Press.

Gotts, N. M. (2007) Resilience, Panarchy, and World-Systems Analysis. *Ecology and Society*, 12, 1, 24.

Gunderson, L. H. and Holling, C. S. (eds.) (2002) *Panarchy: Understanding Transformations in Human and Natural Systems*. Washington, DC: Island Press.

Hanley, N. (1998) Resilience in Social and Economic Systems: A Concept that Fails the Cost-Benefit Test? *Environment and Development Economics*, 3, 244–49.

Hart, K. (2000) *Money in an Unequal World*. New York: Texere.

Harvey, D. (2010) *The Enigma of Capital and the Crises of Capitalism*. Oxford: Oxford University Press.

Hornborg, A. (2001) *The Power of the Machine: Global Inequalities of Economy, Technology, and Environment*. Walnut Creek: AltaMira.

Hornborg, A. (2009) Zero-Sum World: Challenges in Conceptualizing Environmental Load Displacement and Ecologically Unequal Exchange in the World-System. *International Journal of Comparative Sociology*, 50, 3–4, 237–62.

Hornborg, A. (2011) *Global Ecology and Unequal Exchange: Fetishism in a Zero-Sum World*. London: Routledge.

Keil, R., Fawcett, L., Bell, D., and Penz, P. (eds.) (1998) *Political Ecology: Global and Local*. London: Routledge.

Kennedy, M. (1989) *Interest and Inflation Free Money*. Sparr: Permaculture Publications.

Kirchhoff, T., Brand, F. S., Hoheisel, D., and Grimm, V. (2010) The One-Sidedness and Cultural Bias of the Resilience Approach. *Gaia: Ecological Perspectives for Science and Society*, 19, 1, 25–32.

Lélé, S. (1998) Resilience, Sustainability, and Environmentalism. *Environment and Development Economics*, 3, 249–54.

Levin, S. A., Barrett, S., and Aniyar, S. (1998) Resilience in Natural and Socio-economic Systems. *Environment and Development Economics*, 3, 22–35.

Lévi-Strauss, C. (1966) *The Savage Mind*. Chicago: The University of Chicago Press.

McAnany, P. A. and Yoffee, N. (eds.) (2010) *Questioning Collapse: Human Resilience, Ecological Vulnerability, and the Aftermath of Empire*. Cambridge: Cambridge University Press.

Marcus, G. E. and Fischer, M. M. J. (1986) *Anthropology as Cultural Critique: An Experimental Moment in the Human Sciences*. Chicago: The University of Chicago Press.

Nadasdy, P. (2007) Adaptive Co-management and the Gospel of Resilience. In *Adaptive Co-management: Collaboration, Learning, and Multi-level Governance* (ed.) F. Berkes, D. Armitage, and N. Doubleday. Seattle: University of Washington Press, pp. 208–26.

Nelson, A. and Timmerman, F. (eds.) (2011) *Life Without Money: Building Fair and Sustainable Economies*. London: Pluto Press.

North, P. (2007) *Money and Liberation: The Micropolitics of Alternative Currency Movements*. Minneapolis: University of Minnesota Press.

North, P. (2010) *Local Money: How to Make It Happen in Your Community*. Totnes: Green Books.

Park, A. (2011) Beware Paradigm Creep and Buzzword Mutation. *The Forestry Chronicle* 87, 3, 337–44.

Parker, J. N. and Hackett, E. J. (2012) Hot Spots and Hot Moments in Scientific Collaborations and Social Movements. *American Sociological Review*, 77, 1, 21–44.

Paulson, S. and Gezon, L. (eds.) (2005) *Political Ecology across Spaces, Scales, and Social Groups*. Chapel Hill: Rutgers University Press.

Peet, R., Robbins, P., and Watts, M. J. (eds.) (2011) *Global Political Ecology*. London: Routledge.

Peet, R. and Watts, M. J. (eds.) (1996) *Liberation Ecologies: Environment, Development, Social Movements*. London: Routledge.

Peterson, G. (2000) Political Ecology and Ecological Resilience: An Integration of Human and Ecological Dynamics. *Ecological Economics*, 35, 323–36.

Rappaport, R. A. (1979) *Ecology, Meaning, and Religion*. Berkeley: North Atlantic Books.

Reid, J. (2012) The Disastrous and Politically Debased Subject of Resilience. *Development Dialogue*, 58: 67–79.

Schumacher, E. F. (1974) *Small is Beautiful: A Study of Economics as if People Mattered*. London: Abacus.

Schwartzman, D. (2008) The Limits to Entropy: Continuing Misuse of Thermodynamics in Environmental and Marxist Theory. *Science & Society*, 72, 1, 43–62.

Sebeok, T. A. (1994) *Signs: An Introduction to Semiotics*. Toronto: University of Toronto Press.

Sheridan, M. J. (2012) Water: Irrigation and Resilience in the Tanzanian Highlands. In *Ecology and Power: Struggles over Land and Material Resources in the Past, Present, and Future* (eds.) A. Hornborg, B. Clark, and K. Hermele. London: Routledge, 168–81.

Tainter, J. A. (1988) *The Collapse of Complex Societies*. Cambridge: Cambridge University Press.

von Thünen, J. H. [1826] (1966) *Von Thünen's Isolated State*. New York: Pergamon.

Wackernagel, M. and Rees, W. E. (1996) *Our Ecological Footprint: Reducing Human Impact on the Earth*. Gabriola Island: New Society Publishers.

Walker, J. and Cooper, M. (2011) Genealogies of Resilience: From Systems Ecology to the Political Economy of Crisis Adaptation. *Security Dialogue*, 42, 2, 143–60.

Weatherford, J. (1997) *The History of Money*. New York: Three Rivers Press.

Widgren, M. (2012) Resilience Thinking versus Political Ecology: Understanding the Dynamics of Small-scale, Labour-intensive Farming Landscapes. In *Resilience and the Cultural Landscape: Understanding and Managing Change in Human-shaped Environments*, (eds.) T. Plieninger and C. Bieling. Cambridge: Cambridge University Press, pp. 95–110.

Yoffee, N. and Cowgill, G. L. (eds.) (1988) *The Collapse of Ancient States and Civilizations*. Tucson: University of Arizona Press.

13

RESILIENCE, GOVERNMENTALITY AND NEOLIBERALISM

Jonathan Joseph

Introduction

This contribution sets out the case for seeing resilience in the context of contemporary forms of governance. These forms of governance are understood through the notions of governmentality and neoliberalism. This is a straightforward argument to a not so straightforward issue, since the ambiguities of both governmentality and neoliberalism have been highlighted in recent discussions. Nevertheless, this piece follows Walker and Cooper in claiming an intuitive ideological fit with a neoliberal philosophy of adaptation (Walker and Cooper, 2011, p. 154) and examines this philosophy of adaptation through a governmentality lens. This is justified on the basis of the rationality underlying most resilience discourse and on the basis of the various technologies and techniques that resilience helps to sustain. Starting with the philosophical underpinnings, this chapter suggests that resilience presents a particular vision of the world and our place within it that is consistent with neoliberal governance. In particular, it presents an ontology that deprives human agency of the potential to influence the wider world and which focuses attention instead on our ability to govern ourselves. The discussion then moves to the various technologies and techniques that fit with this approach to self-governance. This position is defended against alternative views, whilst recognising that there is certainly something new about resilience that has a modifying effect on existing discourse and practice.

Philosophical underpinnings

Although resilience has a variety of origins, we will concentrate here on its emergence from the ecology literature. This body of work is used to examine the relationship between ecological systems and human societies through ideas of complexity, multiple states and adaptability. Ecological and social components are linked by complex resource systems such as economic systems, institutions and organisations. Resilience is concerned with the ability of these systems to withstand shocks and survive disturbances, but examines this through focusing on complexity, heterogeneity, functional diversity and nonlinear ways of behaving (Gunderson *et al.*, 2002, p. 530). This fits with current thinking about the complexity and uncertainty of contemporary social and political life, while also maintaining an eye on the role of institutions and their adaptive capacities when dealing with crises and risks.

Resilience-thinking, as derived from the ecology literature, is more concerned with how societies and social systems can adapt to external changes, whether these be environmental, political or economic. C. S. Holling argues that rather than promoting a return to a stable equilibrium, the resilience approach emphasises change and heterogeneity (Holling, 1973, p. 17). Crises can be seen as useful opportunities to consider resource management, learning strategies and adaptation (Berkes *et al.*, 2003, p. 14–20). The focus on adaptation is probably the main or most useful characteristic of resilience. We will see that this is key to a governance strategy, but it is underpinned by the philosophical notion of complexity and the view that the wider world is neither understandable nor controllable. Resilience thinking presents a picture of the world that is decidedly fuzzy. Stable and enduring social relations are believed to have given way to complex networks of actors, each with their own individual pursuits. Our social engagements have no necessity to them and to survive the uncertainties of complex and contingent existence, people have to show their own initiative as active and reflexive agents capable of adaptive behaviour.

Moreover, our understanding of the world is unclear, with blurred boundaries between the external world and the knowledge we have of it. There is little consensus on the meaning of the concept of resilience itself because this too is bound up with blurred understanding and the limits of our knowledge. We cannot rely on any clear distinctions between external and internal, subject and object, cause and effect, and other frameworks that previously might have helped make sense of the modern world. Complex life is open-ended and subject to continual reinterpretation. All this would appear to rule out rational planning and intervention. Hence resilience and complexity thinking presents a variation of the globalisation view that the world is now beyond human control. But this leads to a refined understanding of governing which, according to Chandler (2014, p. 35), suggests we have to work 'through' the reality of complex life rather than working 'over' or 'against' it.

All this justifies what might be termed a neoliberal ontology that conceptualises the social world in a way that is consistent with neoliberal practices of governance. A belief in the contingency and complexity of adaptive systems supports the sociological view that society is moving away from enduring social relations based on such things as class and nation-state in favour of a view of the world as comprising individualised consumer-citizens with their own life-pursuits. This requires knowledge, awareness and risk-assessment that allows us to make our own way through the world. However, the world that is of concern to us is to be understood in terms of a shallow, surface ontology of networks, assemblages and contingent social connections. Since there are either no deeper or underlying relations, or we are denied the possibility of knowing anything more than what is immediately present to us, the knowledge we have of the world has to be practical and pragmatic, based on everyday understanding rather than deeper social inquiry.

Thus although resilience-thinking starts with broad ontological assumptions about the wider social world, we end up with the denial of the possibility of knowing anything more than our immediate engagements. While traditional behaviouralist assumptions about social life might be stripped of some of their rationalist underpinnings, resilience remains focused on what it is that people do in their immediate day-to-day activities rather than concerning itself with the deeper and more enduring relations of social life. Although we started with talk of social systems, resilience actually leads us away from such concerns and towards a focus on individual responsibility, adaptability and preparedness. This is consistent with the practices of contemporary forms of governance, as will be outlined in the next section.

Resilience as a form of governmentality

Michel Foucault's idea of governmentality best explains what resilience is and how it works. It does not explain everything there is to know about resilience, as critics have been quick to point out (e.g. Corry, 2014). However, we might follow Foucault's own advice to consider how resilience as an emergent set of practices operating at the local level might become 'invested, colonized, used, inflected, transformed, displaced, extended and so on by increasingly general mechanisms and forms of overall domination' (Foucault, 2004, p. 30). Foucault's own work is frustrating insofar as it does not really pursue this bigger picture but it does at least suggest that we can treat ideas like resilience as coming under the influence of a particular logic. Resilience will be treated as having a dominant neoliberal form throughout this chapter even though it is possible to consider the existence of alternative ways of understanding and practising resilience.

Foucault's genealogical account of governmentality traces its emergence to the development of capitalism across Western Europe and its connection to specifically liberal forms of rule. These develop an increasing concern for the population as the target of governance, with political economy as the appropriate means of knowledge and apparatuses of security as the main technical instrument (Foucault, 2007, p. 108). Foucault draws attention to how these forms of governance operate through promoting the 'natural processes' of the economic sphere. Government must be self-limiting and operate through the liberal principles of political economy and the freedom of economic processes (Foucault, 2008, p. 10). These, however, are not really natural and must be guaranteed by the state and the apparatuses of security.

That 'freedom' is a fabrication that needs to be actively constructed is clearly evident when we look at the emergence of neoliberalism as a governance strategy. First, it engaged in the forceful dismantling of the postwar institutional settlement through privatisation and 'de-statification' of economic life – often accompanied by a strengthening of the state's repressive role. Second, it promoted a new set of norms and values based on competitive conduct and entrepreneurial skill. This was forcefully introduced into various spheres of social life that had previously been protected from such logic, later being embedded through 'softer' notions like public–private partnerships, networked governance and active citizenship. These then appear to be working from a distance through the encouragement of appropriate behaviour. The state 'steps back' and encourages free conduct through an active intervention into civil society and the opening up of new areas to the logic of private enterprise and individual initiative. It helps create neoliberal subjects who are 'free' to take responsibility for their own life choices, but are expected to follow competitive rules of conduct. Neoliberal governmentality works through the social production of freedom and the 'management and organization of the conditions in which one can be free' (Foucault, 2008, p. 63–4).

It should be clear, therefore, why resilience can be seen through this particular lens. In stressing the importance of heightened self-awareness, reflexivity and learning, it encourages the idea of active citizenship where people take responsibility for their own well-being, particularly in the areas of risk and security. Whilst it has been noted that resilience constructs a picture of the world as beyond our control and comprehension, it does so in order to emphasise the virtues of preparedness and adaptability. This fits with neoliberal emphasis on the responsibility of individuals to govern themselves in the most appropriate ways and is therefore best seen as a liberal form of governance that operates from a distance through the means of political economy and the apparatuses of security. Such an approach, as mentioned, is developed in the work of Walker and Cooper as well as others who use a Foucauldian framework such as might be found in O'Malley's (2010) claim that resilience is not just a reactive model that teaches people how to 'bounce back', but should also be seen as a means to create adaptable subjects capable of responding to and exploiting situations of radical uncertainty. This, in a sense, is back to the philosophical underpinnings – it is dependent on the picture of the type of world or system we live in as well as its component parts and how they interact. Resilience, in bringing complexity theory to this understanding, adds something new, but it reinforces established neoliberal ideas about human behaviour and indeed contributes to the further embedding of associated norms and expectations.

This is a picture that applies to what governmentality scholars like Nikolas Rose have called 'advanced liberal societies' (Rose, 1996). We might question whether strategies such as resilience building can work in such a way outside this advanced liberal context (Joseph 2010). However, it is clearly part of the new strategies of global governance being promoted by the advanced liberal states and the leading international organisations. Global governmentality can already be seen across a range of policy areas like development, poverty reduction and humanitarian aid. Like domestic liberal governance, these govern from a distance by shaping the conduct of conduct, but in this case it is the conduct of governments and key personnel that is targeted. These approaches regulate the behaviour of states from a distance through encouraging them to 'freely' act in a responsible way. Poorer states are made responsible through 'ownership' and engaging in 'partnerships' with Western donors, or else they are made to feel accountable to various 'stakeholders' from the international community, civil society and the private sphere. Countries must open up their institutions and practices of governance to external monitoring and scrutiny. As Rita Abrahamsen argues, this process appears to empower poorer countries but is actually a means of conferring various obligations and duties in relation to development targets, levels of performance and objectives of social development (Abrahamsen, 2004, p. 1461).

Global governmentality, like domestic forms, works from a distance through invoking private and civil society actors. It governs through the market and the competences of the private sector. It lowers expectations of what international organisations and Western governments will do directly. Resilience builds on this by emphasising the ideas of responsibility, self-awareness and self-regulation. It remains committed to the capacity-building approach of existing approaches but modifies this by recognising the failings of liberal peace approaches and emphasising a more practical and flexible understanding of particular challenges. Implicit is a critique of liberalism's centralised, anticipated planning though a belief that governance is context-bound and that society is in constant flux. Chandler suggests that resilience is playing a pivotal role in the shift away from classical liberal interventionist discourses and towards greater emphasis on preventive intervention. This means a focus on 'the empowerment and responsibility of agency at the local societal level, rather than upon the assertion of the right of external sovereign agency' (Chandler 2012, p. 223). However, Haldrup and Rosén continue to see this as compatible with a neoliberal view because neoliberalism, at essence, rejects 'hands on intervention' in favour of 'hands off facilitation' (Haldrup and Rosén, 2013, p. 143).

Foucault argues that liberalism works not through the imperative of freedom, but through the social production of freedom (2008, p. 63). Global governance works by problematising the freedom and autonomy of individuals and institutions in poorer countries. If freedom, as Chandler suggests, is defined as the capacity to make the right decisions and respond correctly to external problems (Chandler, 2010, p. 125), then projects such as state-building, development programmes and resilience-building work on the assumption that intervention is necessary because people lack an adequate understanding to cope with freedom and autonomy. Like domestic resilience strategies, this emphasises the idea of the independence of the governed, but in contrast to domestic strategies, these work by highlighting the lack of independence. This has justified a paternalistic (or pastoral) discourse of failed states, trusteeship and capacity building and now helps us understand resilience as 'the capacity [or lack] to positively or successfully adapt to external problems or threats' (Chandler, 2012, p. 217). But as Chandler argues, the resilient subject is no longer conceived as passive or as lacking agency – as was the case in earlier interventions to save 'victims' – but is now understood as an active agent, capable of achieving self-transformation (Chandler, 2012, p. 17). Again, it is worth making the contrast between the situation within the advanced liberal societies, where citizens are appealed to as resilient subjects capable of taking care of their own security and well-being, and the situation in poorer countries, where the resilience strategies of international organisations invoke such resilient subjects and institutions, but use their lack of capacity as the means by which to discipline their governments. We will now look at this in relation to some specific interventions.

The practices of resilience

In the UK the government now promotes resilience as part of its counter-terrorism strategy (CONTEST). The thinking behind this approach is that resilience best enables communities to adapt to new security risks, withstand threats and show continuity in the face of adversity. As noted above, most resilience-thinking is underpinned by a fatalistic view of the wider world, with systemic shocks seen as an inevitability that cannot be stopped but only prepared for:

> The purpose . . . is to mitigate the impact of a terrorist attack where that attack cannot be stopped. This includes work to bring a terrorist attack to an end and to increase our resilience so we can recover from its aftermath.
>
> *(Home Office, 2011, p. 13)*

This fatalism is also clearly present in the UK's 2010 National Security Strategy:

> we cannot prevent every risk as they are inherently unpredictable. To ensure we are able to recover quickly when risks turn into actual damage to our interests, we have to promote resilience, both locally and nationally. Ensuring that the public is fully informed of the risks we face is a critical part of this approach.
>
> *(Cabinet Office, 2010, p. 25)*

The counter-terrorism *Prepare* strategy is therefore focused on informing the public about the risks they face. It is also very business focused, supporting business continuity, helping businesses prepare for disruption and enhancing cooperation between public- and private-sector infra-structure providers (Home Office, 2011, p. 94). Rather than having anything specifically to do with terrorist attacks or disaster response, this approach is better understood as a means of population management through installing a state of mind that emphasises preparedness, self-awareness and willingness to learn and adapt. The CONTEST strategy is perhaps less concerned with making the UK's physical infrastructure more resilient than with building the resilience of communities and businesses to terrorism and disruption. This is about informing the public, sharing information, building community cohesion, working with the private sector and making the necessary plans for business continuity. This is premised on a certain view of the relationship between the state, society and its citizens, promoting an understanding of the duties and responsibilities of each, of the role of government, civil society and the private sector. Resilience introduces a market logic of competitiveness and initiative. It shifts responsibility on to local actors to deal with risk and possible adversity.

In 2011 the UK government published its *Strategic National Framework on Community Resilience*. This makes the roles and responsibilities of government and community very clear – 'the Government role is to support, empower and facilitate; ownership should always be retained by communities who have chosen to get involved in this work' (Cabinet Office, 2011, p. 14). This is a clear expression of a belief in governance from a distance through encouraging communities to be active and responsible. As with current international development discourse, there is talk of local ownership and empowering local communities while the role of government 'is not to dictate or measure what is being or should be done locally' (Cabinet Office, 2011, p. 8). This is presented as encouraging free conduct: 'to support and enable local activity by making existing good practice available to others who are interested, and removing the barriers and debunking the myths which prevent communities from taking local action' (ibid).

The reality is nothing of the sort and shows how this form of neoliberal governance combines an appeal to artificially contrived freedoms with forceful state action. The UK's 2004 Civil Contingencies Act compels local businesses and providers to make risk assessments, draw up contingency plans and run training exercises. People are made to participate in Regional Resilience Forums and Regional Civil Contingencies Committees. It clearly *is* the case that government dictates what should be done locally. Rather than genuinely devolving powers and letting local actors decide for themselves, this represents a devolution of responsibilities, instructing us on how we ought to behave backed up with a strict interpretation of what constitutes 'best practice'. This reflects the reality of neoliberal governmentality with the state's responsibilities shifted onto individuals, communities and the private sector. Rather than the state providing direct protection, the population itself is responsibilised in a top-down manner. This is promoted as an essential strategy in an increasingly complex and uncertain world. In reality, this works to naturalise the neoliberal condition and to install a greater sense of individual responsibility and self-discipline in the context of the state retreating from many of its former obligations.

As has been briefly discussed above, this is not necessarily the case when we switch attention to resilience-building in an international context. The UK government's Department for International Development (DFID) has been instrumental in promoting a resilience strategy as part of its disaster emergencies and development work. It talks of resilience as the ability of countries, communities and households to manage change in the face of shocks and stress (DFID, 2011a, p. 7) and divides this into four areas. Economic resilience is concerned with how economies can withstand shocks, physical resilience refers to vital infrastructure, social resilience builds on DFID's governance work to strengthen institutions, while environmental resilience relates to the ability to cope with natural hazards (DFID 2011b, p. 8). In addition DFID talks of national resilience as 'helping governments and civil society prepare for and respond to disasters through training and equipping the relevant institutions' (DFID, 2011b, p. 8). This is vital in supporting fragile states, replacing a 'substitution service delivery' with a better understanding of how to support weak institutions and maintain life-saving services (DFID 2011b, p. 8). All this points far less to individual and community resilience and more to larger political, economic and security concerns. Of course there are biopolitical issues of concern, such as population vulnerability, leadership capacities and impacts on women and girls (DFID 2012). But global governmentality is more concerned with what goes on at the state level, developing strategies to get governments to behave in accordance with international norms.

In general, we can understand resilience as part of a new phase where the international community does less while expecting more. In the following passage from a DFID strategy document we find the argument that:

> Ultimately, it is a country government's responsibility to help protect its own population's capacity to resist and adapt to shocks. But the international community has a critical role to support national and local governments, civil society and other partners to help build resilience to future disasters. By doing so, we also safeguard our broader aid investments and the progress made in achieving the Millennium Development Goals.
>
> *(DFID, 2011c, p. 1)*

Safeguarding is done by subjecting countries to a system of monitoring and assessment. DFID talks of developing progress indicators for embedding resilience, which objective countries must meet by 2015. Country offices and DFID departments will decide upon appropriate indicators (DFID, 2011a, p. 14). DFID also uses a number of performance indicators to measure its own work (DFID, 2013). Again this indicates governance from a distance and the shaping of conduct through indicators, peer review and good practice, although given the vagueness and ambiguity in the meaning and use of resilience, international organisations are still in the process of deciding exactly how it should be measured. DFID itself has commissioned a report to look at ways to measure aspects of resilience, particularly exposure, sensitivity and adaptive capacity (Brooks *et al.*, 2014).

DFID is indeed pioneering the resilience approach, commissioning reports and embedding resilience into its various regional strategies. This fits neatly with the policies adopted by a range of UK government departments. This is not the case elsewhere. For example, in Germany resilience thinking has not yet made significant advances in domestic politics. However, resilience has been adopted by German development policy. The *Strategy on Transitional Development Assistance: Strengthening Resilience – Shaping Transition* produced by the Federal Ministry for Economic Cooperation and Development even takes its definition of resilience from DFID, while the main themes of the paper are indistinguishable from the DFID papers just mentioned. Here we find the same arguments for strengthening the resilience of individuals, communities, civil society and institutions to face complex crisis situations and to bridge medium- and long-term measures (BMZ, 2013, p. 5) with emphasis on efficiency, effectiveness, coherence and complementarity (BMZ, 2013 p. 9).

These arguments are also prominent in the European Union's external policies. The discourse is also very close to DFID's, with the EU's Action Plan for Resilience using the idea of country-ownership to assert that national governments have primary responsibility for building resilience. National strategies require firm political commitments and accountability, and may require not only technical support but institutional change. It is clearly stated that, ultimately, individual countries have responsibility to progress towards resilience (based on meeting key development standards that are decided by the international community) (European Commission 2013a, p. 3). EU assistance will take the form of development 'partnerships' that operate from a distance through offering advice and expertise. The EU will 'put in place a framework for measuring the impact and results' of this support for resilience (European Commission, 2012, p. 11–12). This relates to two concerns – first in relation to the resilience programmes themselves, and second in relation to coordinating the EU's own activities. As an organisation driven by a logic of coordination and harmonising its methods and policies, the EU's resilience approach continually emphasises the need to strengthen collaboration, improve effectiveness and ensure consistent understanding and application of internationally agreed standards and guidelines in the delivery of aid. The EU strategy will 'systemise lessons learning' on crisis response while maintaining the 'regular programme of external evaluation and audit, thereby contributing to increasing the effectiveness of Community funded aid operations' (European Council 2008, p. 29).

It is clear then that DFID plays a leadership role in international development and disaster reduction that is certainly more difficult in other policy areas. This is possible because international organisations already have a much stronger Anglo-Saxon character, taking their lead from the World Bank and the United Nations, where an Anglo-Saxon influence has long dominated policy thinking. DFID argues that actors such as the World Bank Global Facility for Disaster Reduction and Recovery and the United Nations International Strategy for Disaster Reduction are necessary partners in effective resilience-building, perhaps as convenors who can help network together a range of other actors such as national governments, civil society, communities and the private sector (DFID, 2011c, p. 16). On issues such as this, the EU is in full agreement. However, getting EU member states to implement neoliberal resilience strategies into their domestic policies is another matter. The European Commission does strongly push a neoliberal agenda to restructure social relations and rethink the European social model by promoting labour market flexibilisation, economic competitiveness, privatisation, public–private partnerships, limitations on government involvement and active citizenship. But the EU's own assessment of this is that member states have failed to rise to the challenge (European Commission, 2010).

In comparison to other EU member states, the UK is much further down this neoliberal path and is therefore much more strongly promoting and implementing resilience strategies across a range of policy areas. This partly explains why UK government policy is able to place so much emphasis on community and individual responsibility, learning and awareness. The Strategic National Framework on Community Resilience defines resilient individuals and communities in terms of enterprise and initiative. Resilient individuals are described as people with awareness of their skills, experience and resources and how best to use these during emergencies. They familiarise themselves with the kinds of risks that might affect them and understand their vulnerabilities so they can prepare for the consequences of emergencies. These individuals are members of resilient communities who are actively involved in influencing and making decisions affecting them. This means taking steps to make their homes and families more resilient, taking an interest in their environment and acting in the interest of the community to protect assets and facilities (Cabinet Office, 2011, p. 15).

By contrast, the resilience approach of international organisations like DFID, the EU, the UNDP, the IMF, the World Bank and others is of a somewhat different nature. Rather than devolving power away from states and on to governmentalised populations, resilience is applied to populations in order to governmentalise poorer states into conforming to international norms and expectations. Rather than constituting a break from previous strategy, resilience invokes new notions of uncertainty and complexity in order to intensify the process of institutional reform and monitoring. The language or philosophy of resilience may be a bit different. It may conform to current intellectual trends. But resilience approaches are neither post-liberal nor post-governmentality, but instead use post-liberal language to reinforce (neo) liberal governmentality at all levels.

Conclusion

Resilience is about making individuals, communities and countries better able to respond to crises, threats and shocks. There is currently a debate about whether resilience is about 'bouncing back' and restoring basic structure and functioning or whether it is about a more radical reorganisation and adaptation of means of operating to better deal with a complex environment (see DFID, 2011a, p. 6). The latter approach, now favoured by the World Bank, can be used to attack existing social or institutional arrangements that do not conform to a neoliberal model. David Chandler describes attempts to retain the same basic structure as a 'classical' understanding of resilience, while the emphasis on a changed state is a 'post-classical' understanding (Chandler, 2014, p. 6). There may or may not be philosophical underpinnings to the 'post-classical' approach. The main thing is that it supports the neoliberal restructuring of 'classical' practices.

The restructuring role of resilience is of more urgency in the areas of global governance and European Union politics than it might be in the Anglo-Saxon world, where the key theme is consolidation of existing neoliberal practices. In the UK, resilience is concerned with continuing the process of devolving responsibility and privatising state powers so that governance can occur from a distance through a set of normative assumptions backed up with the threat of enhanced state coercion, which should be considered as the necessary flip-side of neoliberal 'freedom'. Inside the EU, the resilience approach must still engage with the debate about social Europe and the future trajectory of welfare and labour reform. The neoliberal view has yet to gain full ascendency, as the failure of strategies such as the Lisbon Agenda testify. However, the attempt to embed neoliberal governmentality continues, as might be seen from discussions about European counter-terrorism and critical infrastructure protection (European Commission, 2013b). In the case of global governance, the poorer states are in a weak position in relation to the governmentalizing powers of international organisations. However, the resilience agenda might offer some possibilities to challenge or reinterpret neoliberal projects through greater emphasis on local involvement and hybrid forms of compromise.

The dominant resilience approaches embrace a privatised view of the world where the state steps back and allows partnerships to develop between key stakeholders and the most informed sections of civil society. This strengthens the natural appeal of governance from a distance. Resilience-building is consistent with existing capacity-building approaches, albeit with a greater emphasis on the capacities of people premised on a lesser commitment to putting resources into building institutional capacities. Indeed, this presents something of a paradox. Given less inclination to put resources into mediating institutions, the direct encouragement of the freedom of the governed depends on the increased possibility of direct coercive intervention by the state. This may take the softer form of governments such as that in the UK forcing through compliance with resilience-building initiatives, or it may take the harder form of eroded civil liberties and enhanced police and state powers.

Resilience may open some space for negotiation with the local, particularly in the context of scaled-back international interventions. If it is accompanied by enhanced coercive powers, then the alternative may need to be stronger resistance rather than negotiation. By and large resilience is a conservative concept, albeit one that has a shifting meaning depending on the particular context and wider objectives of governance strategies. Understood in its dominant neoliberal form, resilience is a fabrication that relies on active government intervention. Far from giving power back to civil society or to communities, resilience-building depends on the construction of a sphere of governance that is overseen from a distance either by national governments, international organisations or the international community. Rather than representing a bottom-up organic development, resilience is used in a fairly instrumental way as a tool of governance that places particular emphasis on responsible conduct. Contemporary conditions have given rise to certain practices of governance though which the idea of resilience finds a comfortable home. Should these wider practices be challenged, or should they come up against significant contradictions within the socio-economic system – the very conditions that resilience thinking manages to obfuscate – then we might find that the time of resilience has come and gone.

References

Abrahamsen, R. (2004) The Power of Partnerships in Global Governance. *Third World Quarterly*, 25, 8, 1453–67.

Berkes, F., Colding, J. and Folke, C. (2003) Introduction. In Berkes, F., Colding, J. and Folke, C. (eds), *Navigating Social-Ecological Systems: Building Resilience for Complexity and Change*. Cambridge: Cambridge University Press, pp. 1–32.

BMZ (2013) *Strategy on Transitional Development Assistance: Strengthening Resilience – Shaping Transition*. Bonn: BMZ.

Brooks, N., Aure, E. and Whiteside, M. (2014) *Assessing the Impact of ICF Programmes on Household and Community Resilience to Climate Variability and Climate Change*. Evidence on Demand.

Cabinet Office (2010) *A Strong Britain in an Age of Uncertainty: The National Security Strategy*. London: Cabinet Office.

Cabinet Office (2011) *Strategic National Framework on Community Resilience*. London: Cabinet Office.

Chandler, D. (2010) *International State-building: The Rise of Post-liberal Governance*. Abingdon: Routledge.

Chandler, D. (2012) Resilience and Human Security: The Post-interventionist Paradigm. *Security Dialogue*, 43, 3, 213–29.

Chandler, D. (2014) *Resilience: The Governance of Complexity*. Abingdon: Routledge.

Corry, O. (2014) From Defense to Resilience: Environmental Security beyond Neo-liberalism. *International Political Sociology*, 8, 256–74.

DFID (2011a) *Defining Disaster Resilience: A DFID Approach Paper*. London: Department for International Development.

DFID (2011b) *Humanitarian Emergency Response Review: UK Government Response*. London: Department for International Development.

DFID (2011c) *Defining Disaster Resilience: What does it mean for DFID?* London: Department for International Development.

DFID (2012) *Operational Plan 2011–2015 DFID Growth and Resilience Department (GRD)*. London: Department for International Development.

DFID (2013) *2013 Accelerating Progress on Disaster Resilience in DFID Country Programmes: 'Catalytic Fund'*. London: Department for International Development.

European Commission (2010) *Lisbon Strategy Evaluation Document*. Brussels: European Commission.

European Commission (2012) *EU Approach to Resilience: Learning from Food Security Crises*. Brussels: European Commission.

European Commission (2013a) *Action Plan for Resilience in Crisis Prone Countries 2013–2020*. Brussels: European Commission.

European Commission (2013b) *Commission Staff Working Document on a New Approach to the European Programme for Critical Infrastructure Protection: Making European Critical Infrastructures More Secure*. Brussels: European Commission.

European Council (2008) *European Consensus on Humanitarian Aid*. Brussels: European Council.

Foucault, M. (2004) *Society Must Be Defended*. Harmondsworth: Penguin Books.

Foucault, M. (2007) *Security, Territory, Population*. Basingstoke: Palgrave Macmillan.

Foucault, M. (2008) *The Birth of Biopolitics*. Basingstoke: Palgrave Macmillan.

Gunderson, Lance, Holling, C. S., Pritchard, L. and Peterdon, G. D. (2002) Resilience. In Mooney, Harold A. and Canadell, Josep G. (eds), *The Earth System: Biological and Ecological Dimensions of Global Environmental Change*, Volume 2, Chichester: John Wiley and Sons, pp. 530–31.

Haldrup, S. and Rosén, F. (2013) Developing Resilience: A Retreat from Grand Planning. *Resilience: International Policies, Practices and Discourses*, 1, 2, 130–45.

Holling, C. S. (1973) Resilience and Stability of Ecological Systems. *Annual Review of Ecology and Systematics*, 4, 1–23.

Home Office (2011) *CONTEST: The United Kingdom's Strategy for Countering Terrorism*. London: Home Office.

Joseph, J. (2010) The Limits of Governmentality: Social Theory and the International. *European Journal of International Relations*, 16, 2, 223–46.

O'Malley, P. (2010) Resilient Subjects: Uncertainty, Warfare and Liberalism. *Economy and Society*, 39, 4, 488–509.

Rose, N. (1996) Governing 'Advanced' Liberal Democracies. In Barry, A., Osborne, T. and Rose, N. (eds), *Foucault and Political Reason*. London: UCL Press.

Walker, J. and Cooper, M. (2011) Geneaologies of Resilience: From Systems of Ecology to the Political Economy of Crisis Adaptation. *Security Dialogue*, 42, 2, 143–60.

PART V

Environment

14

CLIMATE CHANGE AND SECURITY

From paradigmatic resilience to resilience multiple

Delf Rothe

Introduction

Resilience—a concept with a long history in disciplines such as psychology or ecology—has recently made it to the desks of security practitioners, national policy-makers and IR (international relations) scholars. In a world of complexity the idea of resilience, as the ability of social, economic or ecological systems to autonomously recover after shocks and to adapt to changing environmental conditions, appears promising. Yet, while everybody seems to talk (about) resilience there is hardly any consent about the concrete ontology of resilience (Brassett *et al.*, 2013, p. 222). Being related to things as diverse as the human mind, energy infrastructure, ecosystems, and World of Warcraft characters (as a quick Google search shows) the signifier of resilience becomes increasingly emptied. Resilience seems to be everything—ideology, discourse, governmentality, strategy or assemblage—yet it is anything but a coherent or fixed program. It is continuously transmogrified and deformed by its concrete spatio-temporal context (O'Malley, 2011, p. 55).

In this chapter I give answers to two related questions: First, I seek to explain why resilience could recently become such a prominent political concept. Second, I shed some light on the ontology of resilience by exploring reasons for its heterogeneity. While scholars often acknowledge the ambiguity of resilience (Walker and Cooper, 2011) it is seldom taken into account analytically (Brassett *et al.* 2013, p. 225). Advocates as well as critics of resilience tend to present it as a rather coherent discourse or even a political paradigm, thereby blurring contradictions and fissures in the actual political practices of resilience (see Corry, 2014, p. 260–262; Dunn-Cavelty *et al.*, 2015, p. 8). Other works have instead tried to grasp the heterogeneity of resilience by distinguishing between different ideal-types, such as engineering, ecological, and socio-ecological resilience (see Bourbeau, 2013; Methmann and Oels, 2015). While such approaches have clearly advanced the conceptual debate on resilience, I would argue that resilience in practice often transcends these deductive typologies. In this chapter, I hence explicitly focus on the incoherence and *ambiguity* of resilience *on the ground* and argue that it is one important reason of its success in security politics. Rather than posing a range of resilience ideal-types, which are then filled with empirical evidence, I study the multiple meanings of resilience inductively by tracing the concrete articulations and practices of resilience in the discourse on climate change-related security risks (in the following abbreviated as climate security) in the United Kingdom (UK). Discourses and practices on climate security in the UK represent an extreme case to study the multiplicity of governmental resilience strategies. First of all it's an extreme case, because the UK can be seen as the heartland of resilience discourse (see Joseph, 2013b) and hence we should assume to find a rather coherent governmental take on resilience; and, second, I will decidedly concentrate on official government discourses and practices. Recently, different works have shown that there are counter-projects to a hegemonic, governmental logic of resilience, pursuing hidden scripts and articulating alternative understandings of resilience (Corry, 2014; Grove, 2013). The present contribution goes beyond this claim in that it studies resilience at the level of government strategy and administration and shows that even at that level there is no coherence but rather a strategic ambiguity of resilience.

Besides shedding light on the ontology of resilience, I try to close a second research gap in the IR literature on resilience: this is the relation of resilience to other technologies of governing an insecure future. Scholars working on resilience usually stress that the approach marks a shift away from classical practices of risk-management.[1] Different, sometimes contradicting, terms to describe the relation of resilience to the future have been used.[2] And it appears to be accepted that resilience represents a post-risk approach of governing the future that can be clearly distinguished from other security logics including prevention, preemption, or preparedness (O'Malley, 2011, p. 45). However, in practice the delineations between these concepts are fluid. In this chapter I hence set out to trace the "multiple temporalities of resilience" that Dunn-Cavelty *et al.* (2015, p. 11) postulate in their introduction to the recent *Security Dialogue* special issue on resilience. Considering this multiplicity, I show that—when it comes to the actual practices of resilience—the latter often is not opposed to but actually goes hand in hand with other forms of risk-management and anticipation.

I proceed in three analytical steps: In a first step I outline what I would call the paradigmatic approach to resilience. I develop an alternative to this paradigmatic approach drawing on Stephen Collier's (2009) concept of topologies of power. In a second step, in section three, I turn to the empirical case study of climate security in the UK and start with tracing different *discursive strands*, or storylines of resilience in this discourse. This archaeological approach of studying the discursive deep structure of resilience is complemented by an analysis of *resilience practices* in the governance of climate security risks. I show how resilience becomes enacted in very different ways and how it thereby emerges as a floating signifier—a quilting point that weaves together diverse practices of governing an insecure future in a complex governmental landscape of climate resilience.

From paradigmatic resilience to resilience multiple

Recent critical literature on resilience often resembles what I would call a *paradigmatic approach* to resilience. In a nutshell, a paradigmatic approach understands resilience as a single discourse, governmentality, or paradigm, which has recently become dominant in international politics.

Paradigmatic resilience

There are five core characteristics which are usually ascribed to resilience thinking in international politics. First, the paradigmatic approach stresses that resilience draws on a particular *ontology of emergent or general complexity* (Chandler, 2014, p. 49). Deduced from complex systems research, this ontology revolves around the concepts of non-linear change and connectivity painting a picture of the world politics as an assemblage of complex, interconnected networks (Kaufmann, 2013, p. 54–56). Second, critical authors have argued that resilience thinking includes an *epistemology of limited knowledge*, stressing the limit to prediction in a world of radical complexity and contingency (Kaufmann 2013, p. 58). It is opposed to classical risk-management resilience, hence "does not imagine specific scenarios against which defences (or pre-emptive attacks) must be prepared" (O'Malley, 2011, p. 55). At the level of policy, this leads, third, to the acceptance that certain risks and dangers are unpredictable and ultimately inevitable (Walker and Cooper, 2011, p. 145–149; Zebrowski, 2013, p. 166). Hence, the focus of policies shifts from the mitigation of risks to the *vulnerability* of populations at risk (Evans and Reid, 2013, p. 84). Fourth, it is criticized that under a resilience paradigm the promise of the state to protect its citizens mutates into a responsibility of the vulnerable to adapt themselves to a changing and ever-more dangerous environment (Reid, 2013, p. 362–363). At the same time, the focus of security politics would shift from external threats towards the inner coping capacities of a community (Chandler, 2013b, p. 218; Evans and Reid, 2013, p. 87). As a result, national and international security policies are increasingly modeled along the lines of a *neoliberal market-driven approach*, which seeks to activate the self-help potential of the vulnerable (Joseph, 2013a, p. 49). And finally, such policies require a particular type of institutional design based on *flat hierarchies and connectivity* (Reid 2013, p. 361)—as paradigmatically expressed in the Anglo-Saxon notion of network governance (Joseph, 2013b, p. 254).

The works I have summarized under the label of a paradigmatic approach have provided valuable insights for our understanding of resilience as a political concept and its problems. In particular, these studies have highlighted the convergence of complexity and neoliberal economic thinking (Walker and Cooper, 2011; Zebrowski, 2013) and helped to make sense of the changing understanding of security and a related shift of responsibility from the state to society and the individual (Chandler, 2013a). Such an understanding of resilience as a mode of self-government under complexity is certainly important—for example, it undergirds many self-improvement manuals that have been quite successful in the mid-2000s (O'Malley, 2011, p. 58). However, it is only one version of resilience among others. Understanding resilience as a discourse or governmentality *in singular*, bears the problem that inner contradictions and fissures of resilience practices are systematically ignored. As Brasset *et al.* acknowledge: "common among both managerial approaches that see resilience as positive value and governmentality perspectives [criticizing it] is that resilience works" (Brassett *et al.*, 2013, p. 225).

Resilience multiple

I would suggest starting empirical research from the idea of *resilience "multiple"* (see Randalls and Simon in this volume; also Randalls, 2013), to stress that in international politics there is no single, coherent concept of resilience. Resilience multiple implies that there is more than one rationality or governmental logic of resilience, but less than many (Mol, 1999)—the meaning of resilience is ambiguous, but certainly not arbitrary.[3] I argue that the tendency to overlook incoherence and fissures in resilience strategies is not, lastly, due to the theoretical and methodological commitment of critical resilience studies to a Foucauldian governmentality perspective (Corry, 2014, pp. 262–263). By using governmentality not as an analytical term to study different knowledge-power complexes in an open way, but as a particular neoliberal form of political power drawing on technologies of self-responsibilization and government at-the-distance (Bulley, 2013; Joseph, 2013a), the resulting heuristic inevitably narrows the analytical perspective and blurs empirical findings that do not fit its pre-established categories.

As a way to avoid the harmonization tendency inherent in the governmentality approach, I suggest following Stephen Collier and understanding power–knowledge relations' complex topologies of power. Collier starts from the observation that Michel Foucault in his later work turned away from totalizing epochal analyses of power–knowledge formations. "Instead, increasingly he will examine how existing elements are taken up and recombined" (Collier, 2009, p. 90).

Other than suggested by the notion of neoliberal governmentality, for Foucault there is no overarching rationality or logic of government:

> One technology of power may provide guiding norms and an orienting telos. But it does not saturate all power relations. Rather, it suggests a configurational principle that determines how heterogeneous elements – techniques, institutional arrangements, material forms and other technologies of power – are taken up and recombined.
>
> *(Collier 2009, p. 89)*

For the case under investigation, this implies that the concrete form and substance of resilience is subject to a temporally and spatially specific (re-)combination of governmental rationalities and technologies: "the space of problematization is a topological space, and thinking is a driver of recombinatorial processes" (Collier 2009, p. 96). A topological analysis of power hence seeks to map how various technologies of power coexist, are constantly refined, (re-)deployed and combined in different contexts (Collier, 2009, p.80). Rather than thought of as a new paradigm of governance, resilience should thus be understood as a *configurational principle*, which allows for a reconfiguration and re-definition of already existing governmental technologies and rationalities (see also Methmann and Oels, 2015, p. 58). In this way, I understand resilience as a re-articulation of existing modes of risk-governance and anticipation including precaution, preparedness and preemption and not so much as their conceptual successor.

Opposed to earlier discourse analyses of resilience, I move from genealogy to archaeology, or from discursive surface structure to the deep structure of language.[4] Put more simply, I am not so much interested in what is being said about resilience by whom, but in *how* resilience becomes articulated through collective symbols, including metaphors, iconic symbols, analogies, and tropes such as metonymy, pars-pro-toto, or catachresis (Hajer, 2006). I trace how these collective symbols have been condensed into a set of storylines. In a second methodological step, I turn away from deep structure towards governmental programs and practices. I study how resilience becomes implemented, practiced, or enacted in different institutional contexts. To theorize resilience in a way that accounts for its heterogeneity, I then distinguish between three privileged *logics of resilience*.[5]

Resilience in UK climate security discourse

Climate security discourse, which started to become prominent in the early 2000s, had become hegemonic by 2007. At that time there was broad consent amongst government officials, strategic think tanks, NGOs, the media, as well as bureaucrats from different UK departments about the security risks of climate change for the UK. Resilience entered the stage of climate security discourse by the late 2000s and until today, managed to become the hegemonic demand in that very discourse (Boas and Rothe 2016). However, resilience in UK climate security discourse is far from being a coherent concept. Rather, there are competing storylines of climate security, each of which produces a different political moral and articulates resilience—as an answer to climate insecurities—in a considerably different way. Table 14.1 summarizes the different storylines to show how they differ with respect to their temporality and their problematization of particular limits to knowledge (about the future).

A first observation that one can make by studying UK climate security discourse is that climate change in the UK has been securitized through storylines of risk (see, e.g., Cabinet Office, 2008, p. 15). The discourse on climate security usually distinguishes between primary and secondary risks for the UK (Cabinet Office, 2008, p. 89). Primary risks are those potential harms for the UK

Table 14.1 Different storylines of climate security and their relation to resilience

	Climate risk and climate conflict	Climate catastrophe	Complexity (ideal-typical resilience)
Collective symbols	Mechanistic metaphors; personification	Motional metaphors; metaphor of the tipping point	Network metaphors; motional metaphors
Temporality	Static; clear distinction between past, present, and future	Teleological; development towards an endpoint	Processual; limits between present and future become blurred
Limits to knowledge	Methodological uncertainty: using the right methods the future can be calculated	Epistemological uncertainty: future cannot be known but actively shaped	Epistemological and ontological uncertainty: The world cannot be intentionally shaped

that directly follow from a warming trend, such as an increased risk of flooding. Of particular importance here is the self-understanding of the UK as an island—both in terms of its vulnerabilities and of the importance of self-reliance and self-sufficiency (Cabinet Office, 2009, p. 39). To cope with the direct risks posed by climate change, the UK has implemented a comprehensive climate impacts program including a periodically conducted national climate risk-assessment. The first report from 2012 comprises an assessment of over 700 different climate-related risks for the UK within the time frames of 2020, 2050, and 2080 (DEFRA, 2012, p.viii). The risk-assessment provides the knowledge resources for the development of a National Adaptation Programme (NAP). As the executive summary of the report states:

> Although we do not know the likelihood future changes in the UK's climate, we know enough to present a range of possible outcomes, which can be used to inform adaptation planning. For this purpose potential climate risks to the UK have been categorised according to their magnitude, "confidence" and the "urgency for action."
>
> *(DEFRA, 2012, p. xi)*

Climate risk calculation and the compiling of comprehensive risk registers are seen as a prerequisite to produce a climate resilient UK. The close relation between prediction and resilience is perfectly mirrored in the foreword to the 2013 NAP Report "Making the country resilient to a changing climate". In this foreword the Secretary of State for Environment, Owen Paterson, argued that:

> Britain's expertise in areas such as weather forecasting, flood modelling, infrastructure and insurance are already coming to the fore to prepare us for the kinds of events we might see more often. Indeed, the UK is already one of the global leaders in this *industry of the future.*
>
> *(DEFRA, 2013, p. 1; emphasis added)*

This "industry of the future" as part of climate resilience governance contradicts the picture of resilience as the end of prediction painted by a paradigmatic understanding of resilience.

The first set of risk-narratives focusing on direct climate risks constructs an antagonism between dangerous climate change, presented as an external enemy through metaphors of personification (see also Methmann and Rothe, 2013, p. 109), and the UK as a threatened referent object. Another version of the climate risk narrative, on the other hand, draws on an antagonism—between the UK and its *dangerous environment*. Such articulations are not so much concerned with the direct impacts of climate change but with the "consequences of consequences" (Smith and Vivekananda, 2007, p. 10). Overall, such storylines paint a picture of an increasingly dangerous environment of the UK in a warming world. This picture is then linked to the idea that the UK is a global hub in an interconnected world, which implies that, "it will be difficult for the UK to isolate itself from the global economic and geopolitical shocks that look certain to be experienced in a warming world" (Government Office for Science, 2011b, p. 118). The focus on the *consequences of consequences* thus makes the vulnerability of communities in the "global South" an immediate concern for the UK.

To sum up, climate conflict and risk storylines first of all draw on mechanistic and personification metaphors to identify *linear causalities* between climatic changes and (direct as well as indirect) security risks for the UK. These storylines take the past, the present, and the future as *closed temporal states*. They focus on risks at a particular point of time in the future (e.g. a +2C average warming world or the UK in 2050) and seek to render them present through calculation and assessment, using a completed past as a source of knowledge (about future risks). Limits to knowledge are posed by *methodological uncertainty*, i.e. the uncertainty about the right methods to calculate future developments (which are assessable in principle).

Storylines of climate catastrophe

A second set of storylines revolves around the notion of catastrophe (Aradau and van Munster, 2011). These storylines differ from a logic of risk, primarily due to the particular temporality they construct. Other than a logic of risk the notion of catastrophe is a teleological one, the idea of a progression towards a catastrophic endpoint (Aradau and van Munster 2011, p. 10). This temporality of catastrophe is paradigmatically expressed through the metaphor of the tipping point (Rothe, 2012, p. 249–250). The symbolic representation of climate change through the tipping point and related motional metaphors is particularly important because it helps establish the prominent distinction between a linear climate change and a non-linear, chaotic climate change:

> Many assume that climate change will be a slow, linear process toward a moderately warmer future. But scientists agree there are likely to be elements of the climate system that function like light switches – rapidly changing to a qualitatively different state.
>
> *(Mabey, 2011, p. 16)*

Sometimes the catastrophe is even elevated through apocalyptic or religious collective symbols: "When the apocalyptic horsemen of famine and pestilence appear, war can't be far behind" (Fields quoted in McGhie *et al.*, 2006). The catastrophe poses the universal threat of an absolute endpoint, both in temporal and in spatial terms (Methmann and Rothe, 2012). Storylines of catastrophe put a focus on mitigation: the catastrophe—in this case dangerous climate change—has to be prevented at any cost (Aradau and van Munster, 2011, p. 28). Climate catastrophism is hence a discourse of political leadership and steering (under extreme conditions), as the following quote demonstrates:

> We do not know precisely where particular tipping points lie; we know they exist. Like a ship navigating through the fog we need to make a judgment about how close we go towards the rocks.
>
> *(Mabey, 2011, p. 43)*

Climate catastrophe storylines construct a planetary *teleology*: the development towards an end-point (non-linear climate change), which must be prevented at any cost. At the same time, there are *epistemological limits* to prediction based on climate models concerning the existence of future tipping points (Mayer 2012, p. 171). Mitigating the catastrophe requires an active engagement with the environment—here international climate governance—to shape a desired future and prevent dangerous pathways of climate change, for example by building resilience overseas.

Storylines of climate complexity

Only a third set of storylines stressing the complexity of climatic changes and related dangers comes close to the ideal-typical description of resilience outlined above. Drawing on network metaphors, climate change impacts are presented as complex and incalculable. Starting from the observation that we are living in an "age of uncertainty" (Cabinet Office 2010b, p. 3) global climate change is identified as one major source behind this uncertainty. Illustrative is an MoD (Ministry of Defence) report that presents climate change as a "ring road issue." A ring road issue is understood as "a driver that is so pervasive in nature and influence that it will affect the life of everyone on the planet over the next 30 years" (MoD, 2010a, p. 6). Climate change is not only articulated as a master-threat, but also perceived as a complex system whose secondary impacts are unforeseeable.

What is striking here is the epistemological interplay between climate research and security thinking. On the one hand, climate systems research has informed those notions of complexity that have led to a rethinking in contemporary security policy (Kavalski, 2011; Mayer, 2012; Price-Smith, 2009). On the other hand, strategic thinkers and security officials have articulated climate change itself as a complex security threat: "The climate is a complex system and most forms of human interaction exist in the realm of complexity. [. . .] Ultimately, complexity itself is a significant risk factor that needs to be addressed explicitly" (Mabey 2011, p. 91). The problematization of complexity comes along with the conviction that stagnation or absolute stability in the contemporary world is not possible any more. Under the headline "stationarity is dead" the British think tank E3G, for example, states that "[p]reparing for the future means rejecting stationarity as a guide to future outcomes. The first presumption should therefore be that all critical systems will be vulnerable without adaptive measures" (Mabey 2011, p. 103). Protective security policies must be as versatile as the perceived threats: "In an age of uncertainty, we need to be able to act quickly and effectively" (Cabinet Office 2010b, p. 5). As a result, the complexity discourse fuels skepticism towards centrally planned political steering. Hence, in line with the critical literature on resilience, climate complexity storylines promote forms of neoliberal governance that shift the burden of security policy from the state to the individual citizen (Cabinet Office 2008, p. 59).

Storylines of climate complexity draw on network and emotional metaphors that stress the uncontrollability and radical uncertainty of climate change. The *processual ontology* of resilience implies that the limits between the present and the future become increasingly blurred. Furthermore, knowing or shaping future developments is beyond the scope of human actors, as *radical contingency* here is not a feature of the representation of the world any more but a feature of the world itself.

The governmental landscape of climate resilience in the UK

I use the remaining part of the chapter to show how actors from different governmental departments draw on these storylines when developing and implementing instruments to cope with climate insecurities. I study how the different versions of resilience in these storylines lead to

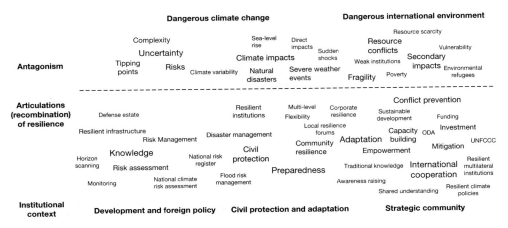

Figure 14.1 Articulations of climate security and resilience in different institutional contexts

a complex governmental landscape of climate resilience policies in the UK. Overall, one can observe that climate security discourse in the UK did not simply translate into a set of clear-cut policy measures. Actors from different institutional backgrounds, among them the Ministry of Defence, the Department for International Development, and the Foreign and Commonwealth Office have adopted climate security discourse, and resilience as a major demand in this discourse, into their own practices. By doing so, however, they have linked the concept of resilience to their own established routines, thereby slightly rearticulating it. As a result, nothing like a coherent UK climate change and security policy could be established. Rather, one can notice the existence of a complex governmental landscape of climate security in which very heterogeneous elements have been recombined. Climate resilience as a hegemonic demand structures this "creative disorder" (Dyer, 2014) *not as a totalizing paradigm*, which would saturate all power relations, but rather as an orienting principle, providing guiding norms but leaving space for creative reinterpretation.

Figure 14.1 gives a good impression of the vast complexity of resilience practices and articulations in the field of climate security. However, despite the vagueness of the term I would argue that its meaning is *not arbitrary* or completely contingent. Rather, there are different privileged understandings of resilience, each of which refers to and rearticulates already established logics in UK climate security policy. Following Anderson (2010) these established security logics that are being rearticulated by resilience are prevention, preemption, and preparedness.[6]

Three logics of climate resilience

The first logic of climate resilience is one of *prevention and risk-assessment*. Hereby, I refer to the ways in which security actors, governmental scientists (Government Office for Science, 2011b), strategic think tanks (MoD, 2010a), and NGOs (non-governmental organizations) (Mabey, 2011) in a broader strategic community become linked in their attempts to render climate change-related threats visible or calculable. Their cooperation and interaction through workshops and research collaborations is behind the growing convergence of methodologies and epistemologies in climate change sciences and strategic thinking. The *currency* of resilience, understood as prevention, is *knowledge,* which is a prerequisite for becoming resilient to future risk. Such future-knowledge is being produced by different methods of calculation, assessing and monetarizing risks, but also more creative approaches of visualizing and imagining the future, for example on the basis of scenario development (MoD, 2010a). Such practices of resilience through risk-management do not follow a discourse of radical complexity, as resilience critics have argued. In a very liberal way, resilience here is based on a series of monitoring and risk-assessment activities including all sorts of "horizon scanning" (Cabinet Office, 2009, p. 44) practices. In short, producing resilience is basically about the generation of knowledge of vulnerabilities and ways to overcome them. Uncertainty is reduced to methodology—by drawing on the right methodologies of anticipation, government intervention becomes possible. Also, resilience practices here follow a liberal discourse, which stresses the role of technology and research for human progress. For example, it is hoped that research on (low-carbon) technologies in the military will increase the resilience of the defense estate in the future (MoD, 2010b, p. 7) and better forecasting technologies will help to improve UK adaptation measures.

A good example of how this logic of resilience as prevention plays out practically is the MoD's Climate Impact Risk Assessment Method (MoD, 2010c). The aim of this approach is to preserve the UK's defence capabilities by increasing its resilience to "the risks to global security presented by the complex geopolitical interactions resulting from a changing climate, as well as the risk to our own establishments and equipment from the impacts of climate change" (MoD, 2010c, p. 2). A resulting "Climate Resilience Risk Register" (MoD, 2010c, p. 5) compiles, prioritizes, and scores any current climatic risk for the MoD's defence estate or infrastructure and combines this risk assessment with scenarios of the UK Climate Projections from 2009. While the paradigmatic approach to resilience describes the latter as an answer to the limits of knowledge (the failure of risk-management), the example of the MoD proves the opposite: knowledge derived from the past is seen as the key to produce resilience in the future. In this sense, a resilient society "understands the risks it faces because it has the scientific capacities to do so" (Smith and Vivekananda, 2007, p. 33). The dominant political metaphor is actually not one of complexity and self-emergence, as resilience critics would argue, but one of UK *climate resilience* as the product of a *political machine* of risk-management. Climate resilience is the product of a series of technical and technocratic adaptation measures that are held together and overseen by the UK government. The fuel that keeps this machine running is risk-knowledge generated by the UK's *"Industry of the Future,"* which was prominently featured in the 2013 NAP Report. Resilience is not so much the answer to limits to knowledge, as has been suggested, but, on the contrary, knowledge is the prerequisite for resilience.

A second logic of resilience articulates the latter in relation to adaptation activities with the aim of producing a resilient UK (Chandler, 2014, pp. 56–57). It can hence be called a *logic of preparedness*. It is in this governmental field that UK resilience practices come closest to the ideal-typical description of resilience outlined above. Activities on climate preparedness recombine established institutions and practices of civil protection with climate adaptation, thereby tearing down departmental dividing lines (Adey and Anderson 2012). The aim is to empower and include local stakeholders and remove the barriers that are faced by established institutions of the state in an "Age of Complexity" (Cabinet Office, 2010a). Drawing on a "multi-level, multi-sector, bottom-up approach to resilience planning" (Cabinet Office, 2009, p. 90) these programs incorporate businesses, communities, and individuals into governmental climate risk management. The rationale behind this strategy is the belief that these actors would be "better placed than government to understand and respond to the needs of the local community before, during and after an emergency" (Cabinet Office 2010a, p. 26). One example of how this networked governance works is the establishment of "Local Resilience Forums," in which local citizens and stakeholders meet regularly and exchange their actions and knowledge with regional administrations and the Civil Contingencies Secretariat (Adey and Anderson 2012, p. 108). Resilience here transcends popular distinctions between interventionist and neoliberal forms of governance by integrating both state-driven as well as market-based adaptation practices into a complex *adaptation assemblage*. The work on preparedness, to sum up, links the practices of very different actors—from disaster planners, to private sector consultancies, resilient subjects, businesses, and communities. It constitutes relations between hitherto unconnected elements, circulates tasks and responsibilities between these elements, and forces political actors into a "continual process of self-reflection upon already existing policy entanglements" as an answer to the limit of knowledge under complexity (Chandler, 2014, p. 57). Rather than the political machine, the ideal-typical metaphors to describe this second resilience-logic are *emergence, adaptability, panarchy, and self-organization*.

A final logic of resilience in the climate security landscape is one of preemption. This logic characterizes the practices of actors that seek to produce a *resilient international environment* of the UK. Cooperation between different actors here follows the aim of preventing secondary climate risks for the UK by *actively shaping* a desired future through diplomacy and development policy. This is perfectly expressed by the notion of an active, or *preemptive* as I would say, *diplomacy* (FCO, 2006). The rationale behind this approach is perfectly expressed in the following quote:

> What happens abroad has never mattered more for our security and prosperity. In an age of rapid global change, the task for Government is to seek to understand and influence the world for the benefit of our people.
>
> *(Blair quoted in FCO, 2006, p. 3)*

Preemptive diplomacy links the UK's mitigation efforts to those of other countries and tries to foster a more integrated approach to mitigate climate-related threats at the international level. Different fora such as the UN Security Council and international conferences are used to raise awareness and to activate the most affected countries (Government Office for Science, 2011b, pp. 90–92). Local stakeholders and communities in developing countries are empowered—to enhance their resilience—and thereby incorporated into the UK's governmental approach in dealing with climate insecurities. A good example is the UK International Climate Fund, established in 2010, which should provide funding for adaptation and mitigation projects in vulnerable countries and regions (DfID et al., 2011). Climate funding here becomes reframed as *investment into resilience* and a preemptive security strategy to produce stability abroad (DfID et al., 2011, p. 2). Another good example for *resilience as preemption* is that of how climate-induced migration recently became reframed, from a potential security threat to a measure of adaptation (Methmann and Oels, 2015, p. 58). The widely recognized Foresight report on "Migration and Global Environmental Change" discusses proactively promoting migration and resettlements in vulnerable regions. The underlying logic is to use planned migration as preemptive measure: "[this] proactive approach can also capitalise on and maximise the benefits from migration, building resilience and transforming adaptive capacity" (Government Office for Science, 2011a, p. 17). The dominant political metaphor undergirding the third resilience-logic is, thus, the figure of a *world in the making*. Other than suggested by the paradigmatic approach to resilience, the latter here does not imply the end of liberal intervention, political steering, and planning. Rather, investment in resilience becomes a possibility for government intervention in the world in spite of complexity and uncertainty. Resilience here follows a very liberal script, which has human progress as its governmental goal and political communities as main governmental addressees. It addresses political subjectivities, which can be shaped and empowered

Figure 14.2 Logics of resilience in the governmental landscape of UK climate security

and which cannot be reduced to self-organizing systems. Figure 14.2 summarizes the different logics of resilience.

Conclusion: resilience as a floating signifier

As I have shown in this chapter, resilience has been interpreted and enacted in many different ways in UK governmental strategies to address dangerous climate change. My study shows that resilience is characterized by a fragility and diversity that a paradigmatic approach to resilience fails to acknowledge. Even in the case of UK governmental strategy, there is no single governmental logic of resilience—for example, in the form of neoliberal governmentality. Drawing on a topological understanding of power I could sketch out a heterogeneous governmental landscape of climate resilience in which different elements were assembled, not only despite their difference but *due to their difference*. Resilience can best be understood as a *floating signifier,* which holds together the diverse practices of climate security, not despite its vagueness but due to its ambiguity. It is precisely because the term is so malleable that different political projects are able to coin it in different ways and it has become so dominant in UK climate security discourse. Certainly, resilience is hegemonic because it resonates well with neoliberal—or better post-liberal—complexity discourse and mistrust in central government. At the same time, however, it easily adopts and integrates oppositional voices and re-interpretations of resilience. In this respect, resilience is different from hegemonic political demands of the modernity project such as democracy, social market economy, or security (e.g. Laclau 1989, p. 70; Nonhoff, 2006). The latter demands constituted particular political communities (Western nation states) by functioning as universal demands of the whole community and establishing a political antagonism—or discursive outside (democratic/non-democratic; capitalism/socialism, etc.), which stabilized the identity of the inner community. In short, political communities revolved around a set of empty signifiers. Resilience, on the contrary, does not produce political communities with fully-fledged political identities. It rather assembles political subjects in a spontaneous and disordered way—linking multiple practices temporarily. And it does not draw on any political antagonism—there is no discursive outside of resilience, no enemy or threat. I would argue that it is exactly this ability of resilience to forge temporary assemblages rather than stable discourse coalitions, or political communities, which makes up the strength of resilience in *late capitalism*. Ambiguity is, hence, at the core of resilience—it is the *conditio resilio*.

Notes

1 Classical risk-management requires the calculability of potential dangers. Resilience, drawing on an ontology of complexity, in the dominant reading of the critical security literature, shifts the focus away from the future (as the external risks are ultimately incalculable) towards the present: the inner vulnerabilities and capabilities of a system (Chandler, 2013b, p. 212).

2 While, for example, Walker and Cooper (2011, p. 143) have called resilience an "operational strategy of risk-management," others understand resilience as "preemptive security" (Bulley 2013, p. 265). Both formulations are at odds with the oft-made assumption that resilience would be "opposed to the preventative paradigm" (Kaufmann 2013, p. 54).

3 This argument goes beyond recent works that have stressed the existence of counter-projects to resilience. For example, Olaf Corry has pointed to the existence of counter-hegemonic projects like the grassroots Transition Towns Movement, whose proponents have articulated a social-ecological notion of resilience that opposes the official neoliberal version of resilience by the UK government (Corry, 2014, p. 263). While this is a valid point, I would even go beyond this argument and claim that ambiguity even is a feature of the official, governmental resilience discourse in the UK.

4 The sample of empirical sources comprised, on the one hand, conceptual defense and security documents: the National Security Strategies (NSS) from 2008, 2009, and 2010 (Cabinet Office, 2008, 2009, 2010b) and the Strategic Defence Review (SDR) 2010 (Cabinet Office 2010a). On the other hand, the sample included concrete policy documents on the implementation of climate change- and security-related policies of the Ministry of Defence (MoD), the Foreign and Commonwealth Office (FCO), and the Department for International Development (DfID), think tank reports and NGO publications from the period 2006–2014.

5 Following Glynos and Howarth, I'm using logics here as an alternative to dominant epistemological concepts including causal laws, causal mechanisms, and contextualized self-interpretations. Logics allow for a certain generalization, but, at the same time, respect the distinctiveness of the case (Glynos and Howarth, 2007, p. 136).

6 However, it is important to note that these logics are ideal-typical and non-exclusive analytical categories. This implies that single technologies or forms of knowledge assigned to one logic can play a role in the other ones as well (but to a lesser degree).

References

Adey, P. and Anderson, B. (2012) Anticipating Emergencies: Technologies of Preparedness and the Matter of Security. *Security Dialogue* 43 (2), 99–117.

Anderson, B. (2010) Preemption, Precaution, Preparedness: Anticipatory Action and Future Geographies. *Progress in Human Geography* 34 (6), 777–798.

Aradau, C. and Van Munster, R. (2011) *Politics of Catastrophe: Genealogies of the Unknown.* Prio New Security Studies. London: Routledge.

Boas, I. and Rothe, D. (2016) From Conflict to Resilience? Explaining Recent Changes in Climate Security Discourse and Practice. *Environmental Politics* 25 (4) forthcoming (accepted for publication).

Bourbeau, P. (2013) Resiliencism: Premises and Promises in Securitisation Research. *Resilience* 1 (1), 3–17.

Brassett, J., Croft, S., and Vaughan-Williams, N. (2013) Introduction: An Agenda for Resilience Research in Politics and International Relations. *Politics* 33 (4), 221–228.

Bulley, D. (2013) Producing and Governing Community (Through) Resilience. *Politics* 33 (4), 265–275.

Cabinet Office (2008) *National Security Strategy of the United Kingdom: Security in an Interdependent World.* Norwich: Crown Copyright.

Cabinet Office (2009) *The National Security Strategy of the United Kingdom Update 2009: Security for the Next Generation.* Norwich: Crown Copyright.

Cabinet Office (2010a) *Securing Britain in an Age of Uncertainty. The Strategic Security and Defence Review.* London: Crown Copyright.

Cabinet Office (2010b) *A Strong Britain in an Age of Uncertainty: The National Security Strategy.* London: Crown Copyright.

Chandler, D. (2013a) International Statebuilding and the Ideology of Resilience. *Politics* 33 (4), 276–286.

Chandler, D. (2013b) Resilience and the Autotelic Subject: Toward a Critique of the Societalization of Security. *International Political Sociology* 7 (2), 210–226.

Chandler, D. (2014) Beyond Neoliberalism: Resilience, The New Art of Governing Complexity. *Resilience* 2, 47–63.

Collier, S. (2009) Topologies of Power Foucault's Analysis of Political Government Beyond "Governmentality." *Theory, Culture & Society* 26 (6), 78–108.

Corry, O. (2014) From Defense to Resilience: Environmental Security beyond Neo-liberalism. *International Political Sociology* 8, 256–74.

DEFRA (Department for Environment, Food and Rural Affairs), Adapting to Climate Change Programme (2012) *The UK Climate Change Risk Assessment 2012 Evidence Report*. London: Crown Copyright.

DEFRA (Department for Environment, Food and Rural Affairs) (2013) *The National Adaptation Programme: Making The Country Resilient To A Changing Climate*. London: Crown Copyright.

DfID (Department for International Development), Department of Energy and Climate Change and Department for Environment, Food and Rural Affairs (2011) *UK International Climate Fund: Tackling Climate Change, Reducing Poverty*. London: Crown Copyright.

Dunn-Cavelty, M., Kaufmann, M., and Kristensen, K. (2015) Resilience and (In)security: Practices, Subjects, Temporalities. *Security Dialogue* 46 (1), 3–14.

Dyer, H. (2014) Climate Anarchy: Creative Disorder in World Politics. *International Political Sociology* 8 (2), 182–200.

Evans, B. and Reid, J. (2013) Dangerously Exposed: The Life and Death of the Resilient Subject. *Resilience* 1 (2), 83–98.

FCO (Foreign And Commonwealth Office) (2006) *Active Diplomacy for a Changing World: The UK's International Priorities*. Norwich: Crown Copyright.

Glynos, J. and Howarth, D. (2007) *Logics of Critical Explanation in Social and Political Theory*. London: Routledge.

Government Office For Science (2011a) *Foresight: Migration and Global Environmental Change. Future Challenges and Opportunities. Final Report*. London: Crown Copyright/Government Office For Science.

Government Office For Science (2011b) *Foresight: The International Dimensions of Climate Change. Final Project Report*. London: Crown Copyright/Government Office For Science.

Grove, K. (2013) Hidden Transcripts of Resilience: Power and Politics in Jamaican Disaster Management. *Resilience* 1 (3), 193–209.

Hajer, M. (2006) Doing Discourse Analysis: Coalitions, Practices, Meaning. In *Words Matter in Policy and Planning: Discourse Theory and Method in the Social Sciences*, Edited By Margo Van Den Brink and Tamara Metze, pp. 65–74. Utrecht: Netherlands Geographical Studies.

Joseph, J. (2013a) Resilience as Embedded Neoliberalism: A Governmentality Approach. *Resilience* 1 (1), 38–52.

Joseph, J. (2013b) Resilience in UK and French Security Strategy: An Anglo-Saxon Bias? *Politics* 33 (4), 253–264.

Kaufmann, M. (2013) Emergent Self-Organisation in Emergencies: Resilience Rationales in Interconnected Societies. *Resilience* 1 (1), 53–68.

Kavalski, E. (2011) From the Cold War to Global Warming: Observing Complexity in IR. *Political Studies Review* 9 (1), 1–12.

Laclau, E. (1989) Politics and The Limits of Modernity. *Social Text* (21), 63–82.

Mabey, N. (2011) *Degrees of Risk: Defining a Risk Management Framework for Climate Security*. London: Third Generation Environmentalism Limited.

Mayer, M. (2012) Chaotic Climate Change and Security. *International Political Sociology* 6 (2), 165–185.

McGhie, J., Migiro, K., Kwatra, A., Pendleton, A., Melby, J., Nutt, D., Wilson, S., and Davison, J. (2006) *The Climate of Poverty: Facts, Fears and Hope. A Christian Aid Report*. London: Christian Aid.

Methmann, C. and Oels, A. (2015) From "Fearing" to "Empowering" Climate Refugees: Governing Climate-induced Migration in the Name of Resilience. *Security Dialogue* 46 (1), 51–68.

Methmann, C. and Rothe, D. (2012) Politics for the Day After Tomorrow: The Political Effect of Apocalyptic Imaginaries in Global Climate Governance. *Security Dialogue* 43 (3), 323–344.

Methmann, C. and Rothe, D. (2013) Apocalypse Now! From Exceptional Rhetoric to Risk Management in Global Climate Politics. In *(De)constructing the Greenhouse: Interpretive Approaches to Global Cimate Governance*. Edited by C. Methmann, D. Rothe and B. Stephen, pp. 105–121. London/New York: Routledge.

MOD (Ministry Of Defence) Development and Doctrines Center (2010a). *Global Strategic Trends – Out To 2040*. London: Crown Copyright/MOD.

MOD (Ministry Of Defence) (2010b) *MOD Climate Change Strategy 2010*. London: Crown Copyright 04/10.

MOD (Ministry Of Defence) (2010c) *MOD Sustainability and Environmental Appraisal Tool Handbook. Section 7: Climate Impacts Risk Assessment Method*. London: Defence Estates.

Mol, A. (1999) Ontological politics: a word and some questions. *Sociological Review* 47, 74–89.

Nonhoff, M. (2006) *Politischer Diskurs und Hegemonie. Das Projekt "Soziale Marktwirtschaft."* Bielefeld: Transcript.

O'Malley, P. (2011) From Risk to Resilience: Technologies of the Self in the Age of Catastrophes. *Carceral Notebooks* 7, 41–68.

Price-Smith, A. (2009) *Contagion and Chaos: Disease, Ecology, and National Security in the Era of Globalization*. Cambridge, Mass: MIT Press.

Randalls, S. (2013) Climate Change Multiple. In *Governing the Climate: New Approaches to Rationality, Power and Politics*, edited by Johannes Stripple and Harriet Bulkeley, pp. 235–242. Cambridge: Cambridge University Press.

Reid, J. (2013) Interrogating the Neoliberal Biopolitics of the Sustainable Development-Resilience Nexus. *International Political Sociology*, 7 (4), 353–367.

Rothe, D. (2012) Security as a Weapon: How Cataclysm Discourses Frame International Climate Negotiations. In *Climate Change, Human Security and Violent Conflict*, edited by Jürgen Scheffran, Michael Brzoska, Hans Günter Brauch, Peter M. Link, and Janpeter Schilling, pp. 243–258. Berlin/Heidelberg: Springer.

Smith, D. and Vivekananda, J. (2007) *A Climate of Conflict: The Links Between Climate Change, Peace and War*. London: International Alert.

Walker, J. and Cooper, M. (2011) Genealogies of Resilience From Systems Ecology to the Political Economy of Crisis Adaptation. *Security Dialogue* 42 (2), 143–160.

Zebrowski, C. (2013) The Nature of Resilience. *Resilience* 1 (3), 159–173.

15

RESILIENCE AND THE NEOLIBERAL COUNTERREVOLUTION

From ecologies of control to production of the common

Sara Nelson

Introduction

The concept of 'resilience', formulated in the early 1970s by ecologist C. S. Holling, has since proliferated far beyond the boundaries of ecosystem science to inform theory and policy in areas as widespread as international development, financial regulation, terrorism risk management, urban planning, and disaster recovery. As 'a pervasive idiom of global governance' (Walker and Cooper 2011, p. 144), 'resilience' reframes the problem of security as a matter of flexible adaptation in an environment (both economic and ecological) characterised by turbulent and unpredictable dynamics. Perhaps not surprisingly, therefore, some of the most innovative contemporary work in resilience theory addresses the possibilities for adaptation to climate change. As the concept has become foundational to contemporary thinking on climate change adaptation (Pelling 2011), resilience has emerged as a strategy for the administration of life on a planetary scale.

This chapter explores the current instantiations of resilience theory (or social–ecological systems (SES) theory) in climate change adaptation, arguing that the forms of power exercised under the rubric of adaptation present new possibilities for resistance and demand new forms of critical engagement. I begin from the proposition that resilience is best understood (in Paolo Virno's (1996) terms) as counterrevolutionary: its emergence as a dominant paradigm for the administration of life was part of the reactive movement, whereby the social upheavals of the 1960s and 1970s were transformed into the basis for a renewed era of capital accumulation in the 1980s and 1990s. These counterrevolutionary origins attest to a critical potential that points beyond – and perhaps undermines – resilience's enrolment in neoliberal strategies of control.

To pursue this argument, I outline two different trajectories for resilience as a strategy for responding to climate change: the first is descriptive of contemporary trends in climate change adaptation, and the second is prescriptive in its suggestion that resilience theory itself can be (re)appropriated in a subversive manner. Following a discussion of the counterrevolutionary origins of resilience, I demonstrate how fostering *adaptability* has come to mean integrating flows of social, natural, and monetary 'capital' in a continuous framework of power, chiefly through markets in environmental financial commodities. If, as this section argues, resilience is aligned with mechanisms of flexible accumulation to operate as a dominant paradigm for the administration of life, consideration of the political possibilities presented by this framework becomes all-important. A final section therefore addresses recent literature on the possibilities for social-ecological *transformation* to explore how the counterrevolutionary origins of SES theory suggest possibilities for its subversion. With an understanding of system potential in terms of a social-ecological common rather than capital, the concept of transformation can inform a radical ecological politics.

Origins of resilience

Resilience theory emerged as part of a renewed era of environmental concern in the 1960s and 1970s. In broad strokes, this literature suggested that both resource scarcity and ecological complexity posed limits to the notions of infinite growth that underpinned the prevailing Keynesian-neoclassical synthesis in economics: not only did the finitude of the Earth entail inescapable material limits to resources, but environmental 'externalities' in the form of pollution and environmental degradation threatened to undermine the reproduction of capital (e.g. Meadows *et al.* 1972; Carson 1962). This resurgence of environmental thought did not signal an isolated set of concerns, but was symptomatic of a widespread crisis of the Fordist-Keynesian regime of accumulation signalled by new social movements, challenges to US industrial power and monetary hegemony, and growing anxieties about energy scarcity (Nelson 2015).

Virno and other autonomist Marxists locate the crisis of Fordist-Keynesianism in the social movements and labour struggles of the 1960s and 1970s. Moreover, they argue that the defining features of neoliberal capitalism – a devolution of governance structures; flexible and adaptive forms of labour management; the centrality of forms of labour formerly relegated to the unwaged sphere of social reproduction – were developed through the co-optation and inversion of workers' self-organization in the context of these struggles. The neoliberal order that emerged in the wake of the crisis was not a necessary outcome, but a contingent series of responses that mobilised 'the very same (economic, social and cultural) tendencies that the revolution would have been able to engage', inverting and reducing these to 'profitable *productive forces*' (Virno 1996, p. 241, original emphasis).

This historical analysis is based on the premise that capitalist innovation is always reactive to the autonomous activity of labour-power. If capital is, for Marx, a social relation of exploitation in which the surplus wealth produced by workers (in excess of the wage) is appropriated by the capitalist as surplus-value, autonomist Marxists contend that labour-power as productive potential always exceeds the measure of surplus-value, destabilising the reproduction of the capitalist relation. This puts capital in a reactive position, such that it is continually forced to adapt to labour-power's autonomous self-organisation.

In this sense, Virno defines counterrevolution as 'literally *revolution in reverse*' (ibid.). Recognising this potential revolution – that neoliberal institutions of decentralised governance and flexible accumulation could have manifested in noncapitalist forms – is crucial, he argues, for locating political possibilities in the present. Historical analysis becomes a matter of mapping a 'future history', or 'the *remembrance* of the potential class struggles that may take place in *the next phase*' (ibid., p. 243).

However, if the crisis of Fordist-Keynesianism was precipitated by the resistance of labour-power, the widespread concern over environmental crisis reveals that it was also catalysed by the failure of existing resource management practices to harness the productivity of ecological systems. This ecological dimension has been largely ignored by Virno and other autonomist thinkers. In order that environmental crisis did not become a crisis *for capital*, the co-optation of environmentalism into new forms of ecological control was, I argue, integral to the broader restructuring that manifested the transformed relation among capital, labour and nonhuman nature in a neoliberal form. Resilience theory, offering a new model of ecological dynamics that demanded a wholesale revision of resource management strategies, was central to this process. Further, following Virno, the counterrevolutionary origins of resilience reveal the contingency of its alignment with neoliberal environmentalism. Locating the potential for resilience to be other-than-neoliberal is a necessary, though by no means sufficient, step toward subverting its neoliberal iterations in the present.

From the beginning, resilience theory was about more than ecological dynamics. Holling's early work was tied up in debates over energy scarcity, environmental degradation and the new forms of risk presented by complex social-ecological relations in late capitalism. In a 1975 volume on energy, Holling argued that '[t]he price and availability of oil are uncertain in precisely the terms that international relations are'. Calling for a resilient energy policy that could 'cope with the uncertain, the unexpected, the unknown', he defined resilience as 'a property that allows a system to absorb *and utilise* (or even benefit from) change' (Holling [1975] 1982, pp. 8, 14).

Resilience implied a fundamentally new approach to resource management – one not concerned with quantifiable outcomes (e.g. flows of resource commodities) but with the support of adaptive capacities under conditions of irreducible uncertainty. Holling argued that conventional management techniques that enforced ecological stability (such as Maximum Sustained Yield in fisheries) ironically reduced resilience, which could only be built through continual exposure to disturbance. In an early volume on global change, Holling argued that the pathological feedbacks between social and ecological systems were not only evident in resource management but were endemic to the spatial and temporal dynamics of modern society, requiring an entirely new and holistic management perspective on social-ecological relations:

> The timing and spatial extent of the pulses [of disturbance that determine a system's resilience] emerge from the interaction between external events and an internally generated rhythm of stability/instability. Industrial societies are changing the spatial and temporal patterns of these external events. Spatial impacts are more homogeneous; temporal patterns are accelerated. An understanding of impacts of global change therefore requires a framework to connect the understanding developed here for ecosystem dynamics to that developed for global biogeochemical changes on the one hand and societal developments on the other hand. There are transfers of energy, material, and information among all three.
>
> *(Holling [1986] 2010, pp. 98–99)*

The disturbances that affect system resilience are not exclusively external, but are generated in the border space between the system and its exterior, a boundary that is itself the product of an interactive relation. From this perspective, the discourse of 'environmental crisis' gains new significance, signalling a crisis of the very boundary between the economy and its reproductive exterior and a transformed relation between the social body and its environment.

In contrast to the stability theory of his contemporaries, Holling's *adaptive management* strategy posed a counterrevolutionary response to environmental uncertainty that harnessed instability as a catalyst for innovation and growth. In his words, it aimed to 'design systems that can absorb and accommodate future events in whatever unexpected form they may take' (Holling 1973, p. 21). In his influential concept of the *adaptive cycle*, Holling modelled the dynamical evolution of social and ecological systems over time through four phases: exploitation, conservation, revolt and reorganization. As social-ecological wealth – here figured as 'capital' – is accumulated during the conservation phase in stable forms, the system becomes less complex and more rigid, making it vulnerable to 'revolt' by internal or external 'agents of disturbance' (Holling 2001, p. 394).

System change occurs through moments of 'creative destruction', in which 'previously accumulated mutations, inventions, external invaders, and capital can become reassorted into novel combinations, some of which nucleate opportunity' (ibid., p. 395). While a more resilient system may reorganise itself on a higher level (maintaining its defining relationships in a changed form), a less resilient system may give way to a fundamentally new configuration.

In the adaptive cycle, resilience is quite literally a counterrevolutionary property that enables controlling elements to maintain and enhance a system's defining characteristics by exploiting crises as adaptive opportunities. Instead of advocating non-growth in response to the evident failures of the Keynesian-neoclassical growth paradigm, Holling reframed growth as uneven and non-linear, and posited that this unevenness that could become the very source of innovation. For Holling, like Virno, the moment of system breakdown is not a dead end but a new beginning. However, while Virno locates the cause of crisis in a fundamental antagonism between labour and capital – in the way that labour-power's potential exceeds its actualisation as surplus-value – in Holling's figuration there is no such distinction. Rather, we have a fetishistic vision of the world as the self-reproduction of capital.

As Walker and Cooper (2011, p. 147) describe, the adaptive cycle offers 'an abstract dynamics of capital accumulation, one that is no longer predicated on the progressive temporality of orthodox political economy but rather on the inherent crisis tendencies of complex adaptive systems'. They analyse the parallels between Holling's ecological theory and Friedrich von Hayek's neoliberal economics, arguing that resilience theory has 'moved from a position of critique (against the destructive consequences of orthodox resource economics) to one of collusion with an agenda of resource management that collapses ecological crisis into the creative destruction of a truly Hayekian financial order' (ibid., p. 157). They argue that these thinkers' shared ontology of complex adaptive systems subsumes all possibility of critique, insofar as a complex adaptive system 'feeds upon deviations from normal reproduction' (ibid., quoting Niklas Luhmann). They therefore conclude that,

> In its tendency to metabolise all countervailing forces and inoculate itself against critique, 'resilience thinking' cannot be challenged from within the terms of complex systems theory but must be contested, if at all, on completely different terms, by a movement of thought that is truly counter-systemic.
>
> *(Ibid.)*

I want to argue, in contrast, that the possibilities presented by SES theory are not exhausted by the neoliberal development regime that they currently inform. Capitalism, like complex adaptive systems, 'feeds upon deviations from normal reproduction'. The expansion of surplus-value requires continual innovation. But these forces of innovation are not capitalist in origin – rather, capital continually subsumes alterity in the service of its own reproduction. Crucially, this subsumption – as Virno reminds us – is never complete: the potential revolution is present, if only latently, in counterrevolutionary forms. This is, in some sense, a classically Marxian insight: the potential for system change is immanent to the system (capitalism) itself, as labour-power is both capital and not-capital, in the service of capital and irreducible to it (Marx 1973, pp. 295–296).

One of the insights of Holling's adaptive cycle is, in fact, to demonstrate that resilience is never guaranteed; even a highly resilient system contains an immanent potential to be radically transformed. Holling stresses that accumulated 'capital' is not exhausted by a system's given form, but 'represents a gradual increase in the potential for other kinds of ecosystems and futures' (Holling 2001, p. 394). 'Capital', for Holling, describes a social-ecological potential that may be actualised in myriad forms, whether 'nutrients [and] biomass' or 'networks of human relationships' (ibid.). In other words, it names a virtual potential immanent to the material embodiments of the system itself.

What resilience theory articulates, though in a counterrevolutionary form, is an ontology of potentiality that resonates with a minor current of Western thought, running through the work of Spinoza, Nietzsche and Marx – an intellectual tradition that enjoyed a strong resurgence in the 1960s and 1970s (e.g. Guerroult 1968; Deleuze 1968; Althusser [1968] 2009; Negri 1991). Sharing a historical conjuncture in the upheaval surrounding the multiple crises of Fordism, these divergent intellectual trajectories are, in very different ways, recognitions of the potential for new forms of life to emerge from the crises of twentieth-century capitalism. But while the Spinozist revival in philosophy and Marxism did not explicitly engage with questions of ecology, resilience theory did not incorporate a critique of political economy. Instead, by adopting a neoliberal ideology that sees capital as the source of innovation, resilience theory turns this notion of potentiality in a counterrevolutionary direction.

Resilience I: ecologies of control

As irreversible climate change has become increasingly apparent, major research and policy institutions such as the Intergovernmental Panel on Climate Change (IPCC), the United Nations Framework Convention on Climate Change (UNFCCC) and the World Bank have focused their attention beyond mitigation to strategies for adaptation (e.g. UNFCCC 2010; Adger *et al.* 2007; World Bank 2013). The shift toward adaptation as an all-encompassing framework for responding to climate change has been strongly influenced by resilience theory, informed by think-tanks such as the Stockholm Resilience Centre and the Resilience Alliance. With adaptability defined as 'the capacity of actors in the system to influence resilience' and widely recognised to result from interrelated social, natural, and monetary 'capital' (Walker *et al.* 2004, p. 1), resilience theory's naturalised understanding of capital has provided a scientific vocabulary that buttresses market-based approaches to climate change. Markets in new environmental commodities, proponents argue, integrate these multiple forms of 'capital' by spreading ecological risk and incorporating the value of 'natural capital' into economic calculus.

Ben Dibley and Brett Neilson (2010, p. 148) have provocatively suggested that the mechanisms of security and securitisation involved in the management of climate risk 'are the current technologies and techniques for the assurance of a population's life', 'render[ing] planetary the biopolitical practices of security that [Michel] Foucault first diagnosed in relation to modern urban administration'. The techniques for producing the adaptive society, however, diverge significantly from Foucault's early descriptions of biopolitics, both in the object they act upon and in the type of threat they seek to mitigate. In Foucault's classic descriptions, biopolitical interventions link disciplinary technologies focused on the individual with 'regulatory mechanisms' at the level of the population, to 'establish an equilibrium . . . and compensate for variations within this general population and its aleatory field' (Foucault 2003, p. 246). In contrast, adaptive management seeks to capitalise on alterity rather than mitigate it. In this way, its mode of operation is more aligned with Deleuze's diagnosis of new technologies of control that succeed discipline: control breaks down the interiors that defined disciplinary society, operating through the 'modulation' of flows in a continuous network of 'open circuits', of which the paradigmatic form is the market (Deleuze 1992, pp. 7, 6). As opposed to discipline's analogical enclosures (the school is like the factory is like the prison), those of control are 'inseparable variations', 'metastable states coexisting in one and the same modulation' (ibid., p. 5). If disciplinary mechanisms are individualising, control operates on 'a "dividual" material' that can be perpetually pulled apart and reconfigured in order to facilitate productive connections between flows (whether financial, ecological or atmospheric) (ibid., p. 7).

Contemporary trends in climate change adaptation suggest that the emergence of technologies of control also involves new forms of biopolitical investment that differ from regulatory power. Stephen Collier (2009, p. 93) has argued that, in Foucault's later lectures, biopolitics does not describe a 'governmental logic', but rather 'a problem space to be analyzed by tracing the recombinatorial processes through which techniques and technologies of power are reworked and redeployed'. Collier posits that thinking receives a new kind of attention in these lectures, as 'a driver of recombinatorial processes' in response to practical urgencies (ibid., p. 96). Rather than emerging out of a stable episteme that provides their conditions of possibility, significant thinkers 'are situated precisely amid upheaval, in sites of problematization in which existing forms have lost their coherence and their purchase in addressing present problems, and in which new forms of understanding and acting have to be invented' (ibid., p. 95). Resilience theory can be understood as a response to just such an urgency, in which the forms of knowledge production that characterise the normalising society (such as statistical prediction and stability theory) proved inadequate to the non-linear dynamics of interconnected social and ecological systems in late capitalism. In this context, Holling and others combined innovations in systems thinking, computer modelling and ecological observation with elements of mainstream economic theory to develop new technologies of ecological management.

If regulatory power views the social body and all threats to it in terms of the biological, seeking to mitigate the risk of 'infection' (Foucault 1990, p. 136), control could be associated with the emergence of the ecological as a primary field of intervention and dominant metaphor for life processes. The reinvention of ecology in the 1960s and 1970s from a taxonomic discipline to a science of complex relations was thereby central to emerging technologies of control. Faced with the overwhelming connectivity of complex social and ecological systems, resilience theory replaced the model of a biological threat of contagion with a model of *catastrophic* threat, the risk that gradual change in system variables could push the system over a threshold into a radically new configuration.

Deleuze (1992, p. 6) describes the passage from discipline to control as a 'mutation of capitalism', associated not only with the dominance of financial capital in the economy but also with the role of financial markets in shaping forms of life. In line with Deleuze's description, in adaptive management financial markets become both models of the supremely adaptive institution, and biopolitical technologies in themselves. As such, they play a privileged role in contemporary efforts to foster adaptation. For instance, Westley *et al.* (2002) argue that financial markets represent the paradigmatic example of the type of forward-looking behaviour necessary for adaptive change (see also Holling 2001, p. 401). Markets in environmental derivatives such as catastrophe bonds, weather derivatives and hurricane futures figure in World Bank, UNFCCC and IPCC literature as exemplary tools for managing non-linear climate risk (e.g. UNFCCC 2007; IPCC 2011; World Bank 2007; see also Cooper 2010 and Johnson 2011). The IPCC's Fourth Assessment Report notes that, 'to date, most adaptation practices have been observed in the insurance sector', through the use of financial markets to 'internalise information on climate risks and help transfer adaptation and risk-reduction incentives to communities and individuals' (Adger *et al.* 2007, sec. 17.2).

As a mode of collective speculation, financial practice also plays an active role in the production of knowledge about uncertain climate futures. This prompts Elsner *et al.* (2009, p. 281) to describe 'catastrophe finance' as an emerging academic discipline 'at the interface of science, finance, and insurance', in which the capital markets serve as 'a real world laboratory to support research and education'. Paul Mills (2008, p. 36) of the IMF argues that, as financial markets become increasingly interconnected, climate risk products present new opportunities for accumulation and risk hedging, such that 'there is likely to be a continuing demand for financial instruments that provide investors a premium to assume weather risk despite climate change'. These products transfer climate risk onto capital markets and enable portfolio diversification through the transfer of financial risk onto climate fluctuations, further integrating financial and ecological dynamics. As Cooper (2010, p. 175) observes, 'trading in weather derivatives has been one of the few markets to survive the credit crunch relatively unscathed'.

In addition to markets in ecological risk, new environmental commodities enable so-called natural capital to circulate in monetary form. The concept of *ecosystem services* now figures prominently in resilience literature, and the cultivation of beneficial ecosystem services – which may include everything from the primary production of soils to flood mitigation, carbon sequestration or cultural values – is often presumed as a general goal of adaptive management. The construction of nature as a 'service-provider' via resilience-based management techniques has enabled a major shift in the way that capital circulates through nonhuman natures, pricing and exchanging ecological *capacities* rather than stocks of material resources (Sullivan 2013). Figured as infrastructural support for the population, efforts to measure and capitalise on the economic value of environmental functions have become fundamental to global environmental governance (Robertson 2012). Ecosystem service commodities are also exchanged in the form of credits or use-rights to a given ecosystem function (e.g. carbon sequestration), through market-based conservation strategies that seek to capture, in commodity form, 'the dynamic capacity of ecosystem life-support as a major "factor of production"' (Deutsch *et al.* 2003, p. 206).

As a biopolitical technology, the trade in ecosystem services establishes the market as the mechanism for fostering the essential life-support functions of the population. But the disconnect between the temporality of exchange and of the production of ecological value, in which the flicker of a credit sold on a computer screen registers, for example, the promised growth of a seedling into a tree, means that ecosystem service commodities essentially create an environmental debt that can be securitised in increasingly complex ways. In wetland markets, environmental advocacy groups have experimented with the use of 'credit stacking' to enable the various individual functions of a wetland (such as flood control, water quality or habitat for threatened flora and fauna) to be 'tranched' and sold separately, in an environmental equivalent of asset-backed securities (Robertson 2012). Similar transactions in 'carbon-backed securities' have already been completed (Chan 2009). The World Bank and the US Commodity Futures Trading Commission have both noted the resemblance between emissions credits and financial commodities, and Michelle Chan has argued that their exchange is 'fundamentally derivatives trading' (World Bank 2011; CFTC 2011; Chan 2009, p. 2). Further highlighting the difficulty of categorising ecosystem services as assets, some proponents have suggested that they could 'be viewed as *natural insurance capital* for spreading risks in the face of uncertainty' (Deutsch *et al.* 2003, p. 214, original emphasis).

Adaptive management disrupts the division between the social body and its environmental exterior on which the normalising society depended. The imperative of biopower to foster life is accomplished not through the stable reproduction of the norm, but by harnessing the aleatory force of the outside as a catalyst for growth. Catastrophe bonds and weather derivatives capitalise on the risk space opened up by the failure of normalising technologies to maintain a stable equilibrium, while new environmental commodities integrate social-ecological dynamics in a continuous framework of control. But while the financialisation of environmental governance changes the relation between the interior of the social body and its environmental exterior, this does not mean that mechanisms of control defy resistance. To follow Deleuze (1992, p. 4), 'there is no need to fear or hope, but only to look for new weapons'.

Resilience II: transformation as production of the common

In its practical instantiation in climate change adaptation, resilience theory informs and is reworked through the complex systems that structure contemporary life. Far from co-opting all possibility of critique, locating the counterrevolutionary tensions within resilience theory may enable us to think the conditions of possibility for resistance from within these structures themselves. As Virno (1996, p. 243) writes, recognising the counterrevolutionary origins of neoliberalism is not only a matter of complicating our understanding of history, but also of recognising that 'that old period of conflict continues still today to represent the other face of the post-Fordist coin, the rebellious side'.

The counterrevolutionary nature of capitalist resilience is manifest in the tension between the desire to foster the aleatory dynamics of social-ecological systems as forces of innovation, and the need to capture and thereby foreclose these forces in the form of surplus-value. As Cesare Casarino (2008, p. 22) writes, capital is 'structurally unable to subsume without at the same time negating and foreclosing that which it subsumes'. The mechanisms of financialisation, discussed above, do not escape this contradiction. Morgan Robertson (2006) has demonstrated, for example, how efforts to isolate and measure ecosystem functions in standardised commodity forms paradoxically undermine the very ecological complexity on which investors seek to capitalise. Despite the sophisticated algorithms and futurological methods involved in pricing weather derivatives, their quantitative value can only ever approximate the over-determined social and ecological risks they seek to price. The success of financialisation is not that it has managed to fully account for ecological complexity, but that it has socialised losses in the form of exacerbated ecological degradation while privatising profits. The political question is how this contradiction might become a crisis *for capital*. The recent literature on transformation in social-ecological systems, I argue, provides an important theoretical tool for framing this question.

Resilience is only one of a broader set of concepts within the general heading of social-ecological systems (SES) theory. If we are to think how SES theory might help us to locate possibilities for resistance within contemporary financial capitalism, we must reject the fetishistic concept of capital presented by the adaptive cycle, which obscures the fundamental antagonism of exploitation that gives the system its motive force. Casarino (2008, p. 23) employs the concept of the *common* to describe a mode of actualising surplus wealth in opposition to surplus-value, understanding capital and the common as 'two radically different ways of materializing the one and only surplus'. By actualising surplus as surplus-value, capital negates and forecloses potential in the form of a quantitative limit, '*living surplus as separation (in the form of value par excellence, namely, money)*'. In contrast, the common names a mode of actualising surplus beyond measure, of '*living surplus as incorporation (in the forms of the common, including and especially our bodies)*' (ibid., original emphasis). Casarino argues that 'the common finds its highest degree of perfection – namely, its own determination beyond capital – in surplus common, that is, in producing its own surplus beyond value' (ibid., p. 35).

The common is the constitutive outside of capital, not only in the sense that capital continually seeks to enclose and privatise the common, but also that capital's own dynamics cause it to continually produce the common as its own internal limit in the form of an excess that cannot be subsumed as surplus-value. This concept of the common is central to Michael Hardt and Antonio Negri's (2009, p. 139) analysis of contemporary capitalism, which they argue increasingly depends upon expropriation of 'common forms of wealth, such as knowledges, information, affects and social relationships' outside of the direct production process through new forms of property right and financial innovation. The productive activity of capital – its role in developing the social forces of production – is thus diminished, and it is increasingly parasitic on the self-organising activity of the 'multitude' (ibid.).

Hardt and Negri (ibid., pp. viii, 139) contrast the ecological common with a social common made up of 'knowledges, languages, codes, information, affects, and so forth', to demonstrate how the latter 'does not lend itself to the logic of scarcity as does the first [ecological commons]'. While they continually point towards a unified conception of a social-ecological common, their conception of material nature in terms of scarcity interrupts these gestures. The preceding analysis suggests the need to expand Hardt and Negri's analysis to account for the ways that contemporary financial capital seeks to capitalise on relations that are irreducibly social and ecological. Indeed, their continual contrast between the social common (as abundance) and the ecological common (as scarcity) is at odds with their own development of the concept. For example, they suggest that a politics of the common involves:

> not only preserving the common but also struggling over the conditions of producing it . . . promoting its beneficial forms, and fleeing its detrimental, corrupt forms. We might call this an ecology of the common – an ecology focused equally on nature and society, on humans and the nonhuman world in a dynamic of interdependence, care, and mutual transformation.
>
> *(ibid., p. 171)*

This ecology of the common resonates strongly with recent SES literature on 'transformability', which describes the 'capacity to create a fundamentally new system when ecological, economic, or social structures make the existing system untenable' (Walker *et al.* 2004, p. 1). The recent emphasis on transformation goes beyond the conservative aspects of resilience (its focus on maintaining existing systems) to explore how crises can be exploited – and even precipitated – as opportunities for revolutionary change. The question posed by the concept of transformability is a question at the heart of revolutionary thought: how do actors in a maladaptive system come to desire, and strive towards, the overcoming of the system of which they are part?

The existing literature on transformation, however, consistently fails to question the naturalised concept of capital incorporated by resilience theory early in its development, and therefore remains unable to articulate the possibility of truly transformative social change. Instead, empirical examples of transformation tend to be limited to discrete conservation areas where, for example, the social-ecological system in question may have transitioned from a city dump to a wetland ecosystem sustained through adaptive management (Westley *et al.* 2013). Moreover, resilience theorists consistently focus on the capacity of the most powerful actors in the system – those with the greatest 'capital' – to effect transformational change (Holling 2010; Westley *et al.* 2013). This poses a troubling paradox for theorists of transformation: why would powerful actors within a system strive to overthrow the very system that sustains their power and influence?

Thinking transformability through the common, rather than capital, would ground the question of transformative change in the fundamental antagonism of exploitation. For Marx, the proletariat is revolutionary precisely in the sense that it strives toward its own overcoming, toward the annihilation of the material conditions that produce it as a coherent subject – the 'working class'. The question of transformation then becomes one of establishing a different system for the actualization of surplus, as common wealth rather than surplus value.

Hardt and Negri (2009, p. 152) suggest that what they call an 'exodus' from capital involves 'a process of *subtraction* from the relationship with capital by means of actualizing the potential autonomy of labour-power'. It involves a radical break precipitated by an eruption of resistance that is neither entirely endogenous nor exogenous to the system itself, but which mobilises existing potential toward new forms of life. The 'event comes from the outside insofar as it ruptures the continuity of history and the existing order, but it should be understood not only negatively, as rupture, but also as innovation, which emerges, so to speak, from the inside' (ibid., p. 59). In describing this notion of the event, they draw on Deleuze's suggestion that resistance to control requires an active 'belief in the world': 'If you believe in the world you precipitate events, however inconspicuous, that elude control, you engender new space-times, however small their surface or volume' (Deleuze, quoted in ibid., p. 61).

In the vocabulary of SES theory, such interventions could be described as transformational changes that '[break] down the resilience of the old and [build] the resilience of the new' through strategic interventions at small scales, that can scale up to have larger system effects (Folke *et al.* 2010, p. 7). The subject of transformation, like the multitude, is characterised by decentralised control. Given conditions of irreducible uncertainty, transformative action requires experimental interventions that facilitate learning and increase the resilience of alternative structures that can become dominant following a crisis of the old order (Westley *et al.* 2013). This is not to posit that transformation lacks purpose or motivation, but rather that the 'desired state' to be achieved is not pre-determined, but emerges through the process of self-organization.

Hardt and Negri (2009, p. 195) write that a project of 'making the multitude . . . must bring the process of exodus together with an organizational project aimed at establishing institutions of common'. Institutions of the common extend the power of the multitude to 'manage their encounters', avoiding negative encounters and fostering positive ones that strengthen the desire to be in common (ibid., p. 357). As Casarino (2008, p. 19) reminds us, recognising the potential to be in common is not sufficient to actualise it: the very desire to be in common cannot be taken for granted, but must be produced – and its production is itself a political project. Transformation, like exodus, requires a collective subject capable of selecting between desirable and undesirable connections, and strengthening the former while weakening the latter. Unlike the multitude, however, the subject of transformation necessarily includes non-human and abiotic natures. By providing a sophisticated understanding of social-ecological dynamics that incorporates nonhumans as 'subjects and forces of change' (Pelling 2011, p. 28), SES theory provides crucial tools for expanding this notion of the common beyond the human.

In drawing on Hardt and Negri's discussion of the common to articulate an alternative direction for transformational change, I do not wish to suggest that their perspective offers a political programme. Not only do they not aim to do this, but I would also argue that they do not sufficiently attend to the question (posed by Virno and others) of the political orientation of the multitude – whether it is necessarily liberatory, or equally regressive in its tendencies.[1] Rather, I hope simply to suggest that SES theory offers theoretical tools both for understanding the capitalist ecologies it currently informs and for developing an exit strategy from them. The founding questions of SES theory are how to effect desirable system change in conditions of radical uncertainty through experimental interventions that facilitate learning, and how local-level interventions can reverberate to have large-scale system effects. By exploring these questions in relation to the dynamics of nonhuman systems, SES theory can offer important tools for anticapitalist ecological politics in the Anthropocene.

Conclusion

This chapter has explored some key trends in adaptation theory and practice, demonstrating how the paradigm of 'adaptability' serves to integrate flows of social, ecological and monetary 'capital' in a continuous framework of power, in part through the establishment of markets in novel environmental commodities such as ecosystem services and environmental derivatives. The point in calling attention to these trends is not, however, to herald the emergence of a flexible and comprehensive planetary system of exploitation. Rather, it is to ask how the forms of control exercised under the rubric of adaptability may present new possibilities for resistance, and demand new forms of critical practice. As we face the prospect of unavoidable climate change and amplified feedbacks among economic and ecological risk, the question of how emergent crises might be leveraged toward alternative ecological futures becomes salient. The shift, in mainstream environmentalism, away from traditional conservationist goals to the question of how to produce desirable social-ecological futures – a shift to which resilience theory has been central – indexes a moment of possibility for transformational change. It would be a mistake for the left to abandon these possibilities by overestimating the resilience of neoliberalism.

Acknowledgements

This chapter is revised and updated from its original version, Nelson, S. (2014). 'Resilience and the neoliberal counter-revolution: from ecologies of control to production of the common', *Resilience* 2(1): 1–17. DOI: 10.1080/21693293.2014.872456. The author would like to thank Bruce Braun for his valuable comments on earlier drafts of this paper, and two anonymous reviewers for their insightful and constructive feedback.

Note

1 See Hardt and Negri, 2009, pp. 167–168 and 176–178 for their response to these critiques

References

Adger, W. N., S. Agrawala and M. Monirul Qader Mirza (2007). Assessment of Adaptation Practices, Options, Constraints and Capacity. In *IPCC Fourth Assessment Report, Climate Change 2007: Working Group II: Impacts, Adaptation and Vulnerability*. New York: Cambridge University Press. Available at: www.ipcc.ch/publications_and_data/publications_ipcc_fourth_assessment_report_wg2_report_impacts_adaptation_and_vulnerability.htm (accessed 15 January 2016).

Althusser, L. ([1968] 2009). Part I: From *Capital* to Marx's Philosophy. In Étienne Balibar and L. Althusser, *Reading Capital*. New York: Verso, pp. 11–75.

Carson, R. (1962). *Silent Spring*. New York: Houghton Mifflin.

Casarino, C. (2008). Surplus Common. In C. Casarino and A. Negri, *In Praise of the Common: A Conversation of Philosophy and Politics*. Minneapolis: University of Minnesota Press.

Chan, M. (2009). *Subprime Carbon? Rethinking the World's Largest New Derivatives Market*. Washington, DC: Friends of the Earth.

Collier, S. (2009). Topologies of Power: Foucault's Analysis of Political Government beyond 'Governmentality'. *Theory, Culture and Society* 26(6), 78–108.

CFTC (Commodity Futures Trading Commission Interagency Working Group for the Study on Oversight of Carbon Markets) (2011). Report on the Oversight of Existing and Prospective Carbon Markets. Submitted to Congress 18 January 2011. Washington, DC: US Commodity Futures Trading Commission.

Cooper, M. (2010). Turbulent Worlds: Financial Markets and Environmental Crisis. *Theory, Culture and Society* 27(2–3), 167–190.

Deleuze, G. (1968). *Spinoza et le Problème de l'Expression*. Paris: Les Éditions de Minuit.

Deleuze, G. (1992). Postscript on the Societies of Control. *October* 59, 3–7.

Deutsch, L., C. Folke, and K. Skånberg (2003). The Critical Natural Capital of Ecosystem Performance as Insurance for Human Well-Being. *Ecological Economics* 44, 205–217.

Dibley, B. and B. Neilson (2010). Climate Crisis and the Actuarial Imaginary: 'The War on Global Warming'. *New Formations* 69, 144–159.

Elsner, J. B., R. K. Burch, and T. H. Jagger (2009). Catastrophe Finance: An Emerging Discipline. *Eos, Transactions, American Geophysical Union* 90(33), 281–282.

Folke, C., S. R. Carpenter, B. Walker, M. Scheffer, T. Chapin, and J. Rockström (2010). Resilience Thinking: Integrating Resilience, Adaptability and Transformability. *Ecology and Society* 15(4), Article 20.

Foucault, M. (1990). *The History of Sexuality, Vol. 1*. New York: Vintage Books.

Foucault, M. (2003). *'Society Must Be Defended': Lectures and the College de France, 1975–1976*. New York: Picador.

Guerroult, M. (1968). *Spinoza, I: Dieu*. Paris: Aubier Montaigne.

Hardt, M. and A. Negri (2009). *Commonwealth*. Cambridge: Belknap Press.

Holling, C. S. (1973). Resilience and Stability of Ecological Systems. *Annual Reviews of Ecology and Systematics* 4, 1–23.

Holling, C. S. [1975] (1982). Myths of ecology and energy. In L. Ruedisili and M. Firebaugh (eds), *Perspectives on Energy: Issues, Ideas, and Environmental Dilemmas*. New York: Oxford University Press, pp. 8–15.

Holling, C. S. (2001). Understanding the Complexity of Economic, Ecological and Social Systems. *Ecosystems* 4(5), 390–405.

Holling, C. S. [1986] (2010). The Resilience of Terrestrial Ecosystems. Reprinted in L. Gunderson, C. Allen, and C. S. Holling (eds), *Foundations of Ecological Resilience*. Washington: Island Press, pp. 67–118.

Holling, C. S. (2010). Coping with Transformation. *Options Magazine* Summer. Vienna: International Institute of Applied Systems Analysis. Available at: www.iiasa.ac.at/web/home/resources/publications/IIASAMagazineOptions/Transformation.en.html (accessed 11 May 2013).

IPCC (2011). *Managing the Risks of Extreme Weather Events and Disasters to Advance Climate Change Adaptation*. New York: Cambridge University Press.

Johnson, L. (2011) Climate Change and the Risk Industry: The Multiplication of Fear and Value. In R. Peet, P. Robbins, and M. Watts (eds), *Global Political Ecology*. New York: Routlege, pp. 185–202.

Marx, K. (1973). *Grundrisse*. M. Nicolaus (trans.) New York: Penguin Books.

Meadows, D. H., D. L. Meadows, J. Randers, and W. W. Behrens III (1972). *The Limits to Growth: A Report for the Club of Rome's Project on the Predicament of Mankind*. New York: Universe Books.

Mills, P. (2008). The Greening of Markets: Financial Markets can play a Valuable Role in Addressing Climate Change. *Finance and Development* 45(1), 32–36.

Negri, A. (1991). *The Savage Anomaly*. M. Hardt (trans.) Minneapolis: University of Minnesota Press.

Nelson, S. (2015). Beyond *The Limits to Growth*: Ecology and the Neoliberal Counterrevolution. *Antipode* 47(2), 461–480.

Pelling, M. (2011). *Adaptation to Climate Change: From Resilience to Transformation*. New York: Routledge.

Robertson, M. (2006). The Nature that Capital Can See: Science, State and Market in the Commodification of Ecosystem Services. *Environment and Planning D: Society and Space* 24(3), 367–387.

Robertson, M. M. (2012). Measurement and Alienation: Making a World of Ecosystem Services. *Transactions of the Institute of British Geographers* 37(3), 386–401.

Sullivan, S. (2013). Banking Nature? The Spectacular Financialisation of Environmental Conservation. *Antipode* 45(1), 198–217.

UNFCCC (2007). Investment and Financial Flows to Address Climate Change. Bonn, Germany: Climate Change Secretariat.

UNFCCC (2010). Report of the Conference of the Parties on its Sixteenth Session, Cancun, 29 November to 10 December. Available at: http://unfccc.int/resource/docs/2010/cop16/eng/07a01.pdf (accessed 15 January 2016).

Virno, P. (1996). Do You Remember Counterrevolution? in P. Virno and M. Hardt (eds), *Radical Thought in Italy: A Potential Politics*. Minneapolis: University of Minnesota Press.

Walker, B., C. S. Holling, S. Carpenter, and A. Kinzig (2004). Resilience, Adaptability and Transformability in Social-ecological Systems. *Ecology and Society* 9(2), Article 5.

Walker, J. and Cooper, M. (2011). Genealogies of Resilience: From Systems Ecology to the Political Economy of Crisis Adaptation. *Security Dialogue* 42(2), 143–160.

Westley, F., S. Carpenter, W. Brock, C. S. Holling, and L. Gunderson (2002). Why Systems of People and Nature Are Not Just Social and Ecological Systems. In Lance Gunderson and C. S. Holling (eds), *Panarchy: Understanding Transformations in Human and Natural Systems*. Washington: Island Press, pp. 103–120.

Westley, F., O. Tjornbo, L. Schultz, P. Olsson, C. Folke, B. Crona, and O. Bodin (2013). A Theory of Transformative Agency in Linked Social-ecological Systems. *Ecology and Society* 18(3), Article 27.

World Bank (2007). *The Caribbean Catastrophe Risk Insurance Initiative. Results of Preparation Work on the Design of a Caribbean Catastrophe Risk Insurance Facility.* Washington, DC: World Bank.

World Bank (2011). *State and Trends of the Carbon Market 2011.* Washington, DC: World Bank.

World Bank (2013). *Turn Down the Heat: Climate Extremes, Regional Impacts, and the Case for Resilience*, a report for the World Bank by the Potsdam Institute for Climate Impact Research and Climate Analytics. Washington, DC: World Bank.

16

THE OPERATIONALIZATION OF RESILIENCE IN PASTORAL REGIONS IN EAST AFRICA AND CENTRAL ASIA

Chuan Liao and Ding Fei

Introduction

Pastoralism has long been considered a resilient livelihood strategy (Moritz *et al.* 2013; Robinson and Berkes 2010) because it is highly adapted to the rangeland ecosystem constantly in disequilibrium (Behnke *et al.* 1993). However, insufficient efforts have been made to operationalize the concept of resilience in the pastoral contexts. In this chapter, we argue that existing resilience research on pastoralism needs to be more cognizant of narratives by pastoralists whose situated knowledge could offer more nuanced understandings of how resilience is manifested and challenged in the real world. Based on empirical evidence from comparative case studies in East Africa and Central Asia, we aim to develop a context-relevant analysis of pastoral resilience.

Resilience is generally considered as an attribute of the socio-ecological system. Its conventional definition emphasizes the system's capacities to absorb disturbance and maintain the state of the system, and to build and increase adaptation through self-organization (Folke 2006; Holling 1973). In order to operationalize such an abstract concept as resilience, a critical task is to identify and specify the resilience of what, namely the subject, and resilience to what, namely the threats (Carpenter *et al.* 2001). For instance, in the field of development studies, resilience has been operationalized as stochastic dynamics of individual and collective human well-being in front of multiple stressors and shocks (Barrett and Constas 2014). Therefore, a practical approach towards quantifying system resilience requires the identification of resilience surrogates and the derivation of quantifiable proxies (Adger 2006; Bennett *et al.* 2005).

Context and perspective are central to resilience research (Bourbeau 2013); however, there is a lack of direct input from pastoralists in terms of the subjective definition of resilience. Scholars have developed their own terms to characterize pastoral resilience, such as seasonal migration (macro-mobility) and rotational grazing (micro-mobility) (Niamir-Fuller 1998). Recent research efforts have proposed the components-relationships-innovation-continuity framework to analyze pastoral resilience (Cumming *et al.* 2005), and have applied context-specific indicators such as mobility, storage, diversification, communal pooling, and reciprocity to operationalize resilience (Agrawal 2010; Fernández-Giménez *et al.* 2015). However, such indicators were largely derived from outsiders' knowledge of pastoralism, which might suffer from an inherent bias in understanding pastoralism. In addition, comparative studies of cross-continental pastoral resilience have remained largely underexplored. Hence, while we have gained substantial knowledge regarding the overall pattern of global pastoralism (Dong *et al.* 2011), resilience narratives from pastoral societies are yet to be sought. Such a knowledge gap might result in an overgeneralization of highly diverse pastoral societies and an oversimplification of the challenges faced by different pastoral populations throughout the world.

Our research thus attempts to bridge the above gaps through comparative empirical analysis of resilience in two distinct pastoral settings: the East African savanna in Borana, Ethiopia and the Central Asian steppe in Altay, Xinjiang, China. Both sites represent the typical resource-use patterns and sociocultural characteristics of pastoral communities in the African and Asian rangelands. Specifically, we aim to answer two research questions: (1) How do pastoralists define resilience in Borana and Altay? (2) What are the surrogate indicators of and threats to pastoral resilience? To answer these two questions, we first developed a subjective definition of resilience from focus group discussions with Boran and Kazak pastoralists. Drawing upon pastoralists' specifications of "resilience of what" and "resilience to what," we investigated mobility, land-use patterns and livelihood diversification as surrogate indicators of resilience. Our research findings suggest that flexible access to different patches of rangelands at strategic locations enhanced resilience, but that the freedom of movement was challenged by a series of socio-environmental risks. Livelihood diversification has been increasingly pursued to smooth household income and cope with socio-ecological stresses. However, unrealistic expectations regarding non-pastoral livelihoods might compromise pastoral resilience.

Study areas and methods

Our empirical research was conducted in the Borana Zone (36.7°–39.7° E, 3.5°–5.3° N) of southern Ethiopia and the Altay District (85.5°–90.5° E, 45.5°–49.1° N) in Xinjiang, China, which are representative of the grazing systems in the savanna of East Africa and the steppe of Central Asia. The similarities and differences of these two sites allow us to compare and contrast how resilience is manifested and operationalized in the pastoral contexts. Extensive livestock herding is practiced in both sites to make use of forage resources heterogeneously distributed in space and time. Both Boran and Kazak pastoralists adopt camp relocation as a key strategy to ensure forage intake and rangeland sustainability. In addition, these pastoralists are perceived as ethnic minority groups who make their livelihoods in the most remote regions of their respective countries. Consequently, these pastoral communities and livelihoods have been subject to various external interventions over the past decades. In Ethiopia, the government and NGOs pushed for the sedentarization of Boran pastoralists by implementing development interventions such as crop cultivation, water facility construction, rangeland fencing, and cash for labor projects (Homann et al. 2008). Similarly, Kazak pastoralists' way of production has also been under substantial government intervention as they went through the era of communes (1960–1980) and subsequent decollectivization (mid-1980s). As the issue of rangeland degradation exacerbates, the central government has recently determined to transform pastoralists' "backward" livelihoods by implementing a new series of sedentarization and development projects (Xinhua 2011).

However, tremendous differences exist between these two pastoral systems. Although both sites are situated in arid and semi-arid lands (ASAL), the Borana Zone is located in a tropical setting in the southernmost region of Ethiopia, while the Altay District in northernmost Xinjiang, China, is in the cold temperate zone of the Earth. The steppe rangeland in Altay is dominated by short grass (Zhang 1992), and the savanna in Borana is increasingly encroached by woody plants that suppress the growth of forage species (Angassa and Oba 2008). Accordingly, Kazak pastoralists in Altay practiced long-distance seasonal migration between the Gobi desert and mountain meadows, while Boran pastoralists herded livestock in a relatively smaller area and relocated between patches of rangelands.

In both Borana and Altay, we conducted focus group discussions and participatory mapping to investigate pastoral resilience. In Borana, our research was conducted in ten communities across the entire zone in the summer of 2013. The number of participants in each group ranged from four to eight, including at least one elder pastoralist, one female pastoralist, and one pastoralist in the local leadership committee. In Altay, we studied pastoralists in six communities in the summer of 2011. Since the pastoralists from the same community were spread out along their migration routes that spanned hundreds of kilometers, we conducted separate investigations in different locations along the annual pastoral migration corridors, namely overwintering villages, transitional pastures, and summer pastures. Such gradients also reflected the ecological differences, as overwintering villages were usually established in the lowlands close to the Gobi desert, while summer pastures were mostly montane alpine meadows situated at higher elevations, with transitional pastures in between.

In each focus group, we asked pastoralists open-ended questions regarding the definition and manifestation of resilience in local contexts. In this way, we were able to infer the local interpretation of resilience. However, asking pastoralists to define resilience was challenging, as a direct translation of resilience into the Oromo and Kazak languages was almost non-existent. Instead, we asked pastoralists to describe their desirable livelihoods, as well as the critical elements in maintaining a desired state of livelihoods. In addition, we discussed the chronic and emerging challenges to pastoral livelihoods, and conducted participatory mapping to investigate household migration activities and land-use patterns. These activities allowed us to derive a set of surrogate indicators of resilience, understand how they contribute to resilience and how they are affected by socio-ecological threats.

Pastoralists' definition of resilience

Both Boran and Kazak pastoralists defined resilience as the capacity to maintain viable livelihoods throughout time. Pastoralists generally believed that decent livelihoods were largely achieved through keeping a viable number of livestock at the household level. Meanwhile, being mobile made it possible to cope with temporary environmental stresses and disturbances in certain geographic locations, to seek forage and water elsewhere. Accordingly, both pastoral societies have developed complex land-use patterns, which allow for sufficient forage intake for livestock on the one hand, and ensure rangeland sustainability on the other hand. Furthermore, both Boran and Kazak pastoralists referred to the diversification of livelihood portfolio as a crucial approach to achieve resilience.

Differences in subjective definitions of resilience in these two pastoral societies largely stemmed from their unique ecological settings. In Borana, the specification of resilience was built on the heterogeneity of spatio-temporal resource distribution on the rangelands. For one, the mosaics of different rangeland types at a fine spatial scale necessitated micro-mobility to make use of these resources effectively. For another, bimodal distribution of precipitation resulted in two rainy and two dry seasons within a year, which made Boran pastoralists adopt macro-mobility (frequent seasonal migration at a broader scale) as a response to uneven rainfall distribution. A combination of micro- and macro-scale mobility strategies allowed pastoralists to keep track of greener pastures, and they were thus able to keep a viable number of livestock in a rangeland ecosystem with high seasonality.

In addition, Boran pastoralists also emphasized the importance of effective rangeland zoning and management to achieve resilience. Rangelands were traditionally divided into *worra* lands (close to settlement) for wet season grazing and *forra* lands (distant from settlement) for dry season grazing (Homewood 2008). However, as pastoralists were getting more sedentarized, such a divide became less common. Since pastoralists in certain communities stopped practicing *forra* herding, they simply divided their *worra* lands into patches for wet and dry season grazing separately. In addition, after the extreme drought that struck the entire Borana in 2011, the pastoralists started to fence more community rangeland reserves to save forage in order to cope with potential droughts.

In contrast, the Kazak pastoralists' definition of resilience focused heavily on following the plant phenology and climate pattern along the gradient from Gobi desert to alpine meadow. The abundant forage in alpine meadows attracted pastoralists to move up to the Altay Mountains in the summer, while heavy snowstorms drove them down to the Gobi desert in the winter. Therefore, the Kazak pastoralists' operationalization of resilience was manifested in the directional and vertical movement along a corridor up to 300 kilometers. In addition, although rangelands in Altay were largely assigned to individual households during decollectivization in the 1980s, fences were not set up to delineate the boundaries. Consequently, each household had their own summer pasture, mid-pasture, lambing pasture and winter grazing land, which served different ecological functions for livestock herding. However, the boundaries of these pastures were vague, and sharing of grazing lands was common among Kazak pastoralists, especially under drought or snowstorm conditions.

As these two study sites were challenged by harsh environmental conditions and faced with external development interventions, both Boran and Kazak pastoralists started to engage in non-pastoral strategies to complement household income in case of poor livestock production. In fact, non-pastoral livelihoods have become a significant part of household income in Kazak. As in 2011, over 31 percent of household income was from crop cultivation, wage labor, hired herding, government subsidy and small business (Liao *et al.* 2015). Pastoralists in Borana also emphasized the importance of non-pastoral livelihoods to smooth household income, and their practice of diversification has also been reported in the literature (Tache and Oba 2010; Tache and Sjaastad 2010).

Overall, pastoralists' definition of resilience largely focused on how to maintain household welfare given the environmental stresses in ASAL. Although resilience in both pastoral contexts was manifested in maintaining a viable number of livestock through flexible access to pastures at multiple locations, pastoralists also highlighted the importance of a diverse livelihood portfolio. Such a definition echoes with the broader theory of resilience. On the one hand, mobility and well-designed land-use patterns allowed pastoralists to absorb the impact of disturbances such as drought and snowstorms and maintain their herd size. On the other hand, flexibility in rangeland management and freedom to diversify into non-pastoral livelihoods reflected the pastoralists' capacity to build and increase adaptation through self-organization and transformation.

Surrogate indicators of pastoral resilience

Numerous factors have been proposed as indictors of resilience, including, for example, governance, civic capacity, natural resources, economic resources, and knowledge sharing (Walsh-Dilley *et al.* 2013). Specific to the pastoral system, indicators such as mobility, communal pooling, diversification, storage, and reciprocity have been applied to analyze resilience (Fernández-Giménez *et al.* 2015). Our research chose three key factors—mobility, land-use pattern and livelihood diversification—as indicators of pastoral resilience, which were the most frequently mentioned surrogates of resilience by Boran and Kazak pastoralists. These three indicators not only characterized resilience in our study sites, but also contained the essence of other factors.

For instance, mobility and land-use patterns suggested whether reciprocity and communal pooling was practiced, because pastoralists commonly sought help from neighbors who were willing to share pastures during drought. Land-use pattern also indicated the concept of storage, as hayfields were designated for winter use in Altay, and community-fenced rangeland reserves were set aside for grazing in dry season in Borana. Due to the above reasons, we believe mobility, land-use pattern, and livelihood diversification are reasonable surrogate indicators of pastoral resilience in our study sites.

Mobility

Mobility is the most important indicator of pastoral resilience because it allowed pastoralists to chase greener pastures and mitigate environmental stresses. The role of mobility has long been recognized in terms of its contribution to pastoral resilience (Fratkin 1997). Pastoralists generally moved their livestock to temporary camps that were closer to areas of underutilized pastures during times of stress (Moritz et al. 2013). Both Boran and Kazak pastoralists believed that greater mobility translated into greater resilience, as a viable number of livestock could only be maintained by a household if they were kept mobile.

Mobility in Borana is manifested at two scales. At a broader scale, seasonal migration is practiced between wet and dry seasonal grazing areas. Wet season grazing is organized around the settlement village. Pastoralists take their animals out for grazing during the day, and bring them back to the corral in the evening. Dry season grazing involves the use of multiple satellite camps, which are set up in places that are dozens of kilometers away from the settlements. Pastoralists typically herd animals at each satellite camp for several weeks. As the forage and surface water start to diminish, they move to another satellite camp location to herd their animals. Such camp relocations can last for months, until the next rain season comes, and then they take animals back to their settlements.

Given increasing human population and government sedentarization policy, traditional extensive herding patterns have been gradually replaced by restricted grazing around settlements, where herding starts and ends on a daily basis. In such cases, pastoralists practice another form of rotational grazing within their constrained herding extent. In wet season, animals are herded on rangeland close to villages, in which the herding loop length is generally less than 12 kilometers. As dry season comes and nearby forage is diminished, pastoralists take their animals to more distant locations for grazing, and their daily herding loop length can reach up to 30 kilometers. Such herding strategy is likely to be observed in communities that are closer to Yabello, the administrative center of the Borana Zone. In these sites, pastoralists have established dense settlements and fenced crop fields in clusters around the villages, resulting in limited migration corridors towards major grazing sites.

In contrast to Boran pastoralists, whose mobility patterns are either nomadic or restricted, the spatial migration pattern of Kazak pastoralists is transhumant, marked by directional and vertical movements. This mobility pattern is a unique adaptation to the ecological context. Pastoralists generally migrate along a southwest–northeast corridor after snowmelt, and follow the same path back to their overwintering villages throughout the year. The seasonal migration distance covers hundreds of kilometers. Although rigorous, conducting such long-distance migration redistributes grazing pressure throughout the landscape. Absence of grazing in winter and spring pastures during the summer time allows forage plants to regrow, which can support animal consumption when they return to these locations for the second time in the year. Summer pastures are also only used in a time window between late June and early September. Resting these alpine meadows in both early and late growing seasons enables rangeland vegetation to recover.

There is less variability in the overall migration pattern of Kazak pastoralists than that of the Boran. The Kazaks generally follow fixed migration routes each year, because their pastures were assigned to individual households in multiple locations. Consequently, the Kazak mobility pattern is more seasonally predictable. In winter, most households stay in the lowland along the Ertix River valley, with an average elevation around 500 meters. In spring, pastoralists start to migrate towards the mountains in the northeast. Along the migration route towards the mountains, they usually travel a couple of days, and then camp in one location for several weeks in their designated herding areas. In summer, they arrive in the mountains to enjoy fresh alpine meadows. In fall, pastoralists follow the same route back to overwintering villages, but with fewer stops on the way (Liao *et al.* 2014a). Even when drought hits the system, pastoralists still follow such a broad migration schedule. However, they can increase the camp relocation frequency and negotiate with their neighbors to access their grazing lands. Most participants in our discussion indicated they were willing to accept visitors herding on their lands, knowing that they might need to rely on such reciprocity to survive the next drought or snowstorm.

Land-use patterns

In order to facilitate rotational grazing and ensure rangeland system sustainability, pastoralists have developed complex land-use patterns. To them, a major concern is flexible access to different pastures at times of need, rather than fixed control of a specific piece of land with varying forage productivity. Both Boran and Kazak pastoralists set specific rules on land use according to their unique ecological endowments.

Boran pastoralists' land-use pattern largely follows the bimodal distribution of annual precipitation for efficient utilization of diverse rangelands (Figure 16.1). Traditionally, pastoralists practiced *worra* herding around their base camp during the wet seasons, which were from March to May and from October to December. As dry season approaches, pastoralists take their animals to graze the underutilized forages away from home, which is known as *forra* herding. *Forra* herding usually takes place from January to February and from June to September. In the communal rangelands, access to grazing lands is largely controlled by the availability of surface water. The lack of water facilities in *worra* pasture in the dry season forces pastoralists to take their animals far away from settlements.

Worra pasture can be further divided into *qaye*, *kalo*, and *mata tika* to achieve a greater degree of rotational grazing. *Qaye* is the area close to the villages, usually within a 1 kilometer radius. Due to the high density of livestock presence in this area, forage is depleted soon after the rain. *Kalo* is the rangeland with fences, which serves as a reserve for livestock consumption in the dry season. In certain communities, *kalo* is only reserved for calves in the dry season. *Mata tika* is the major herding area; however, the exact distance from settlements largely depends on the settlement pattern. In the densely settled communities, *mata tika* can be up to 5 kilometers from base camps. This is because the lands around the settlements have been claimed for other uses such as crop cultivation and rangeland reserves. Therefore, pastoralists have to travel a longer distance to reach

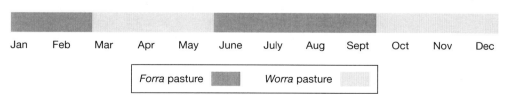

| Jan | Feb | Mar | Apr | May | June | July | Aug | Sept | Oct | Nov | Dec |

Forra pasture   *Worra* pasture

Figure 16.1 Rangeland types and rotational use patterns in Borana, Ethiopia

mata tika on a daily basis. In contrast, *mata tika* for pastoralists in the less sedentarized communities is typically within a distance of 1 kilometer from settlements because the lands are largely left for grazing purposes.

However, broad-scale seasonal migration is undergoing change, as pastoralists become sedentarized and claim patches of rangelands as private crop fields or grazing reserves, leaving the rangelands more fragmented. Consequently, some pastoralists have given up *forra* herding, and stay around their base camp throughout the year. They are now involved in highly restricted movements between their base camp and the major herding areas. Certain areas of *mata tika* are designated as wet season herding areas, while the rest are typically used in the dry season. Such rangeland zoning practices reflect forms of unique adaptation necessary to resolve the conflict between dense settlement and livestock herding.

In contrast to the Boran pastoralists' zoning of rangelands for different purposes of use at a fine spatial scale, Kazak pastoralists' pastures are spread out along a corridor of up to 300 kilometers. These pastures, including winter pasture, lambing pasture, mid-pasture, and summer pasture, serve different functions in pastoralists' annual herding activities from the Gobi desert to the alpine meadows (Figure 16.2). By matching the zoning of rangelands with their associated plant phenology, pastoralists enhance the resilience of both livestock herding and the rangeland ecosystem.

In Altay, winter pasture is generally situated in a transitional area from the Gobi desert to the Altay Mountains Range, with an average elevation of 500 meters. The landscape is mainly desert fodder land. This place is less threatened by snowstorms in winter compared to the mountains in the north, and provides minimal water and fodder that is scarce further south in the desert. There are two kinds of transitional pastures. One is called lambing pasture, which is used for lambing and calving after snowmelt. The other is mid-pasture, which serves as the second transitional zone before they finally reach summer pasture. Vegetation in this area is mainly short and sparse grasses. In fall, pastoralists return there again from their summer pastures. After a whole growing season, the vegetation can support another two months' consumption before they return to over-wintering villages. The vegetation type in the summer pastures is mainly alpine meadows, which are the most productive pasture lands of all. This is the major site for pastoralists to fatten their herds before heading back to overwintering villages.

Livelihood diversification

The practice of non-pastoral livelihoods was often brought up in our discussion with pastoralists. Both Boran and Kazak herders believed that engaging in non-pastoral income-generating activities provided more options, given that livestock herding is becoming increasingly difficult. In pastoral contexts, where the human population increases too fast to allow each household to maintain a viable number of livestock, diversification into other livelihoods seems to be inevitable. In the broader development studies literature, rural livelihoods diversification is generally considered a key focus of poverty reduction strategies in developing countries (Ellis 2000).

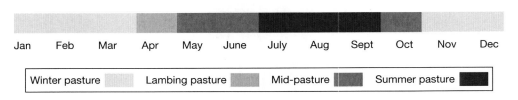

Figure 16.2 Temporal pasture land-use patterns in Altay, Xinjiang, China

204

Diversification is crucial to smooth household consumption and income flow. However, the Boran and Kazak pastoralists debated among themselves regarding the contribution of livelihood diversification to household welfare and beyond. In fact, livelihood diversification in the pastoral contexts has always been controversial. This is not only because the ecological contexts make non-pastoral livelihoods unsuitable, but also due to the fact that pastoralists hold little advantages in non-pastoral livelihoods, over and against their sedentary neighbors (Liao *et al.* 2015).

In Borana, the most commonly practiced non-pastoral livelihood is crop cultivation. Nine out of ten communities were growing tef, maize, and sorghum in their fenced crop fields. In reality, none of the households used the whole fenced area as a crop field. Only half of fenced land was used to grow crops. The remaining part was left as reserved rangeland for individual households. Without livestock grazing inside the fenced lands, the forage plants could grow very well, thus providing valuable support in dry season. However, lands outside of fences were almost barren. Such differences in land cover made some pastoralists believe that the only approach to stop overgrazing and degradation was to fence more rangelands.

In addition to crop cultivation, Boran pastoralists established micro-finance cooperatives to work on saving and credit. The idea was to identify a group of pastoralists who were interested in doing business and willing to contribute a certain amount of money to the group. Anyone in the community could join the group, but that person must have a good reputation. The group typically conducted small business using this money. However, any member could borrow money from the group and do his/her own business, as long as he/she paid back the loan according to the interest rate. There were different forms of saving and credit in practice. The most common activity was to buy livestock in the community and sell them in regional markets. Some cooperatives started a grocery store at the community center. Pastoralists believed that having the extra labor to engage in these non-pastoral livelihoods was crucial to complement their livelihoods.

The Kazaks were also diversifying their livelihood portfolio. The most commonly mentioned non-pastoral source of income in Altay was crop cultivation. According to focus group discussion, about 30 percent of households had crop fields. Popular crops cultivated in Altay were the cash crops such as beans and melons. Pastoralists indicated that they adjusted their cultivated crops each year as an adaptation to changing prices in the regional markets.

In addition, Kazak pastoralists were deriving income from wage labor, hired herding, and small business to complement household income. A substantial proportion of households were engaged in wage labor in cities or townships nearby. Taking care of others' livestock to earn a 'hired herding fee' has also emerged as an income source. This has become prevalent, especially in recent years. Except for a small proportion of hired herders who took care of others' livestock throughout the year, most of them only did so during warm seasons from May to September. In addition, some households sold raw and processed milk products to dairy businessmen or tourists, or ran a small grocery store in their yurts, as access to grocery items was very limited in such remote areas.

Despite the fact that non-pastoral livelihoods were commonly practiced, some pastoralists also pointed out their limited contribution to household welfare and resilience. It might take generations for pastoralists to become professional and efficient in their newly adopted non-pastoral livelihoods. Pastoralists held no advantage in crop cultivation or other non-pastoral livelihoods against their sedentary neighbors. In Borana, there was little evidence that pastoralists have become self-sufficient through grain production. Their yields were only 31 percent of the Ethiopian national average, and grain per capita met only 26 percent of the annual requirement for each household (Tache and Oba 2010).

Wage labor was gaining popularity in both Borana and Altay; however, this was far from being a stable source of income. In Borana, the wage labor position was largely created by NGOs in the pastoral communities. They started "cash for labor" projects and paid pastoralists to clear bushes and construct water facilities. Pastoralists were paid three US dollars for six hours of their labor each day. Such programs were usually phased out in less than three months, so could hardly become a stable source of income. In Altay, nearly 20 percent of participant households are engaged in wage labor (Liao *et al.* 2015). However, due to their lack of schooling and poor Chinese language proficiency, they were mostly hired in low-level office positions, or to work at construction sites and in crop fields based on temporary contracts.

Doing small business in the form of cooperatives was commonly advocated by NGOs in Borana. The development agents taught pastoralists how to establish micro-finance cooperatives. However, due to poor leadership and a shortage of accounting skills, nearly half of these cooperatives were experiencing dropouts. Pastoralists also mentioned that there were quite a number of cooperatives planned several months ago, which never got started due to the lack of seed funds and skilled accountants. In addition, when members could not directly benefit from the cooperatives they refused to continue contributing money and attending regular meetings. Therefore, the effectiveness of micro-finance cooperatives was likely to be compromised.

Challenges to pastoral resilience

Pastoralists' discussions of challenges to resilience revolved around factors that threatened pastoral mobility and land-use patterns. Drought and rangeland degradation were the most frequently mentioned environmental shocks in both Borana and Altay. Social factors that threatened pastoral resilience were largely driven by pastoral policies and external interventions in these two study sites, although the details differed substantially.

Environmental risks

Drought is one of the most common challenges to pastoral livelihoods in ASAL environments throughout the world (Liao *et al.* 2014b). Although pastoralists in Borana experienced dry seasons twice a year, the failure of expected rain usually translated into severe drought. In recent years, drought has hit the pastoral system much more often than before. Therefore, pastoralists have had to adjust their herding practices. Participants used the extreme drought in 2011 as an example to explain how they responded to crisis. Most pastoralists walked several days and took their live-stock to places beyond the Borana Zone to search for water and forage. However, the participants could hardly tell whether those who migrated did better than those who stayed. Despite better forage and water in other places, the increased livestock density caused fierce competition for resources, and a substantial number of livestock died due to disease outbreak. Those who stayed in the communities received support from NGOs and faced less grazing competition from neighbors, which allowed them to (just barely) survive the crisis.

In Altay, most respondents characterized drought as reduced rainfall and less water in rivers; however, under extreme circumstances, drought could also cause a lack of drinking water for both humans and livestock. Drought was least likely to occur on summer pastures, because the Altay Mountains received abundant precipitation throughout the year. In contrast, the transitional pastures received less rain (Zhang 1992). Although winter pastures situated along the Ertix River Valley close to the desert were the driest, pastoralists were typically prepared for the aridity. However, unexpected drought on the relatively humid transitional pastures was more threatening to pastoral livelihoods because pastoralists were usually not prepared to deal with these challenges.

Rangeland degradation was another major ecological challenge to livestock herding, which was manifested in two different forms in Borana and Altay. In Borana, it was woody plant encroachment, which suppressed the growth of herbaceous forage plants in the understory (between the canopy and the forest floor). Once established, bush cover significantly accelerated the decline in grass cover. Fire used to perform an essential ecological role in shaping the structure and composition of vegetation. However, a bush burning ban that lasted for 30 years from the 1970s, accompanied with the intensification of grazing, resulted in a failure to thin the woody plant layer and a depletion of herbs that are highly valuable for cattle grazing (Angassa and Oba 2008). Consequently, some pastoralists changed their livestock portfolio by keeping more camels and small ruminants, but fewer cattle. Moreover, bush encroachment also served as a push factor for people to diversify their livelihoods, because herding livestock on the bush-encroached rangelands was less remunerative.

In Altay, pasture degradation was also identified as a major threat to livestock herding. Kazak pastoralists believed that pasture was the ecological basis of pastoral livelihoods, and its forage availability directly affected income. They considered overgrazing to be the major factor that led to degradation. Pastoralists were fully aware of the imbalance between forage demand and supply on the pastures, as they complained that there were "too many livestock, too few grasses," and "there are too many livestock from households who do not herd in person."

Social risks

Borana, Ethiopia

External interventions in Borana, mostly implemented by NGOs, have had a major impact on pastoral resilience. With more development interventions flowing into this region, the pastoralists have increasingly become dependent on external aid and less likely to develop their own capacity to deal with socio-ecological challenges. As the development agencies have continued to ignore pastoralists' capacities for managing the rangelands, the legitimacy of customary laws have been further compromised in terms of resource management. These changes in civic capacity, institution, and resource-use pattern have gone against the principles of common-pool resource management strategies in Borana that have functioned for centuries.

In general, NGO interventions have been preoccupied with immediate impacts on the targeted population that they could then show to their donors. When their interventions are phased out, the minimal contributions made to the pastoral communities are likely to diminish. In addition, these short-term projects have largely overlooked their negative impacts on the pastoral society and rangeland ecosystem. For example, paying pastoralists to manage rangelands and water facilities has made them increasingly unwilling to organize their own labor to clear the bushes on the communal rangeland or develop and maintain water facilities. Such development interventions have paid little attention to community capacity building, and have instead focused on how programs are perceived by donors.

In the focus group discussions, respondents clearly pointed out that with an increasing human and livestock population, the customary regulation of rangeland management was becoming compromised or being violated. As more pastoralists began to sedentarize, the traditional resource-use patterns were affected, as well as the ability to endure crisis. Moreover, fencing the communal rangelands for private crop fields was likely to cause the disruption of common, property-based rangeland management practice in the pastoral settings. People easily ran into conflicts due to competition for limited forage. In addition, some people took cattle into rangeland reserves at the wrong time of year, and violated the community agreement on fencing.

Water facility management rules were also becoming weaker, largely because the government started interfering by putting pressure on the administrators of the wells, who were no longer permitted to punish those breaking the rules (Watson 2003).

Altay, Xinjiang, China

Social threats to mobility and traditional land-use patterns largely originated from government pastoral policies, which pushed for ecological restoration and development (Liao *et al.* 2014b). Ecological restoration of pastures, which claimed to conserve their biodiversity, was an emerging type of risk that has started to affect pastoralists in recent years. Ecological restoration has been implemented through a number of policies, including fencing off pastures and compensating affected households by government subsidy. However, minimal compensation could hardly support their livelihoods given the increasing price of commodities. As the central government has targeted certain rangelands to become permanently prohibited grazing areas where ecological restoration projects would be given priority, pastoral mobility and access to diverse pastures has become increasingly compromised.

Disturbance from development interventions has also affected the practice of mobile livestock herding. Gold mining in the Altay Mountain Range has grown more intensive and destructive in recent years, with a tremendous impact on the environment. The excavation has devastated the landscape, blocking migration routes and access to rivers. Since the mining has been conducted on these summer pastures in winter over the past several years, pastoralists could hardly stop these practices. The iron mining industry is also burgeoning. Unlike gold mining, which relies primarily on physical extraction of the metal, iron mining requires tons of water and harmful chemicals. As a result, less water is left for pastoralists, and some livestock have died from consuming contaminated river water. With numerous iron mines being discovered, respondents were afraid of the proliferation of iron mining in the future.

Conclusions

This chapter investigated the operationalization of the concept of resilience in pastoral contexts in the Borana zone of Ethiopia and the Altay District of Xinjiang, China. We answered the question of "Resilience of what to what?" by seeking direct input from pastoralists. The results suggested that both Boran and Kazak pastoralists' subjective definition of resilience centered on the maintenance of decent livelihoods throughout time. Three important surrogate indicators of resilience emerged, those of mobility, land-use patterns, and livelihood diversification. Mobility allowed pastoralists to survive and prosper in the ASAL environments. Rangeland zoning was crucial to ensure rotational grazing at multiple scales, while meeting the nutritional demands of livestock. Livelihood diversification was also considered as a crucial smoother for household income, despite its controversial implementation in pastoral settings.

Mobile livestock herding based on flexible access to rangelands in strategic locations at times of need has proven to be successful in both Borana and Altay for centuries. However, such a traditional livelihood strategy has been subject to a series of socio-environmental risks. Forage and water resources were either diminishing or becoming susceptible to change in availability as a result of drought and rangeland degradation, which threatened the feasibility of maintaining a viable number of livestock for each household. In addition, external interventions from government and other agencies strongly affected pastoralists' herding practices and choices of livelihood strategies. These interventions are likely to delegitimize customary institutions in the management of natural resources on both savanna and steppe.

Our empirical research on the operationalization of resilience suggested that mobility and well-designed land-use management schemes allowed the pastoral systems to absorb environmental disturbances, such as droughts and snowstorms, which contributed to the system's overall resilience. However, even among the Boran and Kazak pastoralists themselves, there were divergent perspectives regarding how to balance between the need to maintain livestock herding and the demand to diversify into non-pastoral livelihoods. Future research on pastoral resilience needs to examine the mechanisms to resolve such a dilemma and develop innovative pathways towards pastoral resilience in the long run.

References

Adger, W.N. (2006). Vulnerability. *Global Environmental Change* 16, 268–281.

Agrawal, A. (2010). Local institutions and adaptation to climate change. *Social Dimensions of Climate Change: Equity and Vulnerability in a Warming World*. Washington DC: World Bank, 173–198.

Angassa, A. and Oba, G. (2008). Herder perceptions on impacts of range enclosures, crop farming, fire ban and bush encroachment on the rangelands of Borana, Southern Ethiopia. *Hum. Ecol.* 36, 201–215.

Barrett, C.B. and Constas, M.A. (2014). Toward a theory of resilience for international development applications. *Proc. Natl. Acad. Sci.* 111, 14625–14630.

Behnke, R., Scoones, I., and Kerven, C. (1993). *Range Ecology at Disequilibrium: New Models of Natural Variability and Pastoral Adaptation in African Savannas*. Overseas Development Institute, London.

Bennett, E.M., Cumming, G.S., and Peterson, G.D. (2005). A Systems Model Approach to Determining Resilience Surrogates for Case Studies. *Ecosystems* 8, 945–957.

Bourbeau, P. (2013). Resiliencism: Premises and Promises in securitisation research. *Resilience* 1, 3–17.

Carpenter, S., Walker, B., Anderies, J.M., and Abel, N. (2001). From Metaphor to Measurement: Resilience of What to What? *Ecosystems* 4, 765–781.

Cumming, G.S., Barnes, G., Perz, S., Schmink, M., Sieving, K.E., Southworth, J., Binford, M., Holt, R.D., Stickler, C., and Holt, T.V. (2005). An Exploratory Framework for the Empirical Measurement of Resilience. *Ecosystems* 8, 975–987.

Dong, S., Wen, L., Liu, S., Zhang, X., Lassoie, J.P., Yi, S., Li, X., Li, J., and Li, Y. (2011). Vulnerability of Worldwide Pastoralism to Global Changes and Interdisciplinary Strategies for Sustainable Pastoralism. *Ecol. Soc.* 16(2), 1–23.

Ellis, F. (2000). *Rural Livelihoods and Diversity in Developing Countries*. Oxford University Press, Oxford; New York, NY.

Fernández-Giménez, M.E., Batkhishig, B., Batbuyan, B., and Ulambayar, T. (2015). Lessons from the Dzud: Community-Based Rangeland Management Increases the Adaptive Capacity of Mongolian Herders to Winter Disasters. *World Dev.* 68, 48–65.

Folke, C. (2006). Resilience: The Emergence of a Perspective for Social-ecological Systems Analyses. *Glob. Environ. Change* 16, 253–267.

Fratkin, E. (1997). Pastoralism: Governance and Development Issues. *Annu. Rev. Anthropol.* 235–261.

Holling, C.S. (1973). Resilience and Stability of Ecological Systems. *Annu. Rev. Ecol. Syst.* 1–23.

Homann, S., Rischkowsky, B., Steinbach, J., Kirk, M., and Mathias, E. (2008). Towards Endogenous Livestock Development: Borana Pastoralists' Responses to Environmental and Institutional Changes. *Hum. Ecol.* 36, 503–520.

Homewood, K. (2008). *Ecology of African pastoralist societies*. James Currey; Ohio University Press; Unisa Press, Oxford; Athens, OH; Pretoria.

Liao, C., Morreale, S.J., Kassam, K.-A.S., Sullivan, P.J., and Fei, D. (2014a). Following the Green: Coupled Pastoral Migration and Vegetation Dynamics in the Altay and Tianshan Mountains of Xinjiang, China. *Appl. Geogr.* 46, 61–70.

Liao, C., Sullivan, P.J., Barrett, C.B., and Kassam, K.-A.S. (2014b). Socioenvironmental Threats to Pastoral Livelihoods: Risk Perceptions in the Altay and Tianshan Mountains of Xinjiang, China. *Risk Anal.* 34, 640–655.

Liao, C., Barrett, C.B., and Kassam, K.-A.S. (2015). Does Diversification Improve Livelihoods? Pastoral Households in Xinjiang. *China. Dev. Change* 47.

Moritz, M., Scholte, P., Hamilton, I.M., and Kari, S. (2013). Open Access, Open Systems: Pastoral Management of Common-Pool Resources in the Chad Basin. *Hum. Ecol.* 41, 351–365.

Niamir-Fuller, M. (1998). The Resilience of Pastoral Herding in Sahelian Africa. *Link. Soc. Ecol. Syst. Manag. Pract. Soc. Mech. Build. Resil.* 250–284.

Robinson, L.W. and Berkes, F. (2010). Applying Resilience Thinking to Questions of Policy for Pastoralist Systems: Lessons from the Gabra of Northern Kenya. *Hum. Ecol.* 38, 335–350.

Tache, B. and Oba, G. (2010). Is Poverty Driving Borana Herders in Southern Ethiopia to Crop Cultivation? *Hum. Ecol.* 38, 639–649.

Tache, B. and Sjaastad, E. (2010). Pastoralists' Conceptions of Poverty: An Analysis of Traditional and Conventional Indicators from Borana, Ethiopia. *World Dev.* 38, 1168–1178.

Walsh-Dilley, M., Wolford, W. and McCarthy, J. (2013). Rights for resilience: bringing power, rights and agency into the resilience framework. Atkinson Center for a Sustainable Future (ACSF) – Oxfam Working Paper. ACSF, Cornell University, Ithaca, New York.

Watson, E.E. (2003). Examining the Potential of Indigenous Institutions for Development: A Perspective from Borana, Ethiopia. *Dev. Change* 34, 287–310.

Xinhua, (2011). Complete prohibition of grazing in the eight pastoral scenic spot in Xinjiang. Retrieved from http://news.xinhuanet.com/2011-06/18/c_121552444.htm.

Zhang, X. (1992). Xinjiang. *In Committee on Scholarly Communication with the People's Republic of China* (U.S.) (ed.), National Academy Press, Washington, DC.

PART VI

Urban planning

17

FROM MALADAPTATION TO ADAPTATION

Towards a resilient urban planning paradigm

Jonathan Clarke

Introduction

On 26 October 2012, the tropical cyclone Hurricane Sandy, which had devastated communities across the Caribbean, made landfall on the Mid-Atlantic and Northeastern United States pushing a major storm surge into the city of New York. The city's scant flood walls and defences were overwhelmed, flooding streets, tunnels, subway lines and, most notably, the city's main energy plants at Battery Park, which led to widespread electricity blackouts. This loss of power would prove to be a 'fracture-critical' event, as hospitals lost power and much of the city was without potable water, being reliant upon electricity for pumping.

Whilst only one life was lost within the city, the cost of damage was estimated at over $71.4 billion, and it is widely recognised that New York came close to a much more serious disaster. Significantly, many of these impacts were predicted by a 2011 report, *Responding to Climate Change in New York State* (ClimAID) (NYSERDA, 2011), which highlighted the vulnerability of the city's assets and in particular the poor siting of critical infrastructure. Despite such dire warnings, policy makers had failed to act upon the findings and the city had suffered the consequences. However, the event proved to be a wake-up call for politicians and city leaders; since this time over $50 billion of funding has been invested in resilience initiatives (*International Business Times*, 2014), but, more significantly, this action has been catalytic for urban resilience internationally, with New York emerging as an exemplar for resilient design through a host of innovative and best practice initiatives (Coaffee and Clarke, 2015). It is also illustrative of many of the key arguments raised within this chapter, which reflects upon how cities can be reconfigured, physically, socially and environmentally, to address a range of disruptive challenges and to enhance resilience through learning from maladaptive urban design and planning practice.

In the last 15 years, the concept of resilience has emerged as a key consideration for urban theorists, academics and policy makers, whilst the term is also an important source of discourse in a diverse range of related fields (Coaffee, 2013a, 2013b; Davoudi, 2012; Walker and Cooper, 2011; Cote and Nightingale, 2012). Globally, this period has seen significant shock events, disturbance and volatility with recent disasters, such as the Tohuku earthquake in 2011 or the impact of Hurricane Katrina on New Orleans in 2005; these 'Black Swan' events illustrate the vulnerability and potential weakness within the design, planning and management of contemporary cities, but perhaps also illuminate how we might enhance urban resilience in the future.

Subsequently, the concept of resilience has been utilised as a means to consider a diverse range of contemporary risks and stresses and, within the context of contemporary planning policy and practice, offers a new and increasingly relevant set of ideas, tools and approaches to help understand the complexities of an increasingly urbanised world (Coaffee *et al.*, 2008; Davoudi *et al.*, 2013; Scott, 2013; Stumpp, 2013). In recent years, there has been a gradual shift to an increasingly transdisciplinary concept of resilience that integrates the physical and socio-political aspects of resilience and emphasises 'joined-up' approaches to decision-making. Moreover, the growth in importance of 'resilience' has been underpinned by the political prioritisation of the safety and security of communities against an array of perceived hazards and threats, ranging from terrorism, disease pandemic and global warming-related flooding to stresses which serve to weaken the fabric of everyday life, such as fiscal retrenchment and high rates of unemployment. However, tensions continue to exist regarding the extent to which principles underpinning resilience can become enmeshed within the formal planning processes of vulnerable urban areas.

Despite these issues of operationalising urban resilience in practice, there is a growing consensus that resilience can be understood more broadly as the capacity to withstand and rebound from a range of disruptive challenges, considered from the perspective of an evolving range of contemporary risks (Walker and Broderick 2006; Leichenko, 2011; Scott, 2013; White, 2013; Coaffee and Clarke, 2015). But the concept of resilience also has wider relevance, as Vale (2014, p. 1) elaborates:

> Resilience is, simultaneously, a theory about how systems can behave across scales, a practice or proactive approach to planning systems that applies across social spaces, and an analytical tool that enables researchers to examine how and why some systems are able to respond to disruption.

However, despite the growing prevalence and sophistication of the term, there is also acknowledgement that an 'implementation gap' exists between the theoretical conceptions of resilience and how it can be utilised in practice (Coaffee and Clarke, 2015). Thus, there is a need to further consider how the ongoing practice of urban planning and design practice can bridge this gap.

The resilience turn in urban planning practice

Only in the last decade have ideas of resilience crept into urban policy debates, creating what is termed 'the urban resilience turn' (Coaffee, 2013a; Imrie and Lees, 2014). Importantly, the ways in which ideas and practices of resilience have emerged within such debates – and their relative influence – are highly specific to the institutional contexts and emergent risks faced in particular locations. Notably, international resilience priorities have been increasingly focused on cities because of the particular vulnerability of densely populated political, economic and cultural centres, the interdependencies of networked infrastructures, and as a result of continued and rapid urbanisation (UN-HABITAT, 2011). These trends amplify the pressure upon cities to keep citizens safe, healthy, prosperous and well informed. Whilst urban theorists promote cities' agglomeration of innovation, creativity and economic resources (Glaeser, 2011; Florida, 2002), a variety of threats to life, property and society also converge upon contemporary cities, by virtue of their accumulation of population and critical infrastructure, as well as a lack of foresight in previous developmental regimes (Coaffee, 2009; Edwards, 2009; Fisher, 2012; Bosher *et al.*, 2007).

In evidence of this, an agglomeration of urban risk, Godschalk (2003) identified the worldwide impact of natural disasters in 2001 as resulting in 25,000 deaths, \$36 billion in economic losses and $11.5 billion in insured losses. Recent years have also seen the cost of urban disasters mounting (Zolli and Healey, 2013). Specifically, Fisher (2012, p. 3) highlights the dramatic increase in 'weather-related catastrophes', such as floods, storms and drought, the occurrence of which has increased by over 400 times in the time period from 1900 to 2005. Consequently, issues surrounding water are often the critical vulnerability within the contemporary city; at present there are one billion people living on land vulnerable to flooding, but that figure is set to rise to two billion by 2050, with the cities of the developing world being particularly vulnerable (Fisher, 2012; UN-HABITAT, 2011; Rockefeller Foundation, 2013).

Highlighting these global vulnerabilities to extreme weather, an influential Royal Society report (The Royal Society, 2014, p.7) makes a number of recommendations to address the convergence of population and climate change risks, through planning and preparedness, protecting people and assets, and, critically, using evidence to inform decision-making:

> Societies are not resilient to extreme weather today. To reduce this resilience deficit action needs to be taken by the international community, governments, local policymakers, the private sector and non-governmental organisations. Lessons can be learnt from past events.

Accordingly, the strengthening of the built environment emerges as a critical focus for wider societal resilience. As Helen Molin Valdes (Valdes *et al.*, 2013, p. 50), writing as the Deputy Director of the UNISDR, observed:

> the built environment acts as the core in every city and facilitates the everyday life of human beings. Any destruction to the built environment disturbs the functioning of the human society, and economic and social development of the country due to its strong connection with the human activities.

This quote highlights the importance of the built environment's role in supplying citizens with essential services and this understanding has led to the recent array of philanthropic and commercial attempts to develop strategic evaluation frameworks to assess urban resilience. For example, the UNISDR's *Making Cities Resilient* campaign (UNISDR, 2012) aims to support public decision-making in urban affairs, whilst the World Bank has produced guidance – Building Urban Resilience in East Asia (World Bank, 2012) – which aims to increase the resilience of cities to disasters and climate change impacts by using a risk-based approach in the public investment decision-making process. Moreover, Siemens (2013) and Arup (2014) produced city resilience 'toolkits' that highlight a number of factors that city leaders should consider when making decisions about urban resilience interventions, whilst in 2013 the Rockefeller Foundation launched their 100 Resilient Cities campaign 'dedicated to helping cities around the world become more resilient to the physical, social and economic challenges that are a growing part of the 21st century' (Rockefeller, 2013). Such approaches highlight how an overarching and strategic view of planning-based resilience needs to consider not only the material built environment but also social economic and decision-making processes. It could also be argued that these entrepreneurial or commercial approaches to resilience offer some support to the hypothesis outlined elsewhere within this volume, that resilience is increasingly a tool of global neoliberal forces.

Recent work within the evolving field of urban resilience (Coaffee *et al.*, 2008; Bosher, 2008; Ahern, 2011; Coaffee, 2013b; Bosher, 2014; Chelleri *et al.*, 2015; Coaffee and Lee, 2016) has coalesced around a number of key requirements for implementing enhanced resilience within the built environment. First, the resilience turn has ushered in a greater requirement for foresight and preparedness; this includes making plans and accommodation for foreseeable events, but also building more general capacity for coping with an uncertain future that requires new methods of risk assessment and management. Second, there is a requirement to consider multiple risks and hazards in a holistic fashion; developing planning policy and practice that can respond in a flexible and integrated fashion to multiple risks across a range of scales has been encouraged. Third, a focus upon the changing organisation and institutionalisation of the resilience response has become paramount in embedding resiliency principles within planning policy and practice. As such, new governance approaches to enhancing urban resilience emphasise joined-up and collaborative approaches to decision-making that break down professional and practice silos. Thus where traditional approaches to urban risk have relied upon a narrow range of stakeholders, progressive approaches will need to be more deliberative, drawing a fuller range of professional and community groups into decision-making at a variety of spatial scales, from locally coordinated systems to centralised and sub-national organisations (Coaffee *et al.* 2008, Coaffee and Clarke, 2015). From a spatial planning perspective, resilience is a continuous journey of improvement, but one that helps define the problems at hand and develop planning processes to mitigate emergent issues through adaptation, innovation and cooperation; mirroring Vale's (2014) observations on the multiple utility of the term.

It can thus be said that resilience represents the environmental, social and technical science of persistence and adaptation. Critical to this advancing sophistication of resilience understanding is the engagement with 'complexity', which has moved the conception of resilience beyond ecological theory and shock response to a governance approach that engages and proactively manages our dynamic world (Chandler, 2012; Zolli and Healy, 2013). Governance, according to Healey (1997), is the way we manage common affairs through formal decision-making institutions, complemented by informal networks. But governance also describes a style of governing, where formal power moves away from traditional forms of government towards a network of other stakeholders (Rydin, 2010; Nuissl and Heinrichs, 2011). Within this context, the complexity of engaged stakeholders and the potential for disruptive hazard is a significant challenge to governance operation. In his critique of resilience as a means to manage increased complexity, Chandler (2014) argues that the complexity is a conceptualisation of 'uncertainty' and the limits of what can be scientifically quantified, which has increasingly become important since the 1920s. More widely, he argues that this understanding is itself a critique of liberal forms of 'top-down' government, an alternative to neoliberal approaches, and that an understanding of the medium of complexity offers the secret to new forms of governance. Within the traditionally technical disciplines of engineering and risk management, these notions of social complexity, interdependency and future uncertainty are increasingly challenging traditional, techno–rationale risk management approaches and fostering an interest in more open-ended, forward-looking and socially informed resilience methods (Suter, 2011; Linkov *et al.*, 2014; Baum, 2015).

Designing for resilience

This understanding around the complexity of the potential medium for resilience and thus the need to see resilience enhancement as an ongoing reflexive process, has close parallels to recent developments in urban design and planning; most notably Carmona's (2014) 'place-shaping continuum', which understands urbanism and urban development as part of a much larger and longer-term process. Within this context, celebrated designer and landscape urbanist, James Corner (2004, p. 1) elaborates further on the importance of these corresponding understandings:

> In order to grow and develop, life forms must both persist and adapt, their organizational structures sufficiently resilient to withstand challenges while also supple enough to morph and reorganize. These principles are as topical today in business and management as they are in biology and ecology, urbanism and the design of public space.

Design-based approaches have further relevance within the context of a complex and changeable world, where ongoing learning is critical. Conventionally our ways of knowing and reasoning have followed 'inductive' or 'deductive' approaches; broadly using established theory as a means to explain practice, or using observations of practice as a means to stimulate new theory. However, there is another, more sparsely utilised approach, 'abductive' reasoning, which Walton (2001, p. 143) defines as 'a kind of guessing by a process of forming a plausible hypothesis that explains a given set of facts or data'.

Abductive methods are often associated with approaches that begin with a solution or proposition, and then work backwards towards a rationale or explanation, as is often the case in design practice. This kind of intelligent guesswork or informed intuition is often most applicable when there is incomplete knowledge of the system of study (Walton, 2001), making it particularly relevant for the complex systems that are the medium of resilience work, and in particular the built environment. It could be said that the nature of the design process and the complexity of design factors requiring consideration mean that every new design is a form of experimentation and every design solution is to some extent fallible (Fisher, 2012). In explanation of this Lawson (2005, p. 143) highlights how, in contrast to how conventional rationalities require deductive and interpolative skills, design's unique feature is how it merges these with 'divergent' approaches that utilise 'an open-ended approach seeking alternatives where there is no clearly correct answer'. As Fisher (2012, p. 177) further articulates on the role of abduction within the design process:

> Such lateral or analogical thinking involves a form of induction, in that it draws conclusions from observed phenomena. But unlike induction, it doesn't seek universal laws or general principles, instead it connects particular things in order to solve specific problems in a given time and space.

Therefore, in contrast to the early theoretical conceptions of resilience, which largely utilised a deductive approach based upon ecological models (Holling, 1973, 1986; Gunderson and Holling, 2002), new forms of resilience practice need to focus upon grounded, inductive learning from practice, with the open-ended process of design used as a medium to interrogate different possibilities, and utilising abductive methods to establish different adaptive pathways.

Fracture-criticality and maladaptive planning

Why is it in hindsight that planners are often seen to make poor decisions that increase, rather than reduce, risk to local communities? In his book on the challenge of resilient design, Thomas Fisher (2012) argued that disasters are caused by 'design errors', and thus the key to a more resilient built environment is to learn from these earlier incidents. He (2012, p. ii) uses the 2007 collapse of the I-35W bridge in Minnesota to illustrate a key design problem, which he refers to as 'fracture-critical design': 'This is design in which structures have so little redundancy and so much interconnectedness and misguided efficiency that they fail completely if any one part does not perform as required.'

Fisher's (2012) concept of fracture-critical design describes a development that is vulnerable to linked systematic failures and catastrophic collapse, also vividly illustrated by the events in New Orleans following Hurricane Katrina. However, the examples of design weaknesses identified within the study display a variety of scales of impact and hint that another conception is needed to fully encapsulate ways in which the built environment can lack resilience. Accordingly, the UN-HABITAT (2011) report on global settlement suggests another potentially helpful understanding:

> There are also actions and investments actions and investments that increase rather than reduce risk and vulnerability to the impacts of climate change and these are termed *maladaptation.* . . . Removing maladaptations and the factors that underpin them are often among the first tasks to be addressed before new adaptations (emphasis added).

Within the context of climate change, maladaptation is generally understood to mean an act of adaption that makes the situation worse (Barnett and O'Neill 2010). However, within the term's behavioural sciences origins, maladaptive behaviour is understood to mean simply, 'inappropriate', 'inflexible' and 'counterproductive', and often occurs as a result of adapting to an earlier situation that is now no longer applicable (Supkoff, 2012). Thus design that is no longer fit for purpose, has reached functional obsolescence, and increases wider vulnerability could be said to be maladaptive (Fisher, 2012).

Barnett and O'Neill (2010, p.211) provide five definitions of climate change maladaptation; these are listed in Table 17.1 below, alongside a wider interpretation of the concept.

Notably, these maladaptations within the urban design and development process, most often display a failure to change to new circumstances or a shifting risk landscape, further reinforcing the need to see the design and governance of the built environment as part of a continual process, rather than a one-off action (Carmona, 2014). Accordingly, the concepts of adaptation and adaptive capacity are increasingly recognised as critical to both wider resilience (Zolli and Healy, 2013), and in particular the challenges posed by man-made climate change. The most recent Intergovernmental Report on Climate Change (IPCC, 2014) used the concept of adaptive capacity to represent the ability to adapt to the impacts and changing requirements of climate change. A broader-ranging definition is provided by Jones *et al.* (2010, p. 2), who highlight that:

> adaptive capacity denotes the ability of a system to adjust, modify or change its characteristics or actions to moderate potential damage, take advantage of opportunities or cope with the consequences of shock or stress.

It is notable that this definition also identifies the opportunities inherent in seeking adaption, whilst there is increasing acknowledgement of how adaptive measures are more contextual, site

Table 17.1 Definitions of maladaptation

Climate change (Barnett and O'Neill, 2010)	*Built environment (Author's own)*
Increasing emissions of greenhouse gases	Increases vulnerability
Disproportionately burdening the most vulnerable	Transfers responsibility to vulnerable stakeholders
High opportunity costs	Disproportionate approach
Reduce incentive to adapt	Fails to adapt
Path dependency	Locked-in

specific and relevant at a local level (Galderisi and Ferrara, 2012). These understandings reinforce the importance of challenging maladaptive design at a range of scales, but also the potential benefits of promoting wider adaptation and adaptive capacity building within the urban planning and design professions more locally.

However, in this push to eliminate weakness and failure, there is a danger of stifling the very innovation necessary for building adaptive capacity; if, as Cross (1982) suggests, the central concern of design is 'the conception and realisation of new things', it appears ideally suited to the change paradigm offered by resilience. In this context, we need to find new ways of promoting innovation and adaptive capacity through design, within the complex arena of the built environment.

The behaviour of planners towards the goal of enhancing resilience is, like all planning operations, highly related to organisational context and can have a huge effect on the ability of the planning system, or individual planners, to act effectively to mitigate the impact of disruptive challenge. Sometimes planners fail to act and adapt to changing circumstances where new risk and threats emerge and on other occasions planning responses might be deemed inappropriate or inflexible. If we consider such behaviour to be often maladaptive, then we can see why planning authorities with their often-siloed ways of working, a focus on short-termism, change averseness and fragmentation of roles, combined with the constant necessity for up-skilling and retraining to enhance the knowledge of available options, have struggled to fully absorb and action much-needed resilience requirements.

These understandings reinforce the importance of challenging maladaptation on a range of scales, but also the potential benefits of promoting wider adaption and adaptive capacity building within the urban planning and design professions more locally, so that planners and the planning system can better adapt to changing circumstances by modifying behaviour, actions or plans according to current and future need.

Closing the implementation gap

In the wake of Hurricane Sandy's impact upon New York, there have been a number of publications and reports which have shed further light on the failings that led to the disaster; in particular highlighting that if the recommendations for mitigation contained within the ClimAid (NYSERDA, 2011) report had been acted upon, much of the damage to the city could have been averted (NYS 2012). The maladaptations and design weaknesses highlighted within this study around the location and protection of New York's critical infrastructure, are substantiated by successive publications including Redlener and Reilly (2012), which notes the 'fragility' of the city's power systems as a result of inappropriate siting, before highlighting the massive exposure of healthcare facilities to future flood events. Similarly, a study by Wagner *et al.* (2014) emphasises the problem of poor land uses and unsuitable development locations, which exacerbated the event, driven by flawed risk management processes; it is suggested that the US has been stuck in a 'cost analysis' model for infrastructure investment and that given the low probability of events occurring, decision-makers were unwilling to act, despite the potential exposure of lives and assets.

From the perspective of design, New York's recent *Rebuild by Design* initiative, which aims to promote resilience through transformative design and planning, is both innovative and more widely relevant to future resilience practice. Initially an open ideas competition, it has seen six winning entries developed towards potential implementation, whilst gaining widespread media coverage and critical praise (Rebuild by Design, 2014). Despite the wide-ranging remit and architectural focus of the competition entrants, who include design luminaries such as Rem Koolhaas, all designs utilise some form of green infrastructure.

Amongst the successful entries, the project which has attracted most attention is BIG Architecture's *DryLine*; inspired by the Highline, it aims to convert the ten miles of Manhattan's hard shoreline, with its bridges and infrastructure, into a continuous network of landscape buffers and 'protective parks' (*The Guardian*, 2014a, 2014b; Rebuild by Design, 2014). Developed by Danish architect Bjarke Ingles, the approach is based upon extensive analysis of Manhattan's vulnerabilities and exposure to flood, as well as studies of historic land use that show how the development of Manhattan has encroached onto the shoreline that once buffered against such events. The design incorporates a system of levees, dams and floodwalls, which improves resistance to flood events, integrated within a linear public park that finds imaginative uses for the resultant spaces.

Whilst none of the proposed elements are revolutionary in isolation, the Dryline represents a new relationship with critical infrastructure; developed with an understanding of localised risk, but weaving in new social and environmental benefits in an holistic manner. The Dryline challenges the assumption that flood infrastructure has to be detrimental to urban character and highlights the co-benefits of considering issues of urban design and enhanced resilience in unison.

Despite this notable example, the majority of work in the burgeoning field of urban resilience is seldom grounded within the everyday practices of planners. In the early years of the twenty-first century the rhetoric of resilience has abounded in policy and government narratives surrounding cities and planning – with *Time* magazine famously giving it the distinction of buzzword of the year in 2013 (Walsh, 2013). Here the focus was on the use of resilience as a new form of risk management to cope with the complexities of large integrated systems and reflecting an overall consensus about the necessity of adaptation to the uncertainty of future threats. Now that such a consensus has been reached, it is vital that planners begin implementing resilience rather than just highlighting its merits, and in so doing transforming urban resilience practice.

This point echoes Brown's (2013) analysis of climate change policies, which has highlighted the predominance of incremental approaches that support the status quo, rather than enacting transformative change, which is often necessary to encourage more long-term resilience. In further evidence of this, Pelling and Manuel-Navarrete (2011) observed that the political challenge of adjusting to a changing climate is made more difficult by path dependencies, associated impacts upon development norms and governance structures. Accordingly, UN-HABITAT (2011, p. 27) have found that the response of cities to the new challenges presented by anthropogenic climate have been fragmented, with significant gaps between the rhetoric and the realities of action on the ground. These climate change examples demonstrate the need to integrate more long-term thinking and innovation into transformative urban design and planning practice.

Moving from rhetoric to implementation in urban resiliency is therefore not without its challenges. Today's urban design and planning practice is increasingly seen as a remedy to an ever-increasing array of socio-economic problems, policy priorities and risks facing contemporary society for which resilient responses are required. Yet in an era of austerity, this must be delivered with fewer resources. Despite this, resilience is becoming incrementally embedded as a focus for envisioning future strategic planning and more localised place-making activities, which planners are increasingly adopting as part of their modus operandi. In evidence of this, in the recently released UK National Planning Policy Framework (DCLG, 2012), it is articulated that Local Planning Authorities should:

> work with local advisors and others to ensure that they have and take into account the most up-to-date information about higher risk sites in their area for malicious threats and natural hazards, including steps that can be taken to reduce vulnerability and increase resilience.

In spite of this overarching policy requirement for resilience, the UK's winter flooding of 2015, coming so soon after major flooding in 2013 and 2014, suggests that lessons are not being learned. What is clear from debates about urban resilience is that planners cannot function in isolation and must be part of a more integrated urban management nexus, with design approaches utilised to provide adaptive pathways. Although it is relatively easy to highlight an institutional inertia within a range of built environment stakeholders as a barrier to collaborative working in resiliency until now (Bosher and Coaffee, 2008; Coaffee and Bosher, 2008), we should not forget the key role that education can play in better aligning practice within this crucial area. The importance of training and skills development to raise awareness of options that are available to all built environment professionals involved in the decision-making process, or that hold a stake in developments is vital (Chmutina *et al.*, 2014). This can come through student-centred courses or through continual professional development, where design and adaptive capacity skills can be forged in a multidisciplinary and multi-professional environment, mirroring the complex reality of urban resilience problems on the ground. Whilst the UK and many other countries have been slow to adopt such an integrated approach, we can look to the recently emerging US model to see what might be achieved in training a range of built environment professionals to deliver pre-emptive urban resilience. In May 2014, a collective industry statement on implementing urban resilience was signed by representatives of the US' design and construction industry (including the bodies for planners, architects, chartered surveyors, interior designers, landscape architects, engineering) which noted that:

> contemporary planning, building materials, and design, construction and operational techniques can make our communities more resilient to these threats. . . . Together, our organizations are committed to build a more resilient future.
>
> *(AIA, 2014)*

Within this context, it has been argued that the key to expanding urban resilience praxis is learning and embracing systematic change. Thus within the fields of urban design and planning, this involves learning from practice and past failures as a means to inform future design solutions and transformative adaptation (Fisher, 2012). Similarly, from the perspective of urban governance, there is a growing understanding that earlier policy failures offer learning opportunities about their 'emergent interconnections' in a complex world, an understanding of which allows for more integrative urban policy (Chandler, 2014).

It can be concluded that resilience should be seen as a continuous journey that helps us to define the problems at hand but also to develop more wide-reaching design solutions that mitigate emergent issues through adaptation, innovation and collaboration. Orchestrating a coherently joined-up approach to enhancing the resilience of our cities, to meet the rising threat of anthropogenic climate change and other unforeseen risks, may be the greatest challenge of our generation (Coaffee and Clarke, 2015). It can only be overcome if urban planning and design practitioners come together with academic theoreticians, moving from maladaptation to transformative adaptation.

Acknowledgements

This chapter expands upon themes first published as Coaffee and Clarke (2015), and draws from research conducted during the HARMONISE project (A Holistic Approach to Resilience and Systematic Actions to Make Large Scale Urban Built Infrastructure Secure), which has received funding from the European Union's Seventh Framework Programme for research, technological development and demonstration under grant agreement no. 312013.

References

Ahern, J. (2011) From fail-safe to safe-to-fail: sustainability and resilience in the new urban world. *Landscape and Urban Planning*, 100, 341–343.

AIA (American Institute of Architects) (2014) *Industry Statement on Resilience*. Available at: www.asla.org/uploadedFiles/CMS/Media/News_Releases/Statement.pdf (accessed 28 January 2015).

Arup (2014) *City Resilience Framework*. Available at: www.arup.com/cri (accessed 15 September 2014).

Barnett, J. and O'Neil, S. (2010) Maladaptation. *Global Environmental Change*, 20(2), 211–213.

Baum, S. D. (2015) Risk and resilience for unknown, unquantifiable, systemic, and unlikely/catastrophic threats. *Environment Systems and Decisions*, 35(2), 229–236.

Bosher, L. (2014) Built-in resilience through disaster risk reduction: operational issues. *Building Research & Information*, 42(2), 240–254.

Bosher, L. S. (ed.) (2008) *Hazards and the Built Environment: Attaining Built-in Resilience*. London: Taylor and Francis.

Bosher, L. and Coaffee, J. (2008) Urban resilience: an international perspective, *Proceeding of the Institute of Civil Engineers: Urban Design and Planning*, 161, 145–146.

Bosher, L., Dainty, A., Carrillo, P. and Glass, J. (2007) Built-in resilience to disasters: a pre-emptive approach. *Engineering, Construction and Architectural Management*, 14, 434–446.

Brown, K. (2013) Global environmental change I: a social turn for resilience? *Progress in Human Geography*, 37, 1–11.

Carmona, M. (2014) The place-shaping continuum: a theory of urban design process. *Journal of Urban Design*, 19(1), 2–36.

Chandler, D. (2012) Resilience and human security: the post-interventionist paradigm. *Security Dialogue*, 43(3), 213–229.

Chandler, D. (2014) Beyond neoliberalism: resilience, the new art of governing complexity. *Resilience*, 2(1), 47–63.

Chelleri, L., Waters, J. J., Olazabal, M. and Minucci, G. (2015) Resilience trade-offs: addressing multiple scales and temporal aspects of urban resilience. *Environment and Urbanization*, 27(1), 181–198.

Chmutina, K., Ganor, T. and Bosher, L. S. (2014) Role of urban design and planning in disaster risk reduction. *Proceedings of the Institution of Civil Engineers: Urban Design and Planning*, 167(3), 125–135.

Coaffee, J. (2009) What is the role and responsibility of planners and urban designers? (Board member commentary). *Proceeding of the Institute of Civil Engineers: Urban Design and Planning*, 162(DP1), 35–36.

Coaffee, J. (2013a) Towards next-generation urban resilience in planning practice: from securitization to integrated place making. *Planning Practice & Research*, 28, 323–339.

Coaffee, J. (2013b) Rescaling and responsibilising the politics of urban resilience: from national security to local place-making. *Politics*, 33(4), 240–252.

Coaffee, J. and Bosher, L. (2008) Integrating counter-terrorist resilience into sustainability. *Proceeding of the Institute of Civil Engineers: Urban Design and Planning*, 161, 75–84.

Coaffee, J. and Clarke, J. (2015) On securing the generational challenge of urban resilience. *Town Planning Review*, 86(3), 249–255.

Coaffee, J. and Lee, P. (2016) *Urban Resilience: Planning for Risk, Crisis and Uncertainty*. London: Palgrave.

Coaffee, J., Moore, C., Fletcher, D. and Bosher, L. (2008) Resilient design for community safety and terror-resistant cities. *Proceedings of the Institute of Civil Engineers: Municipal Engineer*, 161, 103–110.

Corner, J. (2004) Not unlike life itself. *Harvard Design Magazine*, 21, 32–34.

Cote, M. and Nightingale, A. J. (2012) Resilience thinking meets social theory: situating social change in social ecological systems. *Progress in Human Geography*, 36(4), 475–489.

Cross, N. (1982) Designerly ways of knowing. *Design Studies*, 3(4), 221–227.

Davoudi, S. (2012) Resilience: a bridging concept or a dead end? *Planning Theory & Practice*, 13(2), 299–333.

Davoudi, S., Brooks, E. and Mehmood, A. (2013) Evolutionary resilience and strategies for climate adaptation, *Planning Practice & Research*, 28, 307–322.

DCLG (2012) *National Planning Policy Framework*. London: HMSO Stationary Office.

Edwards, C. (2009) *Resilient Nation*. London: Demos.

Fisher, T. (2012) *Designing to Avoid Disaster: The Nature of Fracture-critical Design*. London: Routledge.

Florida, R. L. (2002) *The Rise of the Creative Class: And how it's Transforming Work, Leisure, Community and Everyday Life*. New York: Basic books.

Galderisi, A. and Ferrara, F. F. (2012) Enhancing urban resilience in face of climate change. *TeMA – Journal of Land Use, Mobility and Environment. The Resilient City*, 2, 69–87.

Glaeser, E. (2011) *Triumph of the City: How our Greatest Invention Makes US Richer, Smarter, Greener, Healthier and Happier*. London: Pan Macmillan.

Godschalk, D. R. (2003) Urban hazard mitigation: creating resilient cities, *Natural Hazards Review*, 4(3), 136–143.

Gunderson, L. H. and Holling, C. S. (eds) (2002) *Understanding Transformations in Human and Natural Systems*. Washington, DC: Island Press.

Healey, P. (1997) *Collaborative Planning: Shaping Places in Fragmented Societies*. British Columbia: UBC Press.

Holling, C. S. (1973) Resilience and stability of ecological systems. *Annual Review of Ecology and Systematics*, 4, 1–23.

Holling, C. S. (1986) Resilience of ecosystems: local surprise and global change. In Clark, W. C. and Munn, R. E. (eds), *Sustainable Development of the Biosphere*. Cambridge: Cambridge University Press, pp. 292–317.

IPCC (Intergovernmental Panel on Climate Change) (2014) Climate change 2014: impacts, adaptation, and vulnerability. Final draft report, March 2014. USA.

International Business Times (2014) Hurricane Sandy Anniversary 2014: Billions Of Dollars In Federal Aid Still Unpaid. Available at: www.ibtimes.com/hurricane-sandy-anniversary-2014-billions-dollars-federal-aid-still-unpaid-1715019 (accessed 24 March 2015).

Imrie, R. and Lees, L. (2014) *Sustainable London? The Future of a Global City*. Bristol: Policy Press.

Jones, L., Ludi, E. and Levine, S. (2010) Towards a Characterisation of Adaptive Capacity: A Framework for Analysing Adaptive Capacity at the Local Level. Overseas Development Institute, Background Note. Available at: www.odi.org/sites/odi.org.uk/files/odi-assets/publications-opinion-files/6353.pdf (accessed 24 March 2015).

Lawson, B. (2005) *How Designers Think: The Design Process Demystified*. 4th Ed. London: Routledge.

Leichenko, R. (2011) Climate change and urban resilience. *Current Opinion in Environmental Sustainability*, 3(3), 164–168.

Linkov, I., Bridges, T., Creutzig, F., Decker, J., Fox-Lent, C., Kröger, W. and Thiel-Clemen, T. (2014) Changing the resilience paradigm. *Nature Climate Change*, 4(6), 407–409.

Nuissl, H. and Heinrichs, D. (2011) Fresh wind or hot air – does the governance discourse have something to offer to spatial planning? *Journal of Planning Education and Research*, 31(1), 47–59.

NYS 2100 Commission (2012) *Recommendations to Improve the Strength and Resilience of the Empire State's Infrastructure: Executive Summary*. New York: Rockefeller Foundation.

NYSERDA (2011) *Responding to Climate Change in New York State: The ClimAID Integrated Assessment for Effective Climate Change Adaptation in New York State: Final Report*. New York: Blackwell Publishing.

Pelling, M. and Manuel-Navarrete, D. (2011) From resilience to transformation: the adaptive cycle in two Mexican urban centers. *Ecology and Society*, 16(2), 11.

Rebuild by Design (2014) Rebuild by Design website Available at: www.rebuildbydesign.org/ (accessed 18 December 2014).

Redlener, I. and Reilly, M. J. (2012) Lessons from Sandy – preparing health systems for future disasters. *The New England journal of Medicine*, 367, 2269–2271.

Rockefeller Foundation (2013) *100 Resilient Cities website*. Available at: www.100resilientcities.org (accessed 3 September 2013).

Rydin, Y. (2010) *Governing for Sustainable Urban Development*. London: Earthscan.

Scott, M. (2013) Living with flood risk. *Planning Theory & Practice*, 14(1), 103–106.

Siemens (2013) *Toolkit for Resilient Cities*. Available at: http://files.informatandm.com/uploads/2015/4/Toolkit_for_Resilient_Cities_Full_Report.pdf (accessed 22 September 2013).

Stumpp, E. M. (2013) New in town? On resilience and 'resilient cities'. *Cities*, 34, 164–166.

Supkoff, L. M. (2012) Situating resilience in developmental context. In Ungar, M. (ed.), *The Social Ecology of Resilience: A Handbook of Theory and Practice*. New York: Springer, pp. 127–142.

Suter, M. (2011) *Resilience and Risk Management in Critical Infrastructure Protection: Exploring the Relationship and Comparing its Use*. Zürich: Center for Security Studies (CSS), ETH Zürich.

The Guardian (2014a) Will New York's Billion Dollar Design Contest Prevent Future Flooding? Available at: www.theguardian.com/cities/2014/jun/09/will-new-yorks-billion-dollar-design-contest-prevent-future-flooding (accessed 22 March 2015).

The Guardian (2014b) Bjarke Ingels on the New York Dryline: We Think of it as the love-child of Robert Moses and Jane Jacobs. Available at: www.theguardian.com/cities/2015/mar/09/bjarke-ingels-new-york-dryline-park-flood-hurricane-sandy (accessed 22 March 15).

The Royal Society (2014) *Resilience to Extreme Weather*. London: The Royal Society Science Policy Centre Report 02/14.

UN-HABITAT (2011) *Cities and Climate Change: Global Report on Human Settlements 2011*. London: Earthscan.

UNISDR (2012) *How to Make Cities More Resilient – A Handbook for Mayors and Local Government Leaders*. United Nations International Strategy for Disaster Reduction. Geneva: UNISDR.

Valdes, H. M., Amaratunga, D. and Haigh, R. (2013) Making cities resilient: from awareness to implementation. *International Journal of Disaster Resilience in the Built Environment*, 4, 5–8.

Vale, L. J. (2014) The politics of resilient cities: whose resilience and whose city? *Building Research & Information*, 42(2), 191–201.

Wagner, M., Chhetri, N. and Sturm, M. (2014) Adaptive capacity in light of Hurricane Sandy: the need for policy engagement. *Applied Geography*, 50, 15–23.

Walker, C. and Broderick, J. (2006) *The Civil Contingencies Act 2004: Risk Resilience, and the Law in the United Kingdom*. Oxford: Oxford University Press.

Walker, J. and Cooper, M. (2011) Genealogies of resilience: from systems ecology to the political economy of crisis adaptation, *Security Dialogue*, 42(2), 143–160.

Walsh, B. (2013) Adapt or Die: Why the Environmental Buzzword of 2013 will be Resilience. *Time: Science and Space*, 8 January 2013. Available at: http://science.time.com/2013/01/08/adapt-or-die-why-the-environmental-buzzword-of-2013-will-be-resilience/#ixzz2JeE6rFwE (accessed 17 August 2013).

Walton, D. (2001) Abductive, presumptive and plausible arguments. *Informal Logic*, 21(2), 141–169.

White, I. (2013) The more we know, the more we know we don't know: reflections on a decade of planning, flood risk management and false precision. *Planning Theory & Practice*, 14(1), 106–114.

World Bank (2012) *Building Urban Resilience: Principles, Tools and Practice*. Washington, DC: The World Bank.

Zolli, A. and Healy, A. (2013) *Resilience: Why Things Bounce Back*. London: Headline.

18

RESILIENT TERRITORIES AND TERRITORIAL COHESION

Different origins, similar destination

Simin Davoudi

> This time (1970s), however, public trust was all but withdrawn from the political state only to
> be reinvested in the 'invisible hand of the market' – and indeed [. . .] it is the market ability of
> unerring knack for spotting profit chances that would accomplish what the ethics-inspired
> state bureaucrats abominably failed to achieve. 'Deregulation', 'privatization', 'subsidiariza-
> tion' were to bring what regulation, nationalization and the communal state-guided
> undertakings so obviously and abominably failed to deliver. State functions had to be and
> were to be shifted sideways, to the market, that admittedly 'politics-free' zone, or dropped
> downwards, onto the shoulders of human individuals, now expected to divine individually,
> inspired and set in motion by their greed, what they did not manage to produce collectively,
> inspired and moved by communal spirit.
>
> *Zygmunt Bauman (2013, p. 2)*

Introduction

The aim of this chapter is to explore the relationship between two seemingly unrelated concepts of
resilient territories and territorial cohesion. One thing that both have in common is ambiguity.
Despite, or probably because of, their elasticity both have travelled far and fast and risked becoming
buzzwords, or empty signifiers that can be filled with multiple and conflicting agendas. I will unpack
these two concepts by tracing their origins, evolution, multiple meanings and the values that have
been inscribed on them. My aim is to demonstrate that although territorial cohesion and resilience
have different origins, they share a similar destination. Irrespective of their different genealogies and
ideological associations, there is a great deal of overlap in their appropriation by the neoliberal
mentalities, policies and practices. To substantiate this proposition, I draw on previous work
notably, Davoudi (2005, 2007, 2012, 2016) and Davoudi and Madanipour (2015). The chapter is
structured under four sections. After this introduction, the second section unpacks the concept of territorial cohesion and discusses its co-option into neoliberal agendas. The third
section covers similar ground in relation to resilience. The final section concludes the chapter.

Territorial cohesion: from equity to competitiveness

Territorial cohesion has become a pertinent concept in the European policy and spatial planning
discourse. Being translated from the French *Cohesion Territoire*, while leaving behind its wider

systems of meaning, it created a great deal of ambiguity and confusion and, as a result, generated a growing body of literature attempting to define the concept and explore its applications in practice (Faludi, 2004; *Town Planning Review*, 2005; Davoudi, 2005; Faludi, 2007; Kovacs *et al.*, 2013). While the term itself was introduced into the European spatial planning discourse in the 1990s, the values and rationalities that underpin it have a longer history and are rooted in the social democratic ideals of the so-called European Social Model. Indeed, as I will discuss below, territorial cohesion can be seen as the spatial manifestation of the European model. This is a Weberian ideal type model that closely resembles the post-war welfare state in the United Kingdom and the New Deal in the United States. It has been referred to by other names such as, the 'polder model' (by Bill Clinton, the former US President), the stakeholder model, the 'Rhineland model' (by Michel Albert, former director of the French planning agency) and simply the European model (Bolkestein, 1999). All these refer to a new mode of governance that emerged in many Western societies after the Second World War, namely welfarism (Davoudi and Madanipour, 2015, p. 84). In contrast to the classical liberalism of the late nineteenth century, the welfare state rejected the idea that there exists a necessary link between liberty and the private-property-based market; instead, it called for the creation of a 'social market economy' (Lemke, 2010, p. 192) in which the market is not a separate, autonomous domain but rather an integral part of the social relations and has to be regulated and maintained through government intervention.

An influential advocate of the welfare state model was John Maynard Keynes who, in reaction to the 1930s Great Depression, questioned the neoclassical assumptions about the ability of the market to maintain a 'prosperous equilibrium' with full employment. It became clear that, contrary to the liberalist claims, property right is not 'the guardian of every other right' and can indeed generate an unequitable realisation of liberty (Ely, 1992, p. 26). Keynes advocated the need for government intervention to: regulate the market, moderate its boom and bust cycles, and mitigate its adverse effects on vulnerable groups. The emerging welfare state model was, therefore, based on the idea that state intervention, market regulation, and redistributive measures are central for achieving equity and social cohesion. The quest for fairness had another influential supporter, namely John Rawls who set out the principles of social justice in liberal democracies and the need for a fair distribution of resources. Based on these principles, the welfare state assumed both the right and the duty to: correct social and spatial injustices, ensure full employment through Keynesian demand management, provide lifetime social security for people, and reduce disparities between not only individuals and social groups, but also regions and territories. Its goal was to pursue national economic growth and ensure its equitable distribution across national territories and social groups. Under the welfare state model, citizens are considered as free individuals, 'yet firmly bound into a system of solidarity and mutual inter-dependency' (Rose and Miller, 1992, p. 196). Society is understood as a coherent whole, in which solidarity, reciprocity and cohesion prevail.

The ideal of narrowing the gap between the rich and the poor and between the 'core' and the 'peripheral' regions was the underlying rationale for the 1960s regional policies of many European countries, where development opportunities, public funding and private investments were channelled towards the 'lagging' regions through direct state intervention. Similar objectives were also advocated by the European Community (EC). The stated aim of the founding signatories of the 1957 Treaty of Rome was to 'reduce the differences existing between the various regions and the backwardness of the less favoured regions' (Preamble) by promoting a 'harmonious development of economic activities' and 'a continuous and balanced expansion' (Article 2). Although it took nearly ten years for the European Community to adopt its own regional policy, by the mid-1970s, the Community had a dedicated Directorate General for

Regional Policy and a regional development fund; both of which aimed to implement the Community's objective to

> improve the harmony of regional structures in the Community, firstly in order to combat the mechanical effects which tend to develop owing to the mere fact of opening internal frontiers, and secondly in order to permit the implementation of common policies.
>
> *(CEC, 1969)*

At the national level, a classic example of the welfare state regional policy was the construction of the 'growth poles' outside the prosperous regions. While this became a central plank of spatial planning strategies in many European countries, including the UK, perhaps nowhere was it as firmly embedded in the planning culture as in France, where the idea of 'balanced territorial development' became the hallmark of their *amenagement du territoire*. This is a system charac- terised as the 'regional economic approach' to planning (CEC, 1997), where a great deal of emphasis is put on reducing regional disparities through the redistribution of economic development opportunities. A pioneering contribution to this approach was a book published in 1947 by Jean-Francois Gravier, called: *Paris et le desert francais*. Gravier argued that because Paris was sucking the livelihood out of rural France, there had to be a counter-Parisian strategy for the construction of *metropoles d'equilibre*, or growth poles, outside Paris. This was to be implemented by diverting the resources into the French provisional cities and, hence, countering the negative effects of the agglomeration economies (Gravier, 1947). In short, the strategy aimed at creating a *territorially cohesive* France. It was this idea of *Cohesion Territoire* that two influential French officials introduced in the Amsterdam Treaty of the EU in 1997. One was Jacques Delors, the former French Finance Minister and President of the European Commission between 1985 and 1995, and the other was Michel Barnier, the then European Union (EU) Regional Commissioner. Delors' statement is indicative of the rationale behind territorial cohesion. He suggested that:

> Market forces are powerful. If we left things to their own devices, industry would be concentrated in the north and leisure pursuits in the south. But these market forces, powerful though they may seem, do not always pull in the same direction. Man's endeavour and political aspiration is to try to develop balanced economy.
>
> *(quoted in CEC, 2008, P. 9)*

While the French, and the Dutch, officials were instrumental in the promotion of territorial cohesion as an EU goal and a key objective of spatial planning policies, the leverage of the concept was due to its roots in the values that underpin the European Social Model (Davoudi, 2007; Faludi, 2007). Chief amongst these are the provision of greater social protection against economic insecurities, and greater reliance on public institutions and collective choice than what is pro- vided in the arguably contrasting Anglo-Saxon (neoliberal) Model. The concept of territorial cohesion *spatialised* these social values by extending them beyond individuals and groups into places and territories. So, territorial cohesion became the spatial manifestation of the welfare state philosophy and the European Social Model (Davoudi, 2005). As The EU Third Cohesion Report put it:

> The concept of territorial cohesion extends beyond the notion of economic and social cohesion by both adding to this and reinforcing it. In policy terms, the objective is to help achieve a more balanced development by reducing existing disparities, preventing

territorial imbalances and by making both sectoral policies which have a spatial impact and regional policy more coherent. The concern is also to improve territorial integration and encourage cooperation between regions.

(CEC 2004, p. 27)

The spatial turn in the EU Cohesion Policy was largely based on the belief that an individual's life chances are shaped not just by their social standing, but also by the quality of places where they live and work; not just by their 'typical biographical risks (unemployment, disability, poverty, illness, old age) throughout their life course' (Martin and Ross, 2004, p. 12), but also 'by typical spatial risks (such as inaccessibility, isolation, pollution, exposure to natural and technological hazards, place stigma)' (Davoudi, 2005, p.436). This was articulated in the Third Cohesion Report, which offered a simple yet powerful rationale for territorial cohesion by advocating that, 'people should not be disadvantaged by wherever they happen to live or work in the Union' (CEC, 2004). The concept of territorial cohesion, therefore, 'added a *spatial justice* dimension to European spatial policy' (Davoudi, 2005, p. 437 original emphasis) and called for planning intervention in the free markets to reduce regional disparities and seek a more balanced European territory. It extended the idea of solidarity between *citizens* to solidarity between places and *territories*. A 1973 report, known as the Thompson Report, asked for a Community regional policy based on 'moral, environmental and economic grounds' to reduce disparities and structural imbalances (CEC, 1973, p. 4).

The call for territorial cohesion gathered a new momentum following the introduction of the European Single Market and Monetary Union, which were expected to exacerbate place-generated risks and widen territorial disparities. Like the Cohesion Policy itself, which was hailed by some as a 'revolutionary change' (Leonardi, 2005, p. 1), territorial cohesion was meant to counterweigh the negative impacts of European economic integration on the 'peripheral' regions of Europe, especially the less competitive Mediterranean member states that joined the Community in the 1980s. This is reflected in the following statement in the European Spatial Development Perspective (ESDP). ESDP is a pan-European spatial framework that took ten years to be produced by the ministers responsible in all the EU member states before being published by the Commission in 1999.

> Competition in the Single European Market is one of the driving forces for spatial development in the EU and will be intensified even more by European Monetary Union . . . regions . . . compete with each other for economic activities, jobs and infrastructure. . . . However, not all European regions start from a similar point. It is therefore important gradually to aim at *a spatial balance* designed to provide a more *even geographical distribution* of growth across the territory of the EU.
>
> *(CEC, 1999, p. 11; emphasis added)*

However, the European political landscape of the 1990s, into which the idea of territorial cohesion was introduced, was very different from that of post-war Europe. Following the 1970s economic crisis, the ground had been paved for the emergence of a new, neoliberal, mode of governance, especially in the UK. This was based on radically different political rationalities and social values, which were promoted by, among others, Fredrich Hayek – a key architect of neoliberal philosophy – and his fellow Members of the Mont Pelerin Society. They combined the classical liberal moral critique of big government with the economic critique of Keynesianism to denounce the welfare state for its ineffective fiscal interventions and its *dirigiste*, centralized planning and redistributive policies (Davoudi and Madanipour, 2015). Instead, they advocated deregulation, small states and total market freedom. The UK government's response to the 1970s crisis was to trust the 'invisible hand of the market' rather than the regulatory power of the state, as was the case in the 1930s. Since then, these ideas have increasingly colonised politics by 'an unguarded faith in the individual and free market as deliverer of freedom' (Stedman Jones, 2012, p. 19).

Therefore, when the notion of territorial cohesion entered the European policy and planning discourse in the 1990s, the forces of neoliberalisation were making their marks on the European polity, albeit with different intensity, forms and time frames in different member states and certainly not without tensions and contestations. These tensions were heightened in the run-up to the 2004 enlargement of the EU to the 'East', which widened the regional disparities between the 'old' and the 'new' member states and made the latter the net recipients of the Cohesion funds (Molle, 2007). The growing divergence in the political positioning of the member states with regard to these funds is captured by Drevert (2007, p. 152), who argued that,

> the 'East' wants the highest priority, because it suffers obviously from the most acute problems; the 'South' wishes to keep enough funding to tackle the problems not yet solved; and the 'North and the West', which must foot the bill, refuse to pay for both.

The 2004 enlargement was also a watershed in the evolution of territorial cohesion as it marked the shift of emphasis in its underlying principles away from equity and cohesion, towards efficiency and competitiveness (Manzella and Mendez, 2009). Gradually, competiveness and efficiency . . . gained in importance relative to social and redistribution issues (Telle, 2015, p. 215). This was in line with the Lisbon Agenda, which was set out in March 2000 by the European Council to make Europe 'the most competitive and dynamic knowledge-based economy in the world'. The contestations among diverging political rationalities and social values in Europe was further pushed to the fore during the debate about the proposed European Constitution. Amongst the promoters of the reform of the Union was Tony Blair, the former British Prime Minister. In his speech at the World Economic Forum in Davos and just before the Lisbon Submit, mentioned above, he criticised the proponents of the European Social Model by asking:

> does Europe continue with the old social model, that has an attitude to social legislation and welfare often rooted in the sixties and seventies, or does it recognise that the new economy demands a re-direction of European economic policy for the future?

He urged the EU leaders 'to make a definitive stand in favour of market reform' (quoted in *The Economist*, 2000, p. 17). Among the promoters of the European Model were the French and the Dutch 'No Camp' in the referendum who, wary of the creeping neoliberal values, opposed the proposed Constitution on the basis that it was 'too Anglo-Saxon oriented' and 'ultra-liberal', and would lead to the erosion of the European Social Model.

While the contestations continue, the Commission, along with many EU member states, has increasingly adopted the neoliberal mentality and practices that favour market efficiency and competitiveness. This change of direction was confirmed by the Europe 2020 Strategy (CEC, 2010) whose main aim is to 'deliver(ing) growth' framed by mutually constitutive and commensurate adjectives of 'smart, sustainable and inclusive', and measured by a set of quantified targets (Annex 1). Almost reiterating Tony Blair's ideas, the former President of the Commission

José Manuel Barroso, called for a change of direction in the EU policy. Referring to the 2008 financial crisis, he claimed that:

> The crisis is a wake-up call, the moment where we recognise that 'business as usual' would consign us to a gradual decline, to the second rank of the new global order. This is Europe's moment of truth.
>
> *(EC, 2010, Preface)*

The shift in the EU priorities towards growth and competitiveness has changed the principles and values that originally underpinned the Cohesion Policy and provided the rationale for territorial cohesion objectives. While the majority of Cohesion funds are still allocated to less developed 'peripheral' regions of Europe, 'the focus on "Key Growth Priorities" [notably research and innovation] seem to tilt the *spatial selectivity* of the EU Cohesion Policy towards spaces with greater potential to contribute to smart, sustainable and inclusive growth' (Telle, 2015, p. 217; original emphasis). Some have argued that this change of direction might be the reason for the ineffectiveness of the Cohesion Policy in reducing social and spatial polarisation in the new member states (Darvas, 2014). More broadly, Telle (2015, p. 204) suggests that the, 'EU2020 Strategy is . . . an inconsistent policy paradigm or hegemonic project, redirecting the rationale of EU Cohesion Policy towards efficiency/competitiveness objectives', and may 'facilitate socio-spatial polarization'.

Meanwhile, the rhetoric of territorial cohesion has remained an objective of the EU regional policy (now known as the Cohesion Policy) and has become embedded in the European planning discourse. It has also found its way into numerous spatial strategies across Europe to justify the promotion of polycentric and balanced development (Davoudi, 2003). However, its policy goals have been increasingly aligned with the Europe 2020 Strategy. This alignment has gradually stripped away the social democratic values that originally underpinned the concept and turned territorial cohesion into a mere delivery mechanism for the Strategy and its growth and competitiveness agenda. This is clearly indicated in the Strategy itself, as shown below:

> Cohesion policy and its structural funds, while important in their own right, are key delivery mechanisms to achieve the priorities of smart, sustainable and inclusive growth in Member States and regions.
>
> *(EC, 2010, p. 20)*

Emphasis has shifted from directing the resources away from those places which are most *in need of* development, to those which have the greatest *potential for* development (Davoudi, 2003). For example, many of the spatial strategies that advocate polycentric development stay clear from any proactive state interventions to achieve this and instead rely on the mobilisation of local potentials (see the example from the Republic of Ireland in Davoudi and Wishardt, 2005) and 'territorial capital', often defined in European spatial planning literature: "local endowments and territorial characteristics have growing importance for regions in order to cope with and recover from external shocks" (Territorial Agenda of the European Union 2020, 2011: para. 16). This over-emphasis on mobilising the indigenous 'territorial capital' implies that 'peripheral' regions are expected to lift themselves out of decline on their own. So, although territorial cohesion still has discursive currency in the European spatial planning, its policy goals have shifted away from a focus on public services and equity to market competitiveness, territorial self-reliance and resilience. It is here that territorial cohesion meets resilience.

Resilience: from self-organisation to self-reliance

The term 'resilience' has gained an extraordinary reception and almost replaced the term 'sustainability' in many official documents and in popular imagination. The change was captured by a *New York Times* headline, which claimed, 'Forget sustainability. It's about resilience' (Zolli, 2012). Resilience thinking has influenced the work of scholars in regional economics (Simmie and Martin, 2010), socio-technical studies (Janssen *et al.*, 2006), public policy theories (John, 2003), disaster studies (Vale and Campanella, 2005), spatial planning (Davoudi, 2012; Wilkinson, 2012; Coaffee, 2013) and climate change adaptation (Davoudi *et al.*, 2013). It has also found a central place in the rationalities and technologies of contemporary governance, almost colonising multiple areas of public policy discourse. Despite its popularity, like territorial cohesion, it is a contested concept with multiple meanings, as I will argue below. More importantly, the concept of resilience has been increasingly appropriated into the discourses and practices of neoliberal governmentality (Davoudi, 2016).

The literal translation of the Latin origin of resilience is 'to spring back', and that is what the physical scientists and engineers meant by it when they first used it to denote a return to a previous status and to define stability and resistance to external shocks. In the 1960s, resilience entered the field of ecological sciences primarily through the pioneering work of Buzz Holling. In his 1973 article, he made a distinction between engineering and ecological resilience. He defined the former as 'the ability of a system to return to an equilibrium state after a temporary disturbance' (Holling, 1973, p. 17). So, according to *engineering resilience* 'the resistance to disturbance and the speed by which the system' snaps back are 'the measures of resilience' (Davoudi, 2012, p. 300). The main concern is about the return time, 'efficiency, constancy and predictability'; all of which are deemed essential for 'a fail-safe' engineering design (Holling, 1996, p. 31). The emphasis in this perspective is on bounce-back-ability, with the preferred option being a return to 'normal' without questioning the desirability of the normal or seeking a 'new normal'.

This equilibristic perspective has its roots in the Newtonian view of the world, which considered the Universe as an orderly mechanical device with predictable and controllable behaviour. The search for equilibrium has influenced a wide range of disciplines, including the modernist planning ideas of the early twentieth century. For example, the Charter of Athens – a 1930s modernist planning manifesto – was based on a desire to impose order on what was seen as the disorderly cities of the time. A good city, according to its authors, was a city in 'a state of equilibrium among all its respective functions' (CIAM, 1933, n.p.).

Contrasting the engineering resilience, Holling suggested that 'Resilience . . . is a measure of the ability of these systems to absorb changes [. . .] and still persist' (Holling, 1973, p. 17). He later called this *ecological resilience* and defined it as 'the *magnitude* of the disturbance that can be absorbed before the system changes its structure' (Holling, 1996, p. 33). In this perspective, the measure of resilience is 'not just *how long* it takes for the system to bounce back, but also *how much* disturbance it can take and stay within critical thresholds' (Davoudi, 2012). The emphasis is on maintaining the *existence* of function rather than its *efficiency*.

Both engineering and ecological resilience subscribe to the existence of a stable equilibrium, 'be it a pre-existing one to which a resilient system *bounces back* (engineering) or a new one to which it *bounces forth* (ecological)' (Davoudi, 2012, p. 301). The idea of a stable equilibrium has been challenged by new approaches to resilience (Scheffer, 2009) including the more recent work by Holling and his fellow ecologists in the Resilience Alliance – a Stockholm University-based network with global influence, which works closely with the (Beijer) International Institute of Ecological Economics. They now use the term socio-ecological resilience to 'advocate that the very nature of systems may change over time with or without an external disturbance'

(Davoudi, 2012, p. 302). The term also refers to the interdependencies between society and nature (Folke *et al.*, 2010, p. 21). Some scholars have used the term 'evolutionary resilience' (Simmie and Martin, 2010; Davoudi, 2012; Davoudi *et al.*, 2013), suggesting that evolutionary resilience is not about 'a return to normalcy' (Pendall *et al.*, 2010, p. 76), but about 'the ability of complex socio-ecological systems to change, adapt, and crucially, transform in response to stresses and strains' (Davoudi, 2012 drawing on Carpenter *et al.*, 2005). It is about breaking away from undesirable 'normal'.

Evolutionary resilience is rooted in complexity theory, which considers systems as 'complex, non-linear, and self-organising, permeated by uncertainty and discontinuities' (Berkes and Folke, 1998, p. 12). This implies that the very nature of systems may change with or without an external shock and with or without linear or proportional cause and effect. It is based on the idea that complex socio-ecological systems are non-linear iterations of an adaptive cycle with four distinct phases: exploitation or growth; conservation; release or creative destruction; and reorganisation (Gunderson and Holling, 2002). The first loop of the cycle relates to emergence, development and stabilisation of a particular pathway. The second loop relates to its rigidification and decline, while at the same time signals the opening up of unpredictable possibilities, or spontaneous reorganisation, which may lead to a new growth path (Davoudi, 2012 drawing on Simmie and Martin, 2010). This implies that as systems mature, their resilience reduces and they become 'an accident waiting to happen' (Holling, 1986); and when systems collapse, a 'window of opportunity' (Olsson *et al.*, 2006) opens up for alternative pathways. The creative destruction phase is therefore 'the time of greatest uncertainty yet high resilience; a time for innovation and transformation; a time when a crisis can be turned into an opportunity' (Davoudi, 2012, p. 303).

This conceptualisation of resilience has been increasingly advocated by the Resilience Alliance as a *general* systems theory, which can integrate society, economy and ecology. This means that the notion of resilience has been extended beyond its engineering and ecological roots into the realm of society. This 'total complex system' is often dubbed 'Panarchy', and is defined as:

> the structure in which systems, including those of nature (e.g. forests) and of humans (e.g. capitalism), as well as combined human-natural systems (e.g. institutions that govern natural resources use such as the Forest Service), are interlinked in continual adaptive cycles of growth, accumulation, restructuring, and renewal.
>
> *(Gunderson and Holling, 2002, cover text)*

In this panarchy model, systems function in a series of nested adaptive cycles that interact at multiple scales, speeds and timeframes. This means that, 'small scale changes [. . .] can amplify and cascade into major shifts (reflecting Edward Lorenz's idea of "the butterfly effect") while large interventions may have little or no effects' (Davoudi, 2012, p. 303). Therefore, 'past behaviour of the system is no longer a reliable predictor of future behaviour even when circumstances are similar' (Duit *et al.*, 2010, p. 367). The notion of capital is often used to unite everything into a total complex system, defined as 'the inherent potential of a system that is available for change, since that potential determines the range of future options possible' (Holling, 2001, p. 393). This resonates with the notion of 'territorial capital', which is often used in the territorial cohesion literature and was mentioned earlier in the previous section.

As I have suggested, 'the significance of Holling's work lies in his departure from Newtonian and mechanistic assertions of equilibrium – typical of the post-war cybernetics and closed systems theory – and his adoption of complexity science in the field of ecology' (Davoudi, 2016, p.156). Complexity theory suggests that 'contingent outcomes only reveal concrete causality after the event and are impossible to know beforehand' (Chandler, 2014, p. 50). There is, therefore, a need for 'a qualitative capacity to devise systems that can absorb and accommodate future events in whatever unexpected form they may take' (Holling, 1973, p. 21). This way of resilience thinking is a great step forward in systems thinking and a reflection of the paradigm shift in science, where nothing is considered certain except uncertainty itself. However, when it is applied to the social context it is conceptually problematic and normatively contested. Conceptually it is problematic because it ignores human agency, which is manifested in a number of ways such as: our ability to displace the effects of a crisis in time and space; the unequal distribution of power and agency which can disrupt channels of communications and feedbacks; our ability to imagine and perceive 'changes at a larger scale and longer term than our sensory abilities and immediate experience allow' and put in place mitigating measures; and our capacity to undertake organised collective action (Davidson, 2010, p. 1114). It is normatively contested because it raises questions such as, 'resilience from what to what, and who gets to decide?' (Porter and Davoudi, 2012, p. 331).

Furthermore, and related to the above discussion on territorial cohesion, the advocacy for self-reliance resonates closely with the neoliberal mentality and its emphasis on individualisation of responsibility (Davoudi and Madanipour 2015). Indeed, it is this ideological fit with neoliberal mentality which has accelerated the take-up of resilience in public policy (Davoudi, 2016). At the heart of resilience thinking lies the principle that complex systems are self-organising. When resilience is used in the social context, the principle of self-organisation is misguidedly translated into self-reliance, implying that people and *places* should 'pull themselves up by their bootstraps and reinvent themselves in the face of external challenges' (Swanstrom, 2008, p. 10). It is asserted that in order to build resilience, places and territories should be left to their own devices and not expect solidarity from elsewhere or support from the state at times of hardship. A UK government funded report on community resilience, for example, claims that 'if the Government takes greater responsibility for risks in the community, it may feel under pressure to take increasingly more responsibility, thereby eroding community resilience' (RRAC, 2009, p. 6). The principle of self-organization, extracted from the complexity theory, offers a convenient match with both liberal understanding of responsibility and the freedom from state interference and the conservative value of self-help. Furthermore, it creates a platform that can be contingently shared with communitarians' advocacy of self-sufficiency as an alternative to global capitalism. This contingent alliance makes it a powerful concept with a wide-spread appeal. Self-reliance is thus cast as 'a common sense, neutral and universal measure of the resilient self; one that a responsible citizen should aspire to in the face of radical uncertainties' (Davoudi, 2016, p.162). The move from the welfare to neoliberal modes of government, which as discussed earlier began in the late 1970s, has generated and been enabled by a change from 'expectational citizenship' to 'aspirational citizenship' (Raco, 2009) and an emphasis on entrepreneurialism and competitiveness. In the UK, public policy discourse is littered with the liberal advocacy of responsibility, which above all is aimed at entrepreneurship, as stated below.

> What is my mission? It is actually social recovery . . . to mend the broken society. That's what the Big Society is all about . . . *responsibility* is the absolute key, giving people more control to improve their lives and their communities, so people can actually do more and take more power [. . .] But above all, it's *entrepreneurship* that is going to make this agenda work.
>
> *(Cameron, 2011, emphasis added)*

The intuitive fit between this interpretation of resilience and neoliberal values is not coincidental. As Walker and Cooper (2011) show, the ideas that influenced Holling's ecological resilience run in parallel with the birth of neoliberalism. In the 1970s, when Holling was working on his ecological resilience, Fredrich Hayek was developing his theory of 'spontaneous order'. Similar to the idea of self-organization, this theory asserts that social order emerges from the interaction of self-serving individuals who rationally utilise the price systems to adjust their plans (Hayek, 1976). Like Holling, Hayek drew on complex systems theory to criticise 'the state-engineered equilibria of Keynesian demand management' and called for the reform of 'all social institutions in accordance with the self-organizing dynamic of the market' (Walker and Cooper, 2011, pp. 149–150), which, he believed, could better maintain social order.

The over-emphasis on self-reliance overlaps with the liberal view of society and the place of individual within it. As Norberto Bobbio (1990, p. 43) put it, 'liberal individualism' 'amputates the individual from the organic body . . . plunges him into the unknown and perilous world of the struggle for survival'. He distinguishes this from 'democratic individualism', which 'joins the individual together once more with others like himself, so that society can be built up again from their union, no longer as an organic whole but as an association of free individuals' (ibid.). The appropriation of resilience by the neoliberal agenda has turned the concept into a measure of the fitness of people and places to survive in the turbulent world; reiterating 'the Darwinian law of natural selection and its interpretation as the survival of the fittest' (Davoudi, 2016, p. 164). It is claimed that, 'resilience, seen as an innate capacity of the biological species will diminish if people are exposed too much to dependency-inducing state welfare' (Davoudi, 2016, p. 163). Self-reliance is prescribed as a primary measure of resilience and a key 'existential yardstick' (Rorty, 1999). It reproduces the wider process of *existential politics*, by which 'selective meanings and understanding of human subjectivity' are identified and institutionalized (Raco, 2009, p. 437, original emphasis). People are, therefore, expected to 'carry the weight of the world on their shoulders' and become 'responsible for themselves as a way of being' (Sartre, 1957, p. 51). So, 'the resilient subject is a subject which must permanently struggle to accommodate itself to the (ever changing) world' (Evans and Reid, 2013, p. 83).

Conclusion

Territorial cohesion and resilient territories have very different genealogies, but their evolutions appear to have brought them together on a shared platform dominated by neoliberal ways of addressing social problems. Territorial cohesion is a normative concept, rooted in the social democratic ideals of solidarity, equity and balanced development. In some ways, it is the spatial manifestation of the European Social Model and the welfare states. While the rhetoric of cohesion is still alive, the policy goals have shifted from an emphasis on public intervention and welfare to the neoliberal principles of free markets, competition, and places for themselves. Resilience, on the other hand, is a concept rooted in complexity theory. Its application in ecosystems has revolutionised our understanding of ecological dynamics, but its application in the social domain with a misguided translation of self-organisation into self-reliance are reinforcing the neoliberal values of competition and individualisation of responsibility. Therefore, while the origins of these two influential concepts are different, they seem to have arrived at the same destination; one that is a reductionist, yet totalising, neoliberal orthodoxy which disparages the effectiveness of public intervention and celebrates not only the efficiency of markets, but also their morality. Within this climate, complexity and uncertainty are often used to maintain the status quo and justify inaction. However, if there is one lesson to be learned from resilience thinking, it is that uncertainty opens up windows of opportunity and possibilities for alternative action spaces to break away from undesirable 'normal'. How the opportunities for new 'normals' are ceased, and for what purposes, are contested questions that will be framed and reframed by the ongoing struggles over social values. The process will be variegated and differ in different places and times, but at its extremes are two opposing pathways: one is neoliberalisation, social Darwinism, competition and individualisation. The other is social democracy, justice, solidarity and cohesion. One thing is certain; neither territorial cohesion nor resilient territories are value-free, universal or natural; both are highly charged with political and normative questions. As Laclau and Mouffe (2001, p. xvi) suggest 'the present conjuncture, far from being the only natural or possible societal order, is the expression of a certain configuration of power-relations'.

References

Bauman, Z. (2013) *Europe is Trapped Between Power and Politics*. Available at: www.socialeurope.eu/2013/05/europe-is-trapped-between-power-and-politics/ (accessed 15 July 2016).

Berkes, F. and Folke, C. (1998) *Linking Social and Ecological Systems: Management Practices and Social Mechanisms for Building Resilience*. Cambridge: Cambridge University Press.

Bolkestein, F. (1999) The high road that leads out of the Low Countries. *The Economist*, 22 May, 115–116.

Bobbio, N. (1990) *Liberalism and Democracy*. London: Verso.

Cameron, D. (2011) *Prime Minister's speech on Big Society*, 14 February. Available at: www.number10.gov.uk/news/pms-speech-on-big-society/ (accessed 13 May 2014).

Carpenter, S. R., Westley, F. and Turner, G. (2005) Surrogates for resilience of social-ecological systems. *Ecosystems*, 8(8), 941–944.

CEC (Commission of the European Communities) (1969) *A Regional Policy for the Community*, COM (69) 950, 15 October. Brussels: CEC.

CEC (Commission of the European Communities) (1973) *The Regional Problems in an Enlarged Community (The Thompson Report)*, COM (1973) 550 final. Brussels: CEC.

CEC (Commission of the European Communities) (1997) *The EU Compendium of Spatial Planning System and Policies*. Luxembourg: Office for Official Publications of the European Communities.

CEC (Commission of the European Communities) (1999) *European Spatial Development Perspective: Towards Balanced and Sustainable Development of the Territory of the EU*. Luxembourg: Office for Official Publications of the European Communities.

CEC (Commission of the European Communities) (2004) *A New Partnership for Cohesion: Convergence, Competitiveness, Cooperation – Third Report on Economic and Social Cohesion*. Luxembourg: Office for Official Publications of the European Communities.

CEC (Commission of the European Communities) (2008) *EU Cohesion policy 1988–2008: Investing in Europe's Future*, Inforegio Panorama, No. 26. Luxembourg: Office for Official Publications of the European Community.

CEC (Commission of the European Communities) (2010) *EUROPE 2020, A Strategy for Smart, Sustainable and Inclusive Growth*. Brussels: CEC.

Chandler, D. (2014) Beyond neoliberalism: resilience, the new art of governing complexity. *Resilience*, 2(1), 47–63.

CIAM (1933) *CIAM's The Athens Charter*. Available at: http://modernistarchitecture.wordpress.com/2010/11/03/ciam%E2%80%99s-%E2%80%9Cthe-athens-charter%E2%80%9D-1933/ (accessed 18 April 2015).

Coaffee, J. (2013) Towards next-generation urban resilience in planning practice: from securitization to integrated place making. *Planning Practice & Research*, 28(3), 323–339.

Darvas, Z. (2014) *10 years EU enlargement anniversary: Waltzing past Vienna*. Available at: http://bruegel.org/2014/05/10-years-eu-enlargement-anniversary-waltzing-past-vienna/ (accessed 15 January 2016).

Davidson, D. J. (2010) The applicability of the concept of resilience to social systems: some sources of optimism and nagging doubts. *Society and Natural Resources*, 23(12), 1135–1149.

Davoudi, S. (2003) Polycentricity in European spatial planning: from an analytical tool to a normative agenda. *European Planning Studies*, 11(8), 979–999.

Davoudi, S. (2005) Understanding territorial cohesion. *Planning Practice and Research*, 20(4), 433–441.

Davoudi, S. (2007) Territorial cohesion, the European social model and spatial policy research, in A. Faludi (ed.), *Territorial Cohesion and European Model of Society*. Cambridge, Mass: The Lincoln Institute for Land Policy, pp. 81–105.

Davoudi, S. (2012) Resilience: 'A bridging concept or a dead end?' *Planning Theory and Practice*, 13(2), 299–307.

Davoudi, S. (2016) Resilience and the governmentality of unknowns, in M. Bevir (ed.), *Governmentality after Neoliberalism*. New York: Routledge, pp. 152–171.

Davoudi, S. and Madanipour, A. (2015) Localism and post-social governmentality, in S. Davoudi and A. Madanipour (eds), *Reconsidering Localism*. London: Routledge, pp. 77–103.

Davoudi, S. and Wishardt, M. (2005) Polycentric turn in the Irish spatial strategy. *Built Environment*, 31(2), 122–132.

Davoudi, S., Brooks, E. and Mehmood, A. (2013) Evolutionary resilience and strategies for climate adaptation. *Planning Practice and Research*, 28(3), 307–322.

Drevert, J. F. (2007) Chasing a moving target: territorial cohesion policy in Europe with uncertain borders, in A. Faludi (ed.), *Territorial Cohesion and European Model of Society*. Cambridge, MA: The Lincoln Institute for Land Policy.

Duit, A., Galaza, V., Eckerberga, K. and Ebbessona, J. (2010) Governance, complexity, and resilience. *Global Environmental Change*, 20(3), 363–368.

EC (European Commission) (2010) *Europe 2020. A European Strategy for Smart, Sustainable and Inclusive Growth*. COM(2010)2020. Brussels: European Commission.

Ely, J. W., Jr (1992) *The Guardian of Every Other Right: A Constitutional History of Property Rights*. New York: Oxford University Press.

Evans, B. and Reid, J. (2013) Dangerously exposed: the life and death of the resilient subject. *Resilience*, 1(2), 83–98.

Faludi, A. (2004) Territorial cohesion: old (French) wine in new bottles? *Urban Studies*, 41(7), 1349–1365.

Faludi, A. (ed.) (2007) *Territorial Cohesion and European Model of Society*. Cambridge, MA: The Lincoln Institute for Land Policy.

Folke, C., Carpenter, S., Walker, B., Scheffer, M., Chapin, T. and Rockstrom, J. (2010) Resilience thinking: Integrating resilience, adaptability and transformability. *Ecology and Society*, 15(4), 20–28.

Gravier, J. F. (1947) *Paris et le desert français*. Paris: Flammarion.

Gunderson, L. H. and Holling, C. S. (2002) *Panarchy: Understanding Transformations in Human and Natural Systems*. Washington, DC: Island Press.

Hayek, F. A. (1976) *Law, Legislation and Liberty, The Mirage of Social Justice*. Vol. 2. London: Routledge and Kegan Paul.

Holling, C. S. (1973) Resilience and stability of ecological systems. *Annual Review of Ecological Systems*, 4, 1–23.

Holling, C. S. (1986) The resilience of terrestrial ecosystems: local surprise and global change, in Clark, W. C. and R. E. Munn (eds), *Sustainable Development of the Biosphere*. London: Cambridge University Press.

Holling, C. S. (1996) Engineering resilience versus ecological resilience, in Schulze, P. C. (ed.), *Engineering within Ecological Constraints*. Washington, DC: National Academy Press.

Holling, C. S. (2001) Understanding the complexity of economic, ecological, and social systems. *Ecosystems*, 4(5), 390–405.

Janssen, M., Schoon, M., Ke, W. and Borner, K. (2006) Scholarly networks on resilience, vulnerability and adaptation within the human dimensions of global environmental change. *Global Environmental Change*, 16(3), 240–252.

John, P. (2003) Is there life after policy streams, advocacy coalitions, and punctuations: using evolutionary theory to explain policy change? *The Policy Studies Journal*, 31(4), 481–498.

Kovacs, I. P., Scott, J. and Gal, Z. (2013) *Territorial Cohesion in Europe*. Hungarian Academy of Sciences: Prague.

Laclau, E. and Mouffe, C. (2001) *Hegemony and Social Strategy* (2nd edition). London: Verso.

Leonardi, R. (2005) *Cohesion Policy in the European Union. The building of Europe*. Basingstoke: Palgrave.

Lemke, T. (2010) The birth of bio-politics: Michel Foucault's lecture at the Collège de France on neo-liberal governmentality. *Economy and Society*, 30(2), 190–207.

Manzella, G. P. and Mendez, C. (2009) *The turning points of EU Cohesion policy, Report Working Paper, European Policies Research Centre, University of Strathclyde*. Available at: http://ec.europa.eu/regional_policy/archive/policy/future/pdf/8_manzella_final-formatted.pdf (accessed 15 January 2016).

Martin, A. and Ross, G. (2004) Introduction: EMU and the European social model, in Martin, A. and G. Ross (eds), *Euros and Europeans: Monetary Integration and the European Model of Society*. Cambridge: Cambridge University Press, pp. 1–19.

Molle, W. (2007) *European Cohesion Policy*. New York: Routledge.

Olsson, P., Gunderson, L. H., Carpenter, S., Ryan, P., Lebel, L., Folke, C. and Holling, C. S. (2006) Shooting the rapids: navigating transitions to adaptive governance of social-ecological systems,

Ecology and Society, 11(1), 18. Available at: www.ecologyandsociety.org/vol11/iss1/art18/ (accessed 27 February 2012).

Pendall, R., Foster, K. A. and Cowell, M. (2010) Resilience and regions: building understanding of the metaphor. *Cambridge Journal of Regions, Economy and Society*, 3(1), 71–84.

Porter, L. and Davoudi, S. (2012) The politics of resilience for planning: a cautionary note, *Planning Theory and Practice*, 13(2), 329–333.

Raco, M. (2009) From expectations to aspirations: state modernisation, urban policy and the existential politics of welfare in the UK. *Political Geography*, 28, 436–444.

Rorty, R. (1999) *Philosophy and Social Hope*. London: Penguin.

Rose, N. and Miller, P. (1992) Political power beyond the state: problematics of government. *British Journal of Sociology*, 43(2), 173–205.

RRAC (Risk and Regulation Advisory Council) (2009) *Building Resilient Communities, from Ideas to Sustainable Action*. London: RRAC.

Sartre, J. P. (1957) *Existentialism and Human Emotions*. New York: Wisdom Library.

Scheffer, M. (2009) *Critical Transitions in Nature and Society*. Princeton: Princeton University Press.

Simmie, J. and Martin, R. (2010) The economic resilience of regions: towards an evolutionary approach. *Cambridge Journal of the Regions, Economy and Society*, 3(1), 27–43.

Stedman Jones, D. (2012) *Masters of Universe: Hayek, Friedman, and the Birth of Neoliberal Politics*. Princeton: Princeton University Press.

Swanstrom, T. (2008) Regional resilience: a critical examination of the ecological framework, *IURD Working Paper Series*. Berkeley: Institute of Urban and Regional Development, UC Berkeley.

Telle, S. (2015) *European Union Cohesion Policy and the (Re-)production of Centrality and Peripherality through Soft Spaces with Fuzzy Boundaries*. Proceedings of the 29th Annual AESOP 2015 Congress, 13–16 July, Prague, pp: 202–230.

Territorial Agenda of the European Union 2020 (2011) Available at: www.nweurope.eu/media/1216/territorial_agenda_2020.pdf (accessed 15 July 2016).

The Economist (2000) Europe's new left, free to bloom, 12 February, pp. 17–19.

Town Planning Review (2005) Special issue on Territorial Cohesion, 76(1), 1–118.

Vale, L. J. and Campanella, T. J. (eds) (2005) *The Resilient City: How Modern Cities Recover from Disaster*. New York: Oxford University Press.

Walker, J. and Cooper, M. (2011) Genealogies of resilience: from systems ecology to the political economy of crisis adaptation. *Security Dialogue*, 42(2), 143–160.

Wilkinson, C. (2012) Urban resilience: what does it mean in planning practice? *Planning Theory & Practice*, 13(2), 319–324.

Zolli, A. (2012) Learning to bounce back. *The New York Times*, 2 November. Available at: www.nytimes.com/2012/11/03/opinion/forget-sustainability-its-about-resilience.html?_r=0 (accessed 16 January 2016).

19

INSURANCE AS MALADAPTATION

Resilience and the 'business as usual' paradox

Paul O'Hare, Iain White and Angela Connelly

Introduction

Resilience has emerged as central to contemporary political discourse. Whilst espousing positive notions of recovery and adaptability within an interconnected and unpredictable world, resilience has political and managerial dimensions that seek to exert control over uncertainties (White and O'Hare, 2014). Along with allied notions of preparedness and precaution, resilience contains a compelling anticipatory logic 'whereby a future becomes cause and justification for some form of action in the here and now' (Anderson, 2010, p. 778).

Insurance and compensation schemes, long-standing methods of managing risk, have become widely advocated as a means to facilitate resilience. Globally, the marketing, selling and purchase of insurance (and reinsurance) composes a lucrative business; insurers and reinsurers are amongst the largest and wealthiest global corporations. The insurance sector is central to framing and operationalising the broader societal management of risks for two distinct reasons: its integral role in providing a calculative rationality for risk transfer (Dean, 1999; Intergovernmental Panel on Climate Change (IPCC, 2012) and in providing financial recompense (as well as other forms of support) to underwrite recovery and reconstruction. As part of this latter activity, insurers provide services, advice and assistance in the immediate aftermath of a disaster, thereby becoming central to framing response efforts (IPCC, 2012, p. 11). Despite this prominence and the burgeoning academic interest in themes pertaining to adaptive capacity, disaster response and resilience, few accounts offer a critical evaluation of insurance as a dimension of resilience and the broader implications for hazard management (with notable exceptions – see Lamond and Penning-Rowsell, 2014; Penning-Rowsell and Pardoe, 2012; Penning-Rowsell et al., 2014). This becomes ever-more prescient when set within a context of neoliberalisation in which the rollback of centralised states places extra responsibilities on citizens with regard to the risks that they, and their assets, may face.

This chapter contributes to the understanding of the localised impacts of risk transfer (IPCC, 2012, p. 323) through the formal insurance industry in Europe.[1] The chapter initially charts the emergence of the 'risk society' as a feature of late modernity before exploring the links to resilience. We then turn to consider the responsibilities for risk governance and the role of insurance. Lastly, we highlight key operational elements of insurance: risk transfer and moral hazard, betterment and risk pooling, to demonstrate how these may have a detrimental impact upon the ability of insurance to facilitate resilience. There are three key messages of the article. First, long-standing operational norms of insurance, such as the focus on recovery and the restoration of 'business as usual', only deliver resilience characteristics associated with stability (i.e. recovery and coping). In doing so, insurance serves to industrialise, commercialise and reproduce the consequences of risk rather than engendering any system transitions or adaptive behaviour. Second, by consequence, insurance catalyses a cycle of maladaptation enabling individual recovery, but inhibiting adaptation and sustaining exposure. This ultimately reinforces unknowable risk and normalises potentially regressive cycles of exposure and recovery. Third, the pursuance of resilience via insurance effectively conforms to the norms of neoliberalism and holds little transformative power – either with regard to changing the sector itself or altering citizen behaviour and adaptation.

The risk society and neoliberal resilience

The concept of the 'risk society' refers to how society, particularly the institutions of governance and public administration, is organised in response to risk (Beck, 1992; Giddens, 1991). Observers of the risk society propose that the threats emerging from modernity are delocalised (unbounded spatially and temporally), incalculable (hypothetical and based on ways of knowing) and non-compensatable (based on the scientific utopia of making the unsafe controllable), with significant implications for citizens, the market and government (Beck, 1992). Advanced nations are rendered vulnerable by the very catalysts of modernity: science, technology and the highly networked and globalised nature of contemporary society. The boundaries between 'natural' and 'manufactured' risks become blurred, with nature and society now acknowledged to be enmeshed (Beck, 2009). Modern societies have generally tried to defend against risks, meaning that we are less likely to accept fate as an explanatory factor for peril. Rather, the public and decision makers alike demand explanations and mechanisms to manage risk as well as financial compensation (Mythen, 2004). A range of economic and industrial sectors – including those promoting insurance and adaptive technologies – has been stimulated to service the risk society.

Against this context, the rhetorical promise and practical appeal of the concept of resilience has grown. From a political perspective, resilience is cited as a means of governing uncertainty, in particular, anticipated and unanticipated future risks or shocks. The conceptual understanding of resilience is traceable to the work of Holling (1973), who delineated two broad interpretations of the concept: 'engineering' and 'ecological' resilience. The former refers to the ability of an ecosystem to return to a state of stability after a disturbance, or to absorb changes 'and still persist' (Holling, 1973, p. 17). Notably, this interpretation advocates a return to a pre-shock status; 'business as usual' in insurance parlance. In contrast, ecological resilience emphasises systemic change or adaptation to a new normality that may be less vulnerable to risks (see Adger, 2000; Walker and Cooper, 2011 for context). Such approaches to resilience emphasise the potential for reorganisation; not just 'bouncing back' to a previous position following a shock, but evolving, 'bouncing forward' or transforming to a state that is less vulnerable (Maguire and Cartwright, 2008; Shaw and Theobald, 2011).

The concept of resilience now resonates across a multitude of sectors, interests and spatial scales, from the local to the international (see Coaffee, 2013), and a plethora of actors from institutions and professionals to individual citizens, who are encouraged to increase their capacity to cope with shocks. For example, recent studies examine resilient regions (Bristow, 2010), resilient security (Coaffee and O'Hare, 2008), flooding and resilience (White, 2010) and resilient climate adaptation. Many such accounts are united by a desire to evaluate the translation of resilience from rhetoric to reality, yet other accounts have noted the ambiguity surrounding the concept (Brand and Jax, 2007; Davoudi, 2012; Gleeson, 2008; White and O'Hare, 2014). Other critiques propose that manifestations of resilience catalyse individualised citizen–consumers, expanding the availability of market-based 'solutions' or promoting preparedness and self-organisation in the face of hazards, mirroring dominant neoliberal ontologies (Collier, 2014; Joseph, 2013; Shaw, 2012).

Insurance, the resilient subject and 'new prudentialism'

As knowledge about risk expanded amongst both the academic and policy communities in the period of late modernity, 'the various strategies which individuals are required to practise upon themselves to avoid risk have equally proliferated' (Lupton, 1999: 90). Insurance is one such risk management strategy.

Arguing that the risk society is incalculable, Beck (2009, p. 110) cites the insurance industry as instrumental in determining its frontiers. This thesis has been extensively critiqued because insurers continue to indemnify against certain catastrophic loss, not all risks are necessarily 'catastrophic', and advances in mapping and assessments may assist the understanding of risks (see Bougen, 2003; Collier, 2008). Nevertheless, Beck's assertion has resonance for regimes of insurance, as it emphasises how the sector is a core enabler of risk management by distributing risk across space and time (Luebken and Mauch, 2011). In short, insurance allows risk to be 'rendered calculable and governable' (Lupton, 1999, p. 87; also Ericson *et al.*, 2003) through expert knowledges and discourses (Lupton, 2006). The very discourse of risk and the actuarial activities that underwrite insurance essentially aim: 'to master time, to discipline the future' (Ewald, 1991, p. 207). Reflecting previous observations regarding the neoliberalising tendencies of resilience, insurance has a 'special kind of alchemy' (Ewald, 1991, p. 200), whereby catastrophic events become immense business opportunities for insurers and reinsurers (Bougen, 2003).

Regimes of insurance have emerged not only as a technical enterprise that objectifies certain outcomes of complex systems, but a mode of enabling citizens and institutions to be resilient (Ball *et al.*, 2013), or adapt to changing conditions (Wilby and Keenan, 2012). Such initiatives help define civic and social responsibility, ensuring that it becomes a matter of personal provision rather than a collective good (Lemke, 2001; Rose, 1996). Ignoring the responsibilities associated with this agenda is portrayed as foolhardy: 'Risk avoiding behaviour, therefore, becomes viewed as a moral enterprise relating to issues of self-control, self-knowledge and self-improvement' (Lupton, 1999, p. 91; Rose, 2000).

Civic and individual self-reliance is, therefore, increasingly central to risk management, hazard adaptation and preparedness and, by extension, to the realisation of resilience. However, research has expressed scepticism regarding the extent to which these actors are autonomous, or whether, in recognition of the disciplinary potential of resilience policies, it would be more accurate to perceive them as resilient 'subjects' (see Coaffee, 2013; O'Malley, 2010). Citizens may well be encouraged to make informed choices, yet the potential for more empowered outcomes is subservient to the prevailing demands of capital and markets. The citizen is, therefore, at once a neoliberal subject and an instrument of neoliberalism: responsibility becomes not a matter for the state but for individuals and civil society organisations through regimes that equate to a 'new prudentialism' (O'Malley, 1992).

Given the reorientation of individuals toward the centre of risk management, the chapter now examines the specific issue of flooding, the most common natural hazard and a key focus of the resilience discourse (Adger *et al.*, 2005; White, 2010).

The flood resilient citizen

Traditionally, protection from flooding was predominantly provided by state-sponsored, engineered defences. But changes in precipitation and runoff patterns, associated with climatic change and urbanisation, have highlighted the sheer dynamism of flooding, and the difficulties in 'defending' against water based on probabilistic, historical data (White, 2013). This has stimulated an international policy shift from flood 'defence' to flood 'risk management' (Butler and Pidgeon, 2011; Johnson and Priest, 2008), underwritten by a *rescaling* and *rescoping* of flood risk management obligations. For instance, there has been a shift in emphasis from central government management to local scales (e.g. Johnson *et al.*, 2007), with responsibility for flood risk management moving from the state to multiple stakeholders, including the general public (Johnson and Priest, 2008). This has been complemented by policies aiming to prepare citizens to accept the inevitably of flooding, in other words, to 'live' with water (Department for Environment, Food and Rural Affairs, 2005).

Combined, these circumstances foster initiatives that underpin resilience narratives: if floods appear impossible to prevent and risk is unpredictable, then recovery, adaptation and personal responsibility are a logical focus. As part of this 'responsibilisation' agenda, policy makers and citizens are increasingly attuned to technological measures and social initiatives that support resilient adaptation.

The provision and purchase of insurance represent another dimension of individualised risk management. By recompensing for loss, insurance enables recovery and provides security and confidence in the face of potentially devastating disruption. The benefits of insurance are widely recognised – and often promoted – by flood risk managers. One research participant, a UK local councillor, acknowledging that many did not possess cover, stated 'we need to encourage people to engage with insurance'. Floods between 1998 and 2009 in Europe resulted in insurance losses of at least €52 billion (European Environment Agency, 2011), whilst the summer 2007 floods in the UK were estimated to have directly cost the insurance industry around £3 billion from 180,000 separate claims (see Chatterton *et al.*, 2010; Pitt Review, 2008, p. xxi).

Government policy thus encourages citizens to become more responsible for their own resilience. But, as resilience is commodified through the purchase of insurance or flood protection products, issues of acceptability and affordability become prescient. One municipal officer told us that even when fully funded flood resilient technologies were offered to people: 'they still didn't put them in'. The respondent suggested this was heightened in circumstances where local people did not feel responsible for managing flood risk, perhaps where properties were rented from an owner, or where populations were transient. Deeper questions consequently emerged regarding how resilience is not benignly accepted; rather, it is potentially thwarted by wider structural forces. We next analyse three key principles of insurance – risk transfer and moral hazard, betterment and risk pooling – enabling a critique of the notion that insurance is an effective vehicle for resilience.

Risk transfer and moral hazard

Insurance is a strategy of risk transfer from those immediately exposed to a peril to another entity that, through a legal-binding contract, agrees to indemnify in the event of loss. This usually takes the form of an obligation to provide services and/or financial compensation in the aftermath of a hazard. This is commonly a transaction between individuals or businesses and the private sector. However, under particular circumstances and in certain countries, the state may fulfil this remit. For example, the research revealed that in the Netherlands, the state operates as de facto flood insurer mainly due to the nation's threat from potentially catastrophic coastal flooding. Similarly, in Germany, a small proportion of buildings are considered too risky to be insurable. In such cases, insurance for natural catastrophes, including major flooding, has generally been underwritten by public compensation packages (see Botzen and van den Bergh, 2008). Cyprus and the UK provide further examples of this public–private hybrid model, where flood insurance is generally provided as part of private household insurance. However, in the past, flood victims have also been compensated by the government.[2] In these scenarios, the state essentially underwrites the privatisation of resilience when it is uneconomic for the sector to operate under normal market conditions.

Insurance essentially mitigates potentially devastating impacts of risk through the purchase of a smaller, predetermined premium. This process of risk transfer has significant benefits for citizens and businesses, providing a buffer against the impact of hazards and guaranteeing support at a time of great trauma. With regard to hazards such as flooding, depending upon the quality of the cover provided, insurers are responsible for immediate assistance, often providing temporary accommodation, meeting the costs of repair, paying for the replacement of possessions and in the case of commercial clients compensating for lost revenue and/or business continuity. Insurers also become responsible for helping organise recovery, for example, by arranging for favoured contractors to conduct work. Indeed, such services are used to promote insurance schemes as companies vie to provide attractive packages in a fiercely competitive marketplace. Insurers also purport to provide a more intangible 'peace of mind' to those whose lives or livelihoods are vulnerable to threats. In this sense, insurance is an important strategy for providing certainty and security (or 'business as usual'), underwriting citizen, societal and business confidence.

So, insurance promises that the impacts of perils can be ameliorated and where shocks are experienced, there is an efficient return to 'normality'. Similarities with aspects of resilience discourses are striking in this regard. Yet, whilst seemingly synergistic, the fundamental insurance principle of risk transfer, whereby property owners cede power to other agencies, has significant implications for responsibility and autonomy. Despite providing support for policyholders, as a corollary of transferring risk, responsibility is diffused between actors and agencies. This creates a distinction between communities immediately subjected to the potential hazard and those bearing the responsibility to respond and provide recompense. By consequence, the willingness to take measures to reduce risk exposure or to transform behaviour can be eroded, a situation that insurers refer to as 'moral hazard' or 'risk compensation'. Although promoted as a form of risk responsibilisation, the transfer of risk (and the related moral hazard) through the purchase of insurance may therefore partly shelter citizens from aspects of the responsibilisation agenda (Thieken *et al.*, 2006; Treby *et al.*, 2006).

The challenge posed by moral hazard is a long-held concern of the insurance sector (Adams, 1995; Lamond *et al.*, 2009). Some insurance providers make efforts to ameliorate the potential for moral hazard by having contractual clauses that attempt to share or reduce financial exposure to a peril, for instance by having large excess charges or withholding payment if the insured is found to have been grossly negligent. Although moral hazard instinctively appears pejorative, it is not entirely unwanted by insurance companies. In much the same way that Giddens (1998, p. 63) identified an opportunistic or 'positive' dimension of risk, exposure stimulates demand for services and does not automatically equate to a loss if income from premiums is priced accordingly.

The issue of moral hazard remains important when the state acts as an insurer of last resort, either by compensating households or the losses of insurance companies after an extreme event. This situation limits, or even entirely negates, capital exposure and inhibits the self-organisation elements of resilience that lead to transformative change. If the costs of a hazard, such as flooding, fall elsewhere, there may be limited financial incentive for communities to adapt. In this respect, moral hazard can occur between the insurer and the insured or both of these parties and the state, as either entity may be insulated from risk. In the Netherlands and Spain, research suggested that there is not (currently) a market for flood resilience, via insurance or technology, as the state compensates in the event of a flood. Similarly, where awareness of adaptive measures was high, closer analysis demonstrated that the key features of insurance – such as the betterment principle – precluded wider uptake. It is to this issue that the chapter now turns.

The 'betterment' barrier

Multiple research participants including representatives from insurers, civil society and local authority officers, identified the immediate aftermath of a hazard as offering a prime 'window of opportunity' for people to adapt to hazards, such as by installing flood resilient building materials into properties or even relocating. This corresponds with recent research and policy analysis identifying disasters as critical in mobilising agendas (Kingdon, 1995), creating momentum for policy change (Johnson *et al.*, 2004, 2005).

In practice, however, after flooding, the insurer becomes the de facto owner of properties. The 'insured' surrender both responsibility to repair property and a significant degree of autonomy in deciding how property reinstatement should take place. This brings a number of perverse effects that highlight both the power of insurance and insurers in enabling resilience and how its norms of operation inhibit this from being realised. Here, opportunities for individual action are undermined as the operational norms of the insurance sector focus on a return to a pre-shock state as rapidly as possible. A key issue is that insurance schemes commonly adhere to the indemnity principle whereby property 'betterment' (otherwise known as property improvement) is forbidden. Rather, insurers 'promise to put the property back to where it was' (interview with an insurer) and reinstate to the original condition. This frequently excludes the installation of resilient materials, as they may cost slightly more or are not a 'like-for-like' replacement. Properties, though restored, are no better adapted to cope with any future flood, ultimately rendering society no more resilient in the most progressive sense of the concept.

Some insurers do take a progressive stance, but this is limited in the face of repeat flooding. Another property owner, who had suffered from two floods, said that: 'A tiled floor was installed [by their insurer] in the kitchen after the 2008 flood. The insurance company still insisted on it being taken up and re-laid following the 2009 flood'.

In workshops and focus groups with technology innovators, manufacturers and installers, the 'no betterment' principle was consistently identified as a major obstacle to the integration of flood resilient technologies in properties. One manufacturer reflected on how the 'no betterment' principle may drive risk: 'as a result properties can be flooded three or four times'. This correlation between insurance and adaptation was further noted by manufacturers and installers, who broadly agreed that 'no betterment' principles not only prevented the wider use of technologies but also stifled innovation in adaptive technologies. This was, said one manufacturer, a major 'bump in the road to market for adaptation', whilst a policy maker also noted that insurance 'set the context for technology, both in its use in properties and in terms of innovation'. The analysis demonstrates that in the case of property reinstatement, insurance inhibits adaptation to flooding, thus frustrating progressive forms of resilience. The next section examines a further component of this – risk pooling.

Risk pooling

Associated with the transfer of risk is the principle of 'risk pooling' inherent to all insurance schemes. Under normal circumstances, insurance premiums are paid into a shared fund that is used to compensate in the event of a peril occurring. This has the effect of dissipating financial exposure throughout a community of risk shareholders: 'by pooling premiums and insured events, the financial impact of an event that could be disastrous for one policyholder is spread among a wider group' (Insurance Europe, 2012, p. 5). Risk pooling also occurs with regard to individual premiums. For example, in the seven European countries surveyed, it is common for flood insurance to be bundled together with a general household and contents package where separate perils, such as burglary and flooding, are combined and given one price. Whilst convenient for both the insured and the provider, this 'bundling' masks the particularities of any one individual threat, cross-subsidises risks and provides a further hindrance to adaptation. It has been further suggested that future climate change may severely test the ability of certain risk transfer and risk pooling mechanisms to continue to adequately function (Lamond and Penning-Rowsell, 2014).

The extent to which risk pooling and subsidisation occurs has led to insurance regimes falling within one of two broad catagorisations of risk management (O'Neill and O'Neill, 2012). The first is individualist or risk-sensitive insurance, which is provided through highly competitive markets in which individuals' payments are broadly proportional to their level of risk. The second refers to solidaristic insurance regimes that have been described as 'risk insensitive' modes of insurance, whereby those at lower risk subsidise those at higher risk (see Lehtonen and Liukko, 2011 for a discussion). In effect, this model pools exposure within aggregations of policyholders stretching across local, national or even international boundaries. An insurance sector interviewee noted that solidaristic flood insurance schemes provide little compunction to take preventative measures and adapt: 'An owner of a house which has already flooded doesn't pay more than other owners [who were not flooded].' When the state provides standardised cover (or compensation) regardless of individual risk that is similarly solidaristic. Consultees reported that the uptake of flood resilience measures in countries where the state insures as a measure of last resort (such as in Spain and France) is relatively low because of the guarantee that homes will be reinstated by the government.

In the UK, there has been a concerted effort to move toward risk reflective pricing, partly in recognition that this might incentivise personal responsibility. But critically, solidaristic compensation schemes, either provided by the private sector or where the state acts as insurer of last resort, have multiple social and economic benefits. They are generally more socially equitable than competitive market-led configurations of insurance provision, providing at least a basic level of protection to those most exposed to peril, who are often the most socially and economically vulnerable. Detailed analyses of housing markets observe that properties at risk of flood or requiring flood insurance have lower values (Harrison *et al.*, 2001; Sirmans *et al.*, 2005, p. 30). These same citizens may also lack the means to relocate to areas where exposure is limited. Without the intervention that solidaristic regimes bring, blight and inequality would deepen, stagnating housing markets and further suppressing the social and spatial mobility of residents. There is a further injustice in that these people also have the least incentive or financial capacity to 'purchase' risk management, either by partaking in insurance or other resilient measures at the property scale.

This discussion of risk pooling demonstrates that insurance schemes, whether individualistic or solidaristic, may inhibit adaptive behaviours in terms of flood risk. When combined with risk transfer, moral hazard, and 'no betterment', insurance may be considered to be *maladaptive*.

Maladaptive resilience and the 'business as usual' paradox

Insurance regimes not only constitute an essential element of hazard response, but they frame other aspects of resilience in a more general sense by predetermining certain disaster anticipation logics and response pathways. Although insurance is promoted as a facet of resilience and hazard management more generally, some key contradictions became readily apparent through the analysis of flood insurance across Europe. The ambitions of insurance as a mode of resilience are overwhelmingly stability orientated; rebounding to a pre-shock 'normality' where risk is absorbed by a system, but rarely avoided or reduced. Fundamental principles of insurance, such as risk transfer and moral hazard, along with operational norms including risk pooling and betterment, limit the extent to which adaptive behaviour can occur. The responsibilisation agenda – so critical to the pursuit of resilience – is *undermined* by the identification of the insurance sector as a key delivery mechanism, reflecting the assessment that while citizens experience an 'individualized approach to risk', this occurs within 'a politicized social consciousness of the structural underpinnings of risks' (Tulloch and Lupton, 2003, p. 132). Consequently, from an insurance perspective, resilience lacks transformative power, serving to underpin the status quo through adherence to historical norms and structures.

Moreover, insurance represents an outsourcing of resilience to the private sector where risk management is privatised and commodified; a service available for purchase. The commercialisation of resilience in this manner (although solidaristic) has an individualising and fragmenting effect, reducing the concept to a mode of consumption bolstered by general societal and media messages about the pervasiveness of risks and the need to assume personal responsibility. Insurance – and by extension resilience – therefore becomes yet another calculative rationality and a dimension of risk governmentality. Here, insurance regimes extend a very tangible reach beyond actuarial tables, becoming a calculative rationality and political technology bound within neoliberal structures (Collier, 2014). Through surveys and subsequent influence of space, people and behaviours, insurers have disciplinary characteristics, rendering certain activities undesirable or inducing self-regulatory tendencies. The inability of some citizens to secure comprehensive and affordable insurance through the insurer's practice of red lining – the practice by which insurers delineate areas as being of a high or unacceptable risk – may have significant implications for the viability of vulnerable communities and the sustainability of housing markets. The consequences of such punitive action for risk management may, conversely, bring benefits for other risk management strategies. For example, refusing coverage for new development in areas at risk from flooding could curtail building on land that is particularly vulnerable to hazards. However, this contradicts the very essence of an industry predicated on risk management. Here the emphasis is on accurate pricing to prevent loss and consideration of the exposure of portfolios as a whole. After all, a society without risk would have no need for insurance.

The provision of compensation for flood damage, through insurance or through state-sponsored grant aid, creates something of a paradox for resilience. It insulates many from the costs of living with risk, divorces drivers from outcomes, fosters moral hazards and short-term decision-making, and potentially negates measures that can mitigate or adapt to risk. Under this analysis, insurance fosters a cycle of maladaptation: actions (or inaction) that may provide short-term benefits, but ultimately increase vulnerability to future change (see Barnett and O'Neill, 2010). Maladaptation spans a diverse range of sectors and practical dimensions, and is an acknowledged perversion of aspiring climate change adaptation practice (Burton, 1997; McEvoy et al., 2006; Niemeyer et al., 2005). Similar terms of reference have been used to critique the sustainability and equity of adaptive practices, with one account questioning the potentially 'oxymoronic' nature of such initiatives (Brown, 2011). Of particular note to this analysis are maladaptive practices that may limit incentives to adapt, generating a disproportionate burden for particularly vulnerable groups, or that close down or limit choices available to future generations (Barnett and O'Neill, 2010). The inflexibility and lack of reflexivity concerning insurance practices can be used as a framework through which to further examine the intricacies of resilience.

Figure 19.1 illustrates the 'maladaptive cycle' with regard to insurance. Here the general societal message is that risks are pervasive and protection is beyond the means and remit of the state (1). Individuals should take responsibility and manage these risks, for instance through the purchase of insurance (2). Yet, insurance promotes rapid recovery and does not encourage adaptation. This situation has the effect of sustaining overall exposure (3), which then reinforces generic drivers of societal risks. This maladaptive cycle also frames the 'business as usual' paradox: insurance both enables short-term resilience at the individual scale, but simultaneously drives risk and the resultant need to be 'resilient' in the longer term. In other words, it promotes resilience through the diffusion of responsibility, yet abates the incentive to act. This maladaptive cycle reflects dysfunctionality in other ways too. As a market, the provision of insurance or compensation for loss due to flooding and similar hazards is neither always adequate nor is it enjoyed by all exposed to flood risk. Some citizens may not even be able to gain insurance to progress to the recovery stage, which presents critical questions regarding social justice and vulnerability (O'Neill and O'Neill, 2012; Priest *et al.*, 2005). Neoliberal promotions of personal resilience may have regressive tendencies given how financial limitations or a lack of capacity preclude many from participating. Further, many people have unwittingly purchased homes in areas at high risk of flooding, or have had no choice but to live in areas that are exposed to risks, for example social housing tenants. The recent economic downturn has exacerbated these conditions in that spending on flood defences is being reduced, while planning authorities across the EU are realising the value of construction in generating growth. It should be acknowledged that it is not unknown for neoliberal states to propose interventionist policies to circumvent counter-intuitive trends (Castree, 2008), or in this case, to interrupt the maladaptive cycle. For instance, after recent floods in the UK, the government gave each household one-off grants to help make their properties more resilient to floods.

Insurance enables recovery, yet the sector has its own aspirations concerned with profit maximisation rather than adaptive capacity, and indeed benefits from this limited iteration of resilience. By consequence, neoliberal trends of personal responsibility and the marketisation of

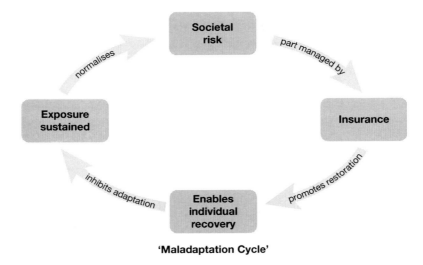

'Maladaptation Cycle'

Figure 19.1   The maladaptation cycle

crisis management are further normalised (Klein, 2007), with society managing and institutio-nalising the very same risks modernity is producing (Beck, 1992, p. 21). The fact that insurance drives demand for its services with a focus on recovery rather than transformation correlates with Beck's (1992, p. 57) argument that the private sector: 'copes with the symptoms and symbols of risks. As they are dealt with in this way, the risks must grow, they must not actually be eliminated as causes or sources'. Recovery is thus prioritised over prevention: rather than insurance engen-dering transformative resilience, it normalises societal risk and recovery from the consequences of risks.

Conclusion – Resilience and the inadequacies of 'business as usual'

Resilience has infiltrated a broad range of policy agendas and practical initiatives as a means to manage change and uncertainty. Presented as proactive and empowering, the emphasising of stability characteristics of resilience has regressive implications. There is no doubt of the important role that insurance has to play, not only in facilitating recovery and in framing the hue of resilience that is adopted by society. The industry is instrumental in framing hazard preparation by con-structing the urban fabric and social conditions that will encounter the 'next' storm or hazard. Yet insurance is ultimately responsive; the emphasis on 'business as usual' and 'like-for-like' restor-ation – so central to the marketing of insurance – is ill-suited to fostering new systemic trajectories or reducing broader sociocultural drivers of risk. Paradoxically, it perpetuates risk, privileges recovery over precaution and promotes limited – if not false – senses of security. Likewise, communities are treated as passive receptacles of risk, 'protected' but potentially locked in a maladaptive cycle of detriment and recovery in a similar vein to the 'safe development paradox' (Burby, 2006) or the 'escalator effect' (Parker, 1995) within floodplain management, whereby defences create a perception of safety. Accessible and comprehensive insurance may mean that developers are willing to continue risky behaviour, for instance building on floodplains, whilst citizens are more willing to live in hazardous areas, as markets for risk management exist and post-event support is available.

   Given how the aspirations of resilience lie at the apex of bureaucratic and policy objectives, there is an urgent need to examine the impact of efforts to create resilient societies. Resilience, though commonly used in the singular, refers to a multitude of strategies that may vie for pre-cedence, that converge or diverge and that can oscillate between being transformational and conservative. As discussed in this chapter, certain articulations of resilience can even be exclusive, with one mode precluding others. This observation becomes all the more pertinent, given that it is now acknowledged that some interpretations of resilience are more progressive than others, necessitating careful reconciliation. Insurance helps society and businesses to withstand shocks. But not only does this do little to reduce future hazards, it may serve to drive overall societal risk in a maladaptive manner. To this extent it can appear temporally and spatially blind, privileging rebound interpretations of resilience, rather than potentially more progressive, adaptive modes. This is ultimately fatalistic, failing to challenge the status quo, leaving current norms that drive risky behaviour unchallenged and embedding potentially maladaptive techno-rational responses to risk.

Acknowledgements

An extended version of this chapter is available: O'Hare, P., White, I. and Connelly, A. (forthcoming) 'Insurance as Maladaptation: Resilience and the "business as usual" paradox', *Environment and Planning C.*, pp. 1–19. This chapter emerged from research derived from the

EUFP7 funded SMARTeST Project (tools, technologies and systems for flood resilience). Further details at http://cordis.europa.eu/result/rcn/155563_en.html and www.smartfloodprot ection.com.

Notes

1 The paper draws on research undertaken between 2009 and 2013 as part of a multidisciplinary European Union (EU) FP7-funded project designed to identify the contribution that small-scale resistance and resilience technologies could make to broader systems of flood risk management. The seven partner countries involved in the research were: Cyprus, France, Germany, Greece, Netherlands, Spain, and the UK.
2 Such government compensation is often on a highly discretionary basis and rarely provides the full cost of damages and recovery.

References

Adams, J. (1995) *Risk*. London: UCL Press.

Adger, W. N. (2000) Social and ecological resilience: are they related? *Progress in Human Geography*, 24(3), 347–364.

Adger, W. N., Hughes, T. P., Folke, C., Carpenter, S. R. and Rockstrom, J. (2005) Social-ecological resilience to coastal disasters. *Science*, 309(5737), 1036–1039.

Anderson, B. (2010) Preemption, precaution, preparedness: anticipatory action and future geographies. *Progress in Human Geography*, 34(9), 777–798.

Ball, T., Werritty, A. and Geddes, A. (2013) Insurance and sustainability in flood-risk management: the UK in a transitional state. *Area*, 45(3), 266–272.

Barnett, J. and O'Neill, S. (2010) Maladaptation. *Global Environmental Change*, 20(2), 211–213.

Beck, U. (1992) *Risk Society, Towards a New Modernity*. London: Sage Publications.

Beck, U. (2009) *World at Risk*. Cambridge: Polity Press.

Botzen, W. J. and Van Den Bergh, J. C. J. M. (2008) Insurance against climate change and flooding in the Netherlands: present, future, and comparison with other countries. *Risk Analysis*, 28(2), 413–426.

Bougen, P. D. (2003) Catastrophe risk. *Economy and Society*, 32(2), 253–274.

Brand, F. and Jax, K. (2007) Focusing the meaning(s) of resilience: resilience as a descriptive concept and a boundary object. *Ecology and Society*, 12(1), 23.

Bristow, G. (2010) Resilient regions: re-'place'ing regional competitiveness. *Cambridge Journal of Regions, Economy and Society*, 3(1), 153–167.

Brown, K. (2011) Sustainable adaptation: an oxymoron? *Climate and Development*, 3(1), 21–31.

Burby, R. J. (2006) Hurricane Katrina and the paradoxes of government disaster policy: bringing about wise governmental decisions for hazardous areas. *The Annals of the American Academy of Political and Social Science*, 604(1), 171–191.

Burton, I. (1997) Vulnerability and adaptive response in the context of climate and climate change. *Climatic Change*, 36(1–2), 185–196.

Butler, C. and Pidgeon, N. (2011) From 'flood defence' to 'flood risk management': exploring governance, responsibility, and blame. *Environment and Planning C*, 29(3), 533–547.

Castree, N. (2008) Neoliberalising nature: the logics of deregulation and reregulation. *Environment and Planning A*, 40(1), 131–152.

Chatterton, J., Viavattene, C., Morris, J., Penning-Rowsell, E. and Tapsell, S. (2010) *Delivering Benefits Through Evidence: The Costs of the 2007 Summer Floods in England*. Bristol: Environment Agency.

Coaffee, J. (2013) Rescaling and responsibilising the politics of urban resilience: from national security to local place-making. *Politics*, 33(4), 240–252.

Coaffee, J. and O'Hare, P. (2008) Urban resilience and national security: the role for planners. *Proceedings of the Institute of Civil Engineers: Urban Design and Planning*, 161, 171–182.

Collier, S. (2008) Enacting catastrophe: preparedness, insurance, budgetary rationalization. *Economy and Society*, 37(2), 224–250.

Collier, S. (2014) Neoliberalism and natural disaster. *Journal of Cultural Economy*, 7(3), 273–290.

Davoudi, S. (2012) Resilience, a bridging concept or a dead end? *Planning Theory and Practice*, 13(2), 299–307.

Dean, M. (1999) Risk, calculable and incalculable. In Lupton, D. (ed.), *Risk and Sociocultural Theory: New Directions and Perspectives*. Cambridge: Cambridge University Press, pp. 131–159.

Department for Environment, Food and Rural Affairs (Defra) (2005) *Making Space for Water: Taking Forward a New Government Strategy for Flood and Coastal Management in England*. London: Defra.

Ericson, R., Doyle, A. and Barry, D. (2003) *Insurance as Governance*. Toronto: University of Toronto Press.

European Environment Agency. (2011) *Mapping the Impacts of Natural Hazards and Technological Accidents in Europe*. Luxembourg: Publications Office of the European Union.

Ewald, F. (1991) Insurance and risk. In Burchill, G., Gordon, C. and Millar, P. (eds), *The Foucault Effect: Studies in Governmentality*. Hemel Hempstead: Harvester, Wheatsheaf, pp. 197–210.

Giddens, A. (1991) *Modernity and Self-Identity: Self and Society in the Late Modern Age*. Cambridge: Polity.

Giddens, A. (1998) *The Third Way: The Renewal of Social Democracy*. Oxford: Polity Press.

Gleeson, B. (2008) Critical commentary. Waking from the dream: an Australian perspective on urban resilience. *Urban Studies*, 45(13), 2653–2668.

Harrison, D. M., Smersh, G. T. and Schwartz, A. L. (2001) Environmental determinants of housing prices: The impact of flood zone status. *Journal of Real Estate Research*, 21(1/2), 3–20.

Holling, C. S. (1973) Resilience and stability of ecological systems. *Annual Review of Ecology and Systematics*, 4, 1–23.

Insurance Europe (2012) *How Insurance Works*. Brussels: Insurance Europe. Available at: www.insuranceeurope.eu/sites/default/files/attachments/How%20insurance%20works.pdf (accessed 26 July 2016).

IPCC. (2012) *Managing the Risks of Extreme Events and Disasters to Advance Climate Change Adaptation: Special Report of the Intergovernmental Panel on Climate Change*. Cambridge: Cambridge University Press. Available at: www.ipcc.ch/pdf/special-reports/srex/SREX_Full_Report.pdf (accessed 20 August 2015).

Johnson, C. and Priest, S. (2008) Flood risk management in England: a changing landscape of risk responsibility?. *International Journal of Water Resources Development*, 24(4), 513–525.

Johnson, C., Penning-Rowsell, E. and Parker, D. (2007) Natural and imposed injustices: the challenges in implementing 'fair' flood risk management policy in England. *The Geographical Journal*, 173(4), 374–390.

Johnson, C. L., Tunstall, S. M. and Penning-Rowsell, E. C. (2004) *Crises as Catalysts for Adaptation: Human Response to Major Floods*. ESRC Environment and Human Behaviour Research Report RES-221-25-0037. Flood Hazard Research Centre Publication 511. Enfield: Middlesex University.

Johnson, C. L., Tunstall, S. M. and Penning-Rowsell, E. C. (2005) Floods as catalysts for policy change: Historical lessons from England and Wales. *International Journal of Water Resources Development*, 21(4), 561–575.

Joseph, J. (2013) Resilience as embedded neoliberalism: a governmentality approach. *Resilience*, 1(1), 38–52.

Kingdon, J. (1995) *Agendas, Alternatives and Public Policies*. New York: Harper Collins.

Klein, N. (2007) *The Shock Doctrine: The Rise of Disaster Capitalism*. London: Penguin.

Lamond, J. and Penning-Rowsell, E. (2014) The robustness of flood insurance regimes given increased risk resulting from climate change. *Climate Risk Management*, 2, 1–10.

Lamond, J. E., Proverbs, D. G. and Hammond, F. N. (2009) Accessibility of flood risk insurance in the UK: confusion, competition and complacency. *Journal of Risk Research*, 12(6), 825–841.

Lehtonen, T. K. and Liukko, J. (2011) The forms and limits of insurance solidarity. *Journal of Business Ethics*, 103(1), 33–44.

Lemke, T. (2001) The birth of bio-politics: Michel Foucault's lecture at the Collège de France on neoliberal governmentality. *Economy and Society*, 30(2), 190–207.

Luebken, U. and Mauch, C. (2011) Uncertain environments: natural hazards, risk, and insurance in historical perspective. *Environment and History*, 17(1), 1–12.

Lupton, D. (1999) *Risk*. London: Routledge.

Lupton, D. (2006) Sociology and risk. In Mythen, G. and Walklate, S. (eds), *Beyond the Risk Society: Critical Reflections on Risk and Human Security*. Maidenhead: Open University Press, pp. 11–24.

McEvoy, D., Lindley, S. and Handley, J. (2006) Adaptation and mitigation in urban areas: synergies and conflicts. *Proceedings of the ICE-Municipal Engineer*, 159(4), 185–191.

Maguire, B. and Cartwright, S. (2008) *Assessing a Community's Capacity to Manage Change: A Resilience Approach to Social Assessment*. Canberra: Australian Government Bureau of Rural Sciences.

Mythen, G. (2004) *Ulrich Beck: A Critical Introduction to the Risk Society*. London: Pluto Press.

Niemeyer, S., Petts, J. and Hobson, K. (2005) Rapid climate change and society: assessing responses and thresholds. *Risk Analysis*, 25(6), 1443–1456.

O'Malley, P. (1992) Risk, power and crime prevention. *Economy and Society*, 21(3), 252–275.

O'Malley, P. (2010) Resilient subjects: uncertainty, warfare and liberalism. *Economy and Society*, 39(4), 488–509.

O'Neill, J. and O'Neill, M. (2012) *Social Justice and the Future of Flood Insurance*. York: Joseph Rowntree Foundation.

Parker, D. J. (1995) Floodplain development policy in England and Wales. *Applied Geography*, 15(4), 341–363.

Penning-Rowsell, E. and Pardoe, J. (2012) Who benefits and who loses from flood risk reduction? *Environment and Planning C: Government and Policy*, 30(3), 448–466.

Penning-Rowsell, E., Priest, S. and Johnson, C. (2014) The evolution of UK flood insurance: incremental change over six decades. *International Journal of Water Resources Management*, 30(4), 694–713.

Pitt Review (2008) *Learning Lessons from the 2007 Floods*. Available at: http://webarchive.nationalarchives. gov.uk/20100807034701/http:/archive.cabinetoffice.gov.uk/pittreview/_/media/assets/www.cabinetoffice. gov.uk/flooding_review/pitt_review_full%20pdf.pdf (accessed 12 July 2013).

Priest, S. J., Clark, M. J. and Treby, E. J. (2005) Flood insurance: the challenge of the uninsured. *Area*, 37(3), 295–302.

Rose, N. (1996) The death of the social? Refiguring the territory of government. *Economy and Society*, 25(3), 327–356.

Rose, N. (2000) Government and control. *British Journal of Criminology*, 40, 321–329.

Shaw, K. (2012) 'Reframing' resilience: challenges for planning theory and practice. *Planning Theory & Practice*, 13(2), 308–312.

Shaw, K. and Theobald, K. (2011) Resilient local government and climate change interventions in the UK. *Local Environment*, 16(1), 1–16.

Sirmans, G. S., Zietz, E. N. and MacPherson, D. (2005) The composition of hedonic pricing models. *Journal of Real Estate Literature*, 13(1), 3–43.

Thieken, A. H., Petrow, T., Kreibich, H. and Merz, B. (2006) Insurability and mitigation of flood losses in private households in Germany. *Risk Analysis*, 26(2), 383–395.

Treby, E. J., Clark, M. J. and Priest, S. J. (2006) Confronting flood risk: implications for insurance and risk transfer. *Journal of Environmental Management*, 81(4), 351–359.

Tulloch, J. and Lupton, D. (2003) *Risk and Everyday Life*. London: Sage.

Walker, J. and Cooper, M. (2011) Genealogies of resilience: from systems ecology to the political economy of crisis. *Security Dialogue*, 42(2), 143–160.

White, I. (2010) *Water and the City: Risk, Resilience and Planning for a Sustainable Future*. London: Routledge.

White, I. (2013) The more we know, the more we don't know: reflections on a decade of planning, flood risk management and false precision. *Planning Theory and Practice*, 14(1), 106–114.

White, I. and O'Hare, P. (2014) From rhetoric to reality: which resilience, why resilience, and whose resilience in spatial planning? *Environment and Planning C: Government and Policy*, 32(5), 934–950.

Wilby, R. L. and Keenan, R. (2012) Adapting to flood risk under climate change. *Progress in Physical Geography*, 36, 348–378.

PART VII

Disaster response

20

A DIFFERENT CUP OF TEA

Learning from enhancing resilience in risk prone communities

Cecile de Milliano and Jeroen Jurriens

Introduction

Humanitarian and development practitioners and donors increasingly regard resilience as a central objective and a fundamental facet of the development path of communities and countries. Between 2012 and 2013, a consortium of European non-governmental organisations of the ACT Alliance set out to strengthen local capacities for enhancing resilience in eight disaster prone countries: a European Union Aid Volunteers Pilot project led by the Inter-Church Organisation for Development Cooperation (ICCO Cooperation). Since resilience is increasingly becoming a central focus of aid organisations, this chapter aims to share lessons that were learned through this project. The first is that multiple interpretations of resilience are being used. This causes confusion amongst practitioners and can result in resilience becoming an empty concept. The second lesson relates to the potential that 'resilience approaches' have to bridge different working fields, where segregated policy and funding architecture, and a lack of unified tools often impede integration. Third, the motivation behind adopting a 'resilience approach' was at times found to be questionable. Fourth, the cases from the eight countries show gaps in organisational and community knowledge, skills, capacities and resources that can hinder enhancing resilience. These gaps signal the need for institutional and governmental commitment and for organisations to network and form partnerships with others.

Both international and national non-governmental organisations (I/NGOs), as well as international donors, are increasingly supporting the idea of undertaking preventive, integrated and holistic approaches (ECHO/Europe Aid 2013; ECHO/Europe Aid 2014; European Communities 2009; Levine *et al.* 2012; Ministry of Foreign Affairs of the Netherlands 2013; OECD 2008). Efforts are made to strengthen resilience by enhancing the ability of people, communities and societies to deal with risks in their environment; by coping with and adapting to hazards and if possible transforming their root causes. It is believed that disaster risk management reduces uncertainty, builds confidence, cuts costs, and, most importantly, saves and improves lives and livelihoods (UNISDR 2013).

Enhancing resilience in theory seems relatively straightforward and understandable. However, for NGO's to enhance the resilience of communities in risk prone areas, is a different cup of tea. The objective of this chapter is to share lessons learned through a case study approach, thereby reflecting on the perspectives of aid practitioners themselves who are directly engaged with enhancing resilience in disaster prone areas. This chapter focuses on two relatively straightforward research questions. First, it explores what activities in the case study were performed to enhance resilience. Second, it analyses the lessons learned.

When mentioning resilience as a concept, the authors refer to

> the ability of a system to accommodate positively to adverse changes and shocks, simultaneously at different scales and with consideration of all the different components and agents of the system, through the complementarities of its absorptive, adaptive and transformative capacities.
>
> *(Béné et al. 2012)*

There is also often a reference to a 'resilience approach', which in this chapter refers to 'those efforts that aim to enhance resilience'.

Before presenting insights on the research questions and drawing conclusions, we provide more details of the case study, the research methodology and the literature on resilience.

The case study

The case study, on which this chapter is based, is the pilot programme coordinated by the Inter-Church Organisation for Development Cooperation (ICCO Cooperation) in the framework of the EU Aid Volunteers initiative of the European Commission (from now on referred to as the EUAVP-ICCO case study). By deploying fifteen advisor volunteers to thirteen implementing local NGO partners, this pilot project (2012–2013) aimed to develop local capacities for enhancing resilience in disaster prone countries.[1] The pilot programme forms an interesting case, as it provided an opportunity to reflect on the experiences and perspectives of a group of people attempting to enhance resilience and operationalise the resilience approach in the humanitarian and development arena.

The pilot programme's overall objective was to contribute to the improved preparation of communities living in areas prone to hazards and to strengthen emergency prevention and mitigation activities, resulting in more resilient communities. It was executed with existing local partners of ACT Alliance members of ICCO Cooperation, Finn Church Aid (FCA) and Diaconia ECCB-Centre of Relief and Development Aid (DECCB-CRD) – in eight different countries in Africa and Asia: the Democratic Republic of the Congo; Ethiopia; Uganda; Liberia; Bangladesh; Cambodia; Indonesia; and Nepal. The local partner organisations participating in the project shared the fact that they:

- are rooted in communities;
- work in areas where hazards frequently occur;
- are involved in activities that contribute to managing risks and increasing resilience;
- are involved in humanitarian and developmental activities and work.

Depending on the country and region, the organisations are struggling with various natural and man-made hazards ranging from flooding, tsunamis, droughts, environmental degradation, cyclones, glacial lake outburst floods and landslides, to fires, epidemics, communal tensions and conflicts (For more information see: ICCO Cooperation and de Milliano 2014; de Milliano and Jurriens 2015).

Methodology

This research builds on a constructionist approach and is what Sarantakos defines as 'exploratory social research' (Sarantakos 2005). The study sets out to explore, explain and evaluate resilience as perceived by humanitarian and development practitioners. Given this stance, reality is perceived as 'constructed', dynamic and evolving. The ontological position implies that social phenomena and categories are believed to not only be produced through social interactions but that they are in constant state of revision (Berger and Luckmann 2002; Goffman 2002; Bryman 2004; Sarantakos 2005). The constructionist interpretation of resilience is less commonly researched and, according to Ungar, is believed to better account for cultural and contextual differences in how resilience is expressed by individuals and groups (Ungar 2004). Ungar emphasises that this interpretation 'explicitly tolerates diversity in the way resilience is nurtured and maintained' (Ungar 2004). Interpretation is seen as the key process that facilitates construction and reconstruction.

The respondents were selected based on their participation in the pilot programme. This was a specific group of individuals, namely staff of thirteen local partner organisations and the fifteen advisor volunteers. As such, a purposive sampling method was employed. Since the sample size was small, this study does not aim to be representative for the humanitarian and development practitioners' community as a whole. Instead, it aims to provide insights into the diversity of people's perception of and experience with enhancing resilience and thus sets out to contribute to a growing knowledge base. As resilience is increasingly becoming a central objective of aid organisations and donors, sharing empirically based insights may assist those setting out to enhance resilience.

The findings are predominantly based on the analysis of qualitative data. This included the outcomes of several formal face-to-face meetings and informal discussions, a survey amongst advisor volunteers (AVs) and their local partner organisations and the study of documents. The formal face-to-face meetings consisted of two separate discussion sessions with the advisor volunteers, a seminar with these AVs and an exchange meeting, during which external NGO practitioners also participated. The study of documents included the revision of reported information from the EUAVP-ICCO Cooperation project such as: mid-term and final evaluation reports, Skype meetings, webinars, monitoring visits by staff, focus group discussions, workshop sessions with the AVs, an online Wiki platform, Facebook group discussions and blogs. As is visible in the following section, we also engaged with some of the key definitions and arguments in the resilience literature, which enabled us to frame our analysis of how resilience has been translated into practice by the aid practitioners in the study.

Resilience – some insights from the literature

What is new about resilience? Reviewing the literature it immediately becomes evident that the word resilience is far from novel. It has historically been used in various senses; for example, referring to: 'to leap', 'to shrink or contract', 'to avoid', 'to retract' or 'to return to a former position' and scholars emphasise that 'resilience is a multi-faceted concept that is adaptable to various uses and contexts, but in different ways' (Alexander 2013). The current popularity of resilience is perhaps not surprising when analysing how the disaster and development paradigms have slowly been moving closer. The focus of the development paradigm has shifted from 'modernisation' between the 1950s and 1970s, through market liberalisation (between the 1970s and 1990s) to sustainable development (1990s–2010s). The disaster paradigm on the other hand, had a technocratic approach between the 1950s and 1970s, followed by a focus on vulnerability between the 1970s and 1990s with resilience receiving a more prominent place since the 1990s (de Milliano *et al.* 2015; Manyena *et al.* 2011).

The contemporary use of resilience strongly draws on theories of complex adaptive systems, which view social systems as organic and self-organised structures that are intricately connected with each other (de Weijer 2013). Subsequently, 'building resilience' is seen to require interventions that strengthen *absorptive* resilience (coping), *adaptive* resilience and/or *transformative* resilience. These capacities can each lead to different outcomes: persistence, incremental adjustment or transformational responses to changes and shocks, at multiple levels (micro, meso and macro) (Béné *et al.* 2012; Newsham *et al.* 2013).

Increasingly, handbooks and principles are being developed which aim to support actors in the humanitarian arena, such as governments and practitioners, in efforts to enhance resilience (PfR 2012; CARE *et al.* 2013; Turnbull *et al.* 2013). Moreover, characteristics of resilient communities or resilient social systems are increasingly being identified. For example, a safe and resilient community can be conceptualised in terms of: being knowledgeable and healthy; being organised; being connected; having infrastructure and services; having economic opportunities; and/or being able to manage its natural assets (IFRC 2012; Twigg 2009). Analysts describe a resilient social system as including numerous characteristics such as high diversity; effective governance and institutions; the ability to work with uncertainty and change; community involvement and the inclusion of local knowledge; preparedness and planning for disturbance; high social and economic equity; robust social values and structures; acknowledging non-equilibrium dynamics; continual and effective learning; and the adoption of a cross-scalar perspective (Bahadur *et al.* 2013; Bahadur *et al.* 2010; IFRC 2012). These multiple, diverse (and perhaps contradictory) guiding instruments and indicators are then advanced as enabling actors in the humanitarian arena to pursue their aims in the light of their individual, communal or organisational interests (Duijsens and Faling 2014; Hilhorst and Jansen 2010).

It is useful to ask why resilience is currently being embraced so positively in the humanitarian arena. Based on the conceptual literature, a key factor would seem to be the fact that the humanitarian arena focuses on risk prone and vulnerable contexts. It is increasingly being acknowledged that the risk of disasters (and the devastation wrought by them) is globally on the rise as, for example, emphasised in the IPCC report of 2014 (Field *et al.* 2014; Guha-Sapir *et al.* 2014). This is held to be a result of the complex interplay of environmental, demographic, technological, political and socioeconomic conditions (de Milliano 2012; Peek 2008). Change and shocks are common in such vulnerable contexts and include natural hazards such as drought, earthquakes and flooding, but also man-made hazards such as violence, ethnic tensions and conflict. Scholars such as de Weijer conclude that 'resilience theory' often views change as 'being unpredictable and non-linear, with positive and negative feedback loops' (de Weijer 2013). The non-deterministic, unpredictable and non-linear characteristics of risks and dangers thereby poses challenges for the application of resilience on the ground as well as stressing the necessity of these projects' success.

Resilience approaches are often embedded in the need to address the underlying causes of vulnerability. As Levine *et al.* point out, years of frustration about repeated external short-term interventions in the same parts of the world show the need to address underlying causes (Levine *et al.* 2012). ECHO, for example, states that:

> Investing in disaster resilience today is more cost effective than responding to a crisis tomorrow. Action now, to reduce future suffering and loss, is vital in order to ensure better results on the ground, in areas of recurring crises and predictable risks. Focusing

on vulnerabilities and addressing root causes rather than dealing with the consequences underpin this approach.

(ECHO/Europe Aid 2014, p. 1)

In addition, it is increasingly acknowledged that small-scale recurrent disasters significantly impact the resilience of local communities and highlight the need to address the root causes of vulnerability (Heijmans 2012).

Finally, resilience is strongly linked to system theory, which assumes that things are intricately connected with each other (de Weijer 2013). Thus it offers a window of opportunity to work across sectors and thematically related areas and employ interdisciplinary and more comprehensive approaches. This is a possible explanation for why resilience is increasingly referred to as an 'umbrella approach'. It then can account for the wide range of risks that communities face in their everyday life or can refer to the integration of fields such as Disaster Risk Reduction (DRR), Climate Change Adaptation (CCA), conflict prevention and eco-system management (CARE *et al.* 2013; Klein *et al.* 2004). It thus may enable bridging between the humanitarian and the development sectors.

These conceptual grounds make it understandable that resilience can appeal across the humanitarian arena, where rapid change and complexity are often the given characteristics. Analysts thereby emphasise that: 'resilience has a bright future ahead of it. . . . However, its success in this respect will depend on not overworking it or expecting that it can provide more insight and greater modelling capacity than it is capable of furnishing' (Alexander 2013, p. 2714; Klein *et al.* 2004). Indeed, a resilience approach cannot be seen as a panacea, although it may have the potential to provide added value. Importance thus lies in learning lessons about how the concept works out in the daily practices within the humanitarian and development arena. In the next section we will present an overview of the resilience-enhancing activities employed in the EUAVP-ICCO Cooperation case study before continuing to the lessons learned section.

Enhancing resilience through the EUAVP-ICCO cooperation project

The EUAVP-ICCO pilot project sought to support the capacities of local organisations in enhancing the resilience of local communities. But how was resilience operationalised in the case study and what efforts and activities were actually done? Within the EUAVP-ICCO pilot project, resilience was operationalised in two ways. First, it was mainstreamed as a *cross-cutting theme* when developing projects and, second, programmes were developed that had a *specific focus* on enhancing resilience.

When analysing the efforts and activities of the pilot programme more closely, five general categories can be identified (see Figure 20.1): the analysis of the risks and governance context; raising awareness and advocacy; design and development of interventions; training and interventions; and measuring progress, learning and changing practice. It should be emphasised that the five categories are a heuristic device; to a great extent the categories are interconnected, overlap each other and are thus not mutually exclusive. However, they are helpful to make the operationalisation of the resilience approach more recognizable and tangible.

The first category of efforts and activities focused on risks and governance contexts. The participatory community risk assessments in Cambodia, Ethiopia and Nepal showed how this can be a useful eye-opener for communities and aid workers, how it had a mobilising/energising effect and that it was a good foundation upon which to develop an action plan. From the project it became evident that in terms of analyses, not only the full scope of risks and root causes needed to be explored, but also that stakeholder and power analysis was pivotal to gain essential insights for action.

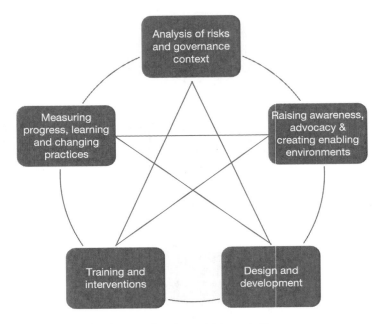

Figure 20.1   Key categories of resilience enhancing activities and efforts

The second category was the focus on raising awareness and creating enabling environments. Examples from DRC, Uganda and Ethiopia included awareness-raising seminars, local radio talk shows organised by the Disaster Risk Reduction Platform and a Disaster Risk Reduction/ Resilience board game. It became evident that awareness-raising should go hand in hand with the analyses of risk and governance contexts. When stakeholders are not aware or informed, they will be unlikely to act. Enough time and effort should be spent on analysing information and identifying which risks are manageable for which actors and subsequently designing appropriate interventions at the right levels.

The third focus was on designing and developing projects, programmes and activities. Insights were gained from Nepal, where a five-Day Training Course on Mainstreaming Climate Change Adaptation (CCA) and Disaster Risk Reduction (DRR) was organised. This resulted in incorporating specific activities (e.g. risk analysis activities) in the planning of new and ongoing projects and programmes. Insights were also gained from Bangladesh and Cambodia, where workshops specifically for thematic programme managers were held. This resulted in adaptations of current organisational policy documents to include aspects of resilience.

The fourth category focused on interventions, training and providing technical expertise for decreasing disaster risks and developing a resilience-enabling environment. The focus was on stakeholders at a national, regional and local level. The programme highlighted that the combination of training and on-the-job coaching by advisor volunteers over a longer period of time proved useful in understanding and incorporating resilience approaches. Furthermore, specific technical expertise was provided, e.g. in the case of Uganda on watershed management, to address highlighted gaps in capacities at the organisational level.

The final category comprised the efforts and activities reflecting on and learning from what has been done. For example, workshops on knowledge management and learning were held in Indonesia and a web-based discussion group was used for learning across countries. From the project it became evident that learning and changing practices can only happen when people and organisations have a critical stance towards their own work, their progress and their environment. This in turn will make them more empowered and better able to engage with the issues at stake, their governments, the donors and other stakeholders.

Lessons learned about resilience

Reflections on the experiences with the implementation of resilience during the EUAVP-ICCO Cooperation pilot project produced several lessons learned. Although they resulted specifically from the project, they generated lessons about opportunities and challenges related to resilience in the humanitarian and development arena. The five key lessons are discussed in more detail below.

Multiple interpretations of resilience

Lesson 1: there are multiple interpretations of resilience. Stakeholders often have a specific scope or thematic focus and interpret and absorb resilience from that perspective. This can create confusion and disillusionment amongst practitioners and it may eventually result in resilience becoming an empty concept.

The first prevailing issue is that multiple interpretations of resilience lead to confusion in practice. Resilience has been understood differently, namely as a goal (or ends) or as an approach (or means), by practitioners and academics alike. The case study shows that resilience is being used by practitioners when referring to a goal – a quality or characteristic – and thus is interpreted as an end in itself, but that it is also being used when referring to an approach and thus as a means to an end (see further Manyena *et al.* 2011; Manyena 2006).

In the case study, it was also found that 'resilience approaches' were being used when specifically referring to integrated risk management approaches. The resilience approach is increasingly being established as a 'novel' strategy. However, this novelty lies not so much in trying to increase resilience as much as the explicit efforts to work towards the integration of different fields. The specific scope (macro, meso or micro) and thematic focus of the adopted resilience approach varies per stakeholder. Examples of fields that are being included are: Disaster Risk Reduction (DRR), Climate Change Adaptation (CCA), Environmental Management and Restoration (EMR), development and conflict resolution. These fields are believed to share a common goal, which is to enhance resilience. At the heart of this interpretation is the aim of making risk management an integral dimension of the design, implementation, monitoring and evaluation of policies and programmes. It entails exploring the wide variety of risks and challenges societies face and identifying suitable and sustainable solutions for them. It was found that, depending on the risks in the communities and the specific scope or thematic focus of the organisations, they interpreted and absorbed resilience from that perspective.

It was felt that the danger of this broad approach towards resilience is not only that it risks being interpreted as 'everything and nothing'; it also causes confusion or disillusionment amongst practitioners. A few examples can be given.

First, practitioners in the case study emphasised that for many of them resilience sounds like 'old wine in new bottles'. Existing strategies and approaches of organisations often contain similarities with, or elements of, resilience approaches. For example, a commonly described starting point of a 'resilience approach' is exploring a risk landscape and questioning what the possible risks and solutions are (CARE *et al.* 2013). Many organisations are doing this already. These organisations realise that much of what they already do fits the 'novel' resilience approach, however they have never labelled it as such.

Second, the approach offers more space for holistic and integrated thinking and for analysing root causes, which has many advantages. However, it is difficult to know what to include and how to include different fields in an integrated manner into current strategies and activities. It brings up practical questions such as: 'What do we include in terms of approaches and how does that translate into practical activities?' 'What is most essential to add to the current approach?' 'To what extent and how can we integrate different issues like climate change, conflict, etc.?'

Finally, the discussions with the practitioners also highlighted the point that initiatives that are financed and 'dubbed' under a resilience header in reality sometimes do not relate to what is usually referred to as resilience in theory. You could, for example, question whether agricultural interventions or interventions focusing on agricultural risk management are resilience or just 'normal' agricultural practice. You could also ask if this discussion is relevant at all. Especially for those organisations that are still caught up in sectoral-based thinking, the resilience approach could bring confusion and contradiction. It was emphasised that more time should be taken to properly support organisations to adopt a more holistic way of thinking and acting, also to know how and to which extent to include and integrate the various issues. Depending on the organisation's scope of work and thematic focus and the levels of risk, organisations should decide on the meaning and implications of the resilience approach for their daily work themselves.

Inadequate linkages

Lesson 2: resilience is often presented as an approach that has the potential to bridge different fields. Research reveals, however, that the different fields often still work in isolation and that there are inadequate linkages to facilitate integration. As one of the respondents in the research emphasised: 'everything in this world is interconnected, so we should know by now that isolated work is unlikely to give long-lasting solutions'. In various of the case study countries, efforts were done to, for example, integrate the fields of Disaster Risk Reduction (DDR), Climate Change Adaptation (CCA), ecosystem management and restoration (EMR), development, emergency response and conflict prevention. Two of the key issues, that were mentioned by the practitioners, that do not facilitate and often even impede integration, are segregated policy and funding architecture. In various countries excellent but separate CCA and DRR policies and strategies exist, which function parallel to each other. It was also mentioned that donor-induced sectoral-thinking has contributed to the development and functioning of different fields as isolated units.

Moreover, the practitioners mentioned that the integration of multiple fields made the application of resilience in practice more difficult. There is often a lack of (practical) knowledge and skills to include and address the different fields integrally. Since the resilience approach is 'new', it still lacks well-researched and documented ways to translate it into practice by offering integrated resilience tools. For example, DRR tools often leave out climate change issues or tackle ecosystem management and restoration issues inadequately. Then again, EMR mainstreaming tools or CCA tools might not pay enough attention to hazards beyond those that are climatically or environmentally induced.

The case study showed that, on the one hand, it is useful and insightful to have separate guidelines for assessing the different risk/hazard/shock/capacity types (DRR, EMR, CCA, conflict sensitivity, and so on). On the other hand, this kind of separated 'box' thinking seems to fit uneasily with the idea of a resilience approach, which is supposed to cover different kinds of shocks and stresses simultaneously – just as they occur in reality – integrated and interconnected. Moreover, organisations often feel overwhelmed by the demands, indicators and checklists, which each approach requires of them.

As a way forward, organisations are now increasingly formulating context-specific guidelines on how to integrate cross-cutting issues and risk management (including all kinds of current and future risks) into their programmes and projects.

Whose agenda is resilience?

Lesson 3: the third lesson relates to the need to analyse the motivation behind adopting the resilience approach. The motivation behind adopting a resilience approach and the promised added value for communities and organisations can at times be questioned. In theory, resilience programmes and strategies strive to address the main risks in a certain context, are based on the communities' needs and thus lead to sustainability (PfR 2012; CARE *et al.* 2013; Turnbull *et al.* 2013). However, the practitioners felt that in the countries in which they worked, the belief in the approach is not always there and that the reason for adopting the approach may be donor driven (See for example: ECHO/Europe Aid 2013, 2014; European Communities 2009; Levine *et al.* 2012; OECD 2008; Ministry of Foreign Affairs of the Netherlands 2013). It was explained that organisations frequently depend on 'Calls for Proposals', which may lead them to design a project more towards the needs of the donor than the actual needs of the communities.

In addition, practitioners felt that donors often put pressure on and limits to putting the resilience approach into practice. The resilience approach may yield sustainable results and save money, however often only in the longer term. Conversely, funding arrangements are normally project-based and time-bound. Familiarising, analysing and understanding risk disablers and resilience enablers demand a great deal of time and money, both of which are usually scarce, especially in local organisations. In that sense, the donor-driven adoption of a resilience approach risks making it into a sustainable problem rather than leading to sustainable solutions. A whole series of concepts have featured, such as 'holistic', 'integrated', 'cluster', 'mainstreaming', and 'community-based approach', which risk being used in proposals as buzzwords only. Thus some organisations in the case study were sceptical about the resilience approach, seeing it as more hype than substance. In this sense, organisations should also be 'resilient' in using donors to reach their own agenda. The issues addressed in the resilience approach should be put on the agenda by communities, supported by local organisations and facilitated by donor funding and not the other way around. To prevent resilience being imposed by donors on local organisations and communities, it was felt valuable for actors to carefully determine why they take resilience on board and how it will be implemented.

Gaps in terms of organisational and community knowledge, skills, capacities and resources to operationalise a resilience approach

Lesson 4: research reveals that it should not be taken for granted that organisations and communities have sufficient expertise, resources and capacities to operationalise a resilience approach.

The experiences from the case study highlighted the tension between the integration of approaches to reach resilience and the specific expertise/capacities of organisations. Successful integration of resilience was felt to require changes at many levels of the organisation, which are not for free and require sufficient human, financial and material resources that are often scarce; especially when organisations are encouraged to manage multiple risks. Some respondents felt that although some organisations should focus on the wider spectrum of potential harmful risks 'it seems more sensible that organisations stick to what they are good at'.

In terms of knowledge, skills and capacities, a common concern raised was that organisations lacked access to 'integrated' knowledge and skills. Practice shows the complexities when assessments bring out risks that are beyond the expertise of the organisation. For example, in Uganda, agricultural field officers performed a participatory risk assessment and HIV/AIDS turned out to be one of the major concerns in that community. It was questioned to what extent the organisation, with limited experience, should now also focus on HIV/AIDS and malaria rather than engage in partnerships with others to cover this specialisation.

In terms of resources, respondents highlighted several issues they experienced. The first relates to projects that have a high visibility factor and that usually attract major funding. Examples are big infrastructure or emergency response projects. However, (small) local NGOs often do not have the capacity to implement and thus apply for these projects. Second, they felt that projects that attract the most funding, and are often most visible, tend to be emergency related. These are normally of a year's duration or less and involve the rapid disbursement of funds. This makes it difficult for local NGOs to think in the longer term.

The EUAVP-ICCO project highlighted the need to identify other stakeholders in or beyond the NGO's network to cover identified issues/gaps that lay outside their area of expertise. By networking and forming partnerships, NGOs could draw on each other's expertise, knowledge, experience and resources and, as much as possible, join forces for common goals. Moreover, in this way NGOs could sometimes come up with creative, affordable and applicable technologies and solutions. One of the respondents felt that:

> By emphasising expensive facilities, not enough focus is put on other measures that could reach the same goal. For example, in Uganda some mitigation strategies against drought and floods are tree planting and adopting sustainable agronomic practices. Village savings and credit associations have also proved to be very useful for people in managing the risk of losing crops.

Respondents, finally, felt that in order to address the organisational gaps needed for a resilience approach, it was crucial that the organisations were receptive to organisational and transformative change.

Not only within the organisations but also when working with communities, challenges were encountered in terms of expertise, resources and capacities to operationalise resilience. Community participation, or community driven action is often seen as pivotal when working towards enhancing resilience (PfR 2012; CARE *et al.* 2013; Turnbull *et al.* 2013). Respondents reported that, although they agree, in practice this posed several challenges. They felt that the importance of providing communities with access to 'integrated' and suitable knowledge and skills was not always acknowledged. For example, if a community doing a risk assessment lacked climate information and forecasts, how could they be expected to come up with suitable solutions? Also strategies of connecting indigenous, practical and scientific knowledge are not always evident. And if, for example, the climate, environment and context is changing, what is, in such a situation, the most suitable tree for massive tree planting? The numerous questions and issues, that organisations struggle with, highlight gaps in terms of knowledge, skills, capacities and resources.

Whose 'responsibility' is resilience? – governmental and institutional commitment

Lesson 5: it is worthwhile asking who is responsible for enhancing resilience and what level of institutional commitment and systematic efforts of relevant stakeholders are required. The case study showed that many projects and local initiatives are well intended and potentially valuable, but that for the resilience approach to be effective a focus on the organisational level is not enough. Respondents felt that without resources or supportive government authorities, it is challenging to work together and take mutual responsibility for risks. Thus the acknowledgment of the importance of a resilience approach and its embrace by the state, institutions, NGOs, research institutes, etc., is pivotal to its success.

Experiences from the EUAVP-ICCO study indicate that a resilience approach requires broad processes of change, including at policy and (higher) institutional levels. The experiences show that getting various institutional actors on board and encouraging them to take responsibility is very challenging, especially in 'fragile states', where relations are often oppositional and the lobbying capacities of the NGOs involved are still limited. As one respondent commented: 'maybe their "acceptance of what is" is a coping mechanism in order to not waste energy on lobbying for an utopia?' This broader contextual question raises fundamental issues that need to be kept in mind by analysts.

Furthermore, the case study highlighted the risk that the resilience approach allows government roles, responsibilities and duties to be shifted onto other stakeholders, such as the communities. As a result, communities can be expected to be 'self-reliant', which can be used as an excuse for non-investment in ordinary government duties and services. In terms of actors and responsibilities, some respondents noted that there were limited incentives for private investment in, for example, climate-friendly technologies. Finally, a practical note that was repeatedly made was the problem of laying responsibility for 'enhancing resilience' upon only a single 'focal person' within the organisation. It was felt to be helpful if there was true institutional commitment and if all staff were made to feel responsible for the resilience approach if it is a cross-cutting issue.

Conclusion

This chapter set out to reflect on the experiences of thirteen implementing local organisations and a group of advisor volunteers who aimed to enhance resilience in disaster prone contexts. Based on this EUAVP-ICCO Cooperation pilot programme, some key opportunities and challenges can be identified when attempting to operationalise resilience. As mentioned, the study does not aim to be representative of the humanitarian and development practitioners' community as a whole. It nevertheless generates some empirical insights that could be helpful for those NGO staff, policy staff and donors who are aiming to enhance the resilience of communities at risk.

This chapter first explored what activities were performed to operationalise resilience. What became evident was that there is no blueprint or a set formula. The case study showed that in order to 'operationalise resilience', organisations developed varying and separate activities to enhance resilience as well as attempting to 'mainstream' resilience as a cross-cutting issue. Resilience-enhancing activities included the analysis of risks and the governance context, but also raising awareness and performing advocacy activities. Furthermore, specific projects were designed and implemented and many training and capacity strengthening activities were provided. Finally, efforts and activities revolved around reflecting and learning.

Second, some key lessons learned when setting out to enhance resilience were drawn out: Lesson 1: there are multiple interpretations of the concept of resilience and this can cause confusion amongst practitioners. Increased clarity could allow tailoring efforts jointly and in the same direction. Lesson 2: the policy and financial infrastructure surrounding the NGOs in daily practice is strongly focused on separate fields. Resilience approaches may have the potential to bridge different fields; however, this would require adequate linkages to facilitate integration. Lesson 3: the motivation behind adopting a resilience approach and the expected added value for communities and organisations should be clarified. For the approach to be sustainable, it should be designed in such a way that it is meaningful to local organisations and communities.

Lesson 4: organisations and communities often require additional support in terms of (access to) knowledge, skills, capacities and resources. In supporting communities, with the multitude of continuously changing risks they need to deal with, it is important to engage in networking and partnership building. Lesson 5: in practice, responsibilities for enhancing resilience are often not clearly defined. This can lead to an insufficient level of institutional commitment and a lack of systematic efforts on the part of relevant stakeholders. The case study shows that it is difficult to achieve specific goals without this explicit institutional commitment and systematic efforts of relevant stakeholders, including government authorities on multiple levels.

It can be concluded that resilience was generally felt to have an added value for the work the local organisations were doing. It allowed organisations to be more aware of, identify and, if possible, focus on the multiple risks faced by the communities they work within. This is especially important since the organisations are operating in complex and interconnected, continuously changing contexts. A focus on resilience encouraged participatory, multi-stakeholder, integrated approaches to their work. However, most organisations felt that long-term commitment and ample time and resources (including human) needed to be allocated to learning about and mainstreaming resilience. In this way, a more holistic manner of thinking and acting could be adopted and could enable organisations to know how, and to what extent, varying risks could be included and integrated. By being aware of the opportunities and challenges of resilience, organisations can then hopefully contribute effectively to enhancing the abilities of communities and societies to positively accommodate adverse changes and shocks.

Acknowledgements

This chapter is revised and updated from de Milliano, Cecile W. J. and Jurriens, Jeroen (2016) 'Realities of resilience in practice: lessons learnt through a pilot EU Aid Volunteer Initiative.' *Resilience*, 4, 3, 79–94. DOI 10.1080/21693293.2015.1094171.

Note

1 The term 'advisor volunteers' was used in the EUAVP-ICCO Cooperation pilot programme to refer to experts who supported local NGOs as advisors, in a setting of voluntary deployment.

References

Alexander, D. E. (2013) Resilience and disaster risk reduction: an etymological journey. *Natural Hazards and Earth System Sciences Discussions*, 1, 1257–1284.

Bahadur, A. V., Ibrahim, M. and Tanner, T. (2010) *The Resilience Renaissance? Unpacking of Resilience for Tackling Climate Change and Disasters*. Brighton: Strengthening Climate Resilience, Institute of Development Studies.

Bahadur, A. V., Ibrahim, M. and Tanner, T. (2013) Characterising resilience: unpacking the concept for tackling climate change and development. *Climate and Development*, 5(1), 55–65.

Béné, C., Wood, R. G., Newsham, A. and Davies, M. (2012) Resilience: New utopia or new tyranny? Reflection about the potentials and limits of the concept of resilience in relation to vulnerability reduction programmes. *IDS Working Papers*, 2012(405), 1–61.

Berger, P. and Luckmann, T. (2002) The social construction of reality. In C. J. Calhoun, J. Gerteis, J. Moody, S. Pfaff and I. Virk, eds. *Contemporary sociological theory*. Oxford, UK: Wiley-Blackwell Publishing.

Bryman, A., (2004) *Social Research Methods*. Second edn, Oxford: Oxford University Press.

CARE, Groupe URD, Wageningen University and Heijmans (2013) *Reaching Resilience. Handbook Resilience 2.0 for Aid Practitioners and Policymakers*. Netherlands: University of Wageningen.

De Milliano, C. W. J. (2012) *Powerful Streams. Exploring enabling factors for adolescent resilience to flooding*. PhD thesis. Groningen, the Netherlands: University of Groningen.

De Milliano, C. W. J. and Jurriens, J., (2015) Realities of resilience in practise: lessons learnt through a pilot EU Aid Volunteer Initiative. *Resilience: International Policies, Practices and Discourses*, 4(2), 1–16.

De Milliano, C. W. J., Faling, M., Clark-Ginsberg, A., Crowley, D. and Gibbons, P. (2015) Resilience: the Holy Grail or yet another hype? In P. Gibbons and H. J. Heintze, eds. *The Humanitarian Challenge – 20 Years European Network on Humanitarian Action (NOHA)*. Switzerland: Springer International Switzerland.

De Weijer, F. (2013) Resilience: a Trojan horse for a new way of thinking? *European Centre for Development Policy Management Discussion Paper*, (139). Available at: www.westafricagateway.org/files/DP%20139_Resilience%20paper_Jan2013_0.pdf (accessed 6 July 2014).

Duijsens, R. and Faling, M. (2014) Humanitarian challenges of urbanisation in Manila: the position of the Philippine Red Cross in a changing disaster and aid landscape. *Resilience: International Policies, Practices and Discourses*, 2(3), 168–182.

ECHO/Europe Aid, (2013) EU approach to resilience: learning from food crises. Fact Sheet. Available at: http://ec.europa.eu/europeaid (accessed 26 July 2015).

ECHO/Europe Aid, (2014) Building resilience: the EU's approach. Factsheet. Available at: http://ec.europa.eu/europeaid (accessed 26 July 2015).

European Communities, (2009) *Overcoming Fragility in Africa: Forging a New European Approach*, Brussels: European Communities.

Field, C. B., Barros, V. R., Mach, K. and Mastrandrea, M. (2014) Climate change 2014: impacts, adaptation, and vulnerability. *Working Group II Contribution to the IPCC 5th Assessment Report-Technical Summary*, 1–76.

Goffman, P. (2002) The presentation of self in everyday life. In C. J. Calhoun, J. Gerteis, J. Moody, S. Pfaff and I. Virk, eds. *Contemporary sociological theory*. Oxford, UK: Wiley-Blackwell Publishing, 46–61.

Guha-Sapir, D., Hoyois, P. and Below, R. (2014) *Annual Disaster Statistical Review 2013: The Numbers and Trends*. Brussels: CRED. Available at: www.cred.be/sites/default/files/ADSR_2013.pdf (accessed 19 July 2015).

Heijmans, A. (2012) *Risky encounters: institutions and interventions in response to recurrent disasters and conflict*. PhD thesis. Wageningen: University of Wageningen.

Hilhorst, D. and Jansen, B. J. (2010) Humanitarian space as arena: a perspective on the everyday politics of aid. *Development and Change*, 41(6), 1117–1139.

ICCO Cooperation and de Milliano, C. W. J. (2014) Realities of Resilience. Reflections on supporting local capacities for resilience. Available at: www.actalliance.org/what-we-do/issues/disaster-risk-reduction-drr (accessed 25 July 2015).

IFRC, (2012) Characteristics of a safe and resilient community. Community based disaster risk reduction study. ARUP International Development – September 2011. Available at: www.ifrc.org/PageFiles/96986/Final_Characteristics_Report.pdf (accessed 23 July 2015).

Klein, R. J. T., Nicholls, R. J. and Thomalla, F. (2004) Resilience to natural hazards: how useful is this concept? *Global Environmental Change Part B: Environmental Hazards*, 5(1–2), 35–45.

Levine, S., Paine, A. B., Bailey, S. and Fan, L. (2012) *The Relevance of 'Resilience'?* London: Overseas Development Institute.

Manyena, S. (2006) The concept of resilience revisited. *Disasters*, 30(4), 433–450.

Manyena, S., O'Brien, G., O'Keefe, P. and Rose, J. (2011) Disaster resilience: a bounce back or bounce forward ability. *Local Environment*, 16(5), 417–424.

Ministry of Foreign Affairs of the Netherlands, (2013) *A World To Gain. A New Agenda for Aid, Trade and Investment*. The Hague: Ministry of Foreign Affairs of the Netherlands. Available at: www.government.nl/documents/letters/2013/04/05/global-dividends-a-new-agenda-for-aid-trade-and-investment (accessed 23 July 2015).

Newsham, A., Béné, C. and Davies, M. (2013) Making the most of resilience. In Y. Azgad and C. Gorman, eds. *In Focus Policy Briefing*, (32). Available at: http://opendocs.ids.ac.uk/opendocs/handle/123456789/2370 (20 May 2014).

OECD (2008) *Concepts and Dilemmas of State Building in Fragile Situations: From Fragility to Resilience*, Paris: Organisation for Economic Co-operation and Development.

Peek, L. (2008) Children and disasters: understanding vulnerability, developing capacities, and promoting resilience – an introduction. *Children, Youth and Environments*, 18(1), 1–29.

PfR (2012) A new vision for community resilience. Available at: www.partnersforresilience.nl/about-us/Paginas/home.aspx (18 March 2014).

Sarantakos, S. (2005) *Social Research*. Third edn, New York: Palgrave MacMillan.

Turnbull, S., Sterrett, C. and Hilleboe, A. (2013) *Toward Resilience. A Guide to Disaster Risk Reduction and Climate Change Adaptation, Warwickshire*, UK: Practical Action Publishing Ltd.

Twigg, J. (2009) *Characteristics of a Disaster-resilient Community. A Guidance Note*. London: Aon Benfield UCL Hazard Research Centre.

Ungar, M. (2004) A constructionist discourse on resilience: multiple contexts, multiple realities among at-risk children and youth. *Youth Society*, 35(3), 341–365.

UNISDR (2013) *GAR Global Assessment Report on Disaster Risk Reduction 2013. From Shared Risk to Shared Value: The Business Case for Disaster Risk Reduction*, Geneva, Switzerland: UNISDR.

21

MANAGING DISASTER RISK AND RESILIENCE IN THE UK

Response vs. prevention in policy and practice

Ksenia Chmutina and Lee Bosher

1. Introduction

The term 'resilience', whilst being surrounded by various debates on its meaning, usefulness and characteristics, has become an integral part of Disaster Risk Management (DRM) terminology. DRM is defined as 'The systematic process of using administrative directives, organizations, and operational skills and capacities to implement strategies, policies and improved coping capacities in order to lessen the adverse impacts of hazards and the possibility of disaster' (UNISDR, 2007).

Within the context of DRM, different approaches to resilience provide different levels of importance to the objectives of avoidance (avoid the shock), recovery (rebound after the shock) and withstanding (resist the shock). Tobin (1999) suggests that resilience is adopted in three ways: as a way to mitigate (emphasising a reduction of exposures and risks); as a way to recover (accepting that not all the shocks can be eliminated and thus embraces actions that are required after them); and as a way to instigate structural changes in society and institutions (based on the importance of situational factors (physical location, age, income, etc.) and cognitive factors (psychological and attitudinal)).

Literature on resilience and its role in DRM also focuses on different aspects. Some concentrate on conceptualising the idea of the resilience metaphor and finding its connections to societies and the environments (e.g. Brand and Jax, 2007; Pelling, 2003). Others focus their attention on local resilience, including urban resilience and local and community-level adaptation to climate change (e.g. O'Brien and Read, 2005; Prasad *et al.*, 2009); emphasis on local resilience rests on the belief that resilience is largely dependent on local action and micro-scale conditions. Some literature argues for a holistic or a broader systems approach to resilience (e.g. Martin-Breen and Anderies, 2011; Lizarralde *et al.*, 2015); this group is based on the *Hyogo Framework for Action 2005–2015* (UNISDR, 2005) and the revised and recently adopted *Sendai Framework for Disaster Risk Reduction* (UNISDR, 2015). These frameworks argue for a broader approach that integrates multiple levels of analysis and intervention (from individual to the national level); multiple time-scales: prevention, emergency, rehabilitation, reconstruction, long-term development; and multiple sectors of intervention, including emergency action, environmental protection and urban development.

However, despite the lack of consensus about what 'resilience' means, the term has in recent years become a central element in policy documents and programmes at international, national and regional levels (Aldunce *et al.*, 2014). In the UK, since the introduction of the Civil Contingency Act (the Act) in 2004, civil protection activity has been conducted under the epithet of 'UK resilience' (HM Government, 2004). As this chapter will explore, 'UK resilience' covers a great variety of areas, from national security to international aid. In this chapter we will demonstrate how resilience policy is implemented in a way that focuses on response rather than on prevention; and also we highlight some of the issues in implementing such policies at the local level.

2. Resilience agenda in the UK

2.1 DRM and resilience

Some sections of the UK government view DRM as one of the key areas that require future attention, as 'important drivers of change could substantially increase future risks of disasters, notably the increasing frequency of extreme weather events due to climate change, and large population increases in cities exposed to natural hazards' (Foresight, 2012, p.5). The main objectives of DRM in the UK are (UNISDR, 2013):

- spotting trouble, assessing its nature and providing warning;
- being ready to respond;
- building greater resilience for the future;
- providing leadership and guidance to resilient communities; and
- effective management.

However, DRM has not always been at the top of the agenda. Since 2001, there has been a shift in how disaster risk has been managed and a dramatic change in purpose and organisation of 'civil protection' in the UK. In place of the Cold War model of civil defence, there emerged a model full of interdependencies and with increased connections to society (Mann, 2007). The UK civil protection plan was significantly restructured to codify existing practices and introduce new statutory duties (O'Brien and Read, 2005), but, whilst doing so, still utilising the agencies and personnel that were largely grounded in a civil defence mentality (Bosher 2014). In 2004, the UK government implemented a legislative and capacity building programme under the banner of UK Resilience. However, as O'Brien and Read (2005) point out, 'the use of the term resilience is an interesting choice' (p. 354), because whilst policy makers increasingly use the term, it was not particularly well defined.

The 'resilience agenda' goes hand in hand with the 'security agenda' in the UK, however whilst the security agenda has traditionally been centralised, the resilience agenda retreats from 'grand planning' and offers 'a legitimate path for disengagement' of the State (Haldrup and Rosen, 2013) by becoming a 'facilitator' instead of a 'builder' of resilience. At the same time, however, whilst it is argued that the resilience agenda is effectively the same as the security agenda, the term 'resilience' only covers particular areas. The traditional security discourse, which focuses on defence, does not use the term but it is used frequently when it comes to the area of DRM, which includes wider security issues such as terrorism and cybercrime, as well as civil emergencies.

UK Resilience takes an 'all hazards' approach, the objective of which is to ensure 'that a robust infrastructure of response is in place to deal rapidly, effectively and flexibly with the consequences of civil devastation and widespread disasters inflicted as a result of conventional or non-conventional disruptive activity' (UK Resilience, 2007 in Rogers, 2011, p. 94).

The Cabinet Office (2012) defines resilience as 'the ability of the community, services, and of infrastructure to detect, prevent, and, if necessary, to withstand, handle and recover from disruptive challenges'. This definition underpins the development of all subsequent resilience-related work, including the Local Resilience Forum (LRF) framework (which will be discussed later in this chapter), the National Risk Register and National Security Strategy, the identification of people who might be vulnerable in a crisis, data protection protocols, cyber-security programmes, and plans for the protection of critical infrastructure and the prevention of violent extremism (Cabinet Office, 2012).

The UK has an established system for emergency planning and engagement between required stakeholders (see Figure 21.1) described in the Civil Contingencies Act (the Act) (Cabinet Office, 2004a). This system is a network of designated governmental, non-governmental and private organisations (typically referred to as 'responders') that can be activated during an emergency and is enacted through exercising and training. This network does not exist permanently (and does not have statutory rights), as the organisations remain formally separate, but is activated if an emergency event occurs. This approach ensures that responders potentially exist at any point in time, based on multi-agency plans that can be changed according to past experiences (Anderson and Adey, 2012).

The Act was the starting point of a new contingencies system that has been developed as a result of various events in the period between 1989 and 2001 (including flooding, terrorist incidents, epidemics and fuel protests). The overarching aim of the Act is preparedness, so all the decisions in the Act are geared towards the negotiation of the potentialities of the event, but, at the same time, opening out the possibilities of response that can be adapted to a specific event. But rather than focusing on the event itself, the Act emphasises the generic consequences of events for human welfare, the environment and the national security (Adey and Anderson, 2011).

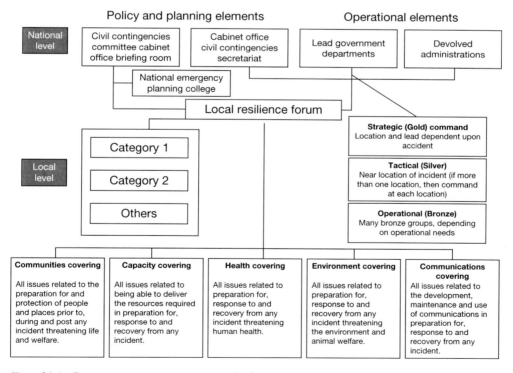

Figure 21.1 Emergency response arrangements in the UK

Source: adapted from Fisher *et al.*, 2014.

Whilst the UK Cabinet Office has ultimate responsibility for civil protection, resilience is carried out through the Local Resilience Forum (LRF), because emergencies typically start at the local level, and most incidents are expected to be able to be dealt with by local responders at this level. The Act describes the duties of appropriate stakeholders to cooperate in a LRF, and formal meetings and allocations of work to responsible stakeholders. It broadens the understanding of civil contingencies activity that now includes planning, preparation, response, recovery and protection, and requires Category 1 and Category 2 responders (Table 21.1) within a given locality to coordinate and prepare for the causes and consequences of various events. The coordination, however, is event-specific and the participation of Category 2 responders and other stakeholders depends on the type, location and scale of the event.

The LRFs, which are defined along Police Constabulary boundaries, typically meet three times a year to discuss emergency planning within their county. In the event of a major emergency, the group would form the Strategic Coordinating Group for that emergency, i.e. it would provide a forum for the coordination of a multi-agency response. A number of sub-groups with specific areas of responsibility meet six times per year and report to the LRF. However, LRFs are neither legal entities nor do they have powers to direct their members, which is often seen as a weakness of such systems (Manyena *et al.*, 2013).

Overall, The UK Civil Contingencies Act places less emphasis on dealing with major catastrophes and more on a range of events that threaten to disrupt, damage or destroy life, thus focusing on preparedness and response to these events – the implications of this will be discussed later in this chapter.

2.2 Resilience policy

Whilst efforts to implement resilience are taken at the local level, the majority of the UK policy documents examined refer to measures and initiatives that have a national/country scope of influence. This is hardly surprising, given that the policy is written by the national government; but at the same time, considering the strong influence that the idea of community and city resilience

Table 21.1 The range of key 'responders'

Category 1 responders	
Local Authorities	All principal local authorities
Government agencies	Environment Agency, DEFRA, Maritime and Coastguard Agency
Emergency Services	Police Forces, British Transport Police, Fire Authorities, Ambulance Services
Health Services	Primary Care Trusts, Health Protection Agency, National Health Service Acute Trusts (hospitals), Foundation Trusts, Port Health Authorities

Category 2 responders	
Utilities	Electricity, Gas, Water and Sewerage, Public communications providers (landlines and mobiles)
Transport	Network Rail, Train Operating Companies (passenger and freight), transport for London, London Underground, airports, harbours and ports, Highways Agency
Government	Health and Safety Executive
Other	Chamber of Commerce, non-governmental organisations and social care charities

has had in literature (Norris *et al.*, 2008; Pelling, 2003; Stumpp, 2013; Tobin, 1999), it becomes clear that UK policy has had to make efforts to redefine the boundaries of the resilience approach.

Resilience is mentioned in documents aimed at foreign affairs, for example: The UK government's humanitarian policy (DFID, 2011), which 'outlines how the UK will help build resilience to crises and respond to humanitarian need resulting from conflict and natural disasters'. One of the programmes is 'Building Resilience and Adaptation to Climate Extremes and Disasters Programme' (BRACED) supported by the Department for International Development. It is also used in relation to terms of data protection (service resilience) and telecommunications (Cabinet Office, 2011a). The definition of resilience therefore resonates with a wider discussion within the UK government on how to handle new forms of risk triggered by a more globalised and interconnected world.

As demonstrated by a recent in-depth policy analysis[1] (Figure 21.2), the policy framework focuses on using a multi-hazard approach, taking into account natural hazards as well as man-made threats (although the term 'resilience' is not used in the Terrorism Act).

All the activities are based around the integrated emergency planning (cycle of emergency planning):

> Central government's approach to civil contingency planning is built around the concept of resilience. This is defined as the ability 'at every relevant level to detect, prevent, and, if necessary, to handle and recover from disruptive challenges'. The processes which underpin resilience form the fundamental elements of civil protection.
>
> (*Cabinet Office, 2003: 1*)

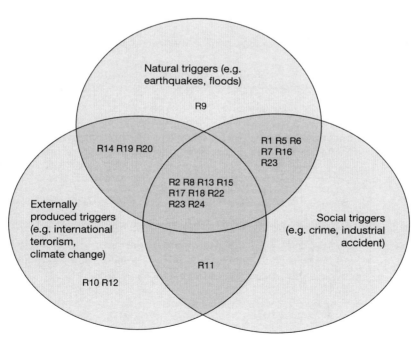

Figure 21.2 'Resilience to what' in UK policy[2]

Source: adapted from Chmutina *et al.*, 2014.

It is appreciated that it is impossible to fully eliminate some risks, therefore resilience is seen by the government as a way of building capacity to respond to emergency events, whilst taking into account the potential interdependencies of services/systems that maybe disrupted; accordingly, resilience in this context primarily refers to the capacity to respond to emergencies and to quickly return to some form of 'normality'.

Unsurprisingly, several representations of community resilience focus on emergency response. One of them argues that resilience corresponds to 'Community and individuals harnessing local resources and expertise to help themselves in an emergency, in a way that complements the response of the emergency services' (Cabinet Office, 2011b, p.11). This representation largely ignores the idea of 'bouncing forward' (Brown, 2011; Birkmann, 2006) and thus is at odds with some theoretical definitions that refer to the importance of producing structural changes in the system, rather than merely returning to previous states of it (Bosher, 2014). In addition, the UK resilience agenda – by encouraging 'active citizenship' – motivates people to engage with situations that are deemed beyond their control; this often leads to a passive attitude from the public (Joseph, 2013).

The Cabinet Office has ultimate responsibility for civil protection; however the main tool through which resilience is carried out are the LRFs, which are non-statutory entities (Birkmann, 2006). Local efforts in enhancing resilience are built on collaboration between organisations, whereas central efforts are based on command and control. The 'resilience agenda' in the UK introduced a number of neoliberal[3] policies that were seen as a way to move away from State-enforced security by adopting an ideology that appears to be on 'the side of laissez-faire' (Amin, 2013, p. 141). The 'command and control' approach was based on the idea that the public entrusts their safety into the hands of an authority, whereas now the resilience agenda is based on a large amount of information, advice, expert opinion as well as 'heroism' stories, where an individual acts in an emergency (Amin, 2013); it emphasises the desirability of personal contingency plans and the importance of public involvement and at the same time makes an emergency a 'shared problem'. This eventually creates tensions, notably when centralised decisions undermine local efforts.

National policy serves as a background for implementation, but a strong emphasis is set on expected capacities at the local level:

> Government can set a framework for sustainable development at a national level, but many changes need to happen through the Big Society at a local level, [. . .] The Big Society puts individuals and groups in the driving seat and Government in an enabling role removing the barriers, where appropriate, which prevent others from taking responsibility.
>
> *(DEFRA, 2011, p. 5)*

The UK government sees resilience as a proactive response to a new unpredictable and unstable world (Aradau, 2014) but these expectations are significantly vague. Thus local stakeholders understand and adjust the principles of resilience differently, holding also several expectations from other stakeholders, notably municipalities and control agencies.

3. Tensions between policy and practice

The definition of resilience provided by the national policy is not strictly accepted at the local level and in addition is reified by the professional remits of those who are 'implementing resilience' (Chmutina *et al.*, 2014). Policy on resilience in the UK has put much emphasis on the capacities expected from other stakeholders in order to achieve 'resilience' and provide an integrated emergency planning approach. This leads to tensions not only among national policy makers and local level policy implementers, but also among those who are directly and indirectly affected by the Resilience Programme. One of the most obvious tensions is created by the focus of policy documents and policy implementation on preparedness and response, thus neglecting the role that can be played by preventative measures.

Whilst UK policy acknowledges the importance of prevention (as it features in its definition of resilience), the majority of policy that emphasises the importance of local level resilience actually focuses on response. This is clearly demonstrated in the terminology: local level *responders* are expected to understand resilience as a way to deal with an event, i.e. being prepared for the event in order to be able to respond to it rather than to eliminate it. The focus on preparedness and response is demonstrated in the choice of wording when it comes to defining resilience, as demonstrated in Figure 21.3. The widespread use of the term resilience in the national policy documents is not reflected at the local level and is often at odds with the practical understanding of resilience. Figure 21.3 illustrates how the understandings of 'resilience' appear to change from policy level to practical implementation level, with the 'prevention' aspects being lost at the local level, which is more focused on coping and being robust.

Unsurprisingly, the definition of resilience provided by the LRF that was at the centre of this study goes in line with the definition provided by the Act, and has permeated into every aspect of emergency services' activities. At the same time, due to the complex nature of the LRF and the diverse profile of professional remits of its members, the LRF adds an extra layer to the definition with regard to the fact that resilience is more about the organisational capacity of the responders. Additionally, their definitions focus on characteristics of resilience rather than the process of implementing resilience (as emphasised by the policy).

Preparedness plays a larger role among the local implementers of resilience. Planners and flood managers see resilience as preparedness and argue that in some cases, when complete safety cannot be achieved due to practical (including financial) reasons, preparedness and protection (which tend to be used as synonyms of resilience) are the best routes. Resilience is understood as preparedness to something that is out of order, although it is seen as a long-term process that will eventually lead to the incorporation of resilience into day-to-day practice. On the other hand,

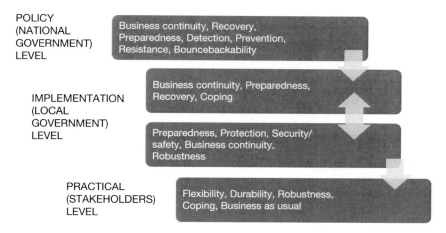

Figure 21.3   Characteristics of resilience within four sectors of intervention

Source: adapted from Chmutina *et al.*, 2014.

emergency services identify resilience with the ability to respond to important events, as officers believe that it is impossible to be fully prepared for all risks. However, they also acknowledge that resilience should be a business-as-usual type of activity; it is an embedded process that does not get acknowledged unless the issues of safety and security are specifically expressed by the client. This understanding of resilience, however, does not sufficiently focus on the more serious low(er) probability types of events. Resilience is a part of day-to-day practice included in business as usual, and its implementation is assumed.

As demonstrated here, the role of prevention is neglected on both national and local levels. Whilst being one of the most important components of Disaster Risk Reduction, in respect of managing the impact of natural hazards and man-made threats, it is also the hardest to implement as it involves a much broader range of stakeholders and requires awareness raising, information distribution and typically financial investment. The main challenge in highlighting the importance of prevention lies in the fact that the UK Resilience Programme is aiming at improving coordination among the emergency services but does not particularly take into account community involvement. The UK policy defines community resilience in a rather restrictive way: 'Community and individuals harnessing local resources and expertise to help themselves in an emergency, in a way that complements the response of the emergency services' (Cabinet Office, 2011b) – as it does not provide any information on the activities that would 'complement the response' nor does it emphasise the importance of self-reliance. To an extent, policy and the actions of LRFs underestimate the ability of the community to respond and instead suggest relying on the Category 1 responders, providing a clear distinction between those who respond and the population that has to be protected (Anderson and Adey, 2012). Curiously, however, when policies are analysed (Figure 21.4), the words such as 'community', 'public' and 'localism' appear much more often in policy documents that in practitioners' vocabulary, the focus of which is on 'planning', 'designing' and 'building' for the event. Even when it comes to business continuity – which plays a much larger role in the resilience agenda compared to community resilience – the emphasis is on preparedness rather than prevention.

4. Discussion and conclusions

Whilst the UK government's definition of resilience is portrayed to be holistic, when scrutinised, it really only focuses on particular aspects of risk that can be managed and thus undermines the more holistic understanding of resilience. The resilience agenda in the UK deals with emergency

Figure 21.4   Ten most frequently used words relevant to resilience among policy documents and practitioners' responses

situations, which, if they occur, could test the limits of capacity and capability of those imple-menting resilience; it focuses on the anticipation of emergency events and the disruptions caused by them. However, as argued by those implementing resilience (such as members of the LRFs), it is impossible to always predict the event and/or the level of disruption it will cause, and this uncertainty leads to a lack of interest or appreciation of the benefits of taking preventive measures. Response activities can be very visible (publicly and politically) actions and thus they can bring hope that such interventions can bring the event and its impact to an end. Therefore preparedness activities can effectively influence public opinions about how the emergency services and local government agencies have handled emergency events. When considering preventative activities, they can be deemed as being expensive, they may never be needed and also there can be political and social concerns that some sections of society are benefiting (i.e. a flood risk area of a town) at the cost of others (areas of the same town that are safe from flooding) (Bosher *et al.*, 2009).

However, whilst the role of prevention is not explicitly addressed in the ways that resilience is defined and implemented, it is a part of the resilience agenda in relation to more day-to-day issues, such as petty crime or terrorism.[4] UK policy clearly states the importance of enhancing resilience, particularly for the complexity of the challenges that the UK faces, thus leading to 'cascading disruptions' (Cabinet Office, 2004b). Thus, preventing the 'cascade' from happening is at the heart of the resilience agenda. However, the current policy does not provide guidance on what is prevention and what are the means of its implementation. Therefore during the process of being translated from policy to practice, prevention often becomes an enhanced preparedness – but without going into a 'state' of emergency; instead it is seen as a continuous preparation embodied in day-to-day activities.

The focus on preparedness results in a situation where there is a distinction not only between the policies and the day-to-day work, but also between those who protect and the population that has to be protected, as highlighted in the previous section of this chapter. Based on best practice, frameworks and guidelines, the resilience agenda in the UK is aimed at coordinating local governments rather than the communities who, it seems, are not trusted enough to be prepared by the policy makers but at the same time are encouraged to be prepared by those implementing the policy at the local level.

The resilience agenda in the UK covers a wide range of issues and can be seen as a solution to a problem where, due to the interconnectedness of the world, many things have to be taken into account simultaneously. It covers every DRM-related activity before, during and after an event, thus making DRM one continuous cycle rather than a phase-based one. However, being pre-paredness and response oriented, the resilience agenda in the UK is neglecting the critical integration of preventative (such as hazard mitigation) considerations into the country's development and planning practices and consequently does not sufficiently mainstream DRM into policy-making.

The statutory role of emergency management practitioners in the UK also contributes to the emphasis on preparedness and recovery rather than on prevention. Playing a central role in all LRFs, local emergency managers probably want to be more cautious and risk-averse, thus making preparedness and recovery a predominant feature. In addition, emergency managers who are in charge of building and implementing resilience plans to respond (rather than be more preventive) to the events because that is the way they have been trained to operate, thus make preparedness and recovery a predominant feature. At this point it should be noted that this is not a problem unique to the UK; the UN's Global Assessment Report on Disaster Risk Reduction (UN 2015) concluded that historically there has been poor proactive management of disaster risk globally, due to an over-reliance on emergency/civil protection expertise and ideologies.

Such approaches, whilst making a shift towards building resilience and encouraging the implementation of resilience as a process rather than a command and control exercise, still remain highly centralised and dominated by prescriptive policy and the technicalities that come with it. Present approaches to resilience rely on implementation by those in charge, whilst excluding those directly affected. Making resilience-related policies more flexible and allowing for the incorporation of prevention could provide an opportunity to develop local frameworks that respond to local needs without being constrained to rather out-dated institutional frameworks.

Notes

1 The methodology used for this chapter consisted of three steps. The first step involved creating a database of documents related to resilience, which included UK national policy documents ranging from 2000 to 2013, published on the UK government web site (www.gov.uk) and written by national agencies such as the Cabinet Office, Home Office etc. Overall, 23 policy documents were thoroughly analysed. The second step involved analysing transcripts from 19 interviews conducted with various stakeholders that are directly or indirectly involved in the implementation of the 'resilience' agenda (including architects, The Head of Regeneration, The Flood Management Officer, emergency planning officers, liaison architectural officers (police), the Fire and Rescue Service Officer, The Counter-terrorism Security Advisor, property developers, an officer of the Civil Contingencies Research Office (police), urban planners). The semi-structured interviews were aimed at identifying the perceptions and representations that stakeholders make of resilience. They were conducted between May and October 2013 and lasted for approximately one hour each. Each interviewee was asked to define resilience and to comment on whether and how resilience is implemented in their day-to-day practice.

   The final step of the study consisted of comparing word uses, frequencies and discourses among policy documents and the transcripts of the interviews. This has been analysed using Nvivo 8 software, enabling patterns and analytical generalisations to be identified.

2 'R' stands for a policy on resilience. The following policies have been analysed:

   R1: Improving the UK's ability to absorb, respond to and recover from emergencies (Cabinet Office, 2013).
   R2: A summary of 2012 Sector resilience plans (Cabinet Office, 2012).
   R3: The National Risk Register of civil emergencies (Cabinet Office, 2012).
   R4: National Security Strategy (HM Government, 2010).
   R5: The National Planning Policy Framework (DCLG, 2012).
   R6: Keeping the country running: natural hazards and infrastructure (Cabinet Office, 2011).
   R7: Civil Contingencies Act (Cabinet Office, 2011).
   R8: The business continuity management standards (BS25999).
   R9: Strategic Framework and Policy Statement on Improving the Resilience of Critical Infrastructure to Disruption from Natural Hazards (Cabinet Office, 2010).
   R10: Protecting the UK against terrorism (Home Office, 2013).
   R11: CONTEST strategy (Home Office, 2011).
   R12: Terrorism Act (Home Office, 2000).
   R13: The role of Local Resilience Forums (Cabinet Office, 2013)
   R14: Improving the flood performance of new buildings (DCLG, 2007).
   R15: Localism Act 2011 (HM Government, 2011).
   R16: Strategic National Framework on Community Resilience (Cabinet Office, 2011).
   R17: Climate resilient infrastructure: Preparing for a changing climate (DEFRA, 2011).
   R18: Building regulations (all relevant parts).
   R19: Adapting to climate change (DEFRA, 2013).
   R20: Flood and Water Management Act (HM Government, 2010).
   R21: Maintaining UK energy security (DECC, 2013).
   R22: Providing regulation and licensing of energy industries and infrastructure (DECC, 2013).
   R23: Strategy for national infrastructure (HM Treasury, 2010).

3 Building resilience is often seen as an agenda that fits perfectly into the neoliberal state (Chandler, 2014) that 'venerates decentralisation, contextualisation, autonomy and independence' (Haldrup and Rosen, 2013: p.143). Whilst liberalism is about hands-on implementation, the approach of neoliberalism is more

towards hands-off facilitation: in a neoliberal state, relocation of authority – and simultaneously of responsibility – from the centre to the periphery takes place.

4 'Prevent' is one of the four strands of CONTEST, the Government's 'Counter Terrorism Strategy' (HM Government, 2006).

References

Adey, P., Anderson, B. (2011) 'Event and anticipation: UK civil contingencies and the space-time of decisions', *Environment and Planning A*, 43, 2878–99.

Aldunce, P., Beilin, R., Handmer, J. and Howden, M. (2014) 'Framing disaster resilience: the implications of the diverse conceptualisations of "bouncing back"', *Disaster Prevention and Management*, 23 (3), 252–70.

Amin, A. (2013) 'Surviving the turbulent future', *Environment and planning D: Society and Space*, 31, 140–56.

Anderson, B. and Adey, P. (2012) 'Governing events and life: "emergency" in UK Civil Contingencies', *Political Geography*, 31, 24–33.

Aradau, C. (2014) 'The promise of security: resilience, surprise and epistemic politics', *Resilience*, 2 (2), 73–87.

Birkmann, J. (2006) *Measuring Vulnerability to Natural Hazards: Towards Disaster Resilient Societies*. Bonn: United Nations University.

Bosher, L.S. (2014) '"Built-in resilience" through disaster risk reduction: operational issues', *Building Research & Information*, 42 (2), 240–54.

Bosher, L., Dainty, A.R.J., Carrillo, P.M., Glass, J. and Price, A.D. (2009) 'Attaining improved resilience to floods: a proactive multi-stakeholder approach', *Disaster Prevention and Management*, 18 (1), 9–22,

Brand, F. and Jax, K. (2007) 'Focusing the meaning(s) of resilience: resilience as a descriptive concept and a boundary object', *Ecology and Society*, 12 (1), 23.

Brown, K. (2011) 'Lost in translation? Resilience ideas in international development. Presentation at Resilience Matters: Seminar Series on Exploring Resilience', Session 3, Durham University.

Cabinet Office (2003) *Dealing with Disaster*. Available at: http://webarchive.nationalarchives.gov.uk/20050523205851/http://ukresilience.info/contingencies/dwd/dwdrevised.pdf (accessed 15 July 2016).

Cabinet Office (2004a) *Civil Contingencies Act 2004: A Short Guide*. London: HMSO.

Cabinet Office (2004b) *Emergency Preparedness: Guidance on Part One of the Act, its Associate Regulations and Non-statutory Arrangements*. London: HMSO.

Cabinet Office (2010) *Emergency Response and Recovery: Non-statutory Guidance accompanying the Civil Contingencies Act 2004*. 3rd ed. London: HMSO.

Cabinet Office (2011a) *Keeping the Country Running: Natural Hazards and Infrastructure*. London: The Stationery Office.

Cabinet Office (2011b) *Strategic National Framework on Community Resilience*. The Stationery Office: London.

Cabinet Office (2012) *Glossary: Revision to Emergency Preparedness*. Available at: www.gov.uk/government/uploads/system/uploads/attachment_data/file/61046/EP_Glossary_amends_18042012_0.pdf (accessed 15 July 2016).

Chandler, D. (2014) 'Beyond neoliberalism: resilience, the new art of governing complexity', *Resilience*, 2 (1), 47–63.

Chmutina, K., Lizarralde, G., Bosher, L.S. and Dainty, A. (2014) 'The reification of resilience and the implications for theory and practice'. In Schrenk, M., Popovich, V.V., Zeile, P. and Elisei, P. (eds), Proceedings of the RealCorp 2014 Conference, Vienna, Austria.

DEFRA (2011) *Mainstreaming Sustainable Development – The Government's Vision and What this Means in Practice*. Available at: www.gov.uk/government/policies/sustainable-development (accessed 15 July 2016).

DFID (Department for International Development) (2011) Defining Disaster Resilience; What does it mean for DFID? Available at: www.gov.uk/government/uploads/system/uploads/attachment_data/file/67451/Defining-Disaster-Resilience-summary.pdf (accessed 15 July 2016).

Fisher, J., Chmutina, K. and Bosher, L. (2014) 'Urban resilience and sustainability: the role of a local resilience forum in England'. In Masys, A.J. (ed.), *Disaster Management – Enabling Resilience*. New York: Springer, pp. 91–107.

Foresight (2012) *Reducing Risk of Future Disasters*. The Government Office for Science: London.

Haldrup, S.V. and Rosen, F. (2013) 'Developing resilience: a retreat from grand planning', *Resilience*, 1 (2), 130–145.

HM Government (2004) *Civil Contingencies Act.* London: HMSO.

HM Government (2006) *Countering International Terrorism: The United Kingdom's Strategy.* London: HMSO.

Joseph, J. (2013) 'Resilience in UK and French security strategy: an Anglo-Saxon bias?', *Politics,* 33 (4), 253–64.

Lizarralde, G., Valladares, A., Olivera, A., Bornstein, L., Gould, K. and Duyne Barenstein, J. (2015) 'A systems approach to resilience in the built environment: the case of Cuba', *Disasters,* 39 (s1), 76–95.

Mann, B. (2007) *Protecting the UK's Critical Infrastructure. Contingency Today.* London: Cabinet Office.

Manyena, S.B., Mavhura, E., Muzenda, C. and Mabase, E. (2013) 'Disaster risk reduction legislations: is there a move from events to processes?', *Global Environmental Change,* 23, 1786–94.

Martin-Breen, P. and Anderies, J.M. (2011) *Resilience: A literature review.* Available at: http://opendocs.ids. ac.uk/opendocs/handle/123456789/3692 (accessed 15 July 2016).

Norris, F.H., Stevens, S.P., Pfefferbaum, B., Wyche, K.F., and Pfefferbaum, R.L. (2008) 'Community resilience as a metaphor, theory, set of capacities, and strategy for disaster readiness', *American Journal of Community Psychology,* 41(1), 127–50.

O'Brien, G. and Read, P. (2005) 'Future UK emergency management: new wine, old skin?', *Disaster Prevention and Management,* 14 (3), 353–61.

Pelling, M. (2003) *The Vulnerability of Cities: Natural Disasters and Social Resilience.* London: Earthscan.

Prasad, N., Ranghieri, F. and Shah, F. (2009) *Climate Resilient Cities: A Primer on Reducing Vulnerabilities to Disasters.* Washington, DC: World Bank Publications.

Rogers, P. (2011) 'Resilience and civil contingencies: tensions in northeast and northwest UK (2000–2008)', *Journal of Policing, Intelligence and Counter Terrorism,* 6 (2), 91–107.

Stumpp, E.-M. (2013) 'New in town? On resilience and "Resilient Cities"', *Cities,* 32, 164–66.

Tobin, G.A. (1999) 'Sustainability and community resilience: the holy grail of hazards planning?', *Global Environmental Change Part B: Environmental Hazards,* 1 (1), 13–25.

UN (2015) *Global Assessment Report.* Geneva: UNISDR.

UNISDR (2005) *Hyogo Framework for Action.* Geneva: United Nations.

UNISDR (2007) Terminology. Available at: www.unisdr.org/we/inform/terminology#letter-d (accessed 15 July 2016).

UNISDR (2013) UK: country profile. Available at: www.unisdr.org/partners/countries/gbr (accessed 15 July 2015).

UNISDR (2015) *Sendai Framework for Disaster Risk Reduction.* Geneva: UNISDR.

22

'BOUNCING BACK' TO CAPITALISM?

Grassroots autonomous activism in shaping discourses of resilience and transformation following disaster

Raven Cretney and Sophie Bond

Introduction

This chapter examines the potential for a radical notion of resilience to challenge hegemonic understandings of everyday capitalist life. Resilience has been increasingly criticised in many fields for focussing on attempts to bounce back or maintain the status quo following a disturbance. Such conceptualisations can uphold the hegemony of discourses of stability and are potentially unhelpful for groups seeking to achieve radical change. Despite this, the concept is fast subsuming sustainability as the latest catch phrase for community organisations wishing to address social and environmental injustices. Grassroots groups are mobilising activism to shape this interpretation through post-capitalist visions – creating alternatives to dominant capitalist narratives in the present. This chapter will discuss the expression of these radical notions of resilience through exploring how activism intersects with experiences of disaster through the example provided by Project Lyttelton, a community organisation at the epicentre of the 22 February 2011 Christchurch earthquake in Aotearoa, New Zealand. By exploring this tension between resilience and post-capitalist activism, this chapter contributes to an emerging area of critique through articulating a more nuanced understanding of the radical potential for what is often expressed as an inherently non-radical concept.

Resilience has become a popular and dominant discourse, not only for disaster recovery and preparedness but also for approaching broader social and environmental challenges (Béné *et al.* 2012; MacKinnon and Derickson 2012; World Bank 2006). The origins of resilience theory speak to a desire to retain the characteristics of an ecological system following a disruption through an ability to absorb and withstand shocks (Holling, 1973). More recent theoretical advances seek to align ecological and social systems through Social-Ecological Systems (SES) resilience, including the introduction of concepts such as adaptation and transformation (Magis 2010). This theoretical framework has become an increasingly popular approach for anticipating and responding to the increasing frequency and intensity of natural disasters (O'Brien *et al.* 2009).

With this rise in popularity, many have called for caution in the use of the term, particularly as it has been appropriated and taken up by top-down and arguably neoliberal politics

(Cote and Nightingale 2012; Walker and Cooper 2011). MacKinnon and Derickson (2012) critique the increase in popularity of resilience, noting that this rise has parallels with the uptake of resilience-based projects and organisations by anti-capitalist activists. While these authors advise against groups using the resilience concept and framework, the fact remains that many community-based organisations are engaging with these ideas. Furthermore, by acknowledging the presence of the resilience paradigm across both grassroots and top-down approaches, it is possible, as shown in this chapter, to build an understanding of how community groups can use the concept in a radical way to counter-act the dominant status quo, particularly following a crisis or disaster event.

Many groups using the idea of resilience, such as Transition Towns,[1] plan for the onslaught of crises that are believed will affect the world during the twenty-first century. Yet few have had the chance to act in a time of crisis and put their plans into practice. But the earthquakes of 2010/11 in the Canterbury region of Aotearoa New Zealand tested one grassroots organisation, Project Lyttelton.[2] This group is a grassroots organisation located in the suburb of Lyttelton in Christchurch, close to the epicentre of the earthquakes.[3] Since the earthquakes in February 2011, Project Lyttelton has been at the forefront of the immediate disaster response and recovery of the town.

In this chapter, we argue that grassroots groups such as Project Lyttelton are mobilising a radical politics of resilience that has the potential to provide valuable and workable alternatives to the political and economic status quo. Through discussing autonomous activism in a disaster zone, we explore the actions and politics of a group that aims to fundamentally (re)work societal relations through their pursuit of resilience.

We first explore the differences between mainstream resilience discourses and those mobilised by more radical discourses of societal change. Following this we discuss the actions of Project Lyttelton and how they occurred in the context of the 2010/11 earthquakes. Finally, we assess the potential of actions by groups such as Project Lyttelton to influence discourses of resilience, prior to, during and following times of crises.

Resilience – to maintain or transform?

There exists widespread ambiguity surrounding a conclusive definition of resilience, despite the rapid uptake of the concept across a wide array of disciplines (Berkes 2007). Original conceptualisations of resilience were instigated in the disciplines of engineering and physics, and referred to the ability for physical strength to be maintained (Norris *et al.* 2007; Pendall *et al.* 2009). In the 1970s, work done by Holling (1973, p. 17) developed the more commonly referred to idea of resilience in relation to biological communities as the 'ability of these systems to absorb changes of state variables, driving variables and parameters, and still persist'.

The main tenants of SES resilience build on this concept of ecological resilience by emphasising the ability of a system to absorb and adapt to uncertainty and shifts in critical thresholds without changing to a different state (Folke 2006). The inclusion of social systems has seen the resilience approach diversify and be applied to varying levels of urban and rural development, including specific communities and cities (Norris *et al.* 2007). The aim of this approach is to interlink systems involving society, the environment and the economy (Gunderson 2010; Walker and Cooper 2011).

Accordingly, traits relating to social systems have been incorporated, such as social learning and memory, various forms of social, human and natural capital, governance and institutions, and adaptive capacity (Folke 2006; Gunderson 2010). Despite numerous papers raising critiques, there exists a distinct lack of a comprehensive framework to understand the relevance of politics and culture to existing SES theories (Cote and Nightingale 2012; Davidson 2010; MacKinnon and Derickson 2012).

To a certain extent, SES resilience does not strictly follow earlier definitions of resilience, which promote a bounce back approach. This is due to a shift in theory that incorporates the concept of adaptive capacity, or the idea of bouncing forward (Berkes 2007). Adaptive capacity involves a framework that acknowledges the multiple, ever changing nature of systems and the need to prepare for uncertainty and make changes in response to disruptions (Engle 2011). Within the context of disaster, these concepts have been important to align SES resilience with a perspective that argues not for the reconstruction of the conditions which produced the disaster, but instead to encourage an adaptive approach that reduces vulnerabilities (Manyena 2006). Nevertheless, there is evidence that discourses that promote the status quo are still expressed through this new perspective, albeit in subtler forms. Pike *et al.* (2010) note that in this case, adaptation can be used to strengthen arguments that advocate for minor changes towards a pre-conceived developmental path.

Despite the many nuances and interpretations of resilience, adaptive capacity and trans-formation, there still remains considerable scope for these concepts to be utilised in a way that justifies and maintains the status quo. As a result, resilience is extensively used to indicate a desire for social systems and crucial infrastructure to either maintain function or quickly recover from disruptions, particularly disasters (Engle 2011). The widespread adoption and popularity of SES resilience by government and international organisations in the past decade is a testament to the broad-ranging interpretations of the framework (Béné *et al.* 2012; MacKinnon and Derickson 2012; Norris *et al.* 2007; Pendall *et al.* 2009). The term 'resilience' is now used as a central element of policy for governments, the World Bank, the International Panel for Climate Change and the European Union (Béné *et al.* 2012; Walker and Cooper 2011). Such expansive development is seen as the infiltration of resilience theory into the arena of mainstream politics and culture.

Several commentators have noted that through this infiltration, resilience theory is being co-opted by those whose interests lie in perpetuating neoliberal discourses and governance that privilege existing power relations and contribute to the maintenance of the current, dominant capitalist system (Joseph 2013; MacKinnon and Derickson 2012; Walker and Cooper 2011). The expression of neoliberal discourses and subjectivities is increasingly represented through contradictory shapes and forms as different manifestations emerge depending on location, culture and governance. Yet Walker and Cooper (2011) have noted that resilience discourses are being widely used as a tool to implement a broad range of these neoliberal ideological projects following a crisis. Such projects are used to justify and motivate actions that increase inequality and disadvantage marginalised communities through the use of market-driven rationale. In this context, disasters are seen as opportunities for furthering projects that selectively restructure urban space and social services. These examples raise questions as to what outcomes state-sponsored resilience programmes are aiming for. Cote and Nightingale (2012) echo this concern, stating that when addressing the use of resilience discourses we must ask questions of resilience of what, and for whom?

Discourses of resilience may also be strengthening government initiatives to de-centralise and roll back the power of the state through emphasising individual and community responsibility (MacKinnon and Derickson 2012). Under the guise of encouraging community resilience, these policies can take an approach that sees populations left with all responsibility and little power or resources (Peck and Tickell 2002). This approach does not address underlying structural issues of power and inequality that may be contributing to the presence of disruptions or vulnerability. Such a dynamic is demonstrated in the British government's 'Big Society' project, as outlined by MacKinnon and Derickson (2012), who argue that this focus on localism and community seeks to further market rationalising discourses and remove the government's role from the provision of state services. Indeed these applications of resilience appear to be used to perpetuate such policies, which may have a negative effect on the resources available to communities.

While this progression of neoliberalism and resilience has been emerging, groups concerned with challenging dominant societal structures and systems have also been mobilising resilience as part of a different ideological approach. In this articulation of resilience, aspects of adaptive capacity and transformation have the potential to defy discourses of bouncing back or forward and lend strength to anti-capitalist, activist projects. Thus resilience is regarded as the strength of communities rather than the aim to maintain dominant economic and political systems. This is considered by some groups as the ability of their alternatively organised community to 'ride out the waves of change' resulting from outside 'shocks' that can occur as a result of unsustainable economic and energy systems (Hopkins and Brangwyn 2010; Transition Towns Totnes 2013).

In order to do so, groups engaged in this alternative articulation of resilience largely carry out localisation activities to improve the conditions of their community and environment such as: establishing systems of co-operative ownership and management, nurturing social capital and networks, encouraging sustainability, and implementing practical projects based around food, energy and care in the community (Hopkins and Brangwyn 2010; North 2010). Through these activities based around resilience, the argument can be made that such organisations are challenging the dominant values and norms of society. Resilience is considered desirable in this context, as it converges with concepts of sustainability to create a platform that addresses the interconnected nature of environmental issues and disasters in a global context (Tobin 1999). The Transition Towns movement is an example of this through their philosophy of relocalisation and the desire to encourage community economies and relations (Hopkins 2009).

One issue that arises from this use of resilience is the limits of the relocalisation philosophy for informing grassroots strategies. Concepts of *local*, *place* and *community* are socially constructed and variable but have risen in prominence as a way of countering the perceived homogenisation and disempowerment associated with globalisation (Feagan 2007). However, it is important not to assume an inherent relationship between the global and negative outcomes and the local with positive. As North (2010) elucidates, there is great complexity underlying the social and environmental costs and benefits of local and global trade and relations.

Project Lyttelton, while not explicitly a Transition Town, follows a similar re-localisation philosophy through working as a democratic grassroots environmental and social change community group. The organisation is self-described as 'an inspiration and a model for communities wishing to build community resilience and sustainability through innovative projects and collective creativity' (Hall 2009). Whilst aiming for these goals, Project Lyttelton has established numerous projects such as a highly successful Farmer's Market, a timebank,[4] a community garden, film nights, a fundraising platform for other community organisations and a community owned and run food co-operative.

As Lyttelton was located directly over the epicentre of the 22 February 2011 earthquake that hit the Canterbury region, the town suffered widespread destruction and disruption, including loss of life. In addition, Lyttelton's transport routes were damaged, geographically isolating the town for several days. During this time the group played a significant role in supporting the community, providing volunteers and engaging with participatory elements of the local government rebuild process. Project Lyttelton has used this experience to learn how to cope and provide support during a disaster and it has established a new project titled the 'Harbour Resilience Project'. This project seeks to improve the resilience of the whole harbour region by focussing largely on food security and building skills in the community.

What emerged from the Project Lyttelton case study represents the multiple engagements of resilience. While the way resilience is being used at a governmental and global level is deeply troubling (see Cote and Nightingale 2012 and Walker and Cooper 2011), the concept is increasingly being used as a key term for strategic purposes by community groups. By drawing on 'resilience', groups can gain access to funding and political buy-in for activities that seek to empower local communities and shift norms and values. More importantly, there is evidence to suggest that the activities promoted in Lyttelton as resilience building do in fact challenge the dominant way that society operates. The following explores interview data that show how Project Lyttelton engaged with resilience in a way that contests power relations and social structures to create and envisage workable alternatives to capitalist society.

The role of autonomous activism in resilience

Grassroots groups, such as Transition Towns, challenge dominant societal discourses by localising social, political and economic interdependencies, in order to respond at a community level to the triple threats of peak oil, climate change and financial crises (Connors and McDonald 2011; Mason and Whitehead 2011). These geographies of autonomous activism are often complex, contested and revolve for the large part around the identities of activists and activist groups (Chatterton and Pickerill 2010).

Autonomous activists desire to use creativity and resistance as tools to imagine and embody alternatives to neoliberal, capitalist lifestyles through the practices of everyday life and challenging discourses of consumption, market provision and work (Chatterton and Pickerill 2010). Gibson-Graham (2006) notes that joining these groups engages individuals in a 'politics of becoming' and discourses of self-transformation as well as the creation of physical projects. They liken the actions these community groups are undertaking to second wave feminism, which offered new practices of the self that resulted in the possibility for new discourses to emerge in the everyday lives of women (Gibson-Graham 2006). Likewise, Transition Towns and groups with similar aims are enacting discourses of transformation and alternative futures that challenge neoliberal values and norms through efforts to strengthen the community, localise food and energy security, and improve local resilience.

Though autonomous movements are often aligned with philosophies that seek to build community resilience through familiar, everyday activities, the disruptions that test resilience constitute the deeply unfamiliar in that they are not usually part of everyday life. Consequently, many groups aiming for resilience have yet to experience their capacities in this manner. However, during the Canterbury 2010/11 earthquakes, Project Lyttelton's resilience capabilities were tested.

Fostering resilience capacities

Despite the hardships experienced in Lyttelton from the earthquake, the town became well known for its community spirit and ability to pull through the disaster. Several Project Lyttelton activities became integral to the disaster response in both formal and informal ways. Indeed, the existence of Project Lyttelton and activities such as the timebank were considered one of the reasons that Lyttelton as a community coped better than other communities: 'It has fared better than other areas . . . because [of] those close knit [relationships], that resilience was already there, it wasn't scrambled together after the earthquakes, it was in place before.'

Here, pre-existing resilience capacity is seen as the ability for people to come together and rally around each other to receive and provide support (Kaniasty and Norris, 1995). The timebank became integrated with the local Civil Defence[5] headquarters, resulting in a network of individuals in the community who provided disaster relief alongside traditional providers such as the Navy and the Fire Service. Thus the timebank created an organised civilian division of the disaster response: 'They'd have these briefing sessions every day . . . and timebanking's skill was being able to have the ability to link people very quickly and so you'd send out broadcasts . . . people would read the broadcasts and then self-select.'

As a result, the timebank was able to check on over 300 elderly people, provide childcare, provide minor household repairs and help establish a 'meals on wheels' system that fed vulnerable people for months following the quakes. These actions, instigated by Project Lyttelton, helped to re-establish community life and showed the value of resilience actions that encourage individuals to regain a degree of control over their surroundings following a disaster (Cicognani *et al.* 2007).

Projects that promote the resilience capacities of social learning and adaptation were also utilised. Social learning involves the ability of societies and communities to retain and build on lessons learnt as a result of disruptive events (Gunderson 2010). Project Lyttelton has addressed this through several projects, which seek to challenge the status quo and provide resilience in the event of future disruptions. The Harbour Resilience Project (HRP) is one such example. Project Lyttelton was able to secure funding for the HRP, which has already established a local food store that runs on a co-operative business model. Furthermore, the HRP plans to set up a resilience centre dedicated to community education and the practical implementation of improving food security for the region: 'The main components [of the resilience centre] would be an organic farm which could then sell produce at the farmers market and the coop and within a community supported agriculture scheme . . . [and] a display of sustainable housing solutions.'

This learning centre will act as a physical repository of social memories and learning from the earthquakes as well as providing practical advice and skills to visitors. The multi-sector approach to the project will be likely to strengthen the community and their responses to future events through collaboration and adaption (Pahl-Wostl *et al.* 2007). In projects such as the HRP and timebank, resilience has provided a useful framework for the organisation to respond to the disaster by focussing on uncertainty, change, social support and adaptation.

Shifting norms and dominant discourses

Project Lyttelton activities combined with the experience of the February earthquake not only provided support for the community but also strengthened the group's motivation to enact alternative futures and further work towards shifting societal norms. For example, timebanks value different strengths and skills in the same way – no one skill is considered more valuable than another (Cahn 2004). This results in skills and roles that are not traditionally valued in a monetary sense, such as domestic child-care, being valued through the collection of time credits that can be 'spent' on other services (Cahn 2004). The Lyttelton timebank appears to have contributed to shifting the norms in the community. One participant noted how important this was after each major earthquake:

> You've already got a community that really knows each other and . . . is used to asking [for] and receiving help. So you can start to get the help that people need really, really, quickly . . . and people can volunteer really quickly and easily. There's no stigma in saying 'oh I'm on my own, can someone come and help me put my house back together' because that's a normal thing to ask before the earthquakes so it just normalised the whole thing.

Gibson-Graham (2006) agrees that these projects can shift dominant societal values by fostering small-scale shifts in the conception of what is possible. These actions do not require higher-level transformations, although they do, in many cases, prelude such patterns. Another example of challenging societal values is the Harbour Resilience Project share stall, where individuals bring excess food or produce and leave it in a covered stall. People then take what they want or need. In a society that values individualism and monetary exchange, these localised economic shifts may indicate a change in values that could potentially challenge dominant discourses around 'help', reciprocity and the provisions of the market. Harris (2009), who analysed alternative food networks, agrees, stating that activism that cultivates thought outside of normalising neoliberal discourses of market rationales and individualism is integral for effective change to be envisioned and realised.

As a result of the earthquakes, Project Lyttelton has also been part of the creation of a food co-operative. The food co-operative is owned by a group of individuals who live in and around Lyttelton. The project was launched following the February earthquake as a result of the single grocery store in the town facing closure due to earthquake damage. After the event, the town had no grocery store for several months. The lack of a supermarket left the town vulnerable in future crisis events as the geographical barriers of the hills could result in the community being isolated for several days without access to food supplies (as occurred on 22 February 2011). Thus, the Harbour Co-op has been established to explicitly enhance the resilience of the town in the case of another earthquake, but also as a wider response to re-localise food supply and production in the region.

In this case, the establishment of the Harbour Co-op has had several outcomes. First, the store is owned and run by the community and the individuals who shop there. This model is significantly different to the dominant neoliberal mode of food production, which relies on globalised corporate supply (Guthman 2008):

> Part of [resilience] is the whole harbour Co-op thing, so that you've got your own food place there that is owned by the community. And it certainly *is* owned by the community. I mean how many people put money into the harbour Co-op? 500 I think . . . that's a big group of people.

The Co-op presents a different way of doing business that runs on democratic organisation, re-localising profits and providing proceeds from the store back to the owners and the community (Harbour Co-op 2016). The store also supports local producers and potentially contributes to lower environmental food footprints through promoting local and sustainably produced food in combination with the Project Lyttelton-run Farmers Market. These autonomous activist projects that radicalise everyday aspects of life show the value that a resilience approach can bring to a community group. Through envisioning the needs and desires of the community through everyday life and the possibilities that arise out of a crisis, the Harbour Co-op established an alternative to the capitalist business model in the community (Gibson-Graham 2006).

Power, autonomy and self reliance

Another trait that Project Lyttelton's activities appear to have nurtured within residents of Lyttelton is that of self-reliance. Participants noted that residents of the town cultivated an atmosphere of autonomy following the earthquakes. Feeling empowered within the community led individuals to take control over elements of the community response without requiring consent from those in power. Examples of this included stories of people who started clearing debris or repairing community assets without 'official' permission. Within Lyttelton these stories cultivated an attitude that suggested that the residents were empowered to take the fate of their community into their own hands. Such actions were generally aimed towards aiding support systems in the community.

However, there is a danger that such a desire for autonomy and control can be used for what Peck and Tickell (2002, p. 386) describe as 'responsibility without power', whereby governments and institutions support policies that roll back the responsibilities of the state. This leaves communities with more responsibility but less funding and resources to carry out previously provided services (MacKinnon and Derickson 2012). This is particularly a concern following a disaster if resilience is mobilised in order to reduce government responsibility and funding without ensuring adequate resourcing for communities to carry out disaster risk reduction and preparedness (Cretney 2016). However interactions between Project Lyttelton, the wider Lyttelton community and government organisations show that rather than accepting sole responsibility for the well-being of the community and shunning the role of the government, individuals are – following the earthquakes – attempting to hold centralised political structures to account and work in negotiation: 'We live here, we know what these things are . . . So people here approached the council and said we don't want to be consulted anymore we want partnership and the council didn't quite know what partnership meant.'

The same participant also acknowledged and linked these political struggles to the wider dominant capitalist discourses of mainstream society that their activities are attempting to challenge:

> People [in Lyttelton] are stroppy they'll go and say no, no we'd don't want that, we want this . . . and I think the way the world has been going through capitalist consumerist society, we've tended to numb people [from] thinking.

Here, the interviewee indicates that far from abdicating responsibility solely to the government or the community, individuals are becoming aware of the power dynamics at play in the complex interactions between politics and everyday communities. In many ways, the group's activities decentralise power in the community resulting in local residents taking action towards their own future post-disaster, while simultaneously seeking to hold government and other centralised power structures to account. This approach takes into consideration a much more nuanced reality of social relations, power and policies in their struggle for resilience.

Obviously Project Lyttelton does not reject the dominant capitalist model in its entirety – the Harbour Co-op and Farmers Market operate as businesses that exchange goods for monetary currency, and the organisation itself hires and employs members of the community. However the difference is that these projects are run democratically as community-owned and operated entities that re-invest profits back into the community. Through engaging in such activities, which are creating tangible alternatives to dominant capitalist practices, Project Lyttelton is using resilience as a platform to extend these ideas and shift societal norms.

The future of resilience?

Community and activist groups engaging with resilience often do so in a way that seeks to build, from the ground up, a transformative alternative to capitalism. Their aim is to create communities which can resist disruptions from environmental, economic or political crises (Hopkins and Brangwyn 2010; Transition Towns Totnes 2013). A disaster as a time of crisis is an opportunity for such groups to take control during a momentary lapse in dominant capitalist life. Through the case study of Project Lyttelton, there are several examples of radical resilience emerging through disaster to be engaged as a framework for building a working alternative to current capitalist norms and discourses.

The first is the implementation of projects such as the timebank that actively shift social relationships and norms from individualism to community and reciprocity. The experiences of participants in these projects during the earthquakes show how ideas of resilience can increase the support available to a community during a crisis. Second, Project Lyttelton's activities are actively building and experimenting with physical and practical alternatives to everyday capitalist life. The experience of disaster, influenced by ideas of resilience, has supported the community in extending these projects following the earthquakes.

Finally, the earthquakes provided an interesting insight into how communities that have already been self-organising respond during a disaster. In the case of Lyttelton an attitude of autonomy was nurtured, which encouraged people to take control in the absence of governing organisations. Following the immediate disaster response phase individuals in the town have been negotiating the restructuring of power relations with government through their participation, or lack thereof, in official processes.

From this case study we can see that despite the worrying application of resilience theory at certain levels of governance and policy, the way grassroots groups are mobilising resilience may prove useful to create workable alternatives to capitalism. The most obvious element of existing resilience theory that co-exists with autonomous desires for societal change is that of social learning and transformation. If a community, nation or organisation does not learn how to adapt and shift with the challenges they face, then it can be argued that their vulnerability to future disturbances will plateau or increase (Tobin 1999). As with most theories, this principle can be interpreted in several ways. The way that Project Lyttelton appears to interpret this is to respond to future concerns through interpreting and identifying the layers of instability in the political and social system as is expressed through the earthquake recovery process. In one participant's view:

> everything else that goes on with the rebuild and recovery is impacting on that ability to be resilient and go forward and for it to be a positive thing and to rebuild better. . . .
> I think that lack of information, that lack of accountability, transparency out of local government and [Parliament] is a real concern [for future resilience].

Project Lyttelton, following disaster, used resilience in a manner that emphasises political and cultural understandings in order to use the concept for its potential to advocate for pre-emptive, transformative change in the face of encroaching social and environmental issues. While theorists and academics debate the implications of using certain frameworks, a number of groups such as Project Lyttelton are working at a grassroots level to interpret resilience in a way that suits their aims – to build alternatives to capitalist society.

Resilience has thus become a term with increasing political and popular buy-in for some community organisations. In Project Lyttelton's case, through pushing an openly resilience-based agenda they have been able to secure funding for projects that subtly yet surely seek to build alternative futures. As a member of Project Lyttelton claimed:

> So [the Ministry for Social Development] start up and go 'so there are different definitions of resilience' and I thought – who cares? . . . Some of the things like resilience, we just use that word because it seems to currently cover what we're doing. We're not that hung up on what it means. . . . We in Lyttelton are quite good at surfing the wave and knowing where we want to go but also knowing what the key words are.

While Project Lyttelton has achieved remarkable success in activities at a local scale, there are likely to be many similar groups operating under resilience visions that do not know about or acknowledge the issues of power and inequalities. It is also likely there are many ways in which Project Lyttelton could improve its activities in the community.

What this case shows is that the verdict on resilience as a framework for grassroots activists is not clear-cut. Critiquing resilience at a theoretical level is indeed a valuable and much-needed process. However, a constructive dialogue with grassroots practitioners is also required. As critical geographers, we want to provide insight that is useful at both the academic and grassroots level. To this end, we believe that there are significant issues with resilience concepts in that they are undoubtedly being used to push a neoliberal policy agenda that sacrifices the well-being of communities and places additional stress on social and environmental concerns.

Despite this, a radical mobilisation of resilience appears to be occurring. As exemplified in this chapter, grassroots groups are using resilience as a way to gain purchase for their actions that aim to deconstruct capitalist norms through radicalising the everyday. Through Project Lyttelton's experiences in the earthquakes in Canterbury in 2010/11, we can see how ideas of resilience mobilised after the experience of disaster have pushed the boundaries of neoliberal norms and contributed to the scaling up of 'resilience' projects that also challenge mainstream societal values such as the Harbour Co-op and the Harbour Resilience Project.

Acknowledgements

This work was supported by the Victoria University of Wellington under the Faculty of Strategic Research Grant 203997. This chapter is an updated and revised version of the previously published piece 'Bouncing back' to capitalism? Grass-roots autonomous activism in shaping discourses of resilience and transformation following disaster, *Resilience*, vol. 2, no. 1, 2014, pp. 18–31. DOI: 10.1080/21693293.2013.872449.

Notes

1 Transition Towns are community groups based around a re-localisation philosophy as a reaction to the threats of peak oil, climate change and financial collapse. Transition Towns often carry out locally based actions such as community gardens, alternative currencies and awareness-raising activities.
2 Canterbury, Aotearoa New Zealand has experienced over 12,000 earthquakes in the past three years. Four major events have occurred, with earthquakes over magnitude 6.0 on the Richter scale, one in 2010 in September of 7.1 magnitude and three in 2011 in February, June and December. The 22 February earthquake was the most destructive, resulting in the loss of 181 lives and widespread damage to buildings and infrastructure.
3 This chapter draws on qualitative research in Lyttelton based on interviews with seven key figures in the community during June 2012. A further eight e-interviews were also carried out using an open-ended questionnaire format to engage individuals in a less time-consuming and intense manner, given the sensitive nature of research in a post-disaster situation (Jensen 2010). The unattributed quotes used in this chapter are taken from these semi-structured and e-interviews. The original notes are with the authors. In addition, websites, social media and a locally published book containing 32 interview transcripts of individuals' experiences of the earthquake were analysed (see Evans 2012).
4 Timebanks are a form of alternative currency, which operates on the basis of earning credits for labour, skills or teaching; credits can then be exchanged by the individual for other services. Timebanks operate on the philosophy that every individual has valued skills and these should be traded at equal value.
5 Civil Defence is the colloquially referred to local emergency management centre and response as part of the New Zealand Ministry for Civil Defence and Emergency Management.

References

Béné, C., Wood, R., Newsham, A. and Davies, M. (2012) Resilience: New Utopia or New Tyranny? Reflection about the potentials and limits of the concept of resilience in relation to vulnerability reduction programmes. *IDS Working Papers*, no. 405, 1–61.

Berkes, F. (2007) Understanding uncertainty and reducing vulnerability: lessons from resilience thinking. *Springer Natural Hazards*, vol. 41, no. 2, 283–295.

Cahn, E. (2004) *No More Throw Away People – The Co-production Imperative* (2nd ed.). Washington, DC: Essential Books.

Chatterton, P. and Pickerill, J. (2010) Everyday activism and transitions towards post-capitalist worlds. *Transactions of the Institute of British Geographers*, vol. 35. no. 4, 475–490.

Cicognani, E., Pirini, C., Keyes, C., Joshanloo, M., Rostami, R. and Nosratabadi, M. (2007) Social participation, sense of community and social well being: a study on American, Italian and Iranian University Students. *Social Indicators Research*, vol. 89, no. 1, 97–112.

Connors, P. and McDonald, P. (2011) Transitioning communities: community, participation and the Transition Town movement. *Community Development Journal*, vol. 46, no. 4, 558–572.

Cote, M. and Nightingale, A. (2012) Resilience thinking meets social theory situating social change in socio-ecological systems (SES) research. *Progress in Human Geography*, vol. 36, no. 4, 475–489.

Cretney, R. (2016) Local responses to disaster: the value of community led post disaster response action in a resilience framework. *Disaster Prevention and Management: An International Journal*, vol. 25, no. 1.

Davidson, D. (2010) The applicability of the concept of resilience to social systems: some sources of optimism and nagging doubts. *Society and Natural Resources*, vol. 23, no. 12, 1135–1149.

Engle, N. (2011) Adaptive capacity and its assessment. *Global Environmental Change*, vol. 21, no. 2, 647–656.

Evans, B. (2012) *The Shaken Heart: Earthquake stories from the Heart of Lyttelton*. Lyttelton, New Zealand: Project Lyttelton.

Feagan, R. (2007) The place of food: mapping out the 'local' in local food systems. *Progress in Human Geography*, vol. 31, no. 1, 23–42.

Folke, C. (2006) Resilience: the emergence of a perspective for social-ecological systems analyses. *Global Environmental Change*, vol. 16, no. 3, 253–267.

Gibson-Graham, J. K. (2006) *A Postcapitalist Politics*. Minneapolis: University of Minnesota Press.

Gunderson, L. (2010) Ecological and human community resilience in response to natural disasters. *Ecology and Society*, vol. 15, no. 2, 1–11.

Guthman, J. (2008) Neoliberalism and the making of food politics in California. *Geoforum*, vol. 39, no. 3, 1171–1183.

Hall, A. (2009) *Project Lyttelton: Our Story*. Christchurch, New Zealand: Project Lyttelton.

Harbour Co-op (2016) *Co-operative Principles*. Retrieved from www.harbourcoop.co.nz/learn-about-us/about-co-ops/co-operative-principles. Retrieved on: 16 July 2016.

Harris, E. (2009) Neoliberal subjectivities or a politics of the possible? Reading for difference in alternative food networks. *Area*, vol. 41, no. 1, 55–63.

Holling, C. (1973) Resilience and stability of ecological systems. *Annual Review of Ecology and Systematics*, vol. 4, 1–23.

Hopkins, R. (2009) *The Transition Handbook: From Oil Dependency to Local Resilience*. White River Junction: Chelsea Green Publishers.

Hopkins, R. and Brangwyn, P. (2010) *Transition Initiatives Primer*. Transition Network. Retrieved from www.transitionnetwork.org/resources/who-we-are-and-what-we-do. Retrieved on: 19 July 2013.

Jensen, H. (2010) The logic of qualitative survey research and its position in the field of social research methods. *Open Journal*, vol. 11, no. 2.

Joseph, J. (2013) Resilience as embedded neoliberalism: a governmentality approach. *Resilience*, vol. 1, no. 1, pp. 38–52.

Kaniasty, K. and Norris, F. (1995) In search of altruistic community: patterns of social support mobilization following Hurricane Hugo. *American Journal of Community Psychology*, vol. 23, no. 4, 447–477.

MacKinnon, D. and Derickson, K. (2012) From resilience to resourcefulness: a critique of resilience policy and activism. *Progress in Human Geography*, vol. 37, no. 2, 253–270.

Magis, K. (2010) Community resilience: an indicator of social sustainability. *Society & Natural Resources*, vol. 23, no. 5, 401–416.

Manyena, S. (2006) The concept of resilience revisited. *Disasters*, vol. 30, no. 4, 434–450.

Mason, K. and Whitehead, M. (2011) Transition urbanism and the contested politics of ethical place making. *Antipode*, vol. 44, no. 2, 493–516.

Norris, F., Stevens, S., Pfefferbaum, B., Wyche, K. and Pfefferbaum, R. (2007) Community resilience as a metaphor, theory, set of capacities, and strategy for disaster readiness. *American Journal of Community Psychology*, vol. 41, no. 1–2, 127–150.

North, P. (2010) Eco-localisation as a progressive response to peak oil and climate change: a sympathetic critique. *Geoforum*, vol. 41, no. 4, 585–594.

O'Brien, K., Hayward, B. and Berkes, F. (2009) Rethinking social contracts: building resilience in a changing climate. *Ecology and Society*, vol. 14, no. 2, 12–28.

Pahl-Wostl, C., Craps, M., Dewulf, A., Mostert, E., Tabara, D. and Taillieu, T. (2007) Social learning and water resources management. *Ecology and Society*, vol. 12, no. 2, Article 5.

Peck, J. and Tickell, A. (2002) Neoliberalizing space. *Antipode*, vol. 34, no. 3, 380–404.

Pendall, R., Foster, K. and Cowell, M. (2009) Resilience and regions: building understanding of the metaphor. *Cambridge Journal of Regions, Economy and Society*, vol. 3, no. 1, 71–84.

Pike, A., Dawley, S. and Tomaney, J. (2010) Resilience, adaptation and adaptability. *Cambridge Journal of Regions, Economy and Society*, vol. 3, no. 1, 59–70.

Tobin, G. (1999) Sustainability and community resilience: the holy grail of hazards planning? *Global Environmental Change Part B: Environmental Hazards*, vol. 1, no. 1, 13–25.

Transition Towns Totnes (2013) *What is Resilience?* Retrieved from www.transitiontowntotnes.org/about/what-is-transition/what-is-resilience/. Retrieved on: 19 June 2013.

Walker, J. and Cooper, M. (2011) Genealogies of resilience: from systems ecology to the political economy of crisis adaptation. *Security Dialogue*, vol. 14, no. 2, 143–160.

World Bank (2006) *Hazards of Nature, Risks to Development: An IEG Evaluation of World Bank Assistance for Natural Disasters* (Independent Evaluation Group Report). Washington, DC: World Bank.

PART VIII

Insecurity

23

THE POLITICS OF SECURITY-DRIVEN RESILIENCE

Jon Coaffee and Pete Fussey

Introduction

This chapter illuminates how, since 9/11, security policy has gradually become more central to a range of resilience discourses and practices whilst seeming to focus upon the everyday needs of populations. Since the early 2000s, the so-called 'resilience turn' (Coaffee, 2013) has seen ideas, discourses and logics of resilience embedded within an array of social and urban policy and practice at a range of spatial scales, driven by an overarching requirement to secure the future from an array of disruptive challenges, threats and events or, more broadly, a general sense of uncertainty about the future (Coaffee, 2010; Walker and Cooper, 2011). In this chapter we argue that practices of security have become the most potent driver and shaper of contemporary resilience practices. In turn, these have served to generate multiple competing 'logics of resilience' identified and explored in this chapter through the concept of 'security-driven resilience' that captures the multi-directional process, where resilience policy becomes increasingly driven by security concerns and, at the same time, security policy adopts the more palatable language of resilience. Such processes hold a range of implications including the narrowing of formerly diverse resilience concerns towards very specific forms of security and, at the same time, generating multiple governmental, scaling and coercive implications.

Specifically, this chapter charts the emergence and proliferation of numerous continually modulating security-driven resilience logics, deployed at different spatial scales within policy and practice, which exist in tension with each other. We exemplify such tensions in practice through the deployment of public surveillance techniques via a detailed case study example from Birmingham, UK: 'Project Champion' – an attempt to install over 200 high-resolution surveillance cameras, often invisibly, around neighbourhoods with a predominantly Muslim population. Here, practices of top-down, security-driven resilience came into conflict with other policy priorities focused upon community centred social cohesion, posing a series of questions about social control, surveillance and the ability of national agencies to construct community resilience in local areas amidst state attempts to label the same spaces as 'dangerous'. We conclude the chapter by arguing that different logics of resilience, which have proliferated across multiple policy domains and scales, generate inherent conflicts in how resilience is realised and operationalised, and produce and reproduce new hierarchical arrangements that in turn, may work to subvert some of the founding aspirations and principles of resilience logic itself.

The 'resilience turn', scales of security and the practice of surveillance

In recent years the emergence, evolution and growth of resilience discourse and practice has become well documented and does not necessarily benefit from a detailed rehearsal here. The concept of resilience incorporates a vast range of contemporary risks and security challenges and, after 9/11, has increasingly become a central organising metaphor within the expanding multi-scalar institutional framework of national security and emergency preparedness (Coaffee *et al.*, 2008).[1] Simultaneously, a growing canon of critical resilience scholarship has generated a number of core debates (see this volume) that serve as critical contexts for this chapter. First among these concerns the futility of searching for a homogeneous definition of resilience. For all the recourse to resilience ur-texts – or conceptual staples such as redundancy and adaptability, notable is the growing acknowledgement that ideological, institutional, socio-cultural and normative considerations shape how resilience is mobilised in different organisational and spatial settings. Instead, it could be contended that focus is better placed on how resilience is enacted, and what its performative roles and implications are. Thus what resilience *is* becomes less important than what it *does*. Increasingly common within this approach is to see resilience in relation to varied forms of neoliberal governance and post-politics (Amin, 2013; Neocleous, 2013). A corollary of this concerns the manifold and localised ways in which resilience becomes interpreted and translated into practice in numerous contexts and across a range of scales (Coaffee and Lee, 2016).

Parallel discourses and practices of security have also followed a number of neoliberalising, diversifying and decentralising tendencies. Notably, since the 1990s, emerging ideas of 'human security' have increasingly come to prominence and tried to pull security away from its institutional bias, focus it on the needs of people and populations, and, in so doing, remap scale in security. This work coincided with a progressive reassertion of the importance of scale in political geography – a shift from traditional Euclidian, Cartesian and Westphalian notions of scale and territory as a fixed stable bounded container, to notions of flexible scalar practices – illuminating the ways in which politics explicitly constrains scale choices (Fraser, 2010). Such a politics of scale has strong resonance with the emerging and fluid geo-political landscape of security which has increasingly highlighted the importance of sub-national and localised responses to new security challenges, 'placing the needs of the individual, not states, at the centre of security discourses' (Chandler, 2012, p. 214). As has been argued, 'security is becoming more civic, urban, domestic and personal: security is coming home' (Coaffee and Wood, 2006, p. 504).

Overall, discourses and practices of resilience and of security have developed in parallel and heavily imbricated ways, becoming more civic-centred and reapplied across a spectrum of multi-scalar socio-economic systems. Further complicating the picture is the way that a broader discursive shift in policy – from security to resilience – has subsequently been used to frame associated practices in the post-9/11 world, attempting to soften the vocabulary of 'emergencies' and focus upon the more positive terminology of resilience (Coaffee, 2006). Yet for all the seeming benignity and diversification of focus implied in resilience discourse, notions of resilience have increasingly adopted and come to resemble security concerns, thus constituting the growth of security-driven resilience. Not only does this signify a narrowing of the polymorphic range of concerns implied by resilience towards those of security and, particularly, counter-terrorism, but it also generates a range of governmental, scaling and coercive implications.

A third operational concept, surveillance, has been a continual feature of human societies with the twentieth century bringing rapid changes in the ubiquity, potency and technological sophistication of surveillance practices and, as the century turned, 9/11 further catalysed these developments and shepherded in many new coercive and automated analytical applications and new forms of dataveillance. This chapter focuses on the role of one particular form, public space surveillance, as a tool of risk and security practice that has become deployed under the wider and more palatable aegis of resilience. In doing so, we argue that it both narrows the possibilities of surveillance applications towards the coercive and draws resilience practice towards more tightly specified security-focused goals.

UK Resilience and security discourse: from hybridity to colonisation?

Prior to 2000, resilience was a term seldom heard within security policy circles. Whereas securing state assets against international terrorism had long been a government priority, this was an agenda that had been almost exclusively delivered by state security services. The events of 9/11, and the concern that key UK sites would be targeted by terrorists, made reform of emergency preparedness a key political priority with national security; policy was thus increasingly focused on the need to respond proactively and develop pre-emptive solutions to perceived security threats. It was at this juncture that the term 'resilience' came to the fore (Coaffee, 2006) and was eventually formalised in policies and practices following the 2004 Civil Contingencies Act (CCA). Following the CCA, the UK government attempted to provide a central strategic direction for developing resilience, based on a cycle of anticipation, prevention, preparation, response and recovery (Cabinet Office, 2005). Subsequent national security and counter-terrorism policies – notably the overarching *Countering International Terrorism Strategy* (CONTEST) (HM Government, 2006),[2] the UK's first national security strategy (*Security in an Interdependent World* – Cabinet Office, 2008)[3] and the initial anti-radicalisation approach (*Preventing Violent Extremism* – HM Government, 2008)[4] – interlinked in various ways with the CCA to form a powerful top-down, state-driven logic for 'resilience' policy. Individually and collectively these policy narratives signified an increasingly complex and fluid landscape, where multiple threats were being faced and which required coordinated responses across a range of scales and stakeholder groups, including local communities. As this range of 'resilience', responses have evolved so a number of different security-driven resilience logics, each encompassing complex relationships between security and resilience, can be identified. As these logics develop and unroll through a range of practices, a series of incompatibilities and tensions within and between different thematic and scalar approaches can be seen to emerge.

The remainder of this chapter charts the surfacing and progression of these different 'logics' of resilience over the last decade. In particular, we accent the prominence of security concerns within such articulations of resilience discourse which, as a corollary, have drawn a number of security practices and infrastructures, such as surveillance, into the delivery of resilience practice. For example, and as we will highlight, the logics underpinning UK resilience policy have responded to the changing targeting preferences of international terrorists, concerns over 'radicalisation' as well as a renewed interest in localism as a means of building enhanced community resilience. As the discussion below relates, surveillance practices have been implicated in the delivery of each of these. Here we pay particular attention to the tensions that have emerged as a result of the simultaneous adoption of security-driven resilience practice at a range of spatial and governance scales.

Security-driven resilience logic 1: state-driven reassurance, resistance and bouncing back

As noted above, in advance of the CCA, and in the wake of 9/11, national government and municipal authorities were forced to confront a widespread fear that the UK would be targeted by international terrorism. This threat gave momentum to the birth of a range of national counter-terrorism and security strategies and the development of what would become specific forms of resilience policy. This prominence of such concerns led to the implementation of measures to counter such threats and elevated emphasis on security couched within broadly conceived notions of resilience. In particular, these measures focused on enhancing the physical robustness of the built environment and furthering human and technological surveillance capabilities.

This first logic of security-driven resilience was materially manifest in a number of ways. Notably, electronic surveillance measures, particularly software-driven systems facilitating automated production, ordering and control of space and everyday life (Lyon, 2003), proliferated throughout public and semi-public spaces. The events of 9/11 in particular proved catalytic for the mass introduction of hi-tech surveillance systems – a surveillance surge – with the intensification and expansion of existing systems and the adoption of ever-more refined tracking technologies (Ball and Webster 2003). Second, security-driven resilience was enhanced through the increased popularity of physical or symbolic notions of the boundary and territorial enclosure, which served a defensive purpose, often through the erection of reinforced security barriers and for the placing of surveillance devices around 'at risk' sites, constructing hermetically sealed exclusion zones (Coaffee, 2004). Under this logic surveillance applications adopt a range of coercive and enforcement-based roles.

This first logic of security-driven resilience has been largely state controlled and implemented by the police and national security agencies.[5] The spatiality of resilience was particularly manifest through highly surveilled and visible fortress-like security at high-risk sites such as government buildings, key financial centres and national embassies.[6] Crucial here is the way in which these avowedly security focused practices have since become articulated in terms of resilience across UK government policy, particularly notable in the latest iteration of the UK CONTEST counter-terrorism strategy (HM Government 2010). Thus, according to this logic, over time the language of security has become recast as that of resilience without changing its fundamental focus and purpose. Such practices reflect a further enduring theme identified within critical analyses of resilience, in particular the way in which resilience planning is often translated into more narrowly conceived measures that seek robustness and stability against potential hazards.

Security-driven resilience logic 2: devolving, preparing and pre-empting

While the first logic of security-driven resilience was inherently reactive, materially focused and sought to mitigate security risk, as the 2000s proceeded increased effort was made to focus on preparedness and preventative aspects of the resilience cycle. The second logic thus moved beyond the ability to absorb shock, to focus on the ability of businesses, governments and communities to *take preventative action*. National government stakeholders increasingly sought to cooperate with regional and local authorities and a range of professional stakeholders through the development of a multi-level system of resilience governance across national, regional and local levels mirroring broader trends in public governance. Such drives towards multi-level action thus may be located among a number of broader processes aimed at devolving central state functions and responsibility onto the local realm, including responsibilities for emergency planning, tackling crime and disorder and, separately, terrorism.

Overall, this second logic fomented a shift in the governance as well as the focus of resilience-enabling security concerns to become further consolidated as the central concern of resilience practice, whilst national security became played out in the local realm under the aegis of resilience and community building. Here, actions of local governments became central in developing tailored resilience strategies against a range of risks, but most prominent among these was terrorism, again underscoring the central role of security in more broadly conceived notions of resilience. Security-driven resilience has thus been enacted through the increasing sophistication and cost of security and contingency planning undertaken by organisations and different levels of government, intended to decrease their vulnerability and increase preparedness in the event of an attack. Thus, resilience practices further coalesced around notions of security.

Notwithstanding the multi-scalar governance established to coordinate resilience practice, the ambient threat of urban terrorist attack and its realisation in London on '7/7'[7] defines the second logic of security-driven resilience. Signifying a further collapse of distinctions between internal and external security, concerns over 'home grown terrorists' focused government attention on the so-called *Prevent* strand of national counter-terrorism policy concerned with 'the radicalisation of individuals'. This became a controversial area of policy, especially with the emotive language often used to describe it and accusations of discrimination against particular racial or ethnic groups.[8] In counter-distinction to the protective and state-led responses to 9/11, after 7/7 there was a refocusing on localised community-based approaches towards counter-terrorism in the UK, with:

> the government acknowledging the need to work in partnership with Muslim communities to prevent young people from being radicalised in the first place and to ensure that communities were resilient enough to respond to, and challenge, extremists from within.
>
> *(Briggs 2010, p. 971)*

The co-option of community level groups into the provision of security-driven resilience practices has been controversial, however, amid accusations that such attempts represented a Trojan Horse for coercive state control to become intensified in local contexts. In the wake of 7/7, the UK government immediately set up the Preventing Extremism Together (PET) Taskforce in August 2005 to underpin this locally focused effort and eventually this fed into enhanced funding, with delivery being coordinated by local police forces and local government in conjunction with community organisations. Overall, *Prevent* was seen as a longer-term objective, where the state and its agencies attempted to tackle the root causes of extremism in a pre-emptive, proactive and community focused way.[9] In the UK, resilience discourses have become further implicated in CVE programmes via the language of *individual* resilience to radicalisation (Home Office 2011). In sum, as security has become the prominent feature of resilience practice, security assets are justified as providing resilience whilst discourses and resources of resilience are deployed to enhance security.

The prominence of this security-driven resilience logic has served to direct the use of specific surveillance and security practices towards pre-emptive and amelioratory ends, whilst, at the same time, such practices have been accompanied by accelerated diversification in the governance of public surveillance (Fussey 2007). Here, responsibility to provide surveillance strategies that meet local concerns, as well as protecting against state-focused transgressions such as terrorism, is devolved 'down' to lower levels of the state and non-state actors. Yet, at the same time, the central state retains its 'trump card' status, potentially overriding local concerns, liberties and rights in areas it defines as the higher national interest. Such composite ensembles of security-driven resilience practice draw a range of competing frames and responsibilities together, generating tensions and collisions elucidated in the empirical case study below. In doing so, the delivery of security-driven resilience animates a particularly important question, long established in critical security studies but only recently gaining prominence in counterpart critiques of resilience: what is being made resilient and for whom?

Security-driven resilience logic 3: towards local and everyday practice

Whereas the first two logics of security-driven resilience have been largely advanced by the state and prescribed through a range of resilience-related national strategies, over time a new logic began to emerge where increased responsibility was devolved to a range of local scales and non-governmental stakeholders, and businesses, governments and communities increasingly sought to anticipate shocks, and to ultimately embed resilience within everyday activities and professional practice in contrast to the traditional command and control approach from central government. In short, the focus of resilience policy has been directed toward smaller spatial scales and everyday activities, which 'is premised on institutions and organisations *letting go*, [and] creating the necessary framework for action' (Edwards, 2009, p.80). Here, resilience is 'coming home' and practices become nested locally, providing a fit with wider UK government ambitions to create a new, more community driven, social contract between citizens and the state. In the UK, principles of resilience underpin the current drive towards enhanced localism with localised resilience approaches becoming realised not through state institutions, but upon localised networked responses, with governance dispersed more widely across key stakeholders and sectors. Enhanced citizen resilience is, however, still articulated through the lens of emergency planning, with the belief that greater resilience will be produced by 'communities and individuals harnessing local resources and expertise to help themselves in an emergency, in a way that complements the response of the emergency services' (Cabinet Office, 2011, p. 4).

Similar to the preceding two logics, security focused initiatives have been central to driving forward this logic of resilience. For example, in March 2010 the UK government released a set of further guidance documents for built environment professionals concerned with enhancing built-in resilience in urban areas. These documents reinforced the message that the threat from terrorist attack was real and imminent, and that in line with the strategic framework – *Working Together to Protect Crowded Places* – a range of key partners including local government, the police, businesses and built environment professionals should work holistically to reduce the vulnerability of crowded places to terrorism (HM Government, 2010). In other respects, a number of police counter-terrorism training schemes, and also public information campaigns, have placed considerable emphasis on encouraging diverse security professionals and the general public to take ownership of, and act upon, feelings of suspicion. Most visibly, untargeted high-profile publicity campaigns such as the Metropolitan Police's 'If You Suspect It, Report It' and Transport for London's 'It's All Up To Us' and 'If Anything Suspicious Catches Your Eye' campaigns. More targeted and formalised measures include government-funded training of security professionals and other public-facing staff working in crowded places (such as shopping malls, stadia and hospitality) in a range of security aspects including identifying and managing suspicious behaviour and materials. As the discussion below illustrates, such processes agitate tensions within the politics of scale as a range of non-state stakeholders and individuals have been increasingly drawn into the delivery of security policy through a process of 'responsibilisation' (Garland, 1996). The governance of resilience, and particularly the interactions between citizen and state, thus progressively place onus for preventing and preparing for disruptive challenge onto institutions, professions, communities and individuals, rather than the state, the traditional provider of citizens' security needs (Coaffee et al., 2008). Propelled by the processes and practices generated by these three dimensions of the securitisation of resilience, a far more pervasive and widespread responsibilisation of citizens may be highlighted than previously acknowledged in much security research.

In sum, as resilience discourse and practice has proliferated, the emergence of three distinct resilience logics can be identified. Within each is a clear gravitation towards the priorities of security and counter-terrorism, which, in turn, draw security infrastructures, organisations and practices into the delivery of resilience. With regard to the specific focus of this chapter, one such form of security practice, technological surveillance, is prominent within all three logics via its deployment to intensify the robustness of systems and infrastructure against shocks, as a tool of anticipatory control, and through its deployment across diverse localised settings. Adding further complexity to the interrelationships between security and resilience is the way security practices have become cloaked in the softer and more palatable language of resilience, thus enabling their non-coercive applications to be foregrounded.

Project Champion: security-driven resilience in practice

As highlighted above, as the state's approach to security-driven resilience has evolved, so different logics have emerged which shape how resilience is put into practice across varied spatial scales. Given the ambiguity surrounding the rhetorics of security-driven resilience, the scalar practices of resilience are thus complicated and fluid and it is therefore not surprising that, as it has grown in scope and usage, 'resilience' has necessarily harboured internal tensions and contradictions as it shifted from a narrative of national protection to one of localised prevention and self-organising, community-led responses. As these diverse approaches and understandings of resilience become operationalised, their discordances become visible. It is these internal tensions that we will unpack through the following case study from Birmingham, UK.

In June 2010 the media reported on a security project to install 290 surveillance cameras in Birmingham. Given the normalisation of surveillance practices within the UK, many aspects of this initiative were not, at first glance, particularly novel. What was exceptional about the adoption of such practices in this instance, however, was the scale, technological sophistication and location of the operation. Of the high-specification surveillance cameras in 'Project Champion', 150 came equipped with Automated Number Plate Recognition (ANPR) capability, which could automatically monitor all vehicles entering and exiting the areas; whilst a further 72 covert cameras became camouflaged within street signs, furniture and other features of the urban landscape. Most controversially, the cameras encircled two predominantly Muslim neighbourhoods of the city, thus articulating elements of the first security-driven logic of resilience outlined above: the use of borders, perimeters and architectures of surveillance. Here, however – with encirclement achieved through technological rather than physical perimeters, and the replacement of defended and valuable intramural spaces with those of containment and crude categorical suspicion – a number of variations on the theme are observable. The subsequent media storm and local community outcry served to exemplify the tension existing in various security-driven logics of resilience around core ideas of protection, prevention, anticipation and localism. In addition, the impact and fallout from Project Champion illustrates the convergence of the three logics of security-driven resilience and how their simultaneous pursuit generates inevitable conflicts and collisions, with one particular fault line converging on the divisive nature of the scheme and attempts by the local state to engage the community in security and crime reduction initiatives. The rise and fall of the project also served to illuminate tensions associated with security-driven resilience; civil liberties and the limits of public acceptability; the material visibility of security infrastructure; the modulation of different scales of resilience and how a range of different actors become involved in resilience governance; and, the labelling of 'dangerous' (and disadvantaged) populations through anticipatory means.

In the UK, counter-terrorism operations have largely concentrated upon a small number of high-density urban areas, with entire security architectures becoming poured into highly specified areas, the focus spilling over from intended subjects, and categorically resting on associates, networks and geographies. Geographical suspicion was a key driver for the inception and intended installation of Project Champion. The scheme was originally conceived after the (narrowly) failed London nightclub and Glasgow airport bombings of 2007, with the siting of cameras determined by the location of several prior high-profile terrorist plots originating from specific parts of Birmingham. These included the first attempted UK-based al Qaeda plot (during 2000), the arrest of a suspected Taliban 'commander' and, perhaps most famously, 'Operation Gamble' – a plot to kidnap and dismember Muslim soldiers serving in the British Army, resulting in five convictions and leading law enforcement professionals applying ecological perceptions of dangerousness to specific parts of the city. These perceptions converged on Sparkbrook and Washwood Heath, two residential areas with high Muslim populations and home to 11 people convicted for terrorist-related activity between 2007 and 2011. These became the neighbourhoods encircled by the 290 Project Champion cameras.

Sparkbrook and Washwood Heath comprise inner-city neighbourhoods of commensurate sizes of just over 30,000 people. Other shared characteristics include high levels of ethnic diversity, and of unemployment and other socio-economic disadvantages. Moreover, both neighbourhoods comprise large concentrations of 'suspect' populations subjected to other forms of law enforcement attention. Beyond describing the demographic composition of each area, such statistics hold important consequences for the way official agencies seek to engage with residents, how variants of security-driven resilience are applied and how they are received, responded to and resisted by communities. In particular, such groups harbour classic characteristics of what UK local authorities have (potentially perniciously) called 'hard-to-reach groups'. Amongst others, these two neighbourhoods also provided the sites for a range of investments targeted at regeneration and 'community building' including the engagement of residents in expressing and setting priorities for crime reduction, activities analogous to the development of 'community resilience' outlined above. Thus, in this setting, the third logic of security-driven resilience engages the same communities that are targeted by the first.

In March 2008, West Midlands Police (WMP) received £3 million in funding to deploy over 200 cameras, many of which were ANPR enabled. Birmingham City Council also agreed to invest £500,000 to assist WMP with running the scheme (Isakjee and Allen, 2013, p. 7). Such a 'ring of steel' vehicle monitoring approach is by no means unique to the UK, having been used within the financial zones of London since the early 1990s (Coaffee, 2003), but the importation of such strategies into a residential area and the enactment of categorical suspicion on such a scale was novel.

From its inception, Project Champion was intended to institute both obtrusive and unobtrusive monitoring regimes, where 'suspicious' subjects were tracked and monitored 'from a distance', ensuring the safety of police officers and allowing recordings to take place unhindered (Fussey, 2013). Such ambitions to 'police from afar' contrast with the public participatory and community engagement remits of Birmingham's municipal crime reduction body (the Safer Birmingham Partnership – SBP), and thus illustrate tensions between different agencies, using the same technologies but with different aims and protocols and thus occupying different positions in the governance of social control. In doing so, they reveal inherent antagonisms between the different logics of security-driven resilience as they are applied in practice. Here, particular tensions exist between the first and the third logics, whereby national security agendas become nested within, and abrade with, local community safety concerns and practices.

Related to this, Project Champion also revealed fundamental questions regarding visibility and transparency in processes of security-driven resilience. Here we need to gain a greater appreciation of the impact of both visible and invisible security measures – how such apparatuses 'transmit' symbolic messages, as well as the variety of ways in which security might be 'received' by its subjects. As Anderson and Möller (2013, p. 203) highlight, this knowledge 'facilitates understanding of the extent to which current societies are penetrated by the ideas and practices of security and surveillance, and furthers investigation of the discursive structures that enable such penetration'. The Project Champion scheme both materially, and in terms of transparent governance, highlights the opacity of many security-driven resilience initiatives. The active concealment of hi-tech cameras, although never activated, symbolically (at least in the eyes of local communities) represented an attempt to introduce espionage-style techniques into the neighbourhood. A key issue here is that whilst the placement and function of overt security measures can be actively contested, those that are more unobtrusive tend to be implemented without reproach. In other words, as Coaffee *et al.* (2009, p. 506) note, 'invisible forms of security may risk becoming an uncontested element of political and public policy'. Moreover, as shown in Project Champion, the concealment of the purpose of security-driven resilience can have major implications for trust between citizens and police at a time when community resilience is expanding in scope and importance within national security policy, with these two groups mutually reliant on each other for the delivery of security and resilience.

From the perspective of Birmingham City Council, Project Champion later became viewed negatively, as it emerged that counter-terrorism concerns were 'hitch-hiking' on the community safety agenda in order to seek justification and legitimation for more controversial proposals. For example, it was reported that the SBP asserted that, at the first meeting between the police and the SBP/local authority, the police never advised that the scheme was a counter-terrorism operation (Birmingham City Council 2010, p. 28). Members of the WMP present at the same meeting claimed the opposite: that there had been 'no confusion that the principle and exclusive objectives of the Project were driven by the counter-terrorism risk' (ibid.). There is evidence to suggest that the police certainly made judicious use of the 'crime' issue, as part of a broader 'drip feed' of information from the police to the local authority and thus viewed their relationship with SBP in instrumental terms. Several other factors support this version of events, highlighting how WMP effectively post-hoc rationalised Project Champion as a solution to high-crime areas and an expedient, politically acceptable and legitimate guise to introduce a more controversial strategy (Thames Valley Police 2010, p. 16), rather than the inherently negative and politically unacceptable labelling of geographical areas as 'hotbeds' of radicalisation. Critical tensions thus emerge between the first and second logics of security-driven resilience. Central and local state responses clash through this instrumental use of local state community safety architectures that were used to deploy highly focused and coercive counter-terrorism initiatives, ultimately undermining the legitimacy of the former.

Thus, the population of particular territories with different logics of security-driven resilience – with a diversity of actors and coalitions – does not necessarily translate into a coherent approach on the ground given the very different use made of high-tech surveillance for anti-crime and counter-terrorism uses. In this sense, heterogeneous elements remain diverse, and diverse logics abrade even when drawn into tentative coalition.

Project Champion was also dislocated from other community focused policing and local authority approaches to security-driven resilience being undertaken in the area. Notably, WMP had established a dedicated department within its Counter Terrorism Unit to focus on developing successful partnerships with a range of local civil society organisations and institutions in order to drive forward the *Prevent* agenda. For example, dedicated 'Security and Partnerships Officers' were working across key neighbourhoods – in schools, mosques, community centres and sports clubs – to encourage community-wide action to defeat violent extremism. This however has proved a problematic relationship to maintain, with a subsequent Institute of Race Relations report noting a parliamentary committee meeting (House of Commons, 2010), which saw the 'embedding' of counter-terrorism police in local services as a major cause for concern for Muslim communities.

The events surrounding this initial phase of Project Champion highlight a series of fissures amongst the approaches used in the delivery of a nationally important, but locally focused, security-driven resilience initiative, placing community approaches at odds with protective logics of security in a way that effectively stigmatised the area (Isakjee and Allen, 2013). This eventually, in response to a media outcry, led to significant resistance to the scheme from local residents amidst complaints that the intentions, and sheer scale of the surveillance deployment, had been masked. Yet despite media representations pitching a Manichean conflict between those applying and those subjected to Project Champion's cameras, initial resistance to the scheme emerged from those less directly targeted by their gaze.

Initial protest began in the more affluent neighbouring district of Mosley, where residents queried the installation of camera stanchions in their street, feeling it diminished the aesthetic appeal of the area. Despite their status as public backers and legitimators of the scheme, representatives of SBP attending the meeting had no knowledge of the location or extent to which counter-terrorism police had rolled out the scheme. In addition to being criticised by the public for the scheme, and excluded by the police from any prospect of utilising the promised integrated system for municipal ends, the origins of this disquiet also signify a further difficulty. Here, it was affluent suburban social movements that managed to mobilise their grievances. Moreover, in addition to highlighting fractures between the local and central state, such events illustrate the limited extent of engagement with local communities under the third logic of security-driven resilience.

Local communities were outraged when Project Champion became public knowledge and, through community leaders, organised a series of public meetings to protest about the initiative as well as to seek clarity as to where the covert cameras were actually sited. With the backdrop of large public meetings, tensions escalated and by June 2010 news of Project Champion reached the national media. As one local protestor noted:

> Now the truth is out, there's a lot of anger. Certain communities have been ring-fenced and saturated with cameras, making it impossible for you to get in or out without being tracked. What's happening here is the government is spying on its citizens covertly in some cases, without their knowledge or consent, and it's a gross invasion of privacy and civil liberties.
>
> *(BBC, 2010a)*

Surveillance had thus become a visible symbol of a pernicious expression of security-driven resilience. A formal public consultation was forced, which led to 'hoods' being placed over the visible ANPR cameras in July 2010 pending 'further consultation', although as the BBC (2010b) noted, at the time, the cameras were not being disabled and the hidden cameras were still, in theory, useable.

The subsequent independent report, led by Thames Valley Police, was highly critical of the Project Champion scheme and WMP, which, it claimed, had done irreparable harm to community–police relations. In the wake of this report, the camera network was dismantled in mid-2011, during which time the Police indicated that the cameras were actually never switched on. Birmingham City Council also carried out its own review into the handling of Project Champion, which indicated that the cameras should be removed. The legacy of the local Project Champion scheme was, however, destined to have national importance with the hardware that was utilised being redeployed in London, and across other areas of the UK, in the policing of the 2012 Olympic and Paralympic Games (BBC, 2011). With the Games hosted in an urban area accommodating Western Europe's most populous Muslim communities, former objections to the cameras become seemingly swept away against the ephemeral and exceptional security demands of the mega-sporting event (Fussey *et al.*, 2011). Another postscript to the Project Champion story further reveals the longevity of conflict and tensions accompanying the scheme. In the wake of convictions of a number of Sparkbrook residents for a failed suicide bomb plot in early 2013, Local Parliamentarian Khalid Mahmood argued that the relaunch of Project Champion 'could ensure the safety and security for people in Birmingham and the whole UK . . . [the cameras] would have been a huge asset and it has been lost. I now want to see a replacement' (*Birmingham Mail*, 2013). Thus, once competing narratives and logics of security-driven resilience are brought together, they may be outlasted by the conflict they generate.

Conclusions: resilience and tensions of devolved state security logics

This chapter has traced the relationship between security and resilience policy and practice that, in the course of which, has led to the dominance of security concerns and the emergence of three distinct security-driven logics of resilience. The prominence of anticipatory and preventative approaches within these logics has served to draw security architectures – particularly those emphasising modes of surveillance – into the practice of resilience. At the same time, the co-purposing of surveillance and other social control strategies towards both security and broader, more seemingly benign, resilience practices enables their deployment under more palatable auspices. Through an analysis of the operationalisation of these security-driven resilience logics via one specific security scheme, Project Champion in Birmingham, we have revealed a number of tensions within and between these logics that become animated as these practices become implemented. These include: the remapping of scale on security; the shift in focus from protection towards local self-organisation; the anticipatory turn in both crime control and national security; and the increasing array of security 'actors', who now have a responsibility for national security and counter-terrorism operations.

Illuminated through the empirical study of Project Champion, the focal argument made is that the modulation between different logics and scales of security-driven resilience exist in perpetual tension and thus do not necessarily translate into any coherent form of social control on the ground. Ultimately, such discordances reveal inherent antagonisms within resilience strategies reliant on co-production and co-delivery between the controller and the controlee. Yet the importance of these frictions goes beyond incoherencies and tensions within broader assemblages of action to reveal a range of processes concerning the governance and scaling of security-driven resilience practice. Project Champion also reveals a number of insights concerning the 'responsibilising' (Garland, 1996) of ever-increasing numbers of local, public-facing individuals and agencies into (security-driven) resilience roles that seek to shift responsibility to general local level governing practices and non-government subjects. Yet for all the focus on local and subjective individual performance of resilience functions (and their absorption of resilience failures), the persistence of state governance from a distance enables multiple extant hierarchies and separations of tasks to remain and exert themselves. At the same time, the proliferation of resilience discourse has led to increasingly broad coalitions of practice and a cluttered organisational landscape.

In many ways, security-driven resilience, and its execution through surveillance practices, is increasingly normalised within modern society and has become a key mode of organising contemporary neoliberal society. Here, we see logics of protection, reassurance, adaptation, preparedness, prevention, pre-managed risk, control and security feeding into an ever-increasing range of national and local policy and practice. Emerging predominantly as a security focused policy connected to countering the threat of international terrorism, resilience is now fully embedded as a policy metaphor for envisioning future local place-making and community building activities alongside broader-scale national security concerns.

Domestic security environments – generated and sustained though the lens of resilience – are heavily mediated by complex and often contradictory practices. These divisions are abundant and serve to underline the fragmented nature of security-driven resilience. As these develop, the contested outcomes, along with the security focused practices that stimulate them, increasingly resemble the antithesis of long-understood principles and conditions of what makes something resilient. In doing so, the realisation of complex, convoluted and contradictory security-driven resilience practices may mutate into practices that ultimately subvert some of the founding principles of resilience logic itself.

Acknowledgements

This chapter is a revised and updated version of Coaffee, J. and Fussey, P. (2015) 'Constructing resilience through security and surveillance: The politics, practices and tensions of security-driven resilience'. *Security Dialogue* 46 (1), 86–105.

Notes

1 The spread of resilience discourse has intimated the simultaneous response to 'all hazards' in which numerous threats and hazards, both 'natural' and human induced, are drawn together.
2 This strategy was developed from 2003 but only made public in 2006. Updated versions were released in 2009 and 2011.
3 See also a revised version in 2010 –*A Strong Britain in an Age of Uncertainty* (Cabinet Office, 2010).
4 See also updated 2011 version.
5 In the UK this involves, for example, the Centre for the Protection of National Infrastructure (CPNI) the National Counter-Terrorism Security Office (NaCTSO) and the Civil Contingencies Secretariat.
6 This reaction was not unique to the UK and characterised the initial international reaction to post-9/11 anxieties (Graham, 2004).
7 In a series of coordinated attacks on London's transport network on 7/7 2005, suicide bombers killed 52 people and injured 770.
8 In a similar way to the UK, other countries have also adopted what Aly (2013) refers to as a 'softer approach' to counter-terrorism – Australia's 'Resilience' approach and the US 'Diminish' being widely cited examples.
9 Likewise, in the US, Canada and Australia, for example, a core approach of localised counter violent extremism (CVE) strategies has been the attempted development of 'community resilience' more generally.

References

Aly, A. (2013) The policy response to home-grown terrorism: reconceptualising Prevent and Resilience as collective resistance. *Journal of Policing, Intelligence and Counter Terrorism* 8(1), 2–18.
Amin, A. (2013) Surviving the turbulent future. *Environment and Planning D* 31, 140–156.
Andersen, R. and Möller, F. (2013) Engaging the limits of visibility: photography, security and surveillance, *Security Dialogue* 44(3), 203–221.
Ball, K. and Webster, F. (eds) (2003) *The Intensification of Surveillance: Crime, Terrorism and Warfare in the Information Age.* London: Pluto Press.
BBC (2010a) Plastic bags to be put over Birmingham 'terror cameras', 17 June. Available at: www.bbc.co. uk/news/10337961 (accessed 2 December 2013).
BBC (2010b) CCTV cameras in Birmingham are covered with hoods, 1 July. Available at: www.bbc.co. uk/news/10477801 (accessed 2 December 2013).

BBC (2011) Birmingham Project Champion 'spy' cameras being removed, 9 May. Available at: www.bbc. co.uk/news/uk-england-birmingham-13331161 (accessed 2 December 2013).

Birmingham City Council (2010) *Project Champion: Scrutiny Review into ANPR and CCTV Cameras.* Birmingham: Birmingham City Council.

Birmingham Mail (2013) Bring back the Project Champion spy cameras in Birmingham, says city's Muslim MP, 23 February 23. Available at: www.birminghammail.co.uk/news/local-news/bring-back-project-champion-spy-1343736 (accessed 2 December 2013).

Briggs, R. (2010) Community engagement for counter-terrorism: lessons from the United Kingdom. *International Affairs* 86(4), 971–981.

Cabinet Office (2005) *Dealing with Disaster (3e).* London: Cabinet Office.

Cabinet Office (2008) *The National Security Strategy of the United Kingdom Security in an interdependent world. Presented to Parliament by the Prime Minister, by command of Her Majesty March 2008 Cm 7291.* London: Cabinet Office.

Cabinet Office (2010) *A Strong Britain in an Age of Uncertainty: The National Security Strategy.* London: Cabinet Office.

Cabinet Office (2011) *Keeping the Country Running: Natural Hazards and Infrastructure.* Available at: www.cabinetoffice.gov.uk/sites/default/files/resources/natural-hazards-infrastructure.pdf (accessed 2 December 2013).

Chandler, D. (2012) Resilience and human security: the post-interventionist paradigm. *Security Dialogue* 43(3), 213–229.

Coaffee, J. (2003) *Terrorism, Risk and the City.* Aldershot: Ashgate.

Coaffee, J. (2004) Rings of steel, rings of concrete and rings of confidence: designing out terrorism in central London pre and post 9/11. *International Journal of Urban and Regional Research* 28 (1), 201–211.

Coaffee, J. (2006) From counter-terrorism to resilience. *European Legacy – Journal of the International Society for the study of European Ideas* (ISSEI) 11.4, 389–403.

Coaffee, J. (2010) Protecting vulnerable cities: the UK resilience response to defending everyday urban infrastructure. *International Affairs* 86 (4), 939–954.

Coaffee, J. (2013) Rescaling and responsibilising the politics of urban resilience: from national security to local place-making. *Politics* 33 (4), 240–252.

Coaffee, J. and Lee, P. (2016) *Urban Resilience: Planning for Risk Crisis and Uncertainty.* London: Palgrave Macmillan.

Coaffee, J. and Wood, D. (2006) Security is coming home – rethinking scale and constructing resilience in the global urban response to terrorist risk. *International Relations* 20(4), 503–517.

Coaffee, J., Murakami-Wood, D. and Rogers, P. (2008) *The Everyday Resilience of the City: How Cities Respond to Terrorism and Disaster.* London: Palgrave/Macmillian.

Coaffee, J., O'Hare, P. and Hawkesworth, M. (2009) The visibility of (in)security: the aesthetics of planning urban defences against terrorism. *Security Dialogue* 40, 489–511.

Edwards, C. (2009) *Resilient Nation.* London: Demos.

Fraser, A. (2010) The craft of scalar practices. *Environment and Planning A* 42, 332,346.

Fussey, P. (2007) Observing potentiality in the global city: surveillance and counterterrorism in London. *International Criminal Justice Review* 17(3), 171–192.

Fussey, P. (2013) Contested topologies of UK counter-terrorist surveillance: the rise and fall of Project Champion. *Critical Studies on Terrorism* 6(3), 351–370.

Fussey, P., Coaffee, J., Armstrong, G. and Hobbs, R. (2011) *Sustaining and Securing the Olympic City: Reconfiguring London for 2012 and Beyond.* Farnham: Ashgate.

Garland, D. (1996) The limits of the sovereign state: strategies of crime control in contemporary society. *British Journal of Criminology* 36(4), 445–71.

Graham, S. (2004) *Cities, War and Terrorism: Towards an Urban Geopolitics.* Oxford: Blackwell.

HM Government (2006) *Countering International Terrorism: The United Kingdom's Strategy.* CM6888. London: TSO.

HM Government (2008) *Preventing Violent Extremism: A Strategy for Delivery.* London: TSO.

HM Government (2010) *Working Together to Protect Crowded Places.* London: TSO.

Home Office (2011) *Understanding Vulnerability and Resilience in Individuals to the Influence of Al Qa'ida Violent Extremis.* London: TSO.

House of Commons (2010) *Communities and Local Government Committee: Preventing Violent Extremism Sixth Report of Session 2009–10.* Report, together with formal minutes, oral and written evidence, 6 March. HMSO: London.

Isakjee, A. and Allen, C. (2013) A catastrophic lack of inquisitiveness: a critical study of the impact and narrative of the Project Champion surveillance project in Birmingham. *Ethnicities* 13(6), 751–770.

Lyon, D. (2003) Surveillance as social sorting: computer codes and mobile bodies, in D. Lyon (ed.), *Surveillance as Social Sorting: Privacy, Risk and Digital Discrimination*. London: Routledge.

Neocleous, M. (2013) Resisting resilience. *Radical Philosophy* 178, 2–7.

Thames Valley Police (2010) *Project Champion Review*. London: Thames Valley Police.

Walker, J. and Cooper, M. (2011) Genealogies of resilience: from systems ecology to the political economy of crisis adaptation. *Security Dialogue* 42(2), 143–160.

24

RESILIENCE AND DISASTER SITES

The disastrous temporality of the 'recovery-to-come'

Charlotte Heath-Kelly

Introduction

This chapter looks at resilience through its application to disaster sites; or rather, the ambiguous position of resilience within disaster recovery. Given the temporality of resilience, such that it focuses on enabling the recovery-to-come, resilience provides no steps by which something broken can be made 'resilient' – rather it works through the anticipation and preparation for the future. 'Recovery' is addressed in only the future tense. The chapter engages with this temporal ambiguity, arguing that while resilience is symptomatic of neoliberal governmentality, as many have suggested (Joseph, 2013; Walker and Cooper, 2011), it is also practically functionless with regard to disaster. It is a chimera that provides the illusion of security by anticipatorily erasing the prospect of disaster (and also retrospectively concealing its horror). Ironically then, despite the centralisation of the disaster event within resilience policy the functionality of resilience is to erase the potential emergency, through discursive containment within anticipatory contingency planning and the retrospective narration of emergencies as stories about recovery. Resilience does not confront the disaster event but rather provides a sophisticated chimera by which insecurity can be ignored. To expose this functionality, it is necessary to explore that which we are supposed to forget – disaster space in the present tense.

Resilience and disaster studies

'Resilience' has been posited, across academic disciplines and policy areas, as the solution to disaster, economic instability, poverty, personal crises – and the list goes on. Wherever there is a problem, the solution seems to lie in resilience. How can one approach solve so many problems? Suspicion regarding the ubiquity of resilience has led to speculation within the fields of Security Studies and International Relations that the concept functions as an 'empty signifier' or 'buzz-word' – its divergent usages across fields of engineering, urban planning, psychology and politics signifying an intensification of neoliberal political discourse (Brassett *et al.* 2013). With this in mind, this chapter addresses the relationship between resilience and the disaster site. The chapter explores how resilience is integrated into the field of disaster recovery, and the consequences of framing disaster sites through resilience discourse.

For a long time, the academic study of disaster has been a project that has flirted with the seeds which grew into 'resilience'. Indeed, a long historical shift has occurred whereby disaster has gradually been reframed through pre-emptive and systemic lenses, eventually culminating in the current 'resilience' agenda within disaster recovery. Since the 1970s the study of disaster has been moving from Marxist-inspired readings of the interconnection of capitalism with the creation of disaster-precarious-populations to the contemporary depoliticised resilience mandate. In recent years it has become clear that the disaster management discipline has been colonised by the assumptions of resilience – such that physical hazards (earthquakes, hurricanes, floods) are no longer understood as disaster 'events'; rather, disaster resides in the lack of contingency planning made around complexly interlinked infrastructural systems. Disaster resides *within* our systems, not the hurricanes and floods which 'shock' them. As I will argue in this chapter, such infrastructural visuality results in assumptions that the disaster exists in the future tense – shifting the focus of practice towards prevention, and away from the mitigation of suffering during disasters.

But it didn't always used to be this way. Before the advent of resilience, disaster management studies used to centralise post-event response. It was occupied with strategies for the mitigation of suffering in disaster areas. The disaster site was extremely prominent, because disaster was understood as the physical event that impacted upon populations. Yet disaster studies has undergone a three stage paradigm shift since the 1970s, whereby post-event, site-centred recovery has been replaced with pre-event mitigation (Grove 2013; 2014). During the 1970s and 1980s, researchers inspired by Marxist political economy problematised the notion of disaster as an exceptional, exogenous event. Critiquing the dominant view that disasters are extremes in geophysical processes (hurricanes, floods, earthquakes), they demonstrated the centrality of capitalism to the impact wrought by hazard events. Geophysical events will always happen, but capitalist processes make sections of populations vulnerable and precarious to the impact of these natural hazards – creating disasters (Hewitt, 1983). This Marxist reframing of 'disaster' as the making-vulnerable of populations by capitalism, rather than just the force of the physical event, provided a critical reframing of the assumptions of disaster management.

A pertinent example of this paradigm shift in disaster studies can be found in Susman *et al.*'s blistering critique of the dominant approaches (of the 1970s and 1980s), which located Africa as a region susceptible to natural disasters. This depoliticised mainstream framing of disaster, they argue, not only misunderstands the composition of disaster (as a hazard event rather than the interface between vulnerable populations and extreme physical events), but also conceals the responsibility of Western imperialist ventures and continuing capitalist exploitation for the creation of vulnerable populations:

> The populations of the underdeveloped areas are becoming more vulnerable. [. . .] Underdevelopment is not just a contemporary phenomenon, nor is it a self-propelled process in isolation. It is an integral part of the process of development of the capitalist countries of the world. As capitalism has evolved, so has underdevelopment. As capitalist penetration reaches the furthest parts of the periphery, the ability of local populations to be self-reliant decreases.
>
> *(Susman et al., 1983, p. 272–3)*

This shift towards viewing disaster as a category constituted through both pre-existing economic structures and the impact of sudden shocks was accelerated in the 1990s through the deployment of 'vulnerability' as the matrix through which to understand disaster. Rather than the interplay of just economic factors and sudden shocks to infrastructural systems, disasters came to be seen as the product of multiple indices – including the precarity constituted for citizens through structures of gender, race, age, class and poverty (Grove, 2014).

These advances in research transformed the mandate of disaster studies from post-event recovery to the critique and problematisation of those structures that make the impact of hazard events imbalanced. This research showed that disasters are more disastrous for some than others, providing a pertinent critique of the dominant technocratic frames within disaster management. But then resilience came to prominence, depoliticising the progress made towards the situation of vulnerability in social structures. Ironically and paradoxically it was critical research that opened the door for resilience, by (in good faith) reframing the disaster as systemic interplay rather than the hurricane, flood or earthquake event.

Resilience doesn't care about the roles of social structures (gender, capitalism, race) in the creation of vulnerability. In resilience discourse, risk and vulnerability are simple and politics is not complicit in their construction. Instead, technocracy is the solution to a problem understood as technocratic. Contemporary mainstream resilience research often points to information technology and big data as tools that can assist risk assessment and mitigate the human cognition bias, which underestimates threats when faced with complex systems (Comfort *et al.*, 2010). Similarly, vulnerability is treated as a technocratic issue. As a depoliticised state of being, vulnerability can be solved through the training of subjects in approved behaviours – not by changing the structure that produces inequality. The UK Community Resilience programme, for example, creates a hierarchy of subject categories from resilience 'champions', 'experts', 'volunteers' and the 'vulnerable'. While 'resilience champions' are local community representatives with the 'energy and enthusiasm' to take leadership roles, the 'vulnerable' are defined as those who have recently had operations, the aged, those without transport, transient groups and those who might find emergency information hard to understand (Bulley, 2013).

Some scholars understand the resilience *oeuvre* as empowering, such that it takes individual agency into account and doesn't posit a determinism of social position (Brown and Westaway, 2011; Milliken, 2013; Murphy, 2007). They argue that resilience provides a better framing of the bottom-up agency that subjects can demonstrate in times of crisis, contra the Marxist-inspired disaster management paradigm of old (where subjects were boxed into socio-economic categories). However, many contemporary scholars disagree. Rather than subscribing to the promise of resilience, they have highlighted the innate neoliberal governmentality at play within its social engineering and the implicit negative categorisation of subjects in terms of their own supposed 'vulnerability' to disaster (Grove 2013, 2014; Joseph, 2013; Welsh, 2014). They are not 'full' subjects, in terms of the hierarchy of subjectivity employed within resilience documentation. They are defined in terms of what they lack (Bulley, 2013). These 'vulnerable' persons and communities are the subject of resilient planning for disaster recovery – not the hazard event; they must be trained to cope with their precarity and to demonstrate resilient behaviours.

The academic position on resilience is thus contested, despite its dominance of the disaster management discipline. However, resilience has colonised the policy world as an unproblematic solution to most problems. Threatened by disaster? Build resilience. Is capitalism causing problems for your economic system? Build resilient financial structures. Worried that your population might be tempted to absorb 'extremist' ideas? Build resilient communities. While this section has explored the paradigm shifts in disaster studies that led to the discursive dominance of the resilience frame in this area, the next section questions the functionality of resilience for policy. Does it actually *do* anything? And should we be suspicious of a concept that can supposedly be applied in equal measure to disaster management, security, psychological treatment and economy? Is resilience actually an empty promise?

The disastrous genius of resilience

Given the extensive deployment of resilience in international disaster management strategies, one would assume that the world is prepared for disaster. For example, the United Nations designated the entire 1990s as the International Decade for Natural Disaster Reduction. Not many concepts get their own decade. Yet despite efforts to proscribe for the local, regional, national and international integration of disaster mitigation procedures, as formulated within the 1994 Yokohama Strategy, the Secretary General of the UN was subsequently compelled to keep disaster reduction on the international agenda. Why? Speaking at the close of the International Decade for Natural Disaster Reduction (IDNDR) in 1999, Kofi Annan acknowledged the irony that efforts to coordinate early warning systems and disaster recovery operations had not sufficiently met the challenge of the upsurge in disasters of 1998 (Annan 1999). Rather than change tack, the international community has extended the 'disaster preparedness decade' into the twenty-first century via the Hyogo Framework for Action 2005–2015, aiming to build the resilience of nations and communities to disaster. But as Annan himself admitted, this extension and repetition of action involves a paradox:

> Ladies and Gentlemen, we confront a paradox. Despite a decade of dedicated and creative effort by IDNDR and its collaborators, the number and cost of natural disasters continues to rise. The cost of weather related disasters in 1998 alone exceeded the cost of all such disasters in the whole of the 1980s.
>
> *(Annan, 1999)*

So does resilient preparation work, or not? The assumption contained within the UN documentation surrounding these decades of international action is that consolidating the multi-scalar integration of disaster preparedness and mitigation policy is useful, yet still in its infancy. It has not *yet* succeeded in the mission of alleviating the cost and frequency of disasters. The complex interconnection of infrastructural systems is only increasing, creating greater costs when disasters occur, and necessitating greater efforts towards building resilience.

The most cynical of commentators could at this point invoke the maxim of Albert Einstein, such that insanity can be defined as doing the same thing over and over again, while expecting different results. The integration of early warning systems and plans for disaster recovery are clearly not working, given the escalation of costs associated with disaster, so why are national and international communities stuck within the discourse of resilience as the answer?

Because resilience contains and deploys a disastrous genius. Resilience is extremely functional – just not in the way it is assumed to be. It provides a new and sophisticated method by which governments and international organisations can problematise issues (terrorism, poverty, hazard events) and perform their resolution, albeit this resolution occurs discursively rather than practically. Resilience doesn't stop events or even mitigate their impact, as we have seen in the UN's own documentation, but it provides a compelling story about the reimagined roles of the state and civil society in the face of unpreventable insecurity. This story involves the neoliberal devolution of responsibility for maintaining security onto the population and local resilience fora, but it also marks a paradigm shift in the goal of security policy regarding the possibility of attaining safety.

The rise of resilience in security policy has involved a recalibration of how governments interact with insecurity. Since Thomas Hobbes' treatise of 1651 on the formation of the modern state, the social contract understanding of state legitimacy has centralised the trade-off between citizens' submission to the law in exchange for the provision of physical security by the state

(Hobbes, 1991). Other canonical figures in the history of liberal political philosophy have focused on the same exchange, highlighting the surrender of 'natural' rights (understood as abilities to do anything of one's choosing) for the physical security provided by the sovereign state – such that others may not use their 'natural rights' against you (Locke, 1821). Leaving aside that the social contract is a fiction, and that no such moment of agreement took place between subjects and rulers, the assertion that the state's primary duty is the provision of physical and territorial security has a long history in statecraft.

The contemporary rise of resilience represents the culmination of two shifts in this tradition. First, state resilience discourse understands that threats might not stem from external or internal enemies: building upon the turn towards Critical Infrastructure Protection, resilient security strategies understand that threat may actually stem from our own infrastructural systems and their complex interdependence. Danger may actually lurk inside the polity – in the tight coupling of complex systems (Perrow, 1984) and the consequences of integrated system collapse (Boin and McConnell, 2007). Disaster is no longer defined as the physical event or the enemy which impacts upon us, but the lack of preparation for such inevitability. As such, we might have to secure against *ourselves* – using technological solutions to outweigh our human cognitive deficits that lead to the underestimation of risk in contexts of complexity (Comfort *et al.* 2010).

Second, in a move that appears to be decidedly neoliberal, the state has now devolved and abrogated its responsibilities to ensure security. It has decided that events cannot always be prevented and, as such, its mandate is not dependent upon the maintenance of physical integrity. In this 'privatisation', citizens become responsible for ensuring their own security (Bulley, 2013; Joseph, 2013; Welsh, 2014). Pre-emptive resilience fora are constituted so that 'resilience champions' may liaise with 'experts' to respond to events, alleviating the responsibility of the state to intervene. Yet this abdication of responsibility does not mean that state involvement with security is dead. Instead, with a cunning sleight of hand, resilience involves the incorporation of insecurity into the remit of security. The disastrous genius of resilience is demonstrated within the appropriation of insecurity. The unpreventable event is now crucial to the performance of security, state and the mandate to rule. The state secures *through* the failure to secure (Heath-Kelly, 2015).

Danger is everywhere, inside the polity and outside, and insecurity has become the method of rule – instead of the promise of security. In the United Kingdom, this transition is often framed within the 'age of uncertainty'. This policy epithet signifies the proliferation of risks in post-Cold War global society, which will inevitably lead to unpreventable events, thus necessitating a turn towards 'resilience' such that their effects can be mitigated. The 'era of uncertainty' is centralised within major policy documents such as *A Strong Britain in an Age of Uncertainty: The National Security Strategy* (Cabinet Office, 2010a) and *Securing Britain in an Age of Uncertainty: The Strategic Defence and Security Review* (Cabinet Office, 2010b). This 'age of uncertainty' is framed contra the 'predictable risks' of the Cold War era which, British policy suggests, came from 'state adversaries through largely predictable military or nuclear means' (Cabinet Office 2010a, p. 19). Lamenting that supposed past, these strategic documents find solace in 'resilience'. While threats may come from unforeseen locations, inside or out, it is possible to remain 'adaptable' and to delegate the responsibility for disaster mitigation to citizens:

> But we cannot prevent every risk as they are inherently unpredictable. To ensure we are able to recover quickly when risks turn into actual damage to our interests, we have to promote resilience, both locally and nationally. Ensuring that the public is fully informed of the risks we face is a critical part of this approach.
>
> *(Cabinet Office, 2010a, p. 25)*

The US Department of Homeland Security has provided a similar reading of the contemporary era in its 2007 National Security Strategy, whereby insecurity is now a fundamental condition which necessitates that we live with risk rather than against it. As such, the resilience era signals the demise of the era of 'security as prevention', and the rise of 'security through inevitable insecurity'. For example:

> Despite our best efforts, achieving a complete state of [. . .] protection is not possible in the face of the numerous and varied catastrophic possibilities that could challenge the security of America today. Recognizing that [. . .] we cannot envision or prepare for every potential threat, we must understand and accept a certain level of risk as a permanent condition.
>
> *(Department of Homeland Security, 2007, p. 25)*

Similarly, Australia has codified its Critical Infrastructure Protection around the concept of resilience as providing security despite (and through) insecurity. Identifying a climate of 'increasing complexity', the Australian government has invoked the necessity of less linear, more adaptive and organic responses to the unforeseeable events which will inevitably shock infra-structural systems (Australian Government, 2010).

Rather than imagining a supposedly unattainable goal of security – characterised as the absence of disruptive events – the resilience discourse advocates the acceptance of insecurity as a fun-damental condition. This acceptance can, it is imagined, lead towards successful mediation of systemic disruption by focusing attention on critical infrastructures and systems rather than on events and/or enemies. Insecurity becomes the explicit condition of security, as security is performed through the unpreventable event.

Crucially, resilience imagines a recovery-to-come to stabilise its deployment of the unpre-ventable event. While we are insecure, in the sense that governments cannot prevent all hazard events from impacting upon us, we are told that we are not *actually* insecure – resilience will save us by mitigating the event through the recovery-to-come. Our recovery is discursively ensured. While events will occur and people will die, and the state cannot save them, the damage will be limited because the deployment of resilience will stop the impact of events cascading across interlinked infrastructural systems. Resilience, then, secures us through our insecurity. This is its disastrous genius. It alleviates the state from the necessity of preventing all terrorist attacks and hazard events, while discursively asserting that the recovery-to-come will ensure that life con-tinues as normal. It doesn't seem to matter that the application of resilience to international disaster management over several decades was determined, by the UN, to have failed to improve the response to disasters. The appeal of resilience is not linked to the ability to prevent or mitigate events; otherwise its failure to improve disaster response would matter. Instead the disastrous genius of resilience stems from its anticipatory erasure of the disaster's consequences. We are promised the recovery-to-come.

Security strategies enact this performance by focusing on 'horizon scanning', risk-mapping and risk registers to identify the future event – exercising resilience through scenario exercises for emergency responders. Ben Anderson and Pete Adey have explored the bizarre temporality of contingency exercises, where health and government officials were gathered together in 2009 to 'exercise' emergency in a hotel room. They were tasked with managing an outbreak of pandemic swine flu and making pressurised decisions about the allocation of limited hospital beds (Anderson and Adey, 2011). The authors contemplate how the exercise of emergency deploys imagined time–space, which is neither present nor future, one which can be understood here as the constitution of the recovery-to-come. In a similar study, Claudia Aradau and Rens Van

Munster have also explored the imagined space–time of the emergency exercise (Aradau and Van Munster, 2012). Focusing on an emergency exercise carried out by the City of Sunderland involving a foreign-registered, and possibly terrorist, lorry carrying suspicious chemicals, they explore the ways in which the conjectural knowledge deployed in such simulations effects the withdrawal of time (this is neither the present nor the future) through the intensive management and scrutiny of public space. These scenario exercises, I argue, also demonstrate the deployment of the recovery-to-come within the resilience frame – enabling the stable appropriation of insecurity by security actors.

Yet to secure through insecurity, disaster sites have to be forgotten, mediated and remade as something else. Otherwise the pretence of security made through the 'resilient recovery-to-come' would be undermined through engagement with the visceral horror of destruction. While insecurity is crucial to resilience discourse and disaster recovery is centralised within policy, the existing bombsite is left unaddressed by resilience policies. Resilience is not applied to the bombsite that exists – rather it is used to think, anticipate and ultimately erase the *future* disruptive event. Even emergency recovery documentation does not address disaster sites except to make future contingency plans for the preparation and restoration of networked systems of transportation, communication, business and infrastructure (Australian Government, 2010; Cabinet Office, 2013, p. 81–7). As such, the temporality of disaster sites in resilience thinking is always pushed towards the anticipation of the future and the promise of the recovery-to-come. The disastrous genius of resilience lies in its anticipatory erasure of the havoc and terror threatened by the next emergency. Security can be performed through insecurity. But does resilience also work backwards? Is it also applied retrospectively to erase the horror of the past disaster?

Effacing the disaster site

As I stated previously, resilience policy does not address the disaster site nor provide guidance for its recovery. However there are instances where resilience is applied retrospectively to contain and efface the horror of the past emergency, even if the present-day disaster is ignored. There are some few texts that engage with resilience in non-anticipatory fashion. Lawrence Vale and Thomas Campanella have produced once such edited volume, entitled *The Resilient City: How Modern Cities Recover from Disaster* (2005). In this text, contributing authors describe the rise of cities from the ashes of devastation – including histories from San Francisco, Chicago, New York, Berlin and Warsaw. While interesting, the volume treats resilience almost as an after-thought. Resilience is treated as the unspoken, unquestioned quality, which must have been evident; otherwise these cities would never have been rebuilt. In the concluding chapter, the editors devise twelve axioms from the preceding descriptions of cities that recovered from dis-aster. Resilience, they suggest, is 'connected to renewal', 'always contested' and 'site specific'. While one of the very few texts which engages with resilience as something which 'has hap-pened', rather than resilience as the recovery-to-come, this approach is unsatisfactory – given that 'resilience' is presumed to have been present in each of these cases, rather than having been postulated and tested.

However, while such academic treatments of non-anticipatory resilience ('resilience must have occurred after the past disaster, because life has continued to exist in this place') are rare, they are much more common during the public remembrance of disaster events. Such retrospective formulation of resilience is very useful for policymakers seeking to consolidate discourses of national identity, renewal and hope. Such statements are often unqualified and offer no insights into how resilience took place. They are simple assertions that life goes on. But their political functionality is revealing – just like anticipatory promises of the recovery-to-come, retrospective assertions of resilience erase the horror of the emergency event.

In my own fieldwork on post-terrorist space I explored the reconstruction and memorialisation of bombsites and grew accustomed to politicians extolling the wonder of resilience. Sites of devastation (caused by attacks they were tasked with preventing) were recast in such resilience-speak as evidence of the nation's resilient spirit and its gritty determination to triumph over adversity – conveniently erasing the failure of security technologies to prevent events. On the tenth anniversary of the Bali bombing, for example, Australian politicians competed with each other to provide the most moving and inspiring reading of the tragedy as evidence of national character – asserting resilience retrospectively and using it for political gain (Heath-Kelly, 2015). Both (the then) Prime Minister Gillard and opposition leader Tony Abbot spoke frequently of the resilient Australian spirit revealed by the bombings, situating this character-trait within the trajectory of the Gallipolli legend of the ANZAC solider (a key component within official depictions of Australian national identity) (Gillard, 2012; see also McDonald, 2010). Despite the historical and contextual distance between trench warfare and a nightclub bomb, the (then) Leader of the Opposition, Tony Abbot, published an editorial in the Sydney Morning Herald on the tenth anniversary of the Bali bombings, which explicitly projected the ANZAC legacy onto the bodies of burnt tourists:

> For many Australians, the abiding image of the 2002 Bali bombing will be Hanabeth Luke helping Tom Singer to escape from the Sari Club. Like the equally emblematic photographs of Simpson at Gallipoli and the fuzzy wuzzy angel leading a blinded digger down the Kokoda Track, it perfectly captured the way we instinctively turn to each other for help and support in the most stressful circumstances. Often, the worst of times can bring out the best in people [. . .] Australians could have railed against the country that harboured their killers. Instead, we worked with Indonesia to find them and Indonesia worked with us to bring them to justice.
>
> *(Abbott, 2012)*

Not to be outdone, Prime Minister Gillard used her speech at the tenth anniversary ceremony of the Bali bombing to incorporate the nightclub disaster into a linear narrative about Australian resilience, grit and fairness – listing examples of Gallipoli, Kokoda, the Bali bombing and the Australian victims of the London bombing (2005) to weave a retrospective story about trauma, heroism, resilient character and national identity.

The horror of the disaster event is discursively erased through its incorporation into memory tropes from previous wars and crises, where the nation has demonstrated its 'resilience'. The retrospective assertion of resilience functions through the 'recovery-that-was', securing through what was once a failure to secure. To put it bluntly, the disastrous media images of burnt bodies are effaced through the re-narration of the emergency as the evidence of resilient national spirit.

Other prominent examples of this retrospective assertion of resilience upon post-terrorist space can be found in the reconstruction of the World Trade Center in Manhattan. On the memorial plaza, which is dominated by Michael Arad's *Reflecting Absence* footwells, visitors are instructed by guides to seek out the 'survivor tree' – planted in the concourse. The 'survivor tree' has become the talisman of retrospective applications of resilience, made iconic through poems and souvenir items on sale onsite. This Callery Pear tree previously stood on the site of the World Trade Center and was buried in the collapse of the twin towers, only to be found a month later by rescue workers in the smouldering rubble. It then recuperated in specialist nurseries, having its genetic material mapped so that its immortality can be ensured through the production of endless descendants (Just, 2013).

The survivor tree is billed as 'a living reminder of resilience, survival and rebirth' on the 9/11 Memorial website and associated promotional material.[1] It is used to perform the 'recovery-that-was' in advertising mailouts and YouTube videos for the memorial (9/11 Memorial, 2014) – asserting retrospective resilience to close the memory of the disaster event. As a symbol used for the performance of hope and recovery, the saplings grown from the survivor tree have been sent to other US disaster sites including the Boston Marathon bombings and areas damaged by Hurricane Sandy (Just, 2013). The tree becomes the focus of retrospective narrations of disaster, erasing the visceral memory of carnage and consolidating a discourse of national pride, tenacity and righteousness.

By asserting retrospective resilience (the 'recovery-that-was'), the curators of destroyed space can smooth over the disruption caused to politics by a disaster. They can discursively mediate the impact of events, silencing their horror, while reasserting a nationalised discourse of tenacity and honour. This retrospective performance also consolidates the anticipatory function of resilience – where the prevention of events is labelled impossible given the contemporary era of complexity and uncertainty. But insecurity is never total because we are promised the recovery-to-come and the recovery-that-was. The retrospective performance of resilience conceals the horror of disaster memory, alongside architectural reconstruction and memorialisation, so that this performance of the recovery-to-come is not destabilised by the visceral evidence of the disaster that broke through.

While resilience policy has no dealings with the disaster site in the present tense, providing no guidance for the making-resilient of destroyed public space, the anticipatory and retrospective applications of resilience are extremely functional. The performance of resilience is a security chimera that functions through anticipatory and retrospective temporalities – erasing the disaster discursively, forwards and backwards, rather than preventing it. By these means, security states can simultaneously disavow their responsibility to prevent all disasters by invoking the unpreventable event while also stabilising their continued claim that we are all still secure. It doesn't matter that some of us are not safe because the promise of the recovery-to-come, bolstered by the assertion of the recovery-that-was, will erase the horror of the disaster. The security edifice is maintained, discursively at least.

Conclusion

This chapter has explored the relationship of resilience to the disaster site, tracing the shifts within disaster studies, which reconstituted 'disaster' from hazard event to its current formulation as under-preparedness. It has argued that the promise of Marxist and critical readings of disaster in the 1970s–1990s has been lost in the turn towards the technocratic approach of resilience. Where disaster studies once contemplated the structural causes of vulnerability to disaster events, it is now dominated by a resilience agenda that focuses on under-prepared subjects as actors-to-be-trained in appropriate behaviours.

Using this history of disaster studies literature as a framing device, the chapter then explored the strange absence of resilience from the disaster site – such that policy provides no recommendations for how to recover destroyed space, despite the centrality of disaster events to the resilience *oeuvre*. It argued that the anticipatory focus of resilience policy on the future disaster and the recovery-to-come prevents nothing, given the UN's own admission that decades of embedding resilience have failed to reduce the costs of disaster events. However, this anticipatory mandate is extremely functional for the discursive stabilisation of security policy. It enables security actors to disavow their responsibility to protect populations under the banner of 'the unpreventable event', while also continuing to promise security through the recovery-to-come. Resilience doesn't actually prevent anything, but it 'secures' through insecurity (Heath-Kelly, 2015). Additionally, the chapter alluded to retrospective applications of resilience such that past disasters are remade as evidence of national character and tenacity. This retrospective assertion of resilience serves to further stabilise the performance of security in an 'uncertain age', where events are unpreventable. The recovery-to-come and the recovery-that-was are the methods by which resilience practices its disastrous genius for the neoliberal age, 'privatising' the responsibility for disaster management in the present tense upon local actors and individuals.

As such, the relationship between resilience and the disaster site is complex but can be summed up in the following way: resilience works forwards, backwards, but is never present at the site of the disaster. It is a chimera that provides no methods by which destroyed space might be made 'resilient'. It only constitutes the illusion that the recovery-to-come will serve as substitute for a politics that cares about human safety.

Acknowledgements

This chapter has been revised and updated and is based on material published by the author as *Death and Security: Memory and Mortality at the Bombsite*. Manchester University Press, forthcoming 2016.

Note

1 See www.911memorial.org/survivor-tree (last accessed 30/10/2012).

References

9/11 Memorial (2014) Survivor Tree. Available from: www.youtube.com/watch?v=JU1rf-481QI (last accessed 10 October 2014).

Abbott, T. (2012) Bombers brought two countries closer in fight against terrorism. *Sydney Morning Herald*, 12 October 2012, 15.

Anderson, B. and Adey, P. (2011) Affect and Security: Exercising Emergency in UK Civil Contingencies. *Environment and Planning D: Society and Space* 29/6, 1092–109.

Annan, K. (1999) Despite Dedicated Efforts, Numbers and Cost of Natural Disasters Continue to Rise. In *Proceedings: International Decade of Natural Disaster Reduction (IDNDR)*, 5–9 July 1999. Available from: www.unisdr.org/files/31468_programmeforumproceedings.pdf (last accessed 30 September 2014).

Aradau, C. and Van Munster, R. (2012) The Time/Space of Preparedness: Anticipating the 'Next Terrorist Attack'. *Space and Culture* 15/2, 98–109.

Australian Government (2010) *Critical Infrastructure Resilience Strategy* (Commonwealth of Australia). Available from: www.emergency.qld.gov.au/publications/pdf/Critical_Infrastructure_Resilience_Strategy.pdf (last accessed 18 July 2016).

Boin, A. and McConnell, A. (2007) Preparing for Critical Infrastructure Breakdowns: The Limits of Crisis Management and the Need for Resilience. *Journal of Contingencies and Crisis Management* 15/1, 50–9.

Brassett, J., Croft, S. and Vaughan-Williams, N. (2013) Introduction: An Agenda for Resilience Research in Politics and International Relations. *Politics* 33/4, 221–8.

Brown, K. and Westaway, E. (2011) Agency, Capacity, and Resilience to Environmental Change: Lessons from Human Development, Well-being, and Disasters. *Annual Review of Environment and Resources* 36, 321–42.

Bulley, D. (2013) Producing and Governing Community (through) Resilience. *Politics* 33/4, 265–75.

Cabinet Office (2010a) *A Strong Britain in an Age of Uncertainty: The National Security Strategy*. London: HM Government.

Cabinet Office (2010b) *Securing Britain in an Age of Uncertainty: The Strategic Defence and Security Review*. London: HM Government.

Cabinet Office (2013) *Emergency Response and Recovery: Non Statutory Guidance accompanying the Civil Contingencies Act 2004*. London: HM Government.

Comfort, L., Oh, N., Ertan, G. and Scheinert, S. (2010) Designing Adaptive Systems for Disaster Mitigation and Response: The Role of Structure. In *Designing Resilience: Preparing for Extreme Events*, edited by Louise Comfort, Arjen Boin and Chris C. Demchak. Pittsburgh: University of Pittsburgh Press, pp. 33–61.

Department of Homeland Security (2007) *National Strategy for Homeland Security*. Washington: Homeland Security Council.

Gillard, J. (2012) Address by The Honourable Julia Gillard MP to the Tenth Anniversary Ceremony for the Bali Bombings, Jimbaran, Bali. Available from: www.youtube.com/watch?v=PdEBzNqcE6g (last accessed 30 October 2012).

Grove, K. (2013) From Emergency Management to Managing Emergence: A Genealogy of Disaster Management in Jamaica. *Annals of the Association of American Geographers* 103/3, 570–88.

Grove, K. (2014) Adaptation Machines and the Parasitic Politics of Life in Jamaican Disaster Resilience. *Antipode* 46/3, 611–28.

Heath-Kelly, C. (2015) Securing through the Failure to Secure? The Ambiguity of Resilience at the Bombsite. *Security Dialogue* 46/1, 69–85.

Hewitt, K. (1983) The Idea of Calamity in a Technocratic Age. In *Interpretations of Calamity: From the Viewpoint of Human Ecology*, edited by Kenneth Hewitt. London: Allen and Unwin, pp. 3–32.

Hobbes, Thomas (1991) *Leviathan*. Cambridge: Cambridge University Press.

Joseph, J. (2013) Resilience as Embedded Neoliberalism: A Governmentality Approach. *Resilience: International Policies, Practices and Discourses* 1/1, 38–52.

Just, O. (2013) World Trade Center 'Survivor Tree' Nurtures Life. *Stamford Advocate* 13 September 2013. Available from: www.stamfordadvocate.com/news/article/World-Trade-Center-Survivor-Tree-nurtures-life-4813814.php (last accessed 10 October 2014).

Locke, J. (1821) *Two Treatises of Government*. London: Whitmore and Fenn.

McDonald, M. (2010) 'Lest we Forget': The Politics of Memory and Australian Military Intervention. *International Political Sociology* 4/3, 287–302.

Milliken, J. (2013) Resilience: From Metaphor to an Action Plan for Use in the Peacebuilding Field. *Geneva Peacebuilding Platform Paper No. 7*, Geneva: Switzerland.

Murphy, B. (2007) Locating Social Capital in Resilient Community-level Emergency Management. *Natural Hazards* 41, 297–315.

Perrow, C. (1984) *Normal Accidents: Living with High Risk Technologies*. New York: Basic Books.

Susman, P., O'Keefe, P. and Wisner, B. (1983) Global Disasters, A Radical Interpretation. In *Interpretations of Calamity: From the Viewpoint of Human Ecology*, edited by Kenneth Hewitt. London: Allen and Unwin, pp. 263–83.

Vale, L. and Campanella, T. (ed.) (2005) *The Resilient City: How Modern Cities Recover From Disaster*. New York: Oxford University Press.

Walker, J. and Cooper, M. (2011) Genealogies of Resilience: From Systems Ecology to the Political Economy of Crisis Adaptation. *Security Dialogue* 42/2, 143–60.

Welsh, M. (2014) Resilience and Responsibility: Governing Uncertainty in a Complex World. *The Geographical Journal* 180/1, 15–26.

25

CIVIC RESILIENCE

Securing "resilient communities" to prevent terrorism

Jessica West

Introduction: securing resilience

Resilience is a common refrain of counter-terrorism and Britons are its quintessential image. But what used to mean fortitude, moral strength and courage—something that was "deeply inscribed in the soul" (O'Malley, 2010, p. 488)—now refers to something that is created through state intervention in response to perceived vulnerability (Furedi, 2007; Howell, 2015b). This study examines the modes of intervention associated with the "building community resilience" approach to preventing terrorism in the United Kingdom (UK) that was deployed following the July 7, 2005 attacks on London by "homegrown" terrorists. Following perceptions of broken communities and broken citizenship that solidified after the riots of 2001, efforts to build community resilience to terrorism emerged in response to what was seen as an ideological threat that spread through social mechanisms. I argue that this approach to resilience involves social interventions aimed at redesigning civil society and citizens to serve the state's counter-terrorism goals, which I refer to as civic resilience. Rather than drawing on the social resilience of Muslim communities as a source of safety, efforts are made to *secure* social spaces and processes by rebuilding civil society and citizens around the values of national security and integrating them into counter-terrorism policing and intelligence methods. The process of building civic resilience works primarily through social and political relations including citizenship, trust and consent. While it appears to decentralize responsibility for security to local communities, it rests on a design logic of integration that seeks to draw the social resources of communities into state-based, counter-terrorism processes. In other words, civic resilience is designed to shore up the capabilities of the state, rather than communities. This experience speaks to the tensions and contradictions between resilience and security, and the challenges of integrating the two—highlighting the social and political effects of this effort, particularly for citizenship—and begs the question, *resilience of what*.

Civic resilience: integrating social resources into the state

Resilience is an amorphous concept that has emerged as a "pervasive idiom of global governance" (Walker and Cooper, 2011, p. 144; Brand and Jax, 2007; Carpenter *et al.*, 2001). Drawing on the approach of Paul Collier and Andrew Lakoff that seeks to "identify specific kinds of security problems and the schemas that have been developed to manage them in a given context," this study seeks to probe beneath its broad surface by examining the origins, policies, programs, and tools of the community resilience approach to counter-terrorism in the UK in order to assess what is being secured, through which kind of interventions, and with what political implications (Collier and Lakoff, 2008, p. 25).

This case shifts the temporal focus of resilience as a future-oriented strategy that operates through anticipatory practices such as preparedness and enactment (Lentzos and Rose, 2009; O'Malley, 2004; Collier and Lakoff, 2008; Aradau and Munster, 2011; Adey and Anderson, 2012) to examine its use in detecting and containing the circulation of present threats that resembles the biological focus of pre-emptive warfare outlined by Melinda Cooper (Cooper 2006). Instead of looking at resilience as a function of individual coping abilities and decision-making skills (Walker and Cooper, 2011; Chandler, 2013; Grove, 2014) I study resilience as a social quality. Closely associated with ecological concepts of resilience, social resilience is defined as the "ability of communities to withstand external shocks to their social infrastructure" (Adger, 2000, p. 361). Echoing familiar concepts such as social capital and cohesion, it emphasizes the social resources that hold societies together with a focus on networks, inclusivity, and trust (Aldrich, 2009). However, in contrast to the exaltation of the social bonds of community popularized in concepts such as social capital (Putnam, 1995) and the common assumption that resilience is a positive characteristic (Walker and Westley, 2011), the focus of resilience as a tool of counter-terrorism recognizes its Janus-faced nature (Aldrich, 2012; Holling, 2001). In this case, the social bonds and resources of Muslim communities are viewed as vulnerable to terrorism and are treated as both a source of danger and safety; as something to be secured. This involves manufacturing what I describe as *civic resilience* by integrating citizens and communities into the values of the state and its security processes through interventions to reshape and claim social resilience on its own behalf.

The manufacturing of civic resilience is an approach to security-by-design that resonates with earlier literature on resilience and safety of dangerous, complex, technological systems (Sagan, 1995; Lovins and Hunter, 1982) and contemporary literature on urban resilience exemplified by Jon Coaffee (Coaffee, 2009; Coaffee, 2004; Coaffee, 2013). Indeed, both Kevin Grove and David Chandler have described resilience as an attempt at social engineering by the state (Chandler, 2013; Grove, 2014). However, while both of these arguments refer to the ability of the state to influence individual decision-making for what Chandler calls "self-securing agency" (Chandler, 2012), civic resilience more closely resembles a technical, systems approach to designing citizens, communities, and their relationship to the state. And while critical scholarship generally assumes that the design logic of resilience involves responsibilized decentralization (Briggs, 2010; O'Malley, 2004; Reid, 2012; Duffield, 2012), even to the point of abandonment by the state (Duffield, 2011), the case of civic resilience demonstrates a parallel process of integration with and control by the state, which Coaffee has likewise noted as a centralizing tendency within urban resilience (Coaffee, 2013). A similar dichotomy has been described regarding the UK's approach to community resilience to disasters and emergencies that was institutionalized in 2011 (Rogers 2013; Bulley 2013). Rather than enhancing the social resilience of communities to respond to terrorism, civic resilience secures the resources of the community to shore up the abilities of the state. This process has been described elsewhere as "in-reach" methods of preventing terrorism (Canadian Association of Chiefs of Police Prevention of Radicalization Study Group, 2008). It reflects writing on resilience from a social-ecological perspective as involving both bottom-up and top-down efforts (Walker and Westley, 2011). But this perspective assumes complementary interests between the top and the bottom, obscuring the political nature of resilience and the often-unasked questions about what is being made resilient and for what purpose. Indeed, as a system-level concept, resilience involves an implicit but understated compromise between the system as a whole and its various parts (Wildavsky, 1988; Longstaff, 2005). In this case, it is the bottom – the communities – that are being redesigned to serve the security imperatives of the state. However, the tensions between resilience and security, communities and the state limit the effectiveness of this approach while creating far-reaching effects on the nature of citizenship and the social contract.

Building resilient communities: from riots to terrorism

Resilience as an approach to pre-empting terrorism emerged as a policy tool in response to the July 7, 2005 'homegrown' attacks on London and in reaction to a particular perspective of terrorism as an ideological threat that spreads through society like a disease (Kundnani, 2012, p. 14; Bartlett *et al.*, 2010). The UK government has described extremism as something which preys on "open spaces in communities and institutions, including mosques, educational establishments, prisons, youth clubs and a wide range of private venues" (HM Government 2009b, p. 88). It built on a conviction of broken communities, civic malaise, and failed multicultural citizenship that solidified in the aftermath of racial riots in 2001, which served as a framework for interpreting the terrorist attacks of 9/11 (Community Cohesion Review Team, 2001; UK Home Office, 2001). Following the attacks on London, the perceived lack of civic integration among Britain's Muslims was further linked to two interrelated security challenges. The first was the failure of Muslim communities to adequately integrate and adopt British values, making them vulnerable to extremist ideology (Brighton, 2007). The second was the failure of British intelligence to penetrate those communities. It was believed that members of the Muslim community had information about the attacks that they were not sharing with police (Anon, 2006) and that the tight social cohesion *within* Muslim communities created a barrier to the ability of the state to gathering community intelligence about potential terrorist threats (Innes *et al.*, 2007). The fear was not that Muslims were "bowling alone" but that they were bowling with terrorists.

In response, then Prime Minister Tony Blair asserted that newcomers to Britain have a duty "to share and support the values that sustain the British way of life"; a duty that was linked to national security through a series of measures that included Muslim citizenship and integration as a central feature of counter-terrorism (Blair, 2005). This was reflected in the new 'community resilience' approach to preventing terrorism. As Peter Rogers notes, resilience is now a metaphor that includes the citizenry and its role in preserving the nation's way of life (Rogers 2008). This approach has been influenced by the work of the British think-tank Demos, which has advocated for a community approach to counter-terrorism that put social resilience "at the heart of national security" (Briggs, 2008, p. 6).

The focus on community resilience grew from a series of policies and programs that broadly aimed to intervene in and rebuild Muslim civil society in order to contain the spread of radicalization and extremist ideology, while also integrating communities into policing and intelligence efforts. The basis of this approach was established through a series of engagement efforts with Muslim communities that convened seven working groups under the umbrella Working Together to Prevent Extremism. Reflecting efforts to build "social cohesion" following the 2001 riots (UK Home Office, 2001; Millie, 2010), the final report noted the importance of "promoting a strong civil society built on shared notions of good citizenship, social cohesion, religious tolerance and peaceful co-existence" (Preventing Extremism Together Working Groups 2005, p. 2). Recommendations focused largely on efforts to rebuild and reorient Muslim civil society by engaging and mobilizing women and youth, educational efforts, and strengthening voluntary and civic organizations. It also included a call to develop a British

Muslim Citizenship Toolkit to "articulate a new vision for a British Islam and equip university Islamic Societies, mosques/imams, parents and the youth to deal with violent/fanatic tendencies" (Preventing Extremism Together Working Groups 2005, Recommendation 11). Finally, it recommended efforts to build stronger partnerships between police and Muslim communities to provide "intellectual and human resources" to policing (Preventing Extremism Together Working Groups 2005, Recommendation 9).

This approach to building community resilience was reflected in the "Prevent" component of the UK's counter-terrorism strategy. It called for greater awareness by and active support of citizens through partnerships with communities with two connected aims: strengthening civil society, and encouraging better cooperation with police (HM Government, 2006). Updated in 2007 (HM Government, 2009b) the strategy was formalized through three interrelated programs: the Preventing Violent Extremism program, run through the Department of Local Government and Communities; the integration of neighborhood policing teams with counter-terrorist policing; and the Channel program, designed to help local communities identify and treat individuals vulnerable to radicalization (HM Government, 2009b). The concept of resilience cut across all three of these programs and served as a measure of success described in National Indicator 35: "Building Communities Resilient to Violent Extremism," which emphasized building the capacity of civil society to resist violent extremism and the state's ability to identify vulnerable individuals (UK Home Office, 2008, Annex C). But rather than shoring up the social resources of communities, implementation of resilience involved interventions into citizenship and civil society to create a vehicle for counter-terrorism that better matched the interests of the state and would facilitate policing and intelligence efforts. Social resilience was transformed into civic resilience.

Building civic resilience: redesigning citizens and civil society

The core of the Preventing Violent Extremism program was delivered through the Department for Communities and Local Government, which is described as a community engagement approach to counter-terrorism (Briggs 2010). However, this program involved more than engagement: state interventions sought to rebuild a version of Muslim civil society that would be both capable of and willing to engage with the state and to contribute to counter-terrorism efforts. A 2007 action plan "Winning Hearts and Minds" focused on two modes of intervention: citizenship education for Muslims, and civic capacity building within Muslim communities (Department for Communities and Local Government, 2007b). It was supported by a Pathfinder fund to rebuild a British brand of social capital within Muslim communities whereby people: identify as part of British society; reject violent extremism; isolate violent extremists and cooperate with police; and develop a capacity to deal with problems (Department for Communities and Local Government, 2007a)

State interventions targeting citizenship and religious education were intended to develop liberal British values among Muslims and promote social cohesion and integration as a guard against extremism (Department for Innovation, Universities, and Skills, 2006). This effort to re-educate citizens was identified as critical for "future national stability" by fostering a "democratic and participative citizenry" that can constructively give voice to their concerns (Department for Innovation, Universities, and Skills 2006, p. 8) Schools were instructed to use curricula as a means of promoting shared values and becoming responsible citizens (Department for Children, Schools and Families, 2007) Specific guidance on Prevent issued to universities and colleges − *Learning Together To Be Safe* − reinforced the importance of promoting shared values, creating space for debate, and listening to and supporting mainstream voices (Department for Children, Schools and

Families *et al.*, 2008). New citizenship studies were tailored for Muslim students aimed at reconciling British citizenship with Muslim values. The Islam Citizenship Education (ICE) project for use in mosque-based educational contexts emphasizes being a British Muslim, equality, active citizenship, community cohesion, and conflict resolution (School Development Support Agency, 2009). Gender equality was a prevalent theme of re-education efforts, serving as a litmus test for British values against "dangerous ideologies and institutions" (Center for Human Rights and Global Justice, 2012; HM Government, 2011c). Citizenship education efforts also a focused on teaching "true" Islam, particularly to "disillusioned" youth, and linking it to a sense of civic responsibility (Waterhouse Consulting Group, 2008).

In this context, citizenship means *active* citizenship based on contributing to counter-terrorism. Citizenship workshops in Birmingham highlighted "the importance of detecting and tackling the signals of violent extremism" (Waterhouse Consulting Group, 2008, p. 27) and "increasing community resilience" through a variety of forums to engage youth and women in particular on the dangers of extremism (Keeley, 2012). Similarly, a training program for women included "the skills and confidence to tackle extremist ideologies" (Department for Communities and Local Government 2008a, p. 41).

The focus on capacity building was intended to reconfigure Muslim civil society into a vehicle against extremism. As stated in a guide issued to local communities: "It is important to reach beyond would-be gatekeepers to the community when seeking strong community voices" (UK Home Office, 2008, p. 17). This reach focused on women and youth. Women because they are viewed as both peaceful and capable of delivering wider social change through their influence over men as mothers and wives; (Waterhouse Consulting Group, 2008; Center for Human Rights and Global Justice, 2012) "resilient communities cannot be built and sustained without their active participation" (Department for Communities and Local Government, 2008b, p. 30). Youth were focused upon because they are viewed as inherently vulnerable. The goal is to redirect disaffected youth toward civic engagement by, "Ensuring young Muslims have access to constructive channels for dealing with concerns and frustrations, so that their voices are heard by policy makers, and they are encouraged to take advantage of opportunities for democratic political engagement" and "active citizenship through volunteering" as a means of "making a difference on issues they feel are important to them" (Department for Communities and Local Government, 2008b, p. 34).

Mosques and Imams—the central hub of Muslims communities—marked a final site of government intervention into civil society (Waterhouse Consulting Group, 2008). As with the broader community, the goal was both reform and building capacity as a vehicle against extremist voices. The Mosques and Imams National Advisory Board was established to provide guidance to mosques, including a steering group to consider issues of accreditation and governance (HM Government 2006). Mosques were also encouraged to formally register as charities with the Charity Commission, which in turn provides information on governance and financial issues and enables greater government regulation (Department for Communities and Local Government, 2007b; Department for Communities and Local Government, 2008b; City of Peterborough, 2009). Resilience-based interventions also focused on training select mainstream or moderate Imams in communication and leadership skills to better reach vulnerable people. The government established a Continuous Professional Development Programme for Faith Leaders aimed at developing their abilities to be effective community leaders (Department for Communities and Local Government, 2007b). Similar programs included the Journey of the Soul project, the Faith Community Development Qualification programme, and the Faith Community (Community Development Foundation, 2005; City of Peterborough, 2009; UK Home Office, 2008; Waterhouse Consulting Group, 2008; HM Government, 2009a). As stated in a review of

Birmingham's local Prevent programming, "Imams are best placed to provide the theological leadership, however, they are not always able to convey their arguments to those vulnerable to violent extremist messages, and because of either language barriers or cultural differences" (Waterhouse Consulting Group, 2008, p. 11). Similarly, Hazel Blears, then Communities Secretary, emphatically claimed in 2007, "making sure in the mosques that imams speak in English and are able to have a proper explanation of what real Islam is, this is very important" (Pinch, 2007).

Building resilience: integrating communities into policing and intelligence

The goal of interventions to rebuild Muslim citizens and civil society was further linked to efforts to secure community support for and participation in policing and intelligence through what have been described as "in-reach" methods of Prevent (Canadian Association of Chiefs of Police Prevention of Radicalization Study Group 2008). Although officials have made clear that "Prevent is not a police program" (HM Government, 2011c) it was and remains part of an integrated counter-terrorism strategy that includes policing, and both the Association of Chief Police Officers and local Counter-Terrorism Units have been key partners in Prevent programming (Lamb, 2012; National Police Chief's Council (n.d.). Moreover, an intended outcome of Prevent includes communities that "support and cooperate with the police and security services" (Audit Commission and Her Majesty's Inspectors of Constabulary, 2008, p. 7) and "supporting intelligence" is a cross-cutting objective of Prevent (Department for Communities and Local Government, 2008b). As detailed in the Prevent Guide to local partners, "Local police have a critical role to play in working with local communities to build their resilience to violent extremism and intervening to support individuals at risk of violent extremism" (HM Government 2009a, p. 47). Indeed, along with resilience, a police role cuts across all three avenues of Prevent programming, including community engagement, community intelligence, and the Channel program.

The *modus operandi* of this police work is social: to build community trust and consent for local counter-terrorism operations. The Muslim Safety Forum – replaced by the London Muslim Communities Forum – was developed as a means of dialogue between local police and Muslim communities (Spalek 2010; Metropolitan Police Service 2012; Spalek *et al.*, 2008). Police also actively engaged community members to explain how and why they act on counter-terrorism information through scenarios such as ACT NOW, Operation Nicole, and DELTA that encourage participants to see through the eyes of counter-terrorism police (HM Government, 2011c; Manchester City Council, Deputy Chief Executive (Neighbourhoods) 2013; Association of Chief Police Officers Prevent Delivery Unit, ACT NOW. Fact Sheet (n.d.); Association of Chief Police Officers Prevent Delivery Unit, Prevent (n.d.). These programs also served as a means of identifying champions for Prevent within the community (Manchester City Council, Deputy Chief Executive (Neighbourhoods), 2013). The longer-term goal of this engagement and consent-building work is to improve community intelligence gathering, and to provide access to the social spaces that intelligence agencies cannot usually penetrate, based on a perceived unwillingness of Muslim communities to facilitate this process (Innes *et al.* 2007, p. 4; Innes, 2006; Kundnani, 2012). This is done by developing knowledge networks within communities and identifying people who can partner with police to serve a public "eyes and ears" function, facilitating a two-way flow of information between police and communities to support police interventions into vulnerable communities and institutions (HM Government, 2009a; Innes *et al.*, 2007).

Initiatives such as the Muslim Contact Unit are an example of this effort. Initially set up through the Special Branch of the Metropolitan police in London in 2002 "to avoid the mistakes made during the IRA campaign of alienating the Irish community," the model went national following the 7/7 bombings and the need for local intelligence (Milne, 2008; Dodd, 2005). While it serves a critical trust-building function in the community (Spalek, 2010; Metropolitan Police Service, 2012), its central purpose is to work with key Muslim leaders to identify and isolate terrorists and to develop intelligence on the emergence of extremism in specific communities (Milne, 2008; Dodd, 2005). Other less formal examples include Gold Groups—"networks of trusted faith and community leaders and other influential persons"—that are "sources of real-time expert advice on crisis management," and community information, and help allay suspicions within communities targeted by counter-terrorism (Canadian Association of Chiefs of Police Prevention of Radicalization Study Group 2008, p. 3).

Similarly, Police Engagement Officers serve to connect counter-terrorism policing, neighborhood policing and communities in an effort to develop community contacts and an understanding of community issues (HM Government, 2011a). More recently, the city of Manchester has described its effort to build Neighbourhood Resilience Networks linked into policing teams to build on existing Key Individual Networks, Community Guardians, volunteers, community leaders, key reps from community organisations etc. to serve as the "eyes and ears in communities" (Manchester City Council, Deputy Chief Executive (Neighbourhoods) 2013, p. 21). Manchester has also created an e-mail-based community tensions network to monitor community tensions that includes Prevent community champions. Prevent counter-terrorism intelligence officers serve as a link between national intelligence processes and community-based information (HM Government, 2009a, p.47).

This process of integrating civil society and social institutions into the policing and intelligence activities of counter-terrorism was formalized by the Channel program, launched as a component of Prevent in 2007 to identify and treat vulnerable people through a community-based referral program (HM Government, 2012, 2011b, p. 201, 2011c). Although focused on the ability of "front-line" social service staff in schools and hospitals to identify specific individuals deemed vulnerable to extremism, it reflects the civic focus of the broader resilience approach; indicators of vulnerability to extremist ideas include the expression of non-British values and opinions, and 'treatment' is likewise based on, *inter alia*, faith guidance and civic engagement, or, in other words, good citizenship (HM Government 2012). Moreover, Channel draws on other community-based resilience efforts including capacity building, trust, and knowledge networks, to identify vulnerable individuals through the use of community intelligence (HM Government, 2012; City of Bradford (n.d.); Innes *et al.* 2007). And, like other elements of Prevent, it involves integrating social institutions into police-led intelligence processes (Choudhury and Fenwick, 2011, p. 24; de Menthon, 2013), further expanding the "eyes and ears" focused on Muslim communities.

Evaluating civic resilience: effects and effectiveness

Despite the language of community resilience that informs Prevent, counter-terrorism in the UK is not about building resilience, but rather securing it. Indeed, it is not the absence of social infrastructure and agency in Muslim communities that is viewed as problematic, but, rather, its suspect quality as a perceived breeding ground for extremism. Rather than drawing on the social resilience of Muslim communities as a source of safety, efforts are instead made to *secure* social spaces and processes by rebuilding civil society and citizens around the values of national security and integrating them into counter-terrorism policing and intelligence methods. In essence, the social resources of communities are being designed and secured for the state. While it decentralizes the responsibility for security to communities, it includes a parallel design logic that is based on control and integration, similar to what Kevin Grove and David Chandler have each described as a process of social engineering (Chandler, 2013; Grove, 2014). And as Chandler argues, this process has implications for the nature of the social contract, (Chandler, 2013) but in this case it is primarily the role of the citizen that has been changed, rather than that of the state.

The process of civic resilience—of securing and integrating the social resources of communities into the state—is deeply implicated in the larger political project of citizenship, extending the reach of security ever deeper into the private, social, and political lives of individuals. Interventions are more profound than what Allison Howell describes as an effort to "enhance" citizens' capabilities (Howell, 2015a). It involves rebuilding the values and responsibilities of citizens. And by combining ideas of social and ideological vulnerability with state interventions into the beliefs and practices that constitute citizens, it creates a new class of ambiguous citizen that is caught in a continual abyss of vulnerability between suspects (Pantazis and Pemberton, 2009; Kundnani, 2012; Benotman, 2012) and citizens. This process resembles efforts to pre-empt pre-insurgent spaces, whereby "the population is targeted as an unstable collective of future friends and future enemies that contains an ever present potential to become (counter) insurgent " (Anderson, 2012). On the surface, resilience clarifies this ambiguity by making it the responsibility of vulnerable groups to transform themselves from suspects to citizens through consent and active support for security efforts within their communities. In other words, citizenship must be enacted through participation in security. This has significant consequences for the nature of the social contract in democratic states. As Peter Rogers has argued in the context of resilience as a mode of emergency management, "these interventions are increasingly moving beyond the realm of managing the impact of a specific event into the deeper, more conceptual understanding of sovereignty, citizenship and the relationship between citizens and the state" (Rogers, 2008, p. 40). Security thus seems to be morphing from a *benefit of* citizenship into a *responsibility* of citizenship. But this is a responsibility unique to the suspect-as-citizen, and it is a task that is never ending, since vulnerability is viewed as inherent—as a state of nature. The ambiguous citizen thus remains suspect, vulnerable, consistently called upon to support security efforts, to denounce terrorism, to do more to counter an ever-present threat.

Tensions in the integrated design logic of civic resilience—combining social resilience with security, and top-down interventions with bottom-up agency—also harm its effectiveness. The pursuit of resilience under the auspice of preventing terrorism has been controversial. As Kevin O'Brien explains, prevention is the most difficult component of counter-terrorism because it requires the ongoing consent and cooperation of the community (O'Brien 2009, pp. 909–910). Securing this cooperation is difficult. Two key ingredients—trust and transparency—are the collateral damage of counter-terrorism efforts that are aimed at entire communities (Jackson, 2008; Lamb, 2013). This breakdown of trust is one of the main casualties of the UK's prevention efforts, which have been mired in mistrust (House of Commons Community and Local Government Committee, 2010). Despite claims to the contrary (Bettison, 2009; HM Government, 2011b), several community organizations claimed that engagement efforts were simultaneously used for surveillance, thus eroding trust in the process (House of Commons Community and Local Government Committee 2010; Dodd 2009). Moreover, the intrusion of security into social spaces can harm the very social infrastructure that counter-terrorism policies claim to be building by eroding trust *within* communities through the combination of social interventions with intelligence gathering. This approach makes communities suspicious of being co-opted into security (Bjeloper, 2012). Further, Rand researchers have discovered that people are reluctant to engage in the type of activities that help to build a community-based response to extremism envisioned by resilience, for fear of casting themselves under the ever watchful eye of counter-terrorism (Helmus *et al.*, 2013). Indeed, it is difficult to envision the type of flourishing civil society and communities that are described as central to resilience when religious, educational, and civic institutions are under constant watch both from within and from without.

The ability of manufactured agency and civic engagement is also limited. Interventions to redesign civil society and practices of selective engagement have led to accusations that the UK government has tried to manufacture a particular, moderate brand of Islam (House of Commons Community and Local Government Committee, 2010; Jackson, 2008). Moreover, this engagement is heavily top-down, focused on imparting messages from the state to the community as part of the effort to secure consent for counter-terrorism measures. This practice has been counter-productive, providing a platform and additional grievances for those who are excluded (Briggs 2008). And similar reports from the US indicate that it can impede police efforts to build good working relations with community groups (Helmus *et al.*, 2013; US House of Representatives Committee on Homeland Security, 2012).

Conclusion

Despite its controversies, government reports have stressed the ongoing need for Prevent programming, and the strategy was revamped again in 2011 based on a bureaucratic separation and renaming of resilience—programs aimed at belonging, integration, cohesiveness and citizenship—as "integration" (HM Government 2011c, p. 20, 2011a, p. 61). In practice, however, the existing resilience-based activities have continued (Manchester City Council, Deputy Chief Executive (Neighbourhoods) 2013; Bradford District Council, 2013). Citizenship reform based on civic integration and British values remains a key government approach to countering violent extremism, focused on changing society to build strong, resilient communities (Communities and Local Government, 2012; Clegg 2011). It is an approach that has since spread to the US and Canada. But the tensions within this design logic of integration— combining social resilience with national security and top-down control with bottom-up agency—present both practical limitations for implementation and troubling political implications for citizenship and the social contract with the state. Resilience does not replace security, but rather it is being *secured*. Indeed, resilience appears to primarily serve as a velvet glove for integrating communities into the more coercive practices of counter-terrorism.

These consequences suggest a lesson about the limits of control and security-by-design, which inform resilience thinking. Kevin Grove argues that the problem is not with resilience per se, but rather the way that it is added to existing approaches (Grove, 2014). But these tensions are embedded in the very concept of resilience. In theory, as a system-level concept, it is inherently about the stability of the system—about the ability of the parts to keep the system whole and functioning. And in practice, it is inherently about the security and stability of the state—in this case about the role of communities in consenting to and contributing to the counter-terrorism goals of the state. Mark Neocleous has described security as a gift from the state (Neocleous, 2008). If that is true, then resilience is the state's way of asking for it back.

Acknowledgements

This research was supported by the Social Sciences and Humanities Research Council of Canada and the Kanishka Project Research Affiliate Program at the Department of Public Safety and Emergency Preparedness, Canada. It represents a portion of a doctoral dissertation on resilience.

References

Adey, P. and Anderson, B. (2012). Anticipating emergencies: technologies of preparedness and the matter of security. *Security Dialogue*, 43(2), 99–117.

Adger, W. N. (2000). Social and ecological resilience: are they related? *Progress in Human Geography*, 24(3), 347–364.

Aldrich, D. P. (2012). *Building Resilience: Social Capital in Post-disaster Recovery*. Chicago: The University of Chicago Press.

Aldrich, R. J. (2009). Beyond the vigilant state: globalisation and intelligence. *Review of International Studies*, 35(04), 889.

Anderson, B. (2012). Facing the future enemy: US counterinsurgency doctrine and the pre-insurgent. *Theory, Culture & Society*, 28(7–8), 216–240.

Anon (2006). Bombers' community may hold clues. *BBC News*. Available at: http://news.bbc.co.uk/2/hi/ uk_news/england/west_yorkshire/4761745.stm (accessed May 26, 2013).

Aradau, C. and Munster, R. van (2011). *Politics of Catastrophe: Genealogies of the Unknown*. London and New York: Routledge.

Association of Chief Police Officers Prevent Delivery Unit, ACT NOW. Fact Sheet (n.d.). Available at: www.npcc.police.uk/documents/TAM/ACTNOWfactsheet.pdf (accessed July 19, 2016).

Association of Chief Police Officers Prevent Delivery Unit, Prevent (n.d.). ACT NOW for Schools - Stop People Becoming Terrorists or Supporting Violent Extremism. Available at: www.acpo.police.uk/ documents/TAM/ACTNOW_ForSchoolsHEFE.pdf (accessed August 31, 2013).

Audit Commission and Her Majesty's Inspectors of Constabulary (2008). *Preventing Violent Extremism: Learning and Development Exercise*, Department for Communities and Local Government.

Bartlett, J., Birdwell, J., and King, M. (2010). *The Edge of Violence*. Demos. Available at: www.demos. co.uk/files/Edge_of_Violence_-_web.pdf (accessed July 31, 2013).

Benotman, N. (2012). Muslim Communities: Between Integration and Securitization. Available at: www. quilliamfoundation.org/wp/wp-content/uploads/publications/free/muslim-communities-between-integration-and-securitization.pdf (accessed July 19, 2016).

Bettison, N. (2009). Preventing violent extremism—a police response. *Policing*, 3(2), 129–138.

Bjeloper, J. P. (2012). *Countering Violent Extremism in the United States*. Congressional Research Service. Available at: www.fas.org/sgp/crs/homesec/R42553.pdf (accessed November 21, 2013).

Blair, T. (2005). Full text: the prime minister's statement on anti-terror measures. *The Guardian*. Available at: www.guardian.co.uk/politics/2005/aug/05/uksecurity.terrorism1 (accessed May 26, 2013).

Bradford District Council (2013). *Working Together to Challenge Extremism: Action Plan for Prevent Delivery 2013–15*. Bradford, UK.

Brand, F. S. and Jax, K. (2007). Focusing the Meaning(s) of Resilience. *Ecology and Society*. Available at: www.ecologyandsociety.org/vol12/iss1/art23/ (accessed May 26, 2013).

Briggs, R. (2008). *Social Resilience and National Security – A British Perspective*. Demos.

Briggs, R. (2010). Community engagement for counter-terrorism: lessons from the UK. *International Affairs*, 86(4), 971–981.

Brighton, S. (2007). British Muslims, multiculturalism and UK foreign policy: "integration" and "cohesion" in and beyond the state. *International Affairs*, 83(1), 1–17.

Bulley, D. (2013). Producing and governing community (through) resilience: producing and governing community. *Politics*, 33(4), 265–275.

Canadian Association of Chiefs of Police Prevention of Radicalization Study Group (2008). *Building Community Resilience to Violent Ideologies*. Canadian Association of Chiefs of Police. Ottawa, Canada.

Carpenter, S., Walker, B., Anderies, M.J. and Abel, N. (2001). From metaphor to measurement: resilience of what to what? *Ecosystems*, 4(8), 765–781.

Center for Human Rights and Global Justice (2012). *Women and Preventing Violent Extremism: The U.S. and U.K. Experiences*. New York: NYU School of Law.

Chandler, D. (2012). Resilience and human security: the post-interventionist paradigm. *Security Dialogue*, 43(3), 213–229.

Chandler, D. (2013). Resilience and the autotelic subject: toward a critique of the societalization of security. *International Political Sociology*, 7(2), 210–226.

Choudhury, T. and Fenwick, H. (2011). *The Impact of Counter-terrorism Measures on Muslim Communities*. Manchester: Equality and Human Rights Commission.

City of Bradford (n.d.). Bradford Metropolitan District Council | A to Z of courses | WRAP (Workshop to Raise Awareness of Prevent). Available at: https://bso.bradford.gov.uk/news/10299-workshop-to-raise-awareness-of-prevent-wrap-training (accessed July 19, 2013).

City of Peterborough (2009). *Building Resilience to violent Extremism: Delivering the Prevent Strategy in Peterborough, an Action Plan for Local Delivery.* Peterborough, UK.

Clegg, N. (2011). Speech: An open, confident society: the application of muscular liberalism in a multicultural society. Available at: www.gov.uk/government/speeches/deputy-prime-ministers-speech-on-the-open-confident-society (accessed February 13, 2016).

Coaffee, J. (2004). Rings of steel, rings of concrete, and rings of confidence: designing out terrorism in central London pre and post September 11th. *International Journal of Urban and Regional Research*, 28(1), 201–2011.

Coaffee, J. (2009). *Terrorism, Risk and the Global City: Towards Urban Resilience.* Farnham England and Burlington VT: Ashgate Pub.

Coaffee, J. (2013). Rescaling and responsibilising the politics of urban resilience: from national security to local place-making: the politics of urban resilience. *Politics*, 33(4), 240–252.

Collier, S. J. and Lakoff, A. (2008). Distributed preparedness: the spatial logic of domestic security in the United States. *Environment and Planning D: Society and Space*, 26(1), 7–28.

Communities and Local Government (2012). *Creating the Conditions for Integration.* UK.

Community Cohesion Review Team (2001). *Community Cohesion: A Report of the Independent Review Team Chaired by Ted Cantle.* UK Home Office, UK.

Community Development Foundation (2005). *Faith Communities Capacity Building Fund for Faith Groups and Organisations: Grants 2006–2007.* UK.

Cooper, M. (2006). Pre-empting emergence: the biological turn in the war on terror. *Theory, Culture & Society*, 23(4), 113–135.

Department for Children, Schools and Families (2007). *Guidance on the Duty to Promote Community Cohesion.* UK.

Department for Children, Schools and Families, Association of Colleges and Department for Business Innovation and Skills (2008). *Learning Together to be Safe: A Toolkit to help Colleges Contribute to the Prevention of Violent Extremism.* Available at: www.education.gov.uk/consultations/downloadable-Docs/17132_DIUS_Learning_Be_Safe.pdf (accessed August 31, 2013).

Department for Communities and Local Government (2007a). *Preventing Violent Extremism Pathfinder Fund: Guidance Note for Government Offices and local Authorities in England.* UK.

Department for Communities and Local Government (2007b). *Preventing Violent Extremism - Winning Hearts and Minds.* UK.

Department for Communities and Local Government (2008a). *Empowering Muslim Women: Case Studies.* UK.

Department for Communities and Local Government (2008b). *Preventing Violent Extremism – Next Steps for Communities.* UK.

Department for Innovation, Universities, and Skills (2006). *The Role of Further Education Providers in Promoting Community Cohesion, Fostering Shared Values and Preventing Violent Extremism.* UK.

Dodd, V. (2005). Special Branch to track Muslims across UK. *The Guardian.* Available at: www.guardian.co.uk/uk/2005/jul/20/religion.july7 (accessed May 27, 2013).

Dodd, V. (2009). Government anti-terrorism strategy "spies" on innocent. *The Guardian.* Available at: www.theguardian.com/uk/2009/oct/16/anti-terrorism-strategy-spies-innocents (accessed December 15, 2013).

Duffield, M. (2011). Total war as environmental terror: linking liberalism, resilience, and the bunker. *South Atlantic Quarterly*, 110(3), 757–769.

Duffield, M. (2012). Challenging environments: danger, resilience and the aid industry. *Security Dialogue*, 43(5), 475–492.

Furedi, F. (2007). The changing meaning of disaster. *Area*, 39(4), 482–489.

Grove, K. (2014). Agency, affect, and the immunological politics of disaster resilience. *Environment and Planning D: Society and Space*, 32(2), 240–256.

Helmus, T. C., York, E., and Chalk, P. (2013). *Promoting Online Voices for Countering Violent Extremism*, Rand Corporation.

HM Government (2006). *Countering International Terrorism: The United Kingdom's Strategy.* UK.

HM Government (2009a). *Delivering the Prevent Strategy: an Updated Guide for Local Partners.* UK.

HM Government (2009b). *Pursue Prevent Protect Prepare: The United Kingdom's Strategy for Countering International Terrorism.* UK.

HM Government (2011a). *Contest: The United Kingdom's Strategy for Countering Terrorism*. UK.

HM Government (2011b). *Prevent Review: Summary of Responses to the Consultation*. UK.

HM Government (2011c). *Prevent Strategy*. UK.

HM Government (2012). *Channel: Protecting Vulnerable People from Being Drawn into Terrorism – A Guide to Local Partners*. UK.

Holling, C. S. (2001). Understanding the complexity of economic, ecological, and social systems. *Ecosystems*, 4(5), 390–405.

House of Commons Community and Local Government Committee (2010). *Preventing Violent Extremism, Sixth Report of Session 2009–10*. London: House of Commons.

Howell, A. (2015a). Resilience as enhancement: governmentality and political economy beyond "responsibilisation": special forum: resilience revisited. *Politics*, 35(1), 67–71.

Howell, A. (2015b). Resilience, war, and austerity: the ethics of military human enhancement and the politics of data. *Security Dialogue*, 46(1), 15–31.

Innes, M. (2006). Policing uncertainty: countering terror through community intelligence and democratic policing. *The ANNALS of the American Academy of Political and Social Science*, 605(1), 222–241.

Innes, M., Roberts, C., Lowe, T. and Abbott, L. (2007). *Hearts and Minds and Eyes and Ears: Reducing Radicalisation Risks through Reassurance Oriented Policing*. Cardiff, UK: Cardiff University, Universities' Police Science Institute. Available at: www.upsi.org.uk/storage/publications/HeartsMinds%202%20 Final%20Release%202011.pdf (accessed August 30, 2013).

Jackson, R. (2008). Counter-terrorism and communities: an interview with Robert Lambert. *Critical Studies on Terrorism*, 1(2), 293–308.

Keeley (2012). Celebrating good practice in Birmingham's Neighbourhoods. *Dash.com*. Available at: www.24dash.com/news/communities/2012-03-20-Celebrating-Good-Practice-in-Birmingham-s-Neighbourhoods (accessed July 19, 2016).

Kundnani, A. (2012). Radicalisation: the journey of a concept. *Race & Class*, 54(2), 3–25.

Lamb, J. B. (2012). Preventing violent extremism; a policing case study of the West Midlands. *Policing*, 7(1), 88–95.

Lamb, J. B. (2013). Light and dark: the contrasting approaches of British counter terrorism. *Journal of Policing, Intelligence and Counter Terrorism*, 8(1), 54–65.

Lentzos, P. and Rose, N. (2009). Governing insecurity: contingency planning, protection, resilience. *Economy and Society*, 38(2), 230–254.

Longstaff, P. H. (2005). *Security, Resilience and Communications in Unpredictable Environments such as Terrorism, Natural Disasters and Complex Technology*. Cambridge, MA: Center for Information Policy Research, Harvard University.

Lovins, A. and Hunter, L. (1982). *Brittle Power: Energy Strategy for National Security*. Andover, MA: Brick House Pub. Co.

Manchester City Council, Deputy Chief Executive (Neighbourhoods) (2013). *Manchester City Council Report for Resolution, Preventing Violent Extremism*. Manchester: Manchester City Council. Available at: www.manchester.gov.uk/egov_downloads/6._Preventing_violent_extremism.pdf (accessed July 19, 2016).

de Menthon, L. (2013). Outline for channel briefing: British Muslims – "The suspect community"? *Islamic Human Rights Commission*. Available at: www.ihrc.org.uk/publications/briefings/10686-outline-for-channel-briefing (accessed August 30, 2013).

Metropolitan Police Service (2012). London Muslim Communities Forum launched. *Metropolitan Police - News and Appeals*. Available at: http://content.met.police.uk/News/London-Muslim-Communities-Forum-launched/1400007687255/1257246741786 (accessed May 26, 2013).

Millie, A. (2010). Moral politics, moral decline and anti-social behaviour. *People, Place & Policy Online*, 4(1), 6–13.

Milne, S. (2008). We need to listen to the man from special branch. *The Guardian*. Available at: www.guardian.co.uk/commentisfree/2008/feb/14/uksecurity.terrorism (accessed May 30, 2013).

National Police Chief's Council (n.d.). What Prevent means to you. Available at: www.npcc.police.uk/NPCCBusinessAreas/PREVENT/WhatPreventmeanstoyou.aspx (accessed February 13, 2016).

Neocleous, M. (2008). *Critique of Security*, Montreal: McGill-Queen's University Press.

O'Brien, K. A. (2009). Managing national security and law enforcement intelligence in a globalised world. *Review of International Studies*, 35(04), 903.

O'Malley, P. (2004). *Risk, Uncertainty, and Government*. London and Portland, Or: GlassHouse.

O'Malley, P. (2010). Resilient subjects: uncertainty, warfare and liberalism. *Economy and Society*, 39(4), 488–509.

Pantazis, C. and Pemberton, S. (2009). From the "old" to the "new" suspect community: examining the impacts of recent UK counter-terrorist legislation. *British Journal of Criminology*, 49(5), 646–666.

Pinch, E. (2007). Blears in pledge to city Muslims. *Birmingham Post*. Available at: www.birminghampost.co.uk/news/local-news/blears-pledge-city-muslims-3971438 (accessed July 19, 2016).

Preventing Extremism Together Working Groups (2005). *Preventing Extremism Together, Working Group Report, August–October 2005*. UK.

Putnam, R. D. (1995). Bowling alone: America's declining social capital. *Journal of Democracy*, 6(1), 65–78.

Reid, J. (2012). The disastrous and politically debased subject of resilience. *Development Dialogue*, (58), 67–80.

Rogers, P. (2008). Contesting and preventing terrorism: on the development of UK strategic policy on radicalisation and community resilience. *Journal of Policing, Intelligence and Counter Terrorism*, 3(2), 38–61.

Rogers, P. (2013). Rethinking resilience: articulating community and the UK Riots. *Politics*, 33(4), 322–333.

Sagan, S. D. (1995). *Limits of Safety: Organizations, Accidents and Nuclear Weapons*. Princeton, NJ: Princeton University Press.

School Development Support Agency (2009). Islam and citizenship education project. Available at: www.theiceproject.com/welcome (accessed February 13, 2016).

Spalek, B. (2010). Community policing, trust, and Muslim communities in relation to "new terrorism." *Politics & Policy*, 38(4), 789–815.

Spalek, B., El Awa, S. and McDonald, L. Z. (2008). *Police-Muslim Engagement and Partnerships for the Purposes of Counter-Terrorism: an examination*. University of Birmingham. Available at: www.religionandsociety.org.uk/uploads/docs/2009_11/1258555474_Spalek_Summary_Report_2008.pdf (accessed December 29, 2013).

UK Home Office (2001). *Building Cohesive Communities: A Report of the Ministerial Group of Public Order and Community Cohesion*. London, UK.

UK Home Office (2008). *Prevent Strategy: A Guide for Local Partners*. London, UK.

US House of Representatives Committee on Homeland Security (2012). *The Radicalization of Muslim-American: The Committee on Homeland Security's Investigation of the Continuing Threat, Executive Summary and Key Findings*. Available at: https://homeland.house.gov/document/radicalization-muslim-americans-committee-homeland-securitys-investigation-continuing/ (accessed July 19, 2016).

Walker, B. and Westley, F. (2011). Perspectives on resilience to disasters across sectors and cultures. *Ecology and Society*, 16(2), 4.

Walker, J. and Cooper, M. (2011). Genealogies of resilience: from systems ecology to the political economy of crisis adaptation. *Security Dialogue*, 42(2), 143–160.

Waterhouse Consulting Group (2008). *Peventing Violent Extremism: An Independent Evaluation of the Birmingham Pathfinder*. Birmingham: Birmingham City Council.

Wildavsky, A. B. (1988). *Searching for Safety*, New Brunswick, NJ: Transaction Books; Bowling Green State University. Social Philosophy & Policy Center.

26

DANGEROUSLY EXPOSED

The life and death of the resilient subject

Brad Evans and Julian Reid

Living dangerously

What does it mean to live dangerously? This is not just a philosophical question or an ethical call to reflect upon our own individual recklessness. It is a deeply political question being asked by ideologues and policy makers who want us to abandon the dream of ever achieving security and embrace danger as a condition of possibility for life in the future. No longer, we are told, should we think in terms of evading the possibility of traumatic experiences. For catastrophic events are not just inevitable but learning experiences from which we have to grow and prosper, collectively and individually. Vulnerability to threat, injury and loss has to be accepted as a reality of human existence (Butler, 2009). The game of survival has to be played by learning how to expose oneself to danger rather than believing in the possibility of ever achieving freedom from danger as such (Reid, 2012).

This belief in the necessity and positivity of human exposure to danger is fundamental to the new doctrine of 'resilience'. The discourse of resilience originated largely in Ecology where it has been deployed, since the 1970s, to describe the capacities of non-human living systems to adapt to dangers which otherwise would threaten their catastrophic failure. Crawford Stanley Holling talked, classically, of resilience as the measure of ecosystems' abilities to absorb changes (particularly sudden catastrophic events) and still go on living (Holling 1973). For learning is said by ecologists to be as much a property of non-human living systems as it is of human life. Resilience, then, describes much more than the mere capacities of species to persist. It describes the ways in which life learns from catastrophes so that it can become more responsive to further catastrophes on the horizon. It promotes adaptability so that life may go on living, despite the fact that elements of it may be destroyed. It confronts all of us living beings, ranging from weeds to humans, with the apparent reality that managing our exposure and vulnerability to dangers is as much as we can hope for because danger is a necessity for our development.

The underlying ontology of resilience, therefore, is actually vulnerability. To be able to become resilient one must first accept that one is fundamentally vulnerable. The political genealogy of the discourse of vulnerability is as complex and fascinating as that of resilience, emerging and developing also since the early 1970s. Significantly the concept developed powerfully within the burgeoning field of disaster studies (Baird *et al.*, 1975). Over time, it has become a fundamental element within discussions concerning the impacts of catastrophic processes on human populations, especially climate change. Reading the 2012 Special Report of the Inter Governmental Panel on Climate Change (IPCC), for example, one encounters its widespread deployment. The IPCC defines vulnerability as 'the propensity or predisposition to be adversely affected' (IPCC, 2012, p. 32). This includes 'the characteristics of a person or group and their situation that influences their capacity to anticipate, cope with, resist, and recover from the adverse effects of physical events' (IPCC, 2012, p. 32). The notion of propensity is significant, since it highlights a progressive orientation that looks *towards* the extreme ends of survivability. And the notion of predisposition is significant since it suggests some *already existing* data (the guiding political presumptions) to confirm the vulnerability that is the precondition of the resilient subject. This brings together the uncertain with the certain as we encounter 'subject-centred events' according to which the event in all its catastrophic permutations cannot be known in advance, while assumptions about the subject's capacities to deal with the occurrence foster behavioural claims to empirical truth. Disaster management, of which much of the social scientific work on climate change is a mere derivative, makes the vulnerable subject the lead actor in the stories it tells as to the catastrophic destinies of human life while rendering that subject, paradoxically, the author of its own endangerment (Evans, 2012).

While there are said to be a number of ways to reduce vulnerabilities, including reduced exposure, transfer and sharing of risks, preparation and transformation, resilience is key to this new ethics of responsibility, defined as:

> the ability of a system and its component parts to anticipate, absorb, accommodate, or recover from the effects of a potentially hazardous event in a timely and efficient manner, including through ensuring the preservation, restoration, or improvement of its essential basic structures and functions.
>
> *(IPCC, 2012, p. 33)*

Significant here is the effective blending of the concept of resilience and resistance:

> This shifting emphasis to risk reduction can be seen in the increasing importance placed on developing resistance to the potential impacts of physical events at various social or territorial scales, and in different temporal dimensions (such as those required for corrective or prospective risk management), and to increasing the resilience of affected communities. Resistance refers to the ability to avoid suffering significant adverse effects.
>
> *(IPCC, 2012, p. 38)*

In other words, resistance here is transformed from being a political capacity aimed at the achievement of freedom from that which threatens and endangers to a purely reactionary impulse aimed at increasing the capacities of the subject to adapt to its dangers and simply reduce the degree to which it suffers. This conflation of resistance with resilience is not incidental but indicative of the nihilism of the underlying ontology of vulnerability at work in contemporary policies concerned with climate change and other supposedly catastrophic processes. What is nihilism, after all, if it is not a will to nothingness as one merely lives out the catastrophic moment? It also alerts us to the fundamentally liberal nature of such policies and framings of the phenomenon of climate change defined, as liberalism has been since its origins, by a fundamental mistrust in the abilities of the human subject to secure itself in the world (Reid, 2011). The function of discourses of both resilience and vulnerability in perpetration of liberal framings of disasters is testified to, as we will see in the following section, in their equivalent valences in US responses, not just to problems of environmental crisis and climate change but, as significantly, the threat of Terror.

Abandoning security

Resilience is premised upon the ability of the vulnerable subject to continually re-emerge from the conditions of its ongoing emergency. Life quite literally *becomes* a series of dangerous events. Its biography becomes a story of non-linear reactions to dangers that continually defy any attempt on its behalf to impress time with purpose and meaning. As the resilient subject navigates its ways across the complex, unknowable and forever dangerous landscapes that define the *topos* of contemporary politics, so the dangerousness of life itself becomes its condition of possibility rather than its threat. In a certain sense, the resilient subject thrives on danger. It lives in a condition of perpetual wakefulness to its reality. It is for these reasons that resilience is very rapidly reshaping the age-old concept of security that has been so fundamental to the policies, international and internal, of liberal states and governments. While the logic of security works on the principle of achieving freedom from dangers, resilience assumes the need to engage with them because their realisation is unavoidable. This instigates a form of collective amnesia. For the historical record is only important insomuch as it affirms some shared experience of the vulnerable to the exposure to danger, the suffering which that exposure entailed, and the eventual resurrection of the vulnerable subject through its discovery of its inner capacities for resilience. Out of this narrative comes an explanation of historical events as always inherently violent and damaging such that the vulnerability of human life is reaffirmed in co-extension with its inherent resilience. The past impresses itself upon the present to provide a reminder as to the radically dangerous nature of life, along with an assurance as to our abilities to nevertheless be able to survive by accepting danger as part of life. Politically qualified life thus begins with the tragedy of its existence that stems from the arbitrary and inescapable violence of the world. The only response in such a predicament is to be better conditioned through some form of exposure to the fact that living is thoroughly dangerous. Juliette Kayeem, policy adviser on Homeland Security to the Obama administration in the United States and Harvard academic summed up this zeitgeist perfectly in recent prose. What we choose to remember should, she argued, be guided by 'less anger' and instead by 'quiet acceptance':

> One day it will be acceptable, politically and publicly, to argue that while homeland security is about ensuring that fewer bad things happen, the real test is that when they inevitably do, they aren't as bad as they would have been absent the effort. Only our public and political response to another major terrorist attack will test whether there is room for both ideologies to thrive in a nation that was, any way you look at it, *built to be vulnerable.*

> *(Kayyem, 2012)*

Offering a claim as to the ontological function of vulnerability in constitution of American and wider liberal societies, discourses such as these present themselves as unproblematic. As such, their power and influence depends on their abilities to divest themselves of their fundamentally aesthetic qualities. We only have to consider, in contrast, Thomas Hoepker's photograph of people in Brooklyn relaxing and enjoying life against the backdrop of the attacks of September 11 to evidence this point. This image was not published until the fifth anniversary of 9/11, their initial publication being held back due to their so-described 'ambiguous and confusing' composition. Moving beyond any judgmental posturing towards the individuals or for that matter sweeping generalisations about cultural insensitivities of an entire nation, Hoepker's photograph is indicative of the contested reality of historical events and experiences of danger and exposure to violence. It provides a powerful antidote to governing discourses perpetrated by the ideologues of vulnerability and resilience, unsettling the dominant aesthetic dialectic of initial vulnerability and subsequent resilience. Instead, it depicts a perfectly normal state of affairs that was permitted by a certain *distancing* from the action. Indeed, as it emphasises, proximity alone offers no such guarantees for the constitution of a shared sense of experience. Many were far more deeply traumatised viewing the unfolding of events thousands of miles away on televised screens than the subjects in Hoepker's frame.

Resilience nevertheless, as New Yorkers can testify, became the defining motif of the tenth anniversary of 9/11 as Americans were encouraged to reflect on, while learning from the experience of the disaster. The media in particular grappled with the need for memorialisation, along with the desire to outlive the trauma of 9/11. *Newsweek* was unequivocal in mapping out the road to recovery. Featuring an image of a passenger jet against cloudless blue sky, it headlined with ever increasing font size 'Ten Years of Fear: Grief: Revenge: Resilience'.[1] The image used was painfully reflective in its normality. While New Yorkers were deeply traumatised by the scarred Manhattan skyline – haunted by the spectre of seeing what was no longer there, on this occasion the visibly animate invoked a tragically normalising complimentary between past memory and the 'business as usual' character of the present. *Time Magazine* was equally reflective, as its 'Beyond 9/11' cover designed by Julian LaVerdiere and Paul Myoda, co-creators of the original 'Tribute in Light' memorial, afforded more than a touch of divine transcendental quality to the idea of resurrection. The impetus being, as Richard Stengel, *Time* magazine managing editor noted, to represent 'something that literally and figuratively moved beyond 9/11'. Whereas *People* magazine's emotional tribute was the 'Legacy of Love –The Children of 9/11- Portraits of Hope', which showed photographs of those who lost fathers that day, sub-headed: 'Their fathers died on that terrible day, before they were born. Today, these 10 kids and their moms have triumphed over tragedy.' All sense of time therefore collapses here in these moments of media aestheticisation, as our sense of immanence is disrupted. As the *New York Times* simply put it: 'Reflect, Remember, Carry On.'

Battery Park in Lower Manhattan was scene to a remarkable aesthetic celebration of the ethos of resilience. Surrounding Fritz Koenig's partially disfigured *The Sphere*, which was formerly located at the Austin H. Tobin Plaza (the area between the Twin Towers), 3,000 whitened flags which featured the names of the deceased symbolically memorialised the past, all the while celebrating the fact that it was possible for certain things to emerge if slightly transformed in design, meaning, and political resonance. *The Sphere* itself became a living symbol of resilience, as it literally provided an optimistic centre for reflection in a sea of tragic memory. In this setting, the memory of the event was both complimentary yet literally paled by the dominant centrifuge, which encouraged the public to concentrate on the positive core. All the while, the *Statue of Liberty* provided an additional background to the aesthetic frame, as if to remind visitors that the values of liberal societies are equally vulnerable yet resilient to the pressure of tyranny in all its forms. Resilience thus defines here the character of a Nation and the freedom of a people that has the strength to carry on in the face of adversity.

Perhaps however it was Marco Grob's *Beyond 9/11: Portraits of Resilience* exhibition, displayed in the Milk Gallery and various additional public spaces across Manhattan, which proves most revealing.[2] Featuring stark black and white photographs of the forty faces said to encapsulate the spirit of recovery, resilience was ubiquitously framed by politicians, the Major, the Admiral, the General, the military hero, the CIA Covert operative, along with the CEO, New York Fire fighters, artists, and everyday survivors. The messages here were poignant. Resilient life was fully inclusive.

It made no distinction. Catastrophe had strengthened the resolve. We learnt more about ourselves by living through the Terror. Shared experience of trauma brought a people together. Despite vast differences in lifestyles (not to mention race, gender and class), resilience was evidently a universal property and capacity of all New Yorkers. Life, however, can only be captured for a moment. Momentarily reflective, we owe it to the victims to face up to the challenge that society must emerge from the ashes and continue its normality apace. With the individual compliant subject therefore becoming the loci for a moment of attention that was delicately poised between past memory and future possibility, so past and future impress upon the present the need to live through the emergency and come out better adapted, and capable of facing up to the next catastrophe on the horizon.

It also pointed to a new political moment in which the trauma of the event shifted from discourses of retribution to a more sombre evaluation of the fragility of life. This was not presented as something to be despaired. Optimism was to be found precisely in the ability to emerge from the ashes of the catastrophic, more appreciative of what it meant to live a finite existence. To be optimistic meant having a more intimate appreciation of the lethality of 9/11, for only then could the trauma of the day be turned around to positively re-enforce the moral surety of liberal ways of life. President Barack Obama's commemorative speech at Ground Zero spoke volumes in this regard:

> These past ten years tell a story of resilience. The Pentagon is repaired, and filled with patriots working in common purpose. Shanksville is the scene of friendships forged between residents of that town, and families who lost loved ones there. New York remains a vibrant capital of the arts and industry, fashion and commerce. Where the World Trade Center once stood, the sun glistens off a new tower that reaches toward the sky. Our people still work in skyscrapers. Our stadiums are filled with fans, and our parks full of children playing ball. Our airports hum with travel, and our buses and subways take millions where they need to go. Families sit down to Sunday dinner, and students prepare for school. This land pulses with the optimism of those who set out for distant shores, and the courage of those who died for human freedom.
>
> *(Obama, 2011)*

As Obama instructs his public, the past can only offer a certain degree of guidance. One thing the future does promise, he indicates, is another catastrophe in some yet to be deciphered guise. While the past therefore remains imperfect, as it was impossible to predict with absolute certainty what came to pass, the future is equally contingent. As finite beings with finite personal qualities in a world of infinite possibility we are then, it seems, somewhat incapable of 'handling the truth'. Indeed, it seems that liberal politicians no longer reason truth to be 'out there' as if it could be captured and settled once and for all. Abandoning the search for fixed essences, truth has become what we make it as we fashion our lives and produce the meaning of our freedoms and liberties as consumable products like any other. There is an important caveat to address here. The liberal fashioning of the truth as conceived in terms of its emergence in the context of our vulnerability is not a courage to speak truth *to* power so that we think different about the political. It is an allegiance to the truth *of* power such that we maintain some allegiance to the truth about the value of political subjects already conceived. In this regard, significant commonality exists between the knowledge of the resilient subject and that of speculative philosophy. Rather than seeking a definitive political rupture with the present, the political subject is tasked to show *fidelity* to the truth – as witnessed in the living out of emerging events – which conforms to some nomologically reducible logic of worlds (see Badiou, 2006). What is wagered, in other-words, is the truth-event of the vulnerable subject, whose very claim to truth arises during the catastrophic moment as a sort of hyper-negative and posthumous 'told you so':

> For a truth to affirm its newness, there must be a *supplement*. This supplement is committed to chance. It is unpredictable, incalculable. It is beyond what is. I call it an event A truth thus appears, in its newness, because an eventful supplement interrupts repetition. . . . An event is linked to the notion of the *undecidable*. Take this statement: 'The event belongs to the situation.' If it is possible to decide, using the rules of established knowledge, whether this statement is true or false, then the so-called event is not an event. Its occurrence would be calculable within the situation. Nothing would permit us to say: here begins a truth. On the basis of the undecidability of an event's belonging to a situation a *wager* has to be made. This is why a truth begins with an *axiom of truth*. It begins with a groundless decision – the decision to say that the event has taken place.
>
> *(Badiou, 2005)*

There is no truth, in other words, other than the truth of the emergent will to know the conditions of our vulnerability. The past is of no relevance here, other than as a contingent moment in time whose passage leaves no contemporary truthfulness from the perspective of the newly emergent truth-event. But what is actually being wagered here? It is not the incalculability of the situation. Neither is it the question of belonging to the situation in all its complexity. It is the ability to excavate something of a pure and unquestionable truth that renders the undecidable decidable, the rupture normalised, the uncertain certain, so that it becomes possible to recover a political truth out of the catastrophic break. To suggest that there are no established rules, then, is the precise point. Vulnerability and insecurity make all claims to established order altogether redundant for there is no truth other than that which has just come to pass and is soon to be forgotten. Collective amnesia thus becomes a default setting for a system of rule that is less about secure principles than it is about axiomatic propositions which, although fleeting, provide the most unquestionable assumptions about the subject's ontological status (vulnerability), its epistemic reasoning (radical uncertainty), and its purely contingent centre of gravity (catastrophic events).

Whose survivability?

Survivability has always been central to the concerns of liberalism. How we might govern ourselves in ways that allow our life to grow and prosper is a question fundamental to the liberal project, and distinguishes its biopolitical origins and remits (Dillon and Reid, 2009). If biopolitics is a key term of art for describing the progressive operations of power that render the modern periodic as such, resilience is a form of biopolitics that produces a conscious awareness of the contemporary bind in which the liberal pursuit of the infinitely possible becomes the basis for the conceptualisation of threats to the finitude of existence (Evans 2012). Resilience, in other words, evidences most clearly how liberal power is confronting the realities of its own self-imposed political foreclosure as the reality of finitude is haunted by infinite potentiality. This brings us to a pivotal moment in the history of liberalism as the project finally abandons its universal aspirations, along with any natural claims to promote all life as a self-endowed subject with inalienable rights. With the outside vanquished to the disappointing realisation of endemic crises, sheer survivability becomes the name of the political game.

Resilience, however, is more than increased vigilance and preparedness against impending attacks. It encourages actors to learn from catastrophes so that societies can become more responsive to further catastrophes on the horizon (Duffield, 2007). It promotes adaptability so that life may go on living, despite the fact that elements of our living systems may be destroyed. And it creates shared knowledge and information that will continually reshape the forms of communities and affirm those core values which are deemed absolutely 'vital' to our ways of living. With this in mind, it is perhaps no accident that the concept of resilience derived directly from ecology. Such thinking foregrounds 'buffer capacities' of living systems; their ability to 'absorb perturbations' or the 'magnitude of disturbance that can be absorbed before a living system changes its structure by changing the variables and processes that control behaviour' (Adger, 2000, p. 349). Living systems are said by ecologists to develop not on account of their ability to secure themselves prophylactically from threats, but through their adaptation to them. They evolve in spite of and because of systemic shocks that register from the minor to the catastrophic. Exposure to threats is a constitutive process in the development of living systems, and thus the problem for them is never simply how to secure themselves, but how to adapt to them. Such capacities for adaptation to threats are precisely what ecologists argue determines the 'resilience' of any living system.

Jeremy Walker and Melinda Cooper (2010) have provided an important contribution here to our understanding of the genealogies of resilience. Drawing upon the number of ways complexity thinking has been shaped, they have exposed the intricate connections between ecological and economical modes of thinking. As they suggest, 'Since the nineties, global financial institutions such as the International Monetary Fund, the World Bank, and the Bank for International Settlements, have increasingly incorporated strategies of "resilience" into their logistics of crisis management, financial (de)regulation and development economics' (Walker and Cooper, 2010, p. 144). Much of this applicability owes to the intellectual contributions of the great Austrian economic theorist Fredric Von Hayek, who understood that shocks to economic systems were caused by factors beyond our control, hence our thinking about such systems required systems of governance that were premised upon insecure foundations. Thus, while Ecology promises to universalise and moralise resilient strategies through the creation of all inclusive catastrophic imaginaries, it is also intuitively in keeping with neoliberalism and its systems of rule:

> [A]s institutions begin to recognize the looming socio-economic effects of climate change, we have seen a rapid uptake of the adaptive model of resource-management offered by resilience science. This has occurred in tandem with calls for the 'securitization of the biosphere': the privatisation and trading of the flow of 'ecosystem services' maintained by intact ecosystems, in recognition that rainforests and watersheds are critical 'natural infrastructure assets' that must to be priced in financial markets in order that corporations can 'capture the value' of biodiversity conservation. In this way, neoliberal environmentalism addresses the depletion of ecosystems as a global security problem, the only solution to which is the securitisation and financialisation of the biosphere.
>
> *(Walker and Cooper, 2010, p. 155)*

So resilience from this perspective is not simply a call to ignite some base-level human instinct for survival. It is an ideological project that is informed by political and economic rationalities which offer very particular accounts of life as an ontological problem, i.e. a problem which emanates from the potentiality of life as ontologically conceived, along with the types of epistemic communities which now scientifically verify the need to become resilient as a *fait accompli*. Resilience in other words is a key strategy in the creation of contemporary regimes of power, which hallmark vast inequalities in all human classifications. Little wonder that resilience is most concerned with those deemed most vulnerable. For it is precisely the inse-curitisation of the most at-risk which politically threatens the security and comforts of those who are sufficiently protected and excluded from the all too real effects of risk-based societies. The following introduction from a joint report on 'The Roots of Resilience', co-sponsored by the United Nations Development Programme, the United Nations Environment Programme, the World Bank and the World Resources Institute, speaks volumes on the political implications:

> Resilience is the capacity to adapt and to thrive in the face of challenge. This report contends that when the poor successfully (and sustainably) scale-up ecosystem-based enterprises, their resilience can increase in three dimensions. They can become more economically resilient – better able to face economic risks. They – and their communities – can become more socially resilient – better able to work together for mutual benefit. And the ecosystems they live in can become more biologically resilient – more productive and stable.
>
> *(UNDP et al., 2008, p. xi)*

Living without death

Taken at face value, resilience might seem commonsense. What is wrong with enabling human beings to take responsibility for themselves so that they can face up to dangers, better survive, avoid death, evading violence and insecurity along the way? Rather than investing hope in their governments being able to make their lives more secure, resilient people take ownership of their dangers and face up to their realities. Thus it becomes a question of individual responsibility that demands a reasoned and calculated choice. It is not incidental that resilience has generated a massive popular literature of self-help manuals aimed at enabling people to better secure them-selves not just from terrorism, but from ordinary 'dangers' such as extreme weather, redundancy and divorce. Beneath this veneer of commonsense, however, lurks a dark and dehumanising political agenda.

Fundamental to human beings is our ability to act on our world in ways that enable us to change it. We don't just put up with dangers and threats of harm; we act in ways that protest their very existence. The political describes, for us at least, this fundamental capacity of human beings to resist the conditions of their own suffering and transform worlds in ways that provide security. What resilience preaches is the impossibility and folly of even thinking we might resist danger and, instead, the acceptance of the necessity of living a life of permanent exposure to endemic dangers.

Resilience does not just encourage us to learn from the violence of catastrophic events so that we become more responsive to further catastrophes on the horizon. It promotes our adaptability so that we are also less of a threat politically. Accepting the imperative to become resilient means sacrificing any political vision of a world in which we might be able to live better lives freer from dangers, looking instead at the future as an endemic terrain of catastrophe that is dangerous and insecure by design. Adaptability in the face of crisis emphasises our resourcefulness, our abilities to thrive in times of risk, and our life-affirming qualities that refuse to surrender to all forms of endangerment. It is, then, a form of reasoning that is not objective, but fully compatible with the neoliberal model of economy, its promotion of risk and its emphasis on care for the self. It is a reasoning that conceals a sinister biopolitical partitioning between those who have the ability to secure themselves from risk, against those who are asked to live up to their responsibilities by accepting the conditions of their own vulnerability and asking not of the social.

A notable casualty of this is has been the Utopian ideal. The idea of Utopia has often been tied to modes of representation, as the future becomes an open site for projected fantasies of worlds yet to be realised. Although it has never been a static concept, overshadowed in many periods by more compelling dystopian supplements that seemed to be more in keeping with our profound suspicions about ourselves, the fact that we no longer even entertain the prospect of some utopian ideal is reflective of the political times. As Fredric Jameson has written, 'the waning of the utopian idea is a fundamental historical and political symptom, which deserves diagnosis in its own right—if not some new and more effective therapy' (Jameson, 2004). Central to Jameson's concerns has been the weakening of any sense of history, along with the collapse of the political imaginary that refuses to envisage anything other than the bleak current state of political affairs. Utopia thus conceived has a distinct revolutionary capacity by allowing us to suspend normality for a moment, take 'mental liberties' (which are invariably particu-laristic and not universalistic), thereby transgressing the present, and believe in possible futures to come. Despite our concerns with the totalising metaphysics of utopianism in historical practice, Jameson does offer a compelling diagnosis of the catastrophic imaginary of contem-porary liberal rule:

> [T]he notion of the market as an untrammelled natural growth has returned with a vengeance into political thinking, while Left ecology desperately tries to assess the possibilities of a productive collaboration between political agency and the earth. . . . Ecology seems to count ever more feebly on its power—unless it be in the form of the apocalyptic and of catastrophe, global warming or the development of new viruses. . . . The science-fictional figure for such change is the situation in which a prisoner, or some potential rescue victim, is warned that salvation will be possible only at the price of allowing the entire personality—the past and its memories, all the multiple influences and events that have combined to form this current personality in the present—to be wiped away without a trace: a consciousness will alone remain, after this operation, but by what effort of the reason or imagination can it still be called 'the same' consciousness? The fear with which this prospect immediately fills us is then to all intents and purposes the same as the fear of death.
>
> *(Jameson, 2004)*

Post-utopianism takes on a number of distinct features in which idealised lifestyles are no longer presented as a common good but a matter of *exclusivity*. If there is any resonance to idealism, it is not premised on inclusion but the need to be able to 'opt-out' of the social landscape. Not only do we evidence this in the various newspaper supplements which offer temporary refuge from the maddening crowds upon some idyllic and depopulated retreat, the marked separation of gated lives has increasingly become the new norm for human habitation, as the logic of risk calls forth the creation of local protectorates. Gated communities offer a particularly telling insight into the politics of resilience. Borrowing from Foucault, we may argue that the gated community is in fact a novel expression of a security apparatus that seeks to *distribute* the chance for risk throughout the networked assemblage. The gated individual out-sources the need to be resilient to other elements within the gated system, ranging from barbed fences, physical walls, surveillance technologies, catastrophe-proofed architectures, insurance premiums, to armed guards patrolling the parameters. This is a far cry from Thomas Moore's vision of Utopia as a site of human togetherness and shared access to resources. Indeed, once we broach the problem of gated life biopolitically, i.e. the gates (whether included or excluded) begin with the human subject, it soon becomes apparent how resilience is tied to a neoliberal ideology that clouds racial, cultural and gendered discriminations by the smokescreen of objective risk assessments. And yet, the tragic irony of resilience is that it renders problematic precisely those populations which are *at risk* in order to permit their veritable containment and keep separated from those for whom resilience is seldom entertained.

What, however, is ultimately at stake here is the problem of finitude. How may we survive in the face of all adversity? How is it possible to go on living despite all the evidence that human life remains the biggest threat to its own very existence? What may we remain come the catastrophic?

The question of finitude is, of course, personally and intellectually daunting. How may we come to terms with a passing into the absolute unknown? None of this is incidental. In fact, it brings us back to the original problematic of philosophy as we confront what it means to die. How is it possible to learn to live with death? Cornel West, in the acclaimed documentary *Examined Life* has provided a telling insight. 'You know', West argues,

> Plato says philosophy's a meditation on and a preparation for death. By death what he means is not an event, but a death in life because there's no rebirth, there's no change, there's no transformation without death, and therefore the question becomes: How do you learn how to die?
>
> *(Taylor, 2008)*

From this perspective, to philosophise is precisely the ability of coming to terms with death while living. As West further explains:

> You can't talk about truth without talking about learning how to die because it's precisely by learning how to die, examining yourself and transforming your old self into a better self, that you actually live more intensely and critically and abundantly.

Hence, it is only by 'learning how to die', to will what Walter Benjamin called 'the messianic' or subscribe to what Simon Critchley termed a 'faithless faith', through which death is metaphorically read more as an affirmative moment of passage, that it becomes possible to transform the present condition and create a new self by 'turning your world upside down'. Resilience cheats us of this notion of learning to die. It exposes life to danger so that life may live a *non-death*.

Zygmunt Bauman has rightly pointed out that while we are more conscious of our mortality and fragile existence, for the most part, death as experience for philosophical reflection has become a private affair that is generally hidden from the public gaze (see Bauman, 2011). That is to say, while any survey of the headstones of the recently deceased seldom write of a person simply having died a 'natural death' (there is always something that is responsible), to think about the question of death as an ontological condition for subsequent rebirth is relegated to the world of religious pathology and the dangerous attempts to counter liberal reason with violence unto oneself.

So how might we live without death? Such a question we believe is politically and philosophically absurd. It is impossible to live meaningfully without knowing how to die. Abandoning death forces us to give up the prospect of self-renewal, without which we merely learn to accept the catastrophic lot. This is less than acceptable. Not only does this commitment prove politically catastrophic, it is fundamentally nihilistic. What is nihilism, after all, if not a political will to nothingness? If we therefore accept that resilience is another form of nihilism that forces the subject to wilfully abandon the political, any rigorous critique must deal with the conflict between the lethality of freedom and the philosophical question of death, for only then can we begin to question what it means to live.

Notes

1 For full representations, see www.nytimes.com/2011/09/10/arts/magazine-covers-about-911.html?pagewanted=all (accessed 1 February 2013).
2 See www.time.com/time/beyond911/ (accessed 1 February 2013).

References

Adger, W.N. (2000). Social and Ecological Resilience: Are They Related? *Progress in Human Geography*, 24(3), 347–364.

Badiou, A. (2005). *Infinite Thought: Truth and the Return to Philosophy*. London: Continuum.

Badiou, A. (2006). *Being and Event*. London: Continuum.

Baird, A., O'Keefe, P., Westgate, K. and Wisner, B. (1975). Towards an Explanation of and Reduction of Disaster Proneness. Occasional Paper (number 11), Disaster Research Unit, University of Bradford, Bradford, UK.

Bauman, Z. (2011). *Collateral Damage: Social Inequalities in a Global Age*. Cambridge: Polity.

Butler, J. (2009). *Frames of War*. London and New York: Verso.

Dillon, M. and Reid, J. (2009). *The Liberal Way of War: Killing to Make Life Live*. London and New York: Routledge.

Duffield, M. (2007). *Development, Security and Unending War: Governing the World of Peoples*. Cambridge: Polity.

Evans, B. (2012). *Liberal Terror*. Cambridge: Polity.

Holling, C.H. (1973). Resilience and Stability of Ecological Systems. *Annual Review of Ecology and Systematics*, 4, 1–23.

Inter Governmental Panel on Climate Change (IPCC) (2012). *Managing the Risks of Extreme Events and Disasters to Advance Climate Change Adaptation*. Cambridge: Cambridge University Press.

Jameson, F. (2004). The Politics of Utopia. *New Left Review*, 25(January–February).

Kayyem, J. (2012). Never Say Never Again. *Foreign Policy*, 10(9). Available at: www.foreignpolicy.com/articles/2012/09/10/never_say_never_again?page=full#.UFIslAvZ-RY.twitter (accessed 1 February 2013).

Obama, B. (2011). Speech on the 10th Anniversary of 9/11. *Wall Street Journal*. Available at: http://blogs.wsj.com/washwire/2011/09/11/obamas-speech-on-the-anniversary-of-911/ (accessed 1 February 2013).

Reid, J. (2011). The Vulnerable Subject of Liberal War. *South Atlantic Quarterly*, 110(3), 770–779.

Reid, J. (2012). The Disastrous and Politically Debased Subject of Resilience. *Development Dialogue*, (April), 67–80.

Taylor, A. (2008). *Examined Life*. New York: Zeitgeist Productions.

UNDP, United Nations Environment Programme, World Bank, and World Resources Institute (2008). *World Resources 2008: Roots of Resilience – Growing the Wealth of the Poor*. Washington, DC: World Resources Institute.

Walker, J. and Cooper, M. (2010). Genealogies of Resilience: From Systems Ecology to the Political Economy of Crisis Adaptation. *Security Dialogue*, 42(2), 143–160.

PART IX

International development

27

RESILIENCE AND DEVELOPMENT AMONG ULTRA-POOR HOUSEHOLDS IN RURAL ETHIOPIA

Brian Thiede

Introduction

This chapter describes subjective understandings of resilience among residents of a community in southern Ethiopia. It also considers the implications of using this term as a mobilizing concept for research and practice in a highly resource-constrained context. Understandings of resilience among ultra-poor households highlight a tension between meeting short-term subsistence needs and taking actions that contribute to building resilience against future shocks and stresses. Responses also underline the need to think beyond resilience-building at the individual or household level, and consider the structural conditions that limit the efficacy of micro-level interventions and contribute to the shocks and stresses that resilience is to be built against. The need to think critically about the spatial and temporal scales at which resilience is enhanced or constrained is also manifest in a brief analysis of a development intervention taking place in Kejima. This intervention addressed a number of the household-level needs identified by respondents from the community, but failed to address major structural constraints and sources of risk, likely reflecting both epistemic positions and practical concerns among development practitioners.

The concept of resilience is increasingly used to motivate research and interventions targeting households and communities in ecologically volatile contexts. In many places in which such resilience thinking is applied, however, prevailing systemic conditions constrain households' ability to access sufficient material resources to meet basic needs, much less accumulate other resources that can be used to withstand future shocks or challenges. Building upon mixed-methods research in rural southern Ethiopia, this chapter examines how the concept of resilience is understood and operationalized within a context of severe resource constraint. Here, seasonal hunger is experienced by nearly all members of the community, inter-annual variability in ecological and economic conditions stymie resource accumulation, and, as a result, the temporal frames for decision-making are decidedly short-term. In what ways do such conditions shape the potential for resilience knowledge and programming?

I address this question by analyzing subjective understandings of resilience among individuals from chronically poor and food insecure households in a rural Ethiopian community. Examining these local understandings of resilience reveals constraints to development in the community, as well as important strengths and limitations of resilience as an analytic concept. I also consider the conceptual framing and implementation of a resilience-building intervention in the community and surrounding area, and explore the implications of using resilience as an organizing concept for programming.

Overall, the evidence presented in this chapter suggests that the concept of resilience, as understood and described by participants in this research, has the potential to highlight the tensions between short- and long-term needs, and identify the structural constraints that limit the ability of some actors to move beyond addressing short-term needs and sustainably accumulate resources over long periods of time. However, this chapter also provides evidence that this potential is not always realized, due to a tendency of reducing resilience to a question of individual resources.

Defining resilience

Given a lack of agreement regarding the precise definition of resilience among development scholars and practitioners, I begin by clarifying how the term resilience is employed throughout this chapter. Many existing papers trace the genealogy of the concept and put forward new, if only slightly modified definitions of the term to contribute to (and perhaps further complicate) the literature (e.g. Adger 2000; Barrett and Constas 2014; Bené *et al.* 2014; Brown and Westaway 2011; Davidson 2010; Folke *et al.* 2010; Frankenberger *et al.* 2014; USAID 2012, Walsh-Dilley *et al.* 2013).

The focus here is upon how resilience is understood subjectively among individuals in the study community, and framed by a resilience-building intervention taking place in that community. However, the study from which the data analyzed below are drawn was motivated by a particular definition of resilience put forward by Marygold Walsh-Dilley and colleagues (2013). According to these scholars, resilience is defined as:

> The process of learning, organization, and adaptation taking place across scales that enable people to respond to and cope with internal and external stresses in ways that allow them to build and defend healthy, happy, and meaningful lives and livelihoods.
> *(Walsh-Dilley et al. 2013, p. 33)*

As well, in individual and group interviews, resilience was translated into a word in the local Sidaminya language that back-translates to English as "strength in the midst of challenges." This broad definition of the term provided participants with an opportunity to define and describe resilience more concretely as they understood it. The opportunity for valorizing such subjective definitions may be an underappreciated benefit of the concept of resilience, which arguably requires context-specificity to describe or measure.

Fieldwork and data

This research draws upon approximately four months of fieldwork in the community described in this chapter, which occurred between March and July 2013. This fieldwork included over thirty semi-structured interviews, numerous unstructured background interviews with key informants, community observations, and a survey of all households living in the community at that time. Broadly, this project was focused on understanding how multiple forms of social differentiation contributed to and were shaped by unequal responses to ecological stress.

For the purposes of this chapter, I draw mainly upon data from twelve individual and two group semi-structured interviews, which were focused specifically on understanding notions of and correlates to resilience in the community. These interviews took place in July 2013 as a part of a rural resilience assessment organized by Oxfam America and Cornell University's Atkinson Center for a Sustainable Future. The purpose of this assessment was, "to facilitate a participatory process of community reflection contributing to resilience building, to generate unique community-level data regarding local resources for resilience, and to inform the development of a national-level indicator of resilience capabilities" (ACSF-Oxfam 2013). The individual and group interviews conducted during this assessment queried respondents' perceptions of governance, civic capacity, natural resources, economic resources, and social learning in their community. Respondents were also asked to describe the characteristics they associated with a resilient household, real or imagined. Responses to this latter prompt constitute the main body of data considered in the analyses below. Background information regarding the social, demographic, and agricultural profile of the community is based on the analysis of data from a household survey unless otherwise noted. This part of the study was implemented between March and May of 2013.

Context

This study took place in a community that I refer to as Kejima, which is located in the Sidama zone of the Southern Nations, Nationalities, and Peoples' Region (SNNPR) of Ethiopia (Figure 27.1). A total of ninety-five households lived in Kejima at the time of the study, nearly 10 percent of which are headed by women. Households range in size from two to twelve persons, and include between one and three generations (i.e. grandparents, children, grandchildren).

Livelihoods among community members are uniformly centered around rain-fed agricultural production. All households that participated in the study reported planting maize and haricot beans, and many also plant some combination of potatoes, cabbage, *ensete* (false banana), and peppers in other parts of their plots. The combination of crops that a given household plants

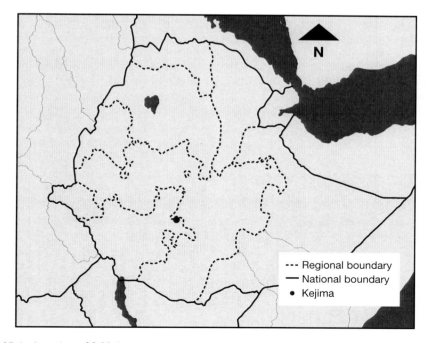

Figure 27.1 Location of field site

is usually contingent upon the size of their landholdings and monetary savings—which are necessary to purchase seeds and fertilizer. With the exception of the very destitute, most households in Kejima also raise at least one kind of livestock. However, average livestock holdings per household are estimated to be less than half of comparable estimates in other parts of Ethiopia.[1] The high levels of deprivation in Kejima are consistent with surrounding communities, which are located in a relatively resource-poor and vulnerable area compared to some other parts of the country.

In most households, at least one person engages in a food or income-generating activity beyond their own agricultural production (Ellis 1998). These activities are highly gendered. Men frequently work on other households' fields for wages or foodstuffs, trade or broker livestock, operate a local donkey taxi, or trade agricultural goods. Women also engage in trade and are often responsible for selling any surplus household agricultural production in the market. As well, women commonly process foods (e.g. *ensete* flour, butter) to sell in the market, or may process food directly for other households. More than a third of households receive government food and monetary transfers for six months of the year through a program called the Productive Safety Net Program (PSNP).

Land is arguably the single most important natural resource in the area, given the centrality of agriculture to livelihoods in Kejima. Legally, the government and people of Ethiopia own all land in the country, and households hold usufruct rights that are typically passed down from fathers to their sons at the time of marriage. The current distribution of land is the result of historical settlement patterns and government land allocations, land appropriations during previous periods of social and political unrest, and family demographic trends. There is currently no unclaimed land in or around the community—so landholdings are essentially fixed among households, and fragmented with each intra-generational transfer between fathers and their son(s). Household land plots range in size from one-quarter to two hectares per household, with one household effectively landless. Approximately 70 percent of households have access to less than one-half hectare of land—small plots that sociologist Dessalegn Rahmato has called "starvation plots" (Rahmato 1994).

In addition to the small and decreasing size of agricultural plots, respondents unanimously reported declining land quality and agricultural production, which they attribute to overuse and erosion. Nearly all land in the community is put under production each year—no respondent or key informant reported fallowing their land. Moreover, households uniformly plant maize as their primary crop each year, which likely has soil-depleting effects above and beyond the fact that land is used year-on-year without lying fallow.

While these temporal declines in land quality are rather consistent across households, there is significant spatial variation in actual levels of land quality. Agricultural plots in parts of the community are subjected to significant water runoff and erosion from the surrounding hillside. Deforestation over recent decades has increased the severity of this problem by reducing barriers to downhill water streams (i.e. increasing flood risk) and exposing loose topsoil to the elements. Frequent, violent flows of water leech nutrients from the soil and cause significant physical erosion, which is evident in large ravines that now divide parts of the community. Indeed, a number of households in this area have lost upwards of one-quarter hectare of land as a result of ravine formation.

Kejima is also subject to frequent weather shocks, which combine with local agro-ecological and economic conditions to adversely affect agricultural production and food security. For example, a 2011 assessment from the Famine Early Warning Systems Network (FEWSNET) suggested that the area faced crisis or emergency conditions, reporting:

> [SNNPR] has also been significantly affected by poor rainfall over the past four months. Despite some rains since April, shortages of water and pasture remain serious in some

lowland areas. . . . Information from ongoing monitoring and recent rapid assessments indicate widespread increasing trends in the prevalence of acute malnutrition. . . . Staple food prices, particularly maize, have been displaying abnormal rising trends in the last few months. . . . Deteriorations in food security . . . [are] expected to keep thousands of poor households in the most affected zones of the region in Crisis (IPC Phase 3) until the next *Meher* harvest begins in October.

(FEWSNET 2011)

Such situations are not uncommon in Kejima, and reflect a combination of climatic volatility and vulnerable agro-ecological systems.

This description of the study community is necessarily cursory, but should nonetheless make clear that households in Kejima are among the most resource poor in Ethiopia, where the average standard of living is already below most places in the world. Community members face the challenge of meeting subsistence needs via rain-fed agriculture in a context constrained by small and decreasing landholdings, declining soil quality, limited access to inputs, and climatic volatility. As such, the results from this study provide insight into how the concept of resilience helps to understand, and perhaps design interventions to help, the world's most poor and vulnerable.

Perceptions of resilience

To explore the subjective understanding of resilience among community members, each study participant was asked to describe the characteristics of a resilient household or person, either real or hypothetical. As mentioned above, during interviews the term resilience was translated into a Sidaminya word that back-translates to "strength in the midst of challenges." These subjective understandings of resilience are valuable in a number of respects. For example, they reveal the resources respondents believe are necessary to deal with frequent shocks or stresses, as well as the conditions experienced by those that are able to successfully do so. What respondents do not say—and cannot imagine—may also reveal insights into the limitations they face. Examining subjective understandings of resilience is also valuable for scholars and practitioners interested in measuring or building resilience. Evidence of how resilience is understood among the subjects of analysis or intervention in a particular context is presumably necessary to accurately identify what resilience actually means in that setting—a requisite to resilience measurement or building that many practitioners aspire to.

In Kejima, respondents' descriptions of resilience largely center on a set of resources needed to support robust agricultural production, such as land and resources to purchase agricultural inputs. Descriptions also focus on conditions or experiences that would result from high and stable levels of production, such as inter- and intra-annual stability in food access, a lack of fear, and autonomy.

Large landholdings are perhaps the most frequently mentioned correlate to resilience. According to many responses, households with large landholdings are more likely to realize surplus production during years with good environmental conditions, and meet subsistence requirements during years with adverse conditions. One respondent described his own experience during a recent period when rainfall was poor and agricultural conditions suffered, saying,

> In our case we have a very small plot of land and we didn't get any production. For those who have a bigger plot of land, they told us that they got at least some small amount of production last year.

The size of landholdings also shapes the composition of crops that households grow. In particular, those with relatively large plots of land are generally more likely to plant large *ensete* plots, which respondents often associated with resilience due to the plant's drought-resistant properties. This plant is a seen as a main source of insurance against environmentally induced food insecurity in the area. One person described a resilient individual, saying,

> He can use his land or his cattle, selling them to the market and having money. And if there is no food at home even, he can buy larger amounts of food from the market than others. . . . And having larger false banana, when a drought comes he can consume that one also.

However, *ensete* takes multiple years to mature, during which time the land allocated toward growing the plant is effectively taken out of production. As a result, those with the smallest plots and closest to the margins of subsistence are unlikely to sacrifice annual maize production to grow *ensete*. Such households prioritize short-term needs at the expense of growing what respondents identified as a resilience-building crop. The association that respondents draw between *ensete* and resilience may therefore suggest that they believe resilience is, in part, about the ability to actively deal with and mitigate both short-term shocks and long-term risks. Resilient households are able to plan and act over relatively long temporal frames, while those who are not resilient tend to be oriented toward dealing with short-term crises only.

A number of respondents also argued that the geographic diversity of landholdings enhanced resilience. Given relatively high levels of heterogeneity in micro-climatic conditions and land quality in this part of Ethiopia, agricultural plots across relatively short distances may experience markedly different conditions and productivity. For example, one community member explained, "The production of the land which is nearest to me failed completely. But I have got some production from the land that is thirty minutes away from me."

Given the structure of land tenure in this context, however, respondents' association between the geographic diversity of landholdings and resilience underscores a major constraint toward resilience building. With the exception of an informal land rental and sharing market, the size, spatial distribution, and quality of households' landholdings are fixed, the result of decades-long social, political, and demographic processes shaping the distribution of land.

Respondents also indicated that wealth—in the forms of livestock and monetary savings—is a characteristic of resilient households. For example, one respondent said,

> In my opinion, resilience describes the one who has a bigger plot of land, the one who has a bigger cow, and bigger false banana. And the one who has enough food in his house, and the one who has extra money from a business. . . . Those people are considered as resilient people in our area.

Likewise, another person described a hypothetical resilient person as,

> One who has good access to land—big land—many resources, and the one who sends his children to school . . . And the one who has deposits in the bank. Because he or she, when a problem comes, they can protect themselves from that problem.

Both livestock and monetary wealth may provide key buffers against crop failures, related food insecurity, and economic challenges. Stored wealth allows such households to meet food consumption needs during periods of stress without engaging in potentially harmful coping behaviors, such as restricting food consumption, discontinuing children's education, and engaging in debt relations.

A number of respondents linked resilience to ownership of two specific assets—corrugated iron houses and motorcycles. One respondent described a hypothetical resilient man as one, "Having a good house that is built from iron sheets. And if he can buy motorbikes too, then he can build different houses in the different towns." While these items are clearly a reflection of household wealth, they may also contribute to resilience directly. For example, houses built with corrugated iron are more sturdy and sanitary, and require less time to maintain. This may improve the health of household members, and increase the time available for productive or meaningful activities. Likewise, motorbikes provide their owners with autonomy, mobility, and the ability to engage in income-generating activities that would otherwise not be possible, as the respondent quoted above suggests.

In addition to identifying specific characteristics of, and resources controlled by resilient households, many participants also discussed feelings, experiences, and relationships that they associated with resilience. Foremost was a lack of fear: resilient households do not fear for what may come in the future. A respondent contrasted their feelings during periods of environmental stress with those of a hypothetical resilient household, saying,

> When something like the dry time happens, his family passes that time without any fear. . . . When I see my life, when drought time comes, I am afraid because I have many children who need food. And those who are resilient people have a small household . . . have good land, good production, and a good cow. Whenever something comes, they don't fear. But right now we are fearing.

These fears and related perceptions of insecurity reflect households' structural positions and levels of risk in the community, and again emphasize issues of temporality. Whereas a previously quoted response highlights the link between resilience and long-term planning and investments, here the respondent suggests that it is the most resource-poor and vulnerable who hold a long-term perspective; but in this case, it is a matter of fearing or anticipating future shocks for which they are unprepared to respond.

Many respondents also suggests that resilient households are unaffected by the seasonal fluctuations in food access that characterize the calendar for most households in the area. As one respondent put it, "When you go to [the resilient person's] house, everything is full, whatever time, rainy season or drought season, he is the same." This is consistent with the responses that emphasize the association between resilience and land, wealth, and other factors affecting food access. Such responses also suggest that resilient households are able to experience stability over time with respect to certain key outcomes, such as food access and asset ownership. This link between stability and resilience is consistent with an observation by Christophe Bené and colleagues (2014) in their review of literature on resilience and development. They state: "Capacity to maintain stability is as important as the ability to adapt, or to transform. . . . It is during periods of . . . stability that households and societies accumulate assets, specialize, create wealth and enhance human wellbeing" (Bené *et al.* 2014, p. 603).

In addition to independence from inter- and intra-annual variability in environmental and economic conditions, many participants suggested that resilient households also maintain independence from other community members. Such households are able to avoid relying upon other community members for wage labor opportunities or other assistance to secure subsistence resources, which often comes with significant obligations and costs. As one respondent put it,

"The one who is resilient . . . is the one who is independent . . . the one who does not need any help from the other people. He who stands by himself. He who faces a problem by himself."

The autonomy described in this response may also represent a form of stability, since resource-allocating social networks are often fluid and contested in the African context, among other places (Berry 1993). Indeed, Bernstein and Woodhouse (2001) suggest that such networks may constitute a source of instability similar to the environmental fluctuations so often highlighted in the resilience literature. They explain, "The 'fluid, dynamic, and ambiguous' nature of institutions/networks . . . provides a sociological counterpart to notions of ecological variability, complexity, and unpredictability of outcomes" (Bernstein and Woodhouse 2001, p. 301). This observation suggests that certain forms of social relations may in themselves represent a source of risk or uncertainty to those whose resources are intertwined in them.

Of course, the perception that resilience is associated with autonomy does not mean resilient households are socially isolated. Instead, respondents suggested that resilient households are positively engaged with other community members, providing support for others and leadership. Speaking of a hypothetical resilient household, one respondent explained,

> He can help other people with that false banana. Just calling over some of the poor and giving them that false banana. He says, "please take this one and when you pass this bad time you will pay me the next time." That is the one who is resilient.

Another respondent suggested that a resilient person was, "The one whose voice is heard by the community, and the one who hears the other's voice." These responses indicate that resilience is not simply a matter of more or fewer social networks, but of a particular type of social status or position within the community.

The responses discussed above suggest that among community members in Kejima, resilience is understood mainly as a matter of how much, how many, and the quality of social and economic resources a household owns or has access to, as well as the conditions, processes, and feelings that are made possible with these resources. In some respects, these accounts describe resilience in a highly circumscribed manner: resilient households are those that own or have access to large bundles of the resources that would be needed to reproduce currently existing agrarian livelihoods in a more sustainable manner, or resources and conditions that would result from more robust agricultural production. However, these subjective understandings of resilience also provide more nuanced insights into the temporal frame through which resilient households make decisions and perceive their interactions. As such, they highlight the tension faced by the ultra-poor between meeting drastic short-term demands relative to their resources and opportunities and, on the other hand, the need to acquire or accumulate resources to achieve long-term resilience as they understand it.

The overarching focus on food security that pervaded nearly all responses likely reflected the high levels of food insecurity in the area. That responses were often framed in negative terms (e.g. *not* subject to food insecurity, *not* fearing) is likely a result of widespread risk and deprivation in the community. Resilience was described vis-à-vis what was perceived as normal in this context. Even during years with relatively good climatic and agricultural conditions—including the one in which the interviews took place—residents are often concerned with recovering from previous shocks, preparing for what are seen as inevitable future shocks, or both. The negative framing of resilience stands in contrast to the definition of resilience used in the interviews, as well as that motivating the study more generally (Walsh-Dilley *et al.* 2013), which emphasized strength, meaningfulness, and other positive terms. Indeed, the framings observed in Kejima stand in contrast to many other academic definitions of the term that underline notions of capabilities, rather than merely freedom from deprivation (i.e. poverty reduction). This again highlights the tension observed among respondents in this community between meeting short-term needs associated with resource deprivation and addressing longer-term challenges and risks.

The nature of these responses may reflect a perceived (and likely real) lack of potential for structural change, which could range from the incremental (e.g. construction of irrigation systems) to the transformational (e.g. changes in land tenure, labor market restructuring). Responses may also reflect a lack of knowledge of what would be possible under other conditions. Indeed, the political situation in the region may stifle imaginations of structural change. Governing ideology promotes, if not romanticizes, the idea that national development is linked to smallholder farming based on a traditional package of agricultural inputs. Further, through political structures in each village and neighborhood, leaders may monitor households' agricultural practices, limiting the potential for basic experimentation, much less thoughts of dramatic change. Finally, these responses also reflect the limited ability of households in this community to shape the climatic and other environmental conditions that affect their agricultural production.

A more limited set of respondents did, however, describe resilience in more radical terms—as a condition contingent upon exit from Kejima. For these individuals, discussing resilience in such terms is necessary because they believe no one in their community is resilient. As one person put it, "We can't say that someone is resilient in our area because everybody needs help." Among this set of responses, nearly all described resilience in terms of non-agrarian livelihoods in towns and cities, where ecological changes and shocks pose far less direct threats than in Kejima. For instance, one respondent described her aspirations for her children saying, "I want them to become a government official in the future, to live a good life in the towns." There, respondents perceive that it is possible to have secure employment that is not contingent upon uncontrollable factors such as rainfall, patronage systems, and government-controlled aid. Respondents identified other amenities associated with urban living. For example, one person stated,

> I consider that a good life is having enough food in the house, enough clothes, and having enough capital for business, and moving from a rural area to the town, constructing a good house there and living there. That is what I consider a good life.

Respondents also suggested that social life is different in urban settings, with clear implications for households' economic standing and prospects. For example, one respondent described the difference between children who are and are not sent to school in the cities, saying,

> Because when they reach to grade seven, eight, their fathers send them to Hawassa or other big towns. Then they will stay there and they don't see anything good about marriage, about farming. Because that is the town, people are not interested in getting married earlier, they just continue their education there.

Towns and cities are also sites of government employment. These jobs were perhaps the most cited correlate of resilience—despite complaints about corruption and abuse of power by current officials—due largely to perceived good pay, stability, and power. The latter is important, given many respondents' powerlessness against environmental conditions and dependence upon sometimes-unreliable government safety net programs. In one example of the observed emphasis on government employment, a respondent said, "Even though the government is not looking after me, or acting in our interest, I want my children to go and work for the government. Because if they are there working for the government, they may recognize us here." Another said,

> If they become a government official they can have a good car, and . . . they will have a nice place to live in good towns. . . . And they have their salary on time, and they can also help us when they get that salary.

Finally, a number of respondents drew a link between resilience and access to transportation. Rather than framing motorbike or car ownership as a means of diversifying income within Kejima, however, these responses associated such assets with autonomy and the ability to exit. One respondent explained, "If a boy has a chance to get a driving license, he can go somewhere, he can drive and he can leave, and survive by himself."

Overall, this group of responses suggested that resilience is contingent upon exit from agrarian livelihoods. That is, resilience can only be achieved by leaving—or at least having access to—urban areas and sources of livelihood outside of the agricultural sector. Respondents emphasized the constraints, in terms both of livelihoods and ecology, as well as a lack of opportunity available in their community and similar agrarian contexts. The implication is that resilience at the individual or household level requires a fundamental change in the community or place in which it is embedded. In this particular case, remaining on the farm, as it were, is considered a dead end due to a lack of educational opportunities, demographic pressures, land fragmentation, and ecological volatility.

Resilience in ultra-poor contexts

Given that households in this community are highly resource constrained and dependent on rain-fed agriculture, discussions about resilience—"strength amidst challenges"—drew overwhelming attention to environment-related food crises, and other factors, such as land fragmentation, poor land quality, and asset poverty, that shape the impact of such crises. That is, concerns about food insecurity—in both the short and long term—and related economic deprivation appear to be so pervasive that notions of wellbeing or a good life are conflated with food security and meeting relatively basic material needs.

On the one hand, this predominant focus on basic material conditions suggests that most of the insights gained in this study could have been discussed using other already common concepts in the development discourse: food security (Barrett 2010), chronic poverty (Hulme and Shepherd 2003) or poverty traps (Barrett and Carter 2013), seasonality (Khandker 2012), and vulnerability (Watts and Bohle 1993), to name a few. However, asking respondents about resilience arguably provided community members with the opportunity to provide more holistic accounts and, in sum, a more diverse set of data than could have been gleaned with a focus on food security, poverty, or another more narrowly defined concept.

Understandings of resilience among households in Kejima also drew attention to households' capacity—or lack thereof—to deal with risk and change across multiple time horizons. Many respondents suggested that, given severe resource constraints in the community, few households are resilient there. The lack of resilience manifests itself in a short-term decision-making orientation and a longer-term outlook that anticipates, or fears, frequent shocks with uncontrollable results.

Indeed, many responses highlighted broader structural constraints to development and resilience-building. These constraints include climatic variability, land degradation, landholding fragmentation, weak or flawed markets, and limited off-farm livelihood opportunities. Discussion of these factors suggests that resilience is about much more than building individual or household resilience, but rather also requires asking about how these people or households come to be in such difficult positions. Why are markets in the community so sensitive to local climatic and agricultural dynamics? Why is rainfall increasingly erratic? These questions demand that scholars resist the tendency evident in some resilience thinking to assume, or at least imply, that shocks, stresses, and changes are exogenous or given. Such assumptions may be particularly tempting at the current time, when the political will to mitigate climate change appears to have diminished greatly, to be replaced by a discourse focused on adaptation.

Building resilience

As a coda to the discussions above, I also briefly consider how the notion of resilience has been operationalized in development planning in the community, and elsewhere in Ethiopia. One prominent example is Ethiopia's Productive Safety Net Program (PSNP), which was designed specifically to promote development in food insecure, high-poverty contexts. As one report describes it:

> The Government of Ethiopia, WFP [World Food Programme] and development partners work together to increase families' long-term resilience to food shortages. Established in 2005, PSNP is aimed at enabling the rural poor facing chronic food insecurity to resist shocks, create assets and become food self-sufficient.
>
> *(World Food Programme 2012)*

In exchange for manual labor on public works projects, PSNP beneficiaries receive predictable food and monetary transfers for a combined six months during the year. These resources are intended to provide a safety net for the worst-off households in the community by filling production–consumption gaps during years with poor agricultural production, and thereby diminishing the need to engage in short-term coping strategies with long-term negative consequences. And, in years with good agricultural production, PSNP presumably helps these households accumulate savings or invest in productive activities, such as improved seed and fertilizer purchases and children's education. The public works requirement is intended to mobilize community labor to improve public goods that may enhance productivity across the community, such as roads or erosion-mitigating forests.

Considered in relation to how participants from Kejima described resilience, this intervention's operationalization of the concept rightly focuses on basic material resources and productive assets—factors emphasized among nearly all respondents. Furthermore, it attempts to lessen the commonly described tension between meeting households' short-term needs and engaging in activities to increase their ability to withstand future stresses and changes. As the WFP describes it, the program aims to help households "avoid depleting their productive assets while attempting to meet their basic food requirements" (World Food Programme 2012).

On the other hand, the program's focus on developing resilience to household food shortages appears to take those seasonal and, in some cases, annual shortages as a given. Rather than interrogate the structural conditions that create such deficits in the first place—as many respondents' accounts alluded to—the program seeks to attenuate the negative household-level consequences of systematic and ecological conditions (and often does so very successfully). This micro-level focus is not unique, but rather ubiquitous across contemporary development practices, which tend to draw upon the seemingly apolitical insights of microeconomics. This is likely a question of both the epistemology upon which contemporary development interventions rest, and the practical demands that international non- and inter-governmental organizations face when operating interventions in foreign, often undemocratic countries where ideas of structural change may be unwelcome.

Conclusion

This chapter has described subjective understandings of resilience among residents of a community in southern Ethiopia. It also considered the implications of using this term as a mobilizing concept for research and practice in a highly resource-constrained context, where notions of wellbeing are often conflated with simply securing basic resources. The evidence considered in this chapter suggests that understandings of resilience among ultra-poor households capture a tension between meeting short-term subsistence needs and taking actions that contribute to building resilience against future shocks and stresses. Responses also underlined the need to think beyond resilience-building at the individual or household level, and consider the structural conditions that both limit the efficacy of micro-level interventions and contribute to the shocks and stresses that resilience is ostensibly to be built against. The need to think critically about the spatial and temporal scales at which resilience is enhanced or constrained was also manifest in a brief analysis of a development intervention taking place in Kejima. This intervention addresses a number of the household-level needs identified by respondents from the community, but fails to address major structural constraints and sources of risk, likely reflecting both epistemic positions and practical concerns among development practitioners. While the broadly defined nature of resilience makes sometimes-problematic interpretations and operationalizations of the concept possible, it also holds the potential to identify important tensions in development thinking and practice.

Acknowledgments

This chapter was revised and updated from Brian Thiede (2016) "Resilience and development among ultra-poor households in rural Ethiopia," *Resilience*, vol. 4, no. 1, 1–13. DOI: 10.1080/ 21693293.2015.1094166. The research this study draws upon was supported by Oxfam America, the Atkinson Center for a Sustainable Future at Cornell University, CARE-Ethiopia, the Rural Sociological Society, the Cornell University Graduate School, and the Louisiana Board of Regents through the Board of Regents Support Fund. A previous version of this paper was presented at the Cornell Workshop on Resilience and Development on October 24, 2014 in Ithaca, New York. Many thanks to Marygold Walsh-Dilley, Sara Keene, and Hyojung Kim for their constructive comments on drafts of this paper. All substantive and editorial errors or shortcomings are mine alone.

Note

1 According to the community census, the average household in Kejima owned the equivalent of 1.97 Tropical Livestock Units (TLUs) of livestock. The most recent analysis of households in the widely used Ethiopian Rural Household Survey (Van Campenhout and Dercon 2012) found that the average household in those communities owned 4.6 TLUs of livestock.

References

ACSF-Oxfam (2013) *Researcher Reference Guide*, June, ACSF-Oxfam, viewed January 14, 2016, at: www. acsf.cornell.edu/Assets/ACSF/docs/collaborations/oxfam/Researcher%20Reference%20Guide.pdf.

Adger, W. N. (2000) Social and Ecological Resilience: Are They Related? *Progress in Human Geography*, vol. 24, 347–64.

Barrett, C. B. (2010) Measuring Food Insecurity. *Science*, vol. 327, 825–8.

Barrett, C. B. and Carter, M. R. (2013) The Economics of Poverty Traps and Persistent Poverty: Empirical and Policy Implications. *Journal of Development Studies*, vol. 49, 976–90.

Barrett, C. B. and Constas, M. A. (2014) Toward a Theory of Resilience for International Development Applications. *Proceedings of the National Academy of Sciences*, vol. 111, 14625–30.

Bené, C., Newsham, A., Davies, M., Ulrichs, M., and Godfrey-Wood, R. (2014) Resilience, Poverty, and Development. *Journal of International Development*, vol. 26, 598–623.

Bernstein, H. and Woodhouse, P. (2001) Telling Environmental Change Like It Is? Reflections on a Study in Sub-Saharan Africa. *Journal of Agrarian Change*, vol. 1, 283–324.

Berry, S. (1993). *No Condition is Permanent: Social Dynamics of Agrarian Change in Sub-Saharan Africa*, University of Wisconsin Press, Madison, WI.

Brown, K. and Westaway, E. (2011) Agency, Capacity, and Resilience to Environmental Change: Lessons from Human Development, Well-Being, and Disasters. *The Annual Review of Environment and Resources*, vol. 36, 321–42.

Davidson, D. J. (2010) 'The Applicability of the Concept of Resilience to Social Systems: Some Sources of Optimism and Nagging Doubts'. *Society and Natural Resources*, vol. 23, 1135–49.

Ellis, F. (1998) Household Strategies and Rural Livelihood Diversification. *Journal of Development Studies*, vol. 35, no. 1, 1–38.

FEWSNET (2011) *Ethiopia Food Security Outlook Update: Below-Average February to May Rains Increase Food Security Concerns*, May/June, FEWSNET, viewed September 25, 2013, at: www.fews.net/sites/default/files/documents/reports/ethiopia_FSOU_0506_2011.pdf.

Folke, C., Carpenter, S. B., Walker, B., Scheffer, M., Chapin, T., and Rockström, J. (2010) Resilience Thinking: Integrating Resilience: Adaptability and Transformability. *Ecology and Society*, vol. 15, 20–8.

Frankenberger, T. R., Constas, M. A., Nelson, S., and Starr, L. (2014). *Nongovernmental Organizations' Approaches to Resilience Programming*, 2020 Conference Brief no. 7, International Food Policy Research Institute, Washington, DC.

Hulme, D. and Shepherd, A. (2003) Conceptualizing Chronic Poverty. *World Development*, vol. 31, 403–23.

Khandker, S. R. (2012) Seasonality of Income and Poverty in Bangladesh. *Journal of Development Economics*, vol. 97, 244–56.

Rahmato, D. (1994) Land Policy in Ethiopia at the Crossroads: Proceedings of the Workshop of Land Tenure and Land Policy. *Proceedings of the Second Workshop on the Land Tenure Project,* Addis Ababa, Ethiopia.

USAID (2012) *Building Resilience to Recurrent Crisis: USAID Policy and Program Guidance*, U.S. Agency for International Development (USAID), Washington, DC.

Van Campenhout, B. and Dercon, S. (2012) *Nonlinear Dynamics of Livestock Assets: Evidence from Ethiopia*, IFPRI discussion Paper no. 1215, International Food Policy Research Institute (IFPRI), Washington, DC.

Walsh-Dilley, M., Wolford, W., and McCarthy, J. (2013) 'Rights for Resilience: Bringing Power, Rights, and Agency into the Resilience Framework', Unpublished Manuscript, Cornell University, Ithaca, NY.

Watts, M. J. and Bohle, H. G. (1993) The Space of Vulnerability: The Causal Structure of Hunger and Famine. *Progress in Human Geography*, vol. 17, 43–67.

World Food Programme (2012) *Ethiopia: Productive Safety Net Program*, World Food Programme, viewed September 25, 2013, at: www.wfp.org/sites/default/files/PSNP%20Factsheet.pdf.

28

DEVELOPING RESILIENCE

A retreat from grand planning

Søren Vester Haldrup and Frederik Rosén

Introduction

This chapter examines the rise of resilience as a concept in international development. It links the resilience concept to changing ideas of capacity and argues that the entwined concepts of resilience and capacity increasingly frame the ways Western donors address societal fragility in the Global South. The study argues that 'the turn to resilience' indicates a new pragmatism and a retreat from grand planning as a response to a crisis in the international community's approach to handling fragility. Increasingly, Western donors take on the role of facilitators: responsibility for implementation and project success – in the name of local ownership and bottom-up approaches – is put on to local partners and the recipient state. Triangularly organised South–South cooperation on 'coaching and mentoring for capacity' is highlighted as a mode whereby donors attempt to create resilience and, it is argued, this type of programming encapsulates in a paradigmatic manner key features of, and challenges posed by, this agenda.

In a 2012 speech, the United Nations Development Program's (UNDP) Administrator, Helen Clark, argued that resilience must be put 'at the heart of the development agenda' (Clark 2012). Her statement expresses well how the concept of resilience has grown into an organising concept for international development. This chapter argues that the 'turn to resilience' marks an important shift in how societal fragility in the Global South is viewed and addressed. The shift is claimed to be a more 'realistic' approach, based on a 'lessons learned' view of fragility and development. This 'realism' reflects a move away from the era where Western democracies believed that 'failed' or 'fragile' states could be fixed by grand and ambitious state-building projects. The financial and political costs of such engagement, and their limited success, induced Western states to disengage from such direct involvement. Putting resilience at the heart of the development agenda paves the way for a more pragmatic approach to fragility, where ambitions are downscaled, and goals of installing Western-like governance institutions are substituted by a focus on realisable 'best fit' and 'achieveable' solutions. A management of local volatilities now seems to be a 'good enough' goal.

As the idealism of the good governance era fades, pragmatism has emerged both as a necessity, to contextualise 'best fit' solutions, and as an excuse to compromise old ideals. The shift from good governance to resilience and concurrent calls for local ownership, contextualisation, 'bottom-up' and 'inside-out' approaches, demand Western states not to entirely disengage but to change donor modality towards discrete adaptive and iterative programmes owned by the receiver state. By shifting the lead to the Global South, the responsibility for failure and success also shifts. The responsibility of the donor is now primarily one of choosing the right implementing partner.

To see how the concept of resilience signals a 'realism' and a retreat from grand planning, as well as offering a legitimate path for disengagement, it is necessary to understand how the concept of capacity provides the lens through which fragility and resilience are perceived. The concept of resilience rests centrally on a notion of capacity – the capacity to resist or recover from crisis and conflict. The overall argument of this chapter is that what we suggest calling the 'resilience–capacity paradigm' of current development aid recasts the role of the Western state from builder to facilitator; and it hands over the ultimate responsibility to those who are facilitated for, thus offering a convenient exit from direct donor responsibility. By donor we mean a state, which allocates development aid to another country or engages directly in development or development-related activities. Responsibility could be vis-à-vis the receiver state, the donor state's political base at home or towards the international community at large. Responsibility issues could typically be about failure in project design and management, wasted finances or negative side effects. The retreat from responsibility is to be understood as the framing of development aid by the entwined concepts of resilience and capacity, which imply lower ambitions and place much greater responsibility for project implementation on local actors.

To make this argument, we first outline the rise of resilience in international development discourse. The following sections investigate the intimate connection between resilience and capacity, and clarify how 'lessons learned' have changed our concept of capacity in international development and how it has become a lens for appreciating resilience. A subsequent section situates the emergence of resilience against the backdrop of an increasing unwillingness on behalf of Western donors to intervene due to financial and political costs. Following this, the chapter explores how triangularly organised South–South cooperation on 'coaching and mentoring for capacity' can be viewed as one example of how the resilience–capacity paradigm translates into concrete programming. In essence, triangularly organised South–South cooperation on 'coaching and mentoring for capacity' embodies both a 'realism', with regard to how capacity may be developed, as well as the resilience discourse's pragmatism and retreat from grand projects and responsibility. We will argue that the turn to coaching and mentoring epitomises key aspects of the resilience–capacity paradigm, and that its exploration can help us gain a greater understanding of some of the practical and political challenges this paradigm confronts us with. Following this, a concluding section discusses some of the practical challenges posed by resilience thinking.

The turn to resilience

Main protagonists of the international development agenda, such as the UN, the World Bank, the Organisation for Economic Co-operation and Development's Development Assistance Committee (OECD/DAC) and the UK Department for International Development (DFID), have increasingly adopted the concepts of fragility and resilience as a starting point for addressing governance deficits in the Global South. Derived from the Latin *resilire* meaning 'to rebound, to recoil', the idea of the attribute 'resilience' has been developed in a number of different disciplines (van Breda 2001). In the 1970s, for instance, resilience appeared as a popular notion in psychology (Garmezy 1973, p. 163). The field of ecology has also used it as a key concept. In addition, resilience thinking has been popular in dealing with issues, such as disaster planning and organisational management, health and community resilience (Martin-Breen and Anderies 2011; Caruana *et al.* 2010; Abesamis *et al.* 2006; Chandra *et al.* 2011).

The concept of resilience and the key elements of resilience thinking found their way into international development during the mid-2000s. In early 2005, the influential OECD/DAC publication *Principles for Good International Engagement in Fragile States and Situations* (2007), expressing the attitude of some 25 core states (with the World Bank, the International Monetary Fund (IMF) and UNDP participating as observers), was drafted at the Senior Level Forum on Development Effectiveness in Fragile States. The publication emphasised among other things the need for international actors to take the context as the starting point when engaging with fragile states. The same year, more than 100 signatories endorsed the Paris Declaration on Aid Effectiveness at the Paris High Level Forum on Aid Effectiveness (organised by the OECD). Ownership, alignment and harmonisation were amongst the principles endorsed in the declaration.

The principles found in the Paris Declaration, along with the problem of unrealistic expectations, featured prominently in the early 2005 United Nations Development Group and World Bank publication on Transitional Results Matrices (World Bank and United Nations Development Group 2005). Between 2007 and 2008 the OECD/DAC published a number of documents on state resilience and how to enhance it (OECD/DAC 2007; OECD/DAC 2008a; OECD/DAC 2008b). In 2008 the Accra Agenda for Action was endorsed at the Third High Level Forum on Aid Effectiveness. The Agenda was designed to strengthen and deepen implementation of the Paris Declaration and it focused on issues such as ownership, inclusive partnerships and capacity development. The Paris Declaration and the Accra Agenda both highlighted a change among donors in their approaches to development towards more emphasis on context and ownership and less on 'one-size-fits-all' grand planning.

The World Bank also embraced the notion of state resilience. Before 2009, the word resilience did not effectively feature in any World Development Reports. Resilience, however, became a key concept in the Bank's 2010 and 2011 reports. The 2011 report had an overall focus on institutional resilience and its impact on violent conflict. A number of bilateral donors have also become fond of the concept of resilience in the context of state-building. In 2011, the United States Agency for International Development (USAID) endorsed the OECD–DAC's guidance on state-building, as did the UK DFID, highlighting a general change in the approach to state-building (United States Agency for International Development 2011, p. 2). Altogether, during the last decade, the agenda-setting states and fora of international development aid have all renegotiated and rearticulated their approach to the Global South through the conceptual framework of resilience.

Resilience in the global development agenda

In this agenda, resilience is mostly conceptualised as the opposite of fragility. However, there is little agreement on what exactly constitutes state fragility and how it is to be measured (van Overbeek *et al.* 2009, p. 6; Japan International Cooperation Agency 2008, pp. iv–v). Most definitions include elements, such as low income (Ikpe 2007), the inability of state institutions to provide basic services and a lack of human security. According to the OECD/DAC's influential definition (van Overbeek *et al.* 2009, p. 7), state fragility is present 'when state structures lack political will and/or capacity to provide the basic functions needed for poverty reduction, development and to safeguard the security and human rights of their populations' (OECD/DAC 2007, p. 2).

Resilience is defined by the OECD/DAC as 'a feature of states and more precisely social contracts . . . defined . . . as the ability to cope with changes in capacity, effectiveness or legitimacy'. A resilient state must, it is believed, 'be able to effectively deliver functions that match the expectations of societal groups' (OECD/DAC 2008b, p. 2). It is clear that the use of the two concepts in the international development agenda is closely connected. The 2008a OECD/DAC publication summed up the relationship as follows:

> fragility arises primarily from weaknesses in the dynamic political process through which citizens' expectations of the state and state expectations of citizens are reconciled and brought into equilibrium with the state's capacity to deliver services. Reaching equilibrium in this negotiation over the social contract is the critical if not sole determinant of resilience, and disequilibrium the determinant of fragility.
>
> *(OECD/DAC 2008a, pp. 7, 17)*

The quote expresses the belief that institutional capacity not only depends on formal design but also on the social context within which institutions function. Resilience is not about reaching Western 'standards' of governance. Instead it must take the local context as its point of departure. This leads the OECD/DAC to conclude that: 'whether and to what degree . . . [a population's] expectations entail poverty reduction, development, security or human rights will depend on historical, cultural and other factors that shape state–society relations in specific contexts' (OECD/DAC 2008b, p. 16).

This line of thought automatically provides donor countries with a more indirect role in their engagement in fragile states. The once-popular good governance approach to core state functions is now seen as potentially problematic, since it may generate over-ambitious reform agendas and inappropriate institutional constructs. Donors instead emphasise the need for international actors to align their approaches with local policies and contexts and to coordinate, prioritise and sequence their efforts through international organisations and coordination units on the ground.

Capacity

Capacity and resilience may be viewed as interlinked concepts, which frame the current development agenda's approach to governance deficits in the Global South. Furthermore, the concept of resilience must be understood as intimately connected to the debates about capacity development in international development. Modern approaches to capacity date as far back as the immediate post-World War II period, but the idea of capacity can be traced even further back in the context of the Great Power colonial politics of the late nineteenth century. The basic assumption in international development, as the discipline appeared during the middle of the twentieth century, was that developing countries lacked important skills and abilities and that these could be built by injecting skills and know-how. This line of thought had been bolstered by the Marshall Plan's successful and swift transfer of capital and technical expertise and later by the impressive rise of the East Asian Tigers (Fukuda-Parr *et al.* 2002, p. 3). Consequently, development aid policies in the 1960s were generally conceptualised as 'technical assistance' programmes and, in the 1970s, as 'technical cooperation' (to connote a more equal relationship between donor and recipient). Technical cooperation projects focused, as the name implies, primarily on filling gaps by transferring technical know-how. Typical activities included the dispatching of foreign consultants on short-term contracts, the provision of equipment and supplies and the training of developing country personnel in North America and Europe (Whyte 2004, p. 27).

In the late 1980s and early 1990s, 'capacity-building' emerged as an important buzzword in development aid and was widely recognised as one of its primary goals. The 1991 UN Commission on Sustainable Development, the 1992 Agenda 21 action plan and the 1992 United

Nations Conference on Environment and Development all express this (Kenny and Clarke 2010). Underlying the approach to capacity – and development in general – was the assumption that organisational and individual performance could be enhanced by creating Western-style organisations and administrative structures. Furthermore, it was assumed that individual performance improves when a particular set of skills and technologies are transferred through training activities (Hilderbrand and Grindle 1997, pp. 31–33). This notion is found in Agenda 21, where it is noted that: 'technical cooperation, including that related to technology transfer and know-how, encompasses the whole range of activities to develop or strengthen individual and group capacities and capabilities' (UNEP n.d.). Although the 'country's own strategies and priorities' are noted as important, a range of pre-specified skills are emphasised as key if the recipient country is to reach the goals pre-determined by international donors. This approach aimed at producing institutions, practices and modes of knowledge to 'change the rules of the game', transform the incentives and consequently induce people to act in certain ways (Kahn 1995, p. 72). The yardsticks of capacity and development in this period were Western standards for 'good governance' and 'best practice'.

During the early 1990s, the technical cooperation programmes were the subject of a number of evaluations. The 1991 OECD/DAC report, *Principles for New Orientations in Technical Cooperation*, called for changes in existing practices. Simultaneously, the UNDP embarked upon a review of technical cooperation in Africa. The UNDP report, *Rethinking Technical Cooperation: Reforms for Capacity Building in Africa*, was published in 1993. The approach to capacity in these studies had a narrow focus on one-way technical skills enhancement. The 1993 publication effectively presented proposals on how to 'deliver the existing package more effectively' (UNDP 1993), implying that capacity-building programmes could be designed externally. Efforts to organise 'consultation with user and beneficiary groups', the report noted, should (only) be made 'whenever possible and relevant' (OECD/DAC 1991, p. 7). This thinking translated into grand projects inspired by Western standards of governance. In such projects, Western donors were both the key architects and implementers.

The top-down approach to capacity underwent revision in the early 2000s. The 2001 UNDP project 'Reforming Technical Cooperation for Capacity Development' sought to revise the notion of capacity, and it emphasised concepts such as ownership and sustainability as well as the importance of recipient initiative and local capacity. The book *Capacity for Development, New Solutions to Old Problems*, published by the UNDP in 2002 (Fukuda-Parr et al. 2002) also exemplified the changing approach to capacity. This book, however, still exhibited an understanding of capacity along quite narrow technical lines. During the early 2000s, almost a quarter of Overseas Development Assistance still went to capacity building initiatives mainly through technical assistance (Whyte 2004, p. 13). Interventions in the early 2000s also displayed many of the characteristics of the top-down approach to capacity. Iraq constitutes a prominent example. This intervention was an exercise in external state-building and 'by its very nature, and despite claims to the contrary', Toby Dodge notes, 'external state-building is bound to be "top-down", driven by dynamics, personnel and ideologies that have their origins completely outside the society they are operating in' (Dodge 2006). The Iraq intervention was an example of the type of grand planning that characterised the good governance era – a type of planning that donors slowly began to move away from.

Capacity development and resilience

Around the mid-2000s, a number of important donors began to take more serious steps away from the established top-down approaches. At this point, development as well as state-, peace- and capacity-building had come to be viewed as highly overlapping activities. Local ownership, context and awareness of recipient communities' needs were emphasised as key features of how to approach the question of capacity more effectively. Thus in 2002, the OECD/DAC asked the European Centre for Development Policy Management to carry out a study of developing countries' successes with building capacity and improving performance. Following the trend of the period, the study ended up focusing on the endogenous process of capacity development – what Derick W. Brinkerhoff describes as 'the process of change from the perspective of those undergoing the change'. Capacity was seen as 'an endogenous process that concerns what goes on in a particular country concerning the creation and/or reinforcement of each of the capabilities, apart from whatever donors do' (Brinkerhoff 2007, p. 67).

The emerging ideas of capacity development differed markedly from the way in which donors had previously conceptualised and approached capacity. Capacity-building had until then been a top-down, externally designed and controlled activity aimed at enhancing externally generated and defined technical skills and know-how. In contrast, approaches to capacity development adhered to a focus on nurturing local, indigenous and already existing practices and capacities. They emphasised the importance of country-led and country-owned processes. Enhanced governance capacity – profound and rooted changes in attitudes, behaviour and professional skills – was believed to be obtained only by engaging closely with the motivation, support and aspirations of people within the recipient country (Brinkerhoff 2007). In that way, capacity became understood as intimately connected to what country actors believed and did. From this perspective, outside actors should only play a supporting role in developing and reinforcing capacity. And grand projects in third world countries conceived and led by external actors were increasingly seen as inappropriate, artificial, inauthentic and indeed unsustainable and ineffective.

Capacity development is a process-oriented conception. It implies the facilitation of long-term learning through practice rather than quick impact results. An example that has been used to illustrate this is the abolition of the use of parallel implementation units and the integration of reform teams directly into target organisations in the 2000–2008 Public Service Reform Programme in Tanzania (Brinkerhoff and Morgan 2010; Morgan, Baser and Morin 2010). In this particular case, the shift from the conventional approach to capacity towards capacity development took place in the mid-2000s (Brinkerhoff and Morgan 2010, p. 6). The conceptual change from 'building to developing' is also apparent in the 2008 publication *Capacity Development: Practice Note* (UNDP 2008a). In 2002, the UNDP still employed a capacity-building approach to development though – confusingly – the term 'capacity development' was sometimes used. By 2008 this had changed. The UNDP now explicitly stated that it preferred to use the concept of 'capacity development' rather than 'capacity building' (UNDP 2008a). The conceptual change also manifested itself in project descriptions. A UNDP capacity enhancement project in Kosovo is a case in point. Between 2004 and 2008 the name of this project was Capacity Building Facility for Kosovo. After 2008 the project changed name to Capacity Development Facility (UNDP 2004; UNDP 2008b); a similar change happened with the UNDP CAP project in Afghanistan (Central Statistics Organisation and UNDP 2011, p. 10).

This change in the notion of capacity may seem like a subtle change in wording, but it reflects a major discursive shift in the perceptions and policy practices of major international development agents, such as the OECD/DAC, the UN, DFID, USAID and World Bank. Importantly, the analysis of the 'transformation' of capacity approaches allows us to reflect more fully on the implications of the new focus on resilience. By 2013, all these major international policy actors had increasingly discarded the workability of top-down designs of capacity building in fragile states. The somewhat alchemistic quest for a general and quick fix to fragile states was replaced by an emphasis on contextualised long-term engagement. It is now the policy consensus that responsive and functioning state institutions need to grow out of the local political, social and cultural context – with all the expectations, beliefs, practices and capacities that exist within it. Concepts of local ownership, context and existing practices underpin current ideas about both capacity development and resilience.

Context has become everything, enabling development, state- and peace-building to merge with issues of fragility and resilience. Capacity is now often the lens through which resilience is viewed and measured and capacity development has emerged as the way to achieve resilience. This policy turn may appease some critics of Western 'neo-colonialism', because it reallocates decision-making to the Global South. Nevertheless, it must be acknowledged that the rollback of grand plans and sweeping ambitions also reflects a pragmatic realism and a handover of ownership over failure to the receiver states and local actors. It involves a shift in responsibility from the Western states to the Global South and it may imply a politics of disengagement rather than an increasing recognition of the rights and agency of the Global South.

Unwillingness

The end of the Cold War meant an end to the superpowers' rivalry-based assistance to many third world countries and thus the beginning of an era of increased uncertainty and instability for these countries. During this period, state weakness or collapse was often framed in the context of humanitarian issues. Ten years later, the 'war against terrorism' reframed instability as a matter of global security (Ikpe 2007). Fragile or failed states were now viewed as potential safe havens for terrorist groups, drugs cartels and weapons dealers and thus a major source of global insecurity (Yannis 2002). The international development agenda became increasingly securitised. The notion that development and security were entwined came to underpin the approach of major international development actors, such as the UN, the World Bank, the OECD/DAC, DFID and USAID. In 2009, for instance, one-third of all aid to developing countries went to states labelled as 'fragile', and the 2011 World Development Report emphasised how 'insecurity . . . has become a primary development challenge of our time. One-and-a-half-billion people live in areas affected by fragility, conflict, or large-scale, organised criminal violence.' (World Bank 2011, p. 1).

Before the rise of the resilience agenda, the link between security issues and fragile states provoked a number of interventions situated within the good governance paradigm. The invasions in Afghanistan and Iraq were both big ambitious projects that aimed at building states on the model of a Western ideal type. These engagements have been extremely costly. According to the 'Costs of War', a research project at Brown University's Watson Institute for International Studies, the economic costs of the Afghanistan, Pakistan and Iraq wars range between 3.2 and 4 trillion US dollars (Costs of War 2015). To this figure one needs to add non-economic costs. These interventions did not constitute the average engagement in fragile contexts, but their costs – and limited success – have had an immense impact in terms of how Western donors understand their involvement in fragile states. Since the latter part of the 2000s, such donors have therefore been hesitant towards extensive involvement. Other previous engagements have also contributed to the engagement fatigue. The post-conflict cases of Somalia and Kosovo are cases in point.

Altogether, a lack of success combined with financial burdens has made Western states reluctant towards involvement in grand state-building projects. The financial crisis from 2008 onwards only rolled back ambitions further. The approach now stresses modesty, 'good enough governance', resilience and stability. This has led to more focus on 'value for money' and increased involvement through regional and international organisations, such as the African

Union and the UN (Chandler 2010, pp. 141–142) as well as multilateral donor trust funds, and it has also resulted in aid increasingly being channelled through and aligned with local government policies (Japan International Cooperation Agency 2008). The stated aim is now to ground institutions and capacities nationally and to facilitate an image of service delivery that can add legitimacy to local political regimes.

It should also be noted that the multilateral donor modalities have weakened and undermined direct relations of association between donor and implementer. Consequently, the responsibility for failure shifts in the direction of recipient states or merely vanishes in the haze of multilateralism. The package of resilience, capacity development and multilateralism offers a convenient exit in the context of a growing unwillingness to bear the burden and responsibility of direct involvement: even if one would, in principle, still be willing to embark on another big state-building project, the ideas of local ownership, contextualisation, bottom-up and inside-out approaches associated with the 'resilience–capacity paradigm' more than excuse any reluctance.

In summary, the rise of the concept of resilience marks how the emphasis of development aid has gradually shifted from ambitious and comprehensive interventions, with the purpose of building Western-like state institutions, towards helping fragile states, societies and regions develop the capacity to be 'resilient'. Rather than assuming the universal applicability of best practice standards, focus is increasingly being turned towards context, local needs, local capacity, coordination, alignment and facilitation. Yet the turn to resilience is more than anything else a symptom of a retreat from ambitious grand projects by the West, a retreat that at its core holds pragmatism – not idealism – and a desire to escape responsibility.

Coaching and mentoring

The notion of triangular South–South cooperation has mostly been used by policymakers and academics to describe the exchange of resources, technology and knowledge between less-developed countries in the Global South. It describes a set-up where the UN, another international organisation or a single donor, funds, instigates, facilitates or supports cooperation between two countries of the Global South. With the growing focus on the importance of motivating cooperation among developing countries, the concept of triangular South–South cooperation has become a central concept. Over the last years, triangular South–South cooperation has occupied an increasingly prominent role in the international state- and peace-building community and their policy documents, including The UN Secretary General's 2011 report on South–South cooperation, the Bogota statement, the G7 agenda and the UN civilian capacity review (UNGA/A/66/229). In this context, triangularly organised South–South cooperation on capacity development has emerged as a model for creating resilience. This attitude was endorsed by the 2013 United Nations Security Council Resolution 2086 on multidimensional peacekeeping, which encourages the use of civilian expertise for peace-building in the immediate aftermath of conflict, including from countries with relevant experience in post-conflict peace-building or democratic transition (UNSC 2013, p. 10). Countries emerging from conflict are today urged to request specialised capacity-building from countries with cultural, linguistic and administrative resemblances that have undergone similar transitions.

South–South organised capacity development ties perfectly into the resilience–capacity agenda. It offers cheap – compared with the sourcing of Western consultants – and instant capacity gains due to the influx of skilled people from the region into the targeted state branches and it facilitates a process of long-term capacity development/resilience building. At the same time, it accommodates calls for local ownership and bottom-up approaches. The focus is not so much on building governance institutions, but on making whatever structures that do exist resilient through propping up the individual capacities of the people running them. Focus lies on the attitudes and behaviour of the civil servants inhabiting the offices. As the UNDP Concept Paper for the Capacity Building Facility in Kosovo notes:

> Soft skills differ from 'hard' technical skills by stressing the nurturing of creativity, initiative, courage, sound judgement and other behavioural norms necessary to lead and leverage public resources for the public good. . . . They are skills that are difficult to teach in the classroom and normally require intimate one-on-one exchanges between a mentor and the beneficiary.
>
> *(UNDP 2004)*

In this regard, triangularly organised South–South cooperation on 'coaching and mentoring for capacity' can be viewed as a concrete example of how donors translate the notions of resilience and capacity development into programming. But again, it also, due to the implied notions of facilitation, help-to-self-help and local ownership, implies a transfer of the ultimate responsibility for success to the receiver. A teacher may be blamed for not teaching properly and thus not capturing the attention of the students. But the general notions of coaching and mentoring build on the idea of the willingness and demands of the coachee/mentee. If such willingness is lacking, success will not happen, no matter the instructiveness of the coach or mentor. In this way, the turn to coaching and mentoring in international development illustrates an approach where responsibility for success at the bottom line rests with the recipient – far away from Western donors.

Coaching and mentoring and the resilience–capacity paradigm

Looking at the workings and theoretical perspectives of this specific 'tool' makes it easier to come to terms with the nature of the resilience-based approach to state fragility and the logic underpinning it. Recent management literature differentiates between coaching and mentoring (Parsloe and Wray 2000; Ives 2008). No significant differentiation is, however, really made between the two concepts in the context of capacity development in fragile states. It is a rather general conception of coaching and mentoring that can be seen to set the agenda for its practice in this area.

Coaching and mentoring implies the idea of long-term and fairly intimate person-to-person relationships. Typically, the coachee/mentee is seen to develop skills, personality attributes and knowledge of their own capabilities, career socialisation and interpersonal skills by being under an informal and friendship-like personal guidance of the coach/mentor – as opposed to more prescribed forms of teaching and supervision. The basic purpose of coaching/mentoring is to unlock existing human potential (Parsloe and Wray 2000; Ives 2008). It suggests help-to-self-help rather than imposed policies. In state-and peace-building, coaching and mentoring represent an approach that takes the individual rather than institutions as the entry point for reform. It implies working on the contextualised individual's personal capabilities and dispositions as the primary instigator of organisational and societal change. These features parallel a general move towards decentralisation and embeddedness in current theorising of capacity and resilience.

Coaching and mentoring does, in this way, not implement; it facilitates. Coaching and mentoring, as practised in state-building (Rosén and Haldrup 2013, p. 46; da Costa *et al.* 2013), presents itself as an inherently process-oriented approach. Key is the idea that the role of the coach/mentor is not that of a 'doer' of line functions. Coaches are supposed to facilitate their coachees or mentees in a process of learning-by-doing. This gives the approach a long-term perspective in line with current ideas about capacity and resilience development because the coachees' personal development and future capacity takes precedence over short-term organisational outputs. The job of the coaches/mentors in settings such as Kosovo (Capacity Building Facility for Kosovo), Afghanistan (The National Institution Building Project) and South Sudan (Initiative for Capacity Enhancement in South Sudan) has therefore been to work with their counterparts to identify existing capabilities and needs and to address these in a nimble and demand-driven manner.

The focus is not on how to create Western-like institutional constructs. In fact, in this type of project, there seldom are clear pre-specified objectives. Grand planning has been replaced by a pragmatic *ad hoc* approach, where the coach works with and for whatever is there in the first place. It implies a form of capacity development, focusing on practical experience through learning-by-doing, and applies a flexible approach, which can address needs and challenges as they emerge – all in line with the resilience agenda's call for plasticity and response enhancement. In accordance with the turn towards capacity development and resilience thinking (the context), existing capacities and local needs are believed to constitute the starting points of coaching and mentoring. The South–South component of these programmes aims at not only utilising cultural similitudes and scaling down project costs, but also at knitting together regional governance structures through the exchange of civil servants as a way of strengthening overall regional resilience. For instance, in the context of the IGAD Initiative in South Sudan, there is a strong sense of regionalism surrounding the initiative.

Conclusion

This chapter has argued that the concept of resilience, with its implied notions of capacity, expresses a 'realism' or a political pragmatism that allows a retreat from ambitious grand state-building projects. Less direct engagement, good enough governance, ownership and context are expressions of a pragmatism born out of a recognition that big ambitious projects so far have not delivered sufficiently, that such projects are way too expensive, and that they ascribe too much responsibility to donors as implementers. The turn to South–South organised coaching and mentoring, we have argued, embodies and evinces the broader move towards a focus on resilience and capacity development.

The shifts in programming following the rise of the resilience–capacity paradigm pose a number of practical challenges. Essentially, resilience thinking – and, in extension, the ethos and practical dynamics of coaching and mentoring – moves project governance away from pre-arranged organisational planning towards decentralised, process-oriented support for vaguely formulated objectives, such as individual development and good 'twin' relations. Such programmes are difficult to accommodate within the development world's conventional frames of project management, which primarily utilise pre-specified implementation schedules and systems of benchmarks and quantitative indicators for monitoring and evaluation. This model is, not least, important for engaging with donors, who usually demand fairly strict reports on what their money has been used for and whether objectives have been met.

Iterative approaches resist by their very nature such forms of project governance. Instead, they stress relational capacities over fixed objectives because project needs and goals have to materialise from the process itself. On a practical level, it is difficult to evaluate such programmes due to the lack of clearly observable and measurable results. How do you, for instance, measure and track personal development? Can you do it in accordance with a pre-defined work plan? How do you measure the success of facilitation? Evaluation is possible but it calls for methods utilising much more qualitative approaches than those usually employed by conventional aid programmes.

New approaches to programming, such as problem-driven iterative adaption attempt to address some of these questions. Implied in this challenge is the broader task of developing adequate concepts of and practical solutions for fragility, resilience and capacity.

References

Abesamis, N.P., Corrigan, C., Drew, M., Campbell, S. and Samonte, G. (2006) Social Resilience: A Literature Review on Building Resilience into Human Marine Communities in and Around MPA Networks. *MPA Networks Learning Partnership.*

Brinkerhoff, D.W. (2007) Capacity Development in Fragile States. Discussion Paper 58D. Maastricht: ECDPM.

Brinkerhoff, D.W. and Morgan, P.J. (2010) Capacity and Capacity Development: Coping with Complexity. *Public Administration and Development,* 30(1), 2–10.

Caruana, V., Stevenson, J., Clegg, S. and Wood, R. (2010) Promoting Students' 'Resilient Thinking'. In *Diverse Higher Education Learning Environments.* Leeds: The Higher Education Academy.

Central Statistics Organisation and UNDP (2011) *Capacity Development Plan (2011–2014).* Kabul: CSO.

Chandler, D. (2010) *International Statebuilding: The Rise of Post-liberal Governance.* Oxon: Routledge.

Chandra, A., Acosta, J., Stern, S., Uscher-Pines, L., Williams, M.V., Yeung, D., Garnett, J. and Meredith, L.S. (2011) *Building Community Resilience to Disasters.* Santa Monica, CA: RAND Corporation.

Clark, H. (2012) Putting Resilience at the Heart of the Development Agenda. *UNDP Website.* Available at: www.undp.org/content/undp/en/home/presscenter/speeches/2012/04/16/helen-clark-putting-resilience-at-the-heart-of-the-development-agenda.html (accessed June 2012).

Costs of War (2015) Economic Costs Summary. Available at: http://watson.brown.edu/costsofwar/costs/economic (accessed July 2016).

da Costa, D.F., Søren Vester Haldrup, S.V., Karlsrud, J., Rosén, F. and Tarp, K.N. (2013) *Friends in Need are Friends Indeed: Triangular Cooperation and Twinning for Capacity Development in South Sudan.* Oslo: NUPI/NOREF Report.

Dodge, T. (2006) Iraq: The Contradictions of Exogenous State-Building in Historical Perspective. *Third World Quarterly,* 27(1), 187–200.

Fukuda-Parr, S., Lopes, C. and Malik, K. (eds) (2002) *Capacity for Development: New Solutions to Old Problems.* New York: UNDP.

Garmezy, N. (1973) Competence and Adaptation in Adult Schizophrenic Patients and Children at Risk. In S.R. Dean (ed.), *Schizophrenia: The First Ten Dean Award Lectures.* New York: MSS Information Corp, pp. 163–204.

Hilderbrand, M.E. and Grindle, M.S. (1997) Building Sustainable Capacity in the Public Sector: What Can Be Done? In Grindle, M.S. (ed.), *Getting Good Government. Capacity Building in the Public Sectors of Developing Countries.* Harvard: Harvard University Press.

Ikpe, E. (2007) Challenging the Discourse on Fragile States. *Conflict, Security & Development,* 7(1), 85–124.

Ives, Y. (2008) What is 'Coaching? An Exploration of Conflicting Paradigms'. *International Journal of Evidence Based Coaching and Mentoring,* 6(2), 100–113.

Japan International Cooperation Agency (2008) *State Building in Fragile States: Enhancing Resilience Against Risk: from Medium- and Long-Term Perspectives.* Tokyo: JICA.

Kahn, M. (1995) State Failure in Weak States: A Critique of New Institutionalist Explanations. In Harriss, J., Hunter, J. and Lewis, C. (eds), *The New Institutional Economics and Third World Development.* London: Routledge.

Kenny, S. and Clarke, M. (eds) (2010) *Challenging Capacity Building: Comparative Perspectives.* Palgrave: Macmillan.

Martin-Breen, P. and Anderies, J.M. (2011) *Resilience: A Literature Review.* New York: The Rockefeller Foundation.

Morgan, P.J., Baser, H. and Morin, D. (2010) Developing Capacity for Managing Public Service Reform: The Tanzania Experience 2000–2008. *Public Administration and Development,* 30(1), 27–37.

OECD/DAC (1991) *Principles for New Orientations in Technical Co-operation.* Paris: OECD Publishing.

OECD/DAC (2007) *Principles for Good International Engagement in Fragile States and Situations.* Paris: OECD Publishing.

OECD/DAC (2008a) *Concepts and Dilemmas of State Building in Fragile Situations: From Fragility to Resilience.* Paris: OECD Publishing.

OECD/DAC (2008b) *State Building in Situations of Fragility: Initial Findings*. Paris: OECD Publishing.

Parsloe, E. and Wray, M. (2000) *Coaching and Mentoring: Practical Methods to Improve Learning*. London: Kogan Page Ltd.

Rosén, F. and Haldrup, S. V. (2013) By Design or By Default: Capacity Development in Fragile States and the Limits of Program Planning. *Stability: International Journal of Security & Development*, 2(2), 46.

UNDP (1993) *Rethinking Technical Cooperation*. Available at: https://books.google.co.uk/books/about/Rethinking_technical_cooperation.html?id=q861AAAAIAAJ (accessed July 2016).

UNDP (Kosovo) (2004) *Capacity Building Facility for Kosovo: Concept Note*. Pristina: UNDP Kosovo.

UNDP (2008a) *Capacity Development: Practice Note*. New York: UNDP.

UNDP (Kosovo) (2008b) *Capacity Development Facility – CDF project*. Pristina: UNDP Kosovo.

UNEP (n.d.) *Agenda 21: National Mechanisms and International Cooperation for Capacity-Building*. Available at: www.unep.org/Documents.Multilingual/Default.Print.asp?DocumentID¼52&ArticleID¼87&l¼en (accessed February 2013).

United Nations Security Council (2013) *Development Plan*, S/Res/2086. Ney York: UN.

United States Agency for International Development (2011) *Statebuilding in Situations of Fragility and Conflict*. Washington, DC: USAID.

van Breda, A.D. (2001) *Resilience Theory: A Literature Review*. Pretoria: South African Military Health Service.

van Overbeek, F., Hollander, T., van der Molen, I., Willems, R., Frerks, G. and Anten, L. (2009) Working Paper I: The Fragile States Discourse Unveiled. Utrecht: Peace Security and Development Network.

Whyte, A. (2004) Landscape Analysis of Donor Trends in International Development. In *Human and Institutional Capacity Building: A Rockefeller Foundation Series*, 2. New York: The Rockefeller Foundation.

World Bank (2011) *World Development Report 2011*. Washington, DC: World Bank.

World Bank and United Nations Development Group (2005) *An Operational Note on Transitional Results Matrices – Using Results-Based Frameworks in Fragile States*. Washington, DC: World Bank.

Yannis, A.B. (2002) State Collapse and its Implications for Peace-Building and Reconstruction. *Development and Change*, 33(5), 817–835.

29

RESILIENCE AND THE POST-COLONIAL

Hidden transcripts of resilience in Jamaican disaster management

Kevin Grove

Introduction

At first glance, the politics of resilience has reached a stalemate of sorts. According to proponents, the rise of resilience thinking in fields such as climate change and disaster studies is inherently political and empowering. Resilience, we are told, focuses on freeing individuals' and communities' agency and empowering them to develop their own coping strategies and adaptations to social, economic, and environmental uncertainties (Brown and Westaway, 2011). Critical readings of resilience offer a more sobering account. In a provocative article, Jeremy Walker and Melinda Cooper (2011) argue that resilience circumscribes the radical possibilities of critique. Their genealogy of resilience draws out how resilience thinking and neoliberal thought share a common comportment to critique's destabilizing effect. In both cases, critique generates crisis that offers possibilities to change for the better and continue current trajectories of growth and development amidst uncertainty. The confluence of resilience thinking with neoliberal governmental rationalities leverages critique's transgressive force to extend and solidify neoliberal rule. For Walker and Cooper, resilience thrives on critique even as it negates critique's political force. Thus, in contemporary neoliberal order, resilience appears to be either inherently empowering or inescapably depoliticizing.

This chapter seeks to develop an alternative critical slant by reading resilience through assemblage theory and post-colonial theory. Bridging these distinct theoretical approaches enables us to analyze how resilience intervenes in, and is inflected by, the variety of contextually specific force relations that comprise everyday life in post-colonial settings. I focus here on ethnographic fieldwork I conducted with Jamaica's national disaster management agency, the Office of Disaster Preparedness and Emergency Management (ODPEM). From June to December 2009, I engaged in a collaborative institutional ethnography in which I assisted ODPEM's Projects Division's efforts to implement two donor-funded resilience programs. Paying attention to the way people tasked with implementing disaster resilience programs take up and use resilience in their everyday practices draws out resilience's diagrammatic qualities. *Diagram* refers to an ideal, virtual set of relations amongst relations (Deleuze, 1988; Massumi, 1992). Diagrams attempt to give direction to the array of economic, cultural, social, and environmental forces whose intersections form the context in which people live. They align bodies and statements with one another, and thus structure the forms of life that can be practiced at any given time and place. Diagrams are political because they attempt—but do not always succeed—to shape the possibilities for socio-ecological life, and, in the process, foreclose on possibilities for *other* ways of life (Povinelli, 2012).

Approaching resilience as one diagram amongst others enables us to recognize how resilience makes possible new ethico-political practices of engaging with the potential for socio-ecological otherness. Because diagrams are virtual, they can potentially be many things at one and the same time. In Jamaican disaster management, resilience attempts to create adaptive, self-organizing cultures of safety that spontaneously adapt to social and ecological surprise in proper ways through programs that encourage individual and community responsibility, freedom, and self-sufficiency. It thus aligns with neoliberal visions of adaptive, self-organizing communities that automatically adapt to social and ecological surprise in proper ways. However, resilience *also* aligns with anti-colonial struggles to advance alternative social projects outside the measure of colonial, bourgeoisie, and neoliberal value systems (Grove, 2013b). Specifically, I will argue here that while disaster resilience solidifies neoliberal socio-ecological relations, it *also,* at the same time, reconfigures the hidden transcripts that maintain the possibility of resistance, and thus politics. Hidden transcripts, following Scott (1990), refer to subaltern peoples' strategic and subversive performances of deference, which maintain the possibilities of resistance in the face of overwhelming force that would crush any outward expression of revolt. This means that a multiplicity of *resiliences* may co-exist in the same subject: disaster resilience creates possibilities for sympathetic state agents to engage in techniques of state practice that enable vulnerable populations to sustain possibilities for alternative forms of life in the face of neoliberal abandonment.

To develop this argument, the second section reviews different strands of thought on resilience and politics, and details how we might approach this question through assemblage theory. The third and fourth sections detail two distinct forms of resilience, neoliberal and subversive, that circulate within Jamaican disaster management assemblages. The fifth section then analyzes how resilience transforms the hidden transcript and enables potentially subversive state practices. A brief conclusion considers the implications of this argument for further research on resilience politics.

Resilience politics?

In the past decade, resilience has become a key theme in the related research fields of both disaster studies and climate change adaptation research (Eakin and Leurs, 2006; Nelson *et al.*, 2007; Brown and Westaway, 2011). However, despite its growing influence, resilience research has only recently begun to engage with questions of power and politics. This has largely taken place through the encounter of resilience thinking with literature on transitions management (Folke *et al.*, 2010). The latter asserts that sustainability may require widespread systemic transformation, such as a shift in production and consumption practices, or the adoption of new beliefs and norms (Smith *et al.*, 2005; Rotmans *et al.*, 2001). Politics becomes an issue here on two fronts. First, formal politics can constrain societies' abilities to adapt in proper ways. Existing institutional structures can be rigid and inflexible, and prevent the transformations societies require to become more sustainable. Second, different interest groups may have conflicting visions of sustainable and resilient futures (Pelling, 2010; Smith and Stirling, 2010). To account for politics conceived as such, resilience approaches increasingly focus on identifying techniques that can overcome the limitations politics imposes on transformability, such as adaptive management, reflexive governance, transformational leaders and collaborative learning.

The confluence of resilience thinking and transitions management reduces politics to an activity to be regulated, managed, and controlled alongside others such as culture or economy. Reducing politics to a technical problem is a hallmark of what Erik Swyngedouw (2009), calls the post-politicization of environmental politics. Swyngedouw, following Jacques Rancière (2010), understands politics as the irruption of novelty: subjectivities, identities, values and so on, that cannot be incorporated into the existing order of things without destabilizing the series of inclusions, exclusions, and divisions that structure this order. From this perspective, resilience is a depoliticizing machine that operationalizes change itself—the motor of politics—as "transformations" that can be rationally managed to produce desired and more-or-less expected outcomes (Evans and Reid, 2014). Of course, a liberal will to truth—a desire to turn everything into an object that can be fully known and controlled—has long been a hallmark of both hazards studies and resilience thinking (Grove 2013a). In an influential essay on the benefits of adaptive management, Kai Lee suggests that:

> Adaptive management recapitulates the promise that Francis Bacon articulated four centuries ago: to control nature one must understand her [sic]. Only now, what we wish to control is not the natural world but a mixed system in which humans play a large, sometimes dominant role. Adaptive management is therefore experimentation that affects social arrangements and how people live their lives.
>
> *(Lee, 1999; no pagination)*

The incorporation of transitions approaches further solidifies this depoliticizing will to truth. The authors of a more recent comparative analysis of resilience and transition management approaches remark that, "An aspiration to create entirely new system states brings the transformability side of socioecological research even closer to the aims in transition management" (Smith and Sterling, 2010, p. 1). Resilience negates the possibility of radical politics. There is no space for the irruption of true novelty, because any attempt to change will be adaptively incorporated into the system through reflexive governance, collaborative learning, and adaptive management.

Thinking the politics of resilience thus requires us to move beyond a modernist political imaginary that enframes politics as a sphere of practice concerned with who holds power, how it is exercised, and how it can be limited. One possible alternative comes from recent work on assemblage theory (Anderson *et al.*, 2012). *Assemblage* refers to contingent configurations of materials and enunciations that are always on the verge of disaggregation (Deleuze and Guattari, 1987). They are similar in form to actor-networks or complex systems, but differ in an important way: assemblages are never stable; they are constantly being dis-aggregated and re-formed by their outside. Assemblages are thus not coherent entities; they are instead defined by the series of affective relations that give rise to individuated bodies and statements with particular meanings, values, and capacities (Massumi, 1992). Gilles Deleuze's (1988) notion of diagrams helps us foreground the political register of assemblages. *Diagrams* are ideal sets of relations between affective relations. They territorialize bodies, statements, and forms of knowledge, drawing them into relation with one another and thereby charging them with certain capacities rather than others. Because they attempt to direct, and thus order, affective relations that comprise assemblages, diagrams are potentially political: they facilitate some capacities, ways of doing, and ways of thinking, and foreclose others. Thus, diagrams make some forms of life more possible and desirable, and make others less possible (Povinelli, 2012). However, diagrams never fully succeed in folding life into calculated arrangements: the affective capacities they engender exceed measure and regulation. These virtual possibilities are a de-territorializing force that can reconfigure assemblages in unexpected ways. A politics of assemblage lies in this constant play of de- and re-territorialization that expresses the virtual potentialities assemblages embody.

From this perspective, we can approach resilience as a diagram that attempts to organize life through a particular relation to an uncertain future. Uncertainty and risk are not conditions to be feared or secured against; instead, they offer the potential for growth, development, and change.

The problem for resilience is to develop the adaptive capacities necessary to live with risk, vulnerability, and insecurity. Techniques such as adaptive management, reflexive governance, and participatory education programs operate on the affective relations between people, their environments, and institutions in order to visualize, objectify, and govern adaptive capacity (Grove, 2014). At this point, politics is no longer about a delimited sphere of action that limits resilience. Instead, politics is immanent to the life-worlds, the *milieus* resilience attempts to engineer. It involves the biophysical, social, and psychic spaces —actual and virtual, extensive and intensive—from which novelty might irrupt without being exhausted in a techno-managerial will to govern. Analyzing resilience's "environmental" politics requires us to map how resilience intersects with place-specific historical trajectories and forces relations to create new capacities for thought and action and new possibilities for domination and resistance. The next two sections detail how disaster resilience intersects, reconfigures, and is reconfigured by, Jamaica's ongoing neoliberalization and its history of anti-colonial struggle, respectively.

Neoliberal resilience

Assemblage theory recognizes that particular contexts are shaped by a series of interlocking force relations that transgress modernist classifications such as culture, economics, society, politics, and environment. These forces condition any practice, even as these practices may reconfigure those same relations. The Jamaican context is indelibly shaped by the 400-year struggle to limit the transgressive, life-forming power of subaltern black populations. Caribbean subaltern scholars have demonstrated that black resistance is the driving force behind long-term historical trans-formations in Jamaican political economic order (Meeks, 2000; Bogues, 2002; Scott, 2003). Throughout Jamaica's history, subaltern existence has been defined by the daily struggle to live outside the race, class, color and gender axes of colonial domination that degrade colonized people's value and humanity. Resistance and freedom are ontological; the grounds of subaltern existence lived in relation to the collective experience and memory of slavery and colonization (Henke, 1997). Autonomy, self-determination, recognition and respect, rather than rights, pri-vileges and responsibilities of liberal democracy, are markers of this more radical form of freedom. James Scott's (1990) concept of *hidden transcripts* is key to understanding how black resistance has shaped Jamaican order. Scott offers a sympathetic critique of Gramscian notions of hegemony that assume subordinate peoples' consent to overwhelming domination. In contrast, he argues, they strategically perform a "public transcript," a series of statements, gestures, and comportments that take the appearance of deference, and are intended to placate dominant elites. At the same time, they also engage in "hidden transcripts" that express quite different sentiments and maintain the continued possibility of resistance. Resistance to hegemony will thus rarely be visible to dominant groups; it is located instead in the hidden transcript, a physical and psychic space of alternative value systems. Faced with the threat of limitless state violence in colonial and post-colonial orders, black resistance in Jamaica circulates through hidden transcripts that have periodically boiled to the surface in explicit expressions of anti-colonial violence and protest (Meeks, 2000). World-deforming events such as the plantation revolts of 1867, the workers' rebellions of 1938, and Norman Manley's democractic socialism of the early 1970s are rare instances where the hidden transcript surfaces. These rebellions have been beaten back by counter-revolutionary forces, such as, respectively, the rise of (brown) bourgeois nationalism, the development of clientelist party politics, and the economic violence of neoliberal structural adjustment programs. In each case, the result has been a progressive restriction on outward expressions of black resistance.

Resilience is the newest fold in this struggle to limit Jamaicans' adaptive capacities. Indeed, the authors of ODPEM's 1999 National Hazard Mitigation Policy recognize that traditional knowledge and practices derive from "a history of autonomously adapting to hazard events and changing environmental conditions" (ODPEM, 1999, p. 5). A 2007 United Nations review of Hyogo's implementation sums up the challenge this presents to disaster management professionals, when its authors suggest that, "capturing and utilizing local knowledge" challenges institutional efforts to build resilience (UN, 2007, p. 54). The problem of autonomous adaptive capacity is the backdrop to the UN's (2005) *Hyogo Framework for Action,* which formally introduced resilience into international disaster management policymaking. In practice, resilience has augmented disaster management's traditional emphasis on pre-event preparedness and mitigation with a focus on governance relations and participatory, community-based programming (Grove, 2013a). These techniques were at the heart of the two donor-funded projects that I worked on with ODPEM: the Building Disaster Resilient Communities (BDRC) project, funded by the Canadian International Development Agency; and the Tropical Storm Gustav Recovery Project, funded by the UK's Department for International Development. The former utilized participatory techniques such as transect walks and education, and training activities to develop a community disaster response plan and build preparedness. The latter offered roofing materials and resilient carpentry training for people across the island whose homes had been damaged by Tropical Storm Gustav in 2008.

Preparedness and mitigation techniques focus on the knowledge, skills, and attitudes of key personnel in various state agencies. In contrast, resilience enables disaster management to target the everyday lives of the population as a whole (Grove, 2013a). Becoming disaster resilient is not the responsibility of the state; it is the responsibility of each individual. Participatory programming inculcates this responsibility through teaching people to become self-sufficient. A member of ODPEM's Training Division, who ran the agency's education activities for the BDRC project, explained to me how participatory education enhances self-sufficiency:

> A lot of [participants] come in and think disaster plans have to be this big, fancy document, but then once we are with them they realize it's something simple that each of us can and must do within the various households. It's being self-sufficient: what do I have, how can I utilize this? . . . I can't afford to change all the roofs, I can't change the walls from wood to concrete, can we do one room first, . . . This info is shared from one group to the next and we facilitate that, we try to get out some other things from them, what they can do to be self-sufficient.
>
> *(interview with ODPEM fieldworker, October 8, 2009)*

Self-sufficiency here requires people to use what is around them in creative ways. The state facilitates this process by collecting and disseminating information on 'best practices' in its participatory education programs.

Resilience approaches have long recognized that diversity, communication, and information exchange are determining factors of adaptive capacity (Gunderson and Holling 2002; see also Dillon and Reid, 2009). However, in Jamaican disaster management, the language of empowerment also justifies these capacity-building activities. A program officer in the Jamaican Red Cross, which frequently assists ODPEM with preparedness training activities, explained to me that:

> We're hoping that eventually we'll saturate communities with training because I think knowledge is power. It gives local community persons the ability to say, 'no, we are not going your way, we know this is wrong.
>
> *(interview with Red Cross officer, October 13, 2009)*

Discourses of self-sufficiency, responsibility, and empowerment are part of neoliberal govern-mental rationalities that seek to fashion entrepreneurial subjects who live with, manage, and profit from risk (Dean 2004). In development and disaster management programming, these categories are the cornerstones of recent post-developmentalist trends in which development, welfare, and aid no longer attempt to reduce poverty and inequality but instead manage the effects of inequality through the production of new subjectivities (Pupavac, 2005). For example, Julian Reid (2012) argues that disaster resilience does not reduce exposure to danger, but rather stra-tegically utilizes this exposure to produce subjects amenable to neoliberal governmental tech-nologies. Resilience reconfigures the institutions, bodies, rationalities, plans, passions, discourses, and statements that make up "disaster management" around principles of self-sufficiency, responsibility, and empowerment. Assemblages of neoliberal disaster resilience do not seek simply to reduce vulnerability and mitigate risk, but, rather, to produce "cultures of safety" (UN, 2005) in which individuals and communities adapt to and live with socio-environmental change, surprise, and uncertainty in ways that are consistent with the security imperatives of Western disaster management and development planning (Grove, 2010; Duffield, 2011).

Resilience thus offers a set of techniques and rationalities that further appropriate subaltern populations' constitutive force. In Jamaica's post-colonial context, the drive to capture, utilize, and share local knowledge appropriates local populations' inherent adaptive capacities and directs them towards the goals of Western disaster management and development professionals (Grove 2014). However, even as neoliberal configurations of resilience narrow the possibilities for both critique and resistance, resilience also reconfigures the physical, social, and psychic spaces of Jamaica's hidden transcripts. The next section examines subversive forms of resilience.

Subversive resilience

The creation of risk-bearing individuals and communities is not the only effect of Jamaican disaster resilience assemblages. As diagrams of resilience touch down in social, political, econ-omic, and ecological contexts, this wider field of force relations charges these diagrams with affective potentials that exceed neoliberal configurations. For example, a disaster management expert in the Ministry of Local Government, who often assists ODPEM with their community outreach efforts, defined empowerment to me in a way that exceeds neoliberal efforts to free oppressed agency:

> What I mean by empowerment is the ability to act independently irrespective of the influence of others, it is being able to make independent decisions. The political process at the start of our development, probably from the 1930s onward, wasn't geared at independent decision making of individuals; it was based on a suggested party. . . . What it sought to do was to create a populist type of politics in which the leader was a saviour, and the leader would provide the resources.
> *(Interview with Ministry of Local Government officer, October 14, 2009)*

His definition situates empowerment within the Jamaican poor's daily struggle for dignity and survival. Here, empowerment stands opposed to a historically and geographically specific form of political practice in Jamaica that operates through a system of patron–client relations of dependency and obligation (Stone, 1983; Meeks, 2000). Jamaica's clientelist system emerged through articulations of European-style parliamentary democracy with patron–client relations of dependence associated with the plantation (Beckford, 1972). Informal patron–client relations were a key technique for structuring social relations on the colonial plantation. Where effective, they constructed relations of psychological and material dependence between colonists and the colonized, who came to rely on entrenched elites and, by extension, the colonial system for their own well-being. This practice extended to the formal political sphere following the 1938 worker uprisings that swept the island. Widespread participation in party and electoral politics, and indeed the systems' legitimacy, is based on popular expectations for material benefit. The state becomes a source of material resources that party elites distribute to their loyal constituents, often through brokers such as neighborhood 'dons' in impoverished inner-city communities.

Set against the backdrop of clientelist party politics, disaster management becomes another tap from which state resources might flow (Grove, 2013b). Clientelism's dependencies and expectations reinforce expectations that the state will provide recovery resources. ODPEM's community-based programming works against this dependency by constructing a variety of responsibilities participants should assume. The Red Cross officer highlighted the importance of inculcating responsibility:

> The first thing is we need to get the person to understand they're responsible for their own well being . . . meaning that when there is a disaster or emergency, they're the ones that will have to take charge as first responders. Whether they're taking charge of their own family or of their neighbor, they're the persons, because there are times when there are different situations that will cause external help to not get in, such as a blocked road.
>
> *(Interview with Red Cross officer, October 13, 2009)*

This is certainly a form of neoliberal responsibilization that makes individuals responsible for the provision of immediate disaster response needs. However, it *also* signals a wider sense of responsibility that draws on an ethic of empathy and care. A fieldworker for the Social Development Commission (SDC), a state-affiliated community development agency that often partners with ODPEM, suggested this in language worth quoting at length:

> Being responsible is understanding how your actions either help, hurt, or hinder the people around you in the community. You understand you are part of a whole, a unity, and how you function: your actions have an impact, a wider impact. So your responsibility as a good citizen is that you don't bring any form of harm to the persons who are around you, your family, and, by extension, community. That's the main thing, you're responsible for your actions fitting with the laws of the community – not just the laws on the books but an overall responsibility to your fellow man, because it's not illegal for you to drive past someone who's on the road begging. It's not illegal, but at the same time, there's a social responsibility: you have to help your fellow man, you understand. You don't have to legally, but when you look at the development of the country and the effect it has, you're your brother's keeper, you understand . . . [trails off]. So that is it, you're your brother's keeper, that sums it up.
>
> *(Interview with SDC fieldworker, September 30, 2009)*

In Jamaica, the assertion that "you are your brother's keeper" resonates with religion—both Christianity and Rastafarianism—and the history of resistance to race-based oppression (Campbell 1987). The juxtaposition of religious, neoliberal and anti-colonial diagrams within Jamaican disaster resilience imbues responsibility with multiple senses of meaning. Disaster management and development practitioners articulate the language of individual responsibility and also, *at the same time, and in the same language*, a responsibility to the other that signals a potentiality to be affected by others' suffering.

A similar doubling is at play with empowerment. The Ministry of Local Government officer discussed how education enables people to push back against clientelism's confines:

> Education enables communities to clearly identify their critical needs. Uneducated communities might identify needs which are influenced by decisions of others, and interests of others. In a well educated community, they will be much better able to identify their critical needs, irrespective of the interests of any other outside group.
>
> *(Interview with Ministry of Local Government official, October 14, 2009)*

At stake in this vision of empowerment is the ability of community members to autonomously define and value socio-ecological phenomena. Empowerment enables community members to enact their own visions of disaster management, and thus exercise greater self-determination over the possibilities for life in an uncertain environment. Jamaican communities' ability to define their own risks relies on a strategic re-appropriation of neoliberal rationalities and practices of security. The SDC fieldworker signaled this re-appropriation as he illustrated empowerment through metaphors of systems theory:

> What we try to do is, instead of top-down, we go to each little cog in the overall wheel and ensure that it's premium, its citizens are empowered to do whatever it is they want to do, whether that's to earn or to learn or to eat. That's why we'll do things like little training centers, because people will be able to not just say, "give a handout," but be able to reach a point where they can generate their own income and they don't have to depend on the government or politics or political persons' handout. That's the whole point, you understand? Empowerment in terms of economy, empowerment on a whole, empowerment on a point where they can actually start making decisions; educated and informed decisions.
>
> *(Interview with SDC fieldworker, September 30, 2009)*

Here, the fieldworker casts empowerment in both the language of complex systems theory and anti-colonial resistance. The object of participatory programming is described through imagery of self-organizing systems made up of efficient little "cogs." At the same time, his specification of empowerment as the ability of each individual cog to "do whatever it is they want to do" exceeds conventional notions of empowerment as individuals' ability to participate in governance regimes and make "proper" adaptation decisions. Resilience approaches suggest that participation gives marginalized subjects more power to define their adaptation choices, and thus produces more just adaptation outcomes. At the heart of this understanding of empowerment is an assumption that participation involves recognition of the self in the other (Pelling 2010, p. 63). This assumption flattens differences between the subjects of participation, for it hinges on the assumption that subjective experiences and intentions can be transparently communicated through language in collaborative negotiation.

In contrast, the SDC fieldworker's use of empowerment draws on a familiar theme in anti-colonial resistance: self-determination is not an essential condition of the subject, but rather is relational and granted through rituals that structure the norms of social recognition. Recognition takes on a variety of linguistic and non-linguistic forms. In a seminal text, Paul Gilroy (1993) re-reads Hegel's master–slave analogy to argue that self-consciousness as slave or master is formed not through verbal exchanges between linguistically-determined subjects, but through non-linguistic expressions such as white overseers' physical violence meted out on recalcitrant black bodies, slaves' duplicitous performances of deference, and slaves' acts of resistant violence carried out on their masters and themselves. Mutual recognition and communication on the plantation do not involve a single, common language but instead involve diverse forms of expression. Gilroy's argument thus destabilizes the foundations of conventional resilience approaches: *there is no common language through which vulnerable people can be granted self-determination.* Like the violence of the slave plantation, the everyday insecurities of the poor and vulnerable in Jamaica are lived, embodied experiences of the systemic violence that sustains neoliberal order (Mullings, 2009). There is no authentic essentialized subject position, whether the slave or the vulnerable, whose experiences can form the basis for a liberal project of betterment—whether emancipation or empowerment. Instead, the subject is an effect of ontologically prior non-linguistic relations between people, things, desires, plans, and strategies that form vulnerable citizens with multiple and potentially conflicting visions of a secure future—visions that are only recognized as "subjective interests" as these citizens are enrolled in participatory networks structured through a modernist political imaginary. Faced with ontologically distinct experiences of vulnerability and insecurity, community members' visions of insecurity, empowerment and resilience—what they "want to do"—may not align with those of policymakers and fieldworkers. Moreover, the absence of a common language means that these differences may not be readily apparent in participatory negotiation.

Rather than situating claims about empowerment in the lives of whole and stable subjects, empowerment here involves an ethos of freedom, a willingness to question the limits of rationality and positively value the presence and possibilities of other forms of individual and collective life. The SDC fieldworker's assertion above that while community members may or may not want to adapt in ways "experts" suggest, what they want is still legitimate and worthy of state support expresses this transgressive ethos. It also signals a second form of resilience: *subversive resilience*, which operates through categories of neoliberal resilience—responsibility, empowerment, self-sufficiency—but mobilizes these categories towards outcomes beyond its measure. Subversive resilience thus mirrors neoliberal resilience at the level of content, but is founded on an ethics attuned to difference and multiplicity. This ethics is key to a politics of resilience: recognizing the incommensurability of different experiences of "vulnerability" and "insecurity" undermines a liberal will to truth that reduces these experiences to properties of pre-formed subjects who can be included within governance processes. Subversive resilience furthers the neoliberalization of socio-ecological relations, but it does so in a way that rehabilitates the cornerstone of Jamaican anti-colonial struggle, the search for recognition and respect beyond the measures of existing order. The next section explores how subversive resilience reconfigures the hidden transcript in ways that sustain the possibility for socio-ecological otherness.

Hidden transcripts of resilience

Neoliberal resilience targets the most intimate reaches of subjectivity, the affective relations between individuals and their social and ecological surroundings (Grove, 2014). However, the deployment of resilience within Jamaican disaster management also de- and re-territorializes the history and techniques of black resistance in a way that reconfigures the hidden transcript and thus maintains political possibilities in an otherwise suffocating neoliberal environment. Specifically, two techniques of subversive resilience – formalization and facilitation – enable empathetic state agents and target communities to perform a public transcript of resilience building while also maintaining the possibility for alternative styles of vulnerability reduction.

First, facilitation involves utilizing the state as a tool of sorts to connect communities with resources they may need to pursue their own goals. Its roots lie in the Jamaican state's local government reform and community development projects (see Osei, 2007). Community-based organizations such as the SDC and the Women's Resource and Outreach Centre (WROC) have been involved in both of these initiatives since the late 1990s. In Jamaica's neoliberal economy, this often involves mediating between communities and international donors that command the bulk of development and disaster management funding (Grove, 2013b). On one level, this is a neoliberal technique that, following the rollback of state funding, promotes competition between communities for scarce development funds. At the same time, when set against the backdrop of black resistance in Jamaica, facilitation also gives communities a degree of autonomy and self-determination within these narrow confines. The SDC fieldworker hinted at this wider resonance when he explained the agency's grant proposal training to me:

> We will teach them [community groups] how to help put together a project proposal. We tend not to help people just write it, we facilitate it to ensure that this is what they want and because . . . if we help you prepare a project proposal in January, we should help you do it so well and teach you how to do it so that in March you don't need to come back to us again so that you're free.
>
> *(Interview with SDC fieldworker, September 30, 2009)*

"Freedom" here is community groups' capacities to interact with donors on their own terms: to identify funding opportunities, translate local needs into fundable projects, and write and submit project proposals. ODPEM has begun deploying techniques of facilitation, in large part through their collaboration with the SDC on community-based disaster resilience projects. For instance, the BDRC project offered grant-writing training sessions to interested community groups. For example, one project ongoing in Trinityville during my fieldwork with the BDRC provided funds to develop guava ketchup production in the community. Community members developed this project with WROC, which helped them attract funding from the European Union and Christian Aid. Importantly, the project was able to frame itself as a resilience program, since it provided the community with an alternative livelihood source to notoriously unreliable banana farming. As such, it illustrates how community members strategically utilized resilience to reconfigure the local economy and ecology (Grove, 2013b). These are small-scale projects that are not revolutionary by any stretch. However, they nonetheless signal the plasticity and multiplicity of resilience that can—although not necessarily will—sustain alternative forms of sociality (cf. Povinelli, 2011).

Second, formalization involves education and training activities that inform communities how to attain recognition and support from international donors. But recognition does not occur solely on donors' terms. Since the colonial era, a key technique of survival and subversive resistance on the part of the Jamaican poor has been their capacity to strategically and creatively identify and exploit dependencies within the existing order of things (see Gray, 2004; Grove, 2013b). Diagrams of resilience extend this capacity to everyday state practice. The post-developmental emphasis on community-based initiatives, and its recent incorporation into disaster risk reduction and resilience programing, enables community members to strategically perform a public transcript of sorts: the role of a "proper" community organization donors seek to support. An SDC fieldworker explained to me how formalization works:

> We encourage community organizations to come together as chartered ones that have a whole bill of laws and a structure, a structure so the development agencies can deal with

a structure they know is not just a random thing. . . . That's what we try to encourage, we encourage them to formalize themselves so it's not just a citizens association, a random citizens association; they transition to the next level where you are recognized as a legal entity and you can deal with development agencies.

(Interview with SDC fieldworker, September 30, 2009)

Donors' insecurities over dealing with "some random thing," a localized and unfamiliar expression of community, opens a space for performance in which communities can strategically adopt the trappings of a formal organization. This public transcript enables communities to gain recognition while still retaining a degree of autonomy and self-determination. The SDC field-worker explained that:

It's really something so that they have a base and they can present something more, I don't want to say "legitimate" to the international community or to the outside community. But it's still the same community, they're still gonna have that spirit that they had in the first place. It's a compromise, there's a little give and take. Give up a little of your quote-unquote "freedom and flexibility" and at the same time you are getting funds and stuff to help you actually achieve your goals. It's a trade-off.

(interview with SDC fieldworker, September 30, 2009)

The "trade-off" expresses a hidden transcript beneath the by-laws, executives, regular meetings with minutes and other elements of the public transcript. In the example from Trinityville above, the hidden transcript can be gleaned as alternative economic arrangements that link communities with national and global markets on their own terms. While this is not a revolutionary, frontal assault on Jamaica's neoliberal order, it nonetheless signals the endurance of socio-ecological multiplicity, and thus the persistent political potential within Jamaican resilience.

Set against the backdrop of both neoliberal development and disaster management, and the country's history of black resistance, facilitation and formalization sustain a space in which a hidden transcript of resilience—alternative practices of community, development, and vulner-ability reduction—might be imagined and practiced. Self-sufficiency, responsibility, and empowerment no longer hold the promise of revolutionary emancipation they did during anti-colonial movements; the neoliberal counter-revolution has significantly hollowed them out. But techniques such as facilitation and formalization enable state agents to engage with communities in a way that maintains rather than forecloses possibilities for novel responses to socio-ecological insecurity. The political potential of resilience lies in this transgressive ethic that infuses Jamaican disaster resilience with the potential to create new worlds out of the violence and insecurities of neoliberal abandonment.

Conclusions

This chapter has drawn on assemblage theory and post-colonial theory to explore the politics of Jamaican disaster resilience. It offers a more complex picture of resilience politics than that found in both critical and applied approaches to resilience. As a diagram of power, resilience is saturated with the potential to be otherwise, and can be both radical and reactionary at one and the same time. Resilience articulates with other cultural, political economic, and ecological trajectories in ways that reconfigure both power and resistance. Thus, while disaster resilience solidifies neoliberal socio-ecological relations, it also introduces new possibilities for resistance to both the depend-encies of clientelism and the violence of structural adjustment. Subversive resilience reinvigorates categories of black resistance that neoliberalism increasingly colonizes. Empowerment, self-sufficiency and responsibility resonate with the history of race-based exclusion and dehumanization, as well as the contemporary economic violence of Jamaica's neoliberal order. While the uncertainties of contemporary social and environmental life are a lever for enacting cultural changes among the poor and vulnerable, these interventions also reconfigure the hidden transcripts that sustain the possibility for resistance to neoliberal socio-ecological orderings.

Linking assemblage theory with post-colonial theories foregrounds the potential ethical and aesthetic dimensions of resilience. The politics of resilience is not simply a matter of competing interest groups to be managed through more and better governance technologies. Instead, it is first and foremost an ethico-political stance towards the potentiality to become otherwise that inheres in the present. Resilience is a life (de)forming practice that operates on the fragile plasticity of socio-ecological existence. Engaging with this potential requires an ethics that values adaptive capacity as the force of socio-ecological creativity, rather than something to be brought in line with Western norms of resilience.

References

Anderson, B., Kearnes, M., McFarlane, C., and Swanton, D. (2012) On assemblages and geography. *Dialogues in Human Geography* 2(2), 171–189.

Beckford, G. (1972) *Persistent Poverty: Underdevelopment and Plantation Economies of the Third World.* Kingston: University of the West Indies Press.

Bogues, A. (2002) Politics, nation, and postcolony: Caribbean inflections. *Small Axe* 11, 1–30.

Brown, K. and Westaway, E. (2011) Agency, capacity, and resilience to environmental change: lessons from human development, well-being, and disasters. *Annual Review of Environment and Resources*, 36, 321–342.

Campbell, H. (1987) *Rasta and Resistance: From Marcus Garvey to Walter Rodney.* Trenton: Africa World Press.

Dean, M. (2004) *Governmentality: Power and Rule in Modern Society.* London: Sage.

Deleuze, G. (1988) *Foucault.* Minneapolis: University of Minnesota Press.

Deleuze, G. and Guattari, F. (1987) *A Thousand Plateaus: Capitalism and Schizophrenia.* Minneapolis: University of Minnesota Press.

Dillon, Michael and Reid, Julian (2009) *The Liberal Way of War: Killing to Make Life Live.* London: Routledge.

Duffield, M. (2011) Total war as environmental terror: linking liberalism, resilience, and the bunker. *The South Atlantic Quarterly* 110 (3), 757–769.

Eakin, H. and Leurs, A. (2006) Assessing the vulnerability of social-environmental systems. *Annual Review of Environment and Resources* 31, 365–394.

Evans, B. and Reid, J. (2014) *Resilient Life: The Art of Living Dangerously.* Cambridge: Polity Press.

Folke, C., Carpenter, S., Walker, B., Scheffer, M., Chapin, T., and Rockström, J. (2010) Resilience thinking: integrating resilience, adaptability and transformability. *Ecology and Society* 15(4), 20.

Gilroy, P. (1993) *The Black Atlantic: Modernity and Double Consciousness.* Cambridge: Harvard University Press.

Gray, O. (2004) *Demeaned but Empowered: The Social Power of the Urban Poor in Jamaica.* Kingston: University of the West Indies Press.

Grove, K. (2010) Insuring "our common future"? Dangerous climate change and the biopolitics of environmental security. *Geopolitics* 15(3), 536–563.

Grove, K. (2013a) From emergency management to managing emergence: a genealogy of disaster management in Jamaica. *Annals of the Association of American Geographers* 103(3), 570–588.

Grove, K. (2013b) Hidden transcripts of resilience: power and politics in Jamaican disaster management. *Resilience* 1(3), 193–209.

Grove, K. (2014) Agency, affect, and the immunological politics of disaster resilience. *Environment and Planning D: Society and Space* 32, 240–256.

Gunderson, L. and Holling, C. (eds.) (2002) *Panarchy: Understanding Transformations in Human and Natural Systems.* Washington, DC: Island.

Henke, H. (1997) Towards an ontology of Caribbean existence (an exchange with Merle Jacob). *Social Epistemology* 11(1), 39–71.

Lee, K. (1999) Appraising adaptive management. *Ecology and Society* 3(2), 3.

Massumi, B. (1992) *A User's Guide to Capitalism and Schizophrenia: Deviations from Deleuze and Guattari*. Cambridge: MIT Press.

Meeks, B. (2000) *Narratives of Resistance: Jamaica, Trinidad, the Caribbean*. Kingston: University of West Indies Press.

Mullings, B. (2009) Neoliberalization, social reproduction and the limits to labour in Jamaica. *Singapore Journal of Tropical Geography* 30, 174–183.

Nelson, D., Adger, W. N., and Brown, K. (2007) Adaptation to environmental change: contributions of a resilience framework. *Annual Review of Environment and Resources* 32, 395–419.

ODPEM (1999) *National Hazard Mitigation Policy: Draft Policy*. Kingston: ODPEM.

Osei, P. (2007) Policy responses, institutional networks management and post-Hurricane Ivan reconstruction in Jamaica. *Disaster Prevention and Management* 16 (2), 217–234.

Pelling, M. (2010) *Adaptation to Climate Change: From Resilience to Transformation*. London: Routledge.

Povinelli, E. (2011) *Economies of Abandonment: Social Belonging and Endurance in Late Liberalism*. Durham: Duke University Press.

Povinelli, E. (2012) After the last man: images and ethics of becoming otherwise. *e-flux Journal*, 35.

Pupavac, V. (2005) Human security and the rise of global therapeutic governance. *Conflict, Development and Security* 5(2), 161–182.

Rancière, J. (2010) *Dissensus: On Politics and Aesthetics*. London: Bloomsbury.

Reid, J. (2012) The disastrous and politically debased subject of resilience. *Development Dialogue* 58, 67–79.

Rotmans, J., Kemp, R., and van Asselt, M. (2001) More evolution than revolution: transition management in public policy. *Foresight* 3, 15–31.

Scott, D. (2003) Political rationalities of the Jamaican modern. *Small Axe* 14, 1–22.

Scott, J. (1990) *Domination and the Arts of Resistance: Hidden Transcripts*. New Haven: Yale University Press.

Smith, A. and Stirling, A. (2010) The politics of social-ecological resilience and sustainable socio-technical transitions. *Ecology and Society* 15(1), 11.

Smith, A., Stirling, A., and Berkhout, F. (2005) The governance of sustainable socio-technical transitions. *Research Policy* 34, 1491–1510.

Stone, C. (1983) *Democracy and Clientelism in Jamaica*. New Brunswick: Transaction Books.

Swyngedouw, E. (2009) Apocalypse forever? Post-political populism and the spectre of climate change. *Theory, Culture & Society* 27(2–3), 213–232.

UN (2005) *Hyogo Framework for Action 2005–2015: Building the Resilience of Nations and Communities to Disasters*. Geneva: United Nations.

UN (2007) *Disaster Risk Reduction: 2007 Global Review*. Geneva: UNISDR.

Walker, J. and Cooper, M. (2011) Genealogies of resilience: from systems ecology to the political economy of crisis adaptation. *Security Dialogue* 42(2), 143–160.

PART X

Conclusion

30

CONCLUSION

International resilience and the uncertain future

Jon Coaffee and David Chandler

In the twenty-first century the political and policy discourse of resilience is everywhere. As Mark Neocleous noted, 'it falls easily from the mouths of politicians, a variety of state departments are funding research into it, urban planners are now obliged to take it into consideration, and academics are falling over themselves to conduct research on it' (2013, p.3). The term has entered into the lexicon of policy communities, the media and academic discourse to not only assess and understand the resistance to disruptive events, both real and imagined, of society, communities and individuals, but also to describe the properties and ability of interconnected and complex ecological, technical, social and economic systems to adapt and change in the midst of disruption and failure. What we think of as 'resilience' is not fixed. As Peter Rogers noted in Chapter 2, resilience is a travelling concept, a conceptual 'rhizome' that has risen to prominence in debates about how we seek to understand the wicked problems of uncertain times. Concomitantly, there is no consensus on how resilience should be theorised and applied (Philippe Bourbeau, Chapter 3).

As many of the chapters in this volume have illuminated, with such a diverse range of applications and flexibility in terminology and use, it is necessary to reflect on the etymology and practices of resilience and whether overuse of the term in so many different contexts is in danger of undermining its meaning and value, and to consider how it might be best applied theoretically and in international policymaking.

Resilience has become an all-encompassing metaphor which can be applied in a variety of national and international contexts – a translation term – that allows connections to be made between different strands of research with common terminology and consistent threads of analysis, without needing to make assumptions that the phenomena under investigation are the product of similar processes that apply regardless of cultural context (Coaffee 2006). Moreover, as Delf Rothe noted in relation to climate resilience, 'resilience can best be understood as a floating signifier, which holds together the diverse practices of climate security not despite its vagueness but due to its ambiguity' (Chapter 14, p. 181). For many others, resilience has become a 'catch-all' phrase used to vaguely express a wide range of responses to threats of many kinds, and pinning down the actual operational meaning of resilience has proved difficult and led to confusion, especially over terminology. This can cause confusion amongst practitioners and can result in resilience becoming an empty concept (Cecile de Milliano and Jeroen Jurriens, Chapter 20), which has led to an 'implementation gap' in the actual operationalisation of resilience in practice (Coaffee and Clarke, 2015).

There is increasingly a broad-brush, yet normalized, notion of resilience that pervades everyday life, tied to a normalised discourse that we are living with constant risk and fear. As Samuel Randalls and Stephanie Simon noted in Chapter 4, the proliferation of resilience-speak is closely tied to the idea that we now live in a 'time of crisis.' This state of affairs poses critical questions regarding the relationship between broader 'resilience policy' for dealing with disruptive challenges (such as flooding), emergent social policies directed at the civic realm (such as community empowerment and counter-radicalisation – now often badged as community resilience), and the qualities of individuals and communities to withstand disruptive events (such as the global economic recession).

Some also view ambiguity over resilience terminology and its use as a progressive and positive feature. For politicians it undoubtedly allows ideological flexibility, offering a new lexicon to make sense of a range of complex disruptive challenges across multiple scales of action (Coaffee, 2013). For research purposes, resilience can be seen as a 'boundary object' (Brand and Jax, 2007) or a 'bridging concept' between the natural and social sciences that can now be applied in a variety of specific national and international contexts. Here, the importance of investigating 'resilience of what to what' is of fundamental importance and thus requires grounded empirical work, as noted by Chuan Liao and Ding Fei whose work utilised direct inputs from Chinese pastoralists (Chapter 16). Here, resilience is not a one-off action but a continuous journey that helps us to define the problems at hand but also to develop solutions that mitigate emergent issues through adaptation, innovation and collaboration (see Chapter 17 by Jonathan Clarke). Moreover, as Brian Thiede noted in Chapter 27, in resource-constrained environments, resilience can have a core advocacy function and is increasingly used to motivate research and interventions.

The application of resilience is specific to context and as this volume has highlighted, the deployment of resilience-like policies in a number of distinct policy arenas – ranging from climate change, disaster-risk reduction, urban planning, territorial cohesion, international development and national security – and across the globe at a range of interlocking spatial scales – from global, to transnational, to national, to local to individual – is testimony to the particularity of operationalising resilience.

Overarching these numerous deployments of resilience is a fundamental quest – a paradigm shift – towards new forms of engagement with new forms of risk and risk management. Whereas in the recent past, ideas of risk management and risk assessment dominated discussions on how society could hope to control the future through probabilistic calculation, a more recent focus upon ideas of adaptability and adaptive capacity and the simultaneous rise of resilience as the policy metaphor of choice for coping with, and managing, future uncertainty – the incorporation of 'the dynamic interplay between persistence, adaptability and transformability across multiple scales and time frames' (Davoudi, 2012) – is now presenting a different paradigm of action. The push for resilience is therefore a response to existential or material vulnerability, insecurity and, ultimately, change (Coaffee *et al.*, 2008) and in the current millennium the scope and importance of enhancing such properties has grown as global society seeks ways of coping and thriving in conditions of greater volatility and uncertainty.

Resilience for whom?

As many of the contributions in this Handbook have showcased, the advance of resilience has not been uncontested and its multiple discourses and practices have been subjected to rigorous critique. At a general level, a key question often asked is whether resilience is a regressive or progressive agenda, posing some fundamental questions of resilience for whom, by whom? Increasingly within such notions of radical and transformative change, there is an appreciation of the need to reflect socio-spatial justice, ethics and power considerations (see for example Fainstein, 2015, and Alf Hornborg, Chapter 12), which address a number of key geo-political questions: How does the rolling out of resilience ensure social justice amidst a post-political landscape that marginalises alternative voices and approaches, diverting attention from questions of justice, power, or alternative futures? And, what are the spatial impacts of resilience policy across different scales and for equitable progress or development? As Charis Boke noted in Chapter 8, resilience might be best framed not merely as a checklist of necessary objects and skills, but rather as a set of relations, grounded in an ethics of care.

Much of the critical assessment of resilience concerns the alleged tarnishing of resilience ideas through 'neoliberal decentralisation' (Amin, 2013) and a post-political landscape understood as the foreclosing of political choice, the delegation of decision-making to technocratic experts, growing public disengagement from politics and, ultimately, the closing down of political debate and agency. As Lennart Olsson and colleagues noted in Chapter 5 (p. 59), 'given the lack of attention to agency, conflict, knowledge and power, and its insensitivity to theoretical development in contemporary social science, resilience is becoming a powerful depoliticising or naturalising scientific concept and metaphor when used by political regimes'.

This emerging canon of work in 'critical resilience studies' has highlighted the ways in which resilience policy and practice indicates a shift in the state's policies, reflecting a desire to step back from its responsibilities to ensure the protection of the population during crises or disruptive challenges and to delegate to certain professions, private companies, communities and individuals. Such a Foucauldian-inspired interpretation argues that resilience encourages individuals to autonomously act in the face of a crisis and precipitates citizens into behaving and adapting according to prescribed moral standards. As Marc Welsh has highlighted, resilience policy is 'a post-political ideology of constant adaptation attuned to the uncertainties of neoliberal economy where the resilient subject is conceived as resilient to the extent it adapts to, rather than resists, the conditions of its suffering' (2014, p. 16). Key concerns with the application of resilience, as highlighted in this Handbook, are multiple but can be broadly grouped around ideas of anticipation, localisation and responsibilisation.

Many resilience policies are increasingly anticipatory and pre-emptive in nature and, for many, come wrapped up in a cloak of unimaginable and impending disaster. Under such a logic of anticipatory governance, 'what if' scenarios have been replaced by 'when, then' scenarios, where the inevitability of further risk is assumed and pre-planned for. Such anticipatory logic often then provides the justification for state-level affirmative and pre-emptive action, with a number of commentators arguing that this emergent politics of fear is being manipulated by governments through, for example, 'planning for emergencies' guidance to citizens or public 'threat assessment levels' (see, for example, Chris Zebrowski, Chapter 6).

For many authors this perpetual fear amounts to a permanent state of emergency where exceptional conditions become normalised as the status quo, and where new discourses – in this case resilience – emerge to reassure the public that they are safe. In essence, resilience doesn't actually prevent anything, but it 'secures' through insecurity (Charlotte Heath-Kelly, Chapter 24). But such anticipatory logic is more often than not driven by government command and control, and, as Claudia Aradau noted in Chapter 7, the promise of security stultifies the future through anticipation and expert knowledge, and disavows the limits of knowledge (and) the transformative capacity of collective political action.

The spreading domestication of exceptional risk and security, considered at one time to be unacceptable or temporary, has become mundane, every day and unchallenged (normalised) in particular spatial contexts and under the rubric of resilience. Such approaches have been operationalised largely through a variety of foresight documents, forward-looking security strategies, future threat assessments and risk registers, and associated simulated practice exercises which, in effect, have attempted to embed the need to be constantly prepared for an array of risks and threats. As Iain White and Paul O'Hare highlight:

> Symbolically, the deployment of resilience discourses reformulates crises and uncertainty as not uncontrollable, but as an opportunity to proactively confront threats and even to provide general betterment. Particularly in circumstances where individuals, communities, and businesses can do little to be immunised from risk, resilience – embedded within a language of assurance and comfort – offers hope and confidence. *Resilience is therefore opportunistically tailored to fill 'policy windows' yielded in the wake of crises or in response to emerging perils.*
>
> (2014, p. 939, emphasis added)

As a number of chapters in this book also testify, the requirement to attempt to anticipate the future through preparedness activities has meant that resilience-thinking has become embedded in a range of interlinked policy objectives – from security to climate change, and from the environment to urban planning – in ways the state had previously found impossible to do. As Neocleous more critically asserts, ' "resilience" is the concept that facilitates that connection: nothing less than the attempted colonization of the political imagination by the state' (2013, p. 4).

Recent years have therefore witnessed considerable evolution and deployment of concepts and practices of resilience at multiple scales of governmental action: on the one hand developing an array of national policy guidance and strategies, whilst on the other hand ostensibly decentralising responsibility to the local scale (see Chapter 23, Jon Coaffee and Pete Fussey, and Chapter 28 Søren Haldrup and Frederik Rosén). As Jonathan Joseph further highlighted in Chapter 13, resilience policy is a process of devolving responsibility and privatising state powers. In most countries that have operationalised resilience-like policies, this is premised on a top-down approach from central government, and actualised through meta-strategies linked to national security or emergency management. Here, central governments can influence their approach through resource allocation and compliance mechanisms and through the development of specific and general plans (Coaffee, 2013). Such ongoing devolutionary processes generate questions about the capacity and connectivity of resilience practice, the degree to which existing hierarchies become translated at the local level and the generation of new hierarchies within newly configured networks of local practice. New agencies and networks populate a growing landscape of resilience practice that, in turn, brings an assortment of organisational priorities and approaches and sub-national and localised responses that mirror broader trends in public governance of the past twenty years, providing a fit with wider government ambitions to create a new, more community-driven, social contract between citizens and the state. Moreover, as Ksenia Chmutina and Lee Bosher noted, understandings of 'resilience' appear to change from the policy level to the practical implementation level (Chapter 21). As a result, resilience approaches often become realised not through state institutions, but localised networked responses, with governance dispersed more widely across key stakeholders and sectors. In a Foucauldian sense, this amounts to state governance from a distance and encourages the development of community or institutional resilience, and of the 'responsible citizen', in accordance with new techniques of governmentality: the replacement of state-centric 'protective' security approaches with those emphasising 'self-organising' human security. But this appears to be an agenda designed for and benefiting the state. As Jessica West argued in Chapter 25 in relation to UK counter-terrorism policy, the focus of civic resilience is designed to shore up the capabilities of the state, rather than communities.

Related to the critique of resilience as rescaled and localised, another common argument made in the critical resilience literature and throughout the contributions to this volume concerns the movement of responsibility for resilience against a range of perturbations towards individual actors and local scales of operation. This shift in emphasis has broader implications for the participation and responsibility of the citizen, as an actor in embedding resilience into everyday life, and demonstrates the ways in which *everyone* is now intended to be involved in the performance of resilience, with modes of behaviour encouraged through the discussion of resilience. As Paul O'Hare and colleagues note in Chapter 19, in relation to flood resilience, civic and individual self-reliance is increasingly central to risk management, hazard adaptation and preparedness and, by extension, to the realisation of resilience. The governance of resilience (and particularly the interactions between citizen and state) is, therefore, progressively 'responsibilising': putting the onus for preventing and preparing for disruptive challenge onto institutions, professions, communities and individuals rather than the state, the traditional provider of citizens' security needs (Coaffee *et al.*, 2008). This, for some, is part of a wider political project where impending crisis and disaster are utilised to subjugate citizens. As Julian Reid and Brad Evans noted in Chapter 26 (p. 338),

> resilience does not just encourage us to learn from the violence of catastrophic events so that we become more responsive to further catastrophes on the horizon. It promotes our adaptability so that we are also less of a threat politically.

Progressive resilience

Despite much of the criticism of resilience and resilience policy – that it draws in an anticipatory and precautionary logic, that it is a depoliticising and reactive tool of government, and that it responsibilises professions, individuals and communities – alternative readings prefer to focus upon how its usage and the implementation of its 'principles' might be repoliticised, so as to illuminate and change the uneven and problematic deployment of much existing resilience policy.

For some, resilience, rather than being debased by neoliberalism, offers an antidote to the vast challenges of coping with and managing future uncertainty and a way to assess the complex challenges that society faces, as well as providing a potential framework by which to respond. As David Chandler highlighted in Chapter 11, the area where resilience-thinking has gone furthest is in the rejection of modernist approaches to governance focused upon 'known knowns', and the embrace of 'known unknowns' or indeed 'unknown unknowns'. As a number of contributing authors and a host of recent international strategies further attest, resilience-thinking and associated processes of enhancing adaptability, flexibility and agility in forward-looking plans are now providing a useful lens through which to view the future. For example, in response to the renegotiation of a number of global development agendas, the discourse and practices of resilience have been both explicitly and implicitly embedded within a set of (post-2015) dialogues aimed at advancing effective global policy.

On 18 March 2015, a revised international framework for risk reduction from disasters (the Sendai Framework for Disaster Risk Reduction – SFDRR 2015–2030) was adopted by UN Member States at the World Conference on Disaster Risk Reduction (WCDRR) held in Sendai, Japan; this was the first major agreement of the post-2015 development agenda.[1] The new framework emphasises a renewed commitment to, and promotion of, the local assessment of disaster risk. It highlights the urgency of building resilience to disasters and ensuring that resilience is embedded within development plans, policies and procedures at all scales so as to complement, not hinder, sustainable development. The SFDRR also highlights the importance of anticipation and preparedness in order to 'more effectively protect persons, communities and countries, their livelihoods, health, cultural heritage, socioeconomic assets and ecosystems, and thus strengthen their resilience' (United Nations, 2015). Moreover, it also recognises the importance of new technologies for warning and informing local communities about risk, urges an increased use of adaptive nature-based solutions for mitigating the impacts of climate change, and encourages greater efforts to be made in measuring and monitoring resilience at the local level.

Following the Sendai agreement, in September 2015 the UN released their much-anticipated Sustainable Development Goals (SDGs), replacing the former Millennium Goals and setting targets in relation to future international development up until 2030. Within the SDGs, the discourse of resilience was utilised to highlight the ability to respond proactively to a range of shocks and stresses and how a range of stakeholders might collectively operationalise a joined-up response. For example, Goal 11 is dedicated to making cities and human settlements inclusive, safe, resilient and sustainable, Target 1.5 focuses upon community resilience, and Target 13.1 seeks to 'strengthen resilience and adaptive capacity to climate-related hazards and natural disasters in all countries'.

The last, and arguably most significant of the UN Post-2015 dialogues occurred at the United Nations climate change conference (COP21), in Paris in December 2015, where the signatories to the UN Convention on Climate Change met to advance an agreement on future climate change adaptation. As with the other 2015 UN dialogues, ideas of resilience were explicit at the conference and in the eventual agreement reached. Notably, on the third day of COP21, dubbed 'Resilience Day', the UN and a number of national governments announced major international partnerships to protect people who are most vulnerable to climate impacts.

Overall, these three post-2015 dialogues highlight the importance and utility of ideas and practices of resilience in tackling the integrated and complex issues of reducing the risk of disasters, advancing sustainable development, and mitigating and adapting to climate change. These core agendas, and their framing in resilience-thinking will ensure that resilience will be a vital area of study for years to come (Coaffee and Lee, 2016).

Increasingly, at national and sub-national scales, resilience is being seen not as a barrier to change but as lens through which to enact it, offering a possibility that resilience processes might contain the possibility of resistance, and thus politics (Kevin Grove, Chapter 29). For example, DeVerteuil and Golubchikov (2016, p. 143) highlight three ways in which the discourse of resilience might be progressed in a positive manner, sitting in counter-distinction to many of the critiques in the literature. First, resilience can sustain alternative and previous practices that contradict neo-liberalism; second, resilience is more active and dynamic than passive; and third, resilience can sustain survival, thus acting as a precursor to more obviously transformative action such as resistance. This reading of resilience, it is argued can 'bring us more closely to a heterogeneous de-neoliberalized reading of resilience, explicitly opening it to social justice, power relations and uneven development, and performing valuable conceptual and pragmatic work that usefully moves us beyond resistance yet retaining (long-term) struggle' (ibid.).

In more recent years, a range of evolutionary approaches to thinking about and enacting resilience have emerged, with a focus upon adaptability and flexibility to cope with an increasingly complex and volatile world. As Simin Davoudi (2012, p. 304) noted, 'evolutionary resilience promotes the understanding of places not as units of analysis or neutral containers, but as complex, interconnected socio-spatial systems with extensive and unpredictable feedback processes which operate at multiple scales and timeframes'. As Davoudi further highlighted in Chapter 18 of this volume, if there is one lesson to be learned from resilience-thinking, it is that uncertainty opens up windows of opportunity and possibilities for alternative action spaces to break away from undesirable 'normal'. Other chapters have also highlighted the potential of adaptive transformation (see, for example, Jessica Schmidt, Chapter 10) and how new forms of control, exercised under the rubric of adaptability, may present new possibilities for resistance, and demand new forms of critical practice (see Sara Nelson, Chapter 15). Others, too, have pointed to the possibilities of 'smart resilience' (Coaffee, 2013), appropriating digital information technologies to stimulate new forms of communication and self-organization during emergencies and for overall resilience planning (see Mareile Kaufmann, Chapter 9). More radical and trans-formative notions of resilience can challenge hegemonic understandings of everyday capitalist life that are generally focused on attempts to bounce back or maintain the status quo following a disturbance (see Raven Cretney and Sophie Bond, Chapter 22).

In short, resilience has the potential to stimulate change in the way we think about the challenges global society faces, both now and in the future:

> Resilience, like sustainability before it, is an idea with potentially transformative power. Resilience is all about our capacity to survive and thrive in the face of disruptions of all kinds. If we were to take resilience seriously (highly recommended in our increasingly disruption-prone world), we would make some far-reaching changes in how we live.
>
> *(Mazur and Fairchild, 2015)*

The future

This Handbook has attempted to deal with resilience as a new conceptual approach to under-standing and addressing complex and uncertain problems, and in so doing has illuminated how resilience-thinking is increasingly transforming international policy-making and government and institutional practices.

The underpinning rhetoric of the need to be resilient is becoming more and more influential in politics and public policy-making, and in community initiatives, as resilience moves from the periphery to the centre of government and non-governmental action. Resilience policy has thus evolved from a rhetoric of absorbing shock towards being more pre-emptive and then on to embedding resilience-thinking as an everyday and localised activity. This has led concomitantly to the dispersion of security and risk management-related responsibilities and to an increasing collaborative network of locally based, resilience-focused professionals and communities that may offer the possibility of transformative and adaptive change.

Note

1 The SFDRR replaced the 10-year international disaster risk reduction plan, The Hyogo Framework for Action 2005–2015 (HFA): *Building the Resilience of Nations and Communities to Disasters.*

References

Amin, A. (2013) Surviving the Turbulent Future. *Environment and Planning D*, 31, 140–156.
Brand, F. S. and Jax, K. (2007) Focusing the Meaning(s) of Resilience: Resilience as a Descriptive Concept and a Boundary Object. *Ecology and Society*, 12, 1, 23.
Coaffee, J. (2006) From Counter-Terrorism to Resilience. *European Legacy – Journal of the International Society for the Study of European Ideas* (ISSEI), 1, 4, 389–403.
Coaffee, J. (2013) Rescaling and Responsibilising the Politics of Urban Resilience: From National Security to Local Place-Making. *Politics*, 33, 4, 240–252.
Coaffee, J. and Clarke, J. (2015) On Securing the Generational Challenge of Urban Resilience. *Town Planning Review*, 86, 3, 249–255.

Coaffee, J. and Lee, P. (2016) *Urban Resilience: Planning for Risk Crisis and Uncertainty*. London: Palgrave.

Coaffee, J., Murakami Wood, D. and Rogers, P. (2008) *The Everyday Resilience of the City: How Cities Respond to Terrorism and Disaster*. London: Palgrave Macmillian.

Davoudi, S. (2012) Resilience, a Bridging Concept or a Dead End? *Planning Theory and Practice*, 13, 2, 299–307.

DeVerteuil, G. and Golubchikov, O. (2016) Can Resilience be Redeemed? *City*, 20, 1, 143–151.

Fainstein, S. (2015) Resilience and Justice. *International Journal of Urban and Regional Research*, 39, 1, 157–167.

Mazur, L. and Fairchild, D. (2015) Is 'resilience' the new sustainababble? *Grist*. Available at: http://grist.org/article/is-resilience-the-new-sustainababble/ (accessed 14 January 2015).

Neocleous, M. (2013) Resisting Resilience. *Radical Philosophy*, 178, 2–7.

United Nations (2015) Sendai Framework for Disaster Risk Reduction 2015–2030, U.N., Geneva, p. 10.

Welsh, M. (2014) Resilience and Responsibility: Governing Uncertainty in a Complex World. *The Geographical Journal*, 180, 1, 15–26.

White, I. and O'Hare, P. (2014) From Rhetoric to Reality: Which Resilience, Why Resilience, and Whose Resilience in Spatial Planning? *Environment and Planning C: Government and Policy*, 32, 934–950.

INDEX

Note: Page numbers in italics refer to figures; numbers in bold refer to tables.